The Road to Renewal

Jeremy Bonner

The Road to Renewal

*Victor Joseph Reed
& Oklahoma Catholicism,
1905–1971*

The Catholic University of America Press
Washington, D.C.

Library of Congress Cataloging-in-Publication Data
Bonner, Jeremy.
The Road to renewal : Victor Joseph Reed and
Oklahoma Catholicism, 1905–1971 / Jeremy Bonner.
p. cm.
Includes bibliographical references and index.
ISBN 978-0-8132-1507-5 (cloth : alk. paper) 1. Catholic
Church—Oklahoma—History. 2. Reed, Victor Joseph,
1905–1971. 3. Catholic Church—Bishops—Biography.
4. Oklahoma—Church history. I. Title.
BX1415.O4B66 2007
282'.7660904—dc22
2007013377

This work is dedicated,

in gratitude and humility,

to my parents, Gerald and Jane,

on the occasion of their fortieth

year of marriage

Contents

Illustrations

Photos of the Reed family in 1920 and 1949 are courtesy of the Reed family. All others are from *The Sooner Catholic*, the biweekly newspaper of the Archdiocese of Oklahoma City.

Acknowledgments

When I was first invited to examine the life of Victor Reed, I was exceedingly grateful that someone was willing to pay for the completion of a work of historical scholarship, but rather inclined to dismiss the project as a somewhat parochial recounting of the story of a minor Catholic diocese in a comparatively unsung part of the United States. As I was to learn, not only was my view of Oklahoma unduly dismissive, but the episcopal career of Victor Reed proved to be anything but insignificant in the context of change within the national—and, indeed, worldwide—Catholic Church.

Without two individuals, this project would never have been completed. Father J. Paul Donovan first conceived the notion that a life of Bishop Reed should be written and was generous enough to fund such an undertaking. Father Donovan played a central role in many of the events described in these pages, but has nevertheless been extremely self-effacing in the process of reconstructing the past and assiduous in not imposing his perspective. Father James White has been a tower of strength, guiding this author through the primary sources, making arrangements for accommodation, setting up critical interviews, providing not one but two editorial critiques of the emerging text, and generally offering the sort of welcome that one could find only in the Midwest. To him, first and foremost, goes the credit for my production of a finished manuscript.

In Oklahoma, there are many people who have given generously of their time. Archbishop Eusebius Beltran of Oklahoma City gave me unprecedented access to the diocesan archives. Staff members at the Archdiocesan Pastoral Center were uniformly welcoming and made my visits to Oklahoma City a delight. In Tulsa, Victor Reed's successor as rector of Holy Family Cathedral, Monsignor Gregory Gier, also provided welcome hospitality and his own brand of entertaining anecdote. Bishop Reed's sister-in-law, Julia Reed, and his niece, Veronica Markey, provided insight into the bishop's early life, while priests, religious, and laity of the diocese spoke about their memories of the bishop during his years in office. Although my research was conducted mostly in Oklahoma, I would be remiss in failing to mention the assistance of Professor John Dick of the American College at Louvain, who kindly scanned and e-mailed me a number of documents relating to the college during the 1930s.

The Catholic University of America trained me as an American historian and I am therefore gratified that the Catholic University of America Press judged my work worthy of publication. I am grateful to David McGonagle, who helped get me over some administrative hurdles, and to Professor Leslie Tentler and also Professor Gerald Fogarty of the University of Virginia, who provided insightful and generous commentaries on my work. I am particularly appreciative of Professor Tentler's contribution, as she has provided much encouragement and critical advice as I carried this project to completion. Established academics who take time from their own work to assist independent scholars are a rare breed, and I consider her a mentor in more ways than one.

An independent scholar, lacking the resources of an academic department, is very dependent on the community in which he resides. I would particularly like to thank the parishes of Mount Calvary Episcopal Church in Baltimore and Trinity Episcopal Cathedral in Pittsburgh, which sustained me over the two years that this project has been under way. Among my academic peers, I have drawn particular encouragement from Mary Beth Connolly and Christopher Gildemeister and thank them for the many useful conversations on religious history that we have shared.

Finally, I would like to pay tribute to my wife, Jennifer, whose entire married life has, to a great extent, been overshadowed by the preparation of this work. Without her love and support, those moments of doubt and uncertainty in the midst of composition would have seemed insuperable.

The Road to Renewal

Introduction

From Catholic American to American Catholic

Change is a profoundly disturbing concept for religious communities. All too often, it is assumed that religious institutions require flexibility only as long as is necessary to establish a missionary foothold. Once that has been achieved, the preference is for consolidation and the establishment of defined parameters of operation. To "step outside the box" may expose an organization to the possibility of discord and force the leadership to make hard choices about the way forward. Beginning in the late 1950s, the Roman Catholic Church in America underwent a series of dramatic transformations that profoundly altered the manner in which its members lived and worshiped. Though intensified as a result of the initiatives of Pope John XXIII and the Second Vatican Council (1962–1965), these transformations were the culmination of a process of change that had been under way within the American Catholic community since the 1930s.

By the close of the 1960s, the religious orders of men and women had been decimated and the priesthood demoralized, while many of the laity radiated a newfound confidence in their ability to direct the future course of the Church. The Church's liturgy had been rendered from Latin into the vernacular, relations with the Protestant denominations were far closer than they had ever been, and the Church enjoyed a reputation for upholding racial equality and opposing war. Perhaps most profound was the "privatization" of Catholic religious identity, such that an American Catholic was no longer obliged to view his confessional identity as in any way in conflict with his citizenship. The era of the Second Vatican Council, then, was the era

I

in which American Catholics ceased to be Catholic Americans. As its distinctive qualities faded, so Catholicism entered the political and social mainstream. It was a profound transformation for those who had grown up in the early twentieth century and could remember the social consequences that stemmed from being Catholic.

Nowhere were these tensions more obvious than in the American Midwest.[1] Historically, Catholicism in the United States had been most culturally distinctive in the cities and on the coast, while a more flexible attitude prevailed among the Church's leadership in the countryside and the interior. "With a different tradition of lay-clergy relations, a less defensive and insular clergy and hierarchy, a more solid place in the community, the Church in the Middle West has been more receptive to the experimental, less attached to the traditional, and more alert to the possibilities of lay initiative and responsibility," wrote one progressive commentator in 1963. "By contrast, in the East and some parts of the South and Far West, the Church is comparatively rigid and fixed in its ways."[2]

Midwestern "experimentation" was the hallmark of the late nineteenth and early twentieth centuries. While metropolitan centers like Chicago, Detroit, and Milwaukee enjoyed sizable Catholic majorities, a much larger proportion (albeit still a minority) of midwestern Catholics lived in rural settings, compared with those in the Northeast. West of the Mississippi River, many Catholic communities had infrequent contact with a parish priest and were forced to fall back on their own spiritual resources. Though replicating the pattern of diverse immigrant enclaves created by Catholics in the Northeast, midwestern Catholics more frequently lived cheek by jowl with their Protestant neighbors. Social interaction and "mixed" marriage—the ultimate measure of religious integration—were not uncommon and were only enhanced by the activities of local bishops who proved to be strong proponents of accommodation with the American system.[3]

---

1. For the purposes of this study, the Midwest should be considered as extending from Ohio to the edge of the Rocky Mountains and from Minnesota to Texas.

2. Callahan, *The Mind of the Catholic Layman*, 114. A comprehensive understanding of the regional distinctiveness of American religious cultures is only now being developed. Marlett discusses the historiographic neglect of the Catholic Midwest in "'There Is a Church West of Buffalo!'" For general regional studies see Lindsey and Silk, *Religion and Public Life in the Midwest* and Slade and Lee, *The Greenwood Encyclopedia of American Regional Cultures*, which includes a chapter on religion.

3. For a regional overview of parish life, see Shaw, "The Cities and the Plains." Oklahoma and Texas are discussed in Nelson, "Modest and Humble Crosses."

During the late nineteenth century, the Midwest was a pivotal setting for the divisive conflict over "Americanism" that would leave the Catholic Church struggling to come to terms with its place in American society for the next half century. Inspired by the writings of Isaac Hecker, the Americanists, led by Archbishop John Ireland of St. Paul (Minnesota), strove to reconcile their Catholic identity with American democracy. The Americanists' efforts to cooperate with the state aroused the concern of Pope Leo XIII who, in January 1899, issued the encyclical *Testem Benevolentiae* repudiating all efforts to soften doctrinal stands or to elevate personal spirituality over the authority of the Church.[4]

In acting as he did, Leo embraced a new vision for the Church that would be enforced by what Gerald Fogarty has called the "Romanization of the hierarchy," beginning with the appointment of William O'Connell as bishop of Portland (Maine) in 1901 and archbishop of Boston in 1907. Between the publication of *Testem Benevolentiae* and the signing of the Lateran Treaty in 1929, the American Church was the most Roman and bishop-dominated in the world, with what David O'Brien has termed a powerful "states' rights" mentality. The influx of ethnic Catholic immigrants from eastern Europe during the 1910s only reinforced the sense of Catholic isolation and kept the fires of anti-Catholicism burning in mainstream Protestant circles.[5]

The defensive stance of Catholicism and its hostility to the American state began to erode after the United States entered the First World War in 1917. The American hierarchy's support for the enlistment of American Catholics in the nation's armed forces was complemented by its decision to establish the National Catholic War Council to coordinate the work of Catholic social agencies in the war effort. The opening of a National Catholic School of Social Service at the Catholic University of America and the drafting by Monsignor John A. Ryan of what became known as the Bishops' Program for Social Reconstruction also signaled the greater openness of the Church to some of the collectivist solutions articulated by many secular social reformers.

---

4. Hennesey, *American Catholics*, 194–203; Fogarty, *The Vatican and the American Hierarchy*, 115–94; McAvoy, *The Great Crisis in American Catholic History*; Curran, *Michael Augustine Corrigan*; Marvin R. O'Connell, *John Ireland*.

5. Fogarty, *The Vatican and the American Hierarchy*, 195–209; O'Brien, *Public Catholicism*, 124–57. On ethnic Catholicism, see Orsi, *The Madonna of 115th Street*; Liptak, R.S.M., *Immigrants and Their Church*, 57–159. On early-twentieth-century anti-Catholicism, see Higham, *Strangers in the Land*, 178–84.

In 1919, a representative of Pope Benedict XV invited the American bishops to establish a permanent body to help implement the pontiff's peace proposals and, under the influence of another reformer, Father John Burke, C.S.P., the National Catholic Welfare Council was established as an annual meeting of all the American bishops, which would elect a standing secretariat to handle business between meetings. When, in 1922, under pressure from Cardinal William O'Connell, the Consistorial Congregation in Rome issued a decree demanding the dissolution of the council, a clear majority of the American hierarchy responded by petitioning for its continuation. As a result, it was retained, though renamed the National Catholic Welfare Conference (NCWC) and with no requirement on the part of any bishop to participate in its deliberations.[6]

As the Church entered the 1920s, it found itself plagued by new social pressures. The end of mass immigration in 1924 was accompanied by a renewed upsurge of anti-Catholic prejudice that buoyed a renascent Ku Klux Klan to successive electoral victories in the South and West. In Oregon, the Klan sought to implement a law compelling all children aged between eight and sixteen to attend public school, a law struck down only by the U.S. Supreme Court in *Pierce v. Society of Sisters* in June 1925. While Catholic politicians made significant advances in areas where their coreligionists represented a majority of the population during the 1920s, the sweeping defeat of Al Smith of New York in the presidential election of 1928 revealed the mountain that Catholic Americans had still to climb to win public acceptance.[7]

Like the fundamentalist Protestants who frequently criticized them, many Catholics concluded from such treatment that it was vital to preserve their communal vision intact from the polluting touch of secular culture, but there were also voices favoring more constructive engagement. From his desk at the NCWC, John Ryan promoted a new interest in Catholic social teaching, being joined in this endeavor by his rural counterpart Bishop Edwin O'Hara, who helped found the National Catholic Rural Life Conference in 1923. At St. John's University in Collegeville, Minnesota, meanwhile, the first stirrings of liturgical renewal were under way under the auspices of the Benedictine Virgil Michel, and a new paper for the Catholic intelligentsia, *Commonweal*, had burst upon the scene.

6. Hennesey, *American Catholics*, 221–33; Fogarty, *The Vatican and the American Hierarchy*, 214–28; McShane, *Sufficiently Radical*; Slawson, *National Catholic Welfare Council*.
7. Higham, *Strangers in the Land*, 291–99; Alexander, *The Ku Klux Klan*; Lay, *The Invisible Empire in the West*.

While none of these undertakings represented a dramatic shift in the institutional monolith that was the Catholic Church in the United States, their discourse steadily permeated the former stronghold of Americanism, the Midwest. In the Midwest, too, the years after the First World War were characterized by the drive of various prelates to "Americanize" the diverse ethnic Catholic communities in their care. This process, while in no way intended to diminish loyalty to the Roman way, involved the elimination of religious practices and rituals peculiar to specific ethnic groups in favor of a common standard. Foremost in this endeavor was Archbishop George Mundelein of Chicago, whose efforts at Catholic Americanization paralleled those of the secular authorities to assimilate immigrants.[8]

The Catholic world underwent a dramatic reorientation, both in Rome and the United States, in 1929. The successful achievement of a concordat between Pope Pius XI and the Italian government of Benito Mussolini subtly shifted the defensive stance adopted by the Church since the liberal revolutions of 1848. The pope's subsequent embrace of the idea of Catholic Action and a committed, albeit subordinate, lay apostolate suggested a departure from the Church's earlier antagonism to lay initiative. The earliest forms of Catholic Action—Young Christian Workers and Young Christian Students— sought to institute notions of a dedicated lay apostolate performed in places of work and dedicated to the transformation of society by the direct application of Christian teaching to the needs of the secular world. A generation of newly ordained priests, exposed to Catholic Action in its Belgian heartland during the 1930s, bore the concept back to the United States. Catholic identity was reaffirmed by such organizations as the Summer Schools of Catholic Action directed by the Jesuit Daniel Lord and Dorothy Day's personalist Catholic Worker movement, which rejected both Marxism and capitalism in favor of a Catholic solution to the problems of economic hardship. The 1930s also witnessed the birth of the Legion of Decency, which rated movies according to whether they conveyed a message suitable for a Catholic audience.[9]

---

8. Hennesey, *American Catholics*, 221–33; O'Brien, *Public Catholicism*, 158–67; Van Allen, *"The Commonweal" and American Catholicism*; Pecklers, *The Unread Vision*; Dolan, *Some Seed Fell on Good Ground*; Cohen, *Making a New Deal*, 83–94. Interestingly, Ryan and O'Hara were both born in Minnesota.

9. Gavin, *Champion of Youth*; Piehl, *Breaking Bread*; Black, *The Catholic Crusade against the Movies*. This argument, it should be noted, is more obviously true for the Catholic Midwest than for other regions of the country.

For all the Church's efforts to continue to emphasize Catholic identity, the coming of the Great Depression posed a severe challenge. The precipitate collapse of the network of enclave Catholic associations impelled the Church toward greater involvement in mainstream American society, albeit on its own terms. With the election of Franklin Roosevelt as president in November 1932, American Catholics found themselves increasingly in harmony with the national administration, at least on economic issues, a state of affairs assisted by the participation of Monsignor Ryan and Bishop Francis Haas in the councils of state and the elevation of Catholic politicians to high office. Their involvement in the labor movement was also enhanced by the succession of Philip Murray to leadership of the Congress of Industrial Organizations in 1940, and many working-class Catholics were incorporated into the new industrial unions.

The leadership of the American Church was now in the hands of the midwestern bishops who dominated the NCWC and generally expressed approval of the Democratic administration's policies. Men like Cardinal George Mundelein of Chicago, Archbishop John T. McNicholas of Cincinnati, and Bishop Robert E. Lucey of Amarillo (later archbishop of San Antonio) rallied to President Roosevelt. While an emphasis on "Catholic" approaches to the problems of industrialization was sustained—and even enhanced in the case of movements like the Catholic Worker—organized labor did much to break down confessional barriers in many American communities. Furthermore, the accelerated demise of ethnically distinct Catholic neighborhoods in much of the Midwest only enhanced the sense of middle-class Catholics as "American" citizens, with the same religious freedom of expression and right to personal conscience.[10]

By the early years of the cold war, the appearance of the Catholic Church in the United States was very different from its 1920s incarnation. Its opposition to Communism helped alleviate the earlier perception of Catholicism as an alien culture within the American body politic. Swelled by the many Catholic ex-servicemen seeking higher education through the G.I. Bill of Rights, Catholic society underwent a dramatic improvement in social status. The newly upwardly mobile fled their former urban enclaves in droves for new lives in the suburbs. Concerned with the stability of the family, many

10. Hennesey, *American Catholics*, 254–79; O'Brien, *Public Catholicism*, 167–94; O'Brien, *American Catholics and Social Reform*; Blantz, *A Priest in Public Service*; Heineman, *A Catholic New Deal*; Broderick, *Right Reverend New Dealer*.

committed middle-class Catholics joined the Christian Family Movement—
the new face of Catholic Action, centered in the Archdiocese of Chicago—
which further developed the notion of the apostolate of the laity. Educated, articulate, and increasingly convinced of their complete integration into
American society, many lay Catholics, particularly in the Midwest, saw this
"Americanization" of the Church as a wholly beneficial event. When Pope
John XXIII announced his intention to summon the first ecumenical council of the Church since 1870, the enthusiasm of most midwestern Catholics
knew no bounds.[11]

A MIDWESTERN BISHOP

How should the process of change within a religious community be approached? There is no question that a change of worldwide proportions requires national and transnational studies that speak to denominational shift.
Such studies, however, frequently focus on religious elites whose identity is
bound up with the Church as an institution. Often, the views of ordinary
laymen, priests, members of religious communities, and bishops who do not
hold national leadership positions are neglected. A valuable corrective may
be provided by a focus on a single diocese and its bishop. The choice here
of the Diocese of Oklahoma City and Tulsa was shaped by three factors: the
desire to offer a biographical study of Bishop Victor Joseph Reed; the appeal
of an understudied region, the Midwest; and, perhaps most important, the
availability of official church records for the 1960s.[12]

The Second Vatican Council had a profound impact on all American
bishops. Accustomed to exercising absolute authority within their dioceses,
they found themselves increasingly challenged from below as the 1960s wore
on, by liberals and conservatives alike. They found the phenomenon of clerical mutiny particularly unsettling. Where the Second Vatican Council had
seemed to promise greater inclusion, it often brought greater division and
factionalism. The bishops' responses to such phenomena ranged from outright resistance to efforts at accommodation, with everything in between.

11. Ward, *Catholic Life, U.S.A.*; Greeley, *The Church and the Suburbs*; Kosa, "The Emergence of a Catholic Middle Class"; Burns, *Disturbing the Peace*.

12. Most diocesan histories, to date, lack access to official records after 1960. Typical
midwestern diocesan histories either conclude before 1960 or rely on published sources for
later events. See Avella, *This Confident Church*; Tentler, *Seasons of Grace*; Fortin, *Faith and
Action*; Avella, *In the Richness of the Earth*.

A few appeared genuinely to believe that the full participation of the laity should be encouraged, and one such who drew considerable national attention was Victor Reed, bishop of Oklahoma City and Tulsa.[13]

A survey of Victor Reed's life provides a valuable opportunity to observe the process of conciliar change from the perspective of a bishop who, while he enthusiastically embraced change, soon discovered that he could not contain it. While one should not discount the successes achieved during Reed's episcopate in such diverse areas as civil rights, liturgical change, and ecumenical dialogue, it is perilous to downplay the tensions of the era, which took their toll both on the Catholic Church in Oklahoma and on the health and well-being of the man charged with its spiritual oversight. "[Bishop Reed] knew intellectually that changes were coming about," declared one of his diocesan priests. "He didn't have a clue how they would come about or what they would look like when they came about and so he didn't give a lot of direction."[14]

Every bishop is unique. Some are bureaucrats, for whom the efficient performance of their official duties is paramount. Some are theorists, who strive to apply the timeless principles of the Church's teaching to the age in which they live. Some are pastors, for whom the bishop's residence is merely a loftier version of their former rectory, from which they minister to those who constitute the living organism that is the Body of Christ. And some, of course, are politicians, whether in the labyrinthine corridors of the institutional Church or in the secular political marketplace.

Victor Reed was certainly no bureaucrat and arguably no politician (had he been that way inclined, he would have avoided some of the controversies that dogged his episcopate). A case might be made for his being a theorist, except that he was perhaps by nature too passive for such a role.[15] While many changes occurred in his diocese on his watch, they came at the initiative of those below him. He permitted them to occur, but he rarely conceived them himself. Ultimately, perhaps, the title of pastor fits him best. As a homegrown bishop of Oklahoma, he retained a sense of identification

13. For national interest in the Oklahoma phenomenon, see Norton-Taylor, "The Catholic Layman Confronts His Changing Church."

14. Gallatin, interview.

15. Monsignor James Halpine described how he and Father Frank Wrigley were in conference with the bishop and asked him for his views on one of the documents emerging from the Second Vatican Council, to which the bishop apologetically responded: "I don't read very much." After the meeting, Father Wrigley exploded: "At least I thought he did that!" Clergy roundtable discussion, June 23, 2005.

Victor Reed with some of his clergy outside the Bishop's House in Oklahoma City. Donated to Bishop Francis Kelley by the founder of Phillips Petroleum in 1939, the property served not only as the bishop's residence but also as the chancery office.

with his people known to few bishops, and that connection was one he enjoyed not only with Catholics but with many Christians throughout the state. There was one other title that described him well, but it was not a functional title. He was, all agree, first and foremost a gentleman.

His clergy called the fourth bishop of Oklahoma City and Tulsa "the Last of the Prince-Bishops." The title was not unearned, for he was, in the words of a former chancellor of the diocese, "everything you would expect a bishop to be in those days," and when he was raised to the episcopate in 1958, the local consensus was that he would revel in the ceremonial and the ritual of high office.[16] He was known to appreciate the finer things in life, including the sumptuous interior of the episcopal residence in Oklahoma City.

Donated to Bishop Francis Kelley in 1939 by local oilman Frank Phillips, the mansion—built by a man who had made his fortune selling mules to the army in World War I—boasted an impressive double staircase with heraldic lions on the newel posts and a pipe organ in a chamber beneath the steps. It served not only as the bishop's residence but also as the chancery office. The bishop made his own additions to the interior and also acquired an extensive art collection. While a devoted pastor and shepherd of his flock, he was hardly an ascetic. "He was a good man," declared one of his progressive critics, but also "an old-school bishop enamored of his fine wine, his art and his spacious mansion and basically compliant with church teaching and the other educational trappings."[17] He also loved the beauties of nature. When he was being driven around the diocese, he would often tell his driver to stop the car in order to dig up a roadside plant or flower that had caught his attention.[18] He threw himself into gardening when on vacation, planting flowers and rose bushes, and reveled in the rose garden that his housekeeper, Sister Mary Joseph, established at the episcopal residence (though he worried about the reaction of the neighbors to the load of cow manure that was brought in to nourish them).[19]

His was an interior life, rarely shaken by external storms. On one occasion a young protégé spent part of a dinner with the bishop inveighing

16. Garthoeffner, interview; Schettler, interview; Halpine, interview.

17. White, "Personal Memories of Bishop Reed"; Robert J. Brousseau, "My Quest for Freedom," in Brousseau, *A Dying Breed of Brave Men*, 189.

18. Schettler, interview.

19. Mies, conversation. "When the news [of his death] reached [me]," wrote one admirer, "I was in the Swiss Alps and as I prayed for his eternal rest I almost could feel his spirit over the lovely mountains—he loved beauty so much!" Sr. Marciana to Revd. Charles H. Schettler, September 12, 1971, Victor Reed Papers.

against what he considered the many failings of the pontificate of Pope Paul VI. When he paused for breath, the bishop smiled gently. "Ah," he said, "we have now heard from Paul of Ardmore [Oklahoma] on Paul of Rome."[20] He could be equally disarming when it came to dodging awkward inquiries. When Father Robert Pickett was appointed to a rural pastorate just after Reed's elevation to the episcopate, he discovered the rectory to be in an appalling state of disrepair. Pickett journeyed to Oklahoma City to appeal to the bishop for funds for renovation but arrived to find the bishop overseeing renovations of the Bishop's House. Reed greeted him graciously but broke off to take a phone call from his upholsterer. After an inconclusive conversation, Pickett prepared to leave. As he escorted him to the door, Reed put an arm round his shoulders. "You know, Bob," he said, "we must all make sacrifices!"[21]

From almost any other bishop, such a comment would have provoked profound resentment, but somehow Reed always managed to get away with it. Perhaps it was because his love of elegant and beautiful things had more to do with aesthetics than with power. His enjoyment of the episcopal lifestyle might at times have been somewhat self-indulgent, but it was never arrogant. The streak of humility that always ran through him prevented him from being a clerical tyrant. Like his predecessor, he attended the Catholic high school sports competitions and presented the trophies, but in contrast to Bishop McGuinness, whose episcopal ring the victorious team members had kissed, Reed deliberately removed his and placed it in his pocket.[22]

Such humility played itself out in his devotional life. Mass was offered daily in the Bishop's House for a community that included several of Reed's relatives and three Precious Blood sisters who performed the domestic duties. Whenever he made a long journey by car, it was his habit to recite fifteen decades of the rosary.[23] While he sympathized with the tribulations of those who abandoned the priesthood, he could never truly empathize with them. "He would not have viewed [laicization] as taking off the shackles, because he wasn't a shackled person," said Monsignor Gregory Gier, whom Reed ordained during the turbulent decade of the 1960s. "That was all from the depths of his soul."[24]

20. Gallatin, interview.
21. Clergy roundtable discussion, June 23, 2005.
22. Clergy roundtable discussion, June 19, 2005.
23. Mies, conversation; Schettler, interview.
24. Gier, interview.

His managerial style was hands-off in the extreme. He was undynamic in the pulpit and rarely raised his voice. At an awards banquet when he was still bishop-elect, he complimented one priest on his delivery of an extemporaneous address, which he admitted he could never have done.[25] He neither typed nor dictated, writing everything in longhand for his aides to render in legible form. An hour before midnight Mass one Christmas Eve, the bishop was writing his homily while, in another room, Father Charles Schettler was frantically typing up the fair copy.[26] When he visited his vacation residence at Texoma, he always took official papers but never worked on them. When asked why, the bishop responded apologetically: "Well, you see, Sister, if I take [them], I don't feel so guilty."[27]

In his personal dealings, he sometimes gave the impression, at least on first acquaintance, of detachment. In stark contrast with his predecessor, he lacked the "hail fellow, well met" style that characterized Bishop McGuinness. "I'm not easy to get to know," he once conceded, "but I wear well."[28] It did not help that, in an age when many of the rising clerical stars of the Catholic Church disdained the leadership of the well-to-do Catholic elite, Reed remained on good terms with many affluent Tulsa Catholic families whose acquaintance he had cultivated as rector of Holy Family Cathedral during the 1950s. "From a purely social standpoint," declared one of Reed's lay acquaintances, "he was at ease drinking wine and cheese at somebody's house as much as he was in the pulpit or among the poor."[29]

The key word here was social for in politics the bishop was increasingly associated with positions that his old friends did not share. When rumors circulated that the bishop was a Republican—something to which his mentor Bishop Francis Kelley had been proud to attest—Reed privately expressed his irritation. "I did rather 'mind' the remark of my good friend Father [James] McNamee about my being a Republican," he complained, "since I am a registered Democrat. Some of my ideas are perhaps more conservative than those of the priests to whom he refers. This, I suppose, explains the 'aside.'"[30]

25. White, "Personal Memories of Bishop Reed"; Clergy roundtable discussion, June 23, 2005.

26. Clergy roundtable discussion, June 19, 2005.

27. Mies, conversation.

28. White, "Personal Memories of Bishop Reed." A Tulsa attorney who first became acquainted with him in 1965 described him as "soft-spoken, reserved, intelligent and gracious." Fox, interview.

29. Fox, interview.

30. Victor Reed to Msgr. William F. Stricker, October 19, 1960, Reed Papers.

Reed was no apologist for the rich and powerful. When Helen Boyle Lauinger, the mother of the publisher of the *Oil and Gas Journal,* industry paper for oil and gas professionals, who had been a stalwart of Holy Family Cathedral, died, Reed returned to Tulsa to conduct her funeral. To an assembled throng of dignitaries, the bishop, no doubt with some relish, remarked that Mrs. Lauinger had been a woman of faith who supported the Church not because she liked its priests or agreed with them, but because she was a good Catholic. What was unusual, Reed concluded, was that she was the only affluent Catholic who never cut off funds to him![31]

Only on rare occasions did Reed indulge in the strictly prophetic style so beloved of Protestant churchmen. "He was not an argumentative type of person," explains Father Charles Schettler, a former chancellor of the diocese. "He would try to dialogue with people and to lead them to what is right and what is true."[32] Perhaps what was most striking, though, was his unwillingness to discipline those priests under his jurisdiction who aspired to prophetic politics, even when they were perfectly happy to critique the perceived shortcomings of their ordinary. "Revenge," declares G. Douglas Fox, a lay representative on the diocesan pastoral board during the 1960s, "was just not part of his makeup."[33] This did not mean that he was unaware of the dangers of letting radical reformers have free rein. "Liberals are good to have around," he once remarked, "but you mustn't give them any authority."[34]

THE CONSEQUENCES AND THE MEANING OF VATICAN II

By the end of the 1960s, the segregated Catholic world into which Reed had been born and in which he had lived for much of his life as a priest had completely collapsed. Bishops who had previously been completely autonomous within their dioceses witnessed a new accretion of power by organizations like the National Conference of Catholic Bishops. Across the nation, Catholic priests and sisters challenged the right of their clerical superiors to demand absolute obedience and employed the discourse of social responsibility and civil rights to vindicate their increasingly independent stance on a variety of issues. At the same time, faithful Catholic laity, after decades of

31. Donovan, interview.   32. Schettler, interview.
33. Fox, interview.
34. Clergy roundtable discussion, June 23, 2005.

adherence to the doctrine of "pray, pay, and obey," began to substitute notions of personal conscience for submission to the authorities of the Church.
A strangely "Protestant" vision of what it meant to be a member of the One
Holy, Catholic, and Apostolic Church began to permeate the outlook of
faithful Catholics throughout the United States.[35]

As the Church passed through the era of debate prompted by the Second
Vatican Council into the era of discord that succeeded it, Reed and his brother bishops found themselves obliged to grapple with issues that had rarely
troubled their predecessors. As the political debate shifted from issues of economic security to such divisive cultural issues as integration, birth control,
and church government, the bishops felt increasingly isolated. Eight years after Reed's consecration, a priestly acquaintance concluded that he had aged
fifteen years in that time. "Any one can conclude that his job is anything but
an easy one," he remarked, a comment that applied equally well to many
members of the Catholic hierarchy.[36]

Most bishops (except in a few self-sufficient cases) fell prey to inner self-
doubt about the conflict between their seminary-instilled belief in the verti-
cal basis of authority of the Catholic Church and the pastoral responsibilities
of a bishop, and the emphasis on a more horizontal conception of authority
that stemmed from the decisions reached by the bishops of the worldwide
Church at the Second Vatican Council. Although often misinterpreted, this
new understanding of authority gave rise to vocal assertions of autonomy by
numerous ordained and lay groups throughout the Church and frequent and
increasingly bitter disputes between them and the hierarchy. Bishops could
openly resist these challenges, as was the case in Los Angeles, Philadelphia,
and San Antonio, or they could play the more mediatory role embraced by
men like Reed, but they could no longer guarantee an end to dissension
solely by episcopal fiat.[37]

35. This was the theme of Bishop Russell McVinney of Rhode Island in an intervention at the Second Vatican Council, when he opined that the "new breed" theologians
seemed to find more of value in Protestant biblical scholarship than in the writings of the
Church Fathers. See Yzermans, *American Participation in the Second Vatican Council*, 256.
Six years later, James Hitchcock echoed McVinney's criticism. "Radical Catholic theology
derives little from Catholic or Orthodox traditions," he wrote, "and much from Protestant
thought of the past 150 years, especially German. Distinctive Catholic devotions and practices have been entirely abandoned in most avant-garde circles." Hitchcock, *The Decline
and Fall of Radical Catholicism*, 21–22.
36. Revd. Jean P. Page to Alta and Charles Heger, May 15, 1966, Reed Papers.
37. A. V. Krebs, "A Church of Silence," *Commonweal*, July 10, 1964; Jones, *John Cardinal Krol*, 355–500; Bronder, *Social Justice and Church Authority*, 100–162. Reed's adapt-

The unfolding nature of these changes helps shape the structure of this book. Chapters 1 and 2 provide not only a biographical sketch of Victor Reed's early life but also the context for the world of the Catholic Midwest—as seen through Oklahoma eyes—and how it contributed to a fundamental reordering of Catholic priorities. (Maps showing the parishes and missions in each quadrant of Oklahoma and the parishes and institutions of Oklahoma City and Tulsa can be found in the appendix.) The role played by one of Reed's closest clerical acquaintances—Father Don Kanaly—in bringing back the concept of Catholic Action from Belgium and helping to propagate it, particularly within the Archdiocese of Chicago, proved especially critical (see chapter 2). True, almost all the bishops during the 1930s and 1940s saw Catholic Action as a lay auxiliary, entirely subordinate to the clergy, but that did not prevent an ever better-educated laity from coming to its own conclusions about the degree of autonomy they should enjoy. While Victor Reed was never an activist regarding Catholic Action, he clearly imbibed some of its philosophy while studying at the University of Louvain, and in the wake of the "midwestern" successes at the Second Vatican Council (discussed in chapter 3), he proved all too willing to give his laity a greater say in the day-to-day operations of their diocese.

Victor Reed's episcopate was shaped by the Second Vatican Council, coming to office, as he did, at the same time as Pope John XXIII. It is only appropriate, therefore, to consider change in Oklahoma in terms of the various aspects of Church life examined by the council. Part 2 explores those areas of life that had traditionally defined what it meant to be Catholic: the bishop and his chancery, the parochial school and the parish community. Here we see an obvious tension between changes prompted by the council and changes driven simply by social and demographic realities on the ground. The failure of a college run by the local Benedictine community obliged Reed to make unprecedented appeals to the laity for financial assistance and may well have impelled him to cultivate a greater degree of lay oversight of diocesan affairs than he might otherwise have done. On the other hand, the establishment of both a diocesan pastoral board—albeit one over which the bishop still exercised the right of veto—and the famous Little Council suggested a commitment to hearing the views of the laity that few other bishops were willing to entertain (see chapter 3).

---

ability should not be overstated. "Am I a liberal?" the bishop once asked one of his younger diocesan priests. The latter quickly reassured him that he was not. Gallatin, interview.

In the field of religious education, too, the pressures on the system were both ideological and practical. The decline of the rural school system would very likely have occurred whether or not the Second Vatican Council had taken place, given the continued growth in the numbers of urban and suburban Catholics. The unfortunate conjunction of these two events, however, led many to see them as related, an impression not dispelled by the hostility of many reformers to the very principle of parochial education. Education, especially at the college level, inevitably became a flashpoint for the culture wars brewing in American society generally and the Catholic community in particular (see chapter 4).

If the parochial school soon became a battleground, the parish proved hardly less of one. Rural-urban tensions played a part, but most striking were the concurrent decline of the principle of the territorial parish and the advent of parish "democracy." The tendency of urban parishes to become more specialized in their ministries and more attuned to the perspectives of a particular group served to reshape the Catholic parish into an institution similar to its Protestant counterpart. This was only accentuated by Reed's support for the establishment of three nonterritorial parishes within his diocese that stressed social outreach and ecumenical dialogue. In ordinary parishes, meanwhile, the bishop's acceptance of the principle of parish councils set the stage for open conflict between priests and laity as to the degree of control the latter should have the right to exert in parish government (see chapter 5).

The changes promoted by the Second Vatican Council are the subject of part 3. They extended into all areas of religious life, embracing liturgical renewal, the development of relations with non-Catholic churches, and engagement with contemporary social problems such as segregation and war. Nothing changed the public face of the local parish church more than liturgical renewal. Changes in the liturgy, however, were not simply a matter of new ceremonies but of making use of liturgy to demonstrate how lay Catholics should behave in their daily life. The new emphasis placed on the Eucharist marked a reassertion of the Church's corporate identity, while the adoption of a vernacular liturgy and encouragement of congregational participation served to break down further the barriers between clergy and laity (see chapter 6).

Ecumenical exchanges also represented a considerable departure from earlier practice. The Second Vatican Council acknowledged the existential reality of the Protestant churches, encouraging their presence as observers at its deliberations. Victor Reed had always had an interest in ecumenism and invited his priests to follow suit. Encouraged by the good relations it enjoyed with the high church Episcopal Diocese of Oklahoma, the Diocese of Oklahoma City and Tulsa pioneered shared services, Christian formation, and common outreach projects. The rising number of mixed marriages during the 1960s also testified to the much-altered attitude on the part of many Catholic laymen toward the Protestant churches (see chapter 7).

For Catholics who embraced the Vatican II ethos, much of the appeal of the council was that it commended engagement with the world's social problems. Many stepped forward to confront the endemic racism evident in both the Church and the wider world. It was in this arena that Bishop Reed took the most proactive role of his episcopate, speaking directly in a wide variety of forums. Inspired by his example, many younger priests carried the banner of civil rights into Oklahoma civil society and even further afield. Tensions inevitably surfaced, however, when their commitment to end the practical segregation of parishes and parochial schools threatened to destabilize parish life (see chapter 8).

A similar change was under way in the conduct of missions. Previously the preserve of clergy and religious, many Catholic dioceses in the 1950s and 1960s moved toward a more lay-oriented mission philosophy directed toward Central and South America. In the case of Oklahoma, the diocesan mission to Guatemala was composed equally of priests and lay members of the Christian Family Movement and achieved a significant hold on the largely Indian population of the Guatemala uplands. The mission also attracted considerable attention from the state's Catholic population, who subscribed substantially to the undertaking. The Catholic obligation to further missionary activity was soon complemented by a belief that a moral obligation to oppose anything other than strictly defensive war was an essential part of the witness of the Church. Hostility to the conflict in Vietnam failed to draw the same level of sympathy as did civil rights, but here again Bishop Reed took center stage with a 1971 pastoral letter deploring the waste of life that the war had provoked (see chapter 9).

The final part of this book turns attention to the basic functional groups in Catholic society: the clergy, the female religious communities, and the laity. For the clergy, Vatican II, while apparently offering great promise, actually served to downgrade their role in parish life. No longer the best-educated men in small Catholic communities, some sought to compensate for their diminution in status by enhancing their role as social activists, while others focused on enhancing their status as professionals. Conflicts over such cultural issues as birth control further widened the gap with the hierarchy, even as many priests also expressed a sense of disdain for those among the laity who failed to embrace all the recent changes with complete enthusiasm (see chapter 10).

For the female religious communities, the tides of change proved equally corrosive, since few were able to see in the theology of lay activism any role for segregated religious society. The fact that most sisters in Oklahoma were engaged in nursing and teaching—activities that brought them into contact with a wide range of laymen—led many of them to conclude that the era of hierarchically ordered communities was over. Some also lamented the fact that their community was insufficiently concerned with the social ethic, leading many to renounce their vows and return to secular life. The statistics for the losses suffered by the religious communities during the 1960s tell their own tale (see chapter 11).

The final two chapters, 12 and 13, seek to address the changing role of the laity during the 1960s. It is clear that Oklahoma Catholics, many of them recent migrants from other parts of the United States, had an extremely positive view of the council's proceedings and endeavored to bring the vision of an empowered laity to life. Ironically, this did not always translate into a specifically "Catholic" countercultural idiom. Instead, many came to conceive of the role of the conciliar Catholic as being that of a Christian raised in the Catholic tradition who was obliged to come to judgments on important moral issues based principally on a reading of his or her own conscience. The inevitable tension that this raised with more traditionally minded Catholics is amply demonstrated in chapter 13, but hostility was not confined to the truly vocal conservatives. Many people found the attitude of diehard proponents of change hard to take, particularly when no aspect of parish life escaped their scrutiny.

The saga of Oklahoma's renewal process throws a revealing light on how one group of midwestern Catholics in a comparatively progressive diocese responded to the Second Vatican Council. In so many areas of Catholic life, the changes were profound enough to excite disquiet in a wide section of the community. That this diocese avoided the conflicts that erupted in many others is testimony to the "permissive" quality that most observers attributed to Victor Reed. "His faith was strong enough to afford him the realization that, despite present anxieties and tensions, and in spite of the failures and foibles of bishops, priests and laymen, it is the Lord's promise that he will guide the Church until the end of time," one priest declared shortly after the bishop's death in 1971:

He was aware of and proud of his being permissive, trying to apply the words of the second century scholar Origen that to err on the side of leniency is far better than to err on the side of harshness. Bishop Reed was fond of saying that while men have many rules, God, in the final analysis, really only has one: adult people, are free to make their own decisions and along with this freedom goes the sure destiny of having to accept the responsibility for all their consequences. Bishop Reed made every effort to challenge the adulthood of all the people he dealt with. He always presumed people's maturity, so that in the fullness of their freedom they could make their own choices and take the responsibilities of their own actions, rather than being able to blame the Church, the Bishop, the establishment, or the parish. . . . More than anyone I know, Bishop Reed fulfilled the definition given by Cardinal Newman of a gentleman[:] a gentleman is one who inflicts no pain. In more than 12 years as a bishop, and in over 40 years as a priest, I have never heard of an incident where he embarrassed anyone. He always tried to relate to people, even in a disciplinary situation, fully aware of the beauty of their human dignity. . . . Perhaps the quality that most greatly impressed me was his constant joy and gladness. He was glad to be alive, to live where and when he did, and to carry out the responsibilities that were his.[38]

In this respect, if in no other, Victor Reed was truly a Vatican II bishop.

38. Sermon of Revd. Thomas L. O'Toole, September 12, 1971, Reed Papers. Reed's "gentlemanly" reputation was all the more remarkable for the criticisms heaped upon him by many of his subordinates, clerical and lay. More than one priest has testified that while the official cause of death might have been reported as a heart attack, "heartbroken" might better have described his condition in 1971. Gier, interview.

part one

Before the Council,
1905–1957

chapter 1

The Roman Way

Early Life, 1905–1934

> *These dangers, viz., the confounding of license with liberty, the passion for discussing and pouring contempt upon any possible subject, the assumed right to hold whatever opinions one pleases upon any subject and to set them forth in print to the world, have so wrapped minds in darkness that there is now a greater need of the Church's teaching office than ever before, lest people become unmindful both of conscience and of duty.*
>
> Leo XIII, Encyclical on Americanism, *Testem Benevolentiae*, January 22, 1899

"Frankly, I had never considered any other career," Victor Reed reminisced in 1963. "I wanted to be a priest from as far back as I can remember, and that was when I was about 10 years old."[1] Such conviction was very much the product of the world into which the future bishop was born, a world that was in a state of flux. Leo XIII's assertion of papal authority in 1899, coupled with fresh waves of Catholic immigrants in the early decades of the twentieth century and a consequent revival of anti-Catholic prejudice, produced a Church that stood apart from the American mainstream and celebrated its "otherness." Catholic identity was a badge of honor and the Catholic parish a haven in a hostile world.

The Reed family's experiences differed somewhat from those of many Catholic immigrants. Victor Reed's father, Victor Larue Reed, was raised in a Protestant household in Pennsylvania, where he developed an interest in

---

1. *Oklahoma Courier*, March 22, 1963.

the region's nascent oil industry and qualified as an engineer. As local oil-fields were exhausted, skilled personnel moved west, in Victor Larue's case to Montpelier, Indiana, a small hamlet incorporated in 1871, where the discovery of local oil deposits had caused the population to swell from nine hundred in 1890 to five thousand in 1896. In Montpelier, Victor Larue met Henrietta Mary Collins, the Canadian-born daughter of Irish immigrants from County Clare. By the time of their marriage, Victor Larue had been received into the Catholic Church and on December 23, 1905, their eldest child, Victor Joseph, was born in Montpelier.[2]

The Reeds would not remain long in Indiana, however, as news of the discovery of major oil deposits in the Oklahoma Territory provoked a great migration of oil industry operatives from the older fields of the Midwest to the seemingly remote and economically backward region of the Great Plains. The towns of Tulsa and Muskogee experienced dramatic increases in population over the next decade as the Glenn Pool field achieved peak production of 117,440 barrels of oil per day in 1907.[3] Such prospects were too attractive to ignore and Victor Larue moved his family, including a daughter, Mary Veronica, and a second son, Collins Gerard, to Bald Hill, Oklahoma, in 1910.

Bald Hill, to the south of Tulsa in Okmulgee County, was an oil camp marking a new stage of development of the Glenn Pool. Conditions were primitive. The economy of Bald Hill was dominated by the saloons and brothels that served the many single men who resided there. Nor can medical facilities have been particularly advanced, judging by Henrietta's decision to stay with her sister in Texas on the occasion of the births of her two youngest children, John Joseph in 1912 and Paul Joseph in 1914. Several years later, the family settled in the nearby town of Mounds, where they would remain until finally moving to Tulsa. Victor Larue worked in the Oklahoma oil industry for thirty-five years: for the Skelly Oil Company, the Producer's Oil Company, and Samedan. During the 1920s, he developed a flow head that prevented an excessive flow of oil from a well during drilling, but he failed to get a patent for it. In working in Oklahoma's oil industry Victor Larue enjoyed an unusual opportunity to see his co-religionists in positions of authority. A sizable minority of oilmen—including W. K. Warren, Joseph

2. "A Short History of Montpelier," www.netusa1.net/~dwalkerw/monthist.html; Reed, Reed Family History; diocesan biographical record on Victor J. Reed, September 10, 1930, Reed Papers. The evidence for Victor Larue's Protestant upbringing comes from an informal conversation with Father J. Paul Donovan.

3. Glasscock, Then Came Oil, 140–43, 165–67; Morgan and Morgan, Oklahoma, 153–56.

The Reed children in 1920, when the future bishop was fourteen. From left: Victor, Veronica, Collins, Joseph, and Paul.

LaFortune, E. C. Constantin, and D. F. Connelly—were Catholics, as were the first three presidents of Tulsa's Exchange National Bank. "If the story of Tulsa is indeed the story of oil," argues Thomas Elton Brown, "then the story of Tulsa Catholics is the story of Tulsa Catholic oilmen."[4]

Although Catholics dominated the economic life of Tulsa, they remained very much an excluded minority throughout Oklahoma and experienced a ghetto existence similar to that of their more numerous coreligionists further east. There was, nevertheless, one important difference. By virtue of their early arrival, the Irish had secured a solid lock on both the priesthood and the episcopate of the American Church. In Oklahoma, however, the clergy

4. Reed, Reed Family History; Reed, conversation; Brown, *Bible Belt Catholicism*, 20.

was heavily Belgian (as late as the 1920s, it was possible to hear only Belgian and Dutch clerical accents at the altars of many Oklahoma parishes). The Diocese of Oklahoma[5] had been raised from an apostolic vicariate to a diocese in 1905, at the urging of Theophile Meerschaert, the Belgian-born vicar apostolic of the Indian Territory, who brought in many of his fellow countrymen to serve the new parishes. Their Catholic constituency included German farmers in the west and northwest of the state, many Osage, Quapaw, and Potawatomi Indians, and sizable—and ethnically diverse—minorities in Oklahoma City and Tulsa, all of whom more or less vigorously proclaimed their loyalty to the Catholic Church.[6]

Even before the coming of statehood in 1907, Meerschaert had moved his residence from Guthrie, the territorial capital, to Oklahoma City, which would become the state capital in 1910. Here he worked to build up Catholic institutions. St. Anthony's Hospital in Oklahoma City—in operation since 1898—was joined in 1914 by St. Mary's Hospital in McAlester, and Benedictine colleges were set up in Shawnee (for men) in 1915 and Guthrie (for women) in 1916. Nor was juvenile education neglected. By 1916, there were fifty-one private and parochial Catholic schools in operation, although most Catholic children continued to be educated in the public school system. Bishop Meerschaert continued to make visits to his far-flung flock to maintain their steadfastness in the faith. Such reassurance was greatly needed in the face of constant financial worries and the antipathy of anti-Catholic lecturers and newspapers.[7]

Loyalty to the Church was inculcated in Victor Reed at an early age. In Bald Hill the nearest church was at least fifteen miles away (which, depending on the roads, could be as much as a three-hour journey in each direction), but no matter what the weather the family would set out every Sunday to fulfill their Mass obligation.[8] Belief in God was associated with the virtues of honesty, integrity, and good citizenship. Henrietta Reed proved to be an especially important influence. An accomplished pianist, she instilled in her son a love of classical and Irish music. She also placed great stress on dinner with white linen tablecloths, the appropriate silverware and china, and proper etiquette, something that enabled Victor to display an ease in select company that would stand him in good stead as priest and bishop. At the same

5. From 1930 to 1973, it was styled the Diocese of Oklahoma City and Tulsa.
6. Brown, *Bible Belt Catholicism*, 7–13; Halpine, interview.
7. Brown, *Bible Belt Catholicism*, 30–55; White, ed., *Diary of a Frontier Bishop*.
8. *Oklahoma Courier*, March 22, 1963.

time, the young Reed displayed his own brand of boyish high spirits. As a youth, he persuaded his sister Veronica to climb into the tub used to get water from a well and both narrowly escaped falling into the well. He was also fond of fishing (a pastime he carried into adulthood) and of riding a horse owned by the family. Oklahoma was a cattle-raising environment, and the Reed children would watch with interest as herds of longhorns were driven across their land, sometimes almost onto the front porch.[9]

Such days of freedom were much reduced in 1912, when the Reed family moved to Mounds and the seven-year-old Victor was sent away to St. Joseph's College in Muskogee, run by the Brothers of the Sacred Heart. The brothers oversaw an intensive regimen of study little different from that of a Catholic seminary. College sessions extended from September to May, with only a short break at Christmas, and students were expected to devote seven and one-half hours to study every day, except Thursdays and Sundays. All incoming and outgoing mail was scrutinized by the college director, and gifts of food were forbidden except at Thanksgiving and Easter. Some recreation—in the form of baseball, football, and athletics—was permitted, but the emphasis was clearly on formation—both educational and moral. As the college's 1912 catalogue explained, a teacher could best assist a pupil by "repressing his youthful vivacity through a wise system of discipline and . . . by overcoming his indolence and indifference through coercive measures, kindly yet firmly applied."[10]

The constraints imposed by St. Joseph's helped cement a close bond between Victor and his sister Veronica. Every Thursday afternoon he would visit her at nearby Nazareth Academy in Muskogee. The Reed family maintained contact with their offspring; every month Victor Larue rode his motorcycle over muddy roads to take his children out to dinner. During the summer, the demands on the children were relaxed. They were allowed to sleep late and stay up late and played games of leapfrog, cowboys and Indians, and cops and robbers, the laughter from the Reed house being audible across town. On the Fourth of July they went to ice cream socials and listened to Mexican bands.[11]

The outbreak of the First World War in August 1914 disturbed the rela-

9. Markey, reminiscences.

10. Reed, Reed Family History; Reed, conversation; *Catalogue of St. Joseph's College, Alamo Heights, 1912*, St. Joseph's College, Muskogee File, box 95.2, Archives of the Catholic Diocese of Tulsa (quotation on 6).

11. Markey, reminiscences.

tive calm in which most Oklahoma Catholics had lived. In the Midwest, sympathy for the Allied cause was lukewarm at best, but in the case of Oklahoma, the bishop and a substantial portion of the clergy of the Catholic Church were citizens of the nation whose neutrality the German Empire had chosen to violate. Bishop Meerschaert took an active part in Oklahoma's Belgian Relief Fund, and several priests made no secret of their pro-Allied sympathies. When President Woodrow Wilson took the fateful decision to enter the war on the side of the Allies in 1917, Oklahoma Catholics moved speedily to demonstrate their patriotic credentials. While the Knights of Columbus opened a recreation hall for soldiers at Ft. Sill, Catholic women's organizations sewed bandages for the Red Cross and Catholic clergy helped organize Liberty Loan drives. Even in the cloistered environs of St. Joseph's, Reed may well have been exposed to the urgings of Church leaders that Catholic teachers persuade their pupils to join the Oklahoma School Children's Patriotic League, whose motto was "My country, may she ever be right, but right or wrong, my country."[12]

Despite such patriotic undertakings, anti-Catholic agitation resurfaced in Oklahoma during the early 1920s. The failure to exempt sacramental wine in the state's newly enacted "Bone-Dry Law" prompted the Church to initiate a test case in October 1917, arguing that the legislation interfered with the free exercise of religion. When the lower courts upheld the law's constitutionality, the Church appealed the case to the state supreme court, which in May 1918 required that the law contain an exemption for religious agencies that used wine in their services.[13] This success only galvanized the Church's critics and prompted the defeat of Catholic oilman James McGraw of Ponca City in the race for Republican national committeeman, largely on the basis of his religious affiliation. Anti-Catholicism extended to the classroom and the school playground, as Catholics became the targets of abuse and even violence.[14]

Church leaders recognized that they could no longer afford to remain detached from events in the political arena. In 1921, an alliance of workers and farmers selected as their candidate for governor John C. Walton, mayor of Oklahoma City, whose wife was a parishioner at Our Lady of Perpetual Help Catholic Church. The alliance also endorsed the two Catholic judicial incumbents running for election. Although its platform of economic reform

12. Brown, *Bible Belt Catholicism*, 56–63.
13. Ibid., 65–87.
14. Ibid., 91–102; Debo, *Prairie City*, 166–67.

might well not have appealed to wealthy Tulsa Catholic laymen, they acknowledged that Walton was the only viable anti-Klan candidate.

In 1921, the diocese established a state branch of the National Conference of Catholic Men to ensure high Catholic turnout in support of Walton and to oppose a proposed constitutional amendment requiring children to attend public school until at least the ninth grade. Moreover, the vicar-general of the diocese instructed Oklahoma priests to see that every eligible Catholic was registered to vote in the Democratic primary and on the Friday before polling called every pastor to inform him of the candidates favored by the Church, information that was then dispersed informally by trusted parishioners. The strategy paid dividends in the election of Walton, although his subsequent term in office was tumultuous and he was later impeached and removed from office.[15]

Such a sequence of events can only have reinforced the belief among Oklahoma Catholics that their security rested in separatism and community solidarity. Political alliances were matters of convenience and were not intended to undermine the integrity of the religious enclave. This philosophy was sustained by Bishop Meerschaert's successor after Meerschaert's death in 1924 at the age of seventy-six. The new bishop, Canadian-born Francis Clement Kelley, had enjoyed a close relationship with the state of Oklahoma for some years as a result of his leadership of the Catholic Church Extension Society. Headquartered in Chicago, Extension directed money and personnel to rural Catholic communities that lacked the means to maintain a parish, and Oklahoma had been a major beneficiary of its assistance.

Kelley swiftly took his diocese in hand, making visitations to all parts of the state and talking with non-Catholics about the importance of religious toleration. At the same time, he emphasized the importance of missions, instituting a special monthly collection to raise funds for this purpose. In Kelley's first year, five new religious orders—the Viatorians, Holy Ghost Fathers (who worked with African Americans), Augustinians, Precious Blood Fathers, and the Redemptorists—established themselves in the diocese. Although Al Smith's presidential campaign in 1928 aroused latent anti-Catholic feeling, Kelley did succeed in curbing somewhat the hostility of Oklahoma Protestants toward the Catholic Church.[16]

15. Brown, *Bible Belt Catholicism*, 103–19. For the wider context of the Walton election, see Goble, "Oklahoma Politics and the Sooner Electorate," 146–50.
16. Brown, *Bible Belt Catholicism*, 124–51; Gaffey, *Francis Clement Kelley*.

THE SEMINARIAN

Victor Larue and Henrietta watched with satisfaction the budding vocation of their eldest son. The cost of pursuing such an undertaking evidently concerned them, however, particularly given that Victor's attendance at St. Joseph's had cost $200 per year, and they consequently turned to their parish priest, Father Joseph Van Eyck, a Belgian missionary priest who had come to Oklahoma in 1908. Van Eyck then appealed to the diocese to bear the costs of Reed's education at St. John's Seminary in Little Rock, Arkansas, citing what he perceived as Reed's call to a religious vocation and the fact that he came from a good Catholic family.[17]

Religious formation in the American seminary system would subject Reed to an essentially Roman discipline. From the 1870s onward, successive popes had sought to institute uniform standards for seminaries throughout the Catholic world and reduce the authority that local ordinaries enjoyed over them. Further steps in this direction occurred in 1924, when Pope Pius XI reinforced the Roman monopoly on biblical studies by requiring all professors of sacred Scripture to hold degrees from the Pontifical Bible Institute or the Pontifical Bible Commission in Rome and imposed a requirement on bishops to submit triennial reports on all seminaries in their dioceses.[18] St. John's certainly conformed to the new standards. Opened in 1911, it was operated by diocesan clergy rather than by a religious teaching order, and despite its comparatively small student body, it was a frequent destination for Oklahoma seminarians, who were then exposed to its emphasis on home missions and catechetics.[19]

Seminary life during the 1920s was characterized by a continual emphasis on personal piety and separation from the world. Leslie Tentler has described conditions at Sacred Heart Seminary in Detroit, where seminarians were virtually segregated, subject to prohibitions on leaving the seminary grounds

---

17. White, *The Souls of the Just*, 324; Revd. Joseph A. Van Eyck to "Right Reverend and Dear Monsignor," September 8, 1924, Reed Papers. A year later, the Reed family moved to Tulsa, where Victor Larue and Henrietta would remain for the rest of their lives. While Van Eyck's letter in the Reed papers is most explicit, Reed's niece has the impression that Victor Larue was quite well off by the time the family moved to Tulsa in 1925; the family had nice clothes, domestic help, and the newest vehicles. Indeed, Henrietta Reed once asked her husband if he would buy her a $300 dress she had seen in a fashion magazine. When he answered that he would if she really desired it, she replied that she did not—she merely wished to see if he would have been willing to purchase it for her! Markey, reminiscences.

18. White, *The Diocesan Seminary*, 67–73.

19. Ibid., 303, 309–10.

or receiving visitors without permission, and liable to expulsion for such of-
fences as smoking, drinking, dancing, or attending unauthorized commercial
amusements. Similar policies of social isolation prevailed at almost all the nation's Catholic seminaries. Seminarians were generally required to wear the
cassock and Roman collar—at least in their final two years—to emphasize the
reality of their future vocation and expected to pursue a rigorous program
of spiritual discipline that included daily Mass, weekly confession, and non-
liturgical devotions, including meditations on the Sacred Heart of Jesus, the
Way of the Cross, and rosaries in honor of the Virgin Mary. "The seminarian," writes Tentler, "had few outlets—other than sports and furtive gossip—
for his restlessness and resentments. He was not much encouraged to dwell
on the emotions that sometimes disturbed his peace of soul. . . . He was expected rather to overcome these difficulties by prayer and acts of will, and by
hewing closely to seminary regulations."[20]

Seminary instruction was intended primarily to provide future priests with
a sound knowledge of church doctrine so that they might profitably instruct
the laity, and most seminaries emphasized dogmatic and moral theology over
instruction in pastoral care. St. John's was no exception, though it made its
students' lives a little more arduous with a 5,215 class-hours requirement, the
highest of all the nation's Catholic seminaries. "It was a pure lecture system
with all textbooks in Latin, modeled after monastic life," declared one former seminarian who studied at the seminary during the 1940s. "In no way
was it geared for parish priests and secular life."[21]

Few seminaries demonstrated great interest in contemporary scholarship.
Latin continued to be the principal language of instruction for dogmatic theology, and many seminaries continued to use Adolphe Tanquerey's *Synopsis
Theologiae Dogmaticae,* published in 1894. After theology, most seminaries
devoted the bulk of their time to sacred Scripture and Church history, with
comparatively little attention to canon law. Again, St. John's stood out by
virtue of its minimum requirement of seventy hours of canon law, the low-
est figure for all American seminaries. Many educators complained that seminary classes were often "overtaught" and required too much memorization
and too little private study, but despite this Reed displayed strong academic
proclivities. On only two occasions did he fail to achieve at least a cum laude

20. Tentler, *Seasons of Grace,* 372–76 (quotation on 374); White, *The Diocesan Seminary,* 341–45.
21. Robert J. Brousseau, "My Quest for Freedom," in Brousseau, *A Dying Breed of
Brave Men,* 174.

(the exceptions were a Latin course, a weakness he always admitted, and a course in pastoral theology). His best subjects proved to be apologetics, philosophy, sacred Scripture, Church history, and dogmatic theology.[22]

One option available to bishops for their more intellectually gifted seminarians was to send them abroad, either to the Catholic University of Louvain (with which Oklahoma enjoyed a singular relationship, given that its first bishop and many of its serving priests were graduates) or to the North American College in Rome. In 1926, Reed raised with Bishop Kelley the possibility of going to Louvain. Admitting his weakness in Latin, the young seminarian nevertheless maintained that the university would be a good place in which to improve it and acquire other languages. Kelley was sympathetic but had no available funds. Eight months later, life in an American seminary was evidently not rewarding enough to deter Reed from trying again. This time, Kelley indicated that he wished his younger priests to acquire a facility in Spanish and hinted that it might be better for Reed to attend the South American College in Rome. If he went to Louvain, Kelley concluded, he would have to be willing to spend his vacations in Spain. Only in May 1928 did Reed finally receive permission from Kelley's vicar-general to proceed to Rome to complete his education.[23]

The North American College in Rome grew out of a recommendation of Archbishop Gaetano Bedini after a visit to the United States in 1853 for the better cultivation of a Roman spirit among American priests, and it won the enthusiastic backing of Pope Pius IX. The college opened in December 1859, with twelve students from eight dioceses. Early life for these students was distinguished by strict discipline and a focus on clerical propriety, with little suggestion that they were being trained for a peculiarly American ministry. The college enjoyed limited financial support from the American bishops, although wealthy laymen were persuaded to contribute to its upkeep, and only in 1884 was responsibility for its administration transferred to a board of American bishops.[24]

Until the mid-1920s, many of the elements of student life retained the old emphasis on clerical discipline. Martin Doherty, who went there in 1923, de-

22. White, *The Diocesan Seminary*, 363-70; Grades of Victor J. Reed from St. John's Seminary, Arkansas, 1925–1928, Reed Papers.

23. Victor Reed to Bp. Francis C. Kelley, August 8, 1926, Kelley to Reed, August 27, 1926, Reed to Kelley, May 1, 1927, Kelley to Reed, May 5, 1927, Msgr. Gustave Depreitere to Reed, May 8, 1928, Reed Papers.

24. White, *The Diocesan Seminary*, 91–99.

scribed tomblike rooms in pastel gray with dull red concrete tiles on the floor
and a bare minimum of simple furniture, a refectory open to the air throughout the year so that students were obliged to wear birettas and capes while
dining, and a regimen of spiritual disciplines that included rising at 5:30 a.m.
each day for prayer, meditation, and celebration of the Mass. Nor was the academic life easy, with four hour-long lectures every weekday at the Urban College of the Propaganda, a mile from the American College, classes of as many
as five hundred students, and periodic scholastic disputations, all conducted
in Latin. It could be an exhausting regimen for even the brightest student.
Student life improved somewhat in the early 1920s with the installation of an
American-style coffee machine, a laundry, and a central heating plant, this last
addressing a very real problem facing students during the winter months.[25]

The American students presented a study in contrasts that often confused
their Roman hosts. "There was a spirit of comradery about them," commented Doherty on his arrival, "that you could feel somehow even though it was
but a spirit. It glowed and sparkled in the air as they exchanged views and
counter-views, repartee and reminiscences. You would know for certain that
these young men would stand by one another to the very jaws of hell." Naturally diverse in ethnic backgrounds, as befitted Catholic America, they were
equally diverse in social origin. Doherty's circle included a music teacher, a
former diplomat, a prizefighter, a butcher, and a native-born Irishman studying for an American diocese. Although they performed well in their classes
compared to students from other national colleges (they usually carried off the
prize of the Hebrew medal), they rarely paraded their knowledge, emphasized
a democratic spirit in their relations with those around them, and tended to
ridicule ceremonial forms that had no relation to any specific religious rite.[26]

It was to this community that Victor Reed came as a midwestern back-
woodsman in the fall of 1928. The college was then presided over by Father Eugene Burke, a former navy chaplain popularly known as "the Skip-
per," who had become vice rector in 1921 and rector in 1925. A tall but portly
priest, Burke was a strong proponent of athletics for the seminarians, and his
plans for a new college building (subsequently undermined by the Great Depression) included a playing field and handball and tennis courts.[27] For one

25. Doherty, *The House on Humility Street*, 70–71, 82–83, 91–93, 101–4, 122–25; McNamara, *The American College in Rome*, 498–500.

26. Doherty, *The House on Humility Street*, 73, 74–79, 97–100.

27. McNamara, *The American College in Rome*, 482–83, 510–12. For Burke's support for
athletic exercises as vice rector, see Doherty, *The House on Humility Street*, 128–30.

whose life had been spent in Oklahoma, Rome must surely have been a liberating experience. "No doubt your trip was most pleasant and at the same
time most instructive," a Texas acquaintance wrote to Reed just after his departure for Europe. "For I believe you learn more by observation than any
one I knew [sic]."[28] Reed found the North American College a congenial
working environment. He must have been acquainted with, if not directly involved in, the Blessed Isaac Jogues Mission Unit, set up in December 1925 at
the urging of Aloysius A. Horn of Toledo, which sought to organize a program of missionary prayer, study, and support. Prayers were regularly offered
before the statue of Our Lady in the college gardens, and money was raised
through intramural lotteries and auctions. On Thanksgiving Day 1928, just
after Reed had reached Rome, the mission unit brought Maryknoll priests
James A. Walsh (the founder) and Francis Ford to the college to speak on
the theme of mission.[29]

Reed was also in Rome for the signing of the Lateran Pact three months
later, which established the Vatican City State to guarantee the spiritual sov-
ereignty of the pope. It marked a new era in papal relations with the outside world, of which Pope Pius XI would take full advantage.[30] There is no
evidence that Reed paid much attention at the time to such external events,
being focused instead on pursuit of his ordination. Other students at the
American College had a similarly inward focus. "Holy Orders!" commented
Martin Doherty a few years earlier. "What could be more interesting to us?
Hadn't we left our homes in America and come to live in this foreign land
just to receive that sacrament? It was the goal towards which we were moving, hour by hour and day by day."[31] Reed passed swiftly through the minor
orders, being ordained a subdeacon on July 14, 1929, and a deacon on October 27 of that year.[32] That fall, Bishop Kelley visited Rome and invited him to
accompany the bishop on a visit to the Vatican, for which he was duly grateful.[33] On December 21, 1929, Victor Reed was ordained a priest for the Diocese of Oklahoma. He felt his new calling intensely. "I am trying to say mass

28. Revd. Ed McCullough to Victor Reed, September 8, 1928, Reed Papers.
29. McNamara, *The American College in Rome*, 507–8. Both men later became bishops.
Walsh was arrested by the Chinese Communists in 1949 and not released until the 1970s.
Francis Ford was murdered in Korea in 1950.
30. Ibid., 516–17.
31. Doherty, *The House on Humility Street*, 233.
32. Diocesan biographical record on Victor J. Reed, Reed Papers.
33. Victor Reed to Bp. Francis Kelley, April 9, 1930, Reed Papers.

at the principal shrines in Rome," he wrote to Monsignor Gustave Depreit-ere in March 1930, "and go out every Thursday and Sunday to the various churches."[34] He hoped to be allowed to remain in Rome for another year to try for a doctorate, but in April he received a summons to return, as Bishop Kelley was experiencing a distinct shortage of priests, and in the summer of 1930 the twenty-four-year-old priest left Rome for Oklahoma.[35]

THE NEW PRIEST

In 1928, when Reed left Oklahoma, the overall economic outlook gave an illusive sense of calm. The prosperity of the 1920s, however, was uneven-ly distributed, with the primarily agricultural regions of the United States (including Oklahoma) suffering from persistently low prices for their prod-ucts and recurring drought. By the time Reed returned in 1930, a general economic malaise had descended, which had particularly dire consequenc-es for the agricultural and oil-producing sectors of Oklahoma's economy. Dust storms blanketed wheat-growing western Oklahoma, while slumping prices for all agricultural commodities pushed farmers' incomes to their low-est level in many years. The proportion of tenant farmers—who constitut-ed the overwhelming majority of the state's farmers in this period—also fell dramatically during the 1930s, and many of those abandoned farming and left Oklahoma altogether.[36] The Depression's impact extended to all sectors of the economy, with the collapse of the oil industry proving particularly damaging to the Catholic Church. "Most of the [Catholic oilmen]," Bishop Kelley reported in 1932, "in fact all of them to my certain knowledge have lost two thirds of their fortunes."[37] Parishes that had expanded during the 1920s on the strength of the oilmen's contributions now found themselves with an accumulated debt of $750,000. Many parishes also lost their funds in closed banks. Parochial schools experienced a decline in enrollments, while the Knights of Columbus lost 50 percent of their membership. One wom-an who renewed her subscription to the diocesan newspaper in March 1932

34. Victor Reed to Msgr. Gustave Depreitere, March 4, 1930, Reed Papers. Reed's cor-respondence does not indicate where or by whom he was ordained.

35. Victor Reed to Bp. Francis Kelley, April 9, 1930, Kelley to Reed, April 26, 1930, Reed Papers.

36. Hale, "The People of Oklahoma," 65–69. See also Debo, *Prairie City*, 206–27; Worster, *Dustbowl*, 99–138; Gregory, *American Exodus*.

37. Kelley to Abp. Arthur J. Drossaerts, February 22, 1932, quoted in Brown, *Bible Belt Catholicism*, 153.

stated that her husband had worked only fourteen days in the past eighteen months.[38]

During the early years of the Great Depression, Reed served as an assistant pastor to Monsignor Gustave Depreitere at St. Joseph's Cathedral in Oklahoma City.[39] Only five months after his appointment, however, the churches of Our Lady of Perpetual Help in Oklahoma City and Holy Family in Tulsa were elevated to the status of co-cathedrals, while St. Joseph's, a small parish church that would have been costly to expand, was affiliated with the Basilica of St. Mary Major in Rome and became known as the "Old Cathedral." The change reflected Bishop Kelley's desire to extend to Tulsa— a city he much preferred—equal episcopal dignity, without the multimillion-dollar burden that a new cathedral would have implied. This "forecasts the eventual uplifting of the State into two dioceses," exulted the diocesan newspaper, but it would be forty years and three subsequent episcopates before that long-desired goal was realized.[40]

The rector of St. Joseph's was no ordinary priest. A nephew of Bishop Theophile Meerschaert, Depreitere came to the United States in 1895 and spent twenty years as a pastor in Enid, where he supervised the erection of churches at Billings, Lenapah, Goltry, and Marshall. In 1905, at the age of thirty-four, he was appointed vicar-general (a post he held for fifty-six years) and served as interim administrator of the diocese on the death of his uncle in 1924. Appointed to St. Joseph's in 1920, he remained there until his death in 1961 at the age of ninety. Under Depreitere, St. Joseph's, which had been erected in 1904, was extensively renovated, with new altars in Italian green and white marble, a new tabernacle, and a large crucifix for the sanctuary. Two of his assistants during the 1930s were destined to become bishops themselves. One was Stephen A. Leven, who served first as auxiliary to the archbishop of San Antonio, then as bishop of San Angelo in western Texas. The other, of course, was Reed.[41]

Reed undertook a variety of duties during his time at St. Joseph's. In May 1931, he was master of ceremonies at a celebration for the fifty-year min-

38. Brown, *Bible Belt Catholicism*, 152–57; *Southwest Courier*, March 5, 1932.

39. Msgr. John B. Dudek to Reed, September 11, 1930, Reed Papers.

40. *Southwest Courier*, February 7, 1931. At the time of his death, Reed was contemplating the division of his diocese, but this did not occur until during the episcopate of his successor, John Quinn.

41. St. Joseph's Old Cathedral Welcome Pamphlet, 1985; White, *The Souls of the Just*, 213.

istry of the Benedictine Dom Ildephonse Lanslots, a former pastor of the cathedral, whom the diocesan newspaper described, with pardonable exaggeration, as a well-known theologian. A month later, Reed sang the Mass of Exposition at the annual Invalids' Mass, where "invalids in wheelchairs and on stretchers filled the whole length of the main aisle and doctors and nurses knelt in pews nearby to administer aid."[42] The following year, he was responsible for the missal class for the laity held on Wednesdays and Fridays at St. Joseph's School, and in October he celebrated the Solemn High Mass of Requiem before the mausoleum of Bishop Meerschaert at Fairlawn Cemetery in Oklahoma City. [43] Reed also received his first extraparochial responsibility when Bishop Kelley appointed him the censor of the *Little Flower Magazine*, published by Oklahoma City's Carmelite Fathers, in 1932.[44]

The political crisis caused by the Great Depression brought into the governor's mansion the indefatigable populist Democrat William H. (Alfalfa Bill) Murray, who was succeeded in 1934 by E. W. Marland, an oil millionaire and philanthropist who had lost his fortune in 1930. More open than Murray to the expansion of government regulation and planning favored by President Franklin Roosevelt, Marland established a state planning and resources board and persuaded the state legislature to allow greater cooperation with New Deal agencies.[45] Many Oklahoma Catholics, however, remained ambivalent toward the New Deal. Critical of Roosevelt's foreign policy toward Russia and Mexico, Bishop Kelley even lent unofficial support to 1936 Republican presidential nominee Alfred Landon. At the state level, Oklahoma Catholics backed Governor Marland, in part because of his generous contributions to Catholic schools, hospitals, and parishes. They also achieved a coup in 1935, when, despite strong anti-Catholic propaganda, John Frank Martin was elected mayor of Oklahoma City by eighty votes out of twenty-nine thousand cast, with strong support from the city's black neighborhoods where Martin's wife had taught catechism in the homes of parishioners.[46]

To discuss the Catholic response solely in terms of state politics, however, would be misleading, given the absence of a two-party system in Okla-

---

42. *Southwest Courier*, May 23, June 20, 1931.

43. *Southwest Courier*, April 16, October 29, 1932.

44. Bp. Francis Kelley to Reed, October 22, 1932, Reed Papers.

45. Morgan and Morgan, *Oklahoma*, 122–32; Goble, "Oklahoma Politics and the Sooner Electorate," 154–59; Bryant, "Oklahoma and the New Deal."

46. Brown, *Bible Belt Catholicism*, 158–69. On national Catholic attitudes toward Roosevelt's foreign policy, see O'Brien, *American Catholics and Social Reform*, 86–96.

homa for much of this period, as well as the comparatively small number of Catholic voters. In his 1931 encyclical, *Quadragesimo Anno*, Pope Pius XI had condemned individualism *and* collectivism in contemporary society and affirmed the need for the redemption of the propertyless proletariat through Catholic social action. He also acknowledged the need for state reform of flawed institutions, though only in cases where no solution could be reached at lower levels of association.

Quadragesimo Anno was warmly received by many Catholic leaders who, as the Depression wore on, increasingly turned to Washington for solutions to the economic crisis. Foremost among the reformers was Monsignor John A. Ryan, who headed the Social Action Department of the National Catholic Welfare Conference during the 1920s. Born in rural Minnesota, Ryan developed an interest in economics and, as a professor at the Catholic University of America, interested himself in the cause of industrial democracy. By 1932, he was recognized as *the* Catholic voice among the band of New Dealers who helped set policy. The midwestern Catholic bishops who controlled the National Catholic Welfare Conference increasingly came to embrace the activist state philosophy propounded by Ryan and his associates. Thus, through Kelley's diocesan newspaper, Oklahoma Catholics learned of the condemnation of the open shop by Bishop Joseph Schrembs of Cleveland and Schrembs's support for unionization, a living wage, and social insurance. They were also treated to an extended discussion of *Quadragesimo Anno* and, at the end of 1931, an attack by Ryan on the indifference of public officials to human suffering.[47]

An election year brought Catholics' attention closer to home. In January 1932, the diocesan newspaper profiled Father James Cox of Pittsburgh, who would become one of the clerical heroes of the union movement in western Pennsylvania. After leading a Jobless March from Pittsburgh to Washington, D.C., which demanded $5 billion in relief expenditures, Father Cox became the first Catholic priest to be nominated for the presidency, on the ticket of the Jobless Party. His running mate was an Oklahoma surgeon and thirty-second degree Mason, V. C. Tisdall of Elk City.[48]

Although the universal economic suffering inflicted by the Great Depression helped many Americans of diverse religious backgrounds to view

---

47. O'Brien, *American Catholics and Social Reform*, 17–21, 47–50, 120–49; *Southwest Courier*, March 21, May 31, June 6, November 14, 1931.
48. *Southwest Courier*, January 16, August 27, 1932. On Cox and his impact on Pittsburgh Catholicism, see Heineman, *A Catholic New Deal*, esp. 11–33.

each other in a more sympathetic light, the earlier defeat of Al Smith in 1928 had served to harden the Catholic "ghetto mentality," with Catholic identity and unity in the face of Protestant opposition once again becoming of paramount importance.[49] "How could any church have any claim to Divine Guidance if its doctrines fell short of perfection?" demanded one *Southwest Courier* reader in January 1931. "Thoughtful persons of every creed must rejoice in the fact that there is one force in the world today that refuses to submit its self [*sic*] to the pressure of so-called modernism. Each century shall bring forth new modernisms but only the unchanging truth of Christ's gospels and teachings shall endure unto eternity."[50] A *Southwest Courier* editorial of September 1931 sought to explain why Catholics were unable to share in the liturgical life of the Protestants among whom they lived: "However unsociable and unfriendly it may appear, we cannot worship with heretics in their churches. . . . It would be an acknowledgement that they and their religions are as pleasing to God as we and our Church, the Church and the only Church He commanded all mankind to hear. We cannot be indifferent to this command and by our presence at their services treat other religions as if they were the equal of the Catholic Church."[51]

Instead of joining the march to interdenominational understanding, many American Catholics proposed to bring their fellow citizens back to membership in the One True Church by means of evangelical witness as passionate as that manifested in any Protestant revival. Their instrument for achieving this would be a new lay apostolate—Catholic Action.

CATHOLIC ACTION

One of the earliest forms of Catholic Action was the Catholic Evidence Guild, founded by Frank Sheed in London in 1918. In 1927, Stephen Leven, a seminarian from Oklahoma studying at the American College at the University of Louvain, visited London, where he experimented with the guild's method of street preaching. Rather than confront often-hostile listeners or "win" arguments with them, Catholic Evidence Guild members sought to demonstrate how Catholic truths "completed" what many listeners already believed and to achieve a genuine dialogue, though always with the aim of eventual conversion. Branches of the guild were organized in New York City

---

49. On the 1928 election, see Lichtman, *Prejudice and the Old Politics.*
50. *Southwest Courier*, January 24, 1931.
51. *Southwest Courier*, September 12, 1931.

in 1928 and three years later in the Catholic Diocese of Albany. In October 1931, Leven, by then an assistant priest at St. Joseph's Old Cathedral, persuaded Bishop Kelley to invite Frank Sheed to speak at St. Anthony's School of Nursing on "Outdoor Speaking for the Church." Six hundred people attended the session and fifty expressed interest in participating.[52]

While Leven drew up plans for Oklahoma's Catholic Evidence Guild, his ordinary was already giving thought to a more comprehensive program. In January 1932, Edward Carr of the Knights of Columbus in Chickasha, Oklahoma, had written to Kelley, praising Sheed's visit and Leven's evident enthusiasm for such work. The bishop needed to take a bold initiative, Carr concluded, in order to shock the majority of Catholics out of their current complacency. Kelley thanked Carr and assured him that his suggestions were in line with Kelley's own thinking on the matter.[53] A week later, he requested the priests of the diocese to subscribe to *Catholic Action*, a periodical then being produced by the National Catholic Welfare Conference, so that they might become acquainted with the initiatives and programs of Catholic Action.[54]

Kelley's interest in the role of the laity increased when he learned of a special parish apostolate founded at St. Margaret's parish in Narbeth, Pennsylvania, after the presidential election of 1928. By designing its own information pamphlets in nonconfrontational language directed toward the sort of questions Protestants tended to ask—"Is the Catholic Mind hide-bound?" or "Are only Catholics saved?"—it achieved remarkably positive feedback, even from local Protestant ministers. Significantly, the Catholic Information Society of Narbeth was a lay apostolate, albeit under the overall supervision of the pastor.[55]

The first example of Catholic Action in Oklahoma, however, depended very much on the contributions of participating priests, particularly Stephen Leven, who was to be one of Victor Reed's closest associates throughout his life. Eight months Reed's senior, Leven was born near Blackwell, and was one of the first two native-born priests to be ordained for Oklahoma, in June

52. Leven, *Go Tell It in the Streets*, 23–25; *Southwest Courier*, January 24, October 31, 1931.

53. Edward Carr to Bp. Francis Kelley, January 19, 1932, Kelley to Carr, January 22, 1932, Catholic Action File.

54. Bp. Francis Kelley to "Reverend and dear Fathers," January 26, 1932, Catholic Action File.

55. Maurice S. Sheehy, "Reaching the Unreachables in a Parish Lay Apostolate: A Study of Catholic Action in Action," *Ecclesiastical Review* 86:3 (1932): 288–91, Catholic Action File.

1928. In August of that year he became an assistant priest at St. Joseph's, where he remained for four years.

On April 11, 1932, Leven addressed a crowd on the lawn of the Oklahoma City courthouse. "This is the first time that a Catholic priest has ever given street talks in the South and West," the *Southwest Courier* proudly declared, "and [Leven is] perhaps the first priest to inaugurate a series of open-air addresses in the United States."[56] The following week, Reed took the spotlight, his topic "The Infallibility of the Pope." The audience of 150 people showed great interest, besieging him with questions ranging from the biblical authority for purgatory and the remuneration of priests to topics more pertinent to his theme, such as the mechanics of papal elections, the question of when the pope was coming to America, and why he was not doing something about the present world crisis. For the rest of the summer Reed and Leven alternated as public speakers. In May, Reed addressed "Do Catholics Worship Mary?" and in June "Do Catholics Worship Idols?" while July's topic involved the weighty "How Shall We Know What to Believe?"[57]

When Leven moved to rural Bristow as pastor in 1932, he achieved striking results. Between May and October 1933, three priests delivered 140 talks in nine towns and communities and distributed five thousand pamphlets. At the end of the summer they launched a "Catholic Revival Movement," a series of talks over a one-week or two-week period, which included prayers, hymn singing and general recitation of the Lord's Prayer. They also operated two religious vacation schools for non-Catholics, one for children only and one for women and children. In September 1934, the Bristow Catholic Evidence Guild reported that 273 non-Catholic families were seeking Catholic instruction. John Frank Martin, the future mayor of Oklahoma City and the first Catholic layman in the United States to be a street preacher, gained experience in Bristow. In Oklahoma City the guild continued to train lay speakers but saw little activity in 1933 and 1934. Its brand of street evangelism appealed much less to the retiring Reed than to the extrovert Leven, but it still must have had an effect on the former. While its end might be conversion, its approach was somehow much more "American" and ecumenical than American Catholicism had previously undertaken.[58]

Bishop Kelley had no intention of leaving the future of his diocese en-

56. Leven, *Go Tell It in the Streets*, 26–27; *Southwest Courier*, April 16, 1932.

57. *Southwest Courier*, April 23, May 7, June 18, July 23, 1932.

58. Leven, *Go Tell It in the Streets*, 28–36; "The Catholic Evidence Guild," September 10, 1934, Reed Papers; Brown, *Bible Belt Catholicism*, 176–80.

tirely to the Catholic Evidence Guild. Early 1934 brought a rash of reports of committed Catholic Action movements arising in Spain, Germany, and England.[59] Kelley responded by issuing a call for a Catholic Action Congress to take place in Oklahoma City in October of that year, which Reed helped to organize.[60] At the opening liturgy, Amarillo Bishop Robert Lucey preached a stirring call to Catholic Action. "When you volunteer to work under the guidance of the organized Catholic Action," he told congress participants, "you are showing a spirit that is more selfless, more ready to do the thing you are told to do . . . when you volunteer your services in an organized social work agency you are doing the thing probably in a more intelligent and better organized way."[61]

In his keynote address, Bishop Kelley warned that he did not regard his successes in the preceding ten years as cause for complacency. Improved finances, more priests and churches, and better relations with non-Catholics could not begin to compensate for the laity's neglect of their sacramental obligations or failure to give their children a Catholic education. "Do you not realize," thundered Kelley, "that your own example is a far more powerful persuader than the eloquence of a thousand priests? Give us a devoted, practicing, and exemplary laity, and the conversions will come not by tens but by tens of thousands. . . . You are what you were ten years ago, a timid minority, fearful to ask for what is yours in right and justice, giving ground before an advancing force that you think is bent on attacking you, but which as a matter of fact, is only wondering why you are afraid of it. Shake off this inferiority complex."[62]

Kelley's address was followed by extensive discussion of specialized Catholic Action ministries. Stephen Leven opened the debate by reminding his listeners that it was necessary to go to places where non-Catholics congregated in order to effect conversions. Street preaching generally attracted a respectful audience in small communities in western Oklahoma where lives were simple, there were few material distractions, and Protestant spiritual-

59. *Southwest Courier*, February 24, March 3, May 26, 1934.

60. Leven, *Go Tell It in the Streets*, 37; *Southwest Courier*, October 13, 1934.

61. "Catholic Action Congress, Oklahoma City–Tulsa Diocese, in Oklahoma City, October 10th–11th, 1934," 3–9 (quotation on 8), Catholic Action File, Archives of the Catholic Archdiocese of Oklahoma City. Lucey had been in Amarillo less than six months when he attended the congress. Saul Bronder insists that Lucey's enthusiasm for Catholic Action in no way implied that he wished to give real authority to the laity. See his *Social Justice and Church Authority*, 49–50.

62. "Catholic Action Congress," 16.

ity was of varying quality. Most non-Catholics took religion seriously and were ready to listen quietly and ask serious questions. In such a setting the guild's emphasis on universal Christian truths could pay dividends: "The Catholic speaker, therefore, can find some of his most successful arguments in the appeal to Catholic doctrines which his non-Catholic listeners hold sacred and the demonstration that these are really Catholic doctrines which the Catholic Church has always taught." In four communities where Leven had preached, non-Catholics had directly requested the holding of services or Sunday schools. His work also improved life for the Catholic minority in such communities. A storekeeper in Terelton—the only Catholic in her community—recounted how Leven's presence had led to people who had previously avoided her store coming in to make purchases. She also noted that the community now had a vacation school that attracted twenty-one Protestant children, of whom fifteen were now saying the rosary.[63]

Speeches on behalf of more indirect methods of communication came from Fathers John J. Walde of Corpus Christi parish in Oklahoma City and Edward Lodge Curran of the International Catholic Truth Society. Walde, a veteran of Catholic radio broadcasting since 1925, praised it as the best medium available to allay anti-Catholic prejudice and expose non-Catholics to Catholic doctrine. The Church, he said, had initially underestimated its value, but few would now deny the impact of the Catholic Hour or the influence of broadcasters like Father Charles Coughlin, then riding a crest of national popularity.[64] "There can be no question," Walde concluded, "that the Catholic Hour is doing one of the finest works of Catholic Action today."[65] Curran attributed a similar potential to the increasingly sophisticated Catholic press, both in renewing the faith of lukewarm Catholics and inspiring the non-Catholic with knowledge of eternal truths. "Remail Every Catholic Newspaper" should be the motto of every priest and layman, Curran suggested, especially if Catholic newspapers all contained an easily read dogmatic page devoted to the doctrines, morality, and history of the Church. In the spirit of the Narbeth movement, Curran also put in a word for effective pamphleteering, grounded in such propositions as the notion that the Bible is in the Catholic Church and the Catholic Church in the Bible.[66]

63. Ibid., 21–30 (quotation on 28).
64. On Coughlin, see Tentler, *Seasons of Grace*, 319–29, 332–42; Brinkley, *Voices of Protest*.
65. "Catholic Action Congress," 51–56 (quotation on 53).
66. Ibid., 62–69.

While the work of conversion was of great importance, Catholic Action also demanded a deliberate personal transformation of its practitioners. A growing Church, Father Daniel Lord, S.J., told the audience, was a mixed blessing if it led to a sense of spiritual alienation. In America, the phenomenon of the growing parish had denuded the Mass of its essentially familial qualities in favor of a hurried weekly routine. Many Catholics lacked the sense of gratitude and belonging that had characterized parish life during the nineteenth century. Catholic Action looked to revive that sense of belonging, which was why it repudiated the current trend toward national organization in favor of a parish-centered life. Cradle Catholics and converts both needed to feel that they were wanted and that their participation was essential to parish life, beginning with their direct participation in the words of the Mass. Pastors should recognize that need, Lord insisted, and tell the laity that they must work *with* them. "I say, Father, sometimes they are not sure that you want them in Catholic Action. And Catholic Action will never make a success until they know that you love them and want them as your faithful workers."[67]

Father James Rooney from Sapulpa echoed Lord's concerns in his discussion of the Catholic Action study club. The Liturgical Movement that had preceded Catholic Action, he pointed out, had been intended to recall the laity to their privilege and duty of participating in the liturgical worship of the Church:

We have imbibed to some extent the doctrine of rugged individualism into our religious life. . . . The spirit of individualism is seen in the multiplicity of popular devotions among us, and to the relegating of the public worship of the Mass to a secondary position. Even the Mass itself is most often valued merely as a private devotion. . . . Religious shrines, too often encouraged and advertised by the Catholic papers, offering rewards, mostly of a temporal nature, seem all too popular. . . . We may boast of our increasing attendance at the Holy Hour and the First Friday devotions, but at the same time must complain of lack of cooperation in promoting the material welfare of the parish. We may boast of the number of Communions but at the same time deplore the miserly contributions toward Catholic Charities and for the Propagation of the Faith. . . . In a word, we are to a very great extent selfish Catholics, and rather unpromising soil in which the study club may thrive.[68]

The congress concluded its work by passing resolutions endorsing vacation schools, study clubs, lay retreats, Young People's Sodalities, extension of

67. Ibid., 69–76 (quotation on 74).
68. Ibid., 87–92 (quotation on 90–91).

the Catholic Evidence Guild, promotion of the papal encyclicals on capital and labor, and support for the Legion of Decency.[69] Kelley clearly intended that the congress should have lasting results, and he soon put his priests on notice that they should take Catholic Action extremely seriously:

Do not think, if I am to have the responsibility of filling important places, that I am going to consider seniority only in the matter. Rather do I intend to select men for important posts who have shown ability and willingness to do what is necessary to keep them important. Seniority is taken, too often, as an excuse for laziness. Let me state, with my usual frankness, that I am sorry I ever paid any attention to Seniority's presumption. Be warned ahead that I am bent only on getting things done, and therefore finding those who can do them. Promotions by seniority, as far as they may have been honored as a policy in the past, are now definitely out. I shall try hard not to embarrass my successor with human problems after I am laid away. It is only fair to you all that you should know my mind on this matter. It would be wise now to begin to like the whole Catholic Action program, for it is going through.[70]

His clergy took note. In Ardmore, Father Francis McCreedy reported that his parish had started an inquirers' class on Mondays and Fridays and two study clubs—one studying the Mass through the Campion-Horan Manual and the other devoted to religion and economics. Across Oklahoma, a drive to encourage every Catholic to subscribe to the diocesan newspaper was taken up with enthusiasm.[71]

As Reed approached his thirtieth year, he found himself exposed to a new and potentially radical strain in American Catholicism, one calculated ultimately to subvert the Roman model with which he had grown up. Though the Catholic Action movement still subordinated the laity to clerical oversight, the initiative in lay spirituality had begun to pass into the hands of laymen. Those who would later denounce Reed's laissez-faire stance as bishop tended to blame the climate of the 1960s for the change in direction, yet the seeds of this transformation had been sown during the early 1930s.

CONCLUSION

Little in the early life of Victor Reed hinted at what was to come. His progress from Catholic school to seminary and ordination mirrored that

69. Ibid., 93–97.

70. Diocese of Oklahoma City and Tulsa, Directions of the Bishop to the Clergy on Catholic Action, October 24, 1934, Diocesan Congress of Catholic Action File.

71. Revd. Francis D. McCreedy to Bp. Francis Kelley, November 1, 1934, Diocesan Congress of Catholic Action File; *Southwest Courier*, November 10, 17, 1934.

of countless priests of the Catholic Church in the United States during the late nineteenth and early twentieth centuries. Perhaps most significant for the future was the setting of Oklahoma. Nowhere, not even in Tulsa, could Oklahoma Catholics ever find themselves living in the insulated and self-contained world of immigrant Catholicism, but were rather constantly obliged to engage with the non-Catholic world on its own terms. Like many southern Catholics, they felt the sting of anti-Catholic prejudice, whether in the form of the overt bigotry of the Ku Klux Klan or the more subtle prejudice of the Protestant ascendancy. While Victor Reed was subject to the discipline of Rome, his upbringing in the rural Midwest and the Belgian influences present in the Diocese of Oklahoma prepared him for something very different in the years ahead.

chapter 2

A Youthful Apostolate

The Heyday of Catholic Action,
1935–1957

Just as a young man leaves home to go to a Maryknoll Seminary because he believes that it is through a missionary life that he can best fulfill his destiny, which is to be a saint, so a person in CFM [Christian Family Movement] should in time see his vocation as union with God in and through the family apostolate. There is no sanctity for the layman without his witness in the lay life to which he is called, and there is no lasting witness unless there are deep roots in the divine life. Just as in the real order grace and nature are never separate, so also are the apostolate and sanctity joined in holy wedlock.

Denis J. Geaney, O.S.A., *CFM and the Priest*

During the early years of the Great Depression, Bishop Kelley had felt obliged to restrict overseas activities by his priests. In 1932, he instructed them not to request funds for a vacation in Europe and to keep their domestic vacations as brief as possible, not least for the sake of good public relations.[1] As the decade wore on, however, the bishop felt a renewed imperative to send some of his students to the American College at Louvain, and Stephen Leven and Victor Reed were obvious candidates for such advancement. Both had shown considerable academic promise during their seminary days (Reed at Rome and Leven at Louvain); both had been involved in the Catholic Evidence Guild and sympathized with Kelley's goal of bolstering Catho-

---

1. Bp. Francis Kelley to "Reverend and dear Fathers," January 26, 1932, Catholic Action File.

lic Action in Oklahoma; and both were part of the new breed of Oklahoma-bred Catholic clergy who sought to effect the transformation of the Church in rural America.[2]

Reed's experiences at Louvain were to be very different from his first visit to Europe, for the American College at Louvain embraced a critical engagement with biblical studies and philosophy not to be found in Roman educational institutions. "The outstanding characteristic of true science," declared one observer of the Louvain scene in 1939, "is that no race, no country, no people nor any particular group of people have a monopoly upon it. In other words science is universal. So is the Catholic Church. Thus at Louvain the universality of science is allied to the universality of Faith and through this alliance the university becomes supranational. Close relations between scholars in the field of social sciences and particularly in the branch of historical sciences is absolutely essential."[3]

By the dawn of the twentieth century, Louvain's Faculty of Theology had become a center of the "historical critical method," which, though rooted in the tradition of the Church and anchored in Scripture and historical texts, saw all theology as developmental just as human understanding was developmental, and which understood theology as existing primarily for the sake of pastoral ministry. The appointment of Albert Cauchie as professor of church history in 1895 helped promote a scientific approach in the fields of exegesis, patristics, and church history, while the 1923 launch of the *Louvain Theological Journal* bore witness to the strength of the faculty's exegetical tradition.[4]

While the University of Louvain traced its origins to the late Middle Ages, the American College at Louvain was scarcely eighty years old. Founded in 1857 at the initiative of Father Peter Kindekens, vicar-general of the Diocese of Detroit, it had trained European clergy for mission work in the United States. It secured the blessing of Pope Pius IX in 1868 and affiliated with the university as a house of studies in 1897 so that its students might attend university lectures. By 1907, it had prepared seven hundred priests for

2. Reed later claimed that Kelley planned to build a minor seminary in Muskogee and intended him to be its rector, though, on the face of it, Leven would have been the more likely candidate. *Oklahoma Courier*, March 22, 1963.

3. Strakhovsky, "The Louvain Concept of a University," 179.

4. Ibid., 179–83. I am indebted to Professor John Dick of the American College at Louvain for information on the college and other matters pertaining to the University of Louvain.

American missions and produced fifteen archbishops and bishops, including Oklahoma's Theophile Meerschaert.[5]

The devastation wrought by the German occupation of Belgium during the First World War raised doubts about the future of the college, particularly as the need for foreign-born priests for the United States lessened. At the initiative of the college's fourth rector, Monsignor Jules De Becker, however, funds were raised in the United States to reconstruct the college, and an American was appointed as vice rector. From 1933 to 1935, that position was held by Father Gerard Schellinger of Wyoming, the first Catholic priest to volunteer as an army chaplain during the First World War and the founder of the college's Catholic Evidence Guild. After 1920, most of the college's students were American-born candidates for advanced degrees and by 1930, the college boasted eighty-six students.[6]

Viewed as a highflyer, Stephen Leven was appointed vice rector in succession to Father Schellinger in 1936 and later taught courses in liturgy and pastoral theology.[7] In addition to Reed, the Oklahoma contingent at the American College formed a tight-knit circle that included Don Kanaly, destined to be one of the leading figures in American Catholic Action during the 1940s, and Raymond Harkin (a lawyer turned priest), vicar-general to Victor Reed from 1964 to 1971. The friendships cultivated at that time would endure for the rest of Reed's life.[8]

Unlike Leven, Reed enjoyed a comparatively leisured existence. Living in a house owned by the college that overlooked its extensive grounds, he reveled in its tennis courts and baseball diamond. He was a great walker, often taking fourteen-mile hikes after lunch.[9] His personal recreation was not confined to the vicinity of the college. In company with three other American priests, he motored through France, saying Mass at Ars and visiting (for the second time) the tomb of his patron below the ruins of the Abbey of St. Victor near Marseilles. He undertook a trip to Monte Carlo but assured Bishop Kelley that neither he nor his companions understood the game![10] A rather

5. Cross and Zoeller, *The Story of the American College*, 3–35.
6. Ibid., 36–42.
7. Leven, *Go Tell It in the Streets*, 39–41; Cross and Zoeller, *The Story of the American College*, 43.
8. Reed and Harkin both assisted at a solemn High Mass conducted by Leven at the college on the occasion of his mother's death in Oklahoma. Leven, *Go Tell It in the Streets*, 43.
9. *Oklahoma Courier*, March 22, 1963.
10. Victor Reed to Bp. Francis Kelley, January 12, March 16, 1936, Reed to Beulah Stafford, December 9, 1936, Reed Papers.

different incident was *not* confessed to his episcopal mentor. While traveling with another friend through southern Germany, eastern France, and Switzerland, they were stopped and the car searched by the French customs. Their surreptitious supplies of cigarettes cost them 578 francs (about $30), an incident that left both of them, the future bishop admitted, "mad as hell."[11]

Reed also attended the 1936 ceremonies surrounding the return to Belgium of the body of Father Damian, missionary to the lepers of Mokolai, who had died on that island in 1889. "The procession was the finest I have ever seen," he later recounted. "There were thousands of persons in it—plenty color in costume and flags—bands and banners." Later that year, he visited Germany to attend a friend's ordination, a pleasant experience "except for too much Nazism—it was just before the elections." He was also invited by the American Legion to deliver prayers at the only American cemetery in Belgium, where 350 soldiers killed during the final offensives of 1918 were buried.[12]

The future bishop enjoyed his academic studies but made slow progress in French. As his academic workload increased, he confessed to a greater sense of pressure. "Steve and I are both quite busy now preparing for the fateful days of July," he told Bishop Kelley in 1937. "It's always about this time I begin to consider how much happier life would be without exams."[13] The crisis passed and Leven and Reed were both advanced to work on their doctoral theses, which entailed exposure to nineteenth-century philosophy of a decidedly non-Catholic hue. Leven had been encouraged by no less prominent a figure than Fulton Sheen, a fellow student at Louvain during the 1920s, to avoid study of nineteenth-century American liberalism. "Don't waste your time on that," America's second most popular radio priest insisted. "Get into something on Socialism or Communism. That is going to be the apostolate of the future." While Leven turned his attention to the British philosophical anarchist William Godwin, therefore, Reed embarked upon a comparative study of John Stuart Mill and August Comte."[14]

11. Victor Reed to James Coffey, November 9, 1936, Reed Papers.

12. Victor Reed to Beulah Stafford, May 28, 1936, Reed Papers.

13. Victor Reed to Bp. Francis Kelley, May 20, 1937, Reed Papers. Leven was equally eloquent in writing of the oral examinations at Louvain: "If there was ever a place for a nervous breakdown, this was it . . . some few broke down and were given another opportunity to take the examinations at the beginning of the next year. If they failed then, they were 'washed out' of the course." Leven, *Go Tell It in the Streets*, 41.

14. Leven, *Go Tell It in the Streets*, 42, 45-49; Victor Reed to Beulah Stafford, December 9, 1936, Reed Papers.

Reed's years at Louvain also exposed him to the developing thrust of Catholic Action in Belgium. "Our present students," commented Monsignor De Strycker in 1938, "living in a country where social difficulties have for years been a matter of public concern, take an eager interest in Belgian Catholic social action. . . . It is precisely the application of Catholic principles in a Catholic way which our students witness here in Belgium. They learn to understand these principles by seeing them applied in a new but strong organization of Young Catholic Workers, the Jocists, and thus are enabled to go back to their homeland not only knowing Catholic social theory but having seen it in practice as well. Each succeeding generation has its way of adapting the old Louvain spirit to its own new problems. The adaptation changes but the spirit is ever the same."[15]

The Young Christian Workers (YCW) were the brainchild of Father Joseph Cardijn, who himself grew up in a working-class family in Brussels. In 1912, as a young priest, he organized his first youth groups, and twelve years later he formally launched his organization, with ecclesiastical approval, seeking to restore the working classes to Christ. "That," wrote one observer, "is what the YCW is—an organization of young apostles thoroughly imbued with an ardent desire to go out into the world and bring the world back to Christ. They are the shock troops, the men in the front line. They are resolved to do battle for their fellow men."[16]

With its motto "See, Judge, Act," the YCW presented a new sort of apostolate, one that deepened the sense of intimate bonds that linked Christians to the Mystical Body. Specialized social action groups, Cardijn taught, should be formed from people in particular callings and organized on the cell principle, with weekly meetings at which all members contributed observations. The cell leader then laid out the Christian principles that should govern the resolution of the issues under consideration and outlined a plan of action for the following week.[17]

An eloquent American practitioner of Jocism was Father Don Kanaly, who returned to Oklahoma in 1938 and was appointed assistant pastor at St. Mary's parish in Ponca City.[18] Backed by Bishop Kelley, Kanaly organized the first YCW cell in an American diocese, consisting of a grocery clerk, an

15. *American College Bulletin* 31 (July 1938): 5–6.
16. Bernard Schumacher, "The Laborers Are Many . . . ," *American College Bulletin* 32 (July 1939): 38–42 quotation on 40.
17. Gleason, *Contending with Modernity*, 159–63.
18. His name at birth was Donel James Kanaly, but he always went by Don.

office worker, a filling station assistant, a mill worker, a restaurant worker, and an accountant. He also helped organize a number of priests' cells in Oklahoma City and Tulsa, and lectured on YCW in various towns in Oklahoma, as well as in Chicago and New Orleans in early 1939.[19] Though YCW would have limited appeal in the United States, it helped lay the groundwork for both the Young Christian Students (YCS) during the 1940s and the Christian Family Movement (CFM) during the 1950s.

In February 1939, Reed advised Bishop Kelley that he needed three more months to complete his thesis, adding parenthetically, "War talk is heard everywhere now and many people here are persuaded that there will be trouble this year." That spring Monsignor De Strycker decided that the college would accept no new American students for the coming academic year and asked all the American bishops to send enough money to ensure safe passage for their seminarians should war break out.[20] The prevailing gloom was only heightened by news of the death of Pope Pius XI. "Everyone is mourning the death of the Holy Father," Reed reported on February 12, "and I'm feeling it will be hard to replace him with an equally capable man."[21] By the middle of August, however, he had successfully completed the requirements for a doctoral degree, and the following month he sailed for home as German tanks crossed the Polish frontier. Although offered a teaching position at the Catholic University of America, Reed chose to return to his native state. "It was a great honor," he explained a quarter of a century later, "but how could I consider the appointment when there was such a great shortage of priests in Oklahoma?"[22]

THE PASTOR OF STILLWATER

Upon his return, Reed was assigned to St. Francis Xavier parish in Stillwater, the home of Oklahoma Agricultural and Mechanical College (OAMC), now Oklahoma State University. The parish had had a troubled existence since 1933 when the hot-tempered Father Clarence McGinty had taken

19. *American College Bulletin* 32 (July 1939): 43–44; Brown, *Bible Belt Catholicism*, 184–85.

20. Victor Reed to Bp. Francis Kelley, February 2, 1939, Reed Papers; Cross and Zoeller, *The Story of the American College*, 45.

21. Victor Reed to Beulah Stafford, February 12, 1939, Reed Papers. Pius XI died on February 10, 1939. His successor, Eugenio Pacelli, who had been Pius's secretary of state, was elected on March 2 as Pius XII.

22. *Oklahoma Courier*, March 22, 1963.

charge. Parishioners felt that McGinty was too doctrinaire in the way he ordered the business and finance of the parish and wished him at least to keep them apprised of prospective repairs and the disposition of money, whether to pay off debt or erect a new church building. They even went to the extent of organizing an informal committee to represent their views, but received short shrift from McGinty. "The Committee has been informed on several occasions that they carry no authority," its members complained to Bishop Kelley in May 1940, "and that things are going to be done the way he, Father McGinty, wants them to be done. This, to say the least, is very embarrassing to the Committee and to the congregation at large."[23]

Although Kelley reminded the committee members that McGinty had ultimate responsibility for the state of the parish and that the laity enjoyed a purely advisory role, he also recognized that relations between McGinty and his flock had gone beyond the point of no return.[24] A few months later, McGinty was transferred to the chaplaincy of St. Mary's Hospital in Enid, and Victor Reed was appointed as his replacement. By extricating his ordinary from a parochial dilemma, Reed certainly won gratitude, but it would seem that he ranked high in Kelley's affections for his own sake. "You helped to make this 1940 Christmas week of mine better than ever," Kelley wrote at the end of the year. "All I can do is to say, as presumably my ancestors of Kilkenny and Wexford, 'Thank ye, kindly.' O yes, and to pray for you, which I did and continue to do."[25]

Stillwater would experience rapid growth after the Second World War, but when Reed arrived it was still an essentially rural community. While rural Catholic parishes accounted for only about one-fifth of total Church membership in the United States in the 1940s, their small size embodied the community atmosphere favored by Catholic Action activists. Rural parishes fortunate

23. The Church Committee, St. Francis Xavier Church to Bp. Francis C. Kelley, May 2, 1940, St. Francis Xavier Church, Stillwater File, box 80.1, Archives of the Catholic Diocese of Tulsa (hereafter ADT). This incident would seem to bear out the contemporary view of one Catholic sociologist: "The effects of homogeneity, stability and dominance of primary social contacts are seen in the development of a distinctly rural mentality. The technique of developing and sustaining the rural parish must take this into account. Tradition has much greater importance, and change occurs slowly. On any problem rural people like time to ponder; they take a personal interest in local problems and are inclined to think they have both a right and a responsibility to solve them." Hynes, "The Parish in the Rural Community," 114.

24. Bp. Francis C. Kelley to K. D. Greiner, May 3, 1940, St. Francis Xavier Church, Stillwater File.

25. Bp. Francis Kelley to Reed, December 30, 1940, Reed Papers.

enough to maintain a parochial school, moreover, were considered more likely to generate religious vocations than their larger urban counterparts. "Any
practical plan to increase the proportion of rural Catholics," Catholic sociologist Emerson Hynes concluded in 1951, "must start with the rural parish.
Planning is needed to prevent the exodus to the city by helping young farmers to procure land and by educating rural Catholics in their responsibility to
maintain Catholic families in the parish area. Planning is also needed to develop methods of bettering the standard of living of rural people, and to develop
sources of nonfarm income, perhaps through decentralized industry."[26]

Such were the objectives of the National Catholic Rural Life Conference,
founded by Father Edwin V. O'Hara in 1923. The small size of the rural parish was viewed as an asset to the pastor, since he was likely to be far more
intimately acquainted with his parishioners, and the homogeneity of a rural
parish gave its members a strong sense of unity. Families also tended to play
a much greater role in the liturgical life and social action of the rural parish
than did individuals. "In the instruction of children, in sermons, and in social contacts," wrote Hynes, "the pastor can assume a common understanding among his parishioners. Very often to know the common problem is to
know the special problem of all parishioners."[27]

Reed undertook substantial community-building work in Stillwater and
apart from John Van den Hende, the chaplain at the new Stillwater Municipal Hospital, he was the sole clerical representative of the Catholic Church
in the area. His responsibilities included the parish church, a mission in Paw-
nee County, a parochial school with forty pupils, and a chapter of Theta
Kappa Phi at OAMC. When a student remarked to him that his first impression of the parish church was that it was an abandoned building, the rector
undertook a restoration that included new windows and paint. Subsequently, Reed rebuilt the rectory, modernized the school, and raised an additional $30,000, which was invested in war bonds for the future construction of
a new church. The rebuilding of the rectory evoked complaints from some
members of the parish board, still smarting from the McGinty years, but
Reed proved more of a diplomat than his predecessor, holding a substantial
dinner for the board, accompanied by fine wines. When all had eaten and
drunk their fill, Reed announced that it was time to show the members the

26. Hynes, "The Parish in the Rural Community," 101–5 (quotation on 104–5). On
O'Hara and the National Catholic Rural Life Conference, see Dolan, *Some Seed Fell on
Good Ground.*
27. Hynes, "The Parish in the Rural Community," 105–19 (quotation on 111).

work that he had had done on the rectory. By this point, however, all were exclaiming that it was amazing how he had done it so cheaply![28]

In 1940, Stillwater opened a new hospital funded both by the city and the federal government through the Public Works Administration. To run the facility, the city reached an agreement with the Sister Adorers of the Most Precious Blood. While it was hardly unusual for Oklahoma hospitals to be operated by Catholic religious communities, the fact that a largely Protestant municipality was willing to take such a step demonstrated that a considerable reduction in anti-Catholic prejudice had occurred since the 1920s. The new pastor lost no opportunity for opening the door to the local Protestant community even further. "Father made friends with everyone," a history of the Stillwater Altar Society testifies, "and people all over town were proud to call him one. Stillwater once again was a parish that could hold its own." Reed encouraged the altar society to erect a nativity scene, which was well received by the whole community; and he joined the town's ministerial alliance, delivering at least one Good Friday address in a local Methodist church.[29]

While Reed devoted himself to parochial life, others continued the work of expanding Catholic Action in Oklahoma. In May 1940, a Catholic Action congress drew twenty-four priests and sixty-five religious to hear presentations on all aspects of Catholic Action, including the Boy Scouts, Catholic Youth Organization, Newman clubs, vacation schools, and Young Christian Workers.[30] One year later, a 1,200-delegate congress, including 177 sisters and 90 priests, met at Holy Family Cathedral in Tulsa, where their bishop warned of the threat to civilization posed by war and the need for renewal of the faith. The highlight of that meeting was an address by Monsignor Luigi Ligutti, executive secretary of the National Catholic Rural Life Conference, who urged that Catholic Action should shift its focus to the rural areas. The more urban America became, Ligutti warned, the greater the maldistribution of material resources and the more the birthrate declined. "We never say back to the land—we say forward to the land!" he told the assembled delegates. "Cities are the graveyard of Catholicity—the graveyard of democracy." Reed's contribution to the congress, by contrast, was a paper entitled "Catholic Action in the University," in which he argued for the need to keep Cath-

28. Clergy roundtable discussion, June 19, 2005.

29. *Official Catholic Directory* (hereafter *OCD*) (1940), 474–5; "History of Stillwater Altar Society," n.d. (prob. 1956), 9–11 (quotation on 11), Reed Papers; Halpine, interview; *Southwest Courier*, February 3, 1940.

30. *Southwest Courier*, May 25, 1940.

olic ideals alive in secular colleges, since they would provide future recruits for the National Councils of Catholic Men and Catholic Women.[31]

The approach of war had cast its shadow over Oklahoma Catholics as early as September 8, 1940, when every American diocese observed a Day of Prayer for Peace (a three-day period of prayers for peace was conducted at Our Lady of Perpetual Help Cathedral in Oklahoma City).[32] Six weeks before Pearl Harbor, a poll of Catholic priests in the United States still revealed considerable opposition to a shooting war. Among fifty-nine Oklahoma respondents, fifty-four were opposed (91.5 percent) and only two in favor. Such figures unquestionably reflected the sentiments of the laity.[33] The news of Japan's attack on Pearl Harbor was all the more unsettling, but Bishop Kelley wasted no time in rallying his flock. "There is no question as to the justice of this war of defense," he told them. "It was settled when we were attacked. We have entered a just war. Catholics know what that means. They will respond as always and do their duty—all their duty; including unselfish support for their President and Congress."[34] Six months later, Kelley warned a YCW rally in Enid of the need to substitute Christ for Hitler and Mussolini in Germany and Italy, for the state in England and for money in the United States.[35]

War transformed the state of Oklahoma, not least because it soon became a center for military training. In 1942, Oklahomans elected as governor the pragmatic populist Robert S. Kerr, who sought to transform the state from one dependent on extractive industries and agriculture to one with its own industrial base. His contacts with national legislators brought in lavish military contracts, making Oklahoma the eighteenth highest beneficiary among the states, while Tulsa and Oklahoma City saw some of the highest increases in job expansion among America's cities. Army camps, Air Corps training centers, and even naval training stations all formed part of this defense buildup.[36]

31. *Southwest Courier*, April 26, 1941. Twenty years later, Bishop Frederick Freking of La Crosse, president of the National Catholic Rural Life Conference, expressed regret that the Constitution of the Church in the Modern World promulgated by the Second Vatican Council devoted insufficient space to the problems of rural laborers and the pressures on them to relocate to the cities. Yzermans, *American Participation in the Second Vatican Council*, 213–14.

32. *Southwest Courier*, September 14, 1940.

33. *Southwest Courier*, October 25, 1941. Oklahoma Catholics were no less isolationist than their Protestant counterparts before December 1941. See Brown, *Bible Belt Catholicism*, 193–94.

34. *Southwest Courier*, December 13, 1941.

35. *Southwest Courier*, December 6, 1941, May 9, 1942.

36. Morgan and Morgan, *Oklahoma*, 132–36; Goble, "Oklahoma Politics and the Sooner Electorate," 162–65.

The Catholic Church in Oklahoma girded itself for the new war effort as it had done a quarter of a century before, opening social centers for military personnel at Lawton, Oklahoma City, and Muskogee. Later that year, Bishop Kelley authorized the first evening Masses in Oklahoma, in an effort to serve the military population more effectively. Eight Oklahoma priests became full-time military chaplains and a further twenty-five—including Reed—served as auxiliary chaplains, ministering to small groups of servicemen as well as to their parish. The Church participated in the United Services Organization fund drive, and Catholic schools conducted bond and stamp drives, with Tulsa's Monte Cassino School selling $1 million in bonds (a higher figure ✗ than any other school except the University of Notre Dame). In 1943, Catholic Activities of Tulsa (a Catholic Action group for young adults) organized a nine-day series of Masses at Holy Family Cathedral on behalf of servicemen and servicewomen. This proved to be something of an ecumenical initiative, since non-Catholics were invited to join in the novena for peace and the safe return of absent friends.[37]

Throughout the war years, Reed devoted considerable energy to enhancing the life of St. Francis Xavier parish. By the spring of 1942, his parish boasted an altar society of sixty members, a unit of the National Council of Catholic Men (NCCM), and two study groups. An increasing number of Catholic students from OAMC also worshipped at St. Francis Xavier, and all three Sunday services were filled to capacity. Reed made himself available to the students and helped organize a Newman club, which had eighty-five members in 1942. By 1944, the altar society had grown to sixty-five and the NCCM unit to thirty-five, although the Newman club had halved in number, owing, no doubt, to the recruitment of students into the armed forces.[38]

One wartime pastoral problem that confronted priests like Reed was the issue of marriages conducted in haste. Within his own tradition, Reed displayed a willingness to take decisive action that belied his laid-back style as bishop. When one Catholic family with a pending military wedding suffered a death, Reed intervened to reschedule the wedding to take place on the Sunday (when it would normally have been prohibited) before the funeral.[39] Such an occurrence, while poignant, did not present the problems posed by

37. Brown, *Bible Belt Catholicism*, 200–3; *Southwest Courier*, July 18, 1942, December 11, 1943.

38. *Southwest Courier*, April 11, 1942, April 22, 1944; "History of Stillwater Altar Society," 9–11; *OCD* (1941), 486–87; *OCD* (1942), 539–40; *OCD* (1944), 556–57; *OCD* (1945), 564–65; *OCD* (1947), 592–93.

39. Clergy roundtable discussion, June 19, 2005.

hasty marriages across denominational lines.[40] While the *Official Catholic Directory* did not distinguish mixed marriages from Catholic ones in Oklahoma until 1945, the proportion of mixed marriages in the diocese rose from 43.9 percent in 1945 to 54.1 percent in 1947.[41] So concerned were the authorities that the diocesan chancery issued a 1943 directive requiring all Catholic marriages (including those involving a non-Catholic spouse) to have two Catholic witnesses, since there had been a spate of cases in which not even one of the witnesses had been a Catholic.[42]

In June 1942, Reed received a letter from a woman, a member of the United Brethren congregation in Stillwater, who was engaged to a Catholic man. Her pastor, she explained, was concerned about the implications of a mixed marriage and she besieged Reed with questions about Catholic belief and practices, including whether a priest had the power to forgive sin; whether a person had to be Catholic in order to be saved; whether it was obligatory to bring up the children of mixed marriages as Catholics; and what views the Catholic Church held on the Second Birth. Sadly, no response by Reed has been located.[43] Eighteen months later, Father Joseph Woucters at Hennessey (Belgian-born and thirteen years Reed's senior) sought his advice about a Methodist soldier engaged to a Catholic woman, who had applied for a marriage license that expired only two weeks later, before he had even consulted Woucters. Another mother asked him to marry her Marine son to a Hennessey girl while on a two-day furlough. The rules issued by the chancery were confusing, Woucters complained, and he begged to delegate such decisions to Reed as the official military chaplain.[44]

40. In historian Angie Debo's mythical Prairie City (based on her hometown of Marshall, Oklahoma), four members of the graduating high school class were married before graduation and many more were engaged. *Prairie City*, 240–41.

41. *OCD* (1945), 566; *OCD* (1946), 589; *OCD* (1947), 594.

42. *Southwest Courier*, August 21, 1943. Father Paul Donovan gives as his opinion that the Church position on the necessity for the non-Catholic partner in the marriage to agree to raise the children Catholic was observed fairly strictly before 1960. To his knowledge, no priest, even in informal conversation, spoke against the rules that were in place. Most young soldiers wanting to get married during the 1940s were getting married for the first time and so the legislation regarding annulments did not apply. Conversation reported by Father James D. White.

43. Maxine Johnson to Reed, June 6, 1942, Reed Papers.

44. Revd. Joseph M. Woucters to Reed, December 23, 1943, Reed Papers. This was not an issue confined to communities where Catholics were in the minority. Similar problems were reported in urban areas, with one Chicago priest even opining that it might be better if a justice of the peace conducted such wartime marriages. If, as seemed likely, many of

Throughout his pastorate, Reed maintained close connections with the students and staff at Oklahoma Agricultural and Mechanical College. "You have won the complete confidence of the undergraduates," one student told him in March 1941. "I do not think that there is any thing that the members of [Theta Kappa Phi] would not do for you, if you asked them. They are enthusiastically behind all your projects."[45] When Reed left Stillwater in 1947, OAMC President Henry Bennett went out of his way to thank him for all the work he had done with the students.[46]

The college connection also enhanced Reed's ecumenical credentials. He won praise for a spiritual meditation delivered at OAMC, which led the pastor of Stillwater's First Baptist Church not only to applaud Reed's emphasis on the primacy of grace but also to express the hope that he and Reed could grow to be "workers together with God."[47] Reed's educational activities were not confined to the Newman club. In 1946, he spoke on the subject of education for the "Forming the Catholic Mind" lecture series at St. Thomas More Bookstore in Oklahoma City, a series designed to help Catholics better conform their lives as well as their minds to the Catholic way.[48]

Reed's relationship with OAMC also enabled him to secure college premises for the June 1944 meeting of the National Catholic Rural Life Conference. Although the constituency of this body had somewhat diminished since its establishment twenty years before, its insistence that higher birth rates were to be found in rural areas than urban areas continued to exercise a powerful hold on the midwestern hierarchy. An early advocate of organic farming and soil conservation, the conference would later take an ecumenical lead in authoring a statement on the stewardship of the soil and a farmer's obligations to future generations, intended to be signed by persons of all faiths. It encouraged rural dioceses to organize retreats for farm families and to appoint a rural life director; during the 1940s it would oppose efforts on a federal level to abolish the Farm Security Administration.

Concern with the physical needs of rural Catholics did not blind the conference to the need to nourish them spiritually. It set precedents for later liturgical renewal, by arguing the need for a greater emphasis on the liturgical

---

them did not endure, the Catholic party would then be able to contract a valid marriage at a later date. Avella, *This Confident Church*, 53.

45. Edward J. Kirchner to Reed, March 24, 1941, Reed Papers.
46. Henry G. Bennett to Reed, April 15, 1947, Reed Papers.
47. C. Dewitt Matthews to Reed, October 21, 1946, Reed Papers.
48. Mildred Stone to Reed, January 22, 1946, Reed Papers.

year, one that reflected the rhythm of the seasons. In 1950, the Sacred Congregation of Rites in Rome declared St. Isidore to be the conference patron, with provision for his feast to be observed on March 22 (17,530 St. Isidore devotional pamphlets were distributed in 1954). Rural priests were also encouraged to celebrate Rogation Days at the end of April and say Mass in fields, barns, and farmhouses (again, a precursor for modernization of the Mass in the 1960s). Extension of access to the sacraments in isolated rural areas, begun by Father Howard Bishop's Catholic Home Missioners of America in 1939 in the Archdiocese of Cincinnati, was advanced by the Glenmary Fathers, who brought the Gospel to those parts of America that had yet to see much evidence of Catholic penetration.[49]

Forty-five Oklahoma priests attended the 1944 meeting, and many non-Catholic college faculty expressed great interest in the proceedings. It fell to Reed to deliver a message of welcome on behalf of the ailing Bishop Kelley, and Monsignor Ligutti was once again in Oklahoma to deliver his message on behalf of the rural apostolate, with a threefold strategy of caring for underprivileged rural Catholics, converting rural non-Catholics, and encouraging a "forward-to-the-land" mentality. The national government, Ligutti complained, was now more interested in developing industry than assisting agriculture. A new push to develop rural life schools was needed; one that would involve the laity as well as priests and religious, and that would involve greater cooperation with other rural life groups and government agencies. Father Urban de Hasque, the unofficial diocesan historian, suggested that the urban trend in Oklahoma was really only twenty years old and that, in its early days, the Catholic Church in Oklahoma had favored church construction in rural areas. The conference concluded that a diocesan rural life conference should be organized.[50]

THE CALL TO HOLY FAMILY

In November 1944, Oklahoma Catholics acquired a new leader when, as a result of the continued ill health of Bishop Kelley (who would die in early 1948), Bishop Eugene J. McGuinness of Raleigh, North Carolina, became coadjutor bishop. In January 1945, McGuinness was installed in Oklahoma

49. Schirber, "Catholic Rural Life"; Ward, *Catholic Life, U.S.A*, 202–20; Fortin, *Faith and Action*, 277–80.
50. *Southwest Courier*, July 1, 1944; Revd. Urban de Hasque to Reed, August 26, 1944, Reed Papers. See also Hynes, "The Parish in the Rural Community," 121–27.

City at a ceremony at which Archbishop Samuel Stritch of Chicago praised Kelley's role as a Catholic leader. Four days later, in Tulsa, McGuinness reminded those in attendance at Holy Family Cathedral that it was the responsibility of every Catholic to propagate the faith.[51]

A year before Bishop Kelley's death, Victor Reed boldly requested a plum assignment to Holy Family Cathedral in Tulsa (which had fallen vacant following the death of its pastor, Father John T. Hall), where his parents worshipped. "Realizing, however, that the good of the Church is the prime factor involved," the aspiring rector assured the new bishop, "I know that your Excellency will understand that I do not wish to prefer myself to anyone else whom you may judge to be better suited to the responsibility." No doubt to the surprise of some, McGuinness granted his request. Reed remained rector of Holy Family until his elevation to the episcopate eleven years later.[52]

The transfer to Tulsa marked an entirely new phase of Reed's career. If Oklahoma City housed the diocesan machinery, it was in Tulsa that Oklahoma's wealthy Catholic elite resided, and over the next decade Reed was to come to know many of them intimately. Holy Family Cathedral was a suitably imposing structure on the corner of Eighth Street and Boulder Avenue, with an attached rectory and school. Erected in 1914, it had been consecrated in 1925 (after it had become entirely debt-free, as Church law then required) and named a co-cathedral in 1930. It offered a remarkably good fit for the forty-one-year-old Reed, and the local community responded positively. "The people of Tulsa have given me a wonderful welcome," he assured McGuinness a year after his arrival, "and I feel that all things will turn out for the best."[53] In his later years at Holy Family, Reed would often take walks around downtown Tulsa, where he would stop and chat to people, though most agreed that he rarely remembered the names of those with whom he conversed. At Mass, he was a meticulous but slightly abstract celebrant, known for his frequent use of the phrase "Holy Mother, the Church" when he preached.[54]

Holy Family was then the most liturgically advanced parish in the diocese.

---

51. *Southwest Courier*, November 25, 1944, January 13, 20, 1945.

52. Victor Reed to Bp. Eugene J. McGuinness, March 19, 1947, McGuinness to Reed, April 11, 1947, Reed Papers; *Southwest Courier*, April 19, 1947.

53. Victor Reed to Bp. Eugene J. McGuinness, November 2, 1948, Holy Family Cathedral, Tulsa File, box 1.1, ADT.

54. Gallatin, interview. He was also fond of the movies, being happy to take in a Walt Disney production from time to time. Msgr. William F. Stricker to Revd. Charles H. Schettler, September 10, 1971, Reed Papers.

A full-range pipe organ had been installed in 1914 and it had acquired a professional music director, Harry Evans, in 1925. An English-born boy soprano who had sung at the coronation of King George V in 1910, Evans steadily built up a choir composed of members of city parishes and nonmember artists who relished the chance to sing professionally. As the choir grew in size and skill, Evans became more adventurous, introducing such works as the Gounod Mass on Christmas Eve, Dubois's *Seven Last Words* on Good Friday, the Silas Mass on Easter Sunday, and polyphonic Masses by Palestrina and Hassler. In later years, an orchestra drawn from the Tulsa Symphony and the University of Tulsa provided music for the Christmas Eve services. Evans also established a series of children's choirs: the boys from the grade school (the Choristers) sang the Sunday evening devotions; the grade school girls (the Girls' Choir) and high school girls (the Girls' Glee Club) sang the First Friday service; while the high school boys (the Boys' Glee Club) sang the Requiem Service and all the Holy Week services, the latter in Gregorian chant.[55]

As rector of Holy Family, Reed's duties included responsibility for one of the more prestigious parochial schools in Tulsa.[56] For the students of the Reed era, the 1950s were a time of international tension and superpower posturing. At such a time, the rector believed, Christians had an even higher responsibility than usual to identify what was of greatest value to them. In an article in the school paper in 1948, he reflected upon this theme at some length. "If, in life, we make the world mean 'everything,'" he told his students, "fight for everything in it and win, we are only making dying harder. . . . Religion is rejected by too many people today, men and women of the type of the age, because they think it is a gloomy thing and gives them no information about what is to them the greatest question—'how to live.' In reality religion is the one great thing they need, because it alone can teach them the essential lesson of living, by teaching them how to die."[57]

Some parents continued to worry that their children lacked the immersion in Catholic culture that had characterized earlier generations. One mother, with five boys at the school, complained to Bishop McGuinness about the lack of facilities or organization for youth recreation outside school hours,

55. "Holy Family Music as remembered by Bob Greer and Tom Evans," n.d., "Musical Biography of Robert M. Greer, n.d., Holy Family Cathedral Papers, box 1.2, Holy Family Cathedral, Tulsa, Oklahoma; *Southwest Courier*, January 11, 1947.

56. Until 1954, Catholic schools in Oklahoma were formally segregated and it was not until the late 1960s that effective integration of Holy Family School would take place. See chapter 8.

57. *Crusader* 2:4 (1948).

The new monsignor with his family in Tulsa in 1949. Back row, from left: Collins, Edward Markey, Joseph, Victor, and Paul. Front row seated, from left: Julia Reed (Joseph's wife), Mary Ann Reed (Paul's wife), Veronica Markey, and the Markeys' daughter, also named Veronica. Standing in front are the children of Joseph and Julia.

compared with Kansas City, which had a Catholic youth organization with offices and a salaried director. "There is so much more to life than teaching the Catechism to them," she insisted. "They need to be taught to live life right and face problems in the world and as you yourself know, a boy is hard to manage through high school age if entirely in the hands of women. . . . If all of us mothers with large families had more time we would band together and try to learn the way to do things but with middle class families like ours there is no money for help so it is impossible to leave the younger ones and all the work to go out and do this."[58]

58. Mrs. James Cremin to Bp. Eugene McGuinness, July 15, 1953, Holy Family Cathedral, Tulsa File, box 1.1.

Traditional Christian virtues and Catholic piety nevertheless remained fundamental elements of the curriculum at Holy Family School, which maintained a Sodality of Our Lady. "You are part of the world-wide Sodality," a student explained to his fellow sodalists, "which numbers among its members the Holy Father himself, cardinals, archbishops, bishops and thousands of priests and religious, and an enormous militant army of Catholic lay men and women of all nations and all ages. You are privileged to be in the Catholic Faith. Your membership in the Sodality will help you to be a stronger and better Catholic as well as a loyal citizen of the United States."[59]

Sodalists were urged to attend daily Mass, to pray for a sense of calling to the religious life, recite the rosary daily during Lent, distribute Catholic literature, and perform works of Corporal Mercy, such as taking food to the needy or visiting convalescent homes.[60] Other signs of active piety included a Rosary Crusade by the eighth grade class, devoted to the conversion of Russia, and a Lenten Mass Chart for the fourth and fifth grade classes.[61] The latter consisted of photographs of each of the forty-two pupils suspended on strings, above which was placed an image of Christ with his Crown of Thorns. For every Mass a child attended, his or her picture was raised one space up to a maximum of forty. If a child reached the top of the chart, one thorn could then be removed from the picture above the chart.[62]

The Catholic lifestyle was explored in other contexts. In 1948, the Tulsa District of Catholic Youth discussed Christian courtship and marriage.[63] Three years later, Father Vincent McGouldrick addressed the subject of vocation to the religious life with freshmen and sophomores. Many boys thought that they were too stupid to be priests, McGouldrick told them, but this was the wrong attitude. "What would happen," he demanded, "if there were no priests or nuns? Where would the Catholic Church be?"[64] One lay activity that many Church leaders viewed as a vital step on the road to priestly vocation was that of altar boy. In 1956, Bishop McGuinness invested 299 altar boys in the St. John Berchmans Society of Holy Family Cathedral, a body

59. *Crusader* 2:2 (1948).

60. Ibid. The seven Corporal Works of Mercy are (as a paradigm) feeding the hungry, giving drink to the thirsty, clothing the naked, sheltering the homeless, visiting the sick, visiting the imprisoned, and burying the dead.

61. *Crusader* 2:1 (1947).

62. *Crusader* 2:3 (1948). It must be allowed that such devotional exercises may well have been at the initiative of the sisters teaching in the school rather than the rector.

63. *Crusader* 2:3 (1948).

64. *Crusader* 5:4 (1951).

that encouraged altar boys to be faithful in their duties and prayerfully consider a vocation to the religious life. "You who serve the priest at Mass are the church of tomorrow," the bishop assured them, "and on your shoulders will be placed the support of the church."[65]

The catholicity of Holy Family School was tempered by a new sense of inclusion in American daily life. "Even in school," declared the caption to one class picture in the 1958 yearbook, "Sputnik captures a prominent place in the attention and discussion of American citizens. Commercial geography, a class composed entirely of sophomores, furnishes an ideal setting for originality in the expression of opinions based on facts. A modern touch, the use of cartoons, is added to enliven the presentation of material."[66] National, regional, and religious pride was summed up in a 1948 student essay on "Courage": "I was with the doughboys in the first World War and with the G.I.s in the second. I was with Father Dunne when he fought poverty in New York. I have been in all parts of the world. I inspired the Pilgrims to come to America and the Pioneers to go West. I am Courage. When I die out of men's hearts, the world will not be worth living in."[67] The admonition to gain greater knowledge of contemporary social life and its discontents suggested a more sophisticated Catholic community than had been envisaged prior to the Second World War and one, moreover, that was now able to offer its own cultural artifacts to the wider world and have them taken seriously. "Twentieth-century Catholic magazines with modernistic art and current hard-hitting articles are flooding the market," reported a student, noting that no less an authority than Walter Winchell had recommended Fulton Sheen's "The Fifteen Mysteries" in the *Catholic Digest* to all Americans.[68]

Aside from the school, Reed was responsible for the well-being of the entire Holy Family community. An early test of his administrative skills came with the renovation of the cathedral and rectory in 1948, in preparation for the celebration of the golden jubilee of the parish in 1949. Bishop McGuinness, a staunch budgeter, kept a careful eye on proceedings and demanded frequent updates. In his reminders about his abhorrence of "luxury" for the priests who lived at Holy Family, McGuinness indicated that he would con-

65. *Southwest Courier*, December 22, 1956. St. John Berchmans (1599–1621) was a Belgian-born Jesuit novice who died at twenty-two, after having lived a life of great holiness. He was canonized in 1888 and was named the patron of altar boys.

66. Holy Family Cathedral School, *Spires* (1958): 39.

67. *Crusader* 2:2 (1948).

68. Holy Family Cathedral School, *Spires* (1953): 56; Mary Kay Dunn, "Catholic Press, Alive, Truth-Centered," *Crusader* 5:3 (1951).

sider the installation of an elevator for the four-story building to fall into that category. By December 1948, the builders had taken up permanent residence, and Reed reported that he and his assistants had been living under plaster dust for the past few weeks. So chaotic was the repair situation that he even suggested that the Pontifical Mass scheduled for the Cathedral's patronal feast on January 9 be postponed.[69] The decorative changes approved by Reed led one interior designer to comment that he had unusual taste for a man, but they do not seem to have entirely charmed Bishop McGuinness. "Last month," he told his long-suffering secretary of a stay at Holy Family, "there were no towels, this month there was no heat, next month we stay at Christ the King [rectory]."[70]

While pleased with the final results, many parishioners might have welcomed greater consultation about what proved to be a substantial financial outlay. In 1951, the cathedral still owed $135,000, but the rector was unbowed. "I sincerely feel that the debt has done the parish good," he declared. "The people are giving more and working much better. There is much more interest in parish offices and some of the long accumulated lethargy has been shaken."[71] Sometimes, the future bishop's meticulousness could be annoying. Father Bill Ross recalled an occasion when, while an associate priest at Christ the King parish, he asked Reed to check his draft summary of a meeting for which he had taken the notes. To Ross's fury, Reed produced a red pencil and proceeded to go through the draft line by line rather than simply giving a verdict on the content.[72]

One parish ministry that experienced a renaissance was the Cathedral Women's Club.[73] In the apparatus of parish organizations, the club existed to harness the talents of the many active Catholic women connected with Holy Family, but it broadened its membership rules in 1950 to include both the non-Catholic wives of Holy Family parishioners and women who belonged to

69. Bp. Eugene McGuinness to Reed, November 2, 1948, Reed to McGuinness, December 14, 1948, Holy Family Cathedral, Tulsa File, box 1.1.
70. White, "Personal Memories of Bishop Reed"; Clergy roundtable discussion, June 23, 2005.
71. Victor Reed to Bp. Eugene McGuinness, February 12, 1951, Holy Family Cathedral, Tulsa File, box 1.1.
72. Clergy roundtable discussion, June 19, 2005.
73. Reed had personal affection for the Cathedral Women's Club, whose members selected his mother as nominee for Mother of the Year in 1950 and gave him much-needed emotional support at the time of her death in 1953. See Minutes of Cathedral Women's Club, March 2, 1950, Reed to Cathedral Women's Club, January 8, 1953, Holy Family Cathedral Papers, box 4.1.

other Tulsa parishes. By 1957, it included four circles—St. Ann's and St. Teresa's, which were geographic; St. Gerard's for young mothers; and St. Teresa's for businesswomen. The club held monthly meetings and fostered greater devotion to the Blessed Sacrament, maintained the altar and sanctuary, organized social activities, and attempted to further the cause of Catholic Action. "The Cathedral," a summary of one meeting read, "being the only downtown Catholic Church, serves as many non-parishioners as parishioners, particularly for confessions and on Holy Days of Obligation. But it faces a constant loss of members as the business district expands and the older residential areas are abandoned."[74]

The club combined the traditional duties of a Catholic women's organization with outreach to the wider Tulsa community. In 1950, at Reed's request, it conducted a church census and compiled a comprehensive list of practicing Catholics. Reed also recommended the establishment of study clubs to review the text of a new pamphlet, "We Offer the Mass." In 1952, the club furnished a room for the newly established Associated Catholic Charities at a cost of $250. It was also eligible for plenary indulgences, if all its members attended Mass in a body, made their confession, and recited five Our Fathers and five Hail Marys for the special intention of Pope Pius XII.[75]

Club members did not see their role as a purely auxiliary one, but also sought to be representatives of the new spirit of vocal Catholic identity that marked the 1950s. They greeted with excitement the decision of the local television station to broadcast the *Light of Life* program, which allowed various denominations, including the Catholic Church, to present their beliefs to interested viewers, and they successfully pressed for the station to carry Bishop Fulton Sheen's television series, which had attracted almost as much interest as Billy Graham's crusades.[76] Club leaders praised Tulsa's mayor for supporting the decision to dismiss municipal employees on Good Friday so that they could attend religious services, and joined forces with civic decency organizations to protest such films as Roger Vadim's *And God Created Woman*, which had been condemned by the Legion of Decency. "It is very disheartening," Marguerite Gavin told the city manager of Tulsa, "to be-

74. Minutes of Cathedral Women's Club, March 2, 1950, April 6, 1950, "The Cathedral Women's Club—Tulsa, Oklahoma," n.d. (prob. 1957), Holy Family Cathedral Papers, box 4.1.
75. Minutes of Cathedral Women's Club, March 2, 1950, July 23, 1952, September 12, 1957, Holy Family Cathedral Papers, box 4.1.
76. Mrs. J. C. Altman to KOTV Television Station, November 15, 1952, March 4, 1953, Holy Family Cathedral Papers, box 4.1.

lieve the decency of mankind must suffer to afford patrons for the Independent Theatres."[77] Cooperation with the civic authorities extended to matters of civil defense in 1956, when the club agreed to allow the basement of Holy Family to be used to practice how refugees and injured people might be cared for in the event of a nuclear strike. While the Catholic patriotism of the 1950s was carrying the Church in interesting directions, within a decade Catholic pacifism would have become the theology du jour.[78]

Other Catholic groups spoke both to new social trends and old-style devotional practices. An example of the former was the Catholic Business and Professional Women's Club of Tulsa, for which Reed became spiritual moderator in October 1950.[79] The latter was represented by the Legion of Mary, whose first praesidium at Holy Family (Our Lady, Help of Christians) was launched on November 21, 1952, with Father Finton McMahon as spiritual director. Its early activities included placing Mass schedules in hotels, contacting Catholic students in public schools, visiting prisoners in jail, inviting non-Catholics to instruction classes, and conducting parish censuses. By 1954, there were five local praesidia—Holy Family; St. Francis Xavier, Tulsa; St. Anthony's, Okmulgee; St. William's, Skiatook; and the Chapel of the Little Flower, Collinsville—available to form the Tulsa Curia. A separate praesidium for women—Our Lady of Lourdes—was organized in 1957, at Reed's request, to visit patients in hospitals and rest homes, but in 1960, membership in Our Lady, Help of Christians was opened to women, and two years later the Our Lady of Lourdes praesidium was dissolved.[80]

THE EPISCOPATE BECKONS

While Reed fostered the spiritual life of Holy Family, the scope of Catholic Action in the diocese continued to grow, initially through an increased

77. Josephine Middleton to Mayor C. C. Clark and City Commission, April 11, 1955, Marguerite Gavin to Carl Flynn, April 1, 1958, Marguerite Gavin to J. C. Duncan, April 1, 1958, Holy Family Cathedral Papers, box 4.1.

78. Minutes of Cathedral Women's Club, June 13, 1956, Holy Family Cathedral Papers, box 4.1.

79. Anne Curren to Bp. Eugene McGuinness, October 2, 1950, McGuinness to Curren, October 3, 1950, Holy Family Cathedral Papers, Tulsa File, box 1.1.

80. Larry Erman to Revd. James D. White, March 27, 1974, Holy Family Cathedral Papers, box 1.2; Victor Reed to Bp. Eugene McGuinness, October 23, 1956, Holy Family Cathedral Papers, Tulsa File, box 1.2. The Legion of Mary was founded in Dublin in 1921 and combined outreach activities with individual and community prayer. In its own way, it could be considered a form of Catholic Action.

number of branches of Young Christian Students. The focus of meetings like one held for Tulsa high school students in February 1953 was more on personal spiritual growth, Mass attendance, and spiritual reading than on the influence a member of YCS could bring to bear on friends and neighbors, in stark contrast with Bishop Kelley's earlier emphasis on evangelism and the conversion of non-Catholics.[81] Holy Family School had its own YCS unit, which collected food for the underprivileged, observed the triduum for President Eisenhower and Pope Pius XII, took part in a Christmas pageant at Central High School, and sold cookies and candy to raise money for mission work.[82] Perhaps the greatest publicity for Oklahoma's YCS came in June 1953, when Father William Nerin, an assistant at Christ the King parish, accompanied three YCS leaders from Tulsa to the White House to deliver a petition signed by twelve thousand Tulsans pledging two days of prayer for peace in Korea. The delegation met President Eisenhower in person, who told them of his own belief in the power of prayer and asked them to go back home and spread the idea farther afield.[83]

The 1940s marked the high point of the early Catholic Action movements—Young Christian Workers and Young Christian Students. The 1950s and early 1960s were distinguished by a new force, the Christian Family Movement, which attained considerable popularity among Oklahoma Catholics. "The Fifties were a very delightful time but they were also very naive," declares an Oklahoma-born former assistant national chaplain of CFM, "so our work was trying to awaken in Catholics a sense of responsibility for their lives and what was going on around them."[84]

CFM began in the late 1940s as an initiative of Pat and Patty Crowley, who had helped launch the Cana Movement (then known as Family Renewal) in Chicago in 1944 to offer a family apostolate to the new class of suburban Catholics that was emerging in the postwar years. Aiding the Crowleys was Monsignor Reynold H. Hillenbrand, first among equals in Catholic Action in the Archdiocese of Chicago. Since Hillenbrand's understanding of the concept of Catholic Action had been radically enhanced by contact with Father Don Kanaly, the bond between Oklahoma and Chicago was a strong one. The Christian Family Movement, Kanaly told its coordinating commit-

81. *Southwest Courier*, February 21, 1953.

82. Holy Family Cathedral School, *Spires* (1953): 70.

83. *Southwest Courier*, June 20, 1953. Nerin afterward commented that it was one of the outstanding experiences of his life.

84. Halpine, interview.

tee, "is the university of Catholic mothers and fathers. You are educators, and it is your lifelong vocation to develop the mind of Christ in its totality. In doing that you are the reformers of all things. You are the purifiers of art, literature, drama, economics, recreation, marriage and the family."[85]

The extraordinary upturn in marriages and childbearing that characterized the early years of the cold war proved a blessing to the fortunes of CFM. "Family life was not only a mission of the church *to* and for the family," the director of the Family Life Program in New York City observed, "but it was a movement *by* Church families for the Church and for the nation."[86] From a mere twenty-five hundred couples nationwide in 1952, CFM grew to sixteen thousand in 1955 and thirty-two thousand in 1957. At the parish level were action groups—consisting of six couples and a chaplain—and a section—containing the leader couple from each action group. Above this were the federation (diocesan level), the area (a group of federations), and the National Coordinating Committee. Oklahomans played leading roles in the early phases of the Christian Family Movement, including the National Coordinating Committee's program committee, whose first chair couple were James and Peggy Cockrell of Oklahoma City, and its executive committee, whose members included Joseph and Kay Trimble of Tulsa.[87]

In October 1953, a CFM-YCS workshop in Tulsa drew contributions from the Crowleys, the Trimbles, the Cockrells, and Fathers Don Kanaly and William Nerin. Those attending heard the Crowleys explain that they worked for CFM because it was concerned with family-oriented people, because the movement sought to establish the father as bishop of the home, and because it enabled them to travel across the United States and meet many other similarly minded Catholics. "[CFM] brings families closer to one another and closer to God," Patty Crowley declared, "thus establishing the much needed unity." The meeting concluded that new recruits from CFM came largely from active members of YCS, emphasizing the need for coordination between the constituent elements of Catholic Action.[88] The future lay with CFM, Father Nerin later concluded. "I should say that in Oklahoma (where I speak most experientially), whenever you go to NCCIJ [National Catholic Conference for Interracial Justice] meetings or political or social meetings, percentage-wise the greatest number of Catholics will be CFMers. The grass

85. Avella, *This Confident Church*, 39–41. Kanaly is quoted in Burns, *Disturbing the Peace*, 49–50.

86. Kelly, *Inside My Father's House*, 71.   87. Burns, *Disturbing the Peace*, 39–44.

88. *Southwest Courier*, October 3, 24, 1953.

roots support for interracial justice will be given by CFMers. The laymen pushing the liturgy, Cana conferences, couples retreats, lay school boards, adult education classes, YCS groups, are CFMers to a significant degree."[89] Nerin here identified the divisive potential inherent in this latest phase of Catholic Action. As CFM moved away from its family-centered origins toward a more involved social agenda, its members would find themselves more divided over possible solutions and less and less driven by the essentially hostile attitude to the prevailing secular culture that had underpinned Cardijn's original conception. By the mid-1960s, CFM would find it increasingly difficult to keep its members united.

CFM's phenomenal growth, however, was not what principally caught people's attention during the 1950s, for Bishop McGuinness had a far more neutral view of Catholic Action than his predecessor. Known as a "brick and mortar man," as were so many of his fellow bishops in the 1950s, he was a builder who sought to emulate the buoyant, optimistic growth, both in adherents and institutions, achieved by so many of his episcopal colleagues. Having ridden out the Great Depression and the Second World War, Catholic leaders of all persuasions welcomed the promise of the new decade. Conservative prelates like Archbishop James McIntyre of Los Angeles and Archbishop Samuel Stritch of Chicago oversaw substantial expansion. McIntyre raised sufficient funds to erect eighty-three new schools between 1948 and 1953, in a community of 1.5 million Catholics that was adding 1,000 new believers every week, while the Archdiocese of Chicago was generating an average of six to eight new parishes each year from 1948 to 1958, all with schools and large plants. Progressives like Archbishop Joseph Alter of Cincinnati were also caught up in the spirit of the times. Alter oversaw a massive expansion of the archdiocesan elementary and high school system—already one of the most extensive in the nation—and promoted the $5 million renovation of St. Peter in Chains Cathedral.[90]

McGuinness's first priority was the steady expansion of religious vocations and the diocesan institutions they served. During the 1940s, he encouraged the establishment of various burses to provide financial support to men seeking to enter the ministry.[91] He was a "one-person vocation program,"

---

89. William Nerin, "What is CFM?" Xerox copy, CFM Papers, University of Notre Dame, quoted in Burns, *Disturbing the Peace*, 3.

90. A. V. Krebs, "A Church of Silence," *Commonweal*, July 10, 1964, 467; Avella, *This Confident Church*, 79–80; Fortin, *Faith and Action*, 282–83, 322–24.

91. *Southwest Courier*, April 14, August 18, September 15, 1945, April 13, 1946.

one of the products of his drive for priestly vocations later explained, who called on Oklahoma Catholics to contribute not merely their time and money but "their flesh and blood."[92] The bishop was also a constant booster of those who pursued a clerical calling: "[He] was an outgoing, affable Irishman. . . . He was tough, but they all thought he was the greatest guy in the world and he thought they were the greatest guys in the world and used to tell everyone in the world that. He would go back home to Philadelphia and tell [them] that he had the best goddamn priests in the United States."[93]

Young Oklahomans responded to the bishop's appeal. Joseph Dillon, the child of an Irish father and a German mother, raised in Christ the King parish in Tulsa and educated in its parochial school during the 1930s, was inspired by the examples of the Benedictine sisters who taught him and of the assistant pastor, Father Cecil Finn, who organized the school's athletic programs. A protégé of McGuinness, Dillon was sent to the North American College in Rome in 1950.[94] A pious widowed mother raised another high-flyer, Robert Brousseau, after his father died when he was three. Educated by the Augustinian priests of Cascia Hall in Tulsa, Brousseau developed a love of learning and an excellence in sports. Indeed, his friendship with McGuinness began when, on first meeting him, the bishop recalled an occasion when Brousseau had been dismissed from a basketball semifinal game for fighting, an incident McGuinness found humorous. Brousseau attended St. John's Seminary in Little Rock, but lost his promised place at the North American College to Dillon.[95] William Garthoeffner, also raised in a traditional Catholic household in Oklahoma City, attributes his former vocation to the influence of Monsignor John Connor of Our Lady of Perpetual Help Cathedral and his assistant, Father Charles Buswell. Although he initially attended Mount St. Mary's Seminary in Emmitsburg, Maryland (Connor's alma mater), he found the intellectual atmosphere stifling and transferred to St. Thomas Seminary in Denver.[96]

Such men and others recruited through the efforts of McGuinness ensured for the diocese a steady stream of new vocations. Most were intellectually gifted and well versed in the new debates sweeping through the Church,

92. Joseph D. Dillon, "Reflections on My Life," in Brousseau, *A Dying Breed of Brave Men*, 51; Monsignor Raymond F. Harkin, interview.

93. Donovan, interview.

94. Dillon, "Reflections on My Life," 47–53.

95. Robert J. Brousseau, "My Quest for Freedom," in Brousseau, *A Dying Breed of Brave Men*, 164–75.

96. Garthoeffner, interview.

particularly the issue of liturgical reform. Monsignor James Halpine, whose interest in this subject was sparked while he was a seminarian in St. Louis and Rome, became the director of liturgy for Christ the King parish on his return to Oklahoma, where he taught the congregation how to join in the hymns. (This would inspire one parishioner to protest: "Oh, Halpine's in there teaching them to sing again. Let's go to the Cathedral!") Halpine directed the music for the celebration of the fiftieth anniversary of the diocese in 1955, which included a performance of the Kyrie in Greek, and composed a schola for the requiems of deceased priests that was written up in the liturgical journal *Orate Fratres* and so impressed Bishop John Cody that he asked for a copy for use in the Diocese of Kansas City.[97]

On an administrative level, McGuinness was an individualist who preferred to rely on close friends in the diocese rather than officials at the chancery. His secretary (and Reed's future vicar-general), Monsignor Raymond Harkin, once described himself as "the best-dressed chauffeur in the state of Oklahoma." McGuinness's appointment of the inexperienced Father Garthoeffner as chancellor testified to his own desire to micromanage, even though many of the older priests in the diocese viewed the appointment as a mistake. "I don't think he was very impressed with the importance of administrative levels," Garthoeffner concludes today.[98]

Certainly, when McGuinness embarked upon building projects, he kept consultation to a minimum. In February 1955, he announced a campaign to raise $1.5 million to build a junior seminary for the diocese. Dedicated in 1959, after the death of McGuinness, the St. Francis de Sales Seminary was to prove one of the more short-lived and costly investments embarked upon by Oklahoma Catholics. "It was always a financial drain on the diocese," its erstwhile rector admits. "The priests of the diocese never wanted it built, but Bishop McGuinness built it."[99] Even more financially damaging was the authorization that the bishop gave the Tulsa Benedictines to establish a women's college for which they believed they could secure generous lay support. In the early 1960s, Benedictine Heights College was to become one of the *N.B.* diocese's greatest financial liabilities.[100]

---

97. Halpine, interview; Revd. James F. Halpine to Bp. Eugene McGuinness, November 4, 1957, Christ the King Church, Oklahoma City File, Archives of the Catholic Archdiocese of Oklahoma City.

98. Garthoeffner, interview.

99. *Southwest Courier*, February 12, March 19, 1955; Donovan, interview.

100. *Southwest Courier*, April 23, 1955. For details of the financial crisis that resulted from the decline of Benedictine Heights College, see chapter 3.

By 1957, Reed was held in high regard by many of his peers. In 1949, he became a papal chamberlain, and four years later he was raised to the status of domestic prelate.[101] On November 10, 1954, he celebrated his silver jubilee as a priest, with Bishop McGuinness and a hundred priests in attendance. Delivering the homily on this occasion was his old friend Monsignor Stephen Leven, soon to be appointed an auxiliary to the archbishop of San Antonio, Robert Lucey.[102] Reed's relations with his own ordinary, however, were cordial rather than warm. "They were such different personalities," recalls William Garthoeffner, who notes that McGuinness preferred to stay with other pastors rather than at Holy Family Cathedral when he visited Tulsa.[103] Relations were further strained after the bishop requested Reed to review the sisters' proposed academic plan for Benedictine Heights College in 1957. Reed's warning that it was the financial condition of the project, not its curriculum, that should raise concerns was received frostily by McGuinness, who told him to leave such matters to the bishop.[104]

In such circumstances, the announcement on December 5, 1957, of Reed's appointment as titular bishop of Lamisa and auxiliary bishop of Oklahoma came as no small surprise to many in the diocese, though the diocesan newspaper concealed this with aplomb. "Bishop Reed," it declared, "will always be known for his tolerance and his understanding. The clergy will continue to love him, as they have always. The laity will know him as a friend, a prudent servant of God."[105]

Within a month of Reed's appointment, however, McGuinness was admitted to the hospital and on December 27, 1957, the third bishop of Oklahoma City and Tulsa died suddenly at the age of sixty-seven.[106] Speculation was rife as to his successor, for while McGuinness had succeeded to the office on the death of the incumbent, he was both an established bishop and an outsider. The disinclination of the Vatican to appoint priests as bishops of their diocese of origin was hinted at by the apostolic delegate when he called Reed to assure him that he would receive a bishopric but failed to specify where that might be.[107]

Nevertheless, on January 29, 1958, Pope Pius XII named Victor Reed to

101. Bp. Eugene McGuinness to Reed, September 21, 1949, March 11, 1953, Reed Papers. Both honorifics carried the title of monsignor.
102. *Southwest Courier*, November 20, 1954.
103. Garthoeffner, interview. 104. Donovan, interview.
105. *Southwest Courier*, December 21, 1957. 106. *Southwest Courier*, January 4, 1958.
107. Garthoeffner, interview.

succeed McGuinness. "I am not without a definite sense of wonderment," the bishop-elect admitted, "that I have been chosen the successor of Bishop Meerschaert, our first shepherd, who confirmed me, of Bishop Francis C. Kelley, who brought luster and prominence to the Catholics of our state, and of Bishop Eugene J. McGuinness, whose leadership of clergy and laity was crowned by the remarkable progress of the Church in Oklahoma which we know today. . . . You know me as one of your own. I consider this a great blessing and my knowledge of you makes me proud of being your Bishop. Need I say more?"[108]

On March 5, 1958, Victor Reed was consecrated by the apostolic delegate, Archbishop Amleto Cicognani, Jeremiah Minihan, auxiliary bishop of Boston, and Stephen Leven in Holy Family Cathedral, where he had shepherded Tulsa's Catholic community for over a decade.[109] Two weeks later, he was installed at Our Lady of Perpetual Help Cathedral in Oklahoma City by Archbishop Robert Lucey of San Antonio, assisted by Stephen Leven and the bishops of Amarillo and Corpus Christi. In his sermon, Archbishop Lucey offered for consideration a model of episcopal leadership that would soon be overtaken by events:

Bishop Reed will rule over you in all justice and charity. The little people of his flock, the least of all the brethren, will be close to his heart. . . . They are the brethren of Christ, made to the image of God. The reverend clergy will look upon Bishop Reed as their spiritual leader with power to command, with a desire to assist and advise them in all their labors. . . . We need not remind him that he assumes the heavy duties of his exalted office in a period of history when all that we hold dear as followers of Christ and citizens of America is placed in jeopardy. Grey days have come to Church and State. The enemies of God and religion have succeeded all too well in the dark designs of their treachery. If human society is to be saved from chaos and climb once more the heights of moral grandeur, that can be achieved only by a return to the good, the beautiful and the true. It is the glorious mission of the Church to accomplish just that.[110]

With Lucey's injunction ringing in his ears, the new bishop was poised to steer his people through the uncharted and choppy waters of the 1960s.

---

108. Statement given to the *Oklahoma City Times*, January 29, 1958, Reed Papers.
109. *Tulsa Daily World*, March 6, 1958.
110. *Southwest Courier*, March 22, 1958.

CONCLUSION

Victor Reed's study in Louvain during the late 1930s can be considered a critical turning point in his clerical career. Exposed to the work of Joseph Cardijn—and its deep influence on close friends such as Don Kanaly—the future bishop returned to Oklahoma with a far deeper understanding of the budding liturgical renewal movement and the drive for active ministries of the laity. A gradualist rather than an activist by temperament, he was nonetheless fully convinced of the need for ecclesiastical adaptations to suit the character of the postwar American Catholic middle class. Both at St. Francis Xavier and later at Holy Family, he sought to model a form of clerical leadership that acknowledged the narrowing intellectual gulf between priest and people. Such a style was conspicuously at odds with his ordinary, and Reed's almost accidental elevation to the episcopate can be considered little short of miraculous, but for the Oklahoma Catholic community, 1958 might well be considered the year when the man and the hour had finally met.

part two

The Institutional Church,
1958–1971

chapter 3

On Being a Bishop

Renewing Diocesan Structures

Among the collaborators of the bishop in the government of the diocese are numbered those presbyters who constitute his senate, or council, such as the cathedral chapter, the board of consultors or other committees according to the circumstances or nature of various localities. These institutions, especially the cathedral chapters, should be reorganized wherever necessary in keeping with present day needs. Priests and lay people who belong to the diocesan curia should realize that they are making a helpful contribution to the pastoral ministry of the bishop. The diocesan curia should be so organized that it is an appropriate instrument for the bishop, not only for administering the diocese but also for carrying out the works of the apostolate. It is greatly desired that in each diocese a pastoral commission will be established over which the diocesan bishop himself will preside and in which specially chosen clergy, religious and lay people will participate. The duty of this commission will be to investigate and weigh pastoral undertakings and to formulate practical conclusions regarding them.

Second Vatican Council, Decree concerning the Pastoral Office of
Bishops in the Church, *Christus Dominus,* October 28, 1965

"Pope John's decision to convene a general Council has already done much to clarify the proper image of the Church," editorialized Oklahoma's diocesan newspaper in July 1962. "As the primary purpose of this Council is the internal condition of the Church, the reform of institutions and procedures where reform is necessary, the Church is compelled to take a scrutinizing view of herself, to look into a mirror under a very bright light. Blemishes are apparent now that were hardly noticed before."[1] Few of the American bishops, including Victor Reed, recognized the prescience of Father John Joyce, the editorialist. The renewal process within the Church would unleash forces that would seriously compromise the authority of the Vatican in the United States and of American bishops in their dioceses.

When Cardinal Joseph Ritter of St. Louis rose to defend the principle of a vernacular liturgy at the council, he demonstrated that the body of American bishops was far more open to liturgical and institutional reform of the Church than many in Europe had previously imagined. "He spoke Latin as a Mid-Westerner would, and his ideas, to a large extent, reflected the liturgical thinking that had been developing for a generation in the heartland of the United States," declared Monsignor Vincent Yzermans in 1967. "He spoke, too, as a representative of the 'new' kind of thinking taking place within the minds of many younger members of the American hierarchy who had only a small voice on the national scene."[2] The importance of the midwestern prelates—who dominated the National Catholic Welfare Conference—had been confirmed as early as 1958, when two products of the Diocese of Cleveland (Ohio) had been elevated to high office. While John Dearden took charge of the Archdiocese of Detroit, Paul Hallinan became bishop of Charleston, a short step on his road to succession to the Archdiocese of Atlanta in 1962. Both men would play key roles in liturgical reform and ecumenical outreach during the council. Other 1958 elevations included the transfer of Albert Meyer from the Archdiocese of Milwaukee to the Archdiocese of Chicago and his replacement by William Cousins. These new archbishops joined Joseph Ritter (a ten-year veteran) and Karl Alter (archbishop of Cincinnati since 1950) to form a progressive bloc that would shape the approach of the American episcopal delegation to Rome between 1962 and 1965.

While considerably junior to such midwestern leaders, Reed was unquestionably a loyal supporter of their point of view. For all four sessions of the council, he lodged with the Marist Fathers at Villa Santa Maria in company with Charles Buswell, the Oklahoma-born founder of Christ the King parish in Oklahoma City, who had become bishop of Pueblo (Colorado) in 1959. Both men pursued a rigorous schedule, with Mass at 6:00 a.m., discussions in the council hall in the morning, study of proposed documents during the afternoon, benediction and the rosary at 7:00 p.m,. and supper at 7:30 p.m.

1. *Oklahoma Courier*, July 6, 1962.
2. Yzermans, *American Participation in the Second Vatican Council*, 136–37.

Bishop Reed with Pope John XXIII in Rome during the Vatican Council, which played an important role in the shaping of Reed's vision.

At times, Reed admitted that he found the pace wearing. "This listening to Latin speeches is more tiring than I would have imagined beforehand," he complained in November 1962. "Of course when I did it as a student I was much younger."[3]

While many of the American bishops were regarded by their European counterparts more as administrators than as theological specialists, they quickly came into their own as the council proceeded.[4] American representation on conciliar commissions exceeded that of all other countries except

3. *Oklahoma Courier*, October 26, November 2, November 16, 1962.
4. "[Bishop] McGuinness told me this, that what [his predecessor Bishop Kelley] did do, you know, the Romans would never give him credit for—because, well, he wasn't an Italian and he wasn't a Frenchman, and no American bishop in the eyes of the Romans

France and Italy, and three cardinals—Francis Spellman of New York, Lawrence Shehan of Baltimore, and Albert Meyer of Chicago—served on the
council presidency.[5] Every Monday the American bishops gathered at the
North American College for strategy sessions that helped consolidate a North
American caucus dominated by the midwestern prelates.[6] The same was true
for the American Bishops' Committee on the Liturgy, which had a decidedly
regionalist appearance, with four bishops from the Midwest—including Victor Reed and Charles Buswell—two from the South, and only one (an auxiliary) from the Northeast. This committee organized a systematic program to
inform the other American bishops on all aspects of liturgy and secured the
election of Archbishop Hallinan of Atlanta as American representative on the
Liturgical Commission.[7]

As the American bishops turned to discussion of liturgical renewal, the
first internal divisions surfaced. Cardinal Spellman insisted that lay participation might unduly extend the duration of the Mass to the disadvantage of
those with limited leisure time, and contended that administering Communion under both kinds would prove a great inconvenience to many priests.
His former auxiliary, James Cardinal McIntyre of Los Angeles, vocally defended the principle of Latin universalism. "Protestant sects turned to the
vernacular," he warned, "and dissolved into numerous factions."[8] Their midwestern counterparts would not let such statements pass. Cardinal Ritter reminded delegates that even the Council of Trent had allowed for changes in
the administration of the sacraments to assist the faithful. "[O]nly a liturgy
which exists in conformity with daily life of man is able to work as an integral element and integrate that same life," Ritter insisted. Archbishop Hallinan, who oversaw a community that was only 2 percent Catholic (compared
to Oklahoma's 5 percent), argued that greater lay participation would reso-
nate with many non-Catholics: "In the United States, as in the rest of the
world, our Christian people and others, too, live in an atmosphere of isolation. They are victims of an excessive spirit of individualism. . . . The liturgy

---

could ever be capable, in those days at least, of any small diplomatic coup because they just
were regarded as bush league." Harkin, interview.

5. Yzermans, *American Participation in the Second Vatican Council*, 7.

6. Rynne, *Vatican Council II*, 62, 70. Rynne attests to the development of regional
groupings among both the African and South American contingents (129).

7. Yzermans, *American Participation in the Second Vatican Council*, 130–34. For the
development of liturgical renewal in the United States, see chapter 6.

8. Ibid., 149–51, 155–56, 158–59 (quotation on 159); Rynne, *Vatican Council II*, 61–62, 72.

of the Church must be public, but this can have real meaning for our people only if they understand enough of it to be a part of it. They must be united to God not alone as in private prayer, but together with the whole Church in our Head who is Christ."[9]

More junior bishops like Reed and Stephen Leven (the Oklahoma-born auxiliary bishop of San Antonio) felt encouraged to take a public stand, with Leven insisting that the words of Scripture exerted a power over the mind—Catholic as well as Protestant—that nothing else could equal. Reed's intervention on November 12, 1962, while more technical, had much the same objective. He sought to minimize the repetition of scriptural texts at weekly Masses (so that the laity could be exposed to as many of the teachings of Christ as possible) and to reduce observance of saints' feast days to those of "universal significance."[10]

By the time of the second session of the council, Reed was clearly identified with those who favored a great emphasis on the biblical heritage of the Christian faith and the greater understanding that this fostered with the Protestant churches. With Cardinal Cushing of Boston, he agreed that American bishops needed to downplay their administrative expertise in favor of more pastoral traits. "We must teach and sanctify first," he explained, "and let administration follow."[11] One potential instrument for such teaching was the periodic letter that Reed sent home from Rome to be published in the diocesan newspaper. "The things the history books will miss recording . . . we have," one Oklahoman enthusiastically told her ordinary in 1963. "It is this sort of thing which made the formal pronouncements of the council relate to everyday life for me."[12] It is sad to relate that Reed's letters from the later council sessions conveyed little in the way of theological insight and were far more concerned with recounting the many and varied Roman eating establishments that he had patronized.

As the focus of debate shifted from the liturgy to ecumenical relations with the so-called separated brethren and the related issue of religious freedom, many midwesterners embraced an issue that they considered pecu-

---

9. Yzermans, *American Participation in the Second Vatican Council*, 151–53, 157–58 (quotations on 152, 157).

10. Ibid., 165–66, 168–69.

11. *Oklahoma Courier*, March 22, 1963.

12. Patricia Cochrane to Victor Reed, April 20, 1963, Reed Papers. Cardinal Meyer of Chicago strove to keep members of his archdiocese well informed about the council. Avella, *This Confident Church*, 331.

liarly their own. During the second session of the council, Bishop Charles Helmsing of Kansas City–St. Joseph (Missouri), whose acquaintance Reed had cultivated at the first session, was elected to the Secretariat for Promoting Church Unity. In the floor debates both Helmsing and Cardinal Ritter urged the Church to abandon the harsh rhetoric of the Council of Trent and recognize that Protestantism, however imperfectly, endeavored to realize the full potential of the operation of the Holy Spirit in its life and worship. Ritter insisted that absolute religious freedom, the inviolability of human conscience, and the incompetence of any civil government to interpret the Gospel were all fundamental to any ecumenical declaration. Perhaps the most devastating address came from Bishop Leven, who flayed those Spanish and Italian bishops who still resisted the call to dialogue. "Every day it becomes clearer that we need a dialogue not only with Protestants, but also among bishops," he warned. "The prelates who seek a sincere and fruitful dialogue with non-Catholics are not the ones who show disaffection and disloyalty to the Holy Father. It is not our people who miss Mass on Sunday, refuse the sacraments and vote the Communist ticket. . . . We have not lost the working class. They are the foundation and support of the Church."[13]

During the third session, the bishops were finally given the opportunity to wrestle with the vexed question of religious freedom. Sixty-five years earlier, Pope Leo XIII had proscribed the attempt of the American bishops to compromise with American pluralism, but now the American prelates sought to make certain aspects of such pluralism an integral part of the worldwide Church. Archbishop Robert Lucey of San Antonio called the Declaration on Religious Liberty "*the* American issue" of 1963, and the American bishops carefully planned their strategy for convincing their fellow bishops, both with written submissions and oral interventions.[14] The midwestern bishops loudly echoed the pleas of Richard Cardinal Cushing of Boston, with Archbishop Alter offering reassurance that the liberty expressed in the declaration did not imply the right of a person to teach error. "The human right to immunity from external force in religious matters has been confirmed only as a so-

13. Yzermans, *American Participation in the Second Vatican Council*, 286–88, 305, 310–12 (quotation on 311–12); Rynne, *Vatican Council II*, 239. At a U.S. Bishops press panel in October 1963, Reed objected to the use of the phrase "regrettable separation" of church and state in a conciliar document. "This phrase," he said, "would not be an expression of the true feeling of the American hierarchy or America Catholics." *Oklahoma Courier*, November 1, 1963.

14. Yzermans, *American Participation in the Second Vatican Council*, 623–25, 634–41.

cial and juridical right," Alter insisted, "before civil power and in the temporal order; by no means has the right of a person to religious freedom before God been affirmed." Cardinal Meyer, meanwhile, stressed the need to set an example to civil governments and encourage dialogue with non-Catholics.[15]

At the fourth session, Cardinal Ritter warned that failure to endorse the declaration would undermine many of the other achievements of the council, and Meyer and Ritter were part of a group of fourteen cardinals who directly approached Pope Paul VI about efforts by conservatives to block publication of the declaration.[16] Although Reed did not directly address the council on this issue, he was favorably disposed toward the ecumenical implications of the declaration. "I wish to say that the historical responsibility for religious intolerance cannot be placed entirely at the door of the civil authorities," he told Cardinal Bea, the head of the Secretariat for Promoting Christian Unity, in December 1964. "Certainly the Church and our separated brethren share the responsibility."[17] The American hierarchy greeted the emergence of a revised schema in 1965 with almost universal approbation, with Cardinal Ritter and Archbishop Hallinan warm in its praise, and on September 21, 1965, the Declaration on Religious Liberty received the endorsement of 1,997 bishops, with only 224 opposed.[18] "At long last," writes Gerald Fogarty, "the peculiar tradition of the American Church was Catholic teaching. American democracy and ideas of freedom were no longer construed in terms of nineteenth century European liberalism, but in terms of British and American Common Law, which underlay the twentieth century constitutional forms of government."[19]

"Vatican Council II has been accurately described as one of the greatest events in the life of the Church, and possibly in the present history of the entire world," Victor Reed told his people in February 1963. Leslie Tentler has described the profound transformation undergone by Archbishop John Dearden of Detroit as a result of the council sessions.[20] Could the same be

15. Ibid., 644–46, 651–53, 658–60 (quotation on 651); Rynne, *Vatican Council II*, 299–302.

16. Rynne, *Vatican Council II*, 317–22, 417–20.

17. Victor Reed to Agostino Cardinal Bea, December 31, 1964, Reed Papers. See also Reed's welcome of the declaration and belief that aggiornamento is assured in *Oklahoma Courier*, September 24, 1965.

18. Rynne, *Vatican Council II*, 455–56, 460, 462–65.

19. Fogarty, *The Vatican and the American Hierarchy*, 390–99 (quotation on 399).

20. Victor Reed to "My dear People," February 7, 1963, Reed Papers; Tentler, *Catholics and Contraception*, 257.

said of Victor Reed? Some argue that no such radical reordering of priorities affected Reed because he was already attuned to the intellectual currents that influenced the council's deliberations.[21] On the other hand, his fellow resident at Villa Santa Maria, Bishop Buswell, was convinced that Reed learned a greater appreciation of the idea of freedom within the Church from his time in Rome, an appreciation evidenced in the permissiveness that underpinned the later years of his episcopate.[22]

Perhaps the best indication of the bishop's feelings came in a letter to a member of St. Mary's parish in Tulsa penned in September 1965. "The process of 'Renewal,'" he wrote, "which happily is taking place in the entire Church under the supreme authority of the Pope and Bishops necessarily involves changes, and changes in anything to which we have become accustomed can be disturbing. But the changes of Christian Renewal of the Vatican Council do not touch upon the essence of the Church."[23] In this respect, Reed's expectation of how aggiornamento would evolve was no different from many of his peers. As he would soon discover, expectations at the grassroots were very different. One of Reed's priests, Father William Garthoeffner, was a canon law student in Rome for much of the council. "It changed everything for me," Garthoeffner later recalled. "Some would say I went to Rome and lost my faith . . . but I never felt that I lost my faith . . . suddenly everything I had studied, everything I had grown up with began to kind of click, began to make sense. Yes, this is the way the Church ought to be structured!"[24]

DIOCESAN RENEWAL

When Reed returned to his diocese after the final council session in 1965, it was to oversee a process of the renewal of diocesan structures that had been under way for several years. "I think there's going to be a battle," warned Thomas Staley, as conflict between the Church's progressives and traditionalists reached a climax in 1968, "between those people who still believe in structures and those people who don't believe in any structures at all any more. . . . I think there's an interesting irony in this in that so many of the

21. Clergy roundtable discussion, June 19, 2005.
22. Clergy roundtable discussion, June 23, 2005.
23. Victor Reed to Robert M. Kinney, September 7, 1965, St. Mary's Church, Tulsa File, box 14.1, Archives of the Catholic Diocese of Tulsa (hereafter ADT).
24. Garthoeffner, interview.

Bishop Reed with Monsignor Raymond Harkin, secretary to three bishops, and after 1961 the vicar general.

people . . . who are for wiping out structures are creating new ones."[25] Staley was a Catholic professor at a nominally Presbyterian institution of higher education; his comment illustrates perfectly the two competing impulses in diocesan administration that characterized the late 1950s and 1960s: centralization and democratic subsidiarity.

The drive to centralize administrative functions in diocesan chanceries

25. "Where Do We Stand?" *Decade of Change: A Supplement to the Oklahoma Courier*, March 1, 1968, 7. Staley was a professor of English at the University of Tulsa.

from 1920 to 1960 reflected an accommodation of the Catholic Church to the American principles of good business practice. The driving force behind the transformation—Cardinal George Mundelein of Chicago—spent much of the 1920s shifting the initiative for building schools and churches from pastors and influential parish laymen to the chancery.[26] His achievement encouraged other bishops to follow suit. A decade later, Detroit's Archbishop Edward Mooney launched an archdiocesan development fund intended to give his chancery greater control over Catholic charitable and educational activities and later chartered a federation to oversee all Catholic charitable agencies within his archdiocese. During the 1950s, Bishop John Wright of Worcester (Massachusetts) also sought to limit the financial autonomy of powerful pastors in his diocese by requiring outside scrutiny of parish accounts and pressuring pastors to deposit surpluses with the chancery and take loans from the diocese for any building work that they wished to undertake.[27]

Such administrative changes, while they might have aided the redistribution of funds from wealthy to poor parishes, were rarely intended to open the process of church governance to lay participation or even outside scrutiny. Most bishops would have strongly denied that they had any obligation to justify their management practices to anyone other than their spiritual superior—the pope. The idea that a bishop's general financial oversight could be distinguished from his spiritual responsibilities revived unhappy memories of the battles over lay trusteeship during the 1840s.[28] One archbishop who partially broke with this pattern was Joseph Ritter of St. Louis, who, during the 1940s, made public an audit of diocesan finances, gave substantial autonomy to his department heads, and consulted with lay experts on education and communications, but Ritter was exceptional. Democratic subsidiarity would only truly come into its own after the Second Vatican Council had redefined the nature of the lay apostolate.[29]

By the standards of the large urban dioceses, Oklahoma's chancery was administratively irrelevant. "We do not have the resources in men or material that we feel necessary even for an adequate carrying of the Church to all parts of Oklahoma," lamented the chancellor in 1960, "let alone for servicing all the areas in the way a mature diocese would with Newman clubs, marriage

26. Kantowicz, *Corporation Sole*, 33–48.
27. Tentler, *Seasons of Grace*, 348–52; O'Brien, "When It All Came Together."
28. On the nineteenth-century conflict over lay trusteeship, see Hennesey, *American Catholics*, 93–99; Carey, *People, Priests, and Prelates*.
29. Faherty, *Dream by the River*, 188–89.

A meeting of the diocesan Pastoral Board, established in 1968 to coordinate decision-making in the diocese and advise the bishop.

counseling and so forth."[30] To further complicate matters, Reed's predecessor had made a point of concentrating power not merely in the chancery but in his own person. This state of affairs had been tolerable while Bishop McGuinness was alive, since he did not have to rely solely on financial support from within the diocese, but it had done nothing to foster good relations between parish priests and the chancery and had undermined the authority of chancery officials and local deans. The sitting chancellor when Reed took office, Father William Garthoeffner, had been appointed one year after his ordination and despite his lack of administrative experience. "Whether the process was gradual or immediate I do not know," Garthoeffner told the new bishop in 1961,

30. *Oklahoma Courier*, April 1, 1960.

"but during [McGuinness's] administration all authority which according to law, usually is to be delegated was removed and centered in himself."[31]

Although Garthoeffner offered to resign in favor of a more experienced priest, Reed evidently felt that the knowledge he had acquired since 1954 was too valuable to waste. With the vicar-general (Monsignor Sylvester Luecke from 1958 to 1964 and Monsignor Raymond Harkin from 1964 to 1971) assigned to parishes in Oklahoma City, the chancellor was the bishop's alter ego, not only undertaking a diverse range of administrative functions but serving as chauffeur and general factotum. Garthoeffner filled this role from 1958 to 1961 (when he was sent to Rome for study) and took up the chancellorship again from 1964 to 1967, when he was succeeded by Father Charles Schettler (who had served as acting chancellor from 1961 to 1964). Office administration was in the hands of a laywoman, the ever-efficient Margaret Navitsky, while the clerical contingent received a boost in 1964 with the arrival of Father Charles Meiser as director of vocations.[32]

Reed's first priority in the early 1960s was to solve the looming financial crisis that confronted the diocese, a process that left little time for other administrative reforms. After his return from the Second Vatican Council, however, it was evident that the bishop had been greatly impressed by the debates over episcopal collegiality and intended to apply the principle in his daily activities. In February 1965, monthly staff meetings to coordinate diocesan activities became a regular feature of chancery life, and a month later the diocese established an antipoverty committee with representatives from each deanery to distribute information about the new Economic Opportunity Act and encourage Catholics at the grassroots level to submit projects for federal funding.[33] The general dynamics of the office were far removed from those under McGuinness, who always cleared his desk after a couple of hours.[34] No micromanager, the new bishop was once heard to remark of his in-tray: "Well, you know, most of these things solve themselves."[35] At the same time, he expected certain standards of behavior from his staff. When his director of vocations took to wearing a turtleneck shirt and no clerical collar when doing paperwork in the office, the bishop kindly but firmly told him: "Charles, I think you ought gradually to work back into a collar."[36]

31. Revd. William C. Garthoeffner to Victor Reed, January 4, 1961, Reed Papers.
32. Schettler, interview; Meiser, interview.
33. *Oklahoma Courier*, February 12, March 26, 1965.
34. Clergy roundtable discussion, June 19, 2005.
35. Gallatin, interview.   36. Meiser, interview.

Chancery reform affected not only the central bureaucracy—such as it was—but also the lower levels of church governance. In December 1965, a new uniform accounting system was introduced for all parishes in the diocese that required the classification of different types of transactions and the systematic gathering of information for a comprehensive annual report to the diocese. This move not only provided a more uniform picture of the financial state of the diocese but also ensured that individual parishes now had a permanent record of income vs. expenditure, something that few of them had previously maintained. Administrative reforms were also applied to the deanery system, with the two oversized urban deaneries reduced in size and the overall number of deaneries increased from seven to eight (the Oklahoma City deanery went from seventy-nine priests to fifty-seven and the Tulsa deanery from sixty-one to thirty-five). Deanery seats were, in some cases, relocated to central locations on major highways, and efforts were made to ensure that each deanery was predominantly urban, small-town, or rural to enable it to focus on the problems peculiar to that environment.[37]

Worthy though such reforms clearly were, they fitted—with the possible exception of deanery reorganization—into the category of centralization rather than that of democratic subsidiarity. None could be said to alter the bishop's authority over the diocese in favor of other interested parties. Advocates of reform at the national level, like Father Joseph O'Donoghue of the Archdiocese of Washington, warned in 1967 that diocesan chanceries continued to be closed systems that discouraged lay participation. New chancery officials, appointed on the recommendation of their predecessors, tended to be conservative in outlook, wedded to established programs, and uninformed about sentiment at the grassroots. It was essential, O'Donoghue concluded, to define the status and function of the new pastoral commissions that had been appointed in the wake of the Second Vatican Council, perhaps even allowing them a say in the appointment of chancery officials. O'Donoghue praised the decision of the archdioceses of Detroit and St. Louis to open up their administrative structures and particularly approved of the attempt by the Diocese of Pittsburgh to train lay officials to conduct canonical investigations of the validity of marriages.[38]

37. *Oklahoma Courier*, December 31, 1965, November 4, 1966.
38. Fr. Joseph O'Donoghue, "Those Faceless Chanceries," *Commonweal*, April 28, 1967, 167–71. Father O'Donoghue was a member of the priests' senate in the Archdiocese of Washington.

While Reed failed to go as far as O'Donoghue probably would have wished, he took an important step in October 1968 with the establishment of a pastoral board to coordinate decision making in the diocese and provide practical expertise in matters of finance. One of the first in the United States, the board consisted of the bishop—with the right to veto any decision—the vicar-general, two elected members (one chosen by the clergy and the other by the delegates to the diocesan Little Council; see below), and two members appointed by the bishop—the treasurer and the secular affairs officer. Under the new setup, all chancery departments—except the marriage tribunal—reported to the pastoral board rather than to the bishop directly, and the eight deans were now treated as the equivalent of regional vice presidents.

The board consulted with interested parties on major decisions affecting the running of the diocese and periodically held open meetings to make clear to the wider Catholic community how its decisions were reached. It oversaw the establishment of parish councils and the diocesan board of education and served as a final court of appeal against decisions to close parochial schools (see chapter 4). In 1969, the board took a cue from earlier diocesan reforms, requiring that all parish financial reports be subject to an audit in order to determine the need for subsidies, the cost of parochial schools, and the assignment of missions to parishes. Since many of the reports submitted in 1969 turned out to be either incomplete or inaccurate, it was clear that such a reform was long overdue. Overall, the day-to-day operations of the pastoral board were generally amicable, and the bishop encouraged frank and full discussion. "He was so open [to hearing other people's points of view]," declared a lay member of the board, "that he was perhaps thought to have [opinions] that he didn't [hold] because he let those views be expressed."[39]

FINANCE

It may well be the case that, had Reed enjoyed the same ability as his predecessor to raise funds from external sources, he might have shown less inclination to devolve power. During the 1950s, the Diocese of Oklahoma City and Tulsa had not been short of capital. The contacts that Bishop McGuin-

---

39. *Oklahoma Courier*, April 26, 1968; *Diocesan News*, Diocese of Oklahoma City and Tulsa, May 1969, Reed Papers; Revd. John J. Sullivan to Revd. Joseph F. Scharrer, C.PP.S., December 7, 1969, St. Catherine's Church, Nowata File, box 61.1, ADT; Fox, interview.

ness had developed in his home area of Philadelphia and during his days at the Extension Society ensured that he always had ready access to outside sources of funding. At his death such sources of financial support soon became unavailable, and this loss was only compounded by news of the precarious financial condition of Benedictine Heights College. By 1960, the Benedictine community in Tulsa, no longer able to make adequate repayment of its debt, faced the ignominious prospect of going bankrupt, and in its extremity turned to the bishop for relief (see chapter 11).

Reed recognized that he faced a choice of evils. He could permit the community to default on its repayments, a move that would protect the diocese but would seriously damage the morale of all the communities of women religious in Oklahoma and compromise the standing of the Catholic Church in the eyes of non-Catholics. Alternatively, he could allow the diocese to shoulder the debt burden, a course that would increase the diocesan debt from around $1.8 million to $4.5 million. His decision in early 1960 to go with the latter option marked the first significant intrusion of Catholic laity into the financial affairs of the diocese, for the board of control he appointed to oversee all female Benedictine institutions in Oklahoma was composed of three laymen and three priests. The board imposed a tight rein on the Tulsa community's operations, developing a new system of internal financing and devoting all fund-raising efforts to debt retirement.[40] "All during [Reed's] administration," explained Father Paul Donovan over forty years later, "this debt was overhanging him and it limited much of what he would have liked to do."[41]

The Benedictine financial crisis obliged the diocese seriously to reassess the way in which it raised money to meet its expenses. In March 1960, a member of the bishop's lay advisory board proposed that the diocese create a central office of finance and replace the annual Bishop's Drive with four quarterly collections.[42] When Reed invited a group of prominent Oklahoma Catholics, including future governor Dewey Bartlett and James Cockrell, the head of the state Catholic Action committee, to discuss the establishment of a diocesan educational fund, the participating laymen rejected such a solution as being too limited to cope with the existing crisis, when what was needed

40. Minutes of the First Meeting of the Board of Control of the Institutions of the Benedictine Sisters in Oklahoma, February 19, 1960, Reed Papers.
41. Donovan, interview.
42. J. A. Padon to Victor Reed, March 2, 1960, Reed Papers.

was "a fund much broader in scope to support all the expansion needs of the diocese on a long range basis, namely, a diocesan development fund."[43]

Echoing earlier calls for a more professional approach to diocesan administration, they urged the establishment of a diocesan finance committee with professional staff, including a business manager and public relations director. Such a committee should determine priorities for future diocesan expansion, establish a plan for liquidating the indebtedness of Benedictine Heights College, and begin study of such issues as an insurance program, central purchasing, and property appraisal. It should also have responsibility for establishing a diocesan development fund (DDF) and appointing a chairman to organize the first diocesanwide campaign. Short-term drives (whether interparish, regional, or diocesan) should eventually be replaced with long-range annual giving to the diocese, a strategy that would relieve the bishop of sole responsibility for setting financial priorities and enable the laity to participate more effectively in the administrative workings of the Church. The post of DDF chairman went to Father Charles Statham, director of the Associated Catholic Charities and founder of Tulsa's Catholic Information Center, who declared his initial priorities to be the liquidation of diocesan debt and expansion of student ministries at Oklahoma's state colleges.[44]

A meeting of the lay advisory board in September 1960 revealed that in addition to diocesan debt—owed mainly on the Catholic high schools in Oklahoma City and Tulsa and the Benedictine debt that it had assumed—parish debts amounted to almost $2.2 million. While structural reforms might well produce some savings, those present urged that Father Statham investigate how feasible it might be to hire a professional fund-raiser to oversee the first year of the DDF. Statham responded with two alternatives. Hiring an expert for a year to create a diocesan program and go out and instruct parishes that were in the process of launching drives would cost around $18,000. A more intensive approach over a six-month period would cost closer to $40,000 but had the potential to raise up to $500,000. A cheaper alternative to both these schemes, Statham added, would be a "homemade" drive conducted through the diocesan newspaper. This would seek to obtain a DDF contribution of at least $25 from every parishioner, over and above the parish contributions. The bishop could contact substantial donors personally in an effort to maximize contributions. "The big advantage of this type of campaign,"

---

43. Memorandum of meeting held at Tulsa, Oklahoma, May 18, 1960, Reed Papers.
44. *Oklahoma Courier*, June 24, 1960. See the profile of Statham in White, 254–55.

Statham concluded, "is that it doesn't cost anything like the amount professional fund people would cost. It forces us as Priests and as people to initiate a hard headed educational program and to follow through with it. A final advantage of this kind of a campaign is that even the parishes who are in the mist [*sic*] of a campaign on their own can be approached since the Christmas collection has always gone to the needs of the diocese anyway."[45]

Reed endorsed Statham's "homemade" formula in the diocesan newspaper, reminding the laity that many existing projects (like Catholic high schools) required a much greater degree of cooperative financing than had been the case in years gone by. There were still at least fifteen parishes in the diocese that couldn't cover their own expenses, the bishop pointed out, and he was concerned to learn that some parishioners had not raised their contribution in twenty-five years. "Surprisingly, some people seem to think the financial resources of the diocese are limitless," Reed concluded. "That is not true at all, the diocese has very little income."[46]

The first DDF campaign was launched in 1961, with an initial goal of $330,550, most of it committed to debt service. The public response was lukewarm, with only one family in five contributing. The bishop acknowledged that the fund's novelty and the lack of work at the parish level had hampered fund-raising efforts, but he still felt moved to administer a pointed rebuke in March 1962: "We all wish to feel we are contributing to progress, to something new. Actually, this is closely tied to the idea I think prevails that . . . contributions [are] buying something, paying for some new effort on behalf of the Church. The better attitude would be the attitude of sharing what we have with God, rather than fixing it on a purchase of a particular piece of property or the construction of a particular building."[47] Reed's reproof evidently changed some minds. A single collection in 1963 raised more on its own than two 1962 collections, although the bishop pointed out that only half the potential contributors in the diocese were actually pledging and that had they all done so, the annual debt burden could have been entirely met.[48]

45. Minutes of the Bishop's Lay Advisory Board, September 20, 1960, Charles M. Statham, "Alternate Proposals for Hiring Professional Fund Raiser for the Bishop's Development Fund," October 17, 1960, Reed Papers.

46. *Oklahoma Courier*, November 25, 1960.

47. *Oklahoma Courier*, March 23, 1962.

48. Paul Sprehe, "Finances," *Decade of Change*, 30; Reed to "Dearly Beloved in Christ," April 1, 1963, Reed Papers.

At a 1963 meeting of the lay advisory board, most members approved of the progress achieved but expressed concern that inadequate emphasis was being placed on debt retirement. With the increasing cost of secondary education, several members pressed for tuition rates for families with children at the two principal diocesan high schools to be based upon income, so that parents rather than the diocese would help subsidize poorer families unable to pay the going rate. While acknowledging the force of their argument, Reed gave it as his opinion that it would take time to persuade parents of the need for higher tuition rates without provoking a decline in enrollment.

Board members also challenged some of Reed's other priorities, including the maintenance of a cash reserve of almost $200,000, which the bishop defended on the grounds that parishes were able to borrow at low rates of interest on the strength of these reserves. Funding for the new diocesan mission to Guatemala ($30,000) was also criticized, but Reed defended this as a necessary exercise of his pastoral responsibilities. A final issue of controversy was the attempt to replace the patchwork of insurance policies that protected parish buildings throughout Oklahoma with a single diocesan policy, which could reduce the overall cost by more than half. The bishop acknowledged that such a move might create problems for local insurance agents, but he accepted that the needs of the time demanded a new approach.[49] That there was a price to pay for such efficiencies was demonstrated by Father Joseph Campbell at Sacred Heart parish in Boise City, who stressed that the loss of such a policy meant far less to a Tulsa insurance firm than to a rural agent, especially when the agent was a member of the parish. "Any and all steps towards centralization of either church or civil affairs," Campbell warned, "are quite unpopular in this area and looked on with distrust."[50]

By 1965, the many hours of labor by priests and designated laity at the parish level seemed to be bearing fruit. From Duncan, Father Ferdinand Strasser reported that the new procedures had led to greater participation and increased pledges by parishioners of Assumption Church.[51] In Decem-

---

49. Minutes of the Bishop's Lay Advisory Board, April 23, 1963, Reed Papers. A similar attempt was made to persuade teachers in Catholic schools to subscribe to the diocesan health insurance plan, on the ground that small-group policies were frequently subject to sudden premium increases. See Herbert Giles to Revd. William T. Swift, June 9, 1970, St. Pius X Church, Tulsa File, box 17.2, ADT.

50. Revd. Joseph R. Campbell to Victor Reed, July 26, 1970, Reed Papers.

51. Revd. Ferdinand J. Strasser to Victor Reed, n.d. (prob. March 1965), Assumption Church, Duncan File, Archives of the Catholic Archdiocese of Oklahoma City (hereafter AAOC).

ber 1965, the Catholic Foundation of Oklahoma was incorporated to allow the people of Oklahoma to invest in the long-term growth of the Church and to build a permanent investment fund. Experienced laymen were given the task of managing the fund. The following year, Reed brought together a group of priests and businessmen to provide expert advice on the budget and operations of the various diocesan departments. After making the alarming discovery that no fewer than eleven separate checking accounts existed, the committee ultimately engaged a professional accounting firm to implement a complete overhaul of the financial system. By the spring of 1967, all departments were required to submit budget requests, paving the way for a detailed budget on which the ensuing Bishop's Fund drive could be based.[52]

Deliberations within the diocesan finance committee revealed Reed to be a bishop who quickly grasped the financial issues at stake. Although he had defended certain expenditures over debt reduction in 1963, he later joined Douglas Fox in his insistence on the need to draft a balanced budget. Fox, who served on the committee from 1965 to 1968, called the bishop "soft-spoken, reserved, intelligent and gracious," noting that as issues became more complicated Reed tended to become more involved, not less, and that he had a good personal understanding of real estate. He took a stance of fiscal responsibility in the face of demands from advocates of social justice programs to shut down all diocesan administrative functions and put the money into their neighborhoods. "Here was a man who was excoriated by many as a raging liberal," noted Fox, "who . . . took the more conservative stand, and that was in order to conserve the institution."[53]

Despite Reed's fiscally prudent approach, some of his lay coworkers clearly hoped that responsibility for financial affairs would fall more and more on them. "I can foresee that within the next year we will move farther up toward the point where the administration of the diocese will be handled more by the laity who have expertise in this particular field," Paul Sprehe, chairman of the diocesan finance committee, declared in 1968. "Specifically, perhaps an administrative lay assistant who will take much of the burden off Bishop Reed that he now has in handling these kind of matters."[54]

"Financial problems are signs of the times," Father Charles Schettler observed in August 1969. "The government (federal, state and local), families, individual persons, and the Church (the diocese as well as the individual par-

52. Sprehe, "Finances," 30.   53. Fox, interview.
54. "Where Do We Stand?" 25.

ishes) are all subject to financial difficulties. . . . One of the joys of heaven will be the absence of finances and financial problems."[55] He probably had debt service ($418,586) and fund-raising ($56,045) in mind, for these constituted the two largest items in the 1967 budget. Only three other departments received more than $40,000: Education ($47,911), the Guatemala Mission ($42,000), and Religious Education ($41,195), the latter supporting programs for adults and for children not in the Catholic school system. In the course of two years, total operating expenses increased by almost 20 percent, from $576,470 in 1965 to $685,353 in 1967. While the total pledge of $650,000 for 1967 represented an increase of over $44,000 on the total pledge for 1965, the passage of two years saw an operating surplus of $29,456 transformed into an operating deficit of $35,353.[56]

As the euphoria of the immediate aftermath of the Second Vatican Council began to dissipate and cultural cleavages became increasingly evident, there was a dramatic decline in the willingness of local Catholics to subscribe to diocesan financial relief. To prevent further leakage, Father Stephen MacAulay (who had replaced Father Statham as DDF chairman in 1964) recommended the use of a movie depicting a visit to a hostile contributor, who initially refuses to give but subsequently allows himself to be persuaded. "To make a 10-minute story short, they are successful Thursday evening—but a lot happens between Sunday and Thursday," MacAulay wrote the bishop. "Cutbacks from our 1967 movie are used frequently and the movie ends with your personal appeal." MacAulay berated the diocesan finance committee for the reduction that it had made in his budget, which hampered efforts to contact the $100-or-more donors, many of whom were holding back on pledges in 1968. "At our conventions of over 40 dioceses conducting DDF campaigns," he complained, "we have heard the speakers ridicule and deride 'basement bargain campaigns.' We are on the threshold of launching one!"[57]

MacAulay's forebodings were not allayed by the 1969 budget, in which most of the cuts fell on the DDF machinery. Between 1967 and 1968, the diocese lost 1,306 contributors and $74,459.02 in pledges. Of this figure, 258

---

55. Revd. Charles H. Schettler to Joseph P. Weaver, August 6, 1969, Sacred Heart Church, El Reno File, AAOC.

56. "1967 Bishop's Fund," Reed Papers.

57. Revd. Stephen A. MacAulay to Victor Reed, November 22, 1968, Reed Papers. The 1967 movie provoked positive responses at the Glenmary mission parish of St. Francis de Sales, Idabel. See Revd. Raymond Berthiaume, Glenmary Missioner Newsletter, May 4, 1967, St. Francis de Sales Church, Idabel File, ADT.

individuals (who pledged at least $100 in 1967 and *nothing* in 1968) account-
ed for $39,318.89. Moreover, while 113 parishes showed a decrease in 1968, a
core group of 28 accounted for over 90 percent of the loss. The two most
dramatic declines occurred in Tulsa at the Church of the Madalene, whose
pledge fell from $19,091.50 to $11,940.50 and Christ the King, whose pledge
fell from $70,791.80 to $63,652.10. Steep declines were also recorded for parishes in Norman, Tulsa (St. Pius X), Oklahoma City (St. Francis of Assisi),
Lawton, and Ponca City. Some churches saw a smaller monetary reduction
but a greater percentage of loss. The parish in Altus saw its pledge fall from
$2,795.25 to just $597.00, a decline of 78.6 percent, while that of Hobart was
close behind, declining from $1,632.00 to $504.00, a decline of 69.1 percent.
Other sizable losers included the parishes of Perry (58.4 percent), Skiatook
(58.2 percent), St. Jude's, Tulsa (53.2 percent), and Ardmore (50.9 percent).

MacAulay maintained that only a minority of pastors failed to support the
DDF, but he also complained about the reluctance of parish finance committees to engage in diocesanwide activities. He further noted that much reluctance stemmed directly from opposition to some of the activities pursued in
the diocese, a fear that the DDF might provide funding to sustain the controversial diocesan newspaper, and the "goings-on" at certain Catholic student centers. "Many Catholics," he concluded, "feel that the only way they
can get the Bishop's attention is to refuse to give."[58] As early as 1963, Father
Elmer Robnett reported that parishioners at St. Mary's parish in Ardmore
were not contributing to the Bishop's Fund to the fullest extent possible,
because of the conviction that "they are building schools in Oklahoma City
and Tulsa."[59]

Four years later, a local Catholic explicitly linked her failure to contribute
to what she considered to be unsound teaching in the diocese. "The chancery office, being aware of these situations," she noted, "has done nothing,
at least publicly, to alleviate them. We have lived in this diocese for four years
and seen the situation go from bad to worse and cannot in good conscience
contribute to anything which will further the causes we are against."[60] In
March 1971, a Cushing lawyer stated that he disagreed with the philosophy
of the DDF and that his requests for information had provoked a threat to
reduce his parish to mission status. Moreover, he claimed that the former

58. Revd. Stephen A. MacAulay to Victor Reed, January 23, 1969, Reed Papers.
59. Revd. Elmer C. Robnett to Victor Reed, March 1, 1963, Reed Papers.
60. Mrs. J. C. Richard to Victor Reed, April 26, 1967, Reed Papers.

chancellor of the diocese had told him that "we don't need to worry about [parish] finances because before long everything will be channeled through the Chancery anyhow."[61]

THE LIFE AND DEATH OF THE *Oklahoma Courier*

A key facet of Catholic administrative reform in the early 1960s was the establishment of diocesan newspapers that would be competitive—at least as regards content—with their secular counterparts and that would be a source of information for the Catholic laity about changes in the modern world. While many papers were owned by dioceses, there was a considerable diversity of editorial opinion among Catholic publications, extending from *Commonweal* and the *National Catholic Reporter* on the left to the *Wanderer* on the right, and none of these papers owed any obedience to the local ordinary. Indeed, when Bishop Charles Helmsing repudiated the progressive stands on birth control and clerical celibacy espoused by the *National Catholic Reporter*, which was based in his Diocese of Kansas City–St. Joseph (Missouri), in 1967, he neither tried to suppress it nor sought to have it remove the word "Catholic" from its title. The Catholic press emerging in the 1960s, therefore, saw itself in large measure as the vanguard of the new order within the Church.[62]

Following a precedent set by another reformer, Archbishop Joseph Ritter of St. Louis, Reed endeavored to bring the new standards of professionalism to Oklahoma's diocesan newspaper, the *Southwest Courier*.[63] In 1960, he appointed Father John Joyce, fresh from graduate studies at the Catholic University of America, to manage the paper, subsequently renamed the *Oklahoma Courier*. Joyce fervently embraced the new ethos of the Catholic press, replacing hometown news and folksy columns with extended analysis of the national scene and biting social commentary. Joyce was trying to create "a real newspaper," declared Father Bill Ross, "not a house organ."[64] Haldan

61. D. O. Cubbage to A. A. Burkey, March 9, 1971, Sts. Peter and Paul Church, Cushing File, box 36.1, ADT. For Cubbage's role in challenging his pastor over parish finances, see chapter 5.
62. Greene, "The Catholic Press in America." When Helmsing sought a change of name some years later, the editors ignored him.
63. For the changes in St. Louis, see Faherty, *Dream by the River*, 193–94.
64. Clergy roundtable discussion, June 19, 2005. One problem with Joyce's strategy was that some of what he printed may well have been above the heads of the average reader. A Midwest City resident drew attention to this problem after the *Courier* reprinted an

Tompkins, music director of Christ the King parish in Oklahoma City, described the paper as a "burst of fresh air in a smoke filled room":

The Oklahoma Courier, as it stands, represents to [my] mind, the greatest contribution the Church in Oklahoma has and can contribute to the people of this nation. This is one of the few examples of a break-through by contemporary Christian thought in this country at the diocesan paper level. . . . Anyone can support a paper which sticks carefully with what, to Catholics, have been so often, nice "safe" topics: birth control, aid to education, observance of Sunday, anti-Communism, etc. Few papers today have the courage to discuss the un-popular but equally un-Christian mess in their own front yards: the damnable practice of segregation in *all* its forms, even within the Church; migrant workers scandals, change in the liturgy and the Church, scripture problems, religious art . . . or for example the danger to a free society of *any* type of thought control—whether from the radical right or left. . . . The Courier does not approach, by any stretch of the imagination, the form of thought-control its critics would impose upon it (providing of course, they did the controlling).[65]

Rarely did the *Courier* evoke neutral sentiments, something that probably greatly cheered Joyce, who gleefully printed acerbic letters on his correspondence page. His philosophy was aggressively on show in a 1963 editorial on change. "All tradition is not dogma," he told his readers, "every custom is not sacrosanct, even if both are orthodox and beneficial. New points of view on the Christian mystery, new ways of translating it into life must make their appearance if the living organism established by Christ is to do His will. To do otherwise would be sloth."[66]

These were fighting words. When the new paper had first appeared, readers had raised objections to the inclusion of a column by Walter Lippmann and the neglect of local news, but these proved to be mild indeed compared with the confrontation over Oklahoma's right-to-work legislation.[67] Joyce's 1961 editorial was only the last in a long line of pronouncements opposing moves to end the union shop that had provoked a storm of protest, particularly from well-to-do Catholics.[68] "In my college days," declared Lloyd

---

article by the theologian John Courtenay Murray. "If the Courier is, in any sense, a paper for the titillation of the intelligentsia," she concluded, "it has no right to consider itself the diocesan organ." *Oklahoma Courier*, June 16, 1961.

65. Haldan D. Tompkins to Victor Reed, June 19, 1961, Reed Papers.

66. *Oklahoma Courier*, December 6, 1963.

67. Letters attacking the Lippmann column appear throughout the *Courier*'s existence. For an early example, see *Oklahoma Courier*, February 19, 1960. For a plea for more local news, see *Oklahoma Courier*, March 11, 1960.

68. *Oklahoma Courier*, April 7, 1961.

Freese of Tulsa, "I had the privilege of studying under Dr. [John A.] Ryan
. . . and even in the wildest days of Dr. Ryan espousing the labor cause, never once would he have said 'all Catholics who do not agree with me are
wrong,' or 'all Baptists who do not agree with me on this political situation
are wrong.'"[69] For the next three years a running battle with the *Courier*'s
editors ensued, as conservative Catholics invoked "leading Catholic scholars"
in support of a statewide referendum on a right-to-work law in 1964, while
accusing priests who opposed the measure—including Reed's vicar-general,
Monsignor Sylvester Luecke—of getting involved in politics.[70]

Conservatives did not confine protest to complaining to the bishop about
the editor of the *Courier*—they actively sought to dissuade advertisers from
purchasing ads there, arguing that it promoted Communism. They also encouraged people to cancel their subscriptions, even supplying them with post-
cards to send to the paper, their pastor, and the bishop indicating their desire
not to receive it. After the 1964 election, Joyce hit back at such tactics, arguing that there had to be limits on "loyal opposition." He had never claimed
that his views were always shared even by the bishop, Joyce contended, and
while he considered that his opponents had the right to try to replace him as
editor, it was inappropriate for them to try to undermine financially a diocesan institution.[71]

After the 1964 elections, Joyce pledged to stay out of state politics, but
he demonstrated no similar inclination to avoid criticism of Catholic institutions.[72] Frank Wallace, a former parishioner at Holy Family Cathedral, was
outraged by the paper's description of the Latin Mass as "mumbo jumbo."
The *Courier*, he warned, was fomenting discord throughout the wider Catholic community. "It is forming a massive undercurrent of resentment, and I
hope the diocesan leaders are aware of it."[73] Declared another of Reed's cor-

---

69. M. Lloyd Freese to Victor Reed, February 23, 1961, Reed Papers.

70. Victor E. Bailey to Victor Reed, March 3, 1964, Anthony F. Keating to Victor
Reed, August 29, 1964, "Extreme Right Wingism in Oklahoma," n.d., 3, Reed Papers. For
a representative editorial opposing the referendum, see *Oklahoma Courier*, May 1, 1964.

71. "Extreme Right Wingism in Oklahoma," 12; *Oklahoma Courier*, November 20,
1964. Conservatives were not uniformly critical. Governor Dewey Bartlett's wife strongly disagreed with the *Courier*'s editorials against her husband. "I am, however, especially
pleased that our paper is interested in our state and in our responsibilities in our government," she told Reed in April 1967. "I think the fact that it doesn't allow us to be too comfortable for long is one of the main reasons that the paper is good for us." Ann Bartlett to
Victor Reed, April 11, 1967, Reed Papers.

72. John E. Rooney to Victor Reed, August 20, 1964, Reed Papers.

73. Frank A. Wallace to Victor Reed, April 12, 1964, Reed Papers.

respondents: "I am not going to sign my name—after reading the last Courier, I know how mean your liberal friends can be to the people who disagree with them. They have no love, charity or tolerance."[74]

By 1967, many readers suspected that Joyce had become convinced that to ensure a spirit of freedom within the Church, it was not only necessary to expose all its failings but also to avoid excessive criticism of the prevailing secular culture. Some of the most strident criticism to date was generated by a 1967 editorial, authored by Joyce, that called for the abolition of sin laws. "Priests like Joyce and [John] Vrana," Al Kavanaugh complained to Reed, "backed by you indicate public concern with the damage the religious ideas of moral children as expressed in prayer might have on pagan children, and then Joyce publicly editorialized in the Catholic Diocesan paper, that the obscenity peddlers have a right to publicly contaminate the minds of all children with filthy pictures and magazines."[75] The following year, William Suliburk expressed similar sentiments. "Is the Courier aiming at the sensationalism of the secular press," he demanded, "or is it dedicated to providing newsworthy material which allows the reader a dispassionate appraisal of world events as they affect his religion—or more particularly his faith in God?"[76] Robert Tompkins, chief of staff at Tulsa's St. Francis Hospital, poured fuel on the fire by criticizing the *Courier*'s practice of unsigned editorials: "If the editorials and feature articles were explanations and presentations of 'orthodox' dogma and teaching, we could safely assume that they represented the authentic magesterium in our ordinary. The Courier's editorial policy has differed so markedly from this course, even skirting the edges of outright heresy, that the reader is entitled to know whose opinion is being foisted upon him. A non-Catholic, like Mr. Bickham, should not write on Catholic doctrine in a Catholic publication, particularly when hidden behind the veil of 'editorial policy.'"[77]

At the heart of such complaints was the more fundamental question of whether a diocesan paper should be subject to the same principles of free speech enjoyed by secular publications and, if so, whether it should be per-

74. "A Catholic Mother" to Victor Reed, April 25, 1966, Reed Papers.
75. Al J. Kavanaugh to Victor Reed, July 10, 1967, Reed Papers._
76. William M. Suliburk to Victor Reed, February 25, 1968, Reed Papers.
77. Robert G. Tompkins to Victor Reed, August 16, 1968, Reed Papers. Reed had already required Joyce to implement a policy of signed editorials. See *Oklahoma Courier*, August 9, 1968. Jack Bickham, a journalism professor at the University of Oklahoma, was the paper's managing editor.

mitted to adopt a particular viewpoint, even if that might be at odds with the expressed position of Church leaders. Such controversies were by no means peculiar to Oklahoma. In August 1967, Bishop Michael Hyle of Wilmington (Delaware) sacked the editor of the *Delmarva Dialog* at the request of a majority of the priests in his diocese. The action provoked heated exchanges between the bishop and influential local laymen, with the former insisting that the poor financial condition of the paper was to blame and the latter accusing Hyle of attempting to stifle editorial freedom. While the truth was probably somewhere in between, there was no question that the sympathies of the new Catholic press were far more inclined to innovation than to the preservation of stability.[78]

For one who cherished a desire to be viewed as a professional newspaper editor, Father Joyce often displayed a surprising degree of contempt for those who paid his bills. The *Courier* was funded not by individual subscription but by diocesan parishes, which were expected to purchase a number of copies proportionate to their membership and pay for them out of the parish budget. This could present difficulties if a large number of parishioners moved away and had no desire to continue to subscribe to the paper, as Father Bernard Loftus of St. Francis Xavier, Stillwater, attested in 1960.[79] By 1967, resistance to subscriptions had risen dramatically. "Many people of this parish do not agree with the many editorials and articles published in the Courier," read one letter to Reed. "They feel these articles are derogatory towards the United States Government actions in Vietnam and other American principles. . . . The parish should not have to pay for subscriptions to those who do not wish to receive it."[80]

Joyce's manner toward his fellow clergy only exacerbated preexisting resentments. "The Courier has not received much from you during the past year," he complained in April 1962 to Monsignor John Connor of Oklahoma City's Cathedral of Our Lady of Perpetual Help, "except abuse, a commodity that appears to be a finely nurtured specialty of yours." An infuriated Connor hit back a few days later in a letter to the bishop: "After careful consideration, I have decided not to answer the impudent and insolent letter of

78. *Oklahoma Courier*, July 21, 1967; John Deedy, "Dialog but Blandly," *Commonweal*, August 11, 1967, 484–86. For a defense of Hyle's actions, see the letter of Joseph R. McMahon of Wilmington in *Commonweal*, September 8, 1967, 539.

79. Revd. Bernard Loftus to Revd. John M. Joyce, December 28, 1960, St. Francis Xavier Church, Stillwater File, box 80.1, ADT.

80. Holy Trinity Justithe Council to Victor Reed, December 1, 1967, Reed Papers.

Father Joyce.... I do think it is only fair that you should know that I consider the Courier pretty much a failure as a Diocesan newspaper.... It has an appeal to a certain group of pseudo intellectuals but I fear that the vast majority of the folks in the Diocese neither like nor read it."[81] Father Frederick Beckerle of St. Mary's Church in Tulsa was equally incensed by Joyce's demands. "If you would have bothered checking the records of the 'Oklahoma City Courier,'" he complained in 1966, "you would have found that we have always paid every cent of the unjust assessment to the Courier. We deeply resent your having the Bishop send us a personal dun for this assessment. Fortunately or unfortunately—we of St. Mary's are old-fashioned Catholics, and we still believe in heeding the requests of our Bishop."[82]

In February 1969, the pastoral board announced the closing of the *Courier*, effective April 9.[83] This followed the decision of the diocesan Little Council (see below) in 1968 to discontinue parish support, which, in turn, owed much to a curious alliance of conservatives—who objected to the paper's editorial stance—and liberals—who opposed the idea of compelling people to pay for something with which they disagreed. Conservatives hailed the *Courier*'s demise with undisguised glee. "If one were to wish to know what the people feel," Father Philip Wilkiemeyer remarked, "all he need do is look at the number of subscriptions to the Courier that have been paid for freely by the laity and not the forced subsidy list of every parish."[84] Even priests who had doubts about the wisdom of democratic governance for the Church welcomed this particular decision by the "people," arguing that pastoral letters were all that was necessary to communicate with members of the diocese.[85]

Reed made no secret of the fact that he regretted the Little Council's decision. "Father Joyce and his excellent staff have worked untiringly and courageously to produce one of the best Catholic papers in the country," he declared in February 1969, "[but] the fact is that the Catholics of our diocese have said a very loud NO to *The Oklahoma Courier* by not voluntarily subscribing."[86] The bishop's closest clerical aides agreed. Father Paul Donovan

81. Revd. John M. Joyce to Msgr. John M. Connor, April 27, 1962, Connor to Victor Reed, May 2, 1962, Reed Papers.

82. Revd. Frederick W. Beckerle to Revd. John Joyce, December 31, 1966, St. Mary's Church, Tulsa File, ADT.

83. *Oklahoma Courier*, February 21, 1969.

84. Revd. Philip Wilkiemeyer to Revd. David L. Jones, November 25, 1968, Reed Papers.

85. Revd. Ferdinand F. Meis to Victor Reed, February 28, 1969, Reed Papers.

86. Victor Reed to the People of Oklahoma, February 19, 1969, Reed Papers.

admitted that the *Courier* was expensive, one-sided, and displayed a dislike for "nuns, Catholic schools, bishops, Popes and authority in general," but insisted that it had been well received on the national scene and had been a useful means of communicating with Catholics throughout Oklahoma.[87] Father William Garthoeffner (no longer chancellor of the diocese but still an influential figure) echoed Donovan's arguments, accepting that the *Courier* had been "guilty at times of apparent disregard for and condescension towards those with whom the editorial staff comes in contact in preparation of stories," but he still maintained that it should be subsidized. "If we lose the paper—or if it is cut back so far as to become ineffectual—how will the Church in Oklahoma do any effective 'preaching'?" he asked. "Through the Sunday sermons, an adult education class (so poorly attended), an occasional circular letter, or sporadic reporting in the secular press or a national news magazine? That is all we would have left!"[88]

Radical pastors and laymen shared Garthoeffner's belief in the value of the *Courier* but had little sympathy with any critique of its motivations. Father William Skeehan at Tulsa's Church of the Resurrection maintained that the paper had been willing to address the issues of the day, including the corrupt bureaucracy of the Church. The fact that "our illiterate laity" had voted down the involuntary subscription program only proved the need for its presence in every home, Skeehan concluded.[89] Tulsa layman James McUsic argued that the paper needed a year to build up a subscription base, having been subsidized since its inception. It had been the only newspaper to ignore the rosy images presented by the Chamber of Commerce and critique the failings of Oklahoma, McUsic told Reed, and it had been one of the best adult education tools in existence.[90] Michael Ward, who served on the parish council of the Church of the Assumption in Muskogee, also regretted its demise. "Regardless of one's attitude toward the Courier," he insisted, "it was an outstanding, if not the outstanding Catholic weekly in the United States. It was our only source of diocesan Catholic views and it was read."[91]

That these events were followed beyond state lines was confirmed by a letter to Reed from Father Peter Hereley, who ran the Catholic campus par-

87. Revd. J. Paul Donovan to the Pastoral Board, November 18, 1968, Reed Papers.
88. Revd. William C. Garthoeffner to Revd. David L. Jones, November 24, 1968, Reed Papers.
89. Revd. William Skeehan to the Pastoral Board, November 5, 1968, Reed Papers.
90. James M. McUsic to Victor Reed, March 6, 1969, Reed Papers.
91. Michael S. Ward to Victor Reed, March 15, 1969, Reed Papers.

ish at South Dakota State University in Brookings: "I respect the decision of your Diocesan Pastoral Council as a decision of the people of the Church in Oklahoma. One of the great accomplishments of the renewal in the Church is the opening up to the Laity of a role in the decision making processes of the Church. But I cannot endorse this particular decision as being wise or prudent. Having followed the agonizing developments leading to the final establishment of the Council through the reporting of the events in the 'Courier', I find it depressingly ironic that one of the agencies most influential in the promotion of the Pastoral Council should be the sacrificial victim of the same Council."[92]

THE LITTLE COUNCIL

No transformation of diocesan structures more reflected the new involvement of the laity in Church governance than the establishment of the Little Council. In March 1964, Father Paul Donovan privately warned that there was a lesson to be learned from the fact that the bishops rather than the papal curia had determined policy at the Second Vatican Council. If subsidiarity (the notion that every activity should be undertaken at the most basic organizational level possible) were taken to its logical conclusion, Donovan insisted, the influence over policy exercised by Oklahoma's diocesan administrators should be replaced by a greater reliance on the deliberations of ordinary pastors and the people. The conciliar documents encouraged bishops to form pastoral councils to examine conditions at the diocesan level, and Donovan advocated such an approach for Oklahoma. Such a council should be composed of both clergy and laity and, while it might draw on the advice of experts, any initiatives should come from the grassroots.[93]

Following Archbishop Ritter's establishment of a similar council in St. Louis in December 1964, Reed announced that he intended to establish a "Little Council" to implement the reforms emerging from the deliberations

92. Revd. Peter J. Hereley, O.P., to Victor Reed, February 26, 1969, Reed Papers.

93. Revd. J. Paul Donovan to Revd. William C. Garthoeffner, March 9, 1964, Ecumenical Council and Council of Churches Papers. While it is tempting to view the Little Council (and, indeed, some of Reed's other reforms) as a resurrection of the "power-sharing" arrangement adopted by Bishop John England under the Charleston constitution of 1822, the Little Council appears to have been an entirely local and present-minded initiative, whose progenitors—several diocesan priests and active lay members of the Christian Family Movement—made no allusion to historical precedents. On England, see Carey, *An Immigrant Bishop*.

in Rome. "This appeals to me," he explained, "as a particularly appropriate method of advising the people of the work of Vatican Council II and of its results."[94] Reaction was mixed, though the proposals for the Little Council caught the attention of audiences ranging from the student body at Bishop McGuinness High School in Oklahoma City to an Episcopal laywoman who regretted that her own denomination had not initiated something similar.

Father Ernest Flusche, diocesan superintendent of schools, warned that it might be difficult to mesh a democratic structure with the hierarchical nature of the Church, while Father Joseph McGurk more optimistically hoped that it might be a means of reuniting liberals and conservatives in the diocese. Elsia Bibb of Tulsa suggested that more regular meetings between the bishop and the deans of the diocese would be preferable to any deliberative body, while Elizabeth Carr of Ponca City favored the Little Council proposal but worried that lay Catholics might be unwilling to criticize the Church publicly. Carr suggested that a survey of parish opinion be conducted using questions with a yes/no/undecided response formula, which could be tabulated to give a true picture of the views of individual parishes and the diocese as a whole and avoid subversion of the democratic process.[95]

Following the selection of chairmen for parish discussion groups in September 1965, Reed issued a series of pastoral letters for these groups to consider. James Cockrell, the head of the diocesan Catholic Action committee, ordered the preparation of two thousand discussion manuals, but received requests for three thousand in the first three days. Ultimately, between five thousand and ten thousand people would meet during the fall of 1965 to study the Constitution of the Church. By no means all laymen were equally confident in their new role. Father Joseph LaBarge at Christ the King parish in Oklahoma City thought that some parishioners were apprehensive about not having a priest to guide them through the discussion process.[96]

Elsewhere, there was more enthusiasm. "Our parish has caught the ball and is running with it," exulted Mrs. Arthur Boniface of St. Mary's parish in Tulsa. In Lawton, 160 laymen met at Blessed Sacrament parish and 162 at St. Barbara's parish, while 300 took part in the discussions at St. Mary's parish

94. *Oklahoma Courier*, February 12, 1965.

95. *Oklahoma Courier*, February 26, 1965; Elsia Bibb to Victor Reed, March 12, 1965, Elizabeth M. Carr to James L. Cockrell, August 31, 1965, Ecumenical Council and Council of Churches Papers.

96. "The Little Council of the Diocese of Oklahoma City and Tulsa," n.d. (prob. 1968), 3, Reed Papers; *Oklahoma Courier*, October 29, November 5, 1965.

in Ponca City. These discussions generated over three thousand suggestions, including the implementation of a uniform standard for celebration of the Mass, better adult education, more ecumenical exchanges, and a greater role for the laity in the temporal affairs of the parish.[97]

Oversight of the Little Council fell to James Cockrell, who testified both to Reed's personal concern with the Little Council and the high level of public interest in it. Cockrell initially recommended three investigatory commissions: Religious Education, Clergy, and Religious (members of religious orders, male and female) (see chapters 10 and 11). In an effort to limit the influence of diocesan administrators, a rule was imposed barring persons with defined diocesan responsibilities from serving on the Little Council commission dealing with their area of expertise. "Of course," Father William Garthoeffner pointed out, "the real decisions of the Little Council will be made by the Body of Delegates [later the Board of Delegates; the representative body of the Little Council]. There is no policy barring members of diocesan groups from becoming delegates to that body."[98]

Early in 1966 the Christian Education Commission, composed of seven laymen, four priests, and two nuns, began to draft outlines for the parish discussion groups. As a result of the 1965 parish discussions, seven additional commissions were organized later that year—Liturgy, Ecumenism, Social Action, Family Life, Parish Structure and Activity, Communications, and Diocesan Organization—each with the same number of delegates as the Christian Education Commission. Reed warned participants that any topic raised for discussion must carry an indication from him as to whether it was one on which he was willing to follow majority opinion or one where he wished to know the "consensus of the people" but reserved the right of final decision.[99]

"We expect some fireworks next week," declared William Garthoeffner in April 1966, "[when] parish discussion groups will take up, in three meetings, the nature of the parish. Some of our old crusty guys aren't going to like this—one told me that it had taken him 18 years to get his people under

97. *Oklahoma Courier*, November 12, November 26, 1965.

98. "The Little Council of the Diocese of Oklahoma City and Tulsa," 4; James L. Cockrell to *National Catholic Reporter*, October 26, 1965, Revd. William C. Garthoeffner to Revd. Ernest A. Flusche, December 14, 1965, Ecumenical Council and Council of Churches Papers.

99. "The Little Council of the Diocese of Oklahoma City and Tulsa," 4; Revd. William C. Garthoeffner to Revd. Ernest A. Flusche, December 14, 1965, Ecumenical Council and Council of Churches Papers.

control and now we wanted to come in and upset everything." Garthoeffner had his own concerns about the proposed structure for the Board of Delegates. While clerical and lay representatives were elected separately, they were to meet and vote as one unit, a move intended to improve communication between priests and laity but which might well provoke an alignment of the priests against the bishop. (This model was ultimately dropped in favor of a bicameral structure.) Garthoeffner also drew a less than flattering conclusion about his clerical brethren from the recommendation of most parish discussion groups for more adult education. "So the lay people recognize their shortcomings," he mused. "I am not so sure the priests do."[100]

In August and September of 1966, parishes and diocesan institutions began to select delegates for the Board of Delegates, although this proved to be a slow process, especially in the rural parishes. The Board of Delegates met for the first time in October for a business meeting to certify the 441 delegates and elect a Board of Presidents composed of two priests and three laymen. The bishop then appointed one priest, one religious, and two laymen to the Board of Presidents, making it a nine-member executive with a lay majority.[101] It was this action, more than any other, that guaranteed national publicity for the Diocese of Oklahoma City and Tulsa, as the only jurisdiction to be actively pursuing such a participatory model. While there had been an attempt at a Little Council in St. Louis, Cardinal Ritter had subsequently had second thoughts, and the project soon became enmeshed in layers of diocesan bureaucracy. In December 1966, the magazine *Fortune* printed an eight-page account of the changes sweeping through Oklahoma and St. Louis and the opposition that they had generated.[102]

The first working session of the Little Council took place on May 6, 1967, at Bishop McGuinness High School, where a draft constitution was approved. Although a number of amendments were put forward, the requirement of a two-thirds majority meant that only one—a proposal by Frank Martin that the clause stating that the Little Council functioned "at the pleasure of the bishop" should include the phrase "and the people of the dio-

100. Revd. William C. Garthoeffner to Revd. Bertram Griffin, April 10, 1966, Ecumenical Council and Council of Churches Papers.

101. *Oklahoma Courier*, September 23, October 21, 1966; "The Little Council of the Diocese of Oklahoma City and Tulsa," 4; Revd. William C. Garthoeffner to Revd. William J. Swift, August 23, 1966, Ecumenical Council and Council of Churches Papers.

102. Norton-Taylor, "The Catholic Layman Confronts His Changing Church." For the fate of the Little Council in St. Louis, see Faherty, *Dream by the River*, 208–10.

cese"—was approved. Among the rejected amendments were one giving extra representation to rural areas and one that would have eliminated the two houses of clergy and laity in favor of a unicameral structure.

A full-time Little Council office was established, and in August the council's various commissions were asked to carry out a survey of existing diocesan policy in their area of expertise by interviewing department heads and securing statements of policy. A modified principle of executive accountability to the people was thus established. The commission summaries were then distributed to Little Council delegates at a series of deanery meetings across the state. In December, department heads were invited to comment on any commission statement or delegate resolution proposed for the forthcoming Little Council session.[103]

Candidates for the Board of Presidents in 1967 overwhelmingly represented a generation born during the 1930s and 1940s—committed, educated Catholics deeply involved in the life of the wider community and the promises of Vatican II. Thus, James Goodwin, a twenty-eight-year-old attorney from St. Monica's, Tulsa, who served on the City-County Health Board, declared that he wished to participate in the Little Council in order to further the work of ecumenical dialogue; while Lee Ann Kennedy, a thirty-one-year-old music teacher, who served on the Norman Civic Improvement Council and the Norman Municipal Hospital Auxiliary, pledged to ensure that decisions of the Little Council would be implemented as rapidly as possible. Barbara Hayes, a youthful CCD (Confraternity of Christian Doctrine) teacher from Oklahoma City, perhaps caught the optimistic spirit of the delegates most eloquently. "Oklahoma with its Little Council is in a position to make great contributions to Christianity," she declared. "The whole nation waits for its success or failure. It is at this level where the fate of the Vatican Council lies. . . . Since I'm originally from the East, I can fully appreciate the large responsibility Oklahoma laymen have in their church."[104]

On April 19, 1968, the Little Council met at St. Gregory's College in Shawnee for its third session, with 167 resolutions already approved for consideration at the deanery level. "Most of the priests and people thought it was a healthy idea," Paul Donovan argued. "Some thought it was nuts because we didn't decide anything, hardly, and some of the things we decided

103. *Oklahoma Courier*, May 12, 1967; "The Little Council of the Diocese of Oklahoma City and Tulsa," 5–7.
104. Nominating papers for candidates for Board of Presidents, 1967, Ecumenical Council and Council of Churches Papers.

. . . the *bishop* couldn't decide . . . and he told them that. He said: 'Even if you pass this . . . I won't accept it, but . . . even if I accepted it, it couldn't be done.'"[105] Donovan illustrates once again what was to be one of the fundamental problems of the Little Council—the manner in which an ostensibly democratic process was obliged to coexist with traditional conceptions of ecclesiastical authority.

"At times," an Episcopal clergyman observing the session remarked, "the tedious and somewhat repressive rules of order and voting seemed to defeat spontaneous expression; yet as the council session continued, it became apparent that the difficulties were being resolved and true democratic exchange of ideas was occurring."[106] Early in the session, too, it became clear that the more conservative elements had learned something about parliamentary procedure. The votes to abolish mandatory subscriptions to the *Oklahoma Courier* and to reject a proposal for the diocese to immediately join the Council of Churches were key liberal defeats, although liberals later secured a strong vote in favor of an open housing covenant.

On the liturgy, Little Council delegates stressed the need for controlled experimentation and took no action on modification of the Sunday Mass obligation. Changes that they endorsed included pulpit exchange with Protestant churches on Reformation Sunday and during Lent, a relaxation of canon law in relation to mixed marriages, Communion under both forms, and authorization of general confession. In addition, delegates stressed the need for a governing lay board for all parishes and supported optional celibacy for the clergy. Even if they knew that no action of theirs could force Reed's hand, his willingness to attend and listen was in itself little short of miraculous. "One had to marvel," wrote Elise Hamm of Lawton in a letter to the *Courier*, "at the sight of our bishop, dressed like all his priests, unobtrusively sitting in the Little Council audience and attentively listening to the debates."[107]

After the 1968 session, the momentum generated by the Little Council largely evaporated. Many in the liberal camp shared the concern expressed by Joe Coulter of Norman after the 1967 session that the structure of the Little Council favored the bishop's agenda, which had a strong element of

105. Donovan, interview.

106. Revd. John T. Jackson to Little Council, April 24, 1968, Ecumenical Council and Council of Churches Papers; *Oklahoma Courier*, April 26, 1968. Jackson included a copy of his article "Only in Oklahoma," which appeared in several Episcopal publications, in his communication.

107. *Oklahoma Courier*, April 26, 1968.

truth since Reed had no legal obligation to respect any Little Council resolution.[108] Of equal concern to rural delegates was the suspicion that it was the large urban parishes that set the agenda. "Many delegates in my area," declared Don Gallagher of Mother of Sorrows parish in Apache, "are making the statement that this is truly the Diocese of Oklahoma City and Tulsa with the rest of the state left out or just ignored. I find that in surveying the delegates and Parish Councils in this area that the Board of Presidents did not consult anyone about what is the most pressing need in this area." Gallagher's accusation that the Little Council was monopolizing power was echoed by Father Daniel Perlinski of Blessed Sacrament parish, Coalgate, who pointed out that the deanery meetings held in major urban centers were hard for rural delegates to attend. "I was wondering," he remarked to Father David Jones, the executive director of the Little Council, "if any thought had been given to the small and DISTANT Parishes in trying to come to these meetings."[109]

Some priests even suggested that the views of the delegates were unrepresentative of ordinary Catholics. "I would suggest," declared Father William Saulnier to a colleague in San Francisco in 1970, "that every effort be made to make sure that the 'grass roots level' will be well informed as to what the Council is and hopes to do, and can effect. One of our problems in Oklahoma has been that the delegate assembly does not always represent the attitudes of its constituency."[110] The following year, the bishop reminded delegates to the General Assembly of the Diocesan Council (as the Little Council had come to be known) that they should not think of themselves as a strictly "legislative body," but should try to represent the sentiments of everyone in the diocese. At the same meeting, Father Saulnier urged that the council should meet more frequently. "The direction is going to be much more on a local level than on the grand scale of a meeting a year. There's much more to the Council than attending a meeting a year and then taking the rest of the year to digest it. There must be more work on the local level if the General Assembly is to bear fruit that we would like it to."[111]

While Reed praised the achievements of the Little Council, he sometimes

---

108. *Oklahoma Courier*, May 19, 1967.

109. Don Gallagher to Fr. ?, December 15, 1970, Revd. Daniel A. Perlinski to Revd. David Jones, January 31, 1968, Ecumenical Council and Council of Churches Papers.

110. Revd. William P. Saulnier to Revd. William R. Burns, September 12, 1970, Ecumenical Council and Council of Churches Papers.

111. *Catholic News*, May 1971, 4.

admitted that he regretted the slow pace at which business was conducted. "In the beginning," he declared in March 1968, "I thought that the work of the Little Council would be a matter of perhaps a year or two. But it wasn't very long until I realized that the work of the Little Council is probably a work that is going to go on and on. I don't know just how long. I feel that I expected too much of it too soon. I expected people to throw themselves into it more wholeheartedly than they have done. I felt that they would be able to assimilate things faster than they are able to do."[112] Reed's frustration was shared by the Glenmary priest stationed in rural Idabel. "We had 4 people present for our parish Little Council meeting," he wrote in May 1967, "which show [*sic*] the parish is just not interested in contributing to the renewal of the Roman Catholic Church (tho doubtless they will gripe about what has been done after the fact)."[113]

CONCLUSION

By assuming the Tulsa Benedictine debt, the Diocese of Oklahoma City and Tulsa found itself obliged to implement professional standards of administration during the early 1960s. Since this administrative modernization took place at a later date than in other midwestern dioceses and since Victor Reed proved more open to the active participation of laymen in diocesan administrative life, the adoption of these new standards was accompanied by a high degree of lay oversight, most notably in relation to the pastoral board. Reed's acknowledgment that the laity would play a greater role in the life of the diocese also led him to encourage the transformation of the diocesan newspaper to make it a means of education for those lay Catholics who would ultimately participate in the work of the Little Council. These changes, while they appeared to be in the service of democratic subsidiarity, did not substantively increase the voice of the laity. Indeed, in the case of the *Courier*, Father Joyce's zest for subsidiarity declined markedly when more conservative laymen disagreed with him, something that, ironically, may have precipitated the "democratic" decision to kill the paper.

Only with the Little Council did a modified form of democratic subsidiarity come into its own. A rarity even among midwestern dioceses, the Little Council enjoyed a peculiar freedom both in the way in which its members

---

112. Jack M. Bickham, "An Interview with Bishop Reed," *Decade of Change*, 6.
113. Berthiaume, Glenmary Missioner Newsletter.

were chosen and in its ability to debate contentious issues and pass resolutions. The paradox of the Little Council, however, was that ultimately all decisions rested with Reed. Oklahoma Catholics enjoyed only as much freedom as their ordinary chose to permit, a confusing concept to Americans schooled in the philosophy of popular rule refracted through a system of checks and balances. By the end of the 1960s, the diocese's reliance on lay advisors had unquestionably increased, but it remained open to question whether those in the best position to exert influence were necessarily most representative of those at the grassroots. Ultimately, it was the believers in centralized structures, not their opponents, who would be the victors at the end of the Reed episcopate.

chapter 4 ∽⌒◯

Educated Catholics

The School Question Revisited

> *A Christian education . . . has as its principal purpose this goal: that the baptized, while they are gradually introduced to the knowledge of the mystery of salvation, become ever more aware of the gift of Faith they have received, and that they learn in addition how to worship God the Father in spirit and truth especially in liturgical action, and be conformed in their personal lives according to the new man created in justice and holiness of truth; also that they develop into perfect manhood, to the mature measure of the fullness of Christ and strive for the growth of the Mystical Body; moreover, that aware of their calling, they learn not only how to bear witness to the hope that is in them but also how to help in the Christian formation of the world that takes place when natural powers viewed in the full consideration of man redeemed by Christ contribute to the good of the whole society.*

> Second Vatican Council, Declaration on Christian Education,
> *Gravissimum Educationis,* October 28, 1965

On March 11, 1960, a letter from a professor of history at St. Gregory's College in Shawnee appeared in the diocesan newspaper urging Oklahoma Catholics to acknowledge how many of their children had been consigned to the public school system. "Let's face it," the priest concluded, "the public schools are ours too . . . a child from a solidly Christian or Catholic family may become a very representative Catholic lay man—even if the public school were his only opportunity for formal education."[1]

---

1. *Oklahoma Courier*, March 11, 1960.

The implications of such a declaration were ominous for those convinced that the parochial school system was the lifeblood of the Catholic Church, but worse was to come. Three weeks later (ironically enough on April Fool's Day) the superintendent of Bishop McGuinness High School, Father Ramon Carlin, proposed that, in the age of an active lay movement, it was worth inquiring whether the parochial school system could any longer be justified from either a philosophical or an economic point of view. He called for a serious comparative study of students in Catholic and secular educational institutions to see if the latter could do as good a job of producing spiritually and morally competent young adults.[2]

That the head of a flagship Catholic school could make such a declaration shocked many in the wider educational community. A Benedictine sister teacher, who had worked with Carlin some years before, derided the superintendent's fixation with modernity: "I hoped at last that [Father Carlin] might begin to perceive that Holy Mother Church might have known human nature years before the [Young Christian Students] or [Christian Family Movement] or McGuinness High or Father Carlin were born, and that in so knowing, She had passed Canon Law No. 1374 that states specifically that Catholic children must not attend public schools. I understand Father Carlin is a graduate of a public school. Is he the prototype of public school leader and apostle we Catholic schools have failed to produce?"[3] Although many other correspondents were equally critical, Carlin was not entirely without allies. On April 22, the *Oklahoma Courier* published a letter from a woman who sympathized with his general conclusions and insisted that despite twelve years of Catholic schooling, most of her peers had left with "a timid faith based upon memorized catechetical answers that are difficult, if not impossible, to apply to the stress and strains of everyday life."[4]

During the 1960s, the debate over religiously segregated schools burst onto the national scene for the first time since the 1890s. Then on the defensive, American Catholics had viewed the parochial schools as a vital element in their cultural survival. During the first half of the twentieth century, they took pride in giving their financial all to the upkeep of such institutions. As they began to enter the cultural mainstream and as their children increasingly attended secular colleges for their higher education, however, middle-class Catholic parents increasingly demanded a say in the management of their

2. *Oklahoma Courier*, April 1, 1960.   3. *Oklahoma Courier*, April 8, 1960.
4. *Oklahoma Courier*, April 22, 1960.

parochial schools at the expense of pastors and clerical bureaucrats, seeking greater lay representation at both diocesan and parish levels.

When the Catholic sociologist Father Andrew Greeley conducted just the sort of survey recommended by Ramon Carlin, however, he still did not find most middle-class parents desirous of ending the Catholic education system. "Upward mobility," he concluded, "has made Catholics more concerned about religious education and more able to finance a rapid growth in the system of religious education that they happen to have at hand." Most did not seem to be affected by considerations of costs, and Greeley found little sense of a "revolt" against the principle of a Catholic education.[5] The struggle over the future of the Catholic education system, however, would prove to be as intense a cultural battleground, in its way, as the coincidental debates over renewal of the liturgy and the Church's stance on artificial birth control.

Few Oklahoma Catholics were aware of the tensions bubbling beneath the surface during the 1950s. Just as the prelates of Chicago and Cincinnati were pressing ahead with expansion, so Oklahomans saw similar progress at home.[6] While a few small schools in the rural west were obliged to close, the face of the future was exemplified by St. Anne's parish in Broken Arrow. Located in a growing outer suburb of Tulsa, the parish saw its student body swell from sixty-five in 1958 to one hundred in 1959, leading its pastor to request permission to expand the parochial school. Ironically, given that within a few years parochial schools would be under attack for lacking the facilities enjoyed by public schools, the parish planned to include a kindergarten in the next phase of expansion, something that the Broken Arrow public school lacked.[7]

The general rule also continued to prevail in Oklahoma that if there was an accessible parochial school, Catholic parents had a moral obligation to

5. Greeley and Rossi, *The Education of Catholic Americans*, 199–218. Greeley included a sample of readers of *Commonweal* (212–15) as representative of the extreme integrationist position. These proved even more likely to send their children to Catholic school than the average Catholic parent, but those who did *not* send their children to Catholic school often expressed criticisms of the Catholic school system quite as vigorous as any secular liberal intellectual. *Commonweal* readers tended to be more interested in modifying teaching methods than improving school facilities, but only 7 percent of them expressed the view that parents should have a greater role in the management of schools.

6. On Chicago, see Avella, *This Confident Church*, 88–92; and on Cincinnati, see Fortin, *Faith and Action*, 322–25. Avella notes that it was hard to raise money even in wealthy suburbs, where the middle class was burdened with mortgage and car payments.

7. Revd. Robert Dabrowski, O.F.M.Cap., to Victor Reed, September 3, 1959, St. Anne's Church, Broken Arrow File, Archives of the Catholic Diocese of Tulsa (hereafter ADT).

send their child there. While priests' attitudes varied, some took this parental duty extremely seriously. In 1961, Father Julian Grehan bluntly stated that
few Okmulgee Catholics had any excuse for sending their children to public school at the elementary level. Any financial problems could be resolved,
he reassured chancery officials, and transportation was easily available. Moreover, all the school's teachers were state accredited, which should alleviate
any concerns about children's ability to transfer to a public high school.[8]

When Catholic children were placed in the public schools—and their parents almost always requested the bishop's permission for this—it was generally because the choices available beyond elementary school, especially outside
Oklahoma City and Tulsa, were too limited. One of the leaders in the protest
against Father McGinty at St. Francis Xavier in 1940 (see chapter 2) spoke
for many when he complained to Bishop Reed that while the first six grades
at Stillwater's parochial school were excellent, its teaching of math and science at the higher grades was simply not reflective of the new techniques
employed in the public schools, and it failed to stream by ability. Given the
small number of teaching staff employed by many of these schools, this can
hardly have come as a surprise to anyone.[9] Parishioners of St. Mary's, Ardmore, faced a similar dilemma after their local air force base closed in 1958,
leaving a single child in the parochial school's eighth grade and only two in
the seventh grade. Wishing them to be able to associate with children their
own age, their parents sought permission to enroll them in public school.[10]

Parents who requested exemptions were assiduous in requiring children
who attended public school to take part in parish education and religious
correspondence courses. It was rare for Reed to question their estimation as
to the educational needs of their children.[11] A notable exception to this rule

8. Revd. Julian S. Grehan, C.SS.R., to Revd. William C. Garthoeffner, August 29, 1961,
St. Anthony's Church, Okmulgee File, ADT. Grehan's predecessor was accused of punish-
ing parents for putting their children in public school by denying their offspring First Com-
munion on the grounds that they were inadequately prepared. See Mrs. Layton Wilson to
Victor Reed, January 12, 1959, Teresa Jacobs to Victor Reed, January 12, 1959, St. Anthony's
Church, Okmulgee File.

9. K. D. Greiner to Victor Reed, May 10, 1962, Revd. Charles H. Schettler to Revd.
William J. Pace, June 11, 1962, St. Francis Xavier Church, Stillwater File, box 80.1, ADT.

10. Jack Conroy to Victor Reed, August 18, 1958, Reed to Conroy, August 28, 1958,
Dale Trotter to Reed, September 16, 1958, Reed to Trotter, September 17, 1958, St Mary's
Church, Ardmore File, Archives of the Catholic Archdiocese of Oklahoma City (hereafter
AAOC).

11. Lewis H. Coon to Victor Reed, September 9, 1961, Msgr. Raymond F. Harkin to
Coon, September 19, 1961, St. Francis Xavier Church, Stillwater File, box 80.1.

was the case of the Keitz family at Christ the King parish in Oklahoma City, who sought a recommendation from their pastor for their son to attend a summer school run by the Episcopal Church. Although frequent communicants and active members of the Christian Family Movement, the Keitzs had taken their older children out of the parish school without their pastor's permission and enrolled them at the Episcopal Casady School for what one of the teaching sisters called "political and social reasons." Reed made it clear that the pastor should make no recommendation.[12]

A minority of priests in the diocese shared the misgivings expressed by Father Carlin in 1960. "When we built the Madalene," Father James McNamee declared in 1968, "we built the school first because that was considered the correct thing to do. Later, we built the church. Perhaps that was right, and perhaps it wasn't. No one imagined the changes that would come over the world. Today, probably 40 per cent of Catholic children are in church schools and 60 per cent in public schools."[13] McNamee's priorities were evident as early as 1960, when his parochial school could accommodate only half the children in the parish. Rather than try to obtain funding to expand the school plant, both the pastor and his assistant advised parents to use the public schools. "We do belittle the Tulsa Public School system," admitted one of McNamee's parishioners, "which is undoubtedly one of the state's finest, but the fact remains that it is most difficult to give a child a complete religious training with only Saturday morning Catechism classes and home instruction."[14]

ADMINISTRATIVE REFORM

The increasing demand for academic excellence had repercussions for the entire school system. In June 1960, the bishop made it a requirement that no parochial school classroom have more than fifty students, a move that forced several elementary schools in Tulsa (including the Madalene) to close their first grade due to lack of space. Nine months later, the dioce-

12. Revd. Charles J. Johnson to Victor Reed, April 28, 1961, Reed to Johnson, May 1, 1961, Christ the King Church, Oklahoma City File, AAOC. The Casady School was controversial. One *Courier* correspondent reported that all students were required to attend chapel and that one teacher at the school had told his class that there was no such person as Jesus Christ and that the Bible "was merely the story of a fictitious character after whose life we should try to pattern ours." *Oklahoma Courier*, August 12, 1960.
13. *Tulsa Tribune*, May 9, 1968.
14. Robert L. Edlich to Reed, May 31, 1960, Reed Papers.

Father Ernest Flusche, diocesan superintendent of schools, addresses the diocesan Little Council in the late 1960s.

san board of education banned fund-raising—including for civic charitable
drives—from school property, arguing the need for teachers to focus solely
on education.[15]

Structural transformation of the Catholic educational system was an inevitable part of the 1960s. At the prompting of Father Ernest Flusche, the superintendent of schools from 1959 to 1968, Bishop Reed established the first
mixed (clerical and lay) diocesan board of education in the United States in
1960. The board aggressively encouraged parochial schools to secure state
accreditation (largely achieved by 1964) and imposed new safety regulations
in the wake of 1958's devastating fire at Our Lady of the Angels School in
Chicago. It also implemented health and insurance policies for all its teachers
and worked to raise the salaries of sister teachers. In 1963, the bishop trans-

15. *Oklahoma Courier*, June 3, 1960, March 10, 1961.

formed the board from an advisory to a regulatory body, with full control and authority over planning and building schools, consolidations, dropping of grades, and school closings. While laymen held only six of the twenty positions on the board (priests held ten and sisters held four), the laity now had a real voice in the educational process.[16]

The changes were not confined to the diocesan level. Education was increasingly seen as an overriding community concern, which could no longer be the sole concern of the pastor. As early as 1960, Mr. and Mrs. Leonard Bachle had pleaded for a centralized school board for Oklahoma City, which would enable parishes to cooperate on educational matters and make better use of the talents of the laity.[17] In December 1962, Father Flusche urged Reed to establish parish school boards for Oklahoma, composed of two members elected by the parents' organization; one nominated by the pastor; the pastor; and the school principal, with a right of appeal of all decisions to the board of education. While the effectiveness of these boards varied, many parents welcomed the opportunity to play a more direct role in the Catholic education of their children.[18]

The changes in the nature and authority of the school board were complemented by the establishment of the Office of Religious Education in September 1962, apparently the first institution of its kind in the worldwide Church.[19] In 1961, Father Flusche had proposed the creation of a religious education committee to oversee programs of religious instruction for Catholic children, whether in parochial or public schools, and coordinate their efforts. The choice for chairman of this committee fell on the vice rector of St. Francis de Sales Seminary, Father Joseph Dillon, who was dispatched for a year of study in pastoral catechetics at the International Catechetical School, Lumen Vitae, in Brussels, Belgium. On his return, Dillon became director of religious

16. Flusche, interview; "Running Catholic Schools," April 13, 1963, Reed Papers; *Oklahoma Courier*, March 1, 1963.

17. *Oklahoma Courier*, August 26, 1960. No citywide board ever materialized.

18. Flusche, interview. The general recommendation of reformers was that such boards should deal with school policy, not with day-to-day administration. Most felt that while pastors and school principals should still be members of the board, the chairman should be a layman, elected by the board, so that the lay members would feel no impulse to defer to their pastor's opinion. See Murdick, *The Parish School Board*).

19. Father Flusche stated that he had inquiries about the Office of Religious Education from as far away as India. The office organized five-day workshops with international experts in catechetics, including some from the Institut Catholique in Paris, which drew audiences of up to five hundred people. Flusche, interview.

The basketball team at Cascia Hall, Tulsa, receives its trophy.

education for the diocese, presiding over a nine-member office with elementary, high school and youth, and adult departments.

Stressing the need for a professional approach to the educational process, the office helped parishes to design religious education programs, particularly if they were making the transition to catechetical instruction alone after the closing of a parish school. It arranged teacher training and vacation school preparation workshops, developed sacramental programs involving parents, and maintained a lending library of books, tapes, and visual aids. Although it affected to take a neutral stand on the value of parochial schools, it nevertheless made it clear in 1967 that religious education was not just for children: "The aims of the Office of Religious Education are to bring about an equalization of educational facilities since less than fifty percent of Catholic children attend Catholic schools. The Office offers its services on an equal basis, and thus encourages parishes to equalize their efforts and facilities and thus look forward to the day when the parish budget is more evenly distributed toward all its" members as regards education."[20]

The 1960s also brought new challenges for Oklahoma's Catholic educators, as they sought not only to preserve the substance of a parochial education system but also to structure it so as to win the respect of outside observers. A meeting of the diocesan board of education in October 1964 placed much of the blame for the low reputation of the state Catholic education system on the diocesan press, but agreed that it had at least brought into the open the question of how much ordinary Catholics believed in Catholic schools. "It was felt that the ideal of every Catholic child in a Catholic school no longer exists," board members conceded. "We have an obligation to improve the quality of our schools and to do a better job with the children who are attending our Catholic schools." Thus, at least implicitly, even the diocesan school board conceded the point made by pastors like Father McNamee that the era of statewide Catholic education was over. Board members agreed that the diocese should make parents aware of the true costs of education, implement efforts to combat the existing high rate of teacher turnover, and adopt a uniform salary scale for teachers.[21]

The problem of teacher retention, however, was one over which local school boards and the board of education frequently divided. Rural Catholics fiercely resisted proposals that would increase central oversight and consolidate small parochial schools to achieve economies of scale, since such consolidation could easily lead to children in the more remote parts of the state traveling up to twenty-five miles every day. (School district consolidation was also taking place in the Oklahoma public school system and excited the same opposition from small-town residents about to lose their independent school district.) Mike Schlitz of Ponca City pointed out that many rural dwellers, especially farmers, had college degrees but not the income normally associated with higher education, and argued that teachers should be willing to accept a salary commensurate with what the health of the local economy would bear.[22]

Such an argument was increasingly rejected even by the religious teaching orders, which were not willing to see their members used to subsidize

20. "Office of Religious Education: Response to the Little Council's Education Commission Questionnaire," 1–4 (quotation on 4), September 18, 1967, Reed Papers; Joseph D. Dillon, "Reflections on My Life," in Brousseau, *A Dying Breed of Brave Men*, 55–56.

21. Minutes of the Diocesan Board of Education, October 8, 1964, Reed Papers.

22. *Oklahoma Courier*, October 9, 1964.

ailing school systems, but it also cut very little ice with lay teachers, who knew they could expect much better treatment from the public system. A 1965 report conceded that the majority of lay teachers in parochial schools were either older than the average or new teachers just beginning their careers. They received low salaries, few had access to a retirement plan, and there was little opportunity for them to rise into the better-compensated administrative positions, which were still dominated by the religious teaching orders.[23] Even in urban settings, tensions between religious and secular faculty could be intense. In 1965, lay teachers in Tulsa formed the Tulsa Lay Teachers Association, prompting Father Flusche to urge more comprehensive faculty meetings and greater socialization between religious and lay teachers and their families. Any sense of lay teachers as second-class citizens was obviously something to be avoided.[24]

Public acceptance of Catholic schools rested largely on their ability to secure state accreditation, which in turn depended both on teacher certification and on the number of credits offered by schools.[25] The latter requirement, a particular burden for the smaller high schools, could be addressed through "shared time" or dual enrollment, under which Catholic students could attend public high schools for certain courses, especially vocational ones. Discussions at the December 1966 meeting of the board of education focused on the whole philosophy of shared time. Board member Mary Cherry maintained that if a choice *had* to be made, the Catholic schools should derogate subjects such as mathematics and physical education and maintain responsibility for the "value subjects," such as languages and social studies, into which religious themes could more easily be incorporated. She also argued that shared time should not be contemplated before the sixth grade and warned against the desire of young priests to discard the Catholic education system altogether.[26]

Cherry's defense of the existing system was challenged by fellow board members, including Dr. John Renner of the University of Oklahoma. When the diocesan Little Council produced a statement on education in 1967, Renner objected that it seemed more concerned with preserving school

23. *Oklahoma Courier*, February 26, 1965.

24. "Recommendations to the Administration and Faculty of the Tulsa High School," n.d., Minutes of the Diocesan Board of Education, March 11, 1965, Reed Papers.

25. Minutes of the Diocesan Board of Education, November 19, 1964, Revd. Ernest A. Flusche to Victor Reed, June 15, 1967, Reed Papers.

26. Minutes of the Diocesan Board of Education, December 9, 1966, Reed Papers.

buildings than addressing the needs of children generally deprived of educational opportunities. To ignore such issues as the low salaries of many teachers or the failure of most forms of education to meet the needs both of gifted children and slow learners, Renner concluded, was lamentable:

> I feel the Catholic Church should be seeking areas in the cities and remote places where first rate schools can be established to provide God's children, regardless of their communion, educational opportunities they do not now have. I would like to see the Church send persons into the ghetto schools of the cities to seek and identify talented pupils and assist them on their way. . . . As I read the position paper of the Little Council, I felt a little ashamed that this was the best an entire diocese could do. It does well at discussing Catholic education but does a very pathetic job of addressing itself to Christian education. Maybe the well-intentioned persons writing this document were completely unaware of the real need for education conducted by Christians for Christians and the opportunities there are for doing this in today's world.[27]

THE SCHOOL LEVEL: CONTROVERSY AND CONFLICT

While the philosophical debate raged at the diocesan level, local parents were becoming increasingly aware of the price tag attached to twelve years of Catholic education. As early as 1958, Monsignor Bartholomew Murtaugh, who taught at Bishop McGuinness High School, warned Reed that looming deficits made it imperative that families who could afford to do so meet their tuition and book bills. Those children whose families failed to do so should be denied their graduation transcripts, Murtaugh insisted.[28] Father William Skeehan faced a similar problem at Sacred Heart parish in Oklahoma City. An unrealistically low annual tuition charge, coupled with the need to raise lay teachers' salaries to a level comparable with those of the public schools, had produced a $16,000 deficit for the parish. Skeehan consequently raised tuition to $50 for in-parish Catholics, $75 for out-of-parish Catholics, and $100 for non-Catholics. "The degree to which you believe in a Catholic education for your child," he warned parents in July 1965, "will be the measure of acceptance regarding this proposal."[29]

27. John W. Renner to Revd. Richard Sneed, October 16, 1967, Reed Papers.

28. Revd. Bartholomew A. Murtaugh to Victor Reed, May 10, 1958, Reed Papers. This was never done: it would have been illegal to do so, in the view of the former superintendent of schools.

29. Revd. William K. Skeehan to parents of children attending Sacred Heart School, July 5, 1965, Sacred Heart Church, Oklahoma City File, AAOC.

Not every priest believed in requiring tuition increases to be borne by parents, since doing so often led to a drop in collections or a massive withdrawal of pupils from the school. Skeehan's solution cushioned the blow somewhat for members of Sacred Heart, but other pastors preferred to place the burden on the shoulders of the whole parish.[30] Some laymen developed this argument even further. Richard Ciskowski, a parishioner at St. Joseph's parish in Blackwell, argued from analogy that since public schools were paid for by the secular community as a whole, so parochial schools should be, at least in part, the responsibility of all parishioners.[31]

Many parents increasingly worried about the extent to which they were expected to subsidize the high school system. A 1965–1966 survey of Catholic high schools in the central United States revealed an annual tuition high of $315 at St. Pius X High School in Albuquerque, New Mexico, and a low of $100 at Bishop Miege High School in Kansas City, Kansas. In Oklahoma, tuition at Tulsa's Bishop Kelley High School ranged from $165 to $195, while Oklahoma City's Bishop McGuinness High School charged $175. Ten of the seventeen schools surveyed enjoyed subsidies from their parish or diocese, including both of those in Oklahoma, but such subsidies came increasingly under attack as the 1960s wore on.[32]

In April 1967, Oklahoma City pastors increased parish subsidies for the city's two high schools (McGuinness and Mount St. Mary's) from $41,000 to $56,100. One option—the "Office Plan"—proposed taxing parishes according to their current income to raise the subsidy, while a second—the "Harkin Plan"—increased the per student assessment from $50 to $60 per year for McGuinness pupils and from $25 to $60 for Mount St. Mary's pupils. Thirteen pastors endorsed the Harkin Plan and only four the Office Plan, largely because the former made parish support for the high schools reflective of the services that they received from them. The following year, Bishop Kelley High School also raised tuition, imposing an average increase in tuition costs for parents of between $205 and $250 per year for each student.[33]

---

30. Minutes of meeting with Sisters of Mercy relative to Mount St. Mary's High School, May 10, 1965, Reed Papers.

31. Richard Ciskowski to Revd. Ernest A. Flusche, September 15, 1964, St. Joseph's Church, Blackwell File, AAOC.

32. Comparative Costs of Catholic High Schools in the Central United States, 1965–66, Reed Papers.

33. Minutes of Pastors' Meeting April 21, 1967, Finance Committee to Bishop Kelley High School, December 2, 1968, Reed Papers.

The rendering of such decisions by clergy alone inclined many parents to seek further enhancement of the power of parish school boards. In 1968, Lawrence Rooney urged that the Muskogee Christian Board of Education (of which he was a member) be granted a greater degree of autonomy. "We feel that Parish priests come and go as the system of rotation dictates," Rooney complained. "Therefore it is important that the board be a viable one and not some sort of mendicant organization that may have its actions voided by a pastor. It would be handy if we could deal with the diocese, the Bishop as Corporate Sole, or whatever, within the bounds of proper procedure considering the legalities of the matter. . . . Also, as evidenced by our by-laws, we propose to cooperate with the diocesan school board (if that is the proper name) for matters of school policy, curricula, etc."[34]

Some parishes also fought back against imposed subsidies. In May 1970, the chairman of the parish council of St. Pius X Church in Tulsa objected to a $10 increase in its per-student subsidy for Bishop Kelley High School, which would add $1,500 to parish costs at a time when the parish was running a $15,000 deficit. He suggested that the high school raise the tuition charges for parents to a level commensurate with other schools run by the Christian Brothers. When school administrators objected to the proposition that there should be a $15 differential between St. Pius X and other Tulsa parishes, the chairman explained that his parish was striving to keep open its grade school and that enrollment at Kelley was directly dependent on the survival of Catholic grade schools. Again, he suggested that the $15 be added to student tuition. Ultimately, Bishop Reed was forced to intervene directly. While he offered to make up the difference for the 1970 school year, he also required that the parish meet the subsidy determined by the high school and approved by the diocesan pastoral board. The school's pastor gloomily promised to convey the bishop's desires to the parish council but stated that he had no idea where the money was to be found.[35]

Parental involvement in school governance was not an exclusively church-centered undertaking. As part of the process of engagement with the secular world, members of the Parent-Teacher Association of Christ the King parish in Oklahoma City proposed that the high school PTA join the national orga-

34. Lawrence F. Rooney Jr. to Revd. Ernest A. Flusche, June 7, 1968, Flusche to Reed, June 12, 1968, Reed Papers.

35. Harrison B. Casey to the Pastoral Board, May 12, 1970, Harrison B. Casey to Brother K. Bernardine, F.S.C., June 18, 1971, Victor Reed to Revd. William J. Swift, July 29, 1971, Swift to Reed, August 3, 1971, St. Pius X Church, Tulsa File, ADT.

nization. Christ the King had been a member of the national PTA since 1959, and the proposal was endorsed by the school superintendent and the director of athletics, Father David Monahan. It was vocally opposed, however, by members of St. Francis of Assisi parish who objected to the national PTA's support for Planned Parenthood and the United Nations. While the McGuinness PTA voted 117 to 51 to affiliate in November 1962, this fell short of the 75 percent vote in favor that was required.[36]

The saga of the PTA proposal demonstrates very well the cultural tensions that would dominate the education debate later in the decade. Oklahoma's flagship Catholic high schools—Bishop McGuinness High School in Oklahoma City and Bishop Kelley High School in Tulsa—also provide a study in contrasts. The McGuinness model reflected the spirit of Catholic engagement with the world and its problems. In March 1960, Beverly Stephens, a McGuinness senior and reporter for the school newspaper, *Chi Rhoan*, won first place in an essay contest with "The Catholic in the World." Through a study of five ordinary Catholics—a steelworker, a stenographer, a young mother, a high school student, and an executive—Stephens sought to demonstrate how members of the Mystical Body of Christ were to seek out their own apostolates. The essay also argued that Christians could not avoid politics and must find an "equally practical" solution to the problem of birth control.[37] Such an approach was clearly in harmony with the views of the school superintendent, Father Carlin, who added to his role as Catholic education's stormy petrel by declaring (in a sermon at Christ the King parish) that the teaching of theology, philosophy, and logic in Catholic schools failed to prepare students adequately for the problems of the outside world.[38]

In June 1962, Father Ernest Flusche, who was already superintendent of schools for the diocese, succeeded Father Carlin as superintendent of McGuinness as well, with Father David Monahan as unofficial principal. Under their leadership, the modular system and free dress were introduced and an emphasis on high scholastic standards was continued. Around 87 percent of boys and 65 percent of girls who graduated from McGuinness in the 1950s and early 1960s went on to college, where a quarter of them did well enough in 1963 to make the dean's honor list. In 1965, the number one ranking student at the University of Notre Dame was junior Kenneth Khoury, a McGuinness graduate, as were the presidents of the Independent Students or-

36. *Oklahoma Courier*, April 13, November 9, 1962.
37. *Oklahoma Courier*, March 18, 1960.
38. Mrs. A. W. Kavanaugh to Victor Reed, May 13, 1961, Reed Papers.

ganizations at the University of Oklahoma and Oklahoma State University. A 1964–1965 McGuinness graduate was one of nine Oklahoma high school students to win a Woodrow Wilson Fellowship, and two other 1965 graduates were selected by the University of Oklahoma as university scholars (a program for which only sixty high school graduates were chosen statewide).[39]

Monahan's admirers insisted that such successes were a product of his openness to free enquiry, but this very openness also made him a target of traditionalist Catholics in the diocese. Although he weathered the storm over a school debate on abortion in 1964 (see chapter 13), controversy continued to dog the school, when a poem by George Parks won the literature contest of the "McGuinness Olympics" and appeared in the April 1965 issue of *Chi Rhoan*. According to Monahan, Parks's poem dealt with "man's degradation by sin and resurrection through his conversion from evil," but Monahan conceded that its themes were probably unsuitable for a high school magazine (Monahan also noted that although the poem won the competition on points, neither of the two teachers at McGuinness on the six-judge panel had voted for it).[40]

One critic declared that the principal's apology for publication, coupled with his personal defense of the poem's literary merits, demonstrated that Monahan, while "always gentle, sweet, kind, pleasant and understanding [is] not an educator." Another suggested that it proved that education at the higher grades increasingly reflected a desire to adopt contemporary benchmarks of literary criticism. Where Monahan had viewed the allusions to masturbation, prostitution, and illegitimacy as marks of a sinful society struggling to emerge into new life, his critics saw merely the urge to push the envelope of cultural excess.[41] Reed responded to the fracas by agreeing that *Chi Rhoan* was not a suitable medium for publication, but endorsing Monahan's handling of the incident. He refused to concede any premise of malign intent. "In view of the fact that [Parks's] 'message' is good," he told the school community, "you must not be 'carried away' to the extent of heeding the unreasonable charges of some who would grossly exaggerate and condemn not only the ideals of the faculty at Bishop McGuinness High School, but those of many priests and religious in the Diocese."[42]

39. Gier, interview; Scholastic Fact Sheet on McGuinness High School, n.d. (prob April 1965), Reed Papers.
40. Revd. David Monahan to "Parents," April 23, 1965, Reed Papers.
41. Tom Tennery to Victor Reed, April 26, 1965, Mrs. Walker P. Sandlin to "Committee," May 2, 1965, Reed Papers.
42. Victor Reed to "Parents," April 26, 1965, Reed Papers.

Thus, in the field of literary criticism, two worlds had collided. If traditionalists erred in attributing a calculated attempt to subvert Catholic principles, they at least recognized that there *was* a cultural clash under way. In his monumental study of John Cardinal Krol of Philadelphia, Michael Jones explores the case of La Salle College High School in Philadelphia, like McGuinness a popular magnet school for talented Catholic children. Jones documents how many of the Christian Brothers who taught at LaSalle, exposed in college to the latest trends in biblical and liturgical studies, had become so obsessed with modernity as to lose contact with notions of Church tradition that had underpinned Catholic education in the past. What was important, argues Jones, "was not pedagogic appropriateness any more than it was the transmission of the faith. The impression one gets was that the freshmen at La Salle High School were being given a crash course in the tropes and methods of modernity. The quicker they adopted them the better off they would be. It was most probably an educational mission which [the teacher] could embark on with compete sincerity."[43]

The problem was not that the information conveyed had no value but rather that it was being imparted to Catholic children as part of a new orthodoxy increasingly detached from the universal perspectives of the Church. Such was the context in which another McGuinness controversy broke in October 1966 over a dramatic performance by students of selected scenes from Lillian Hellman's *The Children's Hour*. That summer, Reed and Father Monahan had held a meeting with some of the critics of the school's teaching philosophy, at which one speaker complained that the play was in complete contradiction to the resolve to avoid "the sex, socialism and civil disobedience policy previously pursued by the instructors," since, in his view, it condoned homosexual behavior.[44] Monahan retorted that the play concerned the impact of a false charge of homosexuality that leads to the destruction of professional and personal reputation. While he had refrained from showing it to the whole school, given its content, the movie version had won an A-3 rating from the Legion of Decency, so it was obviously not completely off limits. Monahan also complained that one critic had attempted to commandeer the microphone during the performance to express her personal objections.[45]

The *Children's Hour* affair prompted Catholic traditionalist Tom Costello

---

43. Jones, *John Cardinal Krol*, 162–68 (quotation on 166).
44. Walker Sandlin to Victor Reed, October 11, 1966, Reed Papers.
45. Revd. David Monahan to Victor Reed, October 13, 1966.

(see chapter 13 for more), no stranger to heated debate, to challenge Monahan directly. On this occasion, Costello embarked upon the unusual step of appealing to the state superintendent of public instruction, Oliver Hodge, arguing that since McGuinness was an accredited school, the state had some interest in its activities. Such a course was ironic, given his oft-expressed views about the dangers of supervision of Catholic education by non-Catholics, but Costello argued that the "atmosphere designed around sex and the perversion of sex" necessitated intervention and promised that he and his supporters would endeavor to set in train a legislative investigation of the school—a suggestion that would have evoked Catholic protest across the ideological spectrum only a few years before. Hodge responded that accreditation related solely to the qualifications of teachers and the adequacy of teaching facilities. Dramatic arts did not fall within his remit. "It seems to me," he told Costello, "that this is a problem concerning people of your religious faith."[46]

Costello's letter-writing campaign included communication with Archbishop Egidio Vagnozzi, the apostolic delegate to the United States, and with Cardinal Alfredo Ottaviani, head of the papal department in charge of doctrinal orthodoxy. This resort to outside authorities in turn provoked criticism of Costello by the McGuinness Parent-Teacher Association, which insisted that he had greatly misrepresented the context of the play. "Our children are growing up in a world that makes being a Christian an ever harder endeavor," PTA officers declared. "Therefore, an educational process which, in its curriculum, completely disregards the current problem of man living with his fellow man would fail as much as would a system which would not teach students about history on the grounds that much history is composed of violence, treachery and immorality." At the same time, they cited the fact that the play had been written up in an issue of *Life* magazine and presented on television.[47] The question was surely begged how this pertained to the matter at hand. If the play was defensible on its merits, then the fact that it had received attention in the mainstream media was neither here nor there. It was only if there was an underlying desire for cultural validation that it became relevant.

Matters were very different in Tulsa, where construction of a central high

46. Tom Costello to Oliver Hodge, October 13, 1966, Hodge to Costello, October 18, 1966, Reed Papers.
47. Statement of McGuinness High School P.T.A. Officers, n.d., Reed Papers.

school to replace the high schools at Holy Family Cathedral and Christ the King parish and a junior high school at St. Francis Xavier parish had begun in 1959. The new facility, which Reed requested should be named after his mentor Francis Kelley, served children from all ten of the city's parishes. It boasted twenty classrooms, science laboratories, and a gymnasium that seated twenty-two hundred. Unlike McGuinness, the school, in its early years, was run jointly by the Sisters of Divine Providence, based in San Antonio, Texas, and the Christian Brothers, based in St. Louis, Missouri. It offered scientific, commercial, and classical courses of study, with a mandatory religion component. The teaching philosophy at Kelley was much more focused on traditional Christian living. The Christian Brothers retained uniforms, favored classroom teaching, and laid particular stress on dissuading teenagers from social vices through the use of films, articles, and the testimony of recovering alcoholics. "Our rules also are external evidences that we don't condone drinking or smoking," the principal declared in 1963. "The school has a sort of passive resistance to both."[48]

The school's emphasis on high academic achievement was not viewed with universal approbation. One mother sought to move her son into the public school system in 1961 because she felt that the standards demanded were too high: "I understand their desire for making it an outstanding school with high educational standards," she told Reed, "but when 35 boys in a class of 42 receive D and F marks for the semester, it seems to me the work is too difficult for the student or the teacher is not getting the subject matter across to the student."[49] Another parent complained about the school's ban on social and recreational clubs and noted that school spirit had declined since Kelley had abandoned the playing of sports to allow more time for academics. "Undoubtedly," he declared, "the emphasis should be placed on study and adjustment to the world affairs, but, on the other hand, no student or graduate will be able to take his place in the business or social world unless he or she can meet their associates on a common ground: viz. friendliness, sociability and full appreciation of their common problems."[50]

48. "Copy proposed for Brochure on Bishop Kelley High School, Tulsa, Oklahoma," n.d. (prob. 1959), Reed Papers; Gier, interview; *Tulsa Tribune*, March 16, 1963.
49. Mrs. Fred Phelps to Victor Reed, January 25, 1961, Church of the Madalene, Tulsa File, box 5.1, ADT.
50. H. J. McNally to Sr. Angelina Marie, C.D.P., March 2, 1961, Reed Papers.

CONSOLIDATION AND CLOSURE

The enduring saga of the post–Vatican II era was the steady closing of parochial schools. Those in rural settings were the first to go, and parents who had expended time and money equipping them watched aghast as unsympathetic priests closed down facilities. In 1959, George Latkovich berated Reed for allowing Father Kevin Devlin of Holy Family parish in Canute to close the only Catholic high school (an extremely small facility) in western Oklahoma. Devlin, he declared, had discouraged pupils from enrolling in the school or returning to it and had blocked parishioners' efforts to present their side of the story to the bishop.[51]

Equally painful was the closing of the parochial school at St. Joseph's parish in Blackwell in 1964, after only five years of operation. Parishioners complained that Father Anthony Dockers had inadequately briefed them as to the need for a tuition increase. Worse still, Dockers then proceeded to give away the schoolbooks to a Catholic school in Guthrie and proposed to transfer the school library to Blackwell's public school. Since parents and pupils had raised the money needed to purchase both, they vehemently protested such an arbitrary disposal of assets and brought angry testimony to the diocesan board of education. While Reed accepted Dockers's insistence that his school had too small an enrollment to continue, he reprimanded him for acting in a unilateral fashion and without proper consultation. Sadly, the closing of the Blackwell school was merely a portent of things to come.[52]

In 1965, attention shifted to St. Michael's Church in Henryetta. Its school was part of an extensive church plant erected by Monsignor Theophile Caudron, a Belgian expatriate who had built up the parish from nothing over a period of more than fifty years. Initially, the authorities recommended that the education program be reduced from twelve grades to six. In a letter to Caudron, the diocesan school superintendent pointed out that in the last ten years the school had been unable to offer the electives in modern languages and the physical sciences that high school graduates would need to function

51. George Latkovich Jr. to Victor Reed, October 27, 1959, Holy Family Church, Canute File, AAOC.

52. Victor Reed to Revd. Anthony A. Dockers, August 18, 1964, Mrs. Jack Cordell to Revd. Ernest A. Flusche, September 8, 1964, Mr. and Mrs. Henry Dempewolf to Revd. Ernest A. Flusche, September 10, 1964, Msgr. Sylvester F. Luecke to Revd. Anthony A. Dockers, September 15, 1964, Mrs. Paul Stegeman to Revd. Ernest A. Flusche, September 16, 1964, Flusche to Stegeman, September 18, 1964, St. Joseph's Church, Blackwell File, AAOC.

at a university level. He further noted that the school was failing to attract more than half the Catholic students in the area at the higher grades, leading to an excessively small pupil-teacher ratio. (There were only a dozen pupils and two sister-teachers in the entire high school.) The Benedictine sisters who staffed the school favored the change but warned that Caudron was unlikely to cooperate in any reduction of his empire.[53]

Criticism of the decision was not confined to Catholics. Lawrence Linesdell complained that the state inspector had accorded St. Michael's full accreditation, while Joe Hardin, also representing part of Henryetta's non-Catholic majority, praised the contribution that St. Michael's had made. "Your schools," he told Reed, "afford a sound, basic Christian education which makes the younger generation good American citizens." St. Michael's, he added, was of particular value to Okmulgee County thanks to its two-year commercial and business course, which allowed many who were unable to attend college to obtain jobs in offices and banks. It was a community asset that should not be squandered.[54]

By October 1966, school enrollment at St. Michael's had fallen to thirty-four Catholic and thirteen non-Catholic children, with a similar number of Catholic children in the public school, and the grade school became a casualty of diocesan efforts to save more viable parochial schools. "Perhaps it is no consolation," Flusche told Caudron's successor, Father William Pace, "but many more parochial schools in the diocese will have to close in the immediate years ahead." The closing was implemented with little warning over the summer of 1967, much to the anger of many Henryetta residents. "All of our life we are preached to about sending children to Catholic schools," complained Magdelina Williams. "[W]hen someone is sent to Public School for any reason, they can be refused Holy Communion if the Priest so desires. Then we try to keep a Catholic School for grade schools at least and then all of a sudden there is a meeting called and we are very bluntly informed the school has been closed; and this only two weeks before the opening of school, and after all contracts have been let."[55]

53. Revd. Ernest A. Flusche to Msgr. Theophile Caudron, n.d., Mother Marie Denise Mohr, O.S.B., to Victor Reed, April 1, 1965, Reed Papers.

54. Lawrence J. Linesdell to Victor Reed, April 30, 1965, Joe Hardin to Victor Reed, April 27, 1965, Reed Papers.

55. Meeting of Bishop Reed and Mr. Kleffner, October 5, 1966, Revd. Ernest A. Flusche to Revd. William J. Pace, July 31, 1967, Magdelina Williams to Victor Reed, August 16, 1967, Reed Papers.

As the pattern of closings was repeated across the diocese, lay resentment swelled. When Sacred Heart School in El Reno was slated for closure in March 1967, the pupils begged Reed to intervene directly. "If you could only share one day, or even one hour with us," they wrote, "you could feel and see the unity, the spirit, the love, that is contained within that 'building'—which to others is just a building made up of bricks and cement—not knowing what is within."[56] In Lawton, Father Flusche was drawn into a row over the forced closure of the junior high school attached to Blessed Sacrament Church. In this case, Father Wade Darnall maintained that he had reached an agreement with the local inspector of schools that allowed the school to retain state accreditation despite falling short of the officially required number of students in 1965 and 1966. Subsequent to this, according to Darnall, Flusche had drawn the attention of the state office to the discrepancy, with the result that accreditation was abruptly cancelled and the ninth grade class forced to transfer to the public schools in the middle of the year. Many parents were now unwilling to enroll their children in the surviving elementary school, the pastor complained, while the parish was burdened with a lay teacher's salary for the remainder of the year. This incident highlighted a belief prevalent in the rural areas that the authorities played favorites when it came to which schools stayed open.[57]

By 1968, the recommendations for closings were coming thick and fast, including such diverse communities as Norman, Enid, Okeene, McAlester, Okarche, Purcell, and Chickasha. (Of Purcell, one report noted: "School is down to less than 50 students—42 to be exact and this is draining the parish as almost all the children have to be bussed; *nothing* is spent for more than 50 children in public school; nothing has ever been spent on adult education.") In Muskogee the parishes of St. Joseph's and Sacred Heart merged their operations, with the former keeping the school and the latter becoming a center for religious instruction.[58]

Closings were rarely amicable. So bitter were parishioners at St. Patrick's parish in Oklahoma City over the closing of their parochial school in 1969 (see chapter 5) that they demanded that Father Gregory Gier, an assistant

56. Students of Sacred Heart High School to Victor Reed, March 13, 1967, Reed Papers.
57. Revd. T. Wade Darnall to Victor Reed, September 6, 1967, Reed Papers. For the relationship between racial integration of the parochial school system and certain school closings, see chapter 8.
58. Agenda for meeting with Bishop Reed, February 14, 1967, Reed Papers.

pastor at the parish who had been teaching freshman religion classes, not be allowed to return to McGuinness High School. Since the head football coach at McGuinness was a parishioner at St. Patrick's, they warned that if Gier *did* return, the school would lose its football team.[59] Also closed in 1969 were the parochial schools of St. James' parish in Bartlesville and Immaculate Conception parish in Pawhuska. In 1970, the Church of the Madalene finally closed its school. Dr. John Kleffner, Flusche's successor as superintendent of schools, endeavored to put a positive spin on the closings in July 1970, but his air of quiet resignation was all too evident: "The Catholic schools have, throughout history, reflected the current thinking of the Church. It is, therefore, impossible to hope that schools will be free of turmoil, confusion, and doubt. It is just as difficult to predict the type of private school in existence 25 years from now as it is to predict the type of rapid transportation, or any other major facet of our society. The question is not whether private parochial schools will be in existence, but what format they will have and how many there will be. There has been a great emphasis on quality rather than quantity, and, in my estimation, this is bearing great fruit for Catholic schools in Oklahoma."[60]

Some laymen made a virtue of necessity. When the Madalene restructured its school board to be responsible not only for the parochial school but also for parish children in public school, the elections attracted a 23 percent turnout, compared to only 10 percent in public school board elections. Nor did all parents consider public school attendance as a prelude to apostasy. "Putting our youth in public schools" declared Francis Heinz of Chilocco, "after receiving religious instruction on Sundays should help make lay workers out of them, by their example, friendship and words with their non-Catholic friends, and should work towards Church unity."[61]

HIGHER EDUCATION

Acceptance by the mainstream American academic community had long been a goal of Catholic educators, but it was not until the early 1960s that that goal seemed truly within reach. Despite embracing many of the new dis-

59. Gier, interview.

60. Excerpt from Nell Jean Boggs, "Parochial Problem: Money—Catholic Superintendent Takes Long Look," *Tulsa Tribune,* July 10, 1970, 3, Reed Papers.

61. *Oklahoma Courier*, February 25, 1966; Francis W. Heinz to Victor Reed, May 1, 1966, Reed Papers.

ciplines in the 1920s and 1930s, Catholic colleges were still regarded with suspicion for continuing to assert a Catholic worldview, at a time when most universities that had begun under denominational auspices were shedding what remained of such an ethos in the interests of a presumed "objectivity."[62] Efforts to counter such prejudices included endowed chairs, such as the professorship in Christian Philosophy that the authorities at the University of Oklahoma permitted a wealthy Catholic laywoman to endow in 1961. From this initiative emerged the Skogsberg Foundation, which pledged to raise money to support such a professorship, but ultimately failed to generate the necessary funds.[63]

In 1960, strictly Catholic higher education in Oklahoma was limited to Benedictine Heights College in Tulsa (see chapter 11) and St. Gregory's College in Shawnee. The former was already withering on the vine, and no new students were accepted after 1960. The case of St. Gregory's College was more complicated. Its president, Father Richard Sneed, O.S.B., believed that rising college enrollments in the state during the early 1960s reflected a market that the Benedictines could tap. Sneed embraced a vision of St. Gregory's as an accredited coeducational four-year college with a lay board.

Sneed's approach was welcomed by the State Board of Regents for Higher Education, which agreed to defend his application for federal funds to expand the academic facilities. Sneed further argued that St. Gregory's should have the right to impose a tuition differential for non-Oklahomans, in the same way that state institutions charged higher rates for out-of-state students, to reflect the subsidy that Catholics in Oklahoma had contributed to the college through the diocese.[64]

Sneed's endorsement of a lay board, federal funding, and a tuition differential demonstrated just how far St. Gregory's had come from its Catholic roots. For better or worse, it had entered the mainstream and now proposed to operate just like any other educational establishment. Its student body increased from 162 in 1964 to 600 in 1968, at which point it was the eighth largest of Oklahoma's seventeen junior colleges. It offered courses on

---

62. See Burtchaell, *The Dying of the Light*, esp. 557–716.

63. Revd. Ernest A. Flusche to Victor Reed, February 28, 1961, Reed Papers. The Skogsberg Foundation was not to be an unmitigated blessing for Bishop Reed, since it also drew together a group of conservative academic Catholics who would lead protests against what they saw as the extreme liberalism of the diocese.

64. *Oklahoma Courier*, February 12, 1965; Revd. Richard Sneed to Victor Reed, March 24, 1965, July 15, 1966, Reed Papers.

movie appreciation, Russian, quantitative analysis, and journalism, as well as courses on the theology of Vatican II and ecumenism, that were most unusual for a junior college. Sadly, the educational boom proved fleeting, and the expansion ultimately foundered on a lack of student applications. By 1971, St. Gregory's hopes for baccalaureate-granting status had evaporated.[65]

The goodwill of the state board of regents was not confined to St. Gregory's. In 1965, in a bid to alleviate the problem of an absence of two-year colleges in Oklahoma's metropolitan areas, the board offered to assist the diocese in obtaining accreditation for both St. Francis de Sales Seminary and Benedictine Heights College as full-time junior colleges and to support their applications to obtain federal funds for expansion. Father Sneed, however, objected to any transformation of the seminary, arguing that the State of Oklahoma would eventually open its own colleges, and there were not enough young Catholics to support more than one junior college, so the overall effect would be simply to dilute the pool of potential students for St. Gregory's. This argument, coupled with the financial cost involved, ultimately prevailed.[66]

Unlike St. Gregory's College, St. Francis de Sales Seminary in Oklahoma City was a comparatively recent addition to higher education in the diocese, which Reed had opened in 1959. Embodying the spirit of the optimistic 1950s, the seminary initially included a high school department as well as a two-year course of study for those aspiring to holy orders. The educational atmosphere was comparable with that experienced by Reed at St. John's Seminary during the 1920s or that persisted in seminaries elsewhere in the United States. All incoming mail was reviewed by the rector, and students had few days off.

That said, there were some more progressive elements, including an unusual emphasis on the priest's cultivating personal relationships. "As seminarians," Joe Stine declared in a 1962 article for the seminary newsletter, "we must be interested in such youth groups as YCS, Sodality, Youth Clubs or any other groups in our cities and Towns. . . . It is important to remem-

65. *Oklahoma Courier*, April 26, 1968. In 1997, the college finally became a four-year educational institution, now known as St. Gregory's University.
66. Proposals for Future Use and Development of St. Francis Seminary, n.d. (prob. December 1965), Reed Papers. The problem of accreditation was emphasized by a woman in Yukon who described how her son had spent three years in seminaries in Texas and Oklahoma but after he decided not to pursue the priesthood was not considered to have any college credits since neither of the seminaries was accredited. *Oklahoma Courier*, November 1, 1963.

ber that the interest we take in other people will best help us most of all, and if we do not attempt to develop any kind of interest in others, we will be failures as priests."[67] Some of the faculty worked diligently to inculcate in their students a sense of the transformation of the Church under way in Rome. Father John Vrana, the "tortured intellectual" whose room was always stacked with books and newspapers, took the seminarians to see foreign-language films. The seminary also used the Episcopal Hymnal (1940) because Father Frank Wrigley considered it to be the only decent worship manual in English.[68]

After the high school department closed in 1966, a more relaxed atmosphere prevailed. Scheduled exercises for the seminarians were limited to morning and evening prayers, the daily liturgy, meals, and classes, with mediation, personal prayer, and study left to the students' initiative. They were permitted to visit home every other weekend and to leave campus on Friday evenings, on Saturdays from after the morning liturgy until 5:00 p.m., and on Sundays from after lunch until 5:00 p.m. Recognizing the radical (for the time) freedom expressed by this model of seminary life, the rector, Father Paul Donovan, emphasized the mandatory daily liturgy, in which the whole community—including lay employees—participated, and the mandatory weekly discussion between students, the rector, and other faculty about the nature of spiritual formation and maturation for an aspiring priest. "The faculty realizes that some of these ideas are rather novel," Donovan told Reed, "and yet at the same time if, in our age of great tension, in our age of great development, young men are to be adequately prepared for the priesthood, they must be helped in their maturation. They must come to see that being responsible people is their responsibility and not someone else's. They must come to see that their own life of prayer and their own relationship to Almighty God, while always considered within the framework of the Christian community, is, nevertheless, something in which they must take great personal and serious responsibility."[69]

By 1967, it was clear that the diocese, already burdened with debt because of the Benedictine Heights College debacle, considered the seminary to be an unjustifiable luxury. Alternative uses for St. Francis de Sales were being contemplated as early as 1965, including one of making it a center of

67. Joe Stine, "The Importance of a Seminarian's Summer," *St. Francis de Sales Newsletter*, July 9, 1962, 4–5.
68. Clergy roundtable discussion, June 19, 2005.
69. Revd. J. Paul Donovan to Victor Reed, September 27, 1966, Reed Papers.

clergy education.[70] The superintendent of schools continued to favor a more educationally centered approach, either the junior college program suggested by the state board of regents or a formal tie with Oklahoma City University that would involve the establishment of a chair of philosophy (as at the University of Oklahoma) and permission for seminarians to take their senior year as OCU students. He dismissed Father Sneed's concerns about the former proposal by arguing that St. Gregory's drew most of its students from outside the metropolitan areas, while the latter proposal would still provide some benefit to education in the Oklahoma City area.[71]

In the event, a precipitous decline in the number of seminarians in 1967 took most options out of the diocese's hands. Compared with the early 1960s, when there had been 150 students registered, only 14 had applied for the 1967–1968 academic year, and it could not be considered financially prudent any longer to maintain a seminary within the diocese. "We have no other alternative but to send [our seminarians] elsewhere for the present time," Reed told the press. "The problem of decline [*sic*] vocations is one which faces all of us—Bishop, priests and people alike." The St. Francis de Sales plant, occupied by the Office of Religious Education since September 1966, eventually became the location for the chancery offices, and in the years that followed, the hope also was realized that some free space could be made available to local Protestant churches on a "shared time, shared cost" basis for conferences, workshops, and education programs, thus meeting one of the ecumenical objectives of the Second Vatican Council.[72]

THE NEWMAN APOSTOLATE

If Catholic higher education appeared doomed in the 1960s, the apostolate to students at state colleges and universities had to take on an ever-increasing importance. Since his days at Stillwater, Victor Reed had believed strongly in the potential for good of the Newman club.[73] Named after John

70. "This need for scholarship and the availability of scholarship to all priests today is a *felt need.* This could develop into seminars on certain days of the week on Scripture, church history, liturgy, ecumenism, social thought, dogma, moral etc. It would have the advantage of a school of theology in our midst without the burden of a structured graduate school." Proposals for Future Use and Development of St. Francis Seminary, 6.

71. Revd. Ernest A. Flusche to Study Committee on St. Francis Seminary, October 7, 1966, Reed Papers.

72. Press Release—St. Francis de Sales Seminary, June 26, 1967, Reed Papers.

73. See Reed's letter emphasizing the need for the pastor of St. Francis Xavier Church

Henry Newman, one of the most famous English converts to Catholicism during the nineteenth century, whose writings had dealt at length with the relationship between the university and the believing Christian, the clubs were part of a national movement and were devoted to sustaining the religious commitment of impressionable young Catholics in a secular college environment. As the number of Catholics attending such colleges swelled in the early 1960s, it became all the more important to provide the material resources necessary to keep the Newman clubs vital and active.

Parents of these Catholic students were understandably incensed when they discovered that substandard provision had been made for their children's religious formation. One mother, whose daughter was obliged to attend Oklahoma State University in 1961 for financial reasons, had pinned her hopes on the local Newman club as a place where her daughter could experience the "Catholic atmosphere" lacking from the Protestant community in which they lived. She described the deserted building that she visited as a "run down completely delapidated [*sic*] shack." A good building for Catholic students on a secular college campus should have far greater priority than new Catholic schools, she told Reed. "The eyes of the students of all faiths are turned toward that disgrace that is called the Catholic Student Center and the Catholic students are ashamed and annoyed."[74]

Many of Reed's correspondents, of course, wrongly assumed that the diocese had ample funds available. Oklahoma City and Tulsa was part of the Texoma Newman Province, which also included the dioceses of Amarillo, Dallas–Fort Worth, and San Angelo, and in 1963 the provincial chaplain admitted to Reed that "our Newman effort is just barely toddling along, so numerous are small Colleges and Junior Colleges with even smaller Catholic enrollments." He urged the bishop to allocate more discretionary funds to the diocesan chaplain, Father Clement Pribil, which could be used to assist Catholic professors on secular campuses.[75]

Father Pribil had come to the bishop's attention two years earlier, when

---

to allow his assistant time to carry out his assigned Newman chaplaincy at Tulsa University because the students needed priest-directors. Victor Reed to Revd. Francis E. McGoldrick, July 5, 1962, St. Francis Xavier Church, Tulsa File, box 11.1, ADT.

74. Mrs. Floyd Baldwin to Victor Reed, July 20, 1961, Reed Papers. The problem had still not been fully solved two years later, when a Stillwater farmer told the bishop that he intended to use the money that he was being asked to contribute to the Diocesan Development Fund to support the OSU Newman Club. Michael Schilty to Victor Reed, December 13, 1963, Reed Papers.

75. Revd. George H. Sallaway to Victor Reed, April 7, 1963, Reed Papers.

he warned Reed that Oklahoma was falling behind other states in Newman club activity. Most Newman clubs, Pribil declared, were viewed primarily as marriage marts, and student leadership was generally poor, something exacerbated by the part-time status of most chaplains. At Southeastern State College, which refused to hire Catholic faculty, the local chaplain faced open hostility, while at Central State College in Edmond, most Catholic students were commuters from Oklahoma City who had no time to attend meetings. The University of Oklahoma, heavily dominated by secular fraternities, was little better, and Tulsa University also had low rates of participation.[76]

Somewhat better news came from Southwestern State College in Weatherford, where mathematics professor Lewis Coon reported in March 1961 that students were taking a new interest in leadership positions. Attendance at Wednesday evening Lenten devotions had increased markedly from 1960 to 1961, Coon stated, and the Newman club had become more involved in the life of the college by sponsoring Christmas and Mardi Gras–Valentine's Day dances and entering a float in the homecoming parade for the first time in the college's history. Another bright spot was provided by the OSU Newman club at Stillwater, which, despite the concerns previously expressed, received the award for best club in the Texoma Province in 1961.[77]

Professor Coon attributed much of the success at Southwestern State to a letter from Reed to the diocesan clergy in 1960. In August 1961, therefore, the bishop reissued his memorandum to parish priests obliging them to speak to all students attending a non-Catholic college and to urge them to take part in the meetings, lectures, and devotional activity sponsored by its Newman club. He also encouraged pastors to encourage parents to insist on their children's participation and to display an interest in hearing about the students' experiences when they came home on vacation. Four local colleges, Reed pointed out, even offered credit for religion courses taught by priests.[78]

Newman formation took a variety of forms, often dependent upon the priorities of the local chaplain. At OSU in the early 1960s, Father Pribil commended the increasing numbers of students attending Pre-Cana classes to deepen their understanding of the vocation of marriage, and he urged upon them the value of spiritual disciplines. "Always remember," Pribil told them, invoking the language of Catholic Action, "that we are functioning as the

76. Revd. Clement E. Pribil to Victor Reed, June 1, 1961, Reed Papers.
77. Lewis H. Coon to Victor Reed, March 15, 1961, Reed Papers.
78. Victor Reed to Priests of the Diocese, August 16, 1961, Reed Papers.

Mystical Body of Christ. When you do not do your part, the Body is crippled in fulfilling its mission, the mission of Christ, the Son of God." In the same issue of the Catholic student newsletter, Bill Davis offered his fellow students the story of God's slaying of Onan in Genesis 38 as a scriptural response to those Protestants who asked for the biblical authority for the Church's stand on birth control.[79]

Tulsa University's Newman club also showed clear signs of growth in the spring of 1963. Topics explored by the club in 1963 tended to emphasize the reflective over the active life, despite an address on the diocesan mission to Guatemala and James Cockrell's lecture on "The Role of the Layman in the Catholic Church." Representative offerings included "Original Sin and the Corruption of Human Freedom," "Divine Inspiration in Scripture," "Development of the Old Testament Canon," and "The Church and the Blessed Virgin Mary." A monthly Catholic-Protestant dialogue with Presbyterian and Anglican students was also in place, and members of the Newman club joined with the Canterbury Association (the organization for Episcopal students) to participate in a Passover Seder at the end of March 1963.[80]

By 1965, the new Newman facilities at Stillwater had become a reality, and the Newman apostolate was growing steadily. An emphasis on the active life now pervaded Newman club initiatives, a response to the concern of Father Pribil that specialized Catholic Action attracted the interest of only about 5 percent of Catholic students on campus.[81] The new focus was very different, however, from that of the 1940s and 1950s. The program at St. Thomas More Church in Norman for 1966 featured Michael Novak on "Belief and Unbelief," James Forrest on "Pacifism: Plaything of the Beatniks," Edward Marciniak of the Chicago Commission on Human Relations on "Should the Church Be Involved in Social Problems?" and Dan Sullivan on "Sexuality and Celibacy."[82]

If that were not enough, the selection of film viewings was also calculated to rouse conservative ire, including such offerings as *Room at the Top*, *Long*

79. *Apostolus*, February 21, 1963, Reed Papers. For the decline in use of the Onan story in the battle against artificial contraception, see Tentler, *Catholics and Contraception*, 155, 238.
80. Revd. Thomas Melton to Victor Reed, March 12, 1963, Reed Papers; *Tulsa Tribune*, March 31, 1963.
81. Revd. Clement E. Pribil to Victor Reed, October 27, 1961, Reed Papers.
82. *Oklahoma Courier*, April 2, 1965; Spring 1966 Sunday Night Lecture Series, St. Thomas Moore Church, Norman File, AAOC.

Day's Journey into Night, and Fellini's *Nights of Cabiria* and *La Dolce Vita.*[83] Conservative Catholics increasingly viewed the Newman clubs as hotbeds of political and social subversion. A particular bête noire was Father William Ross at the University of Oklahoma, who sponsored James Forrest to speak at the Student Union, and Father John Vrana, who wrote for the Students for a Democratic Society publication, *Voice.*[84]

Some students nevertheless found such an approach reassuring. Sophomore Beverly Tippett warmed to participation in the new dialogue Mass (see chapter 6). "Our everyday lives can easily become detached from our religious faith," she maintained. "In the dialogue, however, the opportunity to seek a meaningful relationship between the two is tremendous. Also, in our dialogue, older members of the parish have encouraged the college students to communicate their ideas." Several student leaders praised Father William Kelly—another campus radical—as an effective pastor. "The campus minister," they told Reed, "must reinterpret traditional Christian symbols in terms that the 20th century man can relate to, yet he must still maintain a consciousness of the heritage which has created us. The job is one of delicate balance and it requires that the campus minister possess unusual wisdom, love, dedication, and a sense of humor."[85]

Outsiders remained unimpressed. The situation at OSU in the late 1960s was illustrative of the wider problems of campus ministry during this period. When Father Pribil left Stillwater in 1966, an assistant at the Catholic student center expressed her concerns to the bishop:

As I know you are aware, students are pounding away at old values, eager to establish new values and it is, in my opinion, extremely necessary that our leaders, both religious and lay, be not only able to sympathize with their eagerness to change, but also able to present all sides of a question to them, without bias, to enable them to take mature action. In addition, I trust our new pastor will continue the "complex" idea begun under Father Pribil, that of having a total unit of religious, faculty, students and laity working together on campus with effectiveness for the good of all. This, as I know you are aware, will require someone who can administer a physical plant of considerable size, administer a housing situation which will be composed of nuns and priests plus business personnel, administer a parish composed of

83. Fall 1966 Sunday Night Forum and Film Program, St. Thomas Moore Church, Norman File, AAOC.

84. Thomas Costello to Reps. David Boren, Texanna Hatchett, John Miskelly, and Ralph Thompson, October 24, 1967, Reed Papers.

85. Beverly A. Tippett to Victor Reed, May 5, 1969, Doug Caves and Keith McGlamery to Reed, May 5, 1969, Reed Papers.

students and families, and administer a program that meets the needs of all the various kinds of people to be served.[86]

Despite this warning, nine months later the student center was mired in controversy. Some university alumni blamed this on an undue emphasis on involving faculty and graduate students in Newman programs at the expense of the much larger undergraduate student body. Casualties of this new emphasis were social and recreational activities and the student newspaper. A former treasurer of Texoma Province reported in 1967 that he had found the university church and Newman center deserted and that he had been told that most students worshipped in St. Francis Xavier parish.[87]

CONCLUSION

By the early 1970s Oklahoma's Catholic education system was a shadow of its former self. In 1958, there were twenty-five Catholic high schools and seventy-seven elementary schools; by 1971, there were only six high schools and thirty-eight elementary schools. As the number of schools shrank, so the proportion of Catholic pupils in the public schools increased. The diocese reported 22,474 students receiving Catholic religious instruction in 1958, of whom 6,322 were public school pupils (28.1 percent). Thirteen years later, the total number of students was 26,000, but the number in the public school system had increased to 16,610 (63.9 percent).[88]

Equally striking was the change in the composition of the faculty in the Catholic school system. The number of teachers fell 12 percent in the course of Reed's episcopate, a decline largely accounted for by the fact that the religious orders of women more than halved their teaching complement, dropping from three quarters of diocesan educators to only 40 percent. The number of lay teachers steadily increased during the 1960s and represented an absolute majority of the teaching profession by 1971.[89] The loss of sisters and the growing reliance on lay teachers placed such additional financial obligations on the system that many parishes had no choice but to close their schools.

86. Kay Nettleton to Victor Reed, May 24, 1966, Reed Papers.
87. Mr. and Mrs. Dennis Eccleston et al. to Victor Reed, February 28, 1967, Reed Papers; Patrick M. Skees to Reed, n.d. (prob. January 1967), St. John's University Church, Stillwater File, box 81.1, ADT.
88. *Official Catholic Directory* (hereafter *OCD*) (1958), 549; *OCD* (1971): 590.
89. Ibid.

The Catholic population was not the same in 1971 as it had been in 1958. It expected to be consulted on educational matters and yet, when consulted, it wished to retain the local Catholic school system without having to pay the cost that such a system necessarily involved. Under those circumstances, educators like Carlin were spared having to make a sustained intellectual defense of the proposition that secular education supplemented by parish-operated Christian education programs was no worse than parochial education.

Interestingly for a midwestern bishop, education—aside from the Newman apostolate—appears to have been something of only marginal interest to Victor Reed. He largely delegated oversight of the school system to his educational officials and the diocesan school board and rarely made pronouncements on the subject that were not sought by other interested parties. While one can sympathize with his position, and the lack of options open to him, it is perhaps unfortunate that he chose to play such an unobtrusive role. A clear statement either in defense of the existing system—and the lay obligations this would entail—or in favor of a more focused system centered on the metropolitan areas would have lent an intellectual clarity that the piecemeal dismantling of the school system unquestionably failed to convey.

chapter 5

Looking Outward

Parish Life and the Postconciliar Church

The parish offers an obvious example of the apostolate on the community level inasmuch as it brings together the many human differences within its boundaries and merges them into the universality of the Church. The laity should accustom themselves to working in the parish in union with their priests, bringing to the Church community their own and the world's problems as well as questions concerning human salvation, all of which they should examine and resolve by deliberating in common. As far as possible the laity ought to provide helpful collaboration for every apostolic and missionary undertaking sponsored by their local parish.

Second Vatican Council, Decree on the Apostolate of the Laity,
Apostolicam Actuositatem, November 18, 1965

Integral to immigrant Catholic life, the parish remained the cultural center of many Catholic communities well into the twentieth century. Although a substantial minority of parishes had been designated for particular ethnic groups in the early twentieth century,[1] the general principle held that membership in a parish was determined by one's residence, not by a preference for a particular pastor, group of like-minded persons, or specific program undertaken by a parish. The universal quality of Catholic belief was reflected in a Latin liturgy, a consistent pattern of Christian formation—particularly after the adoption of the Confraternity of Christian Doctrine—and, in many cases,

1. Orsi, *The Madonna of 115th Street.*

a parochial school.[2] Familial associations also bound successive generations into the parish community and helped keep neighborhoods stable.

In 1958, there were 93,172 Catholics in the Diocese of Oklahoma City and Tulsa, organized into 124 parishes. The diocese enjoyed the relative luxury of 159 diocesan priests and a consequent priest-to-people ratio of 1:586 (the national average was 1:1,157)—a statistic in which the bishop took particular pride—but the great distance between parishes that prevailed in much of the state rendered this of less benefit than would have been the case further east.[3] The growing social mobility of Catholics after the Second World War, however, stretched parish resources to the limit. The flight of the best and the brightest to the suburbs denuded inner-city parishes of much of their human capital (and the money they brought in), while the rural depopulation that had been occurring since the turn of the century only accelerated after 1950. In much of the United States, the flight to the suburbs prefigured the death of many of the inner-city parishes, but few of Oklahoma's metropolitan parishes (except, ironically, the historically black ones) were closed on Reed's watch, although the bishop did authorize a moratorium on the erection of new churches in Oklahoma City in 1966.[4]

The financial commitment of rural Catholics to their parish compared very favorably with their Protestant counterparts, and they were fiercely opposed to any consolidation of parishes. Members of Sacred Heart parish in Miami raised money for their parish by coming in from the countryside to serve the dinner at conventions that met in town and, in one case, by permanently giving over a portion of their store for rummage sales.[5] When the threat of closure loomed, rural Catholics viewed such action solely as a means of saving money that could then be spent in urban and university settings. The closure of the parish church in Hydro near Weatherford in western Oklahoma prompted one couple to remind their bishop that a local Catholic had recently given $15,000 to the diocese and rubbed salt in the wound by suggesting that Reed's predecessor would never have sold off a rectory or a

2. The Confraternity of Christian Doctrine was a particular project of Bishop Edwin O'Hara of Great Falls (and later Kansas City). Stephen Leven was a director of the National Center of CCD in Washington, D.C., from 1939 to 1940, but most Oklahoma priests did not take the program very seriously in the 1940s and 1950s. Dolan, *Some Seed Fell on Good Ground*, 126–55.

3. *Official Catholic Directory* (1958), 549.

4. See Victor Reed to Revd. John F. Lynch, June 24, 1966, Reed Papers.

5. Father Francis Weiner to Victor Reed, December 6, 1963, Sacred Heart Church, Miami File, Archives of the Catholic Diocese of Tulsa (hereafter ADT).

church. They ignored the fact that Weatherford—a much larger community only one mile distant—still lacked a church and that Bishop McGuinness had always had access to ready money and personnel. They also complained that the resident priest spent too much time ministering to Weatherford's student community, an observation that earned them a rebuke from their former rector, who reminded them that Weatherford was a growing college town and that students, as future community leaders, needed good spiritual directors.[6] Given the shortage of priests, consolidation of facilities was unavoidable.

Far more acrimonious than the suppression of Hydro was the battle to consolidate the three western Oklahoma parishes of St. Joseph's, Elk City; Holy Family, Canute; and St. Francis, Scheidel, which successive bishops had attempted to combine into one parish since the 1920s. In 1966, Reed encouraged local Catholics to consolidate the parochial schools of St. Joseph's and Holy Family (that of St. Francis had been closed in 1960) into one regional parochial school—St. Matthew's—and warned that the sisters who taught in the schools would not remain in the region indefinitely without some action being taken. The creation of a single school was seen as but a first step to parish consolidation. "There are enough people among the three to make a real viable parish," Reed declared on May 13, 1966, "and most of the people are for this solution. However, some of the older generation refuse to consider either the present exigency of the diocese in regard to personnel or the shape of the future in regard to their own community."[7]

The simple truth was that the three parishes were monstrously overburdened with debt (the diocese expended $200,000 between 1967 and 1970 simply to keep them all operational). In November 1970, the consolidation went forward, with the sale of unneeded land and buildings going toward the reduction of the overall debt on the new St. Matthew's Church, although some local Catholics remained unreconciled to the end. Martin Flies told Reed that his grandfather had given $20,000 to the Church in 1927 to the end that future generations could worship in a local church that would endure for at least a century. "[The church] is a memorial to him," Flies declared. "[T]hat is one reason I hate to see it destroyed."[8]

6. Alta and Charles Heger to Victor Reed, April 21, 1966, Revd. Jean P. Page to Alta and Charles Heger, May 15, 1966, Reed Papers.

7. Revd. Philip Donohoe to Revd. William C. Garthoeffner, May 10, 1966, Victor Reed to Most Revd. Egidio Vagnozzi, May 13, 1966, May 17, 1966, Reed to "Reverend Fathers and Devoted Laity of St. Joseph's, Holy Family and St. Francis parishes," May 17, 1966, Reed Papers.

8. Revd. Martin C. Hoehn to Victor Reed, November 9, 1970, Reed to Most Revd.

Inner-city parishes, like their rural counterparts, faced their own crisis of dwindling or mobile populations. Some, like Little Flower parish in downtown Oklahoma City, viewed this as an opportunity to redefine their role. Father Hilary Smith declared in 1963 that his church plant could now be placed at the service of the marginalized, with counseling and social services, and could also serve as a facilitator for discussions between residents of areas of urban blight and advocates of urban renewal. Catholic parishes needed to follow in the footsteps of other Christian denominations, he concluded, and justify their presence among the dispossessed: "Through careful catechism, stressing the Mystical Body of Christ, the parish can enable the laborer to see the importance of his job as a janitor or a waiter in a society that too often holds only entertainers, athletes and millionaires in high esteem."[9]

Suburban Catholics, by contrast, increasingly lacked the visceral commitment of either their urban forebears or their rural peers to the parish for its own sake.[10] New to parishes that were themselves often of fairly recent origin, they manifested their commitment in other ways. The Catholic priests assigned to minister to suburban Catholics in Oklahoma City and Tulsa appreciated that the bonds of Catholic life were weaker than in the era of immigration, and acted accordingly. In 1955, Father Gerald Phee helped establish the parish of St. Pius X in a barn on the far east side of Tulsa and supervised the erection of a modern circular church building that could accommodate eight hundred, with pews arranged in semicircles so that no parishioner was more than fifty feet from the altar.

Phee also attempted to replicate the urban Catholic community by persuading a local builder to erect homes with multiple bedrooms (unusually large for white suburban families) and using parishioners to erect two prefabricated units for a parochial school. By the early 1960s, the parish was offering ten Masses every Sunday and boasted the largest unit of the Christian Family Movement in the state. Its 250 workers included several Protestant couples (and at least one bachelor), and there were a variety of programs, including the Teachers' Program, which trained teachers to provide religious instruction to public school pupils; the Fishers of Men, which welcomed new families to the parish and persuaded fallen-away Catholics to return; the Helpers'

Luigi Raimondi, December 3, 1970, Reed Papers; John F. Flies to Apostolic Delegate, U.S.A., n.d., St. Matthew's Church, Elk City File, Archives of the Catholic Archdiocese of Oklahoma City (hereafter AAOC).

9. *Oklahoma Courier*, March 22, 1963.

10. See Greeley, *The Church and the Suburbs*.

Program, which provided secretarial assistance; the Transportation and Sitters' Program, which assisted the elderly and newlyweds; and the Apostles of Goodwill, who sought to invite non-Catholics to parish functions and CFM meetings. The model for St. Pius X was that of the old urban Catholic parish, but adapted to suburban forms of living.[11]

The waning of an integrated parish life was acknowledged by Bishop Reed as early as 1961. "Not everything needed for living and development can be provided by the parish," he warned, "especially today. Education in college and even in high school, hospital care in time of illness, operations in Catholic Charity, participation in special apostolic works such as Serra Clubs, Catholic Doctors and Lawyers Guilds, the apostolate of the Catholic Press—all of these are extra-parochial activities. The parish is still the unit, but our vision must be raised to see something beyond the parish limits."[12] Given such sentiments, it is unsurprising that progressive elements tended to favor a modification of the strictly territorial understanding of parish membership that still prevailed. Perhaps it was now time to give the laity the opportunity to choose their own parish based on own personal considerations. "Our strictly regulated geographic parishes throw all these kinds of people together in the congregation," a 1962 *Oklahoma Courier* editorial declared, "and present the priest with an impossible task."[13]

Early in his episcopate, however, Victor Reed displayed a markedly ambivalent attitude toward requests for nonterritorial membership in a parish. "I know the Bishop is most aware of the attachments that can grow up with a particular parish church and the priests who staff that church," Father William Garthoeffner told C. D. Taulman of Tulsa's Church of the Madalene who wished to transfer to St. Pius X to give the younger parish some experienced members, "and I am sure that he took these things into consideration in considering your request; however, the division of the diocese into parishes and the requirement that the people participate in the activities of the parish in whose boundaries they live is a centuries old plan adopted by the Church, and through the centuries it has shown itself in most cases to be beneficial to the spiritual needs of the people."[14] Equally unsuccessful was

---

11. *Tulsa Daily World*, March 1, 1963; *Tulsa Tribune*, May 25, 1963.

12. Victor Reed, "The Lay Apostolate in the Life of the Parish," August 28, 1961, Reed Papers.

13. *Oklahoma Courier*, October 19, 1962.

14. C. D. Taulman to Victor Reed, September 9, 1960, Revd. William C. Garthoeffner to Taulman, September 19, 1960, Church of the Madalene, Tulsa File, box 5.1, ADT.

the request of one of Reed's former acquaintances to remain a member of Oklahoma City's Cathedral of Our Lady of Perpetual Help (of which he had been a member for twenty years) despite moving out of the parish. "I feel that the reason," the bishop told him, "although very praiseworthy, is hardly sufficient to make an exception to the general rule of the Church."[15] There was considerable irony in Reed's position since he had, while rector of Holy Family Cathedral, declared his parish "open" to all, in an effort to counteract the depopulation of downtown Tulsa.

Reed did recognize that there were ambiguous situations, particularly where a family lived close to the boundary between two parishes. Mary Humphreys lived just outside the parish of Christ the King, Tulsa, but had been confirmed and married at Christ the King, her children had been baptized there, and her father (who had lived in the parish for forty-one years) had finally joined the Church in 1957. Such a battery of reasons evidently convinced the bishop of the virtue of her petition, for he allowed her to remain a member.[16] Another issue of accessibility was raised by a member of St. Patrick's parish in Oklahoma City who suffered from arthritis; she was permitted to worship at Our Lady's Cathedral, where she found the chairs more comfortable.[17]

Some Oklahoma Catholics successfully pushed the envelope of boundary crossing with justifications that were far more tenuous. No one was blunter than John Mullen of Tulsa, who lived in the Madalene parish but close to the boundary with St. Francis Xavier. Evidently, the activities of Father McNamee and his assistants did not impress Mullen favorably. "Your Excellency," he told Reed in 1958, "to tell you the truth I would just about rather not have my son baptized as to have him baptized in Madalene Church. I do not like the church and do not wish to attend." Reed granted Mullen's request, perhaps fearing that a denial might lead to Mullen abandoning the Church altogether.[18]

Parish programs were also raised as a legitimate cause for boundary crossing. In 1961, Reed approved Father Henry Kelly's request for John Dobel-

15. Jack La Monte to Victor Reed, July 29, 1960, Reed to La Monte, August 1, 1960, Cathedral of Our Lady of Perpetual Help, Oklahoma City File, AAOC.

16. Mary Jane Humphreys to Victor Reed, n.d., Revd. Charles H. Schettler to Humphreys, June 16, 1961, Christ the King Church, Tulsa File, box 2.1, ADT.

17. Mrs. Arthur B. Noll to Victor Reed, September 21, 1959, Reed to Noll, October 12, 1959, Reed Papers.

18. John F. Mullen to Victor Reed, November 11, 1958, Reed to Mullen, November 20, 1958, Our Lady of Guadalupe Church, Tulsa File, box 6.1, ADT.

bower, who had moved into Christ the King parish in Oklahoma City, to remain at Our Lady of Perpetual Help Cathedral to assist with the youth group that he had helped found. Christ the King already had an established youth group, while the cathedral had only just launched its venture.[19] While such an exemption was designed to facilitate effective ministry as much, if not more, than to meet Dobelbower's personal desires, it signaled that blanket denials would no longer be issued. In March 1963, Wendy Harrison of Tulsa inverted the earlier request of John Mullen by asking permission to move from St. Francis Xavier to the Madalene, because the latter used the vernacular liturgy and there were no programs for young married couples in their twenties at St. Francis Xavier. Seven months later, Joan Putnam of Oklahoma City sought to move from Our Lady of Perpetual Help Cathedral to St. Patrick's parish because of the latter's active unit of the Christian Family Movement and because her non-Catholic husband found the liturgy there "more zestful and meaningful."[20] No answer to either of these requests has been located, but it is clear that increasing numbers of Catholics were starting to think like Protestants in terms of "church shopping." By the end of the decade, many were probably not even bothering to request their ordinary's permission.

One factor that may have contributed to this new lay perspective was the emergence of the nonterritorial parish.[21] The brainchild of Father William Nerin, the concept of the nonterritorial parish represented a repudiation of the standard model of parish life in favor of an organic entity that reached *out* to serve man in the world.[22] In August 1966, the bishop approved the consti-

19. Revd. Henry Kelly to Victor Reed, September 8, 1961, John T. Dobelbower to Victor Reed, n.d., Reed to Dobelbower, September 19, 1961, Cathedral of Our Lady of Perpetual Help, Oklahoma City File.

20. Wendy H. Harrison to Reed, February 4, 1963, Reed Papers; Joan M. Putnam to Victor Reed, October 21, 1963, St. Patrick's Church, Oklahoma City File, AAOC.

21. This notion of a nominal geographic parish with a wider participatory community might be compared with the situation of university parishes. In Stillwater, the actual parish boundaries of St. John University parish were extremely small, but students and faculty and their families who actually lived in St. Francis Xavier parish could still belong. However, students living with their parents, noneducational staff, and any person with a child in the St. Francis Xavier parochial school were excluded, so the absolute permission to belong to a nonterritorial parish was a new development. See Revd. Clement E. Pribil to Revd. William C. Garthoeffner, August 10, 1965, Garthoeffner to Pribil, August 11, 1965, Decree of Erection: St. John the Evangelist Parish (Catholic Student Center, Stillwater, Oklahoma), St. John University Church, Stillwater File, box 81.1, ADT.

22. *Oklahoma Courier*, March 18, 1966.

tution of the Community of John XXIII, a nonterritorial parish in Oklahoma City. "We wanted a richer 'parish life,'" explained one organizer, "without building programs, a huge debt, 2,000 unknown faces, and numerous organizations. We were intrigued with the idea of an experimental parish, and we were impatient to get on with the renewal promoted by Vatican II. The knowledge that the Holy Spirit was with us spurred us on, and we continued to investigate the possibility of forming such a parish." While members agreed to designate an area in the north of the city, which included parts of five territorial parishes, as a nominal geographic unit, they urged the bishop to permit any city resident to become a member, and no Catholic living in the designated area was obliged to join. Those who did were expected to make a two-year commitment to support the parish through financial contributions and active participation.[23]

The parish operated on democratic lines and vigorously affirmed lay initiative: "Since this is an experiment we may want to explore procedures based on a growing awareness of the divinity of each person, and the past experience of various Christian and Jewish communities. We are open to any human structure that respects the dignity of man and the divine structure of the Church. We feel that much needs to be explored in this area since our past Catholic experience has been so authoritative leaving the layman little voice in the affairs of the Church." In place of a permanent church structure, the parish rented a building for Sunday services, and a daily Mass was celebrated in members' homes. The entire effort was financed out of members' contributions, and the bulk of parish assets were diverted into social justice, poverty, and international aid programs. Members laid great emphasis on adult education and family-centered juvenile education, with the attendant assumption that children over fourteen would fully participate with adults in the life and work of the parish. They also hoped to develop ecumenical contacts with churches of other denominations and invited priests and laity from elsewhere in the diocese to inform themselves about what was taking place.[24]

In 1967, a group of Tulsa laymen approached Father Henry Kelly about replicating the Oklahoma City experiment. "I do believe these people are

23. L. Mike Sherrod to "Those interested in the Community of John XXIII," n.d., Proposed Outline for an Experimental Christian Community for the Diocese of Oklahoma City and Tulsa, August 8, 1966, Reed Papers.

24. *Oklahoma Courier*, October 28, 1966, March 3, 1967.

honest in their attempt to discover a more relative concept of the Church in today's society," Kelly told the bishop, "that they are quite competent enough to construct a viable kind of Christian community concerned with the larger human city, and that they are generous enough to realize their possibilities."[25] The new Tulsa parish (the Community of the Living Christ) also chose not to own buildings or other material possessions as a parish and strove to avoid economic, geographic, or racial stratification. "We don't conceive of ourselves as a splinter group or an elite corps," declared architect Robert Jones, "and we are not cutting ourselves off from the institutional church as such."[26]

In the space of a single year, the parish grew from ten members to sixty. Kelly favored unstructured worship and the use of guitar accompaniments, took comments on his sermon, and encouraged non-Catholics to attend the services. He also exhorted members to become involved in social action to make Christian witness more meaningful, including interracial work for open housing, the erection of a playground on the north side of Tulsa, and demonstrations against the Vietnam War. At a meeting of the Tulsa Ministerial Alliance, the Community of the Living Christ was praised for having done more than any other organization in Tulsa to bring about communication between African Americans and whites.[27]

Reed made considerable efforts to accommodate the nonterritorial parishes. "I believe [the Community of the Living Christ] helps a generation of well-read, educated young Catholics who are dissatisfied with the slow pace of progress," he told the *Tulsa Daily World*. "I believe it offers them a kind of outlet. I've recommended to several bishops that they could use this type of community to give the people a challenge, an opportunity to do something with their ideas."[28] Such support did not always generate loyalty in response. In 1971, members of the Community of John XXIII threatened to withhold their contribution to the diocesan development fund because they disagreed with one aspect of an unrelated program. "If you really want to show how strong you are on moral values," Father Philip Bryce told them, "why not refuse to pay federal income tax because you disagree with some

25. Revd. Henry Kelly to Victor Reed, August 3, 1967, Reed Papers.

26. *Tulsa Daily World*, September 10, 1967. See also the account of the community in *Oklahoma Courier*, August 18, 1967.

27. Revd. Henry Kelly to Victor Reed, February 12, 1968, Reed Papers; *Tulsa Tribune*, August 31, 1968.

28. *Tulsa Daily World*, September 10, 1967.

governmental programs. That way you can perhaps witness to Christ by suffering imprisonment. As it is now you are fighting the Bishop who won't
fight back, so you won't have to suffer at all."[29]

Although the earliest efforts at "church shopping" tended to come from
liberals, traditionalist Catholics increasingly began to see the merit of crossing parish lines. In April 1966, a group of traditionalist women in Oklahoma
City (including a large contingent from Christ the King parish) decided to
worship at Our Lady of Perpetual Help Cathedral until "anti-Catholic" activities had been eliminated from their home parishes and schools. They resolved to make their offerings in cash so that they could not be traced, study
Church dogma and the encyclicals on their own since "we cannot depend on
most of the priests or the anti-Catholic Oklahoma Courier," and organize
like-minded groups throughout the diocese. Monsignor John Connor's parish proved a natural sanctuary for such a group.[30]

A different clash over parish boundaries occurred in 1971, when Father
Frank Wrigley of St. Joseph's parish in Norman was requested by two of his
more traditionalist parishioners to make provision for a Latin Mass for sixty-
six local Catholics "to encourage those who have stopped attending Mass
and receiving the sacraments to return."[31] Wrigley agreed that such a Mass
might be held at 2:00 p.m. on a Sunday afternoon, provided that the petitioners found a willing priest to celebrate, whose expenses the parish would
pay. However, he insisted that attendance at this Mass be limited to registered parishioners at Norman-area parishes who used weekly contribution
envelopes and supported special collections and the diocesan development
fund. Wrigley's intent was clearly to avoid a situation in which traditionalists
from Oklahoma City could flock to Norman each week, thus denying the efficacy of parish boundaries. He was also aware that many traditionalists regarded abstention from support of the diocesan development fund as a matter of conscience, but did not see why, if they were unwilling to contribute
to the welfare of the diocese, they should be accorded special treatment.[32]

From Wrigley's perspective, the sacraments were no less valid because
they were in the vernacular; the Latin Mass was simply a matter of personal

29. Revd. Philip Bryce to Paul Sprehe, April 8, 1971, Reed Papers.

30. Notes of Women's Meeting, April 11, 1966, Reed Papers.

31. Antoinette Krane and Elizabeth Kovach to the Priests and Executive Council of
St. Joseph's Parish, March 8, 1971, St. Joseph's Church, Norman File, AAOC.

32. Revd. Frank Wrigley to Victor Reed, March 12, 1971, St. Joseph's Church, Norman
File, AAOC.

taste. To the traditionalists, such an approach seemed strangely mercenary. How, in practice, was one to police attendance and why should someone be required to show proof of *any* financial contribution in order to avail him- or herself of the sacraments? At the same time, though, it became increasingly clear that there was a political edge to the traditionalists' request, and they objected to Wrigley having the option of preaching or celebrating at the Latin Mass, despite the fact that he was the parish priest. One of Wrigley's applicants revealed that she had been offered a Protestant church in which the Latin Mass could be held. But a public Mass, the priest gently reminded her, required the permission of the pastor in whose parish it was to be celebrated.[33] Traditionalist Catholics were often no more theologically consistent in such matters than their liberal brethren.

PARISH GOVERNMENT

By the early 1960s, the sentiment was abroad among the laity that the days when a priest ran his parish solely according to his own sense of what was appropriate were over. "Who runs the Parish?" enquired "A Parishioner" in June 1962. "Is it a qualified board of directors; business people who know about finances, budgets, investments, legal and social problems? Why isn't the parish run as a business, which it certainly is, by a board which is elected by the parish?"[34] This notion was developed by Joe Skaggs of Bartlesville, who proposed in 1966 that the town's three parishes—St. John's, St. James, and Our Lady of Guadalupe—establish a central administrative office.

Under such an arrangement, accounting and parish records could easily be updated and a central purchasing plan implemented for the three churches and two parochial schools. With staggered office hours and priests' guests accommodated in local hotels, the need for old-fashioned rectories would disappear. Skaggs touched upon one of the themes of the decade: the transformation of the priest into merely another professional. "At one time, doctors, lawyers and other professional people had offices in their home," he wrote. "They now, for the most part, have offices away from home."[35]

Priests who seemed to take the idea of lay consultation seriously were better placed to weather the new lay militancy. "[F]or seminarians, includ-

33. Ibid.
34. *Oklahoma Courier*, June 1, 1962.
35. Joe Skaggs to Revd. Francis McGoldrick, December 8, 1966, St. John's Church, Bartlesville File, box 23.1, ADT.

Bishop Reed breaks ground for the new church building for St. Patrick's parish in Oklahoma City in the early 1960s. Monsignor Don Kanaly, rector of St. Patrick's and the father of Catholic Action in Oklahoma, is on the far right. In 1969, the parish would be torn apart by disagreements between Kanaly and lay leaders over the future of the parish school.

ing myself, coming out in the late Fifties and early Sixties," declared Charles Meiser, "you looked at people like [Monsignor Don] Kanaly [of St. Patrick's parish, Oklahoma City and thought]: 'This is wonderful . . . he recognizes lay people have a vocation.'"[36] Kanaly's watchword in the early 1960s was complete lay participation, both in the liturgy and in programs that addressed issues of social concern. When the parish began to organize a council in 1965, he sought to foster lay involvement by dividing the parish into fifty-five districts, each of which elected a representative to the parish council.[37]

Less committed pastors than Kanaly could still win broad lay approval. In 1969, Gloria Crotty of St. Michael's parish, Henryetta, contrasted the authoritarian style of her former pastor with his successor's willingness to entertain criticism of his plans from parishioners and to hold parish ballots on contentious issues. "Even though Msgr. Caudron is still interested in St. Michael's," Crotty complained of the retired pastor's efforts to influence parish policy, "how can he possibly have any say in the matter? Isn't this for the people to decide?"[38]

Naturally enough, the principal concern of most laymen was the financial condition of their parish. In December 1960, the diocesan newspaper carried the views of Lawton banker W. F. Wulf and Clifford Sousa of Bartlesville, an influential figure in the state chapter of the National Conference of Catholic Men. Wulf blasted his fellow Catholics for failing to support the Church financially and recommended tithing as a possible solution. Sousa concurred but suggested that "fiveing"—the donation of 5 percent of one's income—was more realistic since Catholics were "half-hearted givers" at best.[39]

In the years that followed, several pastors, including Father Joseph Hoying of St. Catherine's parish, Tulsa, picked up on the idea of the biblical tithe as preferable to more secular and business-oriented fund-raising drives. "This way of giving," Hoying told the *Tulsa Daily World*, "is far preferable to bingo as a means of church support. I have no objection to my people enjoy-

36. Meiser, interview.

37. "The Chronological Development of the Social Action Committee, St. Patrick's Church, Oklahoma City," 1968, St Patrick's Church, Oklahoma City File; *Oklahoma Courier*, February 12, 1965.

38. Gloria Crotty et al. to Victor Reed, February 5, 1969, Grace Donaldson to Reed, March 18, 1968, Reed Papers. Caudron's reluctance to let go is more understandable when one remembers that he was pastor of Henryetta for fifty-two years and that he built every one of the structures, including a high school. Within a few years of his leaving, however, every building was in serious need of repair and had to be razed.

39. *Oklahoma Courier*, December 9, 1960. See the discussion in Pardo, "Parish Finances."

ing themselves, but games and such didn't do a thing for their faith, where-
as tithing is part and parcel of their faith." Other Tulsa pastors, including
Father Kenneth Fulton of St. Jude's and Monsignor William Reid of Holy
Family Cathedral, expressed support for Hoying's methods.[40] Father Philip
Wilkiemeyer of Immaculate Conception parish in Oklahoma City also adopted tithing after a two-year period during which his parish had been unable to pay off any of the principal of its accrued debt. Wilkiemeyer followed
Clifford Sousa's suggestion by defining the tithe as 5 percent of gross income
and pledged that there would be no other types of fund-raising in his parish
except for the bishop's special collections.[41]

By 1964, ten Oklahoma parishes used the Parish Tithing Program in operation in the Archdiocese of Detroit, and its proponents urged Bishop Reed
to make it mandatory throughout his diocese. "The people are taught to
give first for their own spiritual welfare, rather than the laudable but secondary motive of erecting buildings," Richard Meurer assured him. "They learn
that tithing is a way of life and that giving is a repudiation of materialism.
They learn that giving to God is an act of worship. They learn that they are
to offer to God what they *are* and what they *have*."[42] Two years later, many
parishes had begun to set tithing machinery in place and strongly to encourage their parishioners to declare a pledge for the forthcoming year. Even
though it was unusual to get more than one-third of parishioners pledging,
that alone would usually double a parish's income.[43]

In September 1966, the *Oklahoma Courier* published the results of a poll
on parish financing, one of a number that it conducted among its readership during the mid- to late 1960s. Though unscientific (the editor never
disclosed the number of replies or their geographic distribution), these polls
represent the only sampling of Oklahoma Catholic opinion from this period. Respondents supported the *concept* of pledging by 78 percent to 22 percent (although about half expressed some sort of reservation, evidenced by
the fact that only 39 percent actually tithed). More than three quarters of respondents thought their parish was inadequately supported by its members,
with the blame for financial shortfalls being attributed principally to non-

40. *Tulsa Daily World*, February 12, 1961.
41. Revd. Philip Wilkiemeyer to "Parishioner," n.d., Victor Reed to Parishioners of Immaculate Conception Parish, October 21, 1961, Immaculate Conception Church, Oklahoma
City File, AAOC.
42. Richard Meurer to Victor Reed, November 2, 1964, Reed Papers.
43. *Oklahoma Courier*, February 18, 1966.

contributors (49 percent), and to a lesser extent to unnecessary expenditures (19 percent), pastoral incompetence (15 percent), and the parochial school (5 percent). A mixture of systems of financial oversight was reported: in 36 percent of cases, the pastor was solely responsible for financial management; in another 34 percent, the pastor worked jointly with a lay committee; while in a mere 16 percent of cases, the pastor had approved a lay committee to operate independently.[44]

Issues of financial management were bound to increase tensions between clergy and laity, especially as the latter began to see themselves more and more as jointly responsible for the parish's financial well-being. Such was the case at St. Mary's parish in Tulsa in the spring of 1967. Five years before, Father Frederick Beckerle had established a parish finance board and asked Albert Rutkowski to help prepare an annual financial report. Rutkowski, seeing this as an example of lay participation, had happily agreed to participate until 1966, when he discovered that the receipts and disbursements from the bank accounts for the parish school and its cafeteria had not been included in the report to the diocese. "[T]he parish funds are public funds in character," Rutkowski insisted, "and misleading financial reports are, to me, inexcusable."[45]

Furthermore, Rutkowski discovered that Father Beckerle had established a "special" bank account and instructed those who counted the weekly collections to withhold $50 each Sunday. While the priest maintained that this was a personal account to provide him with funds to make loans or advances to parish employees, Rutkowski pointed out that the account was still in the name of the parish and should be reported. When Rutkowski declared that the discrepancies must be reported to the parish finance board and to the chancery, the pastor requested him to withdraw from drafting the 1967 report and informed him that he was no longer a member of the finance board. "It is my opinion that if parishioners are to be expected to take more responsibility in church affairs and contribute to church support," a bitter Rutkowski concluded, "the very least to be done is to send them an annual financial report that is adequate and complete."[46]

44. *Oklahoma Courier*, September 2, 1966.
45. Albert S. Rutkowski to Members of Finance Board, St. Mary's Church, February 1, 1967, St. Mary's Church, Tulsa File, box 14.1, ADT.
46. Ibid. Bishop Reed promised to address the concerns raised by Rutkowski in accordance with diocesan policy. Beckerle was subsequently transferred to a church in Collinsville, but renewed controversy over the liturgy led to his assignment as chaplain to Our

Events like those at St. Mary's only heightened the desire of lay Catholics to establish parish councils with teeth. In January 1967, an open meeting of the members of St. Anne's, Broken Arrow, elected a parish board after extensive discussion about the need for financial retrenchment. The new board immediately froze spending until a proper audit could be conducted, assumed responsibility for all future expenditures and purchases, and pledged to take a parish census. While its members issued assurances that its concerns were solely with the material welfare of the parish—spiritual matters would be resolved by the pastor as he chose—they also warned that they would continue to use the rectory as a parish office only "as long as we can perform our duties without interference." Their goals, they declared, were full lay participation and open books.[47]

In September 1968, Father Beckerle's successor at St. Mary's encouraged the establishment of a parish council that would make decisions on all matters that were not reserved to the pastor under canon law. Comprised of the pastor, his assistant, the chairs of the eight parish committees, and four elected members (the chairman was chosen from among the elected members), the council held regular monthly meetings open to all.[48]

As the number of parish councils grew, the diocesan pastoral board felt obliged to produce guidelines for their organization. Members of the diocesan Little Council, while recognizing the legitimacy of both the vestry system (a council elected by the whole parish) and the executive board system (a council composed of members selected by the various parish organizations), declined to favor one model over the other, and the pastoral board followed their lead. Its guidelines emphasized the need for meetings held at least quarterly and open to the entire parish, publication of minutes, and the council's right of access to all parish records. It firmly stipulated that there should be a minimum number of lay members (three for parishes of one hundred families or less, seven for parishes of more than one hundred families) and required that all officers should be laymen. Pastors were to be ex officio members without voting rights but with veto power, while assistant pastors had a vote. A provision that all lay members had to be "freely elect-

Lady of Sorrows Convent in Broken Arrow in 1969. Victor Reed to Rutkowski, February 2, 1967, St. Mary's Church, Tulsa File, box 14.1, ADT.

47. St. Anne's Parish Newsletter, January 22, 1967, St. Anne's Church, Broken Arrow File, box 27.1, ADT.

48. Charles E. Holmes to Herbert Giles, March 25, 1969, St. Mary's Church, Tulsa File, box 14.1.

ed" was included to prevent a pastor from stacking the council with his own nominees.[49]

Some parishes made a surprisingly aggressive assertion of their independence. "I shudder to think that I may have to approach my local parish committee [about an increased diocesan assessment]," admitted a priest in Vinita, "along with the fear that I may be literally scalped for my audacity. . . . I fear it will take some time for our Catholics to get used to the idea of supporting pastors other than their own."[50] In December 1970, the parish council of Sts. Peter and Paul parish in Tulsa voted to keep the funds raised for the Bishops' Campaign for Human Development and use the money for a parish cannery, as their social action committee had no available funds. Here, the bishop intervened and told the pastor that while the parish could apply for a social action grant from the diocese at a later date, the money must be sent to the National Conference of Catholic Bishops.[51]

The writing of parish constitutions also led to discord. Perhaps the most contested clause in the pastoral board guidelines was article 5: "The Parish Council shall be decision-making in all areas of parochial life except where explicitly limited by church law."[52] When St. Andrew's parish in Moore presented its draft constitution to the pastoral board, the phrase "to establish policy" was for the first time used in relation to the parish council, while its board of directors (parish council) was described as "a governing body." The executive secretary of the pastoral board advised parish leaders that a greater distinction needed to be made between the decision-making role of the whole parish and the board of directors. He also recommended that a qualifying phrase should be inserted in relation to policy making such that it should not be inconsistent with diocesan policies.[53] An amendment to the constitution of St. Barbara's parish in Lawton required either the treasurer or the board chairman to be lay cosignatory with the priest for all expenditures over $300. While the laity viewed this merely as "sound business practice," Father James Ross complained that it was a modified form of trusteeism that

49. "Parish Council Guidelines," n.d., Revd. William C. Garthoeffner to Herbert Giles, April 16, 1969, Reed Papers.

50. Revd. Benedict D'Angelo, C.PP.S., to Victor Reed, August 8, 1968, Holy Ghost Church, Vinita, box 84.1, ADT.

51. Revd. Kenneth S. Fulton to Victor Reed, December 8, 1970, Reed to Fulton, December 16, 1970, Sts. Peter and Paul Church, Tulsa File, box 16.1, ADT.

52. "Parish Board Guidelines," Reed Papers.

53. Revd. David Jones to Herbert O. Giles, December 18, 1969, Giles to Robert Lee, March 13, 1970, St. Andrew's Church, Moore File, AAOC.

might make it difficult to issue checks on time and was contrary to the practices of other parishes and the wishes of the bishop. Reed agreed and told Ross to exercise his veto accordingly.[54]

While the parishioners of St. Barbara's appear to have accepted this executive decision without overt opposition, conflicts at Sts. Peter and Paul parish, Cushing, and St. Patrick's parish, Oklahoma City, boiled over into open warfare. Neither of the affected pastors—Father Martin Reid and Monsignor Donald Kanaly—had a previous reputation as a clerical tyrant, and the outlook of their critics was not necessarily driven by a truly "progressive" sense of lay empowerment.

At the preliminary meeting to elect a parish council in Cushing in February 1969, Father Reid requested the election of a three-member council, in accordance with the Little Council guidelines, since the parish had fewer than one hundred families. When a group of petitioners demanded a six-member council, Reid changed the ballot but asked that the parish select three men and three women. This brought local lawyer D. O. Cubbage to his feet in protest and a series of exchanges between himself and Reid followed, with Cubbage at one point informing the Irish-born Reid: "You know nothing about the democratic process here." Ultimately, Reid agreed to put the matter before the parish, which then elected five men and one woman.[55]

The newly elected parish council selected Cubbage as its chairman and proceeded to adopt a constitution that included a clause giving it responsibility for all financial records and account books. After Reid vetoed this clause, the council overrode his veto by a two-thirds majority, and the stage was set for an appeal to the pastoral board. Cubbage insisted that the changes were intended simply to help get parish finances in order and asked what the canonical position was in such a case. The bishop told him that there was no law precluding the placement of the account books in the parish school building rather than the rectory and—in contrast with his later stance—declared that he had no objection to there being a lay cosigner of checks, *if the pastor agreed.* He reminded all those present that the pastor was ultimately responsible for the parish's financial welfare and that the custom of the diocese was for the pastor to be sole signatory. A weary Martin Reid declared he

54. Revd. James H. Ross and Robert E. Broderick to Victor Reed, March 16, 1971, Ross to Reed, March 17, 1971, Reed to Ross, March 24, 1971, St. Barbara's Church, Lawton File, AAOC.

55. Mrs. J. C. Robb et al. to Victor Reed, April 4, 1969, Sts. Peter and Paul Church, Cushing File, box 36.1, ADT.

was willing to go along with such moves, if only to preclude a dramatic resignation by Cubbage.[56]

Although the pastoral board requested that a final decision be delayed until a two-man delegation had visited the parish to negotiate a compromise, Cubbage lost no time in trying to force Reid to move the financial records from the rectory and to get the parish treasurer's signature placed on the official banking records. At a joint meeting between the pastoral board, Reid, and the parish council on April 7, it was agreed that the financial officer would have access to the parish financial records at least one week of every month and that he and the pastor would come to an agreement both on where he would audit them and where they would be stored between audits.[57]

The financial officer had responsibility for making deposits, collecting monies, consolidating bills, and preparing schedules of disbursements. While the pastor was to be sole signatory of checks, only those accompanied by a check voucher signed by the financial officer would be considered valid. A petty cash fund was also to be created for the pastor, with a monthly deposit of $50. It was this last provision that excited Cubbage's ire, since, as he pointed out to the pastoral board's executive secretary, the petty cash fund lacked a designation as to the uses to which it could be put. The battle between pastor and council continued into the summer, with the parish council exploiting the check voucher system to screen even minor purchases and refusing to make payments into the petty cash fund. They even declined an auto repair bill submitted by Reid on the grounds that he had used his car for personal reasons (such as going to the golf course). Incidents like these did much to sour Victor Reed on the principle of lay autonomy on financial matters.[58]

Far more unsettling, since it involved an old and dear friend, was the conflict that erupted at St. Patrick's parish in the spring of 1969 over the future of the parish's parochial school. Although the parish had been running an overall deficit for some years and the bishop had indicated that he was not will-

56. D. O. Cubbage to Victor Reed, March 10, 1969, Minutes of Special Meeting of Sts. Peter and Paul Parish Council with Pastoral Board, March 24, 1969, Sts. Peter and Paul Church, Cushing File, box 36.1.

57. D. O. Cubbage to Revd. Martin E. Reid, March 27, 1969, Herbert O. Giles to D. O. Cubbage, April 2, 1969, Sts. Peter and Paul Church, Cushing File, box 36.1.

58. Herbert O. Giles to D. O. Cubbage, April 10, 1969, Cubbage to Giles, May 2, 1969, Notes of Revd. William C. Garthoeffner, May 14, 1969, Sts. Peter and Paul Church, Cushing File, box 36.1.

ing to allow that state of affairs to continue, the parish leadership still believed that the budget could be balanced. On Sunday, March 16, however, Kanaly announced that he intended to close the parish school and replace the current religious education program with "Total Parish Life," a "family-oriented" visitation program, under which teams composed of religious and laity would visit individual homes to provide instruction. As Kanaly put it, the priests and the Sisters of Charity would be no longer tied up "baby-sitting" the children. He added that he was dissatisfied with lay control and that he would now have to take over and become a "dictator priest."[59]

At an emergency meeting of the parent-teacher council the following day (St. Patrick's Day), bitter exchanges took place, with Kanaly arriving late and accusing his opponents of bringing about the school's demise. A majority of those present voted to fight the closing through a petition and personal letters to the bishop. The school board and the parent-teacher council also called on sympathetic parishioners to withhold, on three successive Sundays, their usual contribution in the event the school closed and then pay that amount as part of their contribution on the fourth Sunday. While the parish would not ultimately be deprived of revenue, it would send a clear message as to the consequences of Kanaly's decision. School board members met with the pastoral board, which also heard testimony from those in favor of closing the school, and on April 3 the pastoral board indicated that the parish council must adjudicate the matter before any outside body could intervene.[60]

Tensions were rapidly rising as the executive committee of the parish council met to discuss the conditions for a meeting of the general council on April 21. Outside the church, 250 parishioners, led by the school's athletic director, Bob Mannix, protested Kanaly's action. The terms for debate were outlined, with only one proposal—that of allowing eligible voting members to vote by proxy—failing to be adopted. Participants agreed that thirty minutes each would be allowed for presentations in support of the existing program and its proposed replacement and twenty minutes each for discussion.[61]

Parishioners articulated a variety of viewpoints. "We feel that the school

59. "Facts concerning St. Patrick's School Issue," *St. Patrick Herald*, April 20, 1969, Reed Papers.

60. "Facts concerning St. Patrick's School Issue," *St. Patrick Herald*, April 20, 1969; St. Patrick's School Board and St. Patrick's Parent-Teacher Council to "Dear Fellow Parishioners," n.d. (prob. March 18–23, 1969), Reed Papers.

61. *Oklahoma Journal*, April 15, 1969; Minutes of Executive Committee, St. Patrick's Council, April 14, 1969, Reed Papers.

is an unnecessary expense," one woman commented. "We can teach our children a broader concept of religion than what they can learn in parochial school anyway."[62] Michael O'Hara, by contrast, complained that he had been persuaded to sign a petition in support of Kanaly on the understanding that a petition calling for his ouster was pending. No such petition had materialized, O'Hara explained, and he in no way endorsed the sentiments of those who favored an end to the parochial school. Indeed, the state of the world today suggested a greater need for Catholic elementary schools than in the nineteenth century, when the Church grew, despite incurring heavy debt in building its education system: "The founders of St. Patrick's certainly knew the value of Catholic School education Monsignor, and their foresight was *to give Catholic School education to St. Patrick's children . . . then and in the future . . . at St. Patrick's SCHOOL . . .* and their first 'project' was to build a SCHOOL! They were *not* wrong then . . . are not now . . . and will not be in years to come. As a 'builder' yourself, I for one cannot see how you can change your attitude so late in life Monsignor, or bow to those who might try to change you . . . to do so would be to say all you have done in the past was WRONG . . . certainly THAT is not the case!"[63]

On April 21, 1969, the parish council met for the final showdown. In a meeting that lasted from 8:00 p.m. to 12:30 a.m., the council voted down Kanaly's program by twenty-eight votes to twenty-four and affirmed the continuation of the school by twenty-seven votes to twenty-five. At this point, the pastor rose to veto the resolution on the grounds of financial necessity, something that, the bishop's representative Father William Eichhoff later claimed, had never been properly addressed by the school's advocates. In the face of the veto, the council then voted by thirty-three votes to eighteen and thirty-two votes to eighteen (on an amended resolution) to appeal Kanaly's decision to the pastoral board. To be successful, such a vote required a two-thirds majority (thirty-six votes), and the three members who withheld their votes on the first ballot to override the veto just tipped the scale.[64]

Interestingly, a minimum of four members must have voted to override Kanaly even though they favored closing the school, and only half the council had been willing to preserve the school before Kanaly directly intervened. "The problem here," remarked Monsignor Gregory Gier, then an assistant

62. *Daily Oklahoman,* April 15, 1969.
63. Michael C. O'Hara Sr. to Msgr. Donald J. Kanaly, April 17, 1969, Reed Papers.
64. Notes of Revd. Charles H. Schettler, April 22, 1969, Reed Papers.

at St. Patrick's, "is that for eleven years . . . these people had been told, it's *our* church, it's *our* parish, it's *our* grade school, and now you are telling us that even though we have established very clearly that the mind of the parish is to keep the school open . . . you're going to close it anyway. That tore the heart out of people."[65]

Parishioner Paul Scott later begged Reed to override Kanaly's veto, noting that no one at the meeting had called the excellence of the school into question. "The point that I feel needs to be considered is that this outstanding job by the parishioners has been accomplished at a time when, and under conditions where the total parish leadership has been against them, or at least has been working to replace the system with another form. If the parishioners have developed such an outstanding system against these adversities, just imagine what could be accomplished both spiritually and financially with proper leadership."[66]

Reed, however, was not willing to take such action. The only redress of sorts that the affronted parishioners received was Kanaly's acquiescence in a move to another parish (and even then he insisted on being allowed to name his successor). The supreme irony of all this was that Kanaly seemed utterly oblivious to the fact that by his actions he had set at naught the very philosophy of lay empowerment that he had been at pains to inculcate at St. Patrick's over the course of a decade.[67]

Many of the small rural parishes lacked the passion generated in urban settings like St. Patrick's. "I shall need your assistance in drawing together a constitution for the [parish] Council," Father Francis McGoldrick of St. Mark's parish in Pryor requested of the executive secretary of the pastoral board. "This [is] a far-flung parish territorially and made up largely of ultra-conservative people." In Owasso, the members of the social action committee of St. Henry's parish agreed that there were local needs to be met. They concluded, however, that the laity lacked both experience and time and took the surprisingly old-fashioned view that the pastor was best suited to obtain names and pay home visits and had the experience and time necessary to address social needs. As late as 1971, St. Clements parish in Bixby was still only investigating how to form a council. Were there guidelines from the Second

65. Gier, interview.
66. Paul E. Scott to Victor Reed, April 23, 1969, Reed Papers.
67. Joseph D. Dillon, "Reflections on My Life," in Brousseau, *A Dying Breed of Brave Men*, 62–63. See the cartoon in *St Patrick Herald*, May 25, 1969.

Vatican Council, a parishioner inquired, and could the diocese supply lists of appropriate parish commissions and their functions?[68]

CHRISTIAN FORMATION

The role of the parish in juvenile Christian formation had historically been confined to the parochial school (see chapter 4 for parochial education), but in rural America many small parishes and missions lacked the means to build or maintain such an institution. Oklahoma was no exception. One attempt to provide catechetical instruction for the young was the religious correspondence school, which provided instruction materials for children who were outside the Catholic school system. Students enrolled in the program received a weekly assignment that they completed and returned to the religious correspondence office to be marked. While the program was handicapped both by late enrollments and a need to issue reminders to mail in lessons, the sisters who ran the office believed that their courses helped involve parents and even entire families in study outside the weekly catechism class. In 1960, there were 1,256 students from 694 families enrolled, with the largest enrollments from Guymon (94), Cushing (60), Clinton (55), and Chandler (54), as well as St. Patrick's parish in Oklahoma City, which at the time had not completed its parochial school (86). By 1963, however, total enrollment had fallen to 917, with Guymon still the largest contender (100), followed by Tonkawa (71), Union City (65), Ponca City (42), and Okeene (41).[69]

Another pre-1965 catechetical program was the Confraternity of Christian Doctrine, but this depended on the existence of trained lay catechists, who were in short supply in rural Oklahoma. In 1959, therefore, Father John Sullivan—then pastor of St. Mary's, Guthrie, and later bishop of Grand Island, Nebraska, and Kansas City–St. Joseph, Missouri—suggested that Catholic women's colleges in the East might provide suitable instructors. He subsequently secured commitments from fifteen young women from three colleges—Manhattanville, New Rochelle, and Mount St. Vincent's—to serve for a

68. Revd. Francis E. McGoldrick to Herbert Giles, March 18, 1969, St. Mark's Church, Pryor File, box 71.1, ADT; Memorandum from St. Henry's Executive Board to Revd. Lawrence Lange, August 10, 1969, St. Henry's Church, Owasso File, box 65.1, ADT; Carol Davito to Revd. William M. Eichoff, March 22, 1971, St. Clement's Church, Bixby File, box 24.1, ADT.

69. At least 80 percent of the children completed at least one assignment. Sr. M. Josephine to Reed, April 13, 1961, Sr. M. Julia to Reed, May 14, 1964, Reed Papers; Sr. M. Julia to "Revd. Father (Monsignor)," August 8, 1965, Sacred Heart Church, Alva File, AAOC.

year in rural America. The mother superior of the Victory Noll Sisters (who had a mission at Durant, Oklahoma) agreed that her community would provide a two-week training course for these women, while the priest in whose parish the catechetical volunteers were serving was charged with finding them suitable accommodation.[70]

What began as a local initiative was soon taken up by the Catholic Church Extension Society, whose general secretary pledged in February 1961 to train applicants from across the United States and send them to the mission fields in the South and Southwest; Father Sullivan was soon afterward appointed director of the Extension Lay Volunteer Program.[71] Extension workers were warned to avoid showing any form of superiority to those whom they served and to be loyal to their pastor and coworkers. Learn the history of your assigned parish, the program guidelines stressed; talk to parishioners, learn their names, and take part in parish worship. The guidelines thus revealed an appreciation of the regional variations within Catholicism. Volunteers were reminded about the importance of observing community standards, including avoiding being alone with the pastor, wearing shorts in public, consuming alcohol, keeping late hours, or driving recklessly. While dating was permitted, social interaction with non-Catholics was frowned on. "If you are seen in a non-respectable place," the guidelines warned girls raised in more relaxed East Coast environments, "it will be known immediately to the whole parish and the effectiveness of your work will suffer."[72]

For some volunteers, these regulations, though hardly monastic, must often have seemed cramping, but most displayed as great a zest for their work as those who traveled to more exotic mission locations. In the fall of 1959, thirteen laywomen served as teachers in Enid, Oklahoma City, and McAlester, while two others carried out missionary work in Poteau and its mission, Talihina. The following year, students from Marymount College in Salina, Kansas, conducted a parish census in Buffalo, organized a unit of the Legion of Mary, and inquired of non-Catholics about their relations with the Catholic community, eliciting generally favorable responses. Volunteers were reminded that they were not present primarily to bring about conversions. "The Catholics need [your] effort and love as much as the non-catholics [*sic*]," they were told. "Most of them have very little education in their faith,

70. Minutes of School Committee Meeting, February 19, 1959, Reed Papers; *Oklahoma Courier*, April 1, 1960.

71. Revd. John L. May to Victor Reed, February 28, 1961, Reed Papers.

72. "The Volunteer in the Mission," n.d., Reed Papers.

and live among people hostile to their religion. They will learn a great deal from your example and attitudes. Out here in Oklahoma we call this work 'Christianizing the Catholics.'"[73]

Extension workers performed a variety of other roles. In Skiatook they worked with the Young Christian Students and organized a women's discussion group, while in Frederick they started a Rosary Making Club. In Lawton, Mary McMahon served as president of the local branch of the Legion of Mary. On one visit to a fallen-away army wife, she was almost thrown out of the house, but within two hours was invited to stay to dinner. Declared McMahon: "I'm convinced that Army people have the greatest need for assistance with their religion—especially since they rush into marriage so, and keep putting off getting things straightened out."

The four female catechists assigned to the Poteau area had a hectic schedule traveling to towns in a vast area where only three hundred out of a population of forty thousand were Catholics. Their experiences included the conversion of a man who, a few days after his conversion, received a license to preach in the Protestant church of which he had formerly been a member, and a woman who received the sacraments of penance, Holy Eucharist, confirmation, and extreme unction before being buried in the local Baptist church four days later. "We put the stamp and address on them," their pastor explained, "and the Protestants mail them."[74] As late as 1969, Father Joseph Burger of Sacred Heart parish in Mangum had nothing but praise for the catechetical and social work of the volunteers.[75]

With the establishment of the Office of Religious Education in 1962, new pedagogic methods of catechetical instruction began to emerge. In April 1964, Sister Mary Charles Bryce, O.S.B., a Benedictine teaching at McGuinness High School, produced "Come Let Us Eat," a new catechism for First Communion composed of an instruction booklet for the child and a manual for the parents. "Come Let Us Eat" rejected rote memorization of creedal formulae in favor of a child's experiential understanding of the meaning of the eucharistic act.[76] The office was also concerned that varying standards of instruction prevailed in different parishes. In December 1964, Father Joseph

73. *The Acts of the Apostles,* March 1960, Revd. Joseph W. Burger to Msgr. Sylvester F. Luecke, August 16, 1960, Reed Papers.

74. *The Acts of the Apostles,* January 1962, Reed Papers.

75. Revd. Joseph W. Burger to Msgr. Raymond F. Harkin, March 1, 1969, Sacred Heart Church, Mangum File, AAOC.

76. *Oklahoma Courier,* April 10, 1964.

Dillon complained that the priest in Boise City—one of the most remote towns in western Oklahoma—had discarded the education program favored by the office and combined the first eight grades into one class, rather than developing a year-by-year program.[77]

One proposed attempt at standardization was the creation of religious education centers, staffed by sisters and serving a number of parishes in a particular locality. Under this proposal, the sisters would spend one day in each parochial school (where such existed) and successive Saturdays in the various parishes, working with the local priest and lay CCD teachers.[78] As Catholic schools closed their doors, however, the Office of Religious Education began to take the view that a more intensive Christian education program might be necessary. In November 1964, Father Daniel Allen, diocesan director of youth, raised the prospect of special "unity high schools," where students could receive religious instruction from qualified laymen teaching them at their grade level. With two two-month semesters in spring and fall, the unity high system would cover topics ranging from obtaining a job, choosing a marriage partner, witnessing effectively, and determining one's religious vocation.[79]

By 1965, unity high schools existed in southern Oklahoma City and northwest Oklahoma City (though finding enough lay teachers there presented problems), in Tulsa and in Guthrie, with another planned for Enid. They were composite entities, created at the initiative of local pastors but run by a lay board composed of representatives from the constituent parishes, with a faculty that was equal parts religious and lay. As well as religious instruction on at least one Sunday each month (the model proposed for Enid was that of a session from 1:00 p.m. to 8:00 p.m., with several classes, a demonstration session, Mass, and a short social), the program included an annual activity day, student retreat weekends, and a summer camp. Attendance was the responsibility of parents, and students were dropped from the rolls after missing four consecutive sessions.[80]

Unity high schools enjoyed much higher approval ratings than CCD or adult education programs. A poll of sixty-nine families at St. Mary's Church,

77. Revd. Joseph D. Dillon to Victor Reed, December 21, 1964, St. Philip Benzi Church, Boise City File, AAOC.

78. Victor Reed to Mother Mary Consolatrice, B.V.M., July 19, 1965, St. Mary's Church, Medford File, AAOC.

79. *Oklahoma Courier*, November 6, 1964.

80. Report: Unity High Workshop, January 8–9, 1965, Reed Papers; *Oklahoma Courier*, January 29, 1965.

Ponca City, gave the unity high school a 74 percent fair or good rating, compared to 24 percent for CCD and 18 percent for adult education, although the parish was divided about whether to retain it when financial cutbacks loomed. Unity students called for a greater variety of subjects (including practical courses like drivers' education), more ecumenical outreach, an increased willingness on the part of adults to commit resources, and younger teachers. "CCD students go because they're forced," one student opined. "We want religion."[81]

Some parents were less enthralled with what the unity high school system offered. "Several years ago," declared Jo Anne Parris in January 1969, "when the oldest boy began to come home with different interpretations of Catholic Doctrine, we began to be concerned. As time passed and the other two older children discussed [unity high] religion classes, we were forced to accept that a definite difference of teaching methods was being used. . . . Basic truths notwithstanding, we could no longer deny that our children's minds were being usurped by the Church as 'testing grounds' for the new outlook on Catholicism." Parris cited examples ranging from the downplaying of the notion of divine inspiration of Holy Scripture, a teacher's recommendation of movies unsuitable for a particular age group, such as *The Graduate* (though she also objected to *Guess Who's Coming to Dinner*), and the labeling of the motives of persons in the public eye. No more than parochial school administrators could the unity high school faculty escape the charge of succumbing to the prevailing culture.[82]

An apostolate closely connected with the Office of Religious Education was the Association for Christian Development (ACD), formed in 1961 to allow single laywomen to help develop a deeper and stronger parish life in the areas of liturgy, adult education, leadership training, and catechetical instruction.[83] ACD offered single women the possibility of pursuing work that would in earlier decades have been the preserve of teaching sisters. It reflected the new pedagogic trends in religious education and soon won a national reputation as a religious education program, with Father Joseph Dillon—who oversaw the ACD—leading workshops in a number of American dioceses to explain its mode of operation.

ACD workers prided themselves on their educational background. Most

81. Copy of Report from Ponca City, n.d., Reed Papers.

82. Jo Anne Parris to Victor Reed, January 4, 1969, Reed Papers.

83. Revd. Joseph D. Dillon to Victor Reed, May 1, 1961, Reed to Dillon May 3, 1961, Reed Papers.

had spent part of the year in graduate school at such prestigious institutions as Marquette University, the Loyola Institute of Pastoral Studies in Chicago, and the Catholic University of America. Over time, the focus of the ACD shifted from simple instruction to a greater focus on ecumenical and social outreach projects. It also worked on a course of study for the unity high schools and helped plan an annual youth convention for the diocese.

By 1965, however, the emphasis of ACD was on projects that were less overtly "Catholic" in form. Connie Scott helped transform the former rectory of St. Peter Claver parish into "Children's House," a Montessori school and day care center in Oklahoma City that was operated under a federal poverty program, and she trained twenty African American women in the principles of Montessori education. Another initiative of the ACD was the Walnut Grove Neighborhood Council for Community Action Programs of the Office of Economic Opportunity. Through the council, such projects as preschool day care, a thrift store, and a credit union were established for the minority community in Oklahoma City, and an adult education program with individualized tutoring was created. ACD members also played an active role in ecumenical youth projects. Sharlene Shoemaker belonged to the youth council of the Oklahoma City Council of Churches and participated in an ecumenical study weekend at which poverty and racial problems in Oklahoma City were discussed. The change in the nature of the ACD in large measure reflected changes under way in the Church as a whole. Parish growth was becoming defined less by the standard of juvenile education and more by its willingness to intervene in the needs of the wider community.[84]

The 1960s also marked the beginning of a greater acceptance among American Catholics that Christian formation was a lifelong process. In a general announcement to the American bishops, Bishop Charles Greco, chairman of the Committee on the Confraternity of Christian Doctrine, called for CCD to be brought into "full accord with the spirit of change and experimentation which the Council has opened up to all phases of the apostolate." CCD, Greco explained in 1966, gave the misleading impression of being a child-centered program because it had more children in it than did the parochial school system, but the long-term success of such a program was ultimately dependent on the formation of Catholic parents and adults. Since a national program, dubbed "Operation Understanding"—involving the Na-

84. *Oklahoma Courier*, April 30, 1965; A.C.D. Progress Report, March 5, 1964–May 13, 1965, A.C.D. Progress Report, May 14, 1965–May 5, 1966, Association for Christian Development Annual Report, 1966–1967, Reed Papers; Dillon, "Reflections on My Life,"57–58.

tional Center of CCD, the National Council of Catholic Men, the National Council of Catholic Women, the Newman Apostolate, and the National Liturgical Conference—was getting under way, it seemed appropriate to create a national office for adult Christian education. Not only would such an entity coordinate efforts at the diocesan and parish level but it would also explore ecumenical opportunities with similar bodies in other Christian churches. Such a new format for CCD would be critical to any plan to allow qualified laymen to direct ministries hitherto reserved to priests, such as catechizing, distributing Holy Communion, or leading prayer and worship at services where Mass was not celebrated.[85]

At the diocesan level, adult education began to receive attention in the early 1960s. A 1962 survey revealed that only 2 percent of Catholics were engaged in a religious education program, and these constituted only 6 percent of all American adults in such programs. "[T]he Catholic adult," declared one expert in the field, "was likely to go through life with an immature understanding of faith, rarely if ever confronted with mature, adult questions having to do with religious convictions." The impact of the council deliberations had changed all this, laying the ground for what could be described as "adult theologizing."[86] Oklahomans responded to the challenge. In 1963, a *Courier* correspondent proposed that parish libraries be established to provide the laity with the necessary resources to analyze the changes taking place within the Church.[87]

The following year, adult education programs were launched in Oklahoma City and Tulsa, the former taught largely by the younger priests of the diocese and focusing on the process of renewal.[88] Within a couple of years, these programs were considerably more avant-garde. A 1966 schedule in Tulsa included Father John Vrana's course on the work of Teilard de Chardin,

85. Most Revd. Charles P. Greco, "Report on CCD to American Bishops," March 6, 1967, Reed Papers. Bishop Reed welcomed the thrust of Greco's proposal, including the part-time ministry of the laity, but echoed the sentiment voiced by his director of religious education that CCD might not be the best instrument for implementing such a program, given that it was understaffed and short of funds. See Victor Reed to Bp. Charles Greco, March 25, 1967, Reed Papers. "Anyone who has heard Bishop Greco speak on Religious Education must realize that he has a very limited vision," Father Dillon told the bishop privately. For the similarities between Dillon's critique of the Greco Report and Reed's official response to it, see Revd. Joseph D. Dillon to Revd. William C. Garthoeffner, March 18, 1967, Reed Papers.

86. Scott, *Catholic Adult Education*, 13.

87. *Oklahoma Courier*, November 22, 1963.

88. *Oklahoma Courier*, January 17, January 24, 1964.

Father Frank Manning's course on how the Gospels originated and how more meaning could be derived from specific passages, and Father Edward Jeep's course entitled A New Look at Christian Morality.[89] Such approaches elicited comment, not always favorable. The efforts of Father Edward Kelly to organize an adult education Lenten series in 1966 for southern Oklahoma City were met with disdain by several local pastors, who saw it as an effort by a diocesan office to impose a program upon them.[90]

In May 1966, the diocesan director of education recommended that Father Jeep of Corpus Christi parish, Oklahoma City, be permitted to organize a Continuing Christian Education Program for the diocese, including teacher-training and parent-formation programs, because he knew the personnel and problems involved and was willing to travel.[91] A strong proponent of "relevant" liturgy, Jeep devised programs that certainly represented a shift away from traditional modes of Christian formation. One of his Lenten programs sought to illustrate the theme "Sensitivity to the Demonic Powers in our society and culture, and the role of the Church in driving them out." It employed readings from the Bible and Harvey Cox's *The Secular City*, contrasting pictures of American affluence and third world poverty to be projected on a screen, and recordings of the Beatles performing "Yellow Submarine" and "God Bless America."

Two other programs employed at St. Joseph's Church in Norman aimed to heighten sensitivity to persecution and to the poor and lonely. The former employed a film, *The Hangman*, produced by Mass Media Industries in Baltimore, in which a leader read first from the Passion narrative and then recited examples of typical persons oppressed in each decade from the 1930s to the 1960s. After each recitation, the audience responded with the refrain: "We didn't help actively, of course. We weren't even asked to. We enjoyed and were comfortable, mostly." (It should be noted that, with the arguable exceptions of a farmer in Russia in the 1930s and a "revolutionary" in China during the 1960s, all the examples of the persecuted were victims of right-wing regimes.)

The model designed to heighten sensitivity to poverty transformed the liturgy into the form of a trial in which parishioners were called on to answer charges of "theft" (from the poor) and "neglect" (of the elderly and those

89. *Oklahoma Courier*, February 18, 1966.
90. Revd. Edward L. Kelly to Revd. Joseph D. Dillon, February 7, 1966, Dillon to Victor Reed, February 11, 1966, Reed Papers.
91. Revd. Joseph D. Dillon to Victor Reed, May 24, 1966, Reed Papers.

who didn't fit in). People then offered excuses for these charges and with each excuse a person carrying a sign with this "scapegoat" rationale on it stood up. The liturgy concluded with a short homily on the need for lay Catholics to take responsibility for the world's problems, followed by Communion.[92]

CONCLUSION

During the 1960s, a fundamental transformation of the American Catholic parish took place. No longer was life to be centered in a church building and plant (often out of all proportion to the number of Catholics who regularly attended Mass) but in a community of persons—often like-minded persons—who would live their lives in the naked public square (to borrow a phrase of Richard John Neuhaus). Such a change was only accentuated by a process of formation that tended to emphasize Christian responsibility in the world and to downplay Catholic singularity. The transformation of parish life and the concurrent changes in the perception of the laity encouraged the latter to assert more aggressively their role in temporal oversight of parish institutions. The resulting conflict between priest and laity was an inevitable consequence of the declining organic connection between the Catholic layman and his parish.

For Victor Reed, arbitrating such tensions was an increasingly distasteful exercise. Although he approved the establishment of nonterritorial parishes, it is hard to believe that he did not personally identify more with the old-style parish than the modern one. It must have been exceptionally hard for him to reduce the rural western parishes on the grounds of financial necessity, when they embodied, both positively and negatively, all the aspects of the territorial parish so closely.

"Sometimes, a bishop must make a decision concerning a matter which seems impossible to resolve otherwise," he told the Catholics of Elk City, Canute, and Scheidel in December 1970. "Such a time appears to have arrived in the case of the three parishes involved. I have sincerely tried to be understanding and fair to you and I shall continue to be since I am convinced that such qualities are essential to the episcopal office. However, I wish to remind you that the same two qualities should mark the conduct of the people of the parishes toward their pastor and their bishop because every relationship to be successful must be a two-way street."[93]

92. *Office of Religion Newsletter*, n.d. Reed Papers.
93. Victor Reed to "My Dear People," December 6, 1970, Reed Papers.

part three

The Prophetic Church,
1958–1971

chapter 6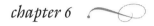

Worship and the Intellect

The Challenge of Liturgical Renewal

But in order that the liturgy may be able to produce its full effects, it is necessary that the faithful come to it with proper dispositions, that their minds should be attuned to their voices, and that they should cooperate with divine grace lest they receive it in vain. Pastors of souls must therefore realize that, when the liturgy is celebrated, something more is required than the mere observation of the laws governing valid and licit celebration; it is their duty also to ensure that the faithful take part fully aware of what they are doing, actively engaged in the rite, and enriched by its effects.

Second Vatican Council, Constitution on the Sacred Liturgy,
Sacrosanctum Concilium, December 24, 1963

As he looked out over the expectant crowd assembled in Oklahoma City in 1961 for the twenty-second National Liturgical Week, Catholic Action stalwart James Cockrell warmed to the task of conveying what the liturgical movement had done for the average layman. The notion that only the priest enjoyed a mediatory role in the Sacrifice of the Mass was outdated, he assured his audience. The priest dispensed God's sacramental grace to the communicant, but it was the communicant "who broadcasts this grace to the neighborhood and to the market place." The layman brought to Mass not only himself and his family but all those with whom he was in relationship in the outside world. In company with other worshippers, he participated corporately in the Sacred Mystery and from it received the Divine Grace that enabled him to be an adequate witness to the unchurched. Such a process dictated a very different type of behavior at Mass from that to which most Catholics were accustomed. "It is not appropriate for the layman to arrive at Mass quietly," Cockrell asserted, "with folded hands and recollected disposition. His piety is to arrive with the bustle of the world, greeting his fellow neighbors with glad shouts and the joy of real accomplishment because he has managed to bring his world to Christ once again in spite of every difficulty."[1]

Cockrell's challenge to lay Catholic understanding of the liturgy was underpinned by 130 years of liturgical renewal in northern Europe and the United States. It owed its origins to Prosper Guéranger and the Benedictine monastery that he founded at Solemnes in 1833. Guéranger's objective had been to restore the Eucharist and the liturgical year to their proper place in Catholic liturgy and to revive the practice of Gregorian chant. More influential on American liturgical thinking, however, were the Belgian foundations of Maredsous and Mont César, which sought to develop participatory liturgical forms that had relevance for parish worship. Dom Lambert Beauduin of Mont César conceived of liturgical prayer as an influential force in the secular world and he and his associates translated the Roman Missal into the vernacular and sought to encourage greater use of the liturgy of the hours and of Gregorian chant by the laity. In 1914, Beauduin published *La piété de l'église*, which supplied the theological basis for his work. The Belgian liturgical movement was solidly pastoral, oriented toward the parish community, and ecumenical in tone.[2]

Virgil Michel, the Minnesota Benedictine credited with launching the American liturgical movement, studied under Beauduin during the early 1920s and carried his vision back to the United States. In 1925, Michel joined with Monsignor Martin Hellriegel and Father Gerald Ellard, S.J., in an effort to conceptualize appropriate liturgical forms for the new European theology of the Mystical Body of Christ. Lamenting the inherently fragmented and individualistic world of Catholic devotionalism and what they perceived as the general lack of lay comprehension of and participation in the actions of the Mass, they founded the journal *Orate Fratres* to popularize their ideas. Liturgical renewal, they argued, was not to be confused with ritual, however, for it was greater *participation* in the liturgy that was seen as the best way to renew the spirit of the Catholic Church. The founders of *Orate Fratres* encouraged use of the missal by the laity as an aid to greater comprehension

1. *Bible, Life, and Worship*, 147–50 (quotation on 149). For another account of the meeting, see *Oklahoma Courier*, August 25, 1961.
2. Pecklers, *The Unread Vision*, 1–23.

(Joseph Stedman's *My Sunday Missal* had become the standard authority by 1932). They recommended frequent reception of Communion at Mass (many Catholics either did not make a weekly Communion or were communicated from the Reserved Sacrament before or after Mass) and they endorsed the *Missa Recitata* (or dialogue Mass) in which the prayers—although still in Latin—were recited alternately between the congregation and a leader. *Orate Fratres*, many of whose subscribers were based in the Midwest, served as a forum for clergy to report on liturgical experimentation at the parish level, successful and otherwise.[3]

Implementing changes at the parish level proved an involved task, but its exponents were persistent. Monsignor Hellriegel took liturgical participation to a high level after he took charge at Holy Cross parish in St. Louis, Missouri, in 1940. The movement also won a hold in about a quarter of the parishes of the Archdiocese of Chicago during the 1940s. After Pope Pius XII mandated observance of a reformed participatory Holy Week liturgy in 1956, a new liturgical vitality could be observed even in remote parishes in such rural communities as Metaline, Washington, and Spring Lake, Michigan. "It is all so different from merely waiting it out," remarked Father Leo Ward in 1959, "sitting and standing up, perhaps with marked fidelity, perhaps in boredom, and it is quite different from the people piously rattling their beads until the welcome blessing ends the Mass." In the Archdiocese of Cincinnati, Archbishop Karl Alter responded to Pius XII's directive by establishing an archdiocesan liturgical commission and encouraging use of the missal and the dialogue Mass.[4]

In Oklahoma, the dialogue Mass had become a fact of life for many parishes by the late 1950s. When Pius XII issued the Instruction on Sacred Liturgy and Sacred Music in September 1958, which formally authorized congregational participation, the move was greeted with enthusiasm at Christ the King parish in Oklahoma City. This parish had been founded by Reed's friend Charles Buswell, who would be named bishop of Pueblo (Colorado) in 1959. Christ the King's second pastor, Father Charles Conley, built up a body of male lay readers as commentators for the dialogue Low Masses, where "direct" congregational participation (the short responses) remained in Latin as required by the Roman Missal, but "indirect" participation (paraphrases of

3. Ibid., 25–55, 158–64.
4. Ibid., 58–61; Avella, *This Confident Church*, 153, 164–65; Ward, *Catholic Life, U.S.A*: 10–31 (quotation on 22); Fortin, *Faith and Action*, 344–47.

Mass texts, such as the *Gloria in Excelsis*, and chants of the Mass) were rendered in English. Conley's approach was not uncontroversial and provoked the charge that women played an inappropriate role in the liturgy, but an investigation ultimately concluded that Conley's critics had confused the role of commentator (who explained the meaning of the Mass to the congregation), which had always been performed by a man, with that of prayer leader, which women could fill if there was no man present.[5] Appreciation for the dialogue Mass was also expressed by laymen like Major Paul Dooley of Norman, who, in good military style, urged dissenters to show greater "obedience" to the sentiments of Pius XII and John XXIII. "Perhaps, in time, the Dialogue Mass will be as familiar to [dissenters] as the Silent Mass now is," Dooley mused. "For they must remember that the Silent Mass was once a change that resulted from the congregation being unable to speak Latin."[6]

Another harbinger of liturgical transformation was Father William Nerin's request for permission to restructure the chancel of his parish church in Owasso in 1958. Nerin wished the altar to face the people, helping "to draw the congregation into the Act of Sacrifice as visibly as it can be done," and he cited a model from a parish in Minneapolis published in the magazine *Jubilee*, where a second altar was located in the sanctuary at a higher elevation than the regular altar. On the rear altar reposed the tabernacle and two candlesticks, keeping the people's focus on the Reserved Sacrament, while allowing Mass to be celebrated with the priest facing the people. Reed approved Nerin's plan with the proviso that Mass should also be said at the rear altar on a regular basis.[7]

Perhaps the most important liturgical innovator in Oklahoma was the diocesan master of ceremonies, Father Joseph Mazaika. Mazaika probably helped draft—if he did not actually write—the report *Our Living Parish*, published in 1959, which indicted contemporary American Catholics for practicing what it called "Capsule Christianity."[8] Invoking Mystical Body of Christ theology, the report warned that no Catholic could afford to be a by-

5. Revd. Charles F. Conley to Victor Reed, April 19, 1963, Revd. Joseph J. Mazaika to Reed, April 23, 1963, Reed Papers.

6. *Oklahoma Courier*, April 21, 1961.

7. Revd. William F. Nerin to Victor Reed, September 21, 1958, Revd. William C. Garthoeffner to Nerin, October 20, 1958, St Teresa's Church (Little Flower), Collinsville File, box 33.1, Archives of the Catholic Diocese of Tulsa (hereafter ADT). Monsignor Gregory Gier has pointed out that as early as 1959, there were experimental Masses facing the students at McGuinness High School. Clergy roundtable discussion, June 23, 2005.

8. *Our Living Parish* (1959), chap. 1, p. 1, Reed Papers. Only a manuscript copy exists in the Reed Papers.

stander in his parish, but must be immersed in parish activities and particularly in the Mass, from which all other activities should derive. The Last Supper, *Our Living Parish* explained, was a community event and the Mass, which mirrored it, was the place where God allowed the communicant to freely offer his or her whole self to the service of other members of the Mystical Body, just as God's Son had done and continued to do. The reality of the average Mass on a Sunday morning, however, was somewhat different: "Three eighth graders are elbowing each other in a back pew. Two high school girls are gaping around to see who's there. One man is looking at the headlines of the Sunday Visitor laying in the pew in front of him. About twenty or thirty will be thumbing their beads monotonously. Of the rest, some will be reading the Missal and some will be doing absolutely nothing. Is this the Mystical Body in its act of greatest union?"[9]

Our Living Parish had harsh words for those who preferred the devotional life. "People of this kind," it insisted, "are the very ones who cannot be persuaded to do anything apostolic, though they can be sold any and every kind of devotion which promises favors, or graces, or relief from hardship. They derive much comfort and emotional release from these devotions and all have their favorites."[10] Although devotionalism seemed healthy during the 1950s, it underwent a transformation as devotions like the family rosary, which focused on the suburban household rather than the parish community, took center stage. "While clearly identifying their practitioners as 'Roman Catholic,'" writes Joseph Chinnici, "they encouraged continual accommodation to the American way of life, thus furthering the unique mixture of congregational allegiance and 'religion-in-general' that had begun to characterize American religious expression." *Our Living Parish* reflected this trend when it acknowledged the value of prayers before the Blessed Sacrament and Forty Hours devotion, but urged that devotional societies be replaced with parish study and social action groups that would help Christians to express their faith and perfect their representation of God's message.[11]

"We live in an era of specialization, in a divided world," explained *Our*

---

9. Ibid., chap. 3, p. 3. Contrast this with the following contention of Father Robert Hovda of the Diocese of Fargo in 1963: "[W]e both see and do not see the Catholic Church at Sunday Mass. We see, if, armed with lore, books and experts, we have become professional liturgists. . . . Otherwise we do not see the Catholic Church when we attend Sunday Mass. Our faith knows that it is there and our faith brings us there. But it is hidden from our eyes." Hovda, "Sunday Mass—Dullsville," 33.

10. *Our Living Parish*, chap. 15, p. 1.

11. Chinnici, "The Catholic Community at Prayer," 52–70 (quotation on 69). There is

Living Parish. "People live and work in isolated existences which rob them of the awareness of the unity of human life. Many are walled-in by self-drawn, prejudice-inflicted, barriers of color, nationality, social and economic standards. But the Eucharistic table recognizes no such barriers."[12] Such barriers could be broken down by a dynamic liturgy. God's Word in Scripture, whether expressed indirectly in the Epistles or directly through Christ's very presence in the Gospel, should be a source of life to Catholics as well as Protestants and not merely a compilation of spiritual instructions and information. Consequently, the Liturgy of the Word, including the too-often ignored resource of the homily, must be given greater prominence in the Mass. Congregational singing, endorsed by no less an authority than Pius XII, should also be encouraged, since it enabled the faithful to follow the ceremony in mind and voice and join with the priest in the act of worship. While many Catholics were unaccustomed to singing, they should be reminded that their voices were a divine gift and that improvement came only with practice. *Our Living Parish* also recommended that all the parishes of the diocese should sing the same hymns at Mass on a particular Sunday of the year.[13]

"It is generally known," Bishop Reed commented in 1964, "that our diocese is among those in the nation which are most advanced in the knowledge and practice of the new liturgy [and] many liturgical events and news items testify to the advanced position of the Diocese of Oklahoma City and Tulsa."[14] It was precisely this advanced reputation that helps explain why the North American Liturgical Conference chose a minor midwestern diocese in which to hold its annual study week in 1961. To an audience that included clerical and lay representatives of many other denominations, Monsignor Frederick McManus, president of the Liturgical Conference, emphasized

---

little evidence about the nature and extent of devotional practices in Oklahoma during the 1950s, but the bishop thought them of some importance. In 1961, he authorized the showing of a special film on Our Lady of Guadalupe in various parishes, and the following year he encouraged Oklahoma Catholics to participate in the Novena of Prayer requested by Pope John XXIII for the success of the Second Vatican Council. He must have been disappointed that subsequent attendance at the novena was only "average." See Revd. Joseph C. Hoying, C.PP.S. to Victor Reed, March 4, 1961, St. Catherine's Church, Tulsa File, box 10.1, ADT; Circular letter from Bishop Reed to Parishes, September 14, 1962, Reed Papers; *Oklahoma Courier*, October 5, 1962.

12. *Our Living Parish*, chap. 9, p. 2.

13. One year later, members of St. Patrick's parish in Oklahoma City were meeting in small groups during the week to practice their singing and dialogue reading as preparation for participation in the dialogue Mass. *Oklahoma Courier*, April 15, 1960.

14. Victor Reed to Msgr. William H. Reid, November 28, 1964, Reed Papers.

the inclusion of "life" in the conference theme, "Bible, Life and Worship." "There is no ivory tower for the worshipper who hears God's Word;" he told them. "[T]he Word of God and the fruits of the liturgical celebration must penetrate our thoughts and deeds, our every social relationship, our place in the society of our fellows."[15] Christ the King's former pastor, Bishop Buswell, took up McManus's theme by urging upon his listeners the value of spontaneous prayer (something that he knew many Catholics were skittish about) for building a more personal relationship with God and bridging the gap between religion and daily life.[16]

The contribution of Oklahoma laymen to the proceedings provided by James Cockrell was supplemented by physician Joseph Evans, who delivered an impassioned plea for use of the vernacular liturgy. Evans maintained that the continued use of Latin hampered the transmission of the message of Christianity to secular society. He adopted a more militant stance than was customary by urging fellow laymen to submit petitions to the Holy See to that effect. The laity, he insisted, had a duty to communicate their views and a right to have those views entertained by the hierarchy with respect.[17] Evans's comments testified to the gains made by the Vernacular Society since its foundation in 1948. In the early 1950s, the society had persuaded the American bishops to prepare a modified version of the Ritual of the Mass with some English. This had been approved by Rome in 1954 and formed the basis for the Masses celebrated at National Liturgical Week, which also used congregational responses.[18]

Support for the vernacular liturgy was strong among Oklahoma clergy. A particularly vocal proponent was Father James McNamee of the Church of the Madalene in Tulsa, who maintained that Latin was a ninth-century innovation that had become a point of principle only after the Reformation. He questioned whether the use of a missal with the English words printed alongside the Latin really conformed to the objective of community worship. "Mass is not supposed to be a dumb affair," McNamee complained in 1962, "where people sit and listen to strange language."[19] Not every priest was

---

15. *Bible, Life, and Worship*, 6.   16. Ibid., 26–27.

17. Ibid., 15–17.

18. Pecklers, *The Unread Vision*, 63–70. Major Paul Dooley of Norman also urged advocates of vernacular worship to sign petitions to their parish priest, Bishop Reed, and the Roman curia and supplied the appropriate addresses to which the latter two should be sent. See *Oklahoma Courier*, September 1, 1961.

19. *Tulsa Tribune*, December 27, 1962. Reed received at least one personal reprimand

quite as self-assured as McNamee. One year later, Father Francis Manning warned of the dangers of treating a love of Latin as solely a matter of child-hood attachment or intellectual snobbery. "It might be found that cultural communion between the human and the Divine has not infrequently been realized in some of its most intense moments through language or other means not easily accessible to the average individual," he pointed out.[20]

IMPLEMENTING THE NOVUS ORDO

"My priestly experience of thirty-three years in the same diocese has been concerned almost totally with the pastoral care of souls," Victor Reed told his fellow bishops in his only oral intervention at the Second Vatican Coun-cil. "I wish to say that the people of my diocese have accepted with en-thusiasm the recent liturgical reforms. Not only do they need liturgical par-ticipation in the Mass and in the sacraments, but they also longed for this participation because today they are better educated and therefore seeking a fuller understanding and appreciation of the riches and fullness of the sa-cred liturgy. In my judgment, this end will be more efficaciously obtained through a fuller use of the vernacular and a greater appreciation of Scripture in the sacred liturgy."[21]

While the Constitution on the Sacred Liturgy—the first fruit of the coun-cil's deliberations—was warmly received by advocates of renewal, many of the American bishops expressed concern about how much liturgical experi-mentation should be permitted and by whom. "In our eagerness to reap the full benefits of the liturgical renewal," warned Archbishop John Krol of Phil-adelphia in January 1964, "we must realize that the legislator who has the right to authorize changes, also has the right to determine what changes are to be made, and how, when and by whom they are to be effected . . . apart from the Holy See, and apart from the bishops acting within the precise lim-

from the apostolic delegate, Archbishop Egidio Vagnozzi, for failing to control the declara-tions of his clerical subordinates. See Abp. Egidio Vagnozzi to Victor Reed, September 12, 1959, Reed to Vagnozzi, October 3, 1959, Reed Papers.

20. *Oklahoma Courier*, May 24, 1963. Manning's views were echoed by a convert op-posed to the vernacular, who insisted that just because something was vocal didn't neces-sarily make it participatory: "Most of us in the diocese have attended 'Dialogue Masses'—with every parishioner reading aloud from his own particular missal translation—and found the results more like the tower of Babel than the community worship of Christians." *Okla-homa Courier*, March 1, 1963.

21. Yzermans, *American Participation in the Second Vatican Council*, 169.

its defined by the Constitution, no one—not even the most expert—should presume to introduce any changes."[22]

The bishops of the United States, Krol noted, had agreed to make the fullest use of the vernacular in "Masses which are celebrated with the people," particularly in relation to Scripture readings, "common prayer," and in chants that pertained to the people, but Latin would remain the language of the canon of the Mass. Any changes in the rites of the Mass, sacramentals, the Divine Office, sacred music, and sacred art should be determined by postconciliar commissions, which should be allowed to pursue their work in an orderly fashion. In the meantime, those charged with teaching ministries in the Church—religious and lay—should read and study the entire Constitution on the Sacred Liturgy and share it with the wider lay community.[23]

Krol's emphasis on postconciliar commissions was lamented by liturgical innovators, many of whom feared that it would accord them little freedom of maneuver. In January 1964, a group of church musicians had proposed the creation of a national board of liturgical and musical experts to research and oversee liturgical experimentation. Although they accepted that some work needed to be carried out at the parish level, they preferred the environment of a seminary or monastic community for experimentation.[24] Haldan Tompkins, music director of Christ the King parish in Oklahoma City, strongly denounced this approach. A national board, staffed by persons with practical experience as well as scholarly credentials, should concern itself solely with the development, coordination, and dissemination of materials, not their control or regulation. This should be vested in the diocesan ordinary to allow for local experimentation. "It is my candid opinion," he told Reed, "that seminaries and religious houses have, to date, proven themselves—on the whole—to be most intransigent and conservative with regard to liturgical progress and development of any kind. In the area of liturgy they are quite often in fact, among the most un-progressive institutions in the Church."[25]

The discovery that Archbishop John Dearden of Detroit, chairman of the Episcopal Liturgical Commission (on which Reed served), had failed to es-

22. Abp. John Krol to "Dear Reverend Father," January 16, 1964, Reed Papers.
23. Ibid.
24. Memorandum of the discussions held by a group of musicians meeting in Pittsburgh between December 27 and 30 at the invitation of the Pittsburgh Music commission and respectfully submitted to the Episcopal Liturgical Commission, December 1963, Abt. Rembert G. Weakland to Abp. John F. Dearden, January 13, 1964, Reed Papers.
25. Haldan D. Tompkins to Victor Reed, January 21, 1964, Reed Papers.

tablish a music review commission and that, consequently, the release of texts for the interim English rite had been delayed, led Tompkins to the conclusion that Dearden had been pressured by "reactionary forces" opposed to vernacular usage. Their strategy, he concluded, was "to let some dioceses go ahead and use unauthorized settings—which they will do—and then get 'jumped on,' thus hoping to discredit and impair the vernacular movement." The overall result would either be the retention of Latin for the High Mass or the elimination of the High Mass in favor of a vernacular Low Mass.[26]

It became increasingly evident that Oklahoma Catholics had begun to take the role of the Bible in liturgy much more seriously. In March 1963, several parishes, most notably St. John's in Yukon and Christ the King in Chickasha, launched a new evening devotion—the Bible vigil. Modeled on the form developed by a Maryland priest, this involved three readings from the Old Testament, Epistles, and Gospels, each followed by a short homily, congregational hymn, or prayer, after which benediction was celebrated. The following year, when the pastor of St. Francis de Sales, Idabel, requested permission to locate his tabernacle to one side of the altar rather than behind it, Father William Garthoeffner, in granting permission, noted that it was now customary for the Bible to be "enthroned" opposite the tabernacle and flanked by two candlesticks. "A place of honor for the Scriptures," he explained, "is becoming fashionable in advanced parishes."[27]

Preparations for implementing the Constitution on the Sacred Liturgy were well advanced by the mid-1960s. In 1960, Reed established a diocesan liturgical commission, chaired by Father Joseph Mazaika, who, a year later, would be instrumental in founding the Southwest Liturgical Conference.[28] As implementation of the Novus Ordo loomed in November 1964, Mazaika conducted workshops for priests, school principals, organists, and choir directors on the first chapter of the Constitution, which dealt with the nature of the liturgy and its reform, promotion of liturgical instructions and liturgi-

26. Haldan D. Tompkins to Victor Reed, n.d., Reed Papers. In fact, there was no music commission at the Vatican level, owing to the opposition of Roman musicians who saw the reforms as threatening everything they had built up over the years. See Bugnini, *The Reform of the Liturgy*, 21–22. My thanks to Father James D. White for the reference.

27. *Oklahoma Courier*, March 15, 1963; Revd. Francis Schenk to Revd. William C. Garthoeffner, December 23, 1964, Garthoeffner to Schenk, December 5, 1964, St. Francis de Sales Church, Idabel File, box 50.1, ADT.

28. *Oklahoma Courier*, October 14, 1960. The Southwest Liturgical Conference—composed of liturgists from seventeen western dioceses—was conceived as a subsidiary of the National Liturgical Conference, but ultimately outlasted it.

cal life, and the pastor and the distribution of roles in worship. For four of these workshops, the bishop was both celebrant and homilist.[29]

In Tulsa, Reed gave the parishes of Christ the King and St. Pius X the status of experimental parishes. Christ the King benefited from the presence of a professional music director, Fred King, who held a degree in music from the University of Chicago. King set the English liturgy to music and worked hard to achieve the goal of full congregational participation. Not only did he organize an adult choir, but he also devoted time before services to the task of teaching the whole congregation how to sing. The experimental parishes were expected to provide reports on the extent of lay participation, the nature of instruction provided, the manner in which Communion was administered (standing or kneeling), and any problems they encountered to the diocesan liturgical commission.[30]

Like many of his contemporaries, Reed lost no opportunity to defend vernacular usage, although he constantly warned that it was merely a first step that would allow clergy and laity "to re-appreciate, you might say, the whole theology and worship of the Church."[31] From New Subiaco Abbey in Arkansas, Brother Donald Price begged the bishop to secure authorization of an English form of the Exultet, which he hoped to sing at the next Easter service. "I have for years hoped that the liturgical movement would accomplish this before it came to be my turn," he declared.[32] Support was also forthcoming from Reed's provincial superior, Archbishop Robert Lucey of San Antonio, who even expressed doubts as to whether the retention of Latin for the canon of the Mass was still valid: "It might seem irreverent if one were to say that the Mass which American Bishops and priests are offering at this time is a hodgepodge of Latin, English, Greek, and Hebrew, but with all propriety it must be said that the language of the Mass in the United States today is quite confusing and the whole complex is quite unworthy of divine

29. Revd. Joseph J. Mazaika to "Dear Father (Monsignor)," March 18, 1964, Reed Papers.

30. *Tulsa Daily World*, November 22, 1964; Minutes of a meeting of the Liturgical Commission, October 6, 1964, Reed Papers. The commission expressed particular interest in any parish that had experimented with a High Mass: "What was the reaction to the music? How was the alternation between the choir and the congregation? Did the people sing? Any particular difficulties? Did the people sing the Lord's Prayer? And were the Propers sung?" For an analysis of the impact of the Novus Ordo, see Mark Massa, "'Into Uncertain Life': The First Sunday of Advent 1964," in *Catholics and American Culture*, 148–94.

31. *Oklahoma Courier*, January 17, 1964.

32. Br. Donald Price, O.S.B., to Victor Reed, December 19, 1964, Reed Papers.

service. . . . Personally, I think that we should be permitted and required either to chant the magnificent words of consecration or at least recite them aloud. I see no logical reason for hiding the very essence of the drama and tragedy of Calvary. The Oriental liturgy is far ahead of us in this."[33] Reed concurred. Most seminarians he knew never acquired sufficient mastery of Latin for it to become a spoken language (perhaps he remembered his own struggles with Latin in the seminary). "To pray with personal understanding and fervor," he told Archbishop Dearden, "a man needs the medium of a language in which he is really proficient. The most pressing need of our seminarians is certainly to learn to pray, to understand and remember the word of God, to appreciate community worship."[34]

At the parochial level, the response to the vernacular liturgy was generally favorable. Former skeptics like Ed Story of Elk City, who were accustomed to the traditional Mass and had learned enough Latin to follow it, commented on the greater participation of the people and their willingness to say the prayers in unison. "Some of the songs are not especially tuneful," Story admitted, "but the words and meaning is very impressive and prayerful, and I am sure pleasing to our Lord."[35] Monsignor Cecil Finn of Tulsa's Christ the King parish declared that his parishioners were more ready to bring non-Catholic neighbors to church now that the latter could understand what was going on. He joined Archbishop Lucey in recommending that the use of English be extended to all parts of the Mass.[36] Interest in extending use of the vernacular to the canon of the Mass was expressed even by children of school age. "Why can't we have the canon in English?" demanded Paul Martin of his ordinary. "My reason is the Mass would be meaningful to the 1st, 2nd, 3rd grades and to us. All the kids of St. Joseph are griping about it."[37]

The diocesan liturgical commission also supported extension of the use of English, but conceded that Rome currently opposed any alteration in the status of the canon.[38] Pleasure in the rendering of vernacular rites was not

33. Abp. Robert E. Lucey to Victor Reed, April 19, 1965, Reed Papers.

34. Victor Reed to Abp. John F. Dearden, February 16, 1966, Reed Papers.

35. Ed J. Story to Victor Reed, April 22, 1966, Reed Papers.

36. *Tulsa Tribune*, November 28, 1964.

37. Paul Martin to Victor Reed, n.d., Reed Papers. Father Joseph Ross recalled an occasion when his younger brother—whose family was on close terms with the bishop—complained to Reed, much to the latter's amusement, that he had just finished training the altar boys in the Latin responses and then "you did away with it." Clergy roundtable discussion, June 19, 2005.

38. Minutes of a meeting of the Liturgical Commission, January 5, 1965, Liturgical Commission meeting, March 1, 1966, Reed Papers.

universal, however. "Terrifying," was the adjective used by Father Francis Weiner, C.PP.S., to describe the new adult rite of baptism in English. "All this talk about making the rite *simpler* and understandable has been met in the reverse," he complained in October 1964. Weiner also described the new profession of faith as long and difficult and declared that he preferred the one drafted by Cardinal Mooney in the 1940s.[39]

Placing reception of the Eucharist at the center of Catholic life obliged the Church authorities to reassess whether to confine celebration of the obligatory Mass to Sunday mornings and holy days. In 1964, Bishop Reed requested Pope Paul VI to authorize a predawn Easter vigil rather than a midnight vigil Mass in parishes that desired it. A midnight vigil imposed considerable hardship on priests in rural areas with a full schedule of services to conduct on the Sunday morning, he explained, and many midnight services were poorly attended. Noting that predawn Easter services were popular in Protestant circles, Reed expressed the belief that perhaps they better captured the symbolism of the event: "The pre-dawn Easter Vigil and sunrise Easter Mass would be in greater conformity with the text and spirit of the Vigil service and the Mass of the Resurrection, the Vigil being held in the waning hour of darkness and the following Mass at sunrise. The spiritual symbolism of 'darkness' and 'light' would thus be much more striking than at midnight."[40] A desire for greater availability of the principal sacrament also lay behind the request of Father Ernest Flusche of St. Francis Xavier parish in Del City for permission to hold a Mass of Obligation on Saturday night. This would enable those in government and the service industries of southeast Oklahoma City who worked on Sunday to still make their weekly Communion.[41]

39. Revd. Francis A Weiner to Revd. William C. Garthoeffner, October 16, 1964, Sacred Heart Church, Miami File, box 57.1, ADT.

40. Victor Reed to Pope Paul VI, February 15, 1964, Reed Papers. In 1960, a priest in Broken Arrow sought permission to celebrate the Easter vigil starting at 9:00 p.m. since many of his parishioners with small children could not attend any later. Reed told him that since he was within the Tulsa metropolitan area he must keep to the proper observance. Revd. Robert Dabrowski, O.F.M.Cap., to Victor Reed, March 24, 1960, Reed to Dabrowski, March 31, 1960, St. Anne's Church, Broken Arrow File, box 27.1, ADT.

41. Revd. Ernest A. Flusche to Victor Reed, August 1, 1966, St. Paul's Church, Del City File, Archives of the Archdiocese of Oklahoma City (hereafter AAOC).

A MASS OF PARTICIPATION

It was not only availability of the Mass that was under scrutiny but also the search for a more intimate eucharistic experience.[42] Father James Ross started the ball rolling by instituting a special family offertory procession at St. Eugene's Church in Oklahoma City. In this rite, the head of the household carried the ciborium while his wife and children carried the cruets and other items. The subsequent offertory prayers related the family to the sacrifice of the Mass.[43] A more radical innovation was witnessed in one Tulsa church a few years later. At the early morning celebration (intended to provide people with an opportunity to receive Communion before going to work), the congregation stood around the altar and the Mass was from time to time interrupted by questions that the celebrant asked of participants to connect them better with the sacrificial act. "No one is a stranger for long at a Togetherness Mass," a parishioner assured the bishop in 1967, "and visitors feel perfectly at home."[44]

A far more common innovation was the home Mass, which became increasingly popular after 1965. In June of that year, the Christian Family Movement chapter of Tulsa's Immaculate Conception parish requested permission for a celebration of the Mass in a parishioner's yard followed by a community meal. Father Mazaika ruled that an outdoor celebration might become undignified, especially if conducted in the vicinity of a working barbecue with people present in various states of undress. It might be acceptable, he added, in "a proper and dignified setting, such as in a home, where the Mass can be offered with a neighborhood group attending. As a matter of fact, considering the scattered situation of our parishes, something of this sort could indeed be very helpful in aiding people to appreciate their position as members of the Mystical Body of Christ."[45] Four months later, Father Henry Kelly sought permission for additional home Masses, this time in connection with the meetings of the Little Council discussion groups. Here, the authorities

42. See the general discussion in McGuinness, "Let Us Go to the Altar."
43. *Oklahoma Courier*, January 17, 1964.
44. John A. Riley to Victor Reed, September 26, 1967, Reed Papers. The idea of "intimacy" presumably also lay behind the proposal of one priest to redesign his confessional so that those who wished to sit and talk with the priest face-to-face might do so. See Glenmary Missioner Newsletter, May 4, 1967, St. Francis de Sales Church, Idabel File, box 50.1.
45. Revd. Daniel D. Cawthon to Victor Reed, June 3, 1965, Revd. Joseph J. Mazaika to Revd. William C. Garthoeffner, June 12, 1965, Garthoeffner to Cawthon, June 18, 1965, Reed Papers.

stated that this would be acceptable, provided it did not become a "habitual" celebration.[46]

Much depended, of course, on *how* a priest celebrated a home Mass. In the mission parish of Idabel, Glenmary priest Raymond Berthiaume described an informal celebration in the rectory at which the participants were all invited to make informal remarks after the Gospel, the offertory verse was followed by multiple choruses of the phrase "He's Got the Whole World in His Hands," with the names of the participating families inserted one by one, and the singing of a special verse at the Communion to the tune "Kumbaya."[47] While some may have found this refreshingly open, it is doubtful if all did.

Indeed, the very idea of a house Mass had far less novelty for rural Oklahomans, many of whom had waited years for a proper church building. A member of St. John the Evangelist parish in McAlester objected to celebrations of the Mass for "splinter groups" because they only impaired unity in a rural setting. "Over [in] this section," she told Reed, "people have struggled to build churches, often at great personal sacrifice and to this day in many parishes of this area, the struggle continues to try and pay the interest on the church mortgage; so the whole idea of taking the Mass back to the house, leaving our churches unused for weekdays or experimentation is very disturbing to me as well as distasteful."[48]

Most clergy pressed on with implementation of the new liturgy, which they saw as a reflection of the new pattern of Catholic life. "I had no problems in any parish ever where I was, in bringing the reforms in," declared Father William Swift, "and I think the reason was that wherever I was . . . we made an effort to explain to the people what it was about and only after explaining it and saying that this is why Rome says this is what we should do and it makes sense if we do it this way. . . . If [people had problems], they didn't say anything about it, because I think they saw that we were so for [the reforms] that it wouldn't do any good."[49] At St. John the Baptist parish in Edmond, Father William Nerin affirmed that the Church's essential nature

---

46. Revd. Henry Kelly to Msgr. Raymond F. Harkin, October 31, 1965, Revd. Charles A. Meiser to Kelly, November 3, 1965, Immaculate Conception Church, Tulsa File, box 4.1, ADT.

47. Glenmary Missioner Newsletter, End of August 1966, St. Francis de Sales Church, Idabel File, box 50.1.

48. Mrs. James J. Pezzetti to Victor Reed, October 4, 1967, Reed Papers.

49. Swift, interview.

was revealed in community, expressed spontaneously through prayer and eucharistic sign. "This is a community because you know them and they know you and each other," he told Reed. "It is a community because in a *real* way they study, plan, work, and suffer together for Christ. It is a community because they can relax together and accept each other for what each one is. . . . It is a community because they can rejoice and suffer together over victory and defeat."[50]

Many laymen agreed that fostering a community atmosphere was an essential element, though their proposals tended to be more practical than philosophical. Anticipating the methods of the Protestant megachurches a quarter of a century later, Al Kavanaugh of Oklahoma City proposed using recordings of the world's greatest musicians performing works of sacred music and of the Church's leading teachers and preachers explaining the daily Epistle and Gospel. Films, broadcast on movie screens erected behind the altar, could be used to instruct the congregation in the elements of the Mass, the Stations of the Cross, or recitation of the rosary. "The Church could become a place where people, young and old, Catholic and non-Catholic, would enjoy a visit," Kavanaugh told Reed in September 1964, "and where they would be taught an interesting impressive lesson on every occasion."[51]

Less fascinated with the wonders of modern technology, Ed Story of Elk City noted that it was extremely difficult to get away from a Protestant church after a service without being introduced to the pastor and several members of the congregation. Catholic churches, by contrast, fell far short of their Protestant counterparts when it came to greeting newcomers, conducting follow-up visits, and providing fellowship activities, and they underestimated the importance of ushers. Story warned that non-Catholics were unlikely to make a second visit if they were not properly welcomed or if they sensed an absence of fellowship.[52]

One presumption surrounding the new liturgy was that it would speak more eloquently to a younger generation of Catholics, about whose devotional commitment many pastors had become increasingly concerned. Such was the theme of Monsignor Bartholomew Murtaugh in describing the worship habits of students in Oklahoma City in the late 1950s:

50. Revd. William Nerin to Victor Reed, February 1, 1966, Reed Papers.
51. Al. J. Kavanaugh to Victor Reed, September 9, 1964, Reed Papers.
52. Ed J. Story to Msgr. George W. Casey, October 25, 1966, Reed Papers.

I am much concerned about the deteriorating changes that occur in the lives of some of our young parishioners who attend [Bishop McGuinness] high school. There are those whom neither Father Monahan nor I have seen at the altar rail in months. Some of them miss Mass frequently. The use of missal, prayer book or rosary at Mass seems to be an unheard of practice. Seldom do we see these young people at special devotions such as Lenten exercises, the Forty Hours and the novena. It seems to me that there is a very serious lack in the spiritual life and development of our high school students. This may explain, in part, some of the more serious disciplinary and moral problems that exist in the school.[53]

In seeking to recapture a vital segment of the Catholic community from indifferentism, priests like Father Donald Brooks emphasized that they sought to bring disaffected students into closer relationship with Christ through active participation. Brooks not only favored the maximum permitted use of the vernacular liturgy, but also sought permission for students to compose their own prayers for parts of the service and to select, under direction, the Epistle and Gospel readings, when there was no assigned Mass text. "The student instinctively asks Christ, not so much to descend to his level," he told Reed, "but to speak gently and challengingly in terms which he, at least partially, grasps."[54]

Brooks later joined Father Kenneth King in a unique approach to catechetical instruction. At a summer camp in southeastern Oklahoma, King proposed to cut the throat of a young lamb in order to teach the children about the concept of sacrifice. Brooks found a young lieutenant stationed at Fort Sill to carry the lamb on his shoulders and to slit its throat. Meanwhile, the campers were divided into twelve "tribes" and directed to build an altar with twelve pillars. After administration of an anesthetic, the lamb was sacrificed in proper Old Testament form. However, while it had been intended that all those participating should eat a portion of the lamb (after it was cooked), the day on which this occurred happened to be a Friday (for which the Church laws on abstinence from meat still applied).[55]

One controversial departure designed to appeal to the young was the institution of folk Masses (pejoratively known as Hootenanny Masses), which employed popular musical instruments, such as the guitar, and expressive body language to heighten the intensity of the experience. The *Oklahoma Courier* devoted a 1965 editorial to the phenomenon, pointing out that folk

53. Msgr. Bartholomew A. Murtaugh to Victor Reed, May 10, 1958, Reed Papers.
54. Revd. Donald Brooks to Victor Reed, January 5, 1966, Reed Papers.
55. As told to Father James White by Father Kenneth King.

music and jazz were merely forms of music, like plain chant and polyphony, which had also been "novel" in the past. "What we must get away from," the editors stated, "is the notion that everyone must use the same form. Our traditional hymns and Masses are just as inappropriate for a congregation of teen-agers as their hootenay [*sic*] is for the majority of us."[56]

Pastors who favored the folk Mass still had a considerable fight on their hands. "If the Mass is going to be a meaningful experience for teenagers (and adults)," declared Father William Skeehan in January 1967, "it must incarnate itself into the culture and way of life of teenagers. The Holy See, by the way, has fully approved folk Masses (not jazz) for our young people."[57] Two months later, the bishop experienced his first folk Mass, with guitar accompaniment, at a confirmation service at the Church of the Madalene. "He had a little trouble getting into the swing of things," a local priest reported, "but he left with the remark that it was 'very well done.'"[58] Reed's openness encouraged the people of St. Mary's parish in Tulsa to petition for their own youth Mass with guitar accompaniment and contemporary music. No fewer than 137 parishioners (including forty-two married couples) put their names to the petition. A visitor to the parish a couple of weeks later told the pastor that he believed such worship encouraged the young to become enthusiastic participants in parish life. His own two-year-old child, he added, had been singing alleluias around the house for some time after Mass. On that basis alone, he would favor the greater employment of contemporary music at Mass.[59]

The following year, Father Mazaika instituted a monthly folk Mass in his home parish. "The melodies and words of these Masses," he explained, "enable the young People of God to convey in meaningful language, their emotions, backgrounds and experiences. This is true liturgical renewal: the liturgy becomes relevant and genuinely contemporary. The guitar, too, has become standard equipment for modern American youth. And again, the Church has

56. *Oklahoma Courier*, July 30, 1965. Earlier that month the *Courier* printed a letter from a member of the Young Christian Students who pointed out the popularity of folk Masses among young Catholics throughout the world. "With the Grace of God," he concluded, "we will become the leaders of the Church just as the ones who criticize us now are." *Oklahoma Courier*, July 2, 1965.

57. Revd. William Skeehan to J. J. Brown, January 5, 1967, Reed Papers.

58. *Tulsa Tribune*, March 18, 1967.

59. Parishioners of St. Mary's, Petition for youth Mass, n.d., Revd. Ben Zoeller to Victor Reed, June 28, 1967, Reed to Zoeller, July 5, 1967, St. Mary's Church, Tulsa File, box 14.1, ADT; John W. Berkbuegler to Revd. Ben Zoeller, July 17, 1967, Reed Papers.

recognized the validity of new musical modes by admitting for use in divine worship instruments other than the organ."[60]

Pressure for the contemporary could, however, produce some unusual results. On July 4, 1968, St Patrick's parish in Oklahoma City hosted a most unusual wedding. The bride's father (a jazz musician), who had already written a jazz Mass for Thanksgiving Day, had set the wedding march, offertory, Lord's Prayer, Mass, and recessional to a Dixieland Jazz setting. To further emphasize the "alternative" nature of the ceremony, passages from the works of Kahill Gilbran and Teilhard de Chardin took the place of the traditional Bible readings. "The music admittedly was loud, as you can well imagine," Father Charles Schettler remarked a few days later. "However, I myself did not feel it to be irreverent or sacrilegious for the occasion. The music did have a joyful reverential enthusiasm, quite in accord with the national holiday and the wedding itself."[61]

THE COST OF CHANGE

By the summer of 1966, some of the most avid proponents of the liturgical apostolate were beginning to express concern that the fire had gone out of the movement. "Priests who are uninformed or unaware, or of a conservative or reactionary bent, are allowed to lead parishes and dioceses down irrelevant paths abandoned by the Council Fathers," insisted the executive secretary of the Liturgical Conference. "Certainly we do not see numbers of American bishops pursuing in their own sees the policies and spirit they endorsed so generously in Vatican II." While Father Mannion had praise for the liturgy training programs for clergy in the Archdiocese of Chicago and the Diocese of New Ulm, he urged that individual parishes be given greater flexibility to experiment with worship styles.[62]

Distrust of the bishops for their perceived delaying tactics was evident at the 1966 meeting of the Southwest Liturgical Conference. In the aftermath, Bishop Thomas Gorman of Houston wrote angrily to Reed's fellow Oklahoman Bishop Buswell of Pueblo, complaining that the tone of the conference had been antiepiscopal and anticlerical. "If some of the 'off-the-beam' boys are there," Gorman concluded, "I think there should be somebody on the

60. *What's New from Hill's View*, September 1968, Reed Papers.
61. *Daily Oklahoman*, June 28, July 5, 1968; Revd. Charles Schettler to Msgr. Paul M. Van Dorpe, July 9, 1968, St Patrick's Church, Oklahoma City File, AAOC.
62. John B. Mannion, "A Dull New Day," *Commonweal*, August 19, 1966, 519–21.

program to defend orthodoxy and common sense in the liturgy. There was no such provision made at the Houston convention . . . except for the speech of welcome by Bishop Morkovsky there was no Bishop on the program. My urge—were I to go to another Liturgical Conference as a Bishop—would be to wear a bullet-proof vest."[63]

Archbishop Paul Hallinan of Atlanta, chairman of the Committee on Liturgy for the newly formed National Conference of Catholic Bishops (NCCB), accepted that some response had to be devised to the flurry of unauthorized experiments that were emerging, including such innovations as use of the Dutch canon of the Mass and Communion celebrated using drugstore wine and supermarket bread. "Whether healthy or drained of all reverence and meaning," he concluded, "[such experimentation reveals] an unrest with forms that [the innovators] call 'churchy.'" Hallinan proposed directed experimentation in a university setting, the results of which could be submitted to Rome for analysis, and for some freedom for bishops to designate seminaries or parishes in their diocese for further liturgical experimentation.[64] He found an ally in Reed, who declared in a letter to Hallinan that, while the ideal process of change might be one in which historical study was followed by controlled experimentation, the current situation might not permit this:

I feel that by trying to hold the line on experimentation according to the present plan we are not only exposing ecclesiastical authority to a cumbersome and indefensible role in the judgment of a large number of well-meaning and knowledgeable clerics and laymen but we are thereby injuring the image of bishops as leaders of the People of God. This last observation may appear extreme to some of my fellow bishops but may I submit in its defense that to me the "telling point" is the "frame of mind" which prevails among so many actively progressive people today. . . . I feel that the bishops must lead the way in liturgical experimentation by making legitimate use of those institutions and persons most suited to inaugurate and guide such experiments. The bishops must avoid as much as possible, the image of authority sanctioning almost endless delay if not actually trying to block liturgical progress.[65]

63. Bp. Thomas K. Gorman to Bp. Charles A. Buswell, October 24, 1966, Reed Papers.

64. Paul J. Hallinan, "A Time to Create," *Commonweal*, October 13, 1967, 47–49. Hallinan had particular praise for the liturgical freedom that Bishop Charles Helmsing permitted in the Diocese of Kansas City–St. Joseph. An Oklahoma priest—Father John Sullivan—was to become bishop of that diocese in 1977.

65. Abp. Paul J. Hallinan to Victor Reed, September 8, 1967, Reed to Hallinan, October 2, 1967, Reed Papers.

In March 1967, Reed publicly declared that adoption of the English canon was inevitable, even as he announced approval of new Scripture readings for the daily Mass, with a choice of translation that included the Confraternity of Christian Doctrine version, the Douay-Rheims version, the Catholic Revised Standard Version, and the Jerusalem Bible. At the same time, Father Mazaika noted that the diocesan liturgical commission had asked for the whole diocese to be declared open to liturgical experimentation.[66] This stance, coupled with Reed's strong support for Hallinan's proposals for greater episcopal flexibility, provoked considerable opposition from fellow bishops, who viewed the pressure for experimentation as coming largely from university communities. Many were particularly concerned about the abandonment by priests of clerical vestments and the reception by the laity of Communion in the hand.

At the 1968 meeting of the NCCB Subcommittee on Liturgical Adaptation, Reed accepted that the lack of communication between the bishops and the tradition of episcopal independence militated against any immediate change of attitude, unless and until the bishops came to acknowledge the extent of the liturgical crisis. He also suggested that expressions of interest from the laity might be of great value in transforming episcopal attitudes. Reed was joined in this sentiment by Father John Miller, chairman of the liturgical commission in the Archdiocese of New Orleans, who warned Reed that the trend in clergy experimentation was only accelerating. "While I do not in the least wish to countenance unauthorized tampering with the Sacred Liturgy," Miller declared, "the fact is that many of the things being done now by the priests have sound theological, liturgical, and pastoral reasons behind them. It will be most unfortunate if only years from now the Bishops persuade the Holy See to authorize these things, and people must again suffer reform."[67]

In June 1966, the *Oklahoma Courier* polled its readership on their view of the liturgical changes to date. On the liturgy as a whole, 64 percent approved of the Novus Ordo (20 percent had minor reservations), while 36 percent preferred the silent Mass (7 percent stated that they supported the changes because they were now Church law, but one can assume that this

66. *Oklahoma Courier*, March 24, 1967. Some priests jumped to the conclusion that Reed had been authorized to give individuals *outside* his diocese permission to experiment. See Revd. Henry J. McIntyre to Victor Reed, July 19, 1967, Reed Papers.

67. Minutes of the Subcommittee on Liturgical Adaptation, St. Louis, April 21, 1968, Revd. John H. Miller, C.S.C., to Reed, October 14, 1969, Reed Papers.

implied private dissatisfaction). On congregational singing, respondents were far more evenly divided. One quarter (24 percent) approved without reservation, while another 33 percent favored congregational involvement but wanted better songs. Another quarter (also 24 percent) described such singing as distracting, while 19 percent would have preferred a choir. Overall, 46 percent expressed a desire for one silent Latin Mass every Sunday, and 32 percent favored benediction after Mass (both hallmarks of a more traditional standpoint), while 42 percent wished the canon of the Mass to be rendered in English.[68] These figures demonstrated that even within a progressive diocese and among what may be assumed to have been a somewhat more liberal readership, there was a wide spectrum of opinion. As experimentation increased in the late 1960s, even some who had welcomed the shift to the vernacular began to express reservations about the direction in which liturgical renewal was moving.

A controversial figure in Oklahoma's liturgical experimentation was Father John Bloms, O.S.B., a Benedictine priest who was assigned to St. Joseph's parish in Ada for most of the 1960s. In his capacity as parish pastor, he appeared in a photograph on page 1 of the first issue of the *National Catholic Reporter* in October 1964, on the strength of his decision to employ altar girls. This unsought publicity was a source of considerable embarrassment to Bishop Reed, who found himself subject to unwelcome attention while attending the third session of the Second Vatican Council in Rome, and he quickly made it clear that this was one experiment that should immediately cease. Unlike some priests, Bloms seems to have enjoyed the support of many of his parishioners. A local physician told the bishop that there were simply not enough men and boys interested in being servers at St. Joseph's. "It is our opinion," he told Reed, "that there are few parishes, other than St. Joseph, wherein family worship is an accomplished fact. This is reflected in the number of daily communicants."[69]

The argument was not confined to purely practical considerations, however. One couple told Reed that the use of altar girls was a natural reflection of the fact that half of the Mystical Body of Christ was, in fact, female. On December 10, 1965, the *Oklahoma Courier* printed letters from three third graders at St. Joseph's protesting the ban on altar girls. One boy compared the bishop's prohibition to racial discrimination, but it was the letter of Eliz-

68. *Oklahoma Courier*, June 10, 1966.
69. *Oklahoma Courier*, December 3, 1965; Frank J. Martin to Reed, December 8, 1965, St. Joseph's Church, Ada File, AAOC.

abeth Kemp that really caught people's attention (though one might wonder if it was entirely her own unaided work). "Girl's [*sic*] are a part of God's family aren't we?" Kemp demanded. "If we can't do anything or really be a part of God's family I think we shouldn't even be there. I was really disappointed when I heard girl's [*sic*] couldn't serve. Jesus let girls serve him."[70]

Even after the abandonment of girl servers, controversy continued to swirl around St. Joseph's parish. When some members of his congregation complained about liturgical experimentation, Bloms provided Reed with a detailed list of innovations, including lay participation in the entrance, offertory, and Communion processions, the use of guitar music, and the singing of "Onward Christian Soldiers" at the graduation day Mass. Most parish music, the priest insisted, still came from booklets produced by the parish liturgical commission and the *Hymnal of Christian Unity* published by the Gregorian Institute of America. These, however, were side issues. What had sparked congregational protests was his request that communicants during Holy Week of 1967 take the consecrated Host directly from the ciborium. Bloms admitted to Reed that he favored distribution of the Sacrament by the laity, but that his request was not a surreptitious way to get around official prohibitions on such practice but consequent upon the fact that he had injured his right hand, which was still swathed in bandages.[71]

Communion in the hand was a liturgical fault line that neither the bishop nor delegates to the Little Council wished to cross. In June 1968, two male servers wrote to the *Courier* expressing concern about parishioners reaching into the ciborium. This was despite the defense of priests like Father Paul Gallatin of St. Mary's parish in Ardmore that such a practice in no way diminished reverence for the Sacrament. "I feel that it better stresses the meal nature of the Eucharist, emphasizes the dignity and value of the person, and acts out the relationship between priest and people," he told Reed. "Our prime concern in our relationship to the Body of Christ is always to maintain a deep and sincere reverence for this Holy Sacrament, the visible sign of the Lord's continued presence arising among and in the Community of Faith."[72] Only in 1970, when Paul VI accorded bishops the right to appoint lay eucharistic ministers where necessary, did Communion in the hand begin to make inroads, and even here it was clear that Reed remained uneasy. In 1970, while

70. Mr. and Mrs. Robert B. Bigul to Victor Reed, December 5, 1965, St. Joseph's Church, Ada File; *Oklahoma Courier*, December 10, 1965.

71. Revd. John Bloms to Reed, n.d. (prob. 1967), Reed Papers.

72. Revd. Paul H. Gallatin to Victor Reed, September 12, 1968, Reed Papers.

appointing two sisters and three laymen to serve as extraordinary ministers of Holy Communion at Sacred Heart parish in El Reno, he stressed the necessity of explaining to the congregation that the laity had been allowed to administer Communion in the Early Church.[73]

The parish was "the one place that people always thought they could find refuge," declared Douglas Fox in 2004. "[Change] might have been okay if that had happened ten years later or ten years earlier." Liturgical change and church politics were inextricably intertwined, a not unexpected consequence of the belief that the liturgy should form a channel between the active and the contemplative life. When Fox's Tulsa parish—Christ the King—introduced guitar Masses, many older parishioners withdrew to Cascia Hall, where they were spared singing, handholding, and frequent amens. A similar concern was expressed by a worshiper at the St. John the Evangelist mission in Cookson, where tape-recorded music had been played that "would make good listening on the Glen Campbell or Ed Sullivan shows, but . . . had no business being played during a religious service. All during the time communion was being distributed rock and roll music was loudly blaring from the back of the church."[74] At Immaculate Conception parish in Tulsa, fifty-two members attended a meeting of the liturgy committee (normal attendance was around seven) in February 1967. At that meeting it was agreed to abandon the folk Mass planned for later in the month, end responsive singing of the "Our Father," and abandon the Communion hymn, yet when these propositions were presented to the pastor and his assistant, they were completely ignored.[75]

Many progressive priests were disinclined to listen to complaints. In 1961, Father Ernest Flusche dismissed a professor at the University of Oklahoma as a "talented scholar of English literature," but "liturgically speaking . . . a rigid screwball [who] will, no doubt, bring you his Ordo from the Diocese of Plymouth (England) as proof that we are all wrong."[76] While Flusche may

73. Victor Reed to Revd. J. Neal Towner, February 17, 1970, Sacred Heart, El Reno File, AAOC.

74. Fox, interview; John R. O'Rourke to Victor Reed, July 3, 1969, Reed Papers.

75. George M. Mason to Victor Reed, February 176, 1967, Immaculate Conception Church, Tulsa File, box 4.1. There were some liturgical enthusiasts who showed greater sensitivity to their parishioners' concerns. In 1967, Father William Swift endorsed the decision of his parish council to schedule contemporary liturgies on Saturday evenings so as not to offend the more traditionally minded parishioners. Revd. William J. Swift to Revd. Charles H. Schettler, August 10, 1969, Reed Papers.

76. Revd. Ernest A. Flusche to Victor Reed, April 15, 1961, Reed Papers.

have been irked by the fact that the professor and his wife traveled to Oklahoma City every Sunday in order to attend a parish where the people did not
participate publicly in the liturgy, his choice of words was hardly pastoral.
One unnamed priest ordered members of his congregation to neither kneel
nor sing "O Lord I Am Not Worthy" while receiving Communion, while
another made a point of instructing parishioners to move from their habitual seats to pews closer to the altar. "If [sitting in a family pew] 'bugs' our
priest," Jo Anne Parris told Reed, "then I'm afraid the good man will just
have to learn to 'accept' this fact."[77]

While most complaints came from frustrated traditionalists, the arrival of
a conservative pastor could likewise throw a progressive parish into a tailspin.
After Father Frederick Beckerle was moved to St. Therese's parish in Collinsville, the bishop was soon the recipient of a petition signed by ninety-eight
members of the parish who expressed concern that all their advances in liturgy and religious instruction would be undermined by Beckerle's desire to
return to the Baltimore Catechism. An evidently irritated Reed (who had
had to move Beckerle from his previous parish because of a dispute over parish finances) was uncharacteristically outspoken in rebuking the pastor: "May
I say, Fred, that I consider it very unwise to interfere in what has been established by your predecessor unless it is clearly against the teaching of the
Church. I feel that we have a competent Religious Education Department in
the diocese and do not wish its effort to be nullified."[78]

Some critics accepted the principle of renewal but criticized the liturgical
instruments used to bring it about. One Oklahoma Catholic voiced concern
about the hymnal *Our Parish Prays and Sings*, not only for its prose style but
also for its implication that non-Catholics could receive Communion, that
confession before Mass was no longer obligatory, and that the souls of the
dead slept until the General Judgment. "I am glad," he told Reed, "that you
are on the commission because I am sure you will want to rectify these er-
rors."[79] Another decried the proposal to eliminate recitation of the *Gloria in
Excelsis* except on major feasts. "We go to church to worship and give glory
to God, and in no place in the Mass do I find this better expressed verbally,"
she reminded the bishop. "I teach my first grade religion class that prayer is

---

77. Mrs. J. C. Richard to Victor Reed, April 26, 1967, Jo Anne Parris to Victor Reed,
January 4, 1969, Reed Papers.

78. Victor Reed to Revd. Frederick W. Beckerle, July 4, 1968, St Teresa's Church (Little Flower), Collinsville File, box 33.1.

79. E. M. Rogers to Victor Reed, July 2, 1964, Reed Papers.

talking to God with love and that we pray to give thanks to God and to tell him that we love Him. . . . In most other parts of the Mass we are begging God's mercy and acceptance of our gifts to Him."[80]

Critics presented more of a challenge when they questioned the very theology that underpinned the new liturgy. "The New Church teaches that God is found by joining a group, by getting involved, by many types of action," argued an anonymous correspondent. "What do the Saints say? They say God is found in prayer and silence and solitude and in the Sacraments. Shall I do what the Saints say, since history proved they were right, or shall I listen to some of your young priests and join a demonstration against the war?"[81] Alice Le Gate, a Los Angeles native visiting Edmond, was appalled at the removal of statuary and votive candles, the relegation of the tabernacle to the sidelines, and the "sacrilege" of communicants crying "Hallelujah, Praise the Lord" at Communion and standing to receive the Host. "Everyone knows Edmond is a bigoted, narrow minded Baptist town," she complained to Reed, "but surely the Catholic Church is not going to make a mockery of the Mass just to be recognized in an area." Many Edmond Catholics, she added, now went to Oklahoma City when they wanted to go to Mass.[82]

Le Gate's comments illustrate how much more unsettling the liturgical revolution could be for Catholic communities with but a single parish. If the priest appointed to a particular community was a zealous reformer, he could impose changes that the community had no choice but to accept if they wished to attend Mass at all. In Tulsa and Oklahoma City, by contrast, the greater number of parishes meant that there would always be some that kept contemporary worship to a minimum. Despite the traditional opposition to Catholics worshipping in a parish in which they were not geographically resident, urban Catholics would increasingly come to behave like Protestants, selecting a parish on the basis of the worship and services it offered or refrained from offering. Thus, while it was the innovations of some urban Oklahoma parishes that drew the greatest criticism from conservatives *outside*

80. Mrs. Joseph L. Barthel Jr. to Victor Reed, April 3, 1965, Reed Papers.

81. "A Catholic who wants to remain a Catholic—so no signature" to Victor Reed, April 24, 1966, Reed Papers.

82. Alice Le Gate to Victor Reed, July 26, 1966, Reed Papers. The changes observed by Le Gate were not received without protest. A flyer for a meeting at St. John the Baptist parish called for the restoration of the tabernacle and the statues of Mary and Joseph, one Latin Mass, benediction, and Marian devotions, and choral singing. Father Nerin had evidently failed to convert everyone to his way of thinking. See "Parishioners—Important!!!" n.d., St. John the Baptist Church, Edmond File, AAOC.

Oklahoma, it was reforming priests assigned to small rural parishes who were likely to excite the most local resentment.

Le Gate was also perceptive in her recognition of how the liturgy had become less "Catholic." Writing to the pastor of Christ the King, Tulsa, one of his parishioners made the same point. "Is there no room in this 'new church' for those who are distressed about the turn events are taking?" she asked. "Why is a prayer any more effective because it is recited by the congregation instead of an individual? The new service is a poor imitation of all that is bad about Protestant services and has none of the dignity of some of them. . . . Somehow, this 'new' church seems to have completely ignored the idea of Christ as a personal, individual Saviour; that only personal reform leads to lasting social reform, and that all of the 'social action' groups you devise will meet with failure without that personal, individual desire to love your neighbor and do the will of God."[83]

CONCLUSION

The Second Vatican Council effected a profound transformation of the day-to-day religious life of ordinary Catholics throughout the United States, to which Oklahoma proved no exception. The council's initial focus on liturgical adaptation guaranteed that within a generation, many Catholics would have no memory of what Tridentine Catholicism had been like. The implementation of a vernacular liturgy stripped away many of the remaining barriers between the immigrant Catholic culture of the early twentieth century and the Protestant mainstream. Perhaps most striking was the eclipse of Catholic devotionalism, which progressive publications like the *Oklahoma Courier* endeavored to bury.[84] "We could not get a dozen people to ask for a weekday Mass or Stations of the Cross during Lent," a Glenmary priest admitted in 1971. "These practices don't seem to mean as much as they once did for Catholics."[85]

The liturgical revolution marked a sea change in the relationship between

83. Mrs. C. W. Eckenwiler to Msgr. Cecil Finn, October 29, 1969, Reed Papers.

84. The American Church, a *Courier* editorial declared, "gives the appearance of a multitude of devotions loosely tied together rather than of one body; and many people busily running from shrine to shrine seem to have forgotten the true nature of the Church." *Oklahoma Courier*, July 22, 1966. According to the *Courier* poll of June 10, only 10 percent of its readers still prayed the rosary during Mass.

85. Glenmary Missioner Newsletter, St. Patrick's Day, 1971, St. Francis de Sales Church, Idabel File, box 50.1.

priest and laity, lifting the latter from their formerly passive role in worship to a more profound level of participation. That at least was the ideal. In practice, liturgical adaptation was not necessarily a process that arose from below but often one imposed from above. The understandable concern voiced by reformers about the inherently passive nature of the devotional life also revealed a fatal miscomprehension of its value, and the adoption of culturally "relevant" worship practices was often marked by the same imposed uniformity that had characterized preconciliar patterns of worship. Reed himself recognized the dangers of liturgical dogmatism and emphasized the duty of his clergy to gently shepherd their people through the intricacies of the new order. "Modifications in the ritual are no reason for putting in or leaving out forms of ceremonial according to one's personal taste," he reflected on one occasion. "Even in the parts of the Mass which are said in English, there are rubrics which must be followed. . . . A priest's first consideration should be the edification of his flock. He should be careful not to introduce any innovation which is likely to shock or scandalize the faithful, whether young or old."[86]

86. Notes on priestly behavior, n.d., Reed Papers.

chapter 7

We Are Our Brothers' Keepers

The Ecumenical Impulse

The Church, then, is God's only flock; it is like a standard lifted high for the nations to see it: for it serves all mankind through the Gospel of peace as it makes its pilgrim way in hope toward the goal of the fatherland above. This is the sacred mystery of the unity of the Church, in Christ and through Christ, the Holy Spirit energizing its various functions. It is a mystery that finds its highest exemplar and source in the unity of the Persons of the Trinity: the Father and the Son in the Holy Spirit, one God. Even in the beginnings of this one and only Church of God there arose certain rifts, which the Apostle strongly condemned. But in subsequent centuries much more serious dissensions made their appearance and quite large communities came to be separated from full communion with the Catholic Church – for which, often enough, men of both sides were to blame. The children who are born into these Communities and who grow up believing in Christ cannot be accused of the sin involved in the separation, and the Catholic Church embraces upon them as brothers, with respect and affection. For men who believe in Christ and have been truly baptized are in communion with the Catholic Church even though this communion is imperfect. . . . It follows that the separated Churches and Communities as such, though we believe them to be deficient in some respects, have been by no means deprived of significance and importance in the mystery of salvation. For the Spirit of Christ has not refrained from using them as means of salvation which derive their efficacy from the very fullness of grace and truth entrusted to the Church.

Second Vatican Council, Decree on Ecumenism, *Unitatis Redintegratio*, November 21, 1964

On August 22, 1961, Charles Scott, a Protestant resident of Duncan, Oklahoma, wrote to Bishop Reed protesting the failure of the Catholic Church to engage in genuine ecumenical dialogue. By way of illustration, Scott cited the case of his own family. After twenty-three years of marriage, his Catholic wife had been to his church on a single occasion and their sons never, while he had attended his Catholic parish church on numerous occasions. Scott concluded:

Sometime ago, in a mild discussion with my wife of this tolerant and intolerant attitude, after reading her church papers and mine; half in jest and half in truth, I offered to give her one dollar for every time she could find one critical or derogatory remark in any of my church papers toward the Roman Catholic Church, provided she would give me ten cents every time I found one in her church papers. She refused to bet! . . . I am definitely of the opinion that the Roman Catholic Church could serve themselves and the cause of Christianity to a remarkable extent by some relaxing of their intolerant attitude toward someone who is seriously and conscientiously attempting to serve the Lord and Christ according to their teachings and their best judgment.[1]

Scott's verdict echoed the views of many Protestants toward the preconciliar Church. Until the 1960s, Roman Catholics held resolutely aloof from the rising tide of transdenominational contacts throughout worldwide Protestantism. Since their tradition was presumed to comprehend the full extent of Christ's earthly ministry, from which all other Christian sects had, to a greater or lesser extent, deviated, there could be no question of a sacramental life outside the Catholic Church. Devout Catholics were expected neither to attend Protestant services nor to participate in non-Catholic religious study groups. Ecumenism, by contrast, conceded that all the Christian churches had some access to divine grace.

The ecumenical debate that came to the fore in the 1960s represented a fascinating story of theological convergence. For a short time, the pontificate of Pope John XXIII seemed to promise that the schisms of the Reformation might be undone and Christian unity in the West finally attained. What distinguished the ecumenical dialogue of the 1960s from that of earlier decades was that it was underpinned by genuine lay enthusiasm. A generation of well-educated American Catholics, inspired by the emphasis of the Second

---

1. Charles W. Scott to Victor Reed, August 22, 1961, Reed Papers. Surprisingly, Scott also noted that his eighty-two-year-old Catholic father-in-law was more tolerant than his daughter, often accompanying Scott to worship services and even donating money to the latter's church.

Vatican Council on the lay apostolate, joined the ecumenical debate. The ecumenical wave swept through the Americanized dioceses of the Midwest like Chicago and St. Louis, with both of which the Diocese of Oklahoma City and Tulsa enjoyed a close relationship. The pressure for an understanding with mainstream Protestantism in Oklahoma, however, would be even more intense, for few Oklahoma Catholics could even begin to sustain the sort of enclave community that their northern counterparts enjoyed. If Methodists, Presbyterians and, above all, Episcopalians were willing to engage in dialogue, they would find Oklahoma Catholics ready to respond.

Prior to 1964, some ecumenical outreach between Catholics and Protestants in Oklahoma did occur. During the 1930s, a Protestant minister had organized Sunday afternoon coffee sessions at the University of Oklahoma at which students could listen to presentations from ministers of various denominations. In Purcell, the local Methodist church adopted a similar approach at one weekly service, while an interdenominational Vespers service was held for the victims of anti-Semitism at a Presbyterian church in Enid (the rabbi who delivered the homily was introduced by a Catholic priest). In 1936, the National Conference of Christians and Jews (NCCJ), an ecumenical body formed in 1928 to seek an end to all forms of religious prejudice, began to organize in Oklahoma. Although it was not an organization generally commended by the American Catholic hierarchy, Bishop Kelley joined several Texas bishops in 1944 to deliver the only official Catholic endorsement that the NCCJ ever received.[2]

With the coming of the Second World War, the American Catholic Church entered upon a period of religious ascendancy that would endure for a quarter of a century. A marked decline began to take place in liturgical practices peculiar to Roman Catholicism, such as novenas and devotions dedicated to the Virgin Mary or a parish's patron saint. Such practices had been a central feature in sustaining immigrant Catholic life in the early twentieth century, but were not favorably regarded in Protestant circles. As Catholic distinctiveness faded and the external Protestant threat receded, American Catholics took note of the increasing willingness of the Vatican to at least contemplate the possibility of ecumenical dialogue. In 1954, Fathers Gustave Weigel and John Sheerin were observers at the first Faith and Order conference to be held in the United States. The year 1960, when John F. Kennedy's presidential can-

2. Brown, *Bible Belt Catholicism*, 188–90. On the early days of the NCCJ, see Curry, *Protestant-Catholic Relations*, 21–24, 28–31.

didacy was giving rise to renewed Protestant unease, was also the year of publication of *An American Dialogue*, a blueprint for the ecumenical movement, written by a Protestant, Robert McAfee Brown, and a Catholic, Gustave Weigel.[3]

Such national trends were mirrored in Oklahoma. "I could, within a year or so, easily start working with and meeting Jewish rabbis of the town and Protestant ministers," Monsignor James Halpine remembered of his arrival in Oklahoma City in 1953, "and gradually became involved in the ministerial alliance of the time and even with the Oklahoma City Council of Churches, and we had discussion groups among Christians and Jews in the Fifties. It was very easy."[4] The same was true both in Tulsa and more rural parts of the state, where Catholic priests increasingly participated in local ministerial alliances and even accepted offices within them.[5] Some of those who did participate still continued to express reservations. Father Julian Grehan admitted complete disinterest in the work of the NCCJ but acknowledged that accepting an invitation to join the Okmulgee branch might be necessary to improve community relations.[6] Such early steps at bridge building were not confined to the clergy. Many young Catholics no longer viewed Protestant culture with the hostility of their parents, especially if they were part of a university environment, whether as students, professors, or chaplains. Suburban Catholics who belonged to the Christian Family Movement also showed enthusiasm for the ecumenical movement, with Oklahoma City's CFM developing ties with St. Elijah's Orthodox Church.[7]

The altered Catholic vision owed much to the 1958 elevation of Ange-

3. Brown and Weigel, *An American Dialogue*, 77–116. For general accounts of Catholic ecumenism during the 1940s and 1950s, see Brown, *The Ecumenical Revolution*, 47–57; Curry, *Protestant-Catholic Relations*, 64–70; Cavert, *The American Churches in the Ecumenical Movement*, 225–26, 232–34.

4. Halpine, interview.

5. Revd. Daniel T. Ray, C.S.Sp., to Victor Reed, April 25, 1958, Reed to Ray, May 1, 1958, St. Monica's Church, Tulsa File, box 15.1, Archives of the Catholic Diocese of Tulsa (hereafter ADT); Revd. Charles H. Schettler to Revd. Howard A. Anthony, December 11, 1962, Immaculate Conception Church, Hugo File, box 49.1, ADT. Some priests also participated in an ecumenical discussion group in Tulsa. *Oklahoma Courier*, July 21, 1961.

6. Revd. Julian S. Grehan, C.SS.R., to Revd. William C. Garthoeffner, September 8, 1961, Garthoeffner to Grehan, September 12, 1961, St. Anthony's Church, Okmulgee File, ADT. Garthoeffner reminded Grehan that Reed had participated in the NCCJ while he was rector of Holy Family Cathedral.

7. CFM report to the Bishop's Catholic Action Committee, March 9, 1961, Reed Papers. Chicago had an Episcopal version of CFM during the 1960s. See Burns, *Disturbing the Peace*, 147–49.

lo Giuseppe Roncalli as Pope John XXIII, perhaps the first occupant of the see of St. Peter for whom the majority of non-Catholic Americans expressed nothing but admiration. His decision to establish the Secretariat for the Promotion of Christian Unity, a body that, although part of the papal curia, was authorized to develop schemata in the same way as the conciliar commissions, was widely welcomed. His grant of permission for Catholic observers to attend the 1961 meeting of the World Council of Churches also signaled a dramatic reorientation of the Church's stance on ecumenical dialogue, and the Oklahoma secular press accorded him an unusually high degree of respect.[8] One Ardmore resident reported that his local paper had praised the new pope for his stand for peace and against Communism, "a most pleasant surprise to one who formerly lived in Ardmore during several years when the great majority of the population there actually was violently anti-Catholic."[9]

The focus of the Second Vatican Council on Catholicism's relationship with other Christian churches helped secure John XXIII's reputation as emissary to the "separated brethren," as Protestants became known in Catholic circles. His death in June 1963, during the second session of the council, was an occasion for genuine mourning throughout the Christian world, not least in Oklahoma. Father Francis McGoldrick of St. Francis Xavier parish in Tulsa recounted how several Protestant clergy had stopped him in the street to express their condolences. Even more striking was the reaction in the secular world. The state legislature passed a bipartisan interfaith resolution praising the late pope, and statewide newspapers offered similar expressions of appreciation and regret. "The Pope's leadership in the ecclesiastical realm helped to soften some of the deep differences which divide Christianity into theologically warring camps," declared the *Tulsa Daily World*, while the *Daily Oklahoman* concluded: "The imprint he left is best exemplified in the emergence of the church into a more conciliatory relationship with the rest of the world and its recent tendency toward more active participation in worldly problems." Likewise, the *Muskogee Daily Phoenix* declared that "his various pronouncements were a powerful force for good in an age that desperately needs that influence."[10]

8. Brown, *The Ecumenical Revolution*, 58–67.

9. T. Raymond Higgins to Msgr. Raymond Harkin, November 20, 1958, St. Mary's Church, Ardmore File, Archives of the Catholic Archdiocese of Oklahoma City (hereafter AAOC).

10. *Oklahoma Courier*, June 7, 1963; *Tulsa Daily World*, June 4, 1963; *Daily Oklahoman*, June 4, 1963; *Muskogee Daily Phoenix*, June 4, 1963.

From early in his career, Reed had shown great interest in the ecumenical movement, perhaps because many of his cousins on his father's side were
Protestants. He had engaged in dialogue with his Protestant counterparts
both in Stillwater and in Tulsa, and he continued such activity after becoming bishop. In 1960, he accepted an invitation to an interfaith breakfast organized by the Oklahoma branch of the Council of Churches.[11] The following
year, he encouraged non-Catholics to attend the annual meeting of the North
American Liturgical Conference in Oklahoma City, a move that bore comparison with the invitation of Protestant and Orthodox observers to the Second
Vatican Council. Particularly well represented were the Episcopalians—Bishop
Chilton Powell, a close acquaintance of Reed, requested one hundred registration blanks for his clergy—but many others, including Baptists and Pentecostals, were in attendance. The response was overwhelmingly positive, with
one Presbyterian commenting that advances in biblical scholarship could be
a meeting ground for Protestants and Catholics, while a Pentecostal minister praised Bishop Charles Buswell for his address on improvised prayer. All
agreed that the meeting had demonstrated that Protestants were beginning to
show a greater interest in liturgy, while Catholics were becoming more con-
gregationally participatory.[12]

An active voice in transforming the ecumenical setting was the *Oklahoma
Courier*. One of its first acts was to report the publication of "Rules for the
Dialogue," a possible strategy for practical ecumenism, in both the *Christian
Century* and *Commonweal*, the leading journals of mainstream Protestantism
and progressive Catholicism, respectively.[13] In July 1960, the editor noted the
growing impulse toward Christian unity, as the theologians of both traditions
found less and less over which to disagree. "When we have reunited Christianity into one body," he concluded, "it will not be a uniform body of Latin rite. It will be a living body bearing traces for a long time of its historical
tragedy as the flock that was divided and is now reunited in Christ."[14] One
Presbyterian minister in Chickasha was so impressed by such freedom of expression and thought that he became a regular subscriber to the *Courier*.[15]

11. Earl N. Kragnes to Victor Reed, January 8, 1960, Reed Papers. Kragnes was executive secretary of the Oklahoma Council of Churches.
12. *Oklahoma Courier*, August 18, September 1, 1961.
13. *Oklahoma Courier*, February 19, 1960.
14. *Oklahoma Courier*, July 29, 1960.
15. Joe R. Ross to Victor Reed, April 26, 1961, Reed Papers. The minister declared that
he had previously considered the Catholic Church to be narrow-minded. The approach

A NEW CHRISTIAN FELLOWSHIP?

An early example of interchurch cooperation was the sharing of church facilities. This practice had been common among Protestant denominations in the American West during the nineteenth century, but less so between Catholics and Protestants. In Oklahoma, however, close ties had developed during the twentieth century between the state's Catholic priests and their counterparts in the Episcopal Church, which in Oklahoma was dominated by the High Church party. It was not greatly surprising that Father Kenneth King of Immaculate Conception parish in Poteau should seek permission for the ordination of an Episcopal priest in his church building in November 1964 because the Episcopal church was too small for such a ceremony. King testified to a close friendship with his Episcopal colleague and reported that the latter had always displayed a proper reverence for the Blessed Sacrament when visiting Immaculate Conception. His request was granted, but with the proviso that the Sacrament be removed.[16]

Similar conditional permission was granted in June 1966 for the wedding of two Episcopalians at the Catholic church in Eufala, though Father William Garthoeffner added parenthetically, "I hope it doesn't involve the son or daughter of a prominent Oklahoma businessman or of some Anglican Bishop some place—thus resulting in wide, wide publicity."[17] In December 1966, Garthoeffner thought it necessary to urge the priest at Sacred Heart parish, Mangum, not to give undesirable publicity to the bishop's permission for a dozen Episcopalians to meet for worship there. "There are still some," Garthoeffner noted, "who might misunderstand this degree of cooperation between the Catholics and the non-Catholic denomination."[18] The following year Reed allowed the priest in Collinsville to offer his church to a group of churchless Episcopalians after Mass.[19]

---

taken by the *Courier* suggested to him that it was actually more permissive than many Protestant denominations.

16. Revd. Kenneth King to Revd. William C. Garthoeffner, n.d., Garthoeffner to King, November 23, 1964, Reed Papers. This ordination made headline news and was featured on NBC's *Huntley-Brinkley Report.*

17. Revd. William C. Garthoeffner to Revd. William M. Eichoff, June 16, 1966, Reed Papers.

18. Revd. Joseph W. Burger to Revd. William C. Garthoeffner, December 9, 1966, Garthoeffner to Burger, December 13, 1966, Reed Papers. Burger wrote: "Because of the great respect the members of the Episcopal congregation have for our worship and our churches, and because . . . the use of our church would forward ecumenical cooperation, I believe a great amount of spiritual good would come from their holding services in our church."

19. Revd. Thomas P. Biller to Victor Reed, June 6, 1967, Revd. William C. Garthoef-

Mainline Protestants followed the deliberations of the Second Vatican Council with great interest. In October 1962, Clark Bornfield, rector of Emmanuel Episcopal Church in Shawnee, invited Father Lawrence Spencer of St. Benedict's parish to preach at his church in October 1962: "Our purpose in extending this invitation is to help our people come to a realization of the importance of the meeting of the Second Vatican Council. All too often in the life of the Church, the laity ignore the meetings of the hierarchy, owing to their ignorance as to their importance. Facing as we do the rise of militant secularism here in America and the phenomenon of a proselyting [sic] Judaism, as well as the forces of international communism, we feel it important that the Church on the local level attempt so far as is possible, to understand their common Christian vocation and witness as the people of God in Christ in the world."[20]

While Spencer never took up Bornfield's invitation, local interest did not dissipate. In March of 1963, Reed addressed a meeting of 150 Protestant and Orthodox clergy in Tulsa on the results of the first session, and he laid particular stress on the presence of the 40 non-Catholic observers, including Dr. Albert Outler of Southern Methodist University.[21] A particularly remarkable request was received by Father Julian Grehan for him to address his local ministerial alliance and a summer school Bible class of Okmulgee's First Baptist Church on the deliberations of the council. "I am not one bit enthused over all this 'interdenominational dialoguing,'" Grehan confided in July 1963, "for I feel that it is cheapening our Catholic religion and is causing more of our 'Separated Brethren' to become more convinced than ever that all religions are equally good—some just more strict than others." The acting chancellor encouraged Grehan with the thought that this might be an opportunity to give the Baptists the Catholic side of the story.[22]

By early 1964, Oklahoma Catholics were actively reaching out to their Protestant brethren. A lay congress held in Oklahoma City devoted itself to interfaith cooperation and the fostering of better understanding between

fner to Biller, June 7, 1967, St. Therese's Church (Little Flower), Collinsville File, box 33.1, ADT.

20. Revd. R. Clark Bornfield to Revd. Lawrence Spencer, O.S.B., October 9, 1962, St. Benedict's Church, Shawnee File, AAOC.

21. *Oklahoma Courier*, March 1, 1963.

22. Revd. Julian S. Grehan, C.SS.R., to Victor Reed, July 14, August 24, 1963, Revd, Charles H. Schettler to Grehan, July 16, 1963, St. Anthony's Church, Okmulgee File, ADT.

Catholics and Protestants. Later that spring, Father Gerald Brousseau helped organize a lecture series in Tulsa entitled "The World of the Bible," the speakers for which included two rabbis and pastors from the Baptist, Eastern Orthodox, Episcopalian, Lutheran, Methodist, and Presbyterian traditions, with a final address delivered by Bishop Fulton Sheen. "Let it be known," the publicity material declared, "that the Roman Church seeks to reform no other religion but its own and only to set an example of religious reform for other churches."[23]

In October, Father Richard Sneed of St. Gregory's Abbey emphasized to members of St. John's Episcopal Church in Oklahoma City the necessity for Christians of all traditions to perceive their common heritage in the Bible rather than focus on the theological positions that distinguished one from another. Doctrinal differences had to be discussed, he acknowledged, but in the context of common prayer and transdenominational works of corporate mercy, such as the St. John's Hospice for single girls, with which St. Patrick's parish was also involved. "The cold war of the clergy has ended—I hope," Sneed declared. "But this is hardly even a beginning. The cold war of the laity has got to stop. We need to stop fearing our neighbors on the score of Christian conviction."[24]

Bishop Reed also authorized another significant ecumenical step when he permitted Tulsa's Church of the Madalene to become the first Catholic parish in the United States to affiliate with the local branch of the Council of Churches. On this occasion, the strongest criticism came from conservative Catholics outside the diocese. "Would it not have been better; and be now wiser to change, to unofficial support of the Council of Churches (if you must), but without membership, which implies full support?" complained John Grady of Arcadia, California. "If, as a Catholic, I am not permitted to attend a Protestant Church Service to refrain from support of error, how infinitely more serious for a Catholic Church to join a Protestant organization." In a personal reply to Grady, Reed insisted that the Tulsa Council of Church-

23. *Tulsa Tribune*, January 11, 1964; The World of the Bible: A Tulsa Church Unity Movement, Sponsors an Address by Bishop Fulton J. Sheen, "The Shape of the World's Heart," New Tulsa Assembly Center, April 8, 1964, St. Joseph's Monastery Archives, Tulsa, Oklahoma. This series apparently attracted the interest of the Church authorities, since Reed was obliged to assure Cardinal Alfredo Ottaviani three months later that no organization named "A Tulsa Church Unity Movement" existed. See Victor Reed to Alfredo Cardinal Ottaviani, July 7, 1964, Reed Papers.

24. Revd. Richard Sneed, Address to St. John's Episcopal Church, Oklahoma City, October 25, 1964, Reed Papers.

es was purely a local organization unaffiliated with the National Council of Churches, but he dodged the issue of Protestant affiliation.[25]

Despite such positive advances, Reed remained nervous about the pace of ecumenical dialogue. "We cannot expect too much too soon," he warned in June 1964. "Humanly speaking, I cannot see how the many differences in Christian beliefs and practices can be easily reconciled. The only one who can bring about this reconciliation is God. He can bring unity out of disunity, but in His own time and in His own way. But we as men are not without some contribution to make."[26] Nevertheless, the council's issuance of *Unitatis Redintegratio* (On the Restoration of Unity) on November 21, 1964 promised great things. It acknowledged the existential reality of the non-Catholic churches and accepted that the Holy Spirit could work through them—thus recognizing Protestantism corporately rather than Protestants solely as individuals. It also introduced the Protestant world to the notion of a "hierarchy of truths," thus allowing for universal Christian doctrines, such as the Trinity and the Incarnation, to take precedence over singularly Catholic doctrines. The way was now open not only for dialogue but also for the sharing of a life of common action and even common worship, although the latter was restricted to services concerned with Christian unity.[27]

For the mainline Protestant denominations, *Unitatis Redintegratio* and the Madalene's affiliation with the Council of Churches were equally positive signs. In January 1965, Father Paul Mollan was invited to preach at an Episcopal Communion service at Ft. Sill in Lawton, as part of the Church Unity Octave. The bishop granted permission as long as the address was kept liturgically separate from the service—either preceding or following the worship itself. He also allowed Father Leonard Murray, S.J., from the Jesuit Retreat House in Cushing to conduct a Lenten "quiet evening" at St. Alban's Episcopal Church later that spring.[28] Other denominations quickly followed suit. In Hobart, Father Charles White addressed a Disciples of Christ congregation after the regular worship service, with the pastor of First Christian

25. *Oklahoma Courier*, April 24, 1964; John Grady to Revd. James McNamee, May 3, 1964, Reed Papers; Victor Reed to John Grady, June 2, 1964, Church of the Madalene File, box 5.1, ADT. See also Mrs. Louis Mendiola Jr. to McNamee, May 1, 1964, Margaret Summers to McNamee, May 13, 1964, Reed Papers.

26. *Tulsa Daily World*, June 14, 1964.

27. Brown, *The Ecumenical Revolution*, 189–207, 280–82, 306–12, 325–30, 336–40.

28. Revd. Paul F. Mollan to Victor Reed, December 5, 1964, Revd. William C. Garthoeffner to Mollan, December 7, 1964, Leonard J. Murray, S.J., to Victor Reed, February 9, 1965, Revd. William C. Garthoeffner to Murray, February 13, 1965, Reed Papers.

Church performing the same role a week later at Sts. Peter and Paul Church, while Father Joseph Kolb of Sacred Heart parish in Sapulpa accepted an invitation to deliver the opening prayer at a preaching mission at First Methodist Church.[29]

In April 1965, Father Francis Weiner of Sacred Heart parish reported a proposed exchange with the Episcopal church in Miami that would allow members of both churches to attend Communion services in the other tradition as observers. Weiner also noted that the local branch of the Church of Jesus Christ of Latter-day Saints had asked for several lay Catholics to talk to its (adult) Sunday school class about Catholicism. Reed granted permission for both events, but advised that the Catholics should not participate in the Episcopal Communion, not even in the prayers or readings, and that only "prudent and well-informed Catholics" should be sent to the LDS meeting.[30] Perhaps the climactic moment of 1965 came in July, when Father James McNamee of the Church of the Madalene preached at the first ecumenical service to be held at a Roman Catholic parish in Tulsa. "There is nothing higher in the church than the ecumenical movement," McNamee assured his congregation, half of whom were Protestants. "The solution is the same as it has always been: one law, one Christ, one faith, one church, with many ways of expressing the truth of that faith."[31]

Of course, for some religious groups in Oklahoma, the promise of *Unitatis Redintegratio* was illusory. The largest Protestant grouping in Oklahoma—the constituent churches of the Southern Baptist Convention—called the council the "biggest publicity stunt" of the century and denounced those Protestant observers who had agreed to attend. Particularly galling for the Southern Baptists had been Pope John XXIII's invitation to the Protestant churches to "come home," since they had never considered themselves to have "left home" in the first place. Declared Southern Baptist Convention president Herschel Hobbs, pastor of First Baptist Church, Oklahoma City, in 1962: "Let us march together, but each in his own unit, and all of

---

29. Revd. Charles G. White to Victor Reed, January 11, 1965, Revd. William C. Garthoeffner to White, January 18, 1965, Sts. Peter and Paul Church, Hobart File, AAOC; Revd. Joseph C. Kolb to Victor Reed, February 25, 1965, Revd. William C. Garthoeffner to Kolb, February 27, 1965, Reed Papers. The bishop wanted to know if this was a liturgical ceremony for Methodists (or Protestants) or a nondenominational gathering organized with the theme of Church unity, since he could give permission only for the latter.

30. Revd. Francis A. Weiner to Revd. William C. Garthoeffner, April 26, 1965, Garthoeffner to Weiner, May 2, 1965, Reed Papers.

31. *Tulsa Daily World*, July 12, 1965.

us under the banner of Christ." In 1964, the Southern Baptist state general convention reaffirmed its opposition to ecumenical movements.[32] Another reminder of the limits of ecumenical witness was the response of Lawrence Mack of the Jehovah's Witnesses to an invitation to join an ecumenical breakfast in Frederick. "The proposed union of religions," Mack informed Father Robert Schlitt, "would be however a unity of headquarters only, not a unity in belief, preaching, and teaching. This we believe is true because religions are unwilling to give up traditions and to root out false doctrines."[33]

THE MARRIAGE QUESTION

A matter of increasing concern to many ecumenists was how to deal with the swelling number of marriages between Catholics and non-Catholics. Even in 1958, 386 of the 808 Catholic marriages conducted in Oklahoma were mixed marriages (47.8 percent), a figure that rose to 499 out of 908 in 1964 (55 percent) and a staggering 960 out of 1,330 in 1971 (72.2 percent).[34] The demands of the Church that such ceremonies be conducted only by a Catholic priest and that the non-Catholic spouse sign a pledge promising to raise any children as Catholics began increasingly to seem open to question as the council broke new ground on Catholic relations with non-Catholic religious bodies.

For young Catholics in particular, a refusal to countenance any recognition of their non-Catholic partner's religious beliefs in a marriage ceremony seemed curiously outdated. "It is our sincere hope," wrote Thomas Walker, while seeking permission to marry his Methodist fiancée in the Wesley Foundation Chapel at the University of Oklahoma in December 1966, "that these plans be in keeping with the ecumenical spirit and Christian love professed by the World's Bishops at the Second Vatican Council. Certainly it is in keeping with the spirit of open-mindedness and unity exemplified by this diocese in the precedent established by the Masses for Christian Unity that have commanded my active presence in recent years. . . . Too, the efforts put

32. *Tulsa Tribune*, October 6, 1962; *Tulsa Daily World*, October 21, 1962; *Oklahoma Courier*, November 27, 1964.

33. Lawrence Mack to Revd. Robert T. Schlitt, n.d., St. Helen's Church, Frederick File, AAOC.

34. *Official Catholic Directory* (hereafter *OCD*) (1958), 549; *OCD* (1964), 616; *OCD* (1971), 590.

forth by our own Bishop Reed in the area of inter-faith services is indicative of this new spirit of love that exists in the Church today."[35]

At the beginning of the decade, the issues in contention were generally uncomplicated, involving the regularization of non-Catholic marriages or participation in non-Catholic weddings. In a 1961 case in Durant, the Church authorities agreed to suspend the need for outside testimonials from both parties that they had been free to marry, because the parents of the Protestant spouse were "opposed to anything Catholic," and the girl feared that general knowledge that she had married a Catholic might cause her to lose her job as a schoolteacher.[36] Reed was also willing to show flexibility toward requests for minor participation in non-Catholic ceremonies. Vocalists from Chickasha and Enid were given permission to sing at the marriages of Protestant classmates, and the bishop also allowed nonparental relatives with whom a bride had lived before marriage to play roles such as that of candle lighter at a Protestant ceremony.[37] He was less willing to permit Catholics to serve as bridesmaids or groomsmen (the principal witnesses) at non-Catholic weddings, but he made exceptions in the case of "best friends," when a Catholic belonged to a predominantly non-Catholic family, or when a Catholic lived in a small town with just a few Catholics.[38] In 1961, he permitted a convert in Clinton whose non-Catholic cousin had been his best man to return the favor by serving as an usher at his cousin's wedding. In granting such requests, Reed acknowledged that the realities of Catholic life in rural Oklahoma required a degree of social adaptability.[39]

The bishop firmly opposed any use of nondenominational chapels for wedding ceremonies, however, even in a university setting. Father Marvin Leven of Tulsa was a particularly vocal advocate of flexibility on this point, offering the example of a Catholic varsity football player at the University of

35. Thomas J. Walker to Revd. William C. Garthoeffner, December 3, 1966, Reed Papers.

36. Revd. George Wagner to Revd. William C. Garthoeffner, January 30, 1961, Garthoeffner to Wagner, February 1, 1961, St. William's Church, Durant File, box 39.2, ADT.

37. Msgr. Gavan P. Monaghan to Victor Reed, May 27, 1958, Reed to Monaghan, May 28, 1958, Monaghan to Reed, July 9, 1958, Reed to Monaghan, July 11, 1958, Revd. John G. Titus to Reed, May 25, 1959, Reed to Titus, May 29, 1959, Holy Name of Jesus Church, Chickasha File, AAOC; Nancy Harding to Victor Reed, January 10, 1959, Reed to Harding, January 20, 1959, St. Francis Xavier Church, Enid File, AAOC.

38. Revd. William C. Garthoeffner to Revd. Forrest L. O'Brien, January 22, 1965, Reed Papers.

39. Revd. John L. Garvey to Victor Reed, June 22, 1961, Reed to Garvey, June 23, 1961, St. Mary's Church, Clinton File, AAOC.

Tulsa whose prospective bride showed every indication of ultimately converting. "It is a great opportunity," Leven declared in 1962, "to bring the Catholic Church before the eyes of the students of the University and elevate Catholic esteem above that of tolerated, second-class citizens."[40] Reed refused to
be drawn, however, and after consulting with several priests informed Leven
that he was not willing to create a precedent in this case.[41]

Change was nevertheless burgeoning in the Catholic intellectual community. In early 1963, the controversial theologian Hans Küng expressed his support for allowing Protestant ministers to conduct mixed marriages, prompting a flurry of outraged letters to the *Courier*. "Since Father Küng is getting
so modern," complained one writer, "why not let us practice birth control,
abortion, infanticide, these are all nice modern liberal things?"[42] Priests increasingly expressed puzzlement as to what stance they should adopt in dealing with potential mixed marriages.[43] In 1964, the pastor of Reed's former
parish in Stillwater reported the case of a Catholic girl at Oklahoma State
University engaged to a Lutheran who, though adamant about not converting, had been willing to attend the Catholic Inquirers' Class. The girl wished
to reciprocate by attending the Lutheran Inquirers' Class so that both would
better understand each other's faith prior to marriage. Was he to tell her that
she might not attend? The chancellor responded that while the pastor might
exercise his judgment in the individual case, the diocese would not grant
blanket permission for Catholics to attend Protestant instruction classes and
urged him to continue to emphasize to the non-Catholic partner the requirement to raise any children in the Catholic faith.[44]

Catholic priests increasingly faced requests for clergy from other religious
traditions to attend and participate in their wedding ceremonies. Father John

40. Revd. Marvin Leven to Victor Reed, February 24, 1962, Sts. Peter and Paul
Church, Tulsa File, box 16.1, ADT.

41. Notes of Revd. Charles H. Schettler, n.d. (March 1962), Sts. Peter and Paul Church,
Tulsa File, box 16.1.

42. *Oklahoma Courier*, April 5, 1963.

43. An article on mixed marriages by Bishop John B. Mussio of Steubenville (Ohio)
was cited by a priest in Vinita as being particularly confusing: "Just wonder whether 99% of
priests in the US should go back to the seminary for their theology or the Author of the article . . . Fr. Finney was defrocked for statements less than those made in this article. Confusion never leads to Unity?" Revd. Joseph A. Bigler, C.PP.S., to Revd. Charles H. Schettler, March 31, 1964, Holy Ghost Church, Vinita File, box 84.1, ADT. Bigler was actually
referring to Father Leonard Feeney, S. J., of Boston.

44. Revd. William Naberhaus to Revd. William C. Garthoeffner, December 4, 1964,
Garthoeffner to Naberhaus, December 7, 1964, Reed Papers.

Bloms at St. Joseph's parish, Ada, while not technically conducting a mixed marriage since the bride was a convert from Anglicanism, was aware that her family was deeply disturbed by her conversion. To address their concerns, Bloms requested that the Episcopal priest be present in the sanctuary and also be permitted to read either the exhortation or the instruction before marriage. Reed responded that while the priest might be present, he thought it premature in January 1965 to allow any reading of prayers.[45] A similar injunction was handed down to Father Joseph Kolb of Sacred Heart parish, Sapulpa, for the marriage of a Greek Orthodox man and a Catholic woman. While a Syrian Orthodox priest was allowed to be present for the wedding, he could administer a blessing to the couple only after the Catholic ceremony had been concluded.[46]

Although Reed ultimately abandoned his opposition to nondenominational chapels, he made it clear that non-Catholic churches were still off-limits. In 1964, he approved the chapel at Tulsa University—which he had refused to Marvin Leven two years previously—for the wedding of two Tulsa University students, although he told the priest to keep the ceremony as quiet as possible.[47] The following year, the bishop was confronted with the case of a Methodist woman who intended to convert to Catholicism after her marriage, but whose mother wished her to be married in the Methodist Student Chapel with her grandfather—a Methodist minister—taking part in the service. Reed refused the plea for the Methodist chapel but suggested that a nondenominational one could be used. He also indicated that the grandfather could read a prayer or invoke a blessing, but not as part of the exchange of vows.[48] Eighteen months later, he informed Thomas Walker of the University of Oklahoma that he also must use a nondenominational chapel, not the Wesley Foundation Chapel.[49] The only case in which the bishop went on record in favor of a Protestant chapel as a wedding site was in regard to the

---

45. Revd. John N. Bloms to Revd. William C. Garthoeffner, n.d., Garthoeffner to Bloms, January 25, 1965, Reed Papers.

46. Revd. Joseph C. Kolb to Victor Reed, February 25, 1965, Revd. William C. Garthoeffner to Kolb, February 27, 1965, Reed Papers.

47. The girl's parents were Baptists and strongly opposed to a wedding in a Catholic church. Revd. John W. Lundberg to Victor Reed, July 25, 1964, Revd. William C. Garthoeffner to Lundberg, July 29, 1964, Sts. Peter and Paul Church, Tulsa File, box 16.1.

48. Revd. Charles J. Swett to Victor Reed, June 14, 1965, Revd. William C. Garthoeffner to Swett, June 21, 1965, Reed Papers.

49. Revd. William C. Garthoeffner to Thomas J. Walker, December 5, 1966, Reed Papers.

marriage of a Jewish man and a Catholic woman in 1967. The couple had proposed the Holiday Inn as a "neutral" venue, which the bishop considered to be too secular and nonreligious. "[T]he bishop," declared the chancellor, "is more inclined to permit the use of a Protestant Church in order to impress upon the couple the religious nature of marriage."[50]

Attempts to insinuate a Protestant minister into the formal part of the marriage ceremony also met with firm episcopal rebuff. In January 1969, Father Forrest O'Brien of St. Eugene's parish, Weatherford, requested permission for wedding ceremonies for a Catholic man and a Methodist woman to be held in both churches in order to placate the girl's parents. "I don't feel there will be any scandal in this community by such an arrangement," he opined. "In fact I think it will cause much good will." The bishop made it clear that ecumenism had its limits: "I cannot allow this, as the marriage of a Catholic by a minister is forbidden." The chancellor sought to soften the blow by suggesting that the couple might go to the Methodist church for a blessing after the ceremony, but one thing was clear: there could be no renewal of marriage vows.[51] In taking such a stance, Reed upheld the position confirmed by the 1966 Instruction on Mixed Marriages issued by the Congregation of the Doctrine of the Faith in Rome, which disappointed many ecumenists by reiterating the obligations for baptizing and raising children of such marriages as Catholics and refusing to recognize marriages contracted outside the Catholic Church as valid, a stance that seemed curiously at variance with the Second Vatican Council's treatment of the "separated brethren" elsewhere.[52]

In 1970, Monsignor Paul Van Dorpe, the former head of the diocesan marriage tribunal, nevertheless vigorously argued for maximum flexibility, suggesting that the bishop should give priests general permission to marry Catholic couples in Protestant churches and allow Protestant ministers to conduct mixed marriages in the presence of a Catholic priest, who could perform the required blessings, as long as dispensation, confession, and High Mass had already taken place. "The publicity would be a pastoral boon," Van Dorpe insisted, "because local papers would pick it up and the permission coming from the Bishop and extending everywhere, would eliminate rash

50. Revd. Robert L. Siebs to Revd. Charles H. Schettler, November 28, 1967, Schettler to Siebs, November 29, 1967, St. John's Church, Bartlesville File, box 23.1, ADT.

51. Revd. Forrest L. O'Brien to Victor Reed, January 17, 1966, Revd. William C. Gathoeffner to O'Brien, January 20, 1966, Reed Papers.

52. Brown, *The Ecumenical Revolution*, 284–85.

judgments, criticisms, confusion and strife amongst the flock vis-à-vis their pastors. In fact it would promote ecumenism in a most touchy matter and help the people of God to think, speak and act more civilly with Protestant friends in social matters."[53]

ECUMENICAL RELATIONS AFTER 1965

As the deliberations of the Second Vatican Council faded into history, it became clear that some in Oklahoma's Catholic community viewed its declarations on ecumenism as validating a considerable broadening of the Church's sacramental function. When a woman at St. Matthew's Episcopal Church in Enid, married to a Catholic parishioner at St. Francis Xavier Church, requested a joint baptismal ceremony for her baby in October 1966, Father Garthoeffner was obliged to make it clear that while a vested Episcopal priest might be present and give a blessing before and after the ceremony, the baptism itself must be performed by a Catholic priest, although he did concede that a more liberal policy might eventually come to pass. "The whole ceremony, intricately [*sic*], should be performed by the Catholic priest," the chancellor insisted. "Perhaps as we progress towards unity, the Episcopal priest could in such instances be invited to celebrate some part of the official ceremony—but not now."[54]

On the administration of Communion, too, Reed remained adamant, despite evidence that some of his clergy would have welcomed greater flexibility. In November 1966, Father Frank Helderle of St. Williams's parish in Durant, sought to give Communion to all those present at the midnight Mass in Tishomingo, three quarters of whom would be non-Catholics. Many would choose not to avail themselves of the opportunity, he conceded, but it would foster goodwill. The bishop refused his request.[55]

53. Msgr. Paul M. Van Dorpe to Victor Reed, January 23, 1970, St. Anthony of Padua Church, Okeene File, AAOC.

54. Revd. J. Frank Crow to Bp. Chilton Powell, October 10, 1966, Revd. Frederick F. Krueger to Revd. William C. Garthoeffner, October 14, 1966, Garthoeffner to Krueger, October 18, 1966, Reed Papers. Powell was the Episcopal bishop of Oklahoma.

55. Revd. Frank Helderle to Msgr. Raymond Harkin, November 28, 1966, Revd. William C. Garthoeffner to Helderle, December 3, 1966, Reed Papers. See also Revd. John Bloms to Reed, n.d. (prob. 1967), Reed Papers. On Protestant communicants at St. Joseph's, Ada, Bloms wrote: "Those who have asked me, I have refused, trying to explain to them why, but with the hope that some day we will be able to be thus fully united with Christ. Methodists, Presbyterians and Episcopalians find this refusal hard to take, but some continue to worship with us regularly."

A more controversial incident took place on September 2, 1967 at a wedding at St. Patrick's parish in Oklahoma City, where the assistant, Father Patrick Quirk, having been refused permission to give Communion to the non-Catholic bridegroom, held a "simultaneous dual Communion service" with the Reverend Neil Lindley of First Christian Church. Lindley performed the exchange of rings and gave Communion to non-Catholics, while Quirk performed the exchange of vows (as required by canon law) and gave Communion only to Catholics. Although technically meeting the requirements laid down by the chancery, no permission had been sought for the Protestant minister's participation, and Reed found himself obliged to explain the episode to Archbishop Egidio Vagnozzi, the apostolic delegate in Washington.[56] Under the circumstances, Father Quirk's action seemed unlikely to reassure conservative Catholics about reformers' respect for the principle of evolutionary change in ecumenical relations.

If sacramental worship remained inviolable, ecumenical enthusiasts found ways in which to make combined worship more of a reality. In Oklahoma City, the local Catholic churches sponsored the Prince of Peace Pageant—a series of tableaux on the Old Testament prophecies of the Incarnation and the New Testament accounts of the birth of Christ, with sung psalms and hymns—which drew an audience of around four thousand in 1964 and 1965. While many non-Catholics refused to join in the singing of the *Ave Maria,* they raised no objection to the *Magnificat.* Catholic churches in Oklahoma City and Tulsa participated in a summer worship series, in the course of which different churches took it in turns to be responsible for a Sunday evening service (without Communion) for an entire community. Tulsa's Church of the Madalene went even further by inviting five Protestant ministers to preach Bible vigils as Lenten devotions.[57] Another innovation was an ecumenical Lenten penance vigil with the Episcopalians of Chickasha in 1970 that included common prayer, Scripture readings, a homily, and general examination of conscience. This was followed by Confession for each denominational group conducted by their its priest.[58]

56. Victor Reed to Msgr. Franco Brambilla, September 14, 1967, Reed Papers.
57. "Report to the Bishop on Ecumenical Endeavors in the Diocese of Oklahoma City–Tulsa," n.d. (prob. 1965), Reed Papers.
58. Notes of Revd. Charles H. Schettler, March 16, 1970, Holy Name of Jesus Church, Chickasha File, AAOC. Zins already planned for Catholics and Episcopalians to gather after their respective Holy Thursday services for a Passover-style meal in the Catholic parish hall.

Restrictions on nondenominational worship, however, remained in place. Reed prohibited the participation of Father Wilbur Moore of Alva in a one-day ashram—a supposedly nondenominational exercise designed by E. Stanley Jones, which endeavored, through small discussion groups, to make real the biblical injunctions "Jesus is Lord" and "The Word was made Flesh." Such exercises were, the bishop concluded, too "distinctive and particular" to be considered truly nondenominational.[59] At Immaculate Conception parish in Tulsa, Father Henry Kelly was reminded that a community Thanksgiving service must be clearly nondenominational, without Catholic or Protestant overtones.[60] When Father Raymond Berthiaume—who had responsibility within his ministerial alliance for the 1967 Week of Prayer for Christian Unity—sought permission for a non-Catholic minister to perform the Scripture readings at the votive Mass for Christian Unity in Idabel, he was told that it would be better for him to preach before or after the Mass.[61]

Cooperation at the parish level was not restricted to worship. An ecumenical pamphlet produced by a parish in Hennessey on the 450th anniversary of the Reformation cited the views of various Catholic and Protestant theologians to demonstrate how narrow the gap between Protestants and Catholics had become in the preceding decade.[62] The following year, Clarence Knippa, pastor of Grace Lutheran Church in Tulsa, sent Reed a check for $300, explaining that St. Francis Xavier parish had given his congregation space for fourteen weeks after a fire swept through their building. "Father Wrigley and his parishioners responded to our need in Christian love," he wrote. "This has left its mark on us. We want to respond to the need of others. We read of the mission in Guatemala and enclose a contribution."[63]

Occasionally, the assistance offered could be sacramental. In 1968, the priest at Okmulgee reported the presence of a Greek Orthodox family in the town at a time when the Orthodox church in Tulsa, already twenty-five

59. Revd. Wilbur E. Moore to Revd. William C. Garthoeffner, March 17, 1966, Garthoeffner to Moore, March 21, 1966, Reed Papers.

60. Revd. William C. Garthoeffner to Revd. Henry Kelly, November 7, 1966, Immaculate Conception Church, Tulsa File, box 4.1, ADT.

61. For a Protestant minister to read the lessons, Father Garthoeffner explained, would be *communicatio in sacris* (taking an active role in a Catholic liturgical service). Revd. Raymond Berthiaume to Victor Reed, January 11, 1967, Revd. William C. Garthoeffner to Berthiaume, January 13, 1967, St. Francis de Sales Church, Idabel File, box 50.1, ADT.

62. Ecumenical booklet, November 1967, St. Joseph's Church, Hennessey File, AAOC.

63. Revd. Clarence W. Knippa to Victor Reed, May 8, 1968, Reed to Knippa, June 3, 1968, St. Francis Xavier Church, Tulsa File, box 11.1, ADT.

miles removed from Okmulgee, had no incumbent. Chancery officials told him that under the council's Decree on the Eastern Churches, he was free to offer them the sacraments if they requested them and if no Orthodox priest was available.[64] Some priests were even willing to involve non-Catholics in issues of internal Church controversy. Father Berthiaume of Idabel, a vocal critic of the papal encyclical *Humanae Vitae*, held a special meeting in his rectory to draft a letter of protest to the bishop that included eight married Catholics, a Presbyterian, an Episcopalian, and two Buddhists.[65]

Beyond the parish level, many Oklahoma Catholics displayed a willingness to participate in statewide and national initiatives. A precedent had already been set in St. Louis, where Cardinal Joseph Ritter had established an ecumenical commission in 1964. This body not only authorized local priests to join ministerial alliances but also gave them discretion to administer the sacraments of confession, Communion and anointing to non-Catholics, where charity demanded it. Ritter encouraged the explanation of other faith traditions in parish education programs and publicly expressed the view that, with so many unchurched in the United States, practicing members of other Christian churches should not be considered a high priority for proselytizing.[66]

In 1966, the National Council of Churches (NCC) and the Catholic Bishops' Commission on Ecumenical Affairs formed a joint working group, and Father David Bowman became an associate director of Faith and Order studies at the NCC and its first Catholic employee. Trends in Unity—an ecumenical information service—was launched in 1967, and by the end of that year Catholic parishes in thirty cities had affiliated with the NCC, the most publicized case being the affiliation of the Archdiocese of Santa Fe with the New Mexico Council of Churches. Numerous "living room dialogues" and interparish meetings also took place during the late 1960s, in many of which the Christian Family Movement played a prominent role.[67]

64. Revd. Gregory Lahay, C.SS.R., to Revd. Charles H. Schettler, November 4, 1968, Schettler to Lahay, November 5, 1968, St. Anthony's Church, Okmulgee File, box 63.1. A 1964 interview with the Orthodox priest in Oklahoma City revealed that many Orthodox viewed differences with Rome as juridical rather than theological and that they expected future unity to derive not from incorporation but from Rome's recognition of their equal status. *Oklahoma Courier*, January 17, 1964.

65. Glenmary Missioner Newsletter, October 26, 1968, St. Francis de Sales Church, Idabel, box 50.1.

66. Faherty, *Dream by the River*, 206–8.

67. Curry, *Protestant-Catholic Relations*, 83–85; Cavert, *The American Churches in the Ecumenical Movement*, 235–39; Burns, *Disturbing the Peace*, 149–56.

Reed certainly continued to treat the Oklahoma Council of Churches as an ally. In March 1966, he reminded a meeting in Ponca City that any effective dialogue required a readiness to admit faults not only personally but also on behalf of one's denomination, as Pope Paul VI was then attempting to do.[68] When the former diocesan seminary was rededicated as the Center for Christian Renewal in September 1967, the list of invitees included representatives of fifteen denominations, including groups not known for their ecumenical outlook, such as the Church of God, the Church of the Nazarene, the Pentecostal Holiness Church, and the Southern Baptist Convention. Also invited was the nation's most famous Pentecostal preacher, Oral Roberts, whom Reed had known in the 1950s while he was rector of Holy Family Cathedral.[69] The bishop remained particularly close to certain individuals. A close acquaintance of Episcopal bishop Chilton Powell, Reed attended the consecration of Powell's suffragan, Frederick Putnam, in 1963.[70] Still, not everyone in the diocese agreed that Reed had gone to the limit. "I feel," declared Father Stephen Wells in March 1969, "that the diocesan response to the overtures of the State Council of Churches has been churlish and contrary to the spirit of ecumenism."[71]

One particular ecumenical association developed at the Second Vatican Council was Reed's friendship with the Methodist theologian Albert Outler. In January 1964, their paths had crossed again when Outler was speaking in Tulsa on a day when Reed was also in town. Soon after, when a parish in Muskogee talked of bringing Bishop Fulton Sheen to speak at a fund-raiser, Reed demurred. "I think," he told the pastor, "if they wish to sponsor such a speech, they should ask someone who would have a real 'ecumenical' impact on the community—it would not necessarily have to be a Catholic. Dr. Outler of SMU comes to mind."[72]

68. *Oklahoma Courier*, March 18, 1966.

69. Revd. Daniel Cawthon to "Dear Reverend," August 9, 1967, Reed Papers.

70. *Oklahoma Courier*, May 24, 1963. Putnam was one of the first people to call to express his condolences after Reed's death. Schettler, interview.

71. Revd. Stephen W. Wells to Victor Reed, March 28, 1969, Reed Papers.

72. *Oklahoma Courier*, January 24, 1964. The Outler recommendation is interesting because there are replies from Reed dated March 24 and March 25 that are duplicates except for the final sentence. After noting that Sheen was much involved with his new duties as bishop and that he had visited the state several years ago, the March 25 reply concludes as above, while that of March 24 concludes: "I think that, if they want to sponsor such a speaker, they should ask someone who appears to have a future." Revd. Elmer C. Schwarz to Victor Reed, March 14, 1967, Reed to Schwarz, March 24, March 25, 1967, Assumption Church, Muskogee File, box 58.1, ADT.

Some of the bishop's clergy took an even more hands-on approach to the ecumenical movement, seeing the work of the World Council of Churches as an essential contribution to ecumenical understanding. In 1968, Father John McNamee, associate pastor of St. Pius X, Tulsa, and nephew of the ecumenical activist James McNamee, joined a Presbyterian and an Episcopalian as delegates from Oklahoma to the World Council of Churches meeting in Uppsala in Sweden. Born in Ireland, McNamee received a degree from the University of Louvain and from 1964 to 1967 served in Midwest City, where he was secretary and president of the local ministerial alliance.[73] Members of the diocesan liturgical commission declared satisfaction that the 1969 meeting of the Southwest Liturgical Conference in Tulsa coincided with a meeting of the executive board of the World Council of Churches and expressed the hope that joint activities—particularly an interfaith worship service—would be possible.[74]

Many ecumenical initiatives emerged in university settings, hardly surprising when one considers that students and faculty were more likely to be exposed to discussion of ecumenism and its consequences than the general population. In 1962, Father Ernest Flusche received permission for the Newman center at the University of Oklahoma to host doctrinal presentations by local Lutheran, Methodist, Baptist, Episcopalian, and Presbyterian ministers on five successive Sundays. This marked the start of a joint program of Continuing Christian Education that saw ties established between Catholic youth groups and Newman Society affiliates at Oklahoma's public universities and their Protestant counterparts, including the transdenominational Town and Country Institute at Phillips University in Enid.[75]

Cooperation between Catholic priests and ministers of other denominations also saw a healthy improvement. At Oklahoma State University, Father Clement Pribil had worked with the Protestant chaplains to raise the status of the religion department and the number of courses that it offered which could be taken for credit. When the local Baptist minister objected to the changes because they limited his ability to proselytize in class, Pribil formed a common front with Protestant clerics to resist any attempts to return to

73. *Tulsa Tribune*, June 22, 1968.

74. Minutes of Diocesan Liturgical Commission, September 24, 1968, Reed Papers.

75. Revd. Ernest A. Flusche to Victor Reed, February 15, 1962, St. Thomas More Church, Norman File, AAOC; "Report to the Bishop on Ecumenical Endeavors in the Diocese of Oklahoma City–Tulsa," n.d. (prob. 1965), Revd. Joseph D. Dillon to Victor Reed, May 25, 1966, Reed Papers.

the status quo ante.[76] Enough common ground existed among ministers in Miami to form a joint campus ministry for the local college in 1968. Involving local Methodist, Catholic, Christian, Episcopal, Missouri Synod Lutheran, and United Presbyterian churches of the town, the governing board had three lay representatives from each participating church. The churches paid dues based on the ratio of students affiliated with their denomination to the total number of students at the college.[77]

Interfaith adult religious education had become a reality in Oklahoma City and Tulsa by the late 1960s, while programs for high school students existed in Sulphur, Ponca City, and Enid. In Marshall, members of St. Camillus parish joined with the Christian Church, the Methodists, and the United Church of Christ to form an ecumenical council, with representatives from each church, to oversee religious education, evaluate programs, and coordinate the selection of teachers, facilities, and curriculum materials. A similar vacation school was organized in Norman by local Catholics, Episcopalians, Presbyterians, and members of the Christian Church in 1968, which used a mixture of generic Protestant, Methodist, and Catholic teaching materials to address the theme "Being Human in a Broken World."[78]

The ultimate achievement in ecumenical relations, of course, was the establishment of ecumenical parishes—shared worship spaces within which different denominational traditions could begin to experience the Christian unity that all desired.[79] In March 1964, the Catholic Archdiocese of Baltimore had set a precedent by working with the National Council of Churches on a cooperative Christian ministry in the "new town" of Columbia, Maryland. Organized out of a centrally located complex, this ministry was owned by a

76. Revd. Clement E. Pribil to Revd. William C. Garthoeffner, April 14, 1965, St. John University Church, Stillwater File, box 81.1, ADT.

77. By-Laws of Norse Campus Ministry Inc., June 10, 1968, Articles of incorporation of Norse Campus Ministry Inc., June 28, 1968, Sacred Heart Church, Miami File, box 57.1, ADT.

78. "Report of the Committee on Ecumenism," n.d. (prob. 1969), "Marshall Oklahoma Ecumenical Programming," *Office of Religious Education Newsletter*, n.d., Reed Papers; *Oklahoma Courier*, June 14, 1968.

79. Reed had arguably brought this issue to the fore in 1965 when he asked the ecumenical commission of the National Catholic Welfare Conference if it might be acceptable to open the Catholic cemetery at Shawnee to non-Catholics. While citing the practical issue of the small number of Catholic burials and the problems of upkeep of a large cemetery, the bishop also noted that it might improve relations with the Protestant community. No record of the NCWC's response has been located. Victor Reed to Msgr. William W. Baum, April 12, 1965, Reed Papers.

nonprofit cooperative formed by the participating denominations. As part of the agreement, the Church agreed not to establish a parochial school—symbol of Catholic separatism—in Columbia. Two years later, Tulsa Catholics attended a discussion session, addressed by a Presbyterian pastor, about the proposed St. Mark's Ecumenical Church in Kansas City, Missouri, which was to be built and run jointly by the Catholic, Presbyterian, Congregational, and Episcopal communities in an inner-city poverty pocket containing fifteen thousand African Americans.[80]

Oklahoma Catholics expressed interest in such initiatives. In 1966, a member of the Madalene suggested erecting a "unity church," which could serve a variety of congregations, possibly even Jewish ones.[81] One year later, the Glenmary Missioners proposed the establishment of an "ecumenical chapel," built with funds from cooperating churches and available to Catholic and Protestant groups.[82] In November 1968, Father David Monahan floated the idea that Bishop McGuinness High School should be transformed into an ecumenical education center, operated jointly by the various Christian communities in the city, with a mixture of shared and separate religious education classes and worship services.[83] A similar initiative came from Father Frank Wrigley who, after consultation with the Presbyterians, Methodists, Episcopalians, and Disciples of Christ, sought to establish a nonterritorial ecumenical parish in Norman.[84]

While none of these proposals ever came to anything, one that did achieve some results was a cooperative ministry in Valliant, twenty miles west of Idabel, in the extreme southeast corner of the state, organized to serve the families of construction workers for—and later employees of—a new paper mill. A joint endeavor involving Catholics, Methodists, Presbyterians, Episcopalians, and the Christian Church, the Valliant Cooperative Ministry invited applications for a post that involved making visitations and organizing youth ministry and social service projects, which could be filled by a seminarian, ordained clergyman, deacon, or apostolic layman. Such a person, according to the job description, should be adaptable, devout, have some knowledge of the Bible Belt, dress conservatively, and own his own car.[85]

80. Spalding, *The Premier See*, 419; *Oklahoma Courier*, November 4, 1966.

81. John V. Neff to Victor Reed, September 29, 1966, Reed Papers.

82. Revd. Raymond Berthiaume to Victor Reed, April 17, 1967, Tentative Five-Year Plan for the Church in McCurtain County, Oklahoma, April 17, 1967, Reed Papers.

83. Revd. David Monahan to Victor Reed, November 19, 1968, Reed Papers.

84. Revd. Frank Wrigley to Victor Reed, April 22, 1971, Reed Papers.

85. Revd.. Raymond Berthiaume to "Whom It May Concern," December 14, 1970, St. Francis de Sales Church, Idabel File, box 50.1.

Mainline Protestants responded to such initiatives with incredulous delight. As early as 1964, the pastor of Oklahoma City's Westminster Presbyterian Church described a community worship service at First Christian Church conducted by the clergy of St. Patrick's Catholic Church as a "source of spiritual blessing to those who were there."[86] Ralph Cottier of Tulsa, chairman of the Committee on Ecumenical Relations of the United Presbyterian Synod of Oklahoma-Arkansas, praised Bishop Reed in 1965 for allowing Protestants and Catholics to sing and kneel in prayer together, a move that had, on a personal level, improved relations with his Catholic brother and sister-in-law. Cottier later invited Father William Garthoeffner to address the synod on ecumenism.[87]

Oklahoma's Episcopalians were equally fulsome in their praise. In 1966, a number of Episcopal clergy expressed gratitude for Reed's ecumenical endeavors and also his willingness to allow his priests the freedom to express their personal convictions on pressing social and political issues.[88] John Wagner, an Episcopal lay observer at the 1970 diocesan convention, went even further. "I told Fr. Garthoeffner," he wrote to Reed, "that if the reason for being of the Episcopal Church was to expound the Gospel within a reformed, biblical Catholicism, then the life of the Catholic Church in Oklahoma now makes Anglicanism superfluous."[89]

If Protestants welcomed ecumenical cooperation, some in the Catholic community continued to entertain reservations. Was there no worthy Catholic hymn? a Catholic layman demanded after Martin Luther's *Ein feste Burg* served as the closing hymn for the dedication of the new church building in Owasso in 1965. (The bishop told him that it simply represented the use of "appropriate means to encourage more friendly relations between Christians.")[90] An equally skeptical priest expressed his doubts about participating in a panel discussion on the nature of belief with several of Miami's Protestant ministers. He thought that it might "bring us socially closer, but little else," and Father William Garthoeffner had to struggle to convince him to keep an open mind.[91]

86. Revd. G. Raymond Campbell to Victor Reed, August 24, 1964, St. Patrick's Church, Oklahoma City File, AAOC.

87. Ralph J. Cottier to Victor Reed, July 1, 1965, Cottier to Revd. William C. Garthoeffner, September 24, 1965, Reed Papers.

88. Bennett H. Barnes to Victor Reed, May 9, 1966, Reed Papers.

89. John E. Wagner to Victor Reed, April 6, 1970, Reed Papers.

90. John J. O'Leary to Victor Reed, August 10, 1965, Reed to O'Leary, August 14, 1965, St. Therese's Church (Little Flower), Collinsville File, box 33.1.

91. Revd. Francis A. Weiner to Revd. William C. Garthoeffner, November 16, 1965,

That ecumenical cooperation could have negative theological implications was demonstrated by Father John O'Brien of St. Rose of Lima parish, when he complained about the participation of a number of Catholic youths in a play put on by a Protestant church in Perry: "The theme of the thing is essentially a glorification of Protestantism—that a man can reach great heights of personal integrity (they rarely call it sanctity) merely by his accepting Christ as his personal Savior, and without any benefit from what we believe are the Fountains Of Grace, the Sacraments, especially the Eucharist, and the mediatorship of Christ's priesthood. I'm all for Ecumenism, within the demarcation limits set down by Revealed Truth and Defined doctrine, but I wonder about something like this."[92] Conservative hostility to the diocesan newspaper could also embody a sort of inverted ecumenism. "I even find the periodical 'Decision,' a Billy Graham publication, incomparably superior to our own local 'religious' paper," declared Father Graham Walters of St. Francis of Assisi parish in Oklahoma City in 1967. "At least I find in it something inspirational and truly religious."[93]

CONCLUSION

The story of Catholic ecumenical endeavor in Oklahoma illustrates how American Catholics responded to the established ecumenical movement during the 1960s. While priests played an important role in ecumenism, it is also clear that younger educated Catholics sought to apply the ecumenical principles of Vatican II more extensively than their parents or grandparents might have desired. The transformation of the liturgy and the development of new ecumenical understanding were related phenomena. American Catholics showed themselves to be open to a wide range of ecumenical initiatives, with certain priests essentially willing to embrace the Protestant ecumenical ideal wholesale. In Oklahoma, this phenomenon was aided by the fact that the liturgical tradition of the state's Episcopalians was Anglo-Catholic and so

Garthoeffner to Weiner, November 19, 1965, Reed Papers. Garthoeffner testified that he had enjoyed speaking at a Presbyterian gathering, even though it had meant for him two hours without a cigarette. "I think," he concluded, "they are going to have to do something about this smoking problem if the Ecumenical Movement is to get very far."

92. Revd. John L. O'Brien to Revd. William C. Garthoeffner, July 29, 1965, Garthoeffner to O'Brien, July 30, 1965, Reed Papers. Garthoeffner replied that Reed didn't want the project condemned outright but he did want parishioners to raise any proposed ecumenical project with their pastor before undertaking it.

93. Revd. Graham L. Walters to Victor Reed, November 26, 1967, Reed Papers.

the apparent doctrinal differences were minimal, but the Church also cultivated positive relationships with Methodists and Presbyterians.

Oklahoma Catholics were at the cutting edge of the ecumenical revolution and disinclined to let the gains of the council be lost. Nevertheless, on
the ecumenical issue, their bishop, while open to innovation, fell far short of
being a flaming radical. For Victor Reed, common dialogue and, above all,
common action, ranked much higher than common worship. In September
1970, he urged Father Paul Mollan of St. Eugene's parish in Oklahoma City
to persuade his parishioners to contribute to the Agency for Church Cooperative Ministry, despite the parish's shortage of funds. "When Baptists and
Catholics seek to cooperate in a common social effort," the bishop concluded, "it's worth stretching to make it a success."[94]

94. Victor Reed to Revd. Paul F. Mollan, September 9, 1970, Reed Papers.

chapter 8

A Colorblind Church

The Search for Racial Equality

Therefore, although rightful differences exist between men, the equal dignity of persons demands that a more humane and just condition of life be brought about. For excessive economic and social differences between the members of the one human family or population groups cause scandal, and militate against social justice, equity, the dignity of the human person, as well as social and international peace. Human institutions, both private and public, must labor to minister to the dignity and purpose of man. At the same time let them put up a stubborn fight against any kind of slavery, whether social or political, and safeguard the basic rights of man under every political system. Indeed human institutions themselves must be accommodated by degrees to the highest of all realities, spiritual ones, even though meanwhile, a long enough time will be required before they arrive at the desired goal.

Second Vatican Council, Pastoral Constitution on the Church in the Modern World, *Gaudium et Spes*, December 7, 1965

Nothing defined America in the 1960s more completely than the national campaign for black civil rights. As spokesman for the body of black Protestant religious leaders, Dr. Martin Luther King Jr. impressed upon two presidents and the wider American public the necessity of completing the work of black emancipation that had begun in 1863. Defying the notion of "separate but equal" that pervaded southern society and the less visible residential segregation that characterized other parts of the nation, King articulated a strategy that would culminate in the passage of congressional legislation enforcing both the right to vote and the right to enjoy access to public accommodations, regardless of race. The triumphs of the mid-1960s, however, would swiftly degenerate into chaos, as black, Hispanic, and Native American ethnocentric activists began to articulate a separatist agenda. By 1968, even some of the participants in the first phase of the civil rights revolution had begun to voice misgivings.[1]

American Catholics were in an awkward position. The era of the "national parish," which had lent stability to ethnic Catholic neighborhoods between 1870 and 1940, had been intended to facilitate their transition to a more universal expression of the Catholic faith, but it had also fostered the belief that racial separation promoted greater religious harmony. As Catholics migrated to the suburbs in the 1940s and 1950s, however, the peculiar ethnic Catholic practices that had characterized religious life in the inner city showed little sign of accompanying them. Increasingly, white middle-class Catholics felt united in a Communion that transcended ethnic origin. Such was not the case when it came to dealing with racial minorities who had embraced the Catholic faith. In the case of Native Americans, Mexican Americans, and especially African Americans, the old idea of the national parish endured into the 1950s. Minority Catholics might be equal in theory, but they remained separate in practice.[2]

With the encouragement of early racial progressives like Father John La-Farge—a key figure in the Catholic Interracial Council (CIC)—efforts were made during the 1940s to end the taint of institutional racism that seemed to be present in American Catholicism. In 1947, the newly appointed archbishop of St. Louis, Joseph Ritter, integrated the city's Catholic school system and warned laymen who threatened to institute legal proceedings against him that they risked excommunication. Where Ritter led, others followed, though many of his episcopal colleagues were by no means as racially progressive. In Chicago, Father Daniel Cantwell opposed restrictive housing covenants and organized a branch of the CIC in 1945, bringing together Catholic Church members with civil rights activists. The Chicago CIC spon-

---

1. Branch, *Pillar of Fire*; Findlay, *Church People in the Struggle*; Weisbrot, *Freedom Bound*; Branch, *Parting the Waters*.

2. For a discussion of the racial implications of the Catholic parochial system before 1950, see McGreevey, *Parish Boundaries*, 29–53. "Superimposed upon the Catholic racialist model of a series of geographically and culturally distinct parish neighborhoods," writes McGreevey, "was an alternative system of racial organization. Deeply embedded within the America that Catholic immigrants wished to claim as their own, this racial system emphasized distinctions between 'black' and 'white'" (33–34).

sored eligible black children for Catholic high schools, organized school interracial days, and sent investigators into communities affected by racial tension. In 1952, it hired its first black director.[3]

During the 1950s, some suburban Catholics ceased to regard integration solely as an act pursued by the secular state to redress a fundamental imbalance in the personal freedoms of racial minorities. They came to understand it as a step in the process of making real the theology of the Mystical Body of Christ, expressed in the 1943 encyclical of Pope Pius XII and put into practice by the practitioners of Catholic Action. In 1953, the Christian Family Movement helped integrate the Catholic schools of the Archdiocese of San Antonio (one year before the Catholic schools in Oklahoma), and Archbishop Joseph Rummel, the architect of integration in the Archdiocese of New Orleans, was the keynote speaker at the 1956 CFM national convention.[4] San Antonio's archbishop, Robert Lucey, established one of the first CIC chapters in the Southwest and publicly condemned segregated trade unions and other forms of institutionalized discrimination. In Chicago, the new archbishop, Albert Meyer, launched an open attack on housing segregation in 1959 and the following year required his clergy to adopt a racially neutral stance in all parochial and diocesan institutions. The National Catholic Conference for Interracial Justice was established at a meeting at Chicago's Loyola University in 1958; and in 1960, John McDermott, a product of Catholic Action, became director of the Chicago CIC, shifting its focus from education to direct action.[5] Even bishops with a later reputation for conservatism took a public stand. "Racism," the archbishop of Washington, Patrick O'Boyle, warned at the Second Vatican Council, "which, in various forms and varying degrees, is to be found in almost every region of the world, is not merely a social or cultural or political problem. It is, first and foremost, a moral and religious problem. And one of staggering proportions."[6]

3. McGreevey, *Parish Boundaries*, 55–110; Faherty, *Dream by the River*, 187–88; Avella, *This Confident Church*, 189–96, 289–97.

4. Burns, *Disturbing the Peace*, 119–24. On Rummel's efforts at desegregation in New Orleans, see Friedland, *Lift Up Your Voice Like a Trumpet*, 39-44.

5. Avella, *This Confident Church*, 289–308; Bronder, *Social Justice and Church Authority*, 68–70.

6. Yzermans, *American Participation in the Second Vatican Council*, 240.

FIRST STEPS IN THE CIVIL RIGHTS DEBATE

Oklahoma's small African American community and the even smaller number of black Catholics lived mostly in urban settings. Battle had been joined as early as the late 1940s, when a younger generation of African Americans challenged the social mores that had prevailed since statehood in 1907. In seeking graduate education at the University of Oklahoma rather than accepting a tuition grant to an out-of-state university, black students like Ada Sipuel and George McLaurin brought unwelcome attention to Oklahoma's stance on segregated education. In 1950, the McLaurin case reached the Supreme Court, where it later formed one of the precedents for *Brown v. Board of Education* (1954). In the wake of that decision, Governor Raymond Gary urged all Oklahomans to accept integration of the public school system, warning school districts that to resist would mean the loss of state funds.[7]

That same year, Bishop McGuinness formally prohibited segregation in the state's Catholic schools.[8] Black Catholic parishes like St. Augustine's parish in Tulsa also made strenuous efforts to serve the African American community. In 1959, Father John Strmiska of the Holy Ghost Fathers invited Bishop Reed to address the fifth annual dinner of the Tulsa Urban League, the same year that his parish completed a recreation center that quickly became the talk of the black community and prompted the nearby Baptist and Episcopal churches to start building facilities of their own.[9]

Many white Catholics, however, remained oblivious to the color line that separated black majority parishes from their white counterparts and critics of the Church detected more than a whiff of hypocrisy in its protestations of racial equality.[10] In April 1961, the *Oklahoma Eagle* accused Tulsa priests of falling short of their Oklahoma City counterparts on this score. "They observe the ugly practice of discrimination within their own institutions," the

7. Morgan and Morgan, *Oklahoma*, 138–43. As a result of historical factors pertaining to the origins of Oklahoma itself, there are a number of all-black or mostly black towns in the state.

8. *Southwest Courier*, August 28, 1954.

9. Revd. John A. Strmiska, C.S.Sp., to Victor Reed, January 3, March 9, 1959, St. Augustine's Church, Tulsa File, box 8.1, Archives of the Catholic Diocese of Tulsa (hereafter ADT). Until financial pressures forced it to close, St. Monica's School was also a vital asset of Tulsa's black community.

10. That many were oblivious was the opinion of Monsignor James Halpine, who was a child organist at St. Monica's Church and knew many of the African American parishioners. Halpine, interview.

paper concluded, "and up to now have done nothing but mark time."[11] Local Catholics were incensed. One declared that a black Catholic student who met the prescribed academic standards and whose family could pay the tuition fees would be admitted to any parochial school in Tulsa. "There are priests in Tulsa as well as Sand Springs, Sapulpa and other outlying communities," she added, "who have quietly worked on the racial problem for many years."[12] Another Tulsa Catholic took up the case of St. John's Hospital, noting that the hospital staff was integrated and there were no segregated wards, while new physicians were selected for their professional ability. "This desegregation did not come about because they were forced to it by use of government funds," she insisted, "but because the hospitals serve mankind."[13]

The *Oklahoma Eagle*'s commendation of Oklahoma City's Catholic priests was prompted by the arrest of a Roman Catholic priest for protesting at a restaurant that excluded African Americans—the first such case involving a priest in the United States. Adopting techniques of peaceful protest, civil rights protesters launched a campaign against segregated dining facilities in July 1960, urging owners to make the change en masse so that no one owner would be penalized for doing so. Among their number was Father Robert McDole, who had been close to Bishop Reed since converting to Catholicism under the latter's tutelage while Reed was pastor in Stillwater. McDole was detained on January 14, 1961 for protesting outside the Anna Maude Cafeteria, although a judge dismissed the case "on the assumption that the defendant was on a frolic of his own and his superiors have far more jurisdiction than I." McDole was unrepentant, insisting that no law had been violated by his action, but he swiftly became a lightning conductor for all those who entertained doubts about his methods of protest. Father George Forner, a priest in Skiatook, presumably had McDole in mind when he denounced the predilection of younger priests for pursuing an approach to civil rights characterized by "ostentatious and publicity-getting action," rather than by "working quietly to change the hearts of men to a right way of thinking and acting."[14]

Reed's reaction to McDole's arrest did much to define his episcopate re-

11. *Oklahoma Eagle*, April 6, 1961. The editor of the *Oklahoma Eagle* was James Goodwin, a Catholic and the product of Catholic schooling.

12. Mary E. Carlton to Revd. Ben H. Hill, April 17, 1961, Reed Papers.

13. Mary L. Jordan to Revd. Ben H. Hill, April 15, 1961, Reed Papers.

14. *Oklahoma Courier*, August 19, 1960, January 20, 1961; Revd. George W. Forner to Victor Reed, April 17, 1961, Reed Papers.

garding issues of racial justice. He had already set the tone in August 1960, when he delivered a televised statement approving of the recommendation for immediate and full statewide desegregation by the Governor's Committee on Human Rights.[15] While it seems safe to assume that he did not enjoy the spectacle of a priest on trial for breach of the peace, he was not willing to silence McDole, as many other bishops would have done. While he accepted that McDole's arrest was a matter of concern because it involved violation of the law by a member of the clergy, which might tarnish the reputation of the Church, he maintained that authority for the radical stance of civil rights advocates could be found in papal social encyclicals, most notably Pope Pius XII's *Summi Pontificatus*, which affirmed the essential unity of the human race, and Pope John XXIII's *Mater et Magistra*, which defined the manner in which social doctrine should be transformed into reality. "With secularism trying to seize leadership and seeking to interpret life on every side," the bishop concluded, "the Church cannot delay. Her mission in the world is not to follow but to lead." Some might consider McDole's action to be undignified, but he could not agree. "If a priest must occasionally suffer indignity to call reluctant public attention to the indignity of racial discrimination, then I feel the breach of decorum is justified."[16] In May, he wrote a letter urging Oklahoma City's restaurant owners to follow the lead of Beverly Osborne, who had just opened his establishment to all races.[17]

Social activists welcomed the bishop's stand. Bill Clifford, president of the Young Christian Students in western Oklahoma, insisted that the sit-ins reflected an American belief that all men were created equal in the eyes of the Creator. By their actions, he concluded, the restaurant operators were

15. *Oklahoma Courier*, August 26, 1960.

16. "Statement of Bishop Reed," 1961, Reed Papers. When Reed first witnessed McDole's protest on television, he sent Father John Joyce to the restaurant to tell him that it was inappropriate for a priest to be sitting on the ground. McDole sent back the message that if the bishop wanted him to stand up he should come down and tell him that himself. Gallatin, interview.

17. Victor Reed to Charles L. Bennett, May 31, 1961, Reed Papers. By July, most eating facilities in Oklahoma City and Tulsa (though not the establishment where Father McDole had first been arrested) had desegregated, as had many establishments in smaller communities like Okmulgee and Henryetta. Few African Americans actually chose to take advantage of this new accessibility once it became available. *Oklahoma Courier*, July 7, 1961. Reed may well have drawn some comfort from the proactive approach adopted by Archbishop Robert Lucey of San Antonio, his provincial superior, who authorized the priests of his archdiocese to take an aggressive stand on civil rights. Bronder, *Social Justice and Church Authority*, 100–105.

trampling on the basic dignity and God-given rights of human beings.[18] Father William Nerin of St. John the Baptist Church in Edmond assured Reed that the complaints he was receiving from more conservative Catholics were essentially political in nature:

I hear through the somewhat accurate grape-vine that the *Courier* and you indirectly are being criticized for upholding human rights over property rights in the Negro situation. I would lay 10 to one that the same critics by and large are for Right to Work Laws, anti-Semitic "privileged membership clauses," NAM [National Association of Manufacturers] *laissez faire* propaganda, McCarthyism or any tactic as long as Commies are eliminated. . . . It affords me great honor to know that you are our Bishop exercising genuine moral leadership in the face of opposition from the "strong and mighty" of the world. How better could you resemble the crucified Lord today who severed [*sic*] persecution for the sake of justice.[19]

Encouraged by Reed's declaration, other Oklahoma City priests, including Fathers William Skeehan and Edward Jeep, joined Methodist, Presbyterian, and Christian Methodist Episcopal pastors who agreed to be assigned on a rotating basis as clerical observers for demonstrations on successive Saturdays.[20]

With the bishop clearly committed to the cause, Oklahoma City Catholics, including Father James Halpine and Father Paul Donovan, rector of St. Francis de Sales Seminary, organized the state's first Catholic Interracial Council.[21] The first meeting took place in March 1961 and served as a forum for discussion of conditions in Oklahoma City. Participants were divided over the wisdom of Father McDole's activities. Sit-ins, one speaker warned, were unlikely to persuade Oklahomans who already felt insecure about the civil rights movement and were unready for "intellectualisms." Other speakers stressed the growing needs of the black community and the impermeability of the central ghetto. Progressive whites, they explained, were rarely able to pierce the color line, since mortgage companies would lend only to nonwhites in certain areas. Educated African Americans also had difficulty obtaining positions commensurate with their skills. Although the proportion of black students in majority white schools had risen from 17 percent in 1956 to 50 percent in 1961, there were still no black teachers on staff. A similar problem prevailed in industry. "In Oklahoma City," another speaker stated, "not

18. *Oklahoma Courier*, March 17, 1961.
19. Revd. William F. Nerin to Victor Reed, March 31, 1961, Reed Papers.
20. *Oklahoma Courier*, March 31, 1961.
21. *Oklahoma Courier*, April 1, 1960. The founders of the CIC stressed that racial discrimination in Catholic institutions must be a top priority.

a single Negro youngster is in training for a job nor in an industry sponsored training function." In his keynote address to the CIC, Victor Reed reminded his hearers that Christ had made no racial distinction in his work of redemption and stated that "the fundamental right to life, liberty and the pursuit of happiness takes precedence over property rights."[22] Council members took note of his words as they studied the social encyclicals to determine their potential application to the civil rights debate during the fall of 1961. In the spring of 1962, the CIC protested to Governor Ross Barnett of Mississippi about the arrest of a civil rights campaigner and pledged to undertake a program of diocesan education on racial issues and cooperate with other groups active in the field of interracial justice.[23]

Civil rights agitation gathered pace around the nation as violence flared at the University of Mississippi in October 1962 and in Birmingham, Alabama, in May 1963. The *Oklahoma Courier* pointedly criticized Catholic silence on the mistreatment of civil rights protesters in Alabama.[24] In the spring of 1964, as the Voting Rights Act made its way through its final stages in Congress, white liberals headed for the Deep South to help register previously disenfranchised African Americans.[25] Oklahoma's radical clergy could do no less, and in May 1964, several of them approached Bishop Richard Gerow of the Diocese of Natchez-Jackson in Mississippi for permission to operate in his diocese. "We regret the preachy and self-righteous tone of this letter," they told Gerow. "We realize that every opportunist and pious fraud in the country may be descending on your state, but the injustice lies open and visible for all to see. Not all who come are frauds. Many seek goals not unlike those we all preach. What we are, you may judge. The work, simple as it is, of registering voters is necessary and right. Let us come and do for you what out of respect for your own, you yourselves cannot do. You, in turn, will help us." Bishop Gerow, though unconvinced of the wisdom of their visit, initially requested only that they refrain from participating in public demonstrations. Several weeks later, however, he wrote to Reed, stating that the situation in Mississippi had deteriorated and asking the bishop to exercise his authority to prevent such a visitation.[26]

22. Catholic Interracial Council of Greater Oklahoma City Conference, March 19, 1961, Reed Papers.
23. Minutes of the Catholic Interracial Council, September 11, 1961, A. W. Kavanaugh to Reed, March 27, 1962, Reed Papers.
24. *Oklahoma Courier*, May 31, 1963.
25. McGreevey, *Parish Boundaries*, 209–47.
26. Revds. Paul H. Gallatin, Wilmer T. Rath, Charles Meiser, G Edward Jeep, Daniel

For Father Gallatin, the visit left lasting memories. In Hattiesburg, he worked to train rural African Americans in the mechanics of holding a precinct meeting. In a simple frame Baptist church, decorated with a cross studded with electric light bulbs, half of which had burnt out, Gallatin watched the aging pastor struggle to conceptualize a political process that was beyond him. "My God," he thought, "we've come here to save these people and we are destroying them." But then the pastor's wife came up to stand by him and support him and the young Oklahoma priest thought: "This is what love is." Gallatin's instinctive response to Bishop Gerow's lack of enthusiasm for the presence of himself and his colleagues was that Reed should suspend them and then reinstate them after they returned, but his ordinary made it clear that he was not going to put a black mark on their records.[27]

The Catholic minority in Alabama and Mississippi was obliged to tread a fine line in its civil rights advocacy for fear of provoking a backlash. In Mississippi, Father Bernard Law (the future cardinal-archbishop of Boston), editor of the *Mississippi Register*, was an outspoken advocate of integration, while chancery official Father Lawrence Watts was active in the state poverty program, but many black Catholics were reluctant to join integrated parishes. In the Diocese of Mobile-Birmingham, Bishop Thomas Toolen reacted to the civil rights activism of Father Maurice Ouellet by expelling him from the diocese. Like Gerow, Toolen probably feared that the mix of traditional southern anti-Catholicism with antipathy to civil rights work could prove a lethal combination, although activists accused him of sacrificing Father Ouellet to public opinion.[28]

Oklahoma priests felt a special obligation to support their more beleaguered brethren. In 1965, five priests from St. Francis de Sales Seminary

---

R. Allen, John Vrana, James McGlinchey, and John Dolan to Bp. Richard Gerow, May 5, 1964, Gerow to Gallatin, May 8, 1964, Gerow to Reed, May 26, 1964, Reed Papers.

27. Gallatin, interview.

28. Friedland, *Lift Up Your Voice Like a Trumpet*, 114–17; *Commonweal*, July 9, 1965, 483–84; Sid Sicotte, "The Church in Mississippi," *Commonweal*, July 9, 1965, 487–88. Southern clerical activists were not the only ones to pay for their witness. The Catholic Interracial Council in Los Angeles and its successor, Catholics United for Racial Equality, faced such opposition from Cardinal James McIntyre that Catholics United for Racial Equality even picketed the chancery and the cardinal's residence, while Father Bonaventure O'Brien was removed from his social and civil rights work by Bishop William Scully of the Diocese of Albany (New York) because of his criticism of the local Democratic machine's neglect of the city's poorer neighborhoods. See A. V. Krebs, "A Church of Silence," *Commonweal*, July 10, 1964, 474–76; Thomas Lickona, "Another Priest, Another Ban," *Commonweal*, December 10, 1965, 298–99.

joined Father McDole on Martin Luther King's Montgomery-to-Selma March, where McDole achieved the rare distinction of being the only priest to be invited onto the speakers' stand. Some believed that the presence of white priests helped to reduce the level of violence. "May be the Negro will change the face of the South," Father John Vrana remarked. "They show love toward those who oppress them. This is the Christian way." Another of those present, Father Donald Brooks, later recounted his experiences to parishioners at St. Barbara's Church in Lawton. He described how two Negroes who received Communion at an all-white church were beaten up in the parking lot after the service and that when he and several other priests escorted several Negroes to another church in Selma, obscene remarks were made in his hearing. "The revolution going on now," he concluded, "is as real as the one of 1776 and we are thankful it is being done with love and not with guns. It is not just a race riot. It is a full scale revolution and we must be part of it because it is Christ's."[29]

These were fighting words and prefigured a more confrontational style within the Oklahoma Catholic community. When the board of trustees of St. Monica's parish in Tulsa sent a priest to support the fight for open housing in Milwaukee, Wisconsin, Reed raised no objection. Unlike Bishop Gerow, Archbishop William Cousins of Milwaukee expressed no hostility to outside participation. "Since Milwaukee is a populous part of the country with many Catholics," Reed told his old acquaintance W. K. Warren, "I don't feel that Father [James] Groppi and his parishioners need our help, but if some priests and people of Oklahoma feel called to go and offer him peaceful support, I don't feel that I should attempt to stop them."[30] Reed's attitude was shared by Chicago's Cardinal Meyer, who allowed three of his priests to join the March on Washington and another to be present at Selma.[31]

While he did not stand in the way of clerical witness, Reed never regarded it as ideal. "It really isn't the clergy's place to take the lead in these demonstrations but the laity did not provide the leadership," he declared in June 1964. "When laymen want to take charge the clergy can drop out. Until then, it's our job."[32] The bishop's reluctance to be overly critical of his

---

29. *Oklahoma Courier*, March 19, 1965; Donovan, interview; "I Love You Too, as a Christian, but . . . ," *Barbarian: Newsletter of St. Barbara's Parish*, June 1965, St. Barbara's Church, Lawton File, Archives of the Catholic Archdiocese of Oklahoma City (hereafter AAOC).

30. Victor Reed to William Warren, September 20, 1965, Reed Papers.

31. Avella, *This Confident Church*, 310–12.   32. *Tulsa Daily World*, June 14, 1964.

priests' efforts was clear from his public pronouncements. At the September 1961 meeting of the National Catholic Conference for Interracial Justice, he stated that the Church had no option but to condemn racial discrimination and insisted that local problems should not obscure the search for a solution at the national level.[33] After a hiatus, no doubt occasioned by preparations for the Second Vatican Council, Reed returned to the offensive in the spring of 1963 when he spoke in favor of a fair employment practices bill authored by Senator Fred Harris of Lawton that would create a state human rights commission. He also endorsed an interfaith drive in Tulsa supporting a petition barring racial discrimination in municipal facilities.[34]

In June 1963, the bishop joined a meeting of religious leaders at the White House to discuss the prevailing crisis over civil rights. Much to his satisfaction, the federal authorities indicated that they did not view the Oklahoma community as particularly troubled by racial tensions, but he returned home still determined to start a statewide interfaith racial council that would present racial discrimination as a moral rather than a political issue. His desire was realized the following month when twenty-five religious leaders organized the Oklahoma Conference on Religion and Race. Reed took the opportunity to announce that his diocese would now include an antidiscrimination clause in all contracts. It was not enough for the Church merely to speak, the bishop declared, but it must act corporately and institutionally.[35]

To this end, Reed sought to exert maximum moral pressure on the authorities in Oklahoma City to pass a public accommodations ordinance in April 1964. "In my judgment," he told them, "this ordinance is in the best interest of our community. I can see no serious reason for delay, either from the standpoint of prudence or that of Justice itself." One year later, he called on the state legislature to pass enabling legislation allowing Oklahoma City to take advantage of the Johnson administration's public housing program.[36] Reed also encouraged his pastors to exert moral pressure wherever it might

33. *Oklahoma Courier*, September 1, 1961.

34. *Oklahoma Courier*, April 19, May 31, 1963. A member of the state senate from 1956 to 1964, Harris was elected to the U.S. Senate in a special election in November 1964 to fill the vacancy caused by the death of Robert S. Kerr. Reelected in 1966, he was not a candidate for reelection in 1972, but was an unsuccessful candidate for the Democratic presidential nomination in 1976.

35. *Oklahoma Courier*, June 21, July 12, 1963. On Reed's interest in a nondiscrimination clause in church contracts, see Robert R. Buck to Victor Reed, April 18, 1963, Reed Papers.

36. Victor Reed to Mayor and Council of Oklahoma City, April 30, 1964, Reed to Hon. H. B. Atkinson, March 10, 1965, Reed Papers.

prove effective. Returning from the 1966 Southern Catholic Interracial Meeting in Atlanta, he called on Oklahoma City pastors to back a fair housing statement campaign "in which earnest people of different churches unite in a common work of justice and charity [and which] will definitely help the community spirit of our city." When a public accommodations ordinance once again stalled in Oklahoma City in 1967, the bishop directed local priests to use their Sunday homilies to bring to people's attention "the moral question of open housing and the necessity of passage of the ordinance," and to urge their city councilmen to vote for it "without delay."[37] In Tulsa, several priests took heart from the Oklahoma City initiative to urge their own city council to adopt a fair housing ordinance, threatening to picket city hall.[38]

Despite the declared stance of the bishop, priests were not united on the race issue. One member of an unnamed Tulsa parish complained that his pastor viewed "failure to financially support the Church" as the gravest moral crisis of the day and had removed a petition supporting a public accommodations ordinance signed by 15 percent of the parishioners, which he had initially allowed to be placed in the church vestibule.[39] Some of the laity were even more outspoken. When an inaccurate rumor circulated that Reed planned to invite Martin Luther King Jr. to Tulsa, one woman angrily questioned the wisdom of such a venture: "We do not need rabble rousing troublemakers in our city. If you and your fellow priests feel the need for action, I suggest that you spend your time and money teaching the people to understand the responsibilities of citizenship and good government. . . . Are you so devoid of leadership that you need to engage the services of a comedian in order to communicate with the Negro population? . . . You will lose the support of the responsible white population if you continue in this vein."[40]

Other Catholics proved more open to civil rights activism. A regional meeting of the Christian Family Movement in Lubbock, Texas, in August 1964 adopted seven resolutions on racial issues for their members to pursue, including programs of joint participation in social activities and other personal contact; expressions of support for the national civil rights bill, for the

37. Victor Reed to all Oklahoma City Pastors, May 12, 1966, Cathedral of Our Lady of Perpetual Help, Oklahoma City File, AAOC; Msgr. Raymond F. Harkin to priests of Oklahoma City, November 17, 1967, Reed Papers.

38. Revd. Charles J. Johnson, *Tulsa Catholic Center Newsletter*, September 13, 1967, Reed Papers.

39. Robert L. Jones to Victor Reed, December 16, 1964, Reed Papers.

40. Elizabeth L. Emery to Victor Reed, n.d. (prob. September 1967), Reed Papers.

elimination of racial classifications in employment applications and official records, for the removal of discriminatory real estate practices, for the encouragement of school administrators to hire Negro teachers, and for the cultivation of links between CFM and groups such as the Urban League and the
National Association for the Advancement of Colored People (NAACP). At
the national meeting of CFM's executive committee in 1967, one Oklahoma
couple urged the national organization to make Catholics aware of the racial
problem "and quit spoon-feeding the people."[41]

Priests like Father Wade Darnall of Blessed Sacrament parish in Lawton
enjoyed good relationships with the African American community because
of the active support by Lawton priests for integration of the town's hotels,
restaurants, theaters, and residential neighborhoods. In May 1965, Darnall allowed the local NAACP chapter to meet at Blessed Sacrament and obtained
Reed's permission for the members to meet in the body of the church. He
feared that asking them to meet in the basement would make a poor impression.[42] At Immaculate Conception parish in Tulsa, the assistant pastor, Father Henry Kelly, developed various social justice and adult education programs to address the problems that stemmed from the expansion of the city's
Negro ghetto. Several parishioners praised Kelly for helping to smooth the
path to integration in northwest Tulsa, and when Kelly was transferred in the
summer of 1966, Josephine Woods complained that those who were most
opposed to integration had been the happiest at his departure.[43]

Another parish with a strong record on civil rights was St. Patrick's parish
in Oklahoma City. In the face of a generally lackluster response to a request
from local religious leaders for observance of June 12, 1966, as Fair Housing
Sabbath Sunday, Monsignor Don Kanaly devoted six homilies to the subject, and eighty-six of his parishioners signed a fair housing petition. "I am
very proud of the fact that our response from Catholic laity and clergy far

41. Resolutions accepted by the majority of CFM delegates at the Area 11 Convention
at Lubbock, Texas, August 9, 1964, Reed Papers. For the national organization's efforts to
combat racism, see Burns, *Disturbing the Peace*, 125–38 (the Oklahoma couple is quoted on
137).

42. Revd. T. Wade Darnall to Victor Reed, May 11, 1965, Reed Papers.

43. Lucille and Margaret Collins to Victor Reed, June 23, 1966, Mr. and Mrs. R. J.
Ramsey to Reed, June 24, 1966, Mary E. Tomaney to Reed, July 4, 1966, Josephine Woods
to Reed, July 13, 1966, Reed Papers. Monsignor James Rooney, rector of Immaculate Conception, dismissed the letter-writing campaign protesting Kelly's transfer and complained
about his contempt for the sisters and hostility to the parochial school system. Msgr. James
Rooney to Reed, July 15, 1966, Reed Papers.

surpasses that from any other religious denomination," one Catholic activist reported, "and I have heard it said . . . that 'if the campaign is a success, it will be because of the Catholics.'"[44] Parishioners from St. Patrick's worked to achieve integration on Oklahoma City's east side and carried out open housing marches in the south of the city. One Sunday, Kanaly led a group of 750 people to the home of a city councilman who had rashly stated that anyone was welcome to come and personally discuss the issue with him. On the streets of the neighborhoods through which the marchers passed, local residents parked their cars on the driveways, from where they sounded their horns and blinked their lights. The councilman was not home that day.[45]

INTEGRATING THE CHURCH

Racial liberals held firmly to the belief that what was being demanded of institutions in the wider world must also apply to the institutional Church. Furthermore, they felt that where an informal institutional segregation persisted, even by the wishes of its members, it must be overturned.[46] While formal segregation in Oklahoma's parochial schools had ended in 1954, this imposed upon a pastor only the requirement not to refuse admission to a black Catholic child domiciled in the parish in question. The existence of essentially all-white and all-black schools troubled the bishop, and in July 1965 he warned that he would not permit the transfer of white children from an integrated school to one that was not integrated.[47] In issuing such a statement, Reed was preparing for the struggle developing at Corpus Christi parish in Oklahoma City, the first in the diocese to attempt seriously to integrate its church and school. As African Americans joined the congregation, no fewer than forty white families severed links in the course of 1964, obliging the Corpus Christi school board openly to urge all parishioners to comply with the will of the bishop and help promote an open housing policy in Oklahoma City. The board concluded with a veiled threat: "You are called upon to bear witness to what you believe. You believe that all men are children of

44. Ruth E. Sullivan to Revd. William C. Garthoeffner, July 14, 1966, Reed Papers.
45. Gier, interview.
46. An early *Courier* editorial praised the merger of a black church and a white church in Oklahoma City and hoped that this would be the shape of things to come. *Oklahoma Courier*, July 15, 1960.
47. Victor Reed to Msgr. Raymond F. Harkin, July 30, 1965, St. Joseph's Old Cathedral, Oklahoma City File, AAOC.

God—are your brothers. Are you willing to live according to that principle? If not, you cannot call yourself a Christian in the true meaning of that word and you really do not belong in this parish." Perhaps, board members hinted, those interested in social justice could move into the parish to help compensate for the current losses and alter the tone of the dialogue.[48]

For integration to be successful, Reed could not risk allowing Corpus Christi to become "too" black. In a letter to Monsignor John Connor, rector of Our Lady of Perpetual Help Cathedral, Reed noted that while Corpus Christi parish was 20 percent Negro, the school was already 45 percent. Once it crossed the 50 percent mark, Corpus Christi School would become a case of de facto segregation. "The problem of maintaining a margin of safety at Corpus Christi School," he told Connor, "is not simply the problem of that parish, but of the whole Catholic population of Oklahoma City."[49]

The solution would be to transport Negro children to other all-white schools, something to which Connor had objected, as he wished to keep the classes at the cathedral school small enough to maintain accreditation. Whatever his private views on integration may have been, Connor couched his protest as an objection to admitting out-of-parish Negro children who might not even be Catholic. To this his ordinary responded that "extraordinary situations demand extraordinary solutions."[50] Connor had an ax to grind, but there were others who had reservations when it came to busing. Sister Celine Townsend, who worked for the Oklahoma Community Relations Commission, criticized what she called the white-imposed vision implicit in enforced busing. Not only did such a policy violate the Fourteenth Amendment, she complained, but it also threatened to aggravate social tension, could lead to Negro students being "segregated" in their new schools, and was not necessarily popular even in the black community.[51]

In Tulsa, Father Forrest O'Brien of Immaculate Conception parish in-

48. Revd. Herman J. Foken to Victor Reed, May 19, 1965, Corpus Christi School Board to Reed, May 19, 1965, Reed Papers.

49. Victor Reed to Connor, August 4, 1965, Cathedral of Our Lady of Perpetual Help, Oklahoma City File.

50. Msgr. John M. Connor to Revd. Ernest Flusche, August 2, 1965, Victor Reed to Connor, August 4, 1965, Cathedral of Our Lady of Perpetual Help, Oklahoma City File. The *Courier* provided a report on the busing of black students to all-white parochial schools acknowledging the "artificial" nature of busing but stating that until African Americans could buy homes in all sections of the city, it was a necessary corrective. *Oklahoma Courier*, September 10, 1965.

51. Sr. Celine Townsend to Eugene Welden, February 6, 1968, Reed Papers.

sisted that his parochial school had contributed significantly to the stabi-
lization of his community, since the local public schools were significantly
below par. By 1967, there were 40 black students out of 247 pupils, three-
quarters of whom came from outside the parish. "Immaculate Conception
School," O'Brien declared in an appeal for diocesan financial support, "perhaps uniquely, is in a position to do far more than what is normally expected
of a parish school. It is in a position to serve the poor, both white and black,
by giving them a quality education in an area where quality is rare. It is in a
position to serve the middle class of the area by giving those children an integrated education and instilling in them a social awareness they will carry
for the rest of their lives."[52]

While integration of Holy Family Cathedral School took place with comparatively few problems, the Sisters of Divine Providence—who ran the
school—sought to take matters a stage further in 1967 by integrating their
teaching staff. Through an arrangement with the Sisters of the Holy Family—who were in the process of withdrawing from St. Monica's School—
several black sisters were added to the faculty. The superior of the Sisters of
the Holy Family proposed that one sister from each community should hold
the positions of principal and vice principal, alternating every three years.
"It would give the school a stronger staff . . . and [present] a more balanced
picture to the parents, both Caucasians and Negroes," she declared.[53] Holy
Family's success at integration was confirmed by the state superintendent of
public schools when he asked the principal how she ensured that her children
played together in racially mixed groups. There was no formula, she replied.
The children simply treated each other on the playground in the same way
they were treated by their teachers in the classroom—as equals.[54]

The final component of integration was the dissolution of the small black
parishes of Oklahoma. In 1963, Reed converted St. Peter Claver parish in
Oklahoma City into a mission of Corpus Christi parish, ending the celebration of Mass on Sundays. St. Martin de Porres School continued to operate
for two years until all the children had been shifted to Corpus Christi School.

52. Revd. Forrest L. O'Brien to Diocesan Finance Committee, June 27, 1968, Immaculate Conception Church, Tulsa File, box 4.1, ADT.

53. Mother Marie Anselm to Mother Mary Amata, May 16, 1967, Mother Marie Anselm to Victor Reed, May 16, 1967, Reed Papers. The proposed alternation does not appear
ever to have taken place, but the Sisters of Divine Providence later withdrew entirely from
Holy Family.

54. Gier, interview.

Community reaction was hostile in the extreme for, as Reed reported to the head of the Holy Ghost Fathers, some whites and a very considerable number of Negro parishioners" were actively opposed to integration.[55] One parishioner, a Mrs. McBride complained that integration would ride roughshod over the "Negro heritage" the parish had upheld for forty years: parishioners wished to share their heritage, not lose it. Two weeks later, Father Donald Brooks offered the standard liberal response: "[T]he white parishes—we—need our Negro brothers in Christ, and . . . real Christians have no past to construct but only a future. . . . I hope Mrs. McBride will pray with me that this incorporation in Christ can take place by building upon the true history of God's people but with no temptation to return to the kind of history in which so few have walked with God."[56] On July 4, 1963, several young parishioners from St. Peter Claver sent a petition arguing that the merger would decrease the number of Negro conversions and leave only one parish to serve the northeast side of Oklahoma City, but in 1965 Reed brought forty years' service by the Holy Ghost Fathers at St. Peter Claver to a close.[57]

Among the laity at Corpus Christi, too, the sense of being a social experiment rankled. It was in this parish that Father McDole served as an assistant pastor, and by the middle of 1964 almost every issue at Corpus Christi was seen through the racial lens. Terry Brennan, who attended Corpus Christi School, in later years dismissed Reed's approach as seriously misguided. "In the name of racial correctness," explained Brennan, "the bishop, in my opinion, succeeded in destroying two good parishes: [St. Peter Claver] just didn't exist any more and Corpus Christi just didn't know what hit it. . . . The people of [St. Peter Claver] worked long and hard to build their parish and school. They were, and rightly so, very proud of their parish. That was all taken away from them by Bishop Reed because he said it was wrong for a predominantly black parish to be located next to a predominantly white parish. Bishop Reed managed to create the same thing he didn't want. Now, Corpus Christi is the predominantly black parish."[58]

55. Victor Reed to Vy. Revd. Vernon F. Gallagher, C.S.Sp., June 26, 1963, Reed to Gallagher, July 8, 1963 (quotation), Reed to Sr. Mary Benedicta, O.P., August 17, 1963, Reed to Revd. James P. O'Reilly, C.S.Sp., September 9, 1963, Corpus Christi Church, Oklahoma City File, AAOC.

56. *Oklahoma Courier*, June 28, July 12, 1963.

57. Petition for Preservation of St. Peter Claver Parish, July 4, 1963, Reed Papers; Reed to Vy. Revd. Francis P. Trotter, C.S.Sp., July 6, 1964, Corpus Christi Church, Oklahoma City File, AAOC;

58. *Oklahoma Courier*, June 12, June 19, 1964; Terence T. Brennan to author, February

In McAlester, the black community generally looked with favor on the Catholic presence. Indeed, one black Baptist minister, W. A. Watts, declared in 1965 that he was seriously considering resigning his pastorate and joining the Catholic Church. His only friends in McAlester, he said, were the Catholic priests, whom he had known for less than a year.[59] Even so, it was one of those priests, Father Joseph Boucher, who asked the bishop to reduce the black parish of St. Mary's to a stational church. "I personally feel that this national parish based on racial difference is out of line with the trend of the times and the teaching of the Church," Boucher argued. "Many of the colored people are very immoral, ignorant, and poverty stricken. . . . I expect to have to cope with this, and do not expect to pass the problem of teaching, giving example, and trying to make converts off on anyone else. But the segregation of the good Catholic colored people holds them back. . . . They are denied the consolation that should be had in real unity in the church. As long as we remain a parish apart, this status of isolation must continue." Boucher proposed that his parishioners begin attending the parishes of St. John's and St. Joseph's (in nearby Krebs), whose boundaries took in most of the town's black neighborhoods, while Boucher continued his work of house-to-house evangelization. Integration would thus be achieved by degrees without provoking a mass exodus of white Catholics.[60]

Such priestly initiatives, for all their good intentions, often carried a strong tone of patronage to black audiences increasingly informed both by the Vatican discourse of lay participation and the secular discourse of Black Power. In 1967, when the Holy Ghost Fathers left St. Monica's parish in Tulsa—built for the black community in the 1930s—many parishioners at St. Monica's and St. Augustine's feared that it would only be a matter of time before they met the fate of St. Peter Claver. In a letter to Reed, several St. Monica's parishioners warned that many black Catholics, lacking adequate transportation and feeling themselves to be social outsiders, would not transfer to other Catholic parishes. "Does not the participation of the laity in the affairs of the church," they asked of the bishop, "so strongly promulgated after the Second Vatican Council, apply to St. Monica's Parishioners?"[61]

19, 2004, in author's possession. Reed was, in large measure, responding to the decision of many religious orders to cut back on their commitments. The alternative of making St. Peter Claver the parish and Corpus Christi its mission would have been politically impossible.

59. *Oklahoma Courier*, April 30, 1965.

60. Revd. Joseph Boucher to Victor Reed, July 13, 1963, Reed Papers.

61. Revd. John A. Strmiska C.S.Sp., to Victor Reed, April 24, 1967, St. Augustine's

Many black Catholics also sensed an implicit disdain for the integrity of their community life behind the overt condemnation of segregated worship. "At the 9:00 AM service last Sunday," raged Carl Flick of Muskogee, "Father [Stephen W.] Wells made the asinine statement that St. Augustine had only been built in 1943 merely to keep the races separate. This is not true at all, and is a nasty slap at good people who spent time, money, and sacrifice to build the church."[62] When Father Lee O'Neil, of St. Monica's in Tulsa, ran for public office, many of the parishioners—not to mention the larger black community—expressed resentment. The prevailing sentiment was that social action priests should be training African Americans for such roles rather than entering politics themselves.[63]

INTEGRATING THE WORLD

Perhaps the greatest challenge for urban Catholics was to accept the racial transformation of the neighborhoods in which they lived. Again and again, in cities across the North, white Catholic neighborhoods resisted black incursions into their self-contained neighborhoods. Some of those who resisted were to be found in Immaculate Conception parish in Tulsa. The parish's then assistant pastor joined Neighbors Unlimited, a body established in 1958 to try to stop panic selling of properties as blacks moved into the area. He worked to improve policing and street lighting, got the National Conference of Christians and Jews involved in community relations, and persuaded half a dozen white Catholics to move into the area.[64]

While some Catholics struggled to keep a changing neighborhood stable, Father Edward Kelly carried out this project in reverse in Millwood, in northeastern Oklahoma City. In 1967, Kelly launched an initiative to persuade white families to move into a formerly segregated neighborhood. Although 30 percent Negro, Millwood had a good school, a cooperative school board, and homes ranging in price from $12,000 to $150,000. With difficulty, the core group hunted down loan companies and real estate agents

---

Church, Tulsa, box 8.1, ADT; Parishioners of St. Monica's Church to Victor Reed, May 19, 1967, Reed Papers. Father Lee O'Neil stated his parishioners' sentiments with characteristic bluntness: "Charles[,] these people feel like they have been treated very badly and it would be of considerable help if the Bishop would exert himself and his time to come and say Mass some (any) Sunday morning." Revd. Lee O'Neil to Revd. Charles H. Schettler, July 22, 1967, St. Monica's Church, Tulsa File, box 15.1, ADT.

62. Carl W. Flick to Reed, August 29, 1967, Reed Papers.
63. Gier, interview.   64. *Oklahoma Courier*, April 21, 1961.

that were at least open to finding properties for whites. "We did not change either the loan companies or the real estate agents," admitted Kelly, "but we believe we started them thinking about new possibilities." Twenty white families moved into Millwood in 1967, and another sixty who had planned to move out chose to remain.[65]

Such projects were not carried out without resistance. An anonymous correspondent in Oklahoma City reported that when she and her husband decided openly to offer to sell their home to any buyer, including an African American, one of their Catholic neighbors told them that he was going to ask her husband's employer to put pressure on them, while the other, who had a priest in the family, promised to ask his relative to set them straight.[66] Carl Fritz of Tulsa took many of his coreligionists to task for their lack of commitment in 1964: "Well then, here we are—fresh from our Easter Vigils, hot out of all the CFM and YCS discussions, and supposedly buzzing with the enthusiasm, truth, and conviction of our religion classes—here we are safely shielded in our peaceful homes, respectively, sagely commenting to each other about how fine it would be if everyone did have equal opportunities in every respect."[67]

Catholic outreach to African Americans increased as the Church developed closer ties with the federal government. In Detroit, the archdiocese sponsored the Phoenix Homes project, backed by a Housing and Urban Development grant, to provide low-income housing for Detroit and Wayne counties.[68] As Lyndon Johnson's War on Poverty gathered momentum, Catholic bishops began to appreciate that they could turn to the federal government for resources to implement poverty relief programs. In April 1965, Reed sought assistance for a Montessori Day Care Pre-School Center from the Office of Economic Opportunities (OEO). This formed the heart of the Seventh Street Project, headed by Sister Nativity Heiliger, who also oversaw a program of food distribution and sewing and home economics classes. An arrangement was also reached with the OEO to use the buildings of the closed parochial school at St. Monica's, Tulsa, to host an antipoverty program for north Tulsa, providing both day care and job training.[69] Two years

65. Revd. Edward L. Kelly to Harry A. Pinsky, September 7, 1967, Reed Papers.
66. *Oklahoma Courier*, March 22, 1963.
67. *Oklahoma Courier*, May 15, 1964.
68. Hiley H. Ward, "Pre-Fab Housing and the Church in Detroit," *Commonweal*, September 29, 1967, 602–3.
69. Victor Reed to Sen. Fred Harris, April 9, 1965, Linus J. Thro, S.J., to Reed, August

later, Reed urged the Federal Housing Administration to allow a civil rights suit in federal court to compel the authorities in the city of Lawton to issue a building permit for the Columbia Square low-cost housing project.[70]

Certain parishes also cooperated with state programs. In Lawton, Father Alfred Kelly instructed parishioners of St. Barbara's Church in the workings of the community action committee of Comanche County and encouraged his parishioners to join the committee and the programs that it sustained. These included the National Youth Corps, Headstart—in which several teenagers from the parish served as teachers' aides—and Foster Grandparents, which helped expose children exiting Headstart programs to places of educational and cultural interest. In Ardmore, Father Elmer Robnett faced more resistance in getting members of St. Mary's Church to participate in the local community action program. "I believe that the one thing wrong with this parish is its failure to be concerned with each as other as well as the Community," he told Reed. "This is brought out by the lack of Christian involvement in the community life; in problems facing society, including the racial crisis, youth delinquency, and in other areas."[71] Sponsors of Oklahoma City's Youth Village—a nonprofit community for young men between twelve and twenty-four, which permitted a vulnerable youth to "'mesh gears' with the community by simulating a community atmosphere without the impersonalness he often experiences in the brick and mortar jungle"—also hoped to secure funds from Washington for its operation.[72]

Some antipoverty activities remained more Church centered. When Oklahoma City organized a Summer Youth Program in 1968 to provide opportu-

---

7, 1965, Reed Papers; Victor Reed to Mrs. William Thornton, August 29, 1966, Revd. William C. King to Reed, October 17, 1966, King to Revd. Julian Wrobel, January 27, 1967, St. Monica's Church, Tulsa File, box 15.1; *Oklahoma Courier*, January 31, 1969. By 1969, Reed was so identified with projects of this sort that Thomas Ward, a Tulsa engineer seeking a small business loan to support a school training unemployed men for the construction industry under the Model Cities program, listed the bishop as the only church leader whom he had consulted. Thomas D. Ward to Sen. Henry Bellmon et al., December 6, 1969, Reed Papers.

70. Victor Reed to Philip N. Brownstein, November 4, 1967, Blessed Sacrament Church, Lawton File, AAOC.

71. Father Al Kelly, "Poverty Programs in Lawton Explained," *Barbarian: Newsletter of St. Barbara's Parish*, December 1966, St. Barbara's Church, Lawton File; Revd. Elmer C. Robnett to Victor Reed, September 5, 1967, Reed to Robnett, September 9, 1967, St. Mary's Church, Ardmore File, AAOC.

72. Minutes of the fourth meeting of the Board of Directors, Youth Village, "Why a Youth Village," n.d., Reed Papers.

nities for employment, education, and recreation, the diocese called on city parishes to provide volunteers for both "geographical" and "interest" (specified project) teams and contribute toward the $350 that would allow a sister or seminarian to serve on one of the teams for a period of two months. It would not be appropriate to ask for federal or municipal funds to employ sisters or seminarians for this, diocesan officials explained, because the program was intended to provide jobs for the hard-core unemployed. That same year, St. Patrick's parish formed a social action committee and established a Samaritan Fund to provide speedy one-time help to those in need, a blood bank, school tutors, and collections of playground equipment for preschools and of books for a study center. It also undertook to help revitalize the heavily African American Lincoln school district.[73] The most successful social action project was Tulsa's Neighbor-for-Neighbor. Founded by Father Daniel Allen of St. Jude's parish, its philosophy was that of one family taking on the problems of another, with the latter eventually assisting someone else in need. Neighbor-for-Neighbor had a biracial board of directors composed of clergy and laity, and it drew members from St. Monica's, St. Augustine's, Immaculate Conception, St. Pius X, St. Mary, and the Church of the Madalene, as well as various Presbyterian and Episcopal churches. Its activities included repairing broken-down cars and selling them to needy families for the cost of the repairs, renovating derelict houses, and persuading the Tulsa Task Force Credit Union to establish a bank at St. Jude's that provided low-interest loans and financial advice. It also leased a service station where credit union members could get discounted gas.[74]

Increasingly, Catholics joined in ecumenical social justice activities. As early as 1963, Donald Dallman, the pastor of Prince of Peace Lutheran Church in Tulsa, addressed the CIC; he noted that Bishop Reed had endorsed a program under which the clergy would promote open occupancy pledges in their congregations and introduce African Americans to their congregations.[75] In May 1968, Oklahoma City Catholics joined Lutheran, Unitarian, and Jewish congregations in sponsoring Project Equality, an interchurch pledge by participating churches to adopt fair employment practices within

73. "Community Council Recreation Program," n.d., Reed Papers; "The Chronological Development of the Social Action Committee, St. Patrick's Church, Oklahoma City," 1968, St Patrick's Church, Oklahoma City File.

74. *Tulsa Tribune*, July 8, 1968; *Oklahoma Courier*, February 14, 1969. Neighbor-for-Neighbor is still in existence after some forty years of operation.

75. *Oklahoma Courier*, March 15, 1963.

their institutions and to demand such practices of all those with whom they did business. Oklahoma's Project Equality even won the support of bodies like the Lutheran Church–Missouri Synod, which otherwise frowned on ecumenical undertakings. Reed was so identified with Project Equality that Pastor Dallman invited him to address a meeting of the Missouri Synod's Oklahoma District at the Center for Christian Renewal.[76]

Another ecumenical undertaking was the emergency meeting held between Governor Dewey Bartlett (Oklahoma's first Catholic governor) and representatives of the Oklahoma Conference on Religion and Race, which sought to involve local clergy in plans to contain civil disturbances while at the same time reducing the causes of racial discontent. Police representatives urged the adoption of a model employed in Kansas City, where ministers were stationed at jails, hospitals, and detention centers to monitor treatment of prisoners, and where churches were used to hold curfew violators apart from rioters until they could be released at daybreak. Speaking on behalf of his fellow clergy, Reed agreed that local places of worship would fulfill that role in the event of rioting and appointed a committee of local pastors to liaise with the civil authorities.[77]

As legal segregation slowly receded, some white communities responded by establishing their own private institutions. Reed became personally involved in the case of Heritage Hall, an independent secular school set up in Oklahoma City, which, critics charged, represented an attempt to evade public school integration by creating a whites-only school. When the First Christian Church offered land to allow the school to expand, Reed joined a number of prominent citizens in signing a petition protesting their decision. "The issue before us all is the future," the petition declared, "with its opportunities for a positive implementation of integration and equality of educational opportunity. The stand of the Church must reflect that part of its faith which would support a raceless community."[78] The issue of Heritage Hall hit much closer to home when Mount St. Mary's Catholic High School offered

76. Revd. Donald J. Dallman to Victor Reed, March 13, 1968, Orra G. Compton to Donald Scruggs, May 22, 1968, Reed Papers. For a discussion of Project Equality, albeit from a Presbyterian perspective, see Tom Cutting, "A Presbytery Considers Project Equality," *Chicago Seminary Theological Register*, September 1972, 31–39.

77. Oklahoma Conference on Religion and Race, Minutes of meeting at the Governor's Mansion, June 26, 1968, Reed Papers.

78. Fellow Citizens of Oklahoma City to First Christian Church Members, May 5, 1970, Reed Papers.

to rent its football field to Heritage Hall. Father William Garthoeffner, pastor of Sacred Heart parish, condemned Heritage Hall as a white-flight school and bitterly opposed leasing the field. Some of his parishioners agreed. It was damaging to the parish, the school, and the Sisters of Mercy, Linda Murdock told fellow parishioners, to take money from an institution that stood for disunity in the community.[79]

The Catholic community of Hugo, in far southeastern Oklahoma, became involved in the case of a local swimming pool run by the Epsilon Sigma Alpha fraternity, whose July 1964 warranty deed included a clause barring "persons of the Negro race," which was clearly unconstitutional. Father James Greiner of Immaculate Conception parish was deputed by the Hugo ministerial alliance to find out the situation and to meet with a representative committee of the fraternity. Ironically, the pool manager was chairman of the parish council and the fraternity secretary a parishioner, but fraternity officers told Greiner that since he was not involved in either the construction or operation of the pool, they saw "no reason to seek your services at this time." Greiner retorted that the town's restaurants had integrated peacefully and could not the pool owners do the same?[80]

With the loss of interest by the local Methodists after their pastor was transferred to Oklahoma City, responsibility for pursuing the case fell exclusively on Greiner. After obtaining the promise of financial support from the diocese if a legal action became necessary, Greiner carried out several experiments to assess the nature of "private memberships" at the pool. On June 25, two white girls were admitted after paying admission without holding pool memberships, but five days later an African American who tried to gain entry was told that it was a private pool and he could not swim there. Greiner's attorney told him that he should first put the matter in the hands of the FBI, but if this failed to produce action he would launch a class action suit.[81] Sadly, the documentary record breaks off at this point and Greiner's ultimate success or failure is unknown.

79. Garthoeffner, interview; Sacred Heart Church Bulletin, October 1970, Sacred Heart Church, Oklahoma City File, AAOC.

80. Fr. James A. Greiner to Alpha Knipp, January 12, 1971, Greiner to Charles J. Harrington, January 20, 1971, Harrington to Greiner, January 27, 1971, Swimming Pool Committee to Greiner, February 9, 1971, Immaculate Conception Church, Hugo File, box 49.1, ADT.

81. Harrington to Victor Reed, April 2, 1971, Greiner to Paul V. McGivern, July 1, 1971, McGivern to Greiner, July 6, 1971, Immaculate Conception Church, Hugo File, box 49.1, ADT.

NATIVE AMERICANS AND HISPANIC AMERICANS

While the civil rights debate was most associated with African Americans, the Church in Oklahoma was also obliged to deal with the concerns of other minority groups. The oldest—and perhaps the least troubled—racial apostolate was that to the Native American community, which had begun with Benedictine Father Isidore Robot's Sacred Heart Mission to the Potawatomi Indians in 1877. Ten years later, two additional missions were established, one to the Osages at Pawhuska—who already enjoyed a tradition of Catholic practice—and one for Chickasaw girls located at Purcell. During the 1890s, Father Isidore Ricklin, O.S.B., carried the Gospel to the Kiowa, Comanche, Caddo, and Wichita tribes at Anadarko.[82]

Native Americans Catholics rarely lived in close proximity to their other coreligionists and consequently did not compete with them for spiritual resources. In 1959, Father Edward Bock, O.S.B., offered a generally positive overview of the Anadarko Mission (the last Indian mission in Oklahoma, which closed in 1966), noting that a recent Indian festival had attracted six hundred participants. Bock had organized a club—composed of Catholics and non-Catholics—to promote the welfare of the mission and developed CCD programs to allow small study groups to carry out a more systematic study of the faith. He nevertheless warned that traditional religious practices continued to present a challenge. "We have attempted to emphasize to the Catholic Indians," he told Reed, "that the Mission and they must take the lead in preserving all that is not contrary to Catholicism in their ancient customs and traditions in order to show the Indian that Catholicism is not against them but the only Religion of the White man that is really for them."[83]

Two years later, Bock faced an external threat from Methodist and Mormon missionaries, who were able to offer superior facilities to the local Indian community. Concerned that the Mormons would win out, Bock requested an immediate grant of $35,000 to build an activities center that could serve as the mission gymnasium and host Indian dances, tribal meetings, funeral dinners, and clubs. This would benefit liturgical celebration, Bock concluded, since festival Masses had currently to be held in the open air because

---

82. *One Family, One Century*, 4–6, 12–13, 26–27.
83. *Oklahoma Courier*, April 22, 1960; Revd. Edward C. Bock to Victor Reed, December 10, 1959, Reed Papers.

Bishop Reed and Abbot Philip Berning O.S.B., of St. Gregory's Abbey, are honored at a Kiowa Indian festival in Anadarko, Oklahoma.

of the lack of room in the church building.[84] Protecting the Indian schools
was a growing priority as the decade progressed. In 1961, Father Leo Hardesty told the Sisters of the Blessed Sacrament that closing the parochial school
in Fairfax would be the "death knell" of the parish, which was heavily Indian in character.[85] Five years later, Reed directly intervened to persuade the
community that their efforts in Pawhuska were appreciated: "The Indians do
love and respect the Sisters, although they are often notoriously lacking in
external signs of appreciation. You know this from working among them. It
is really unthinkable at this time to leave the whole Osage area of Oklahoma
without a parochial school. This is one of the most important Indian areas of
the country."[86]

Mission priests continually sought guidance on how to incorporate Indian tradition into Catholic life without indulging in syncretism. In 1961,
Bishop Reed and Abbot Philip Berning, O.S.B., of St. Gregory's Abbey were
received as honorary members of the Caddo tribe following a confirmation
service in Anadarko. Reed was given the name Ha-Dos Ha-Ka-Yu (White
Dove), signifying a dispenser of the Holy Spirit.[87] The following year, Father
John Strmska urged Reed to encourage his fellow bishops to support accelerated canonization of Kateri Tekakwitha and thereby demonstrate that saint-
hood in the Americas was not to be limited by race.[88] Some Indians were
willing to Christianize their own culture: a Catholic Quapaw requested Father Francis Weiner, C.PP.S., to celebrate Mass as part of a tribal celebration
in 1964.[89]

Compared with missionary work among the Indians, the Hispanic apostolate was a comparatively recent phenomenon in Oklahoma. Our Lady of
Mount Carmel–Little Flower parish was organized in Oklahoma City in 1922.
Six years later, St. Francis Xavier parish in Tulsa established a mission for the
city's small Mexican American community. It was not until the 1950s, however, that rural missions to serve migrant workers began to appear in large

84. Revd. Edward C. Bock to Victor Reed, March 27, 1961, St. Patrick's Church,
Anadarko File, AAOC.

85. Revd. Leo Hardesty to Mother Marie Anselm, S.B.S., March 7, 1961, Sacred Heart
Church, Fairfax File, box 41.1, ADT.

86. Victor Reed to Mother M. David, S.B.S., August 11, 1966, Immaculate Conception
Church, Pawhuska File, box 66.2, ADT.

87. *Oklahoma Courier*, April 21, 1961.

88. Revd. John A. Strmska to Victor Reed, February 26, 1962, Reed Papers.

89. Revd. Francis A. Weiner to Victor Reed, May 7, 1964, Reed Papers.

numbers, beginning with establishment of a unit of the Legion of Mary with a special apostolate to Mexican Americans in the town of Hollis in 1957.[90]

Awareness of the growing Hispanic population of the Southwest had led to the establishment in 1945 of the Bishops' Committee for the Spanish Speaking, whose chairman was Reed's provincial superior, Archbishop Robert Lucey of San Antonio. Under Lucey's direction, the committee organized educational and public housing programs, opened clinics and community centers, and supported a unionization drive in the Diocese of Corpus Christi. In 1950, it turned its attention to the problem of migrant labor, after Lucey was asked to serve on a presidential commission investigating the subject. Lucey's work helped make many Americans aware of the parlous living conditions of migrant workers. As a result, the bracero program (which allowed the contracting of Mexican nationals for farm labor at low wages) was officially terminated in December 1964.[91]

By 1960, the focus of the Church had shifted from purely religious instruction to community-level social provision, something more commensurate with the skills of the laity and vital to preserve the standing of the Church among non-Catholics. "In this pluralistic society," declared the executive secretary of the Bishops' Committee for the Spanish Speaking, "it seems that more and more coordination in community projects is necessary with those not of our faith. In taking care of our migratory workers this is especially true since for so long the Church has not really made any organized effort to help these people. In most cases we are not even supplying the sacramental life to these migrants much less helping them with their social and economic needs."[92]

Many Oklahoma counties with large numbers of migrant workers had minimal resources for oversight of housing and public health standards. Church representatives sought to fill this void and urged employers to meet

90. *Tulsa Tribune*, July 20, 1963; Revd. J. J. Regan, O.P., to Bp. Eugene J. McGuinness, October 15, 1957, Our Lady of Guadalupe Praesidium, Legion of Mary, Hollis, Report for October 24, 1957–December 1, 1958, Sacred Heart Church, Mangum File, AAOC. In 1959, Father Robert Schlitt invited Reed to join the Mexican community in Tulsa for celebration of Mexican Independence Day. Revd. Robert Schlitt to Victor Reed, August 31, 1959, Our Lady of Guadalupe Church, Tulsa File, box 6.1, ADT.

91. Bronder, *Social Justice and Church Authority*, 73–83. See the series of articles on migrant workers in the *Oklahoma Courier*, October 6, October 13, October 20, and October 27, 1961.

92. Revd. John A. Wagner to Revd. William C. Garthoeffner, October 29, 1960, Sacred Heart Church, Mangum File.

their responsibilities in such matters. Medical personnel analyzed water sam-
ples from migrant worker barracks and concluded that most sources were
contaminated and the water unfit for human consumption. Medical teams
also gave advice on hygiene and identified workers in need of medical treatment, providing drugs to those who could not afford them and conveying
those who needed hospital care to Oklahoma City.[93]

In September 1965, they organized an immunization clinic in Greer County, in the southwest corner of the state. Extension Lay Volunteers taught the
migrant workers English and provided religious instruction for their children,
and strenuous efforts were made to enroll the children in the public school
system. Several special centers were established to sell used clothing, hold religious education classes, and show films. Such activities were not always received with appreciation in the English-speaking community. When Mangum
Catholics attempted to obtain federal funds for a community housing project, they encountered opposition from city and county government officials,
many of whom rented property to migrant workers.[94]

As farm mechanization increased, no effort to reduce economic privation
could solve the problem of the declining need for casual labor in agriculture.
As a result, job-training courses, including welding and mechanics for men
and home economics for women, were introduced, and a meeting of Catholic social activists in Altus elected to use a $250,000 federal grant awarded
in 1967 to create job-training centers for the benefit of the Spanish-speaking
community. Job prospects were also enhanced by the news that a producer
of flower seeds planned to open a training center in Harmon County next
door, which ultimately would give Hispanic families the means to set up in
business for themselves.[95]

Community self-empowerment was a constant theme in the early 1970s.
Father Paul Gillespie, O.S.F.S., then an assistant pastor at Assumption parish
in Duncan, called for a social action initiative to benefit Hispanics in southern Jefferson County. "There is a need to undertake this work," he declared.

93. Annual report to His Excellency Bishop Victor J. Reed from the Bishop's Committee for Spanish Speaking, Diocese of Oklahoma City–Tulsa, Greer-Harmon and Jackson
Counties, July 8, 1964, Reed Papers.

94. Annual report to His Excellency Bishop Victor J. Reed from the Bishop's Committee for the Spanish-speaking People, Diocese of Oklahoma City–Tulsa (Greer, Harmon &
Jackson Counties), March 27, 1965, Reed Papers.

95. Joseph Brennan and Ray McKernan to Msgr. Raymond F. Harkin, n.d. (prob.
March 1967), Sacred Heart Church, Mangum File.

"It is part of the picture of rural poverty, every bit as disabling as its urban cousin, but it is remote, often invisible from the highways." Gillespie sought to employ a Frenchman who had grown up in Chile and experienced a lay vocation to work with the poor, while Assumption parish and its missions at Rush Springs, Marlow, and Waurika continued to supply nursing and remedial reading assistance.[96]

In Frederick, St. Helen's parish had become 85 percent Mexican American by the early 1970s, and it was these parishioners who sponsored most of the parish activities. The pastor complained that while the white minority supplied most of the operating budget, it only tolerated the Mexican Americans. Viewing his parish's social action programs as an essential element of authentic Christianity, he insisted, with heavy-handed irony, that the white Catholics "want to be firmly assured that none of the funds are used for Christian purposes." Father Darnall consequently turned to the diocesan social action board for funds, proposing to work with two Carmelite sisters to determine the needs of the Mexican American community, as that community saw them, through community action plans, emergency relief, education, and self-help classes. In March 1971, Darnall persuaded the Office of Economic Opportunity to set up a local employment office, which found jobs for the eligible unemployed and directed dropouts to the Job Corps.[97]

Social action was not the sole concern of the Hispanic missions. Attendance at Mass at Our Lady of Guadalupe mission in Hollis increased in 1967, in part because the minister at the Spanish Baptist mission had suffered a heart attack, but also as a result of the focus on Church renewal. The Guadalupe mission organized a unit of the Christian Family Movement and began work on formalizing irregular marriages, while several men volunteered to take a more active role in the liturgy.[98]

In Frederick, Hispanic Pentecostals posed a direct challenge. "I am told that at least half the Mexican families in Southwest Oklahoma have left the Faith and joined Protestant groups," Father Darnall complained. "I would not be happy with this in any case but the intense hatred that many of such

96. Revd. Paul G. Gillespie, O.S.F.S., to Revd. Charles H. Schettler, March 6, 1970, Project—Social Action Committee, Assumption Church, n.d., Assumption Church, Duncan File, AAOC.
97. Revd. T. Wade Darnall to Victor Reed, February 10, 1971, "Description of Project Area," n.d., Revd. T. Wade Darnall to Revd. William Eichoff, March 25, 1971, St. Helen's Church, Frederick File, AAOC.
98. Joseph Brennan and Ray McKernan to Msgr. Raymond F. Harkin, n.d. (prob. March 1967), Sacred Heart Church, Mangum File.

groups engender in the hearts of these people for the Catholic Church, the priests, the Blessed Virgin and the saints whom they have for centuries held dear is little short of tragic. These strong traditions in the Mexican culture have kept these people staunchly religious despite the almost total lack of any attention from priests and even from the Church herself." When Darnall was forced to borrow the Pentecostal church for services in Tipton because he lacked a building in which to say Mass, attendance fell from thirty-five to five. Since many Hispanic Catholics violently resented the anti-Catholicism of Hispanic Pentecostals, Darnall quickly took steps to erect a new church building on donated land.[99]

CONCLUSION

For many American Catholics during the 1960s, the injunctions of the Second Vatican Council obliged them to participate in the civil rights revolution. Some commentators saw a close connection between the conciliar documents and civil rights legislation. "Vatican II's 1963 constitution on public worship invites comparison with our Civil Rights Law of 1964," wrote Father Robert Hovda in *Commonweal.* "Both have a significance which is universal—truly ecumenical. Both witness to their respective societies' capacity for self-criticism and occasional freedom from the tyranny of habit. Both imply that law is more than petrified custom. And both serve a constituency which is 'not ready' for them."[100] Victor Reed's willingness to participate in the struggle and to give his social action priests the freedom to maneuver was critical. The bishop himself admitted that his readiness to give public testimony on such issues also altered public perceptions of how a bishop should behave. "The old concept of an ivory tower bishop is unrealistic today," he declared in 1968. "It lacks the involvement that must be a part of the bishop's life today, and a necessary part of the responsibility of a bishop as the successor of the Apostles."[101]

Oklahoma Catholics joined many of their coreligionists in the Midwest

99. Revd. T. Wade Darnall to Members of the Finance Committee, Diocese of Oklahoma City and Tulsa, February 17, 1971, Revd. T. Wade Darnall to Revd. William Eichoff, March 25, 1971, St. Helen's Church, Frederick File.

100. Fr. Robert W. Hovda, "Reform without Reformers," *Commonweal,* August 21, 1964, 571–73.

101. Jack M. Bickham, "An Interview with Bishop Reed," *Decade of Change: A Supplement to the Oklahoma Courier,* March 1, 1968, 5.

in confronting the racism prevalent outside the Church and within it and linked the largely secular crusade for racial equality with the Church's desire to reconcile men and women of all races through the Cross. The close bonds that grew up between the Church and the federal government were by no means universally negative, but they sometimes tended to obscure the basis on which the Church proposed to renew society. As can be seen in the case of the black parishes, moreover, the adoption of involuntary integration often generated as many problems for the Church as it did for secular society.

chapter 9

Beyond Oklahoma

The Guatemala Mission and
the Vietnam War

Thus it is plain that missionary activity wells up from the Church's inner nature and spreads abroad her saving Faith. It perfects her Catholic unity by this expansion. It is sustained by her apostolicity. It exercises the collegial spirit of her hierarchy. It bears witness to her sanctity while spreading and promoting it. Thus, missionary activity among the nations differs from pastoral activity exercised among the faithful as well as from undertakings aimed at restoring unity among Christians. And yet these two ends are most closely connected with the missionary zeal because the division among Christians damages the most holy cause of preaching the Gospel to every creature and blocks the way to the faith for many. Hence, by the very necessity of mission, all the baptized are called to gather into one flock, and thus they will be able to bear unanimous witness before the nations to Christ their Lord. And if they are not yet capable of bearing witness to the same faith, they should at least be animated by mutual love and esteem.

Second Vatican Council, Decree on the Mission Activity of the Church,
Ad Gentes, December 7, 1965

Men nowadays are becoming more and more convinced that any disputes which may arise between nations must be resolved by negotiation and agreement, and not by recourse to arms. . . . We are hopeful that, by establishing contact with one another and by a policy of negotiation, nations will come to a better recognition of the natural ties that bind them together as men. We are hopeful, too, that they will come to a fairer realization of one of the cardinal duties deriving from our common nature: namely, that love, not fear, must dominate the relationships between individuals and between

268

nations. It is principally characteristic of love that it draws men together in all sorts of ways, sincerely united in the bonds of mind and matter; and this is a union from which countless blessings can flow.

John XXIII, Encyclical on Establishing Universal Peace in Truth, Unity, Justice, Charity, and Liberty, *Pacem in Terris*, April 11, 1963

THE SOUTH AMERICAN INITIATIVE

During the 1950s and early 1960s, the gaze of Oklahoma Catholics increasingly came to be focused on Central and South America, most notably through missionary contact with the nation of Guatemala.[1] The highlands of western Guatemala were the home of the nation's Indian community, which had been largely neglected by the established Church and whose syncretic faith had been described by one observer as "unorthodox orthodoxy." Without frequent contact with Catholic clergy, the religion of the Indians tended to blend Christianity and older pagan practices. Finding classic Christian conceptions of God and Christ too remote from daily existence, Indian theology embraced a system of localized devotions to a village's patron saint and an array of lesser saints. Responsibility for the patron saint's annual fiesta was vested in a body of elders (*cofradiá*), whose members also controlled most aspects of municipal politics. While the church building remained the focal point of worship, Indians also maintained numerous household altars and relied on the services of local soothsayers. Inevitably, the American conception of a separation between religious and public life had very little relevance for the practitioners of the Tradition (*Costumbre*).[2]

During the 1930s, there emerged among the families of a nascent merchant class a regional form of Catholic Action (*Acción Católica*), whose adherents established a network of centers to impart a greater sense of authentic Catholicism to the local Indian population. While nonresident priests had tolerated the power of the cofradiás, Acción Católica challenged their right to oversee religious and social life. Loyal to the episcopal hierarchy and politically active, members of Catholic Action opposed the reformist government of Jacobo Arbenz, which was toppled in a 1954 military coup carried out with

1. *Oklahoma Courier*, April 1, 1960. The cultivation of links with Latin America and South America was actively promoted by Bishop Edwin O'Hara of Kansas City, who viewed it as an extension of his apostolate to rural America. See Dolan, *Some Seed Fell on Good Ground*, 205–16.

2. Whetten, *Guatemala*, 286–310.

the aid of the United States. They increasingly sought the support of the central government in asserting their right to direct Holy Week processions and intervene in the religious and social life of the municipalities. The movement's strength remained dependent, to some extent, on the enthusiasm of local priests, but its rural units proved extremely effective catechizers.[3]

Although the 1954 coup originated in a conservative reaction to land reform, it also had the effect of accelerating the entry of foreign priests into the country, which had begun in 1943 with the arrival of two Maryknoll priests. At the initiative of Archbishop Mariano Rossell y Arellano, the new priests were directed to the poorly served Indian-dominated sections of the nation, whose burgeoning radicalism the archbishop feared. The foreign-born priests (who constituted over 80 percent of the nation's priestly complement in 1966) helped advance a process of decentralization of the Guatemalan Catholic Church begun by the Vatican when it had—in contravention of Rossell's wishes—established three new dioceses in Guatemala and appointed bishops without ties to the existing ecclesiastical establishment. By the late 1960s, foreign-born priests were regarded with suspicion by Guatemala's civil and clerical elites.[4]

Most of the early missionaries to Guatemala were members of religious orders (the Maryknoll Fathers being prominent in this regard). After Pope John XXIII urged greater missionary support for Central and South America to prevent the advance of Communism and the spread of Protestantism, however, Richard Cardinal Cushing, archbishop of Boston, established the Society of St. James the Apostle to recruit diocesan priests to serve in a region notoriously short of resident clergy. A special conference of American bishops was called to coordinate mission work in Latin America in 1959, at which the bishops pledged to fund the erection of two new seminaries in the region and established the U.S. Bishops' Latin America Committee.[5] The pope's call also inspired many religious superiors, including Mother Celine Carter of the Carmelite Sisters of St. Therese in Oklahoma City, who sent three sisters of Mexican ancestry to establish a mission school for the Maryknoll mission in Guatemala in 1962.[6]

---

3. These conclusions are drawn from a study of San Antonio, Illotenango, conducted by a priest-anthropologist between 1969 and 1970. San Antonio lies just to the north of Santiago de Átitlan, where the Oklahoma mission was based. Falla, *Quiché Rebelde*, 170–83. See also Adams, *Essays on Guatemalan National Social* Structure, 294–96.

4. Adams, *Essays on Guatemalan National Social Structure*, 278–84.

5. Garneau, "The First Inter-American Episcopal Conference."

6. *Oklahoma Courier*, January 19, 1962.

The 1960s marked the entry of the laity into many fields from which they had previously been excluded. In the mission field, the relevant Catholic agency was PAVLA (Papal Volunteers for Latin America), established in 1961. The first diocesan program was launched by Bishop Mark Carroll of Wichita (Kansas), and one of his representatives spoke to Oklahomans in February 1961 about the work of PAVLA, particularly its anti-Communist focus. PAVLA proved particularly popular with the membership of the Christian Family Movement—an influential force among Oklahoma Catholics—which provided numerous recruits as well as financial support for families who volunteered to serve as missionaries abroad. Oklahoma's first official PAVLA volunteer was Jerry Arledge, a twenty-four-year-old agronomist and a parishioner at St. Patrick's parish in Oklahoma City, who was assigned to a mission run by the Diocese of Spokane (Washington), where he taught agricultural classes on the radio, worked with individual farmers, and tried to "convert society."[7]

The request of several Latin American bishops for assistance led Bishop Reed to contemplate a mission project that would be maintained solely by the Diocese of Oklahoma City and Tulsa. In 1962, Father Ernest Flusche, the diocesan director of PAVLA, traveled to Guatemala on a fact-finding mission. He returned with the news that the Maryknoll Fathers were willing to offer the diocese an isolated mission on the coast at El Progresso, where it would not be necessary for staff to have to learn a language other than Spanish.[8]

The future mission director, however, desired a more scenic location. "I couldn't stand [the thought of El Progresso]," Father Ramon Carlin later explained, "It was just hot and humid." Carlin favored the mountain village of Santiago de Átitlan, which lay in one of the most remote and technologically backward regions of Central America and already boasted missions supported by the dioceses of New Ulm (Minnesota) and Spokane. Fortunately, Bishop Angelico Melotto of Sololá, in whose diocese the parish of St. James was located, had no objections to a further complement of American missionaries.[9]

7. *Oklahoma Courier*, February 24, June 16, 1961, December 14, 1962; Burns, *Disturbing the Peace*, 65–67. Arledge later married Maria Valdizan, a schoolteacher from Guatemala City. *Oklahoma Courier*, February 19, 1965.

8. Father Ernest Flusche, interviewed by Father James D. White in Enid, July 25, 2005.

9. *Oklahoma Courier*, August 10, 1962; Victor Reed to the Most Revd. Ambrogio Marchioni, September 19, 1962, Don Jerónimo E. Arlege to Revd. James N. Towner, December 31, 1962, Reed Papers; Halpine, interview.

Father Ramon Carlin, superintendent of Bishop McGuinness High School in Oklahoma City and architect of the Guatemala Mission.

The mission faced significant social and religious challenges. The parish comprised forty thousand Tzutuhil Indians, including twelve thousand in the town of Santiago alone. The public school, built in 1960, had a capacity of one hundred students, whom it educated to sixth grade level. No more than 10 percent of the population could read and write, and while most men understood Spanish, few of the women did. Although the town had running water, few residents could afford to take advantage of it. Health care was particularly sparse, with a single dispensary in Santiago and a visiting doctor who offered a weekly eight-hour general sick call. One quarter of the population suffered from malnutrition, and there was a significant incidence of tuberculosis, trachoma, and infectious diarrhea.

The religious problems were scarcely less daunting. The church building, erected during the sixteenth century, could accommodate only six hundred and was badly in need of repair. There were only one thousand practicing Catholics and the eight cofradías exercised considerable sway, keeping the keys to the church and checking the vestments to make sure that the priest hadn't stolen any. Ritualistic dances and blood rites continued to be performed in the church building, and the last permanent pastor had been drowned in 1949 for trying to exclude members of the local cofradiá. "Please understand," Carlin assured the bishop in his report, "this is being related to you simply for the reason of helping you realize that our work will not be without its serious difficulties. It is not being told by way of dramatics, nor is it for publication in any form."[10]

Ramon Carlin was an appropriate choice to lead the mission. Born in Haskell, Oklahoma, of Mexican parents in 1916, he studied at the American College at Louvain before being ordained in 1941. He served various Oklahoma parishes and was twice chaplain at the federal penitentiary at El Reno. From 1958 to 1962, he was superintendent of Bishop McGuinness High School in Oklahoma City, which became a popular meeting place for priests of a more progressive stripe.[11] It was from a post as pastor of St. Cornelius parish in Cherokee that Reed summoned Carlin to his new extradiocesan role, and by October 1962, the new mission leader was in contact with the federal authorities, seeking information on how to get necessary equipment through Mexico and into Guatemala without incurring excessive import duties.[12]

Carlin's nine-day trip through the region enabled him to speak with Father James Curtin, the superior of the Maryknoll Fathers in Guatemala; representatives of the New Ulm and Spokane missions; Padre Restituto, vicar general of Sololá and weekend pastor of Santiago de Átitlan; and Dr. Roberto Rendon, a Guatemalan neurosurgeon trained at the University of Michigan. Rendon, a member of the Christian Family Movement, had organized forty-seven doctors into the Servicio Especial de Salud Publica (Special Ser-

10. Ramon Carlin, "Findings and recommendations resulting from survey trip made February 6–16, 1963," Reed Papers.

11. See the biography of Carlin in White, *The Souls of the Just*, 182–83.

12. Revd. Ramon A. Carlin to Sen. Robert S. Kerr, October 24, 1962, Reed Papers.

vice of Public Health), which provided weekend medical care—both preventive and curative—to regions of the country without doctors, under the leadership of the Church.[13]

To assist Carlin, the Diocese of Oklahoma City and Tulsa organized a Guatemala advisory board which, in January 1963, calculated the basic cost of a mission from figures supplied by the Spokane mission. The board stipulated figures of $50 for fixed expenses, $100 per person for living expenses, and $25–$50 in work project expenses (including education materials), or around $800 per month, with an initial commitment of five years. Board members warned that raising the required funds would be a serious undertaking and that people might forget after the first flush of interest had dissipated. They urged the establishment of a propaganda committee and the publication of a "Guatemala Diary" in the diocesan newspaper and encouraged Catholic schools and altar societies to collect the thirteen hundred books of trading stamps needed to acquire a Jeep Wagoneer for the mission.[14] Carlin also received a boost from the Catholic bishops of West Germany, who pledged to donate a floating clinic, to be staffed with Oklahoma personnel, which would serve the medical needs of the inhabitants of villages on Lake Átitlan.[15]

The various elements of the mission team were pulled together in the spring of 1963. In addition to Carlin, Fathers Thomas Stafford and Robert O'Brien were appointed, and Carlin requested that a fourth priest join them in June 1964, after a course of study of conditions in Guatemala. All three priests undertook to attend the Wycliff Bible Society course in linguistics at the University of Oklahoma, an essential prerequisite to learning the Tzutuhil language. O'Brien was then to attend the Center of Intercultural Formation in Mexico; Stafford, the Maryknoll Training Center in Bolivia; and Carlin, the Maryknoll Training Center in Guatemala. Carlin also requested Reed to approach the Maryknoll Fathers and the Christian Brothers in the hopes of securing a Maryknoll missioner for part of 1964 and two Christian brothers who could assist with the formation of lay catechists. His preferred choice was Father Edmund McClear, one of the original Maryknoll priests in Guatemala and an avid exponent of lay participation.[16]

Carlin did not overlook the all-important lay component of the mission,

---

13. Carlin, "Findings and recommendations."
14. Guatemala Advisory Board Meeting, January 9, 1963, Reed Papers.
15. *Oklahoma Courier*, January 4, 1963.
16. Carlin, "Findings and recommendations."

and medical missionaries were clearly an essential element. For the permanent team, he requested Tulsa dentist Joseph Trimble and his wife, Kay, both
prominent figures in the Christian Family Movement, and a public health
nurse, Marcella Faudree of Coalgate. As far as doctors were concerned, he
believed that a combination of Guatemalan doctors coupled with periodic
visits from Oklahoma practitioners would prove adequate. Carlin also sought
an expert in the formation of credit unions and agricultural cooperatives, initially favoring Frank Farnsworth, a former member of St. Patrick's parish in
Oklahoma City then residing in Dallas, but Farnsworth proved unable to
move his family to Guatemala. As a result, Patrick Pyeatt, a specialist in agricultural economics, was recruited to complete the team, although Carlin also
hoped to make use of the skills of Jerry Arledge.[17]

Establishment

On August 11, 1963, Bishop Reed distributed crosses to the seven members of the Guatemala mission team. "It will be a question not only of building up new economic structures among [the Indians]," he told them in a
homily that perhaps reflected a less than perfect understanding of Indian
spirituality, "of improving their physical health, of new cooperative structures
in trade and credit but we must also reveal Christ to them. This, perhaps,
will be the most difficult task because some of them may possess his spirit
in a greater degree than do we. . . . The Christian 'renewal' of the people
of Santiago Átitlan must come through a 'dialogue' with them—the 'have
nots.' There is much that we can learn from them."[18]

Members of the mission had first to achieve an internal dialogue. The decision of the Trimbles to bring their pet poodle with them was not well received by other members of the mission, who privately hoped that it would
be eaten by the village dogs the first time it got outside. No one was willing,
however, to say anything publicly for fear of upsetting Kay Trimble, who experienced great difficulty in adjusting to life in an Indian village.[19] Conflicts
between Mrs. Trimble and Patrick Pyeatt also came to the surface. "I guess I
could sum it up by saying that Kay is still far from becoming adjusted to this
life," Carlin told Reed after a visit by the bishop, "and Pat is far from being
grown up."[20] When Father O'Brien abruptly quit the mission for personal

17. Ibid.
18. Sermon of Victor Reed, August 11, 1963, Reed Papers.
19. Revd. Ramon Carlin to Revd. James Towner, December 16, 1963, Reed Papers.
20. Revd. Ramon Carlin to Victor Reed, June 26, 1964, Reed Papers.

reasons in June 1964, Carlin urged that his replacement not be the voluble and erratic Father Robert McDole. "We are too afraid of [McDole's] temper with the Indians," he confessed.[21] Another loss came in September 1965, when Patrick Pyeatt left the mission to enter the Seminario de Cristo Sacerdote in Columbia.[22]

With such internal tensions, it was essential that good relations exist between the bishop and the mission director. Carlin had considerable confidence in Victor Reed. "[Father Stafford and I] want you to know things about ourselves and our work here that we might very well be reluctant to tell other 'superiors' because of the authority angle," he told the bishop in June 1964. "Your approach to the use of authority seems to be so much more Christian and adult that we find ourselves actually wanting you to know some of the more hidden things."[23]

While Reed had called on his people to aid the "renewal" of the Indian community, such a transformation could take place only when the power of the cofradiás was broken. Father Carlin denounced the habitual drunkenness of many of the members and their refusal to receive the sacraments and observed that if he had tried to remove the statues representing their patron saints, he would probably have been murdered. "I have explained the history of the *cofradiá* to the peasant groups and invited them to return to the original position within the Church with the studying of the faith," the mission director explained. "Thus far they are not too sure that they must do this."[24] Father Stafford worked to develop a greater degree of Indian participation in orthodox Catholic worship, an approach that provoked much debate in other American and Spanish missions in the area. In July 1965, Carlin was able to report a higher level of participation (and a reduced incidence of drunkenness) at the Mass for the annual Fiesta of St. James, which included a procession with papier-mâché objects as part of the Prayers of the Faithful.[25] Two Oklahoma priests who visited in 1968 were struck by the majesty of the Holy Week liturgies they attended.[26]

The mission also cultivated good relations with their traditional rivals— the Protestant evangelicals. "Father McClear is all excited these days," Carlin

21. Revd. Ramon Carlin to Revd. James Towner, August 7, 1964, Reed Papers.
22. Msgr. Raymond F. Harkin to Laura T. Brown, September 23, 1965, Reed Papers.
23. Revd. Ramon Carlin to Victor Reed, June 26, 1964, Reed Papers.
24. *Oklahoma Courier*, October 23, 1964.
25. Revd. Ramon Carlin to Victor Reed, July 26, 1965, Reed Papers.
26. Donovan, interview.

declared in June 1964. "He met one of the Protestant Ministers here in this town who has a congregation of thirty people. The man is starting to talk to him about learning the Catholic Faith. He said he 'just never knew nothing' about it before. Some have their fingers crossed, but Father McClear is like a kid with a new toy."[27] Another innovation was the decision to offer the Thursday evening Mass on behalf of specified occupational groups, a move that elicited a telegram of appreciation from the military high command in Guatemala City when it was offered on behalf of the local army post. Priests, members of religious orders, Papal Volunteers, Peace Corps workers, and tourists all flocked to Santiago de Átitlan to observe the new liturgical phenomena.[28]

In 1967, Carlin proposed his most far-reaching project: a monastic foundation located in the parish and oriented toward local culture and language studies. Such a foundation was projected to become a catechetical center for an area that would always be short of resident priests. Study of the three principal Indian dialects—Tzutuhil, Cakchiquel, and Quiche—was to be a top priority, so that a liturgy, hymnology, and psalmody could be developed to fit them, but work could also be done on preserving local folk literature and recreational song and dance. "The salvation of Christ will be brought to these Latin Christians primarily by the priesthood of the laity via the service of the Word," Carlin stated. "It is hoped that the Divine Office, traditionally the very heart of the monastery's prayer life, can become—with necessary adaptations—the basic liturgical prayer in priestless areas; a prayer life that will be completely oriented to the Altar and the Eucharist."[29]

Linguistics formed a central thrust of mission strategy. Carlin taught a number of courses in reading and writing to Indians with limited ability, in the hope that they could then convey the information to family members who completely lacked that facility. "It is a real thrill to look into the eyes of these grown primitives," he confessed, "and see the pride they show there when they can read a short sentence."[30] Father Robert Westerman, who arrived in Guatemala in February 1965, was involved in the process of Spanish-language instruction. Working with six bilingual Tzutuhil men, the priests listened to the sounds the men made, converted these into the internation-

27. Revd. Ramon Carlin to Victor Reed, June 26, 1964, Reed Papers.
28. Revd. Ramon Carlin to "Bill," January 7, 1965, Reed Papers.
29. Revd. Ramon Carlin to Victor Reed, March 13, 1967, Reed Papers.
30. Revd. Ramon Carlin to Victor Reed, June 26, 1964, Reed Papers.

al phonetic alphabet, and then taught the Indians to read their own language. Classes in Spanish, mathematics, and local history were then prepared
in Tzutuhil and broadcast on the mission's radio service, with native volunteers taking the receiver into local homes and neighborhoods.[31]

The missionaries also addressed medical concerns. A full-time public
nurse was appointed to treat dysentery and give basic immunizations, while
visits by the public health doctor were extended from one to two days each
week. Marcella Faudree faced an uphill battle with her classes in midwifery
and general sanitation, for the Indians lacked Western standards of hygiene,
and many women would not cooperate with her unless ordered by their hus-
bands. One Oklahoma doctor visiting the mission on the bishop's behalf in
July 1965 noted that there was still little access to proper sanitation, running
water, or electricity and urged greater emphasis on preventive health care
and the isolation of families suffering from tuberculosis. "I believe," he concluded, "that if more Oklahoma doctors were made aware of the mission and
its objectives that the mission would not be lacking in medical personnel."[32]

With the arrival of laboratory equipment and the promise of assistance
from a doctor sponsored by the Alliance for Progress, Carlin set up a combined laboratory and pharmacy, but responsibility for health matters periodically fell on the priests. When the Trimbles moved to Guatemala City in
1965, Father Westerman was pressed into the role of community dentist on
the strength of two days' instruction. Over the next six years, Westerman ex-
tracted five thousand teeth. He never lacked clients, however, since his only
competition—the local carpenter—charged double the mission's price and
did not use anything so effete as Novocain.[33]

Economic self-sufficiency was the third objective of the mission. Carlin
encouraged training in carving and embroidery. When tourists bought $30
worth of goods in one week—"a big amount in this 'centavo' country"—he
toyed with the idea of organizing an art cooperative.[34] A Maryknoll father
had organized a credit union in 1961 and another was established by a local

31. Robert C. Westerman, "A Priest's Story," in Brousseau, *A Dying Breed of Brave
Men*, 31. The success of radio schools set up by American priests in Sololá was phenomenal:
there were forty-two then in operation in that one region by 1966. Adams, *Essays on Guatemalan
National Social Structure*, 302.
32. *Oklahoma Courier*, March 19, 1965; A. C. Finn to Victor Reed, July 24, 1965, Reed
Papers.
33. Revd. Ramon Carlin to Victor Reed, July 26, 1965, Reed Papers; Westerman, "A
Priest's Story," 31.
34. Revd. Ramon Carlin to Victor Reed, July 26, 1965, Reed Papers.

priest in nearby San Antonio, Illotenango, in April 1964, a process that he complemented with the sale of cheap fertilizer to local farmers. Such actions provoked the hostility of local merchants, who forced the priest's removal to Guatemala City, but the cooperative had doubled in size within two years.[35]

In 1966, the priests at Santiago de Átitlan decided to follow suit with a full-fledged agricultural cooperative, which had seventy-five members by the spring of 1968. The cooperative had assets of $40,000, outstanding loans from the mission of $5,800, and had borrowed $15,000 at 5 percent interest on the strength of land that it owned. Its organizers calculated that its cropland would yield crops with a value of $8,000 in 1968 and $10,000 in 1969. The cooperative store did $40,000 worth of business in cement and roofing materials in one year, reducing the local price of nails from 25¢ per pound to 15¢ (compared to 12¢ per pound in Guatemala City).[36]

Consolidation

With priests from fifty dioceses and PAVLA volunteers from seventy dioceses serving in Latin America, efforts to coordinate missionary work and minimize costs began to receive high priority. In 1964, the Bishops' Committee for Latin America established a coordinating service, with Bishop Ernest Primeau of Manchester (New Hampshire) as secretary.[37] Missions in Guatemala were affected by this transition. In February 1965, in addition to the Oklahoma contingent, the region boasted priests from the dioceses of Helena, New Ulm, and Spokane and PAVLA volunteers from the dioceses of Dallas, Fargo, Houston, Lansing, Peoria, and an unidentified diocese in New Jersey.

Problems could arise when an individual sponsored by one diocese developed responsibilities that transcended the operation of a local mission. Such was the case with Frank Farnsworth, whom Carlin had hoped to secure for Oklahoma but who later arrived in Guatemala under the auspices of the Diocese of Dallas. Once in Guatemala City, Farnsworth and his family took responsibility for the Lay Volunteer Center, which provided accommodations for all Papal Volunteers when they first arrived.[38] The Diocese of Oklahoma City and Tulsa paid the rent on the center, while supporters in Minnesota paid for the furnishings. Farnsworth also served as the official PAVLA representative

35. *Oklahoma Courier*, April 5, 1963; Falla, *Quiché Rebelde*, 184–88.
36. Information concerning the Cooperative at Santiago, Átitlan, Guatemala, April 14, 1968, Reed Papers; *Oklahoma Courier*, January 8, 1965.
37. Bp. James McNulty to Victor Reed, October 1, 1964, Reed Papers.
38. For a profile of Farnsworth and his family, see *Oklahoma Courier*, April 23, 1965.

with the U.S. Air Force and the Guatemalan government for all matters concerned with the importation of medical, agricultural, and educational supplies.

In other words, Carlin told the diocesan PAVLA director, "the Diocese of Dallas is making a much bigger contribution to the re-enlivening of the Church in Latin America than it might appear on the surface." Carlin also suggested that there might be merit in the Diocese of Dallas joining forces with the Oklahoma mission, noting the debts already incurred and Oklahoma's loss of eight diocesan priests through death in the previous year.[39] Fifteen months later, Reed personally appealed to the national director of PAVLA for someone to take over the operation of the Lay Volunteer Center in Guatemala City. It was too expensive for one diocese to operate, the bishop insisted, especially for one like Oklahoma City and Tulsa that had comparatively few Papal Volunteers.[40]

Interest in the Guatemala mission was strong among the Oklahoma laity during the 1960s, enhanced by reports in the diocesan newspaper. Catholics in Skiatook and Tulsa were sponsored by their parishes to fly down to Guatemala to participate in the mission for a week.[41] Even those who could not go in person were encouraged to establish channels of communication. In 1968, Sister Elizabeth Nick, then serving in Guatemala, recommended a nineteen-year-old with nine years of schooling (in a region where the average was three), studying to be a Montessori teacher, as a potential pen pal for the fifteen-year-old son of an Oklahoma City schoolteacher who was studying Spanish.[42]

Equally vital were financial contributions to keep the mission afloat. After viewing a film emphasizing that even small contributions could make a difference, the second grade class at Oklahoma City's Sacred Heart School sent Reed their widow's mite in the form of $4.50 in saved treat money.[43]

39. Revd. Ramon Carlin to Revd. Joseph Weinsapfel, February 11, 1965, Reed Papers. In 1966, there were also reported to be diocesan priests from the dioceses of Belleville (Illinois) and Wheeling (West Virginia) in Guatemala. Adams, *Essays on Guatemalan National Social Structure*, 290.

40. Victor Reed to Revd. Raymond A. Kevane, May 17, 1966, Reed Papers. The North American Bishops kept the Trimbles under observation for more than two years in order to determine that their mode of operation was a truly sacrificial ministry. See Joseph and Kay Trimble to Victor Reed, February 23, 1968, Reed Papers.

41. *Oklahoma Courier*, September 23, 1966, January 17, 1969.

42. Donovan, interview; Revd. Charles H. Schlettler to Sr. Elizabeth Ann Nick, October 8, 1968, Nick to Schlettler, November 10, 1968, Reed Papers.

43. Marilyn Gotcher to Victor Reed, April 17, 1967, Sacred Heart Church, Oklahoma City File, Archives of the Catholic Archdiocese of Oklahoma City.

Pupils at nearby St. Eugene's School raised $16.32 in 1966, while students at McGuinness High School presented Reed with a check for $60.54 at the St. Patrick's Day assembly in 1967.[44] Catholic women's groups were also active. The Women's Club at Holy Family Cathedral (many of whose members no doubt viewed the mission as a special project of their former rector) contributed $100 in 1963, while the Tulsa Deanery Council of the National Council of Catholic Women provided a $50 contribution in 1967.[45]

Nor should the generosity of individuals be overlooked. Frederic Rosengarten, the American president of a Guatemalan corporation that operated a facility near the mission, offered a $50 contribution in 1965.[46] Oklahoma contributors included a former pupil of Carlin at McGuinness High School, who sent $15 for his work; a parishioner at St. Peter and St. Paul Church in Cushing, who made regular $5 monthly payments to support a seminarian for several years; and one family that reduced its Christmas expenditures in 1967 and used the money for special offerings, including a $75 contribution to the Guatemala mission.[47]

Despite the willingness of ordinary Catholics to contribute, day-to-day administration proved a continual headache. Communication between the mission itself and the Guatemala advisory board fell off considerably after 1967. The board forced through a proposal to construct a hospital against the wishes of Carlin, who favored restricting expenditures to the erection of a clinic. Tensions were also exacerbated by the appointment of Frank Farnsworth as Oklahoma coordinator of the Guatemala mission after he returned from Guatemala in September 1966. Despite his undoubted talents, Farnsworth proved to be a gadfly, far more intent on his own interests than on the job for which he had been hired, and with a knack for setting board members at each other's throats. It was later revealed that he had collected money in the diocese for his own Guatemala mission and used diocesan funds to promote it.[48]

In May 1968, Father Paul Donovan gave Farnsworth notice, arguing that

44. Janet Costello to Victor Reed, April 15, 1966, Reed to Revd. Ramon Carlin, March 17, 1967, Reed Papers.

45. Mrs. B. E. Horrigan to Victor Reed, January 7, 1963, Mrs. C. F. Ray to Reed, December 27, 1967, Reed Papers.

46. Frederic Rosengarten Jr. to "Bishop's Fund," May 18, 1965, Reed Papers.

47. Mary Tinker to Victor Reed, September 28, 1964, Reed to Anna Dale Murphy, February 25, 1966, Ray Ryland to Reed, December 21, 1966, Reed Papers.

48. Donovan, interview; Francis O. Farnsworth to Revd. William Garthoeffner, September 13, 1966, Reed Papers.

his salary and expenses had been excessive and his work of limited effect.[49] Subsequent events suggested that this had been a wise move. In 1969, Farnsworth, who had been involved with a "Pentecostal prayer group" at St. Patrick's Church in Oklahoma City, accepted a position with a non-Catholic group, a move that his pastor judged incompatible with his commitments as a Catholic.[50]

Quite apart from administrative problems, the sheer cost of sustaining the mission presented a major challenge. Asked for advice, the coordinator of the Spokane mission in Guatemala told Chancellor Charles Schettler that his diocese had spent about $21,000 in 1966. Having exhausted a legacy earmarked for the mission in 1960, the diocese now allocated $10,000 from its annual diocesan development fund and raised the rest from donations, while the radio station and cooperatives were required to be self-financing.[51] It was increasingly clear that the Oklahoma mission needed to keep a close eye on expenditures. In 1968, it exhausted roughly 10 percent of the income from the Bishop's Fund and anticipated even greater costs once work was begun on the clinic-hospital.[52] Other threats were also looming as Guatemala entered the political unrest of the 1970s. In the years following Reed's death, the diocese would pay for its commitment to Central America in the blood of its ordained ministers.[53] The value of the mission was nevertheless incalculable. For Catholics in the Bible Belt, it had opened up a whole new vista on the universal family of Catholic Christians and the bonds that united them.

THE PEACE MOVEMENT

While the Guatemala mission enjoyed support from Catholics across the theological spectrum, liberal Catholics increasingly shrank from applying the principle of "just war" to the escalating conflict in Vietnam, despite their knowledge of the likely fate of devout Catholics under a Communist regime. Opposition to the Vietnam War was largely absent from conservative Oklahoma society until the late 1960s. When Ammon Hennacy, a Baptist convert

49. Revd. J. Paul Donovan to Revd. Charles H. Schettler, May 7, 1968, Reed Papers.
50. Revd. Joseph D. Dillon to Victor Reed, August 26, 1969, Reed Papers.
51. Revd. John A. Rimpa to Revd. Charles H. Schettler, September 16, 1967, Reed Papers.
52. Robert G. Tompkins to Revd. Charles Schettler, February 27, 1968, Reed Papers.
53. In 2003, the diocese withdrew from Santiago de Átitlan at the request of the local bishop, who wished to place his own priests there. A financial commitment continues.

to Catholicism and a member of Dorothy Day's Catholic Worker movement, spoke in Tulsa and Oklahoma City in March 1960, he found it difficult to convince even the small numbers of Quakers and Catholics who attended his meetings of the wisdom of his pacifist and antigovernment views.[54]

Many of Reed's contemporaries had been distinctly hawkish on foreign policy during the 1950s, a position only hardened by revelations of the persecution meted out to their coreligionists in Eastern Europe and Southeast Asia. The publication of Pope John XXIII's encyclical *Pacem in Terris* in 1963 and the deliberations of the Second Vatican Council imparted a somewhat different perspective.[55] Some of the bishops gathered in Rome between 1962 and 1965 concluded that world peace was intimately connected with the rising gulf between the rich and poor nations of the world. Cincinnati archbishop Karl Alter offered wide-ranging proposals for an international court of justice, a code of international law, voting rights at the United Nations based on a state's population and financial contribution, multilateral military disarmament, and the outlawing of saturation bombing and nuclear weapons.[56]

By mid-decade, many Catholics were beginning to be exposed to a much narrower conception of "just war," one that did not include the Vietnamese conflict. Pope Paul VI only exacerbated internal divisions among American Catholics with his "War no more," address at the United Nations in October 1965. In the wake of this papal reproof, the Catholic Peace Fellowship organized speaking tours of colleges and universities, and a number of Catholic students joined others who had begun to burn their draft cards. On November 9, Roger LaPorte, a twenty-one-year-old Catholic Worker, set himself alight outside the United Nations building as a protest and subsequently died of his injuries.[57]

Such rumblings had little impact on Oklahoma Catholics, however. In December 1965, the *Oklahoma Courier* published letters from eighth grade students in Tulsa to a Tulsa National Guardsman in Vietnam, most of which echoed what they had presumably heard from their parents about the dom-

54. *Oklahoma Courier*, March 11, 1960.
55. *Oklahoma Courier*, April 26, 1963.
56. Yzermans, *American Participation in the Second Vatican* Council, 219–21, 241–45, 247–48.
57. Friedland, *Lift Up Your Voice Like a Trumpet*, 157–63. For a fascinating account of the development of a pacifist conscience in the priest son of a prominent member of the American military, see Carroll, *An American Requiem*, 157–200, 223–42.

ino theory and the godless nature of Communism. "If I weren't too young and in the eyes of my parents too immature," wrote one boy, "I would like to organize a demonstration just like the others but in favor of Viet Nam policy."[58] A 1966 poll of *Courier* readers basically confirmed a prevailing climate of opposition to a strictly pacifist stance. By 60 percent to 21 percent, Oklahoma Catholics considered the Vietnam conflict a just war. Support for escalating American commitments stood at 43 percent, while 20 percent favored the status quo. Among the critics, 25 percent favored negotiating the best peace possible, while only 9 percent endorsed an immediate withdrawal.[59]

Within the American hierarchy, some bishops stood firmly in the tradition of the 1950s. Cardinal Spellman of New York, who was Military Vicar of the Armed Forces, was strident in defense of the nation's military, while Cardinal Cody of Chicago braved the wrath of sixty protesting seminarians to bless tanks bound for Vietnam.[60] Others, while less nationalistic in their sentiments, shrank from taking a stand on the conflict, recognizing that the Catholic community was by no means united on the issue. Even the organ of the Catholic intelligentsia, *Commonweal*, which took the bishops to task in April 1966 for dodging what it termed the nation's number one moral problem, conceded that they faced a dilemma: "Whatever the reasons, the bishops have not seen fit to comment about the moral issues involved. . . . Part of the problem is undoubtedly that the bishops see themselves essentially as spokesmen, and as spokesmen rather than individual moral leaders, there is practically nothing decisive they can say on the issue—no American Catholic consensus to reflect, no direct translation of Christian values into political terms that could definitively stand on its own merits."[61] Certain Oklahoma priests were willing to make that translation into political terms. Later that month, Fathers William King, James McGlinchey, and John Vrana participated in the International Days of Protest, calling for an end to bombing of the North, a declaration of American readiness to negotiate, and recognition by the United States of the right of the people of South Vietnam to determine their own future.[62]

58. *Oklahoma Courier*, December 10, 1965.
59. *Oklahoma Courier*, April 8, 1966. Only 6 percent of respondents anticipated a military victory within a year, and 46 percent expected peace within three years, while a significant 34 percent expected the conflict to continue indefinitely.
60. Friedland, *Lift Up Your Voice Like a Trumpet*, 174–75.
61. "The Bishops and Vietnam," *Commonweal*, April 15, 1966, 93–94.
62. *Oklahoma Courier*, April 22, 1966. Father John Vrana was a member of the New

Some of the bishops were nevertheless beginning to shift their ground. In June 1966, Cardinal Shehan of Baltimore issued the first pastoral letter on war by an American Catholic bishop, acknowledging the need for patriotism but urging negotiations with North Vietnam.[63] Shehan's relatively mild statement prepared the ground for a more forceful peace pastoral authored by Bishops Paul Hallinan and Joseph Bernadin, which concurred with Shehan on the need for the means employed to win the war to be as moral as the ends desired.[64] As the Johnson administration ratcheted up its military engagement, however, the relative silence of the hierarchy attracted mounting criticism. Protestant ecumenist Robert McAfee Brown rebuked the bishops for failing to support the efforts of groups like Clergy and Laity Concerned about Vietnam (CALCAV), prompting the retort from Bishop James Shannon that the methods of protest favored by CALCAV, however laudable their object, were "simply not the style of the Catholic bishops."[65] Father William King of Tulsa's Church of the Madalene attended the national CALCAV convention in Washington in February 1967 and expressed the hope that other Catholics would get involved. "Communism has changed," he told the *Oklahoma Courier*. "It isn't all bad."[66]

As a member of the U. S. Bishops' Commission on Justice and Peace, Bishop Reed followed the debates on the war with keen interest. On April 2, his provincial superior, Archbishop Robert Lucey, delivered a sermon praising the Johnson administration for opposing Communist aggression (the president was in the congregation at San Fernando Cathedral in San Antonio), a stance that earned the archbishop opprobrium from the *National Catholic Reporter*.[67] Although Reed's perspective was far removed from that of Lucey, he still sought to reassure his people that he was not inclined to absolute

---

York–based Institute for Freedom, which was initially formed to uphold the right of Father Daniel Berrigan to be an antiwar campaigner. See *Commonweal*, November 25, 1966, 240.

63. Spalding, *The Premier See*, 440–42.

64. Shelley, *Paul J. Hallinan*, 273–74.

65. Robert M. Brown, "An Open Letter to the US Bishops," *Commonweal*, February 17, 1967, 547–49; "More on 'An Open Letter': Catholic Bishops and Vietnam," *Commonweal*, March 17, 1967, 671–73 (quotation on 672); Friedland, *Lift Up Your Voice Like a Trumpet*, 179–82. Hallinan attended a CALCAV symposium in New York, where he criticized American war strategy, accusing the military of practicing a policy that involved the extermination of whole villages. He did not offer an alternative strategy, however. Shelley, *Paul J. Hallinan*, 274–75.

66. *Oklahoma Courier*, February 10, 1967.

67. Bronder, *Social Justice and Church Authority*, 130–31.

pacifist convictions and insisted that, regardless of personal convictions, he would support the decisions of the president and his administration. In June, however, the narrow agreement at the annual Clergy Day not to discuss the subject of the war prompted seventy-nine priests to sign a statement urging cessation of bombing in North Vietnam, to which Reed added his signature.[68] It was a defining moment, and local conservatives immediately took to the airwaves to denounce Reed's foray into national politics.[69]

"In spite of the Church having contended for centuries that armed conflict is a last resort," the bishop declared in July, "both the European countries and their heirs in the 'new world' have seldom, if ever, actually employed it as such. Usually, both we and they have resorted to force rather readily, if it was judged expedient. In this age of atomic power, the Church must keep reminding all peoples that resort to war must *really* be the last resource."[70] While he rejected the idea of unilateral withdrawal, Reed stressed that he feared an escalation of the conflict might lead to conflict with China. He and Bishop John Dougherty (auxiliary of Newark) were the first members of the American hierarchy to sign on to the Negotiation Now petition, which had been organized by John Kenneth Galbraith and Arthur Schlesinger Jr. in May 1967, to be joined by Paul Hallinan and James Shannon the following month. An Oklahoma chapter of Negotiation Now also was formed.[71]

Reed's stance on the war drew him into a number of cases in which young Oklahomans sought to defy the draft. One of the earliest, Vincent Maefesky, was a former seminarian who had been expelled from Cardinal Glennon Seminary in St. Louis in 1964 for his vigorous criticism of the mediocrity of the program. Maefesky later decided to study graduate philosophy at the University of Oklahoma. Awarded a teaching assistantship, he was unable to continue after refusing to sign a loyalty oath. Because he had been exempted from the draft under student deferments, Maefesky immediately became eligible for the draft. Although he filed for conscientious objector status in June 1967, saying that his views on the war had changed in five

---

68. *Oklahoma Courier*, June 9, 1967. Paul Gallatin explains the refusal of a majority of the clergy to discuss the issue as being compounded of patriotic hostility to Communism and resentment of the "brash young men" who were seeking to bring the issue before them. Gallatin, interview.

69. Typewritten note, June 26, 1967, Reed Papers.

70. Victor Reed to Leo J. Starry, July 11, 1967, Reed Papers.

71. Friedland, *Lift Up Your Voice Like a Trumpet*, 184–85; Shelley, *Paul J. Hallinan*, 276–78; *Oklahoma Courier*, July 21, August 18, 1967.

years, the Tulsa draft board maintained that he had left it too late to do so.[72]

An equally striking case affected Norman Catholics in 1968, after Pat Vaught, a twenty-year-old member of St. Joseph's parish and a student at the University of Oklahoma, went on trial. Vaught had been exposed to the philosophy of the Catholic Worker while working in New York and on his return refused to apply for student deferment. He was consequently called up for service, and his application for conscientious objector status was denied. Since he refused to make further appeals or report for duty, legal action quickly followed. "The draft board said I should fill out a statement saying how I justified staying out of the draft," Vaught told the judge at his trial. "It seems to me that the draft board should rather be required to fill out a statement for me, justifying its opinion that I should go somewhere and bomb and shoot people." The judge was unimpressed and sentenced Vaught to a five-year jail term.[73]

The war and draft resistance hit very close to home for parishioners of St. Patrick's parish in Oklahoma City after Father Henry Kelly attempted to hold a meeting there in support of another draft resister, Joe Gilchrist. Members blocked the doors and denied access to those attending the meeting, fearful that news of an antidraft meeting on parish property would lead to a decline in financial contributions. One parishioner stated that they had offered to devote the Mass on the following Sunday to the theme of peace, but Father Kelly and his supporters had turned this down. Her conclusion was that they wanted, above all else, a demonstration. The following week, traditionalists at a parish meeting introduced a motion barring use of the parish by any group dedicated to the overthrow of the Catholic Church or the American government (clearly, they recognized a degree of compatibility between the positions), but by then tempers had cooled and the motion was disallowed. Reed's involvement in the Gilchrist case was not over, however. He joined with several other state religious leaders in a mercy plea at the end of November, but the presiding judge publicly declared that the petitioners should stick with the business of saving souls.[74]

<hr />

72. *Oklahoma Courier*, December 1, 1967.

73. *Oklahoma Courier*, September 27, November 8, 1968.

74. *Oklahoma Courier*, November 15, November 22, November 29, 1968. Reed's involvement in the Gilchrist case attracted national attention and requests for support and encouragement. In 1971, a Catholic student who had served in the ROTC at Notre Dame and received a commission in 1965 went on to graduate studies at Yale, where he developed a strong pacifist outlook. "My soul searches for moral justification for modern warfare and

In 1970, as Richard Nixon desperately sought to end American involvement in Southeast Asia, Reed took it upon himself to issue a pastoral letter
to be read in the churches deploring the waste of life involved in the ongoing campaign. Reaction was not slow in coming, for Oklahoma, with its large
number of military bases, was a naturally hawkish state. One of the earliest
critical responses came from a group of Catholic veterans, who warned that
a Communist victory would ultimately put Reed's own freedom of expression and way of life at risk.[75] A more sophisticated rebuke by retired colonel
George Glassman questioned the wisdom of such a pronouncement at a time
when de-escalation and disengagement were already under way:

No doubt, your action was taken with the best possible intentions. However, it is
extremely discomforting to consider the strange lot of bedfellows you have thus become associated with. . . . Unfortunately, your position also tends to associate you,
and all of us, with those "priests" who seem to feel compelled, as self-ordained experts, to enter the arena of dissention and revolt. It makes my heart heavy to hear
of a priest getting involved in, or preaching on subjects, of which he soon makes it
clear he has no understanding—only very definite opinion. Not only do they display their profound lack of knowledge, but they bring discredit on the Church and
embarrass most Catholics.[76]

In military communities like Lawton (home of a major artillery training base at Ft. Sill), priests who preached pacifism quickly found themselves
in trouble. When Father Frank Manning preached a sermon at St. Barbara's
parish in which he suggested that it might be time to abandon the war since
it was doing more harm than good and was therefore illegitimate according
to just war principles, there was an outcry from the relatives of servicemen.
Manning's pastor responded by arranging for a retired army colonel to deliver a rebuttal sermon the following Sunday, which received a standing ova-
tion from the congregation.[77] Not every serviceman defended the status quo,

---

finds none," he told Reed. While he wished to be discharged as a conscientious objector,
he feared that basing his defense on the New Testament and the council documents would
not be considered adequate: "For example, what can I say if a Colonel tells me he was a
practicing Catholic before I was born, and has consistently fought, with the blessing of the
Church, in three wars?" Thomas F. Heck to Victor Reed, January 4, 1971, Reed Papers.

75. "Some more of the Silent Majority, Catholic Veterans of WWII, Korea and Vietnam" to Victor Reed, June 20, 1970, Reed Papers.

76. George H. Glassman to Victor Reed, July 16, 1970, Reed Papers.

77. Frank V. Manning, "A Religionless Priest," in Brousseau, *A Dying Breed of Brave
Men*, 118–19. Some priests took a different approach. A member of one Muskogee parish reported that his pastor had preached a "vehement and super-patriotic sermon" against the
pastoral. Michael S. Ward to Victor Reed, June 28, 1970, Reed Papers.

however. Alfred Turney, a retired lieutenant colonel who had earned a doctorate in modern history after his service and taught at Southwestern State College in Weatherford, declared that he now considered the war unwinnable.[78]

Outside the military community, there was a similar level of uncertainty both as to the morality of disengagement and the appropriateness of the bishop expressing an opinion on the matter. Nancy Dastalik of Pryor questioned whether it was morally right to abandon South Vietnam to the mercies of Communism, while Thomas Clary of Shawnee developed Dastalik's point by arguing that the United States had provided considerable economic aid to struggling nations and most of the funding for the United Nations, which was, after all, "the type of organization recommended by the prelates at Vatican II long after its inception." Reed was hardly an authority on foreign policy, Clary maintained, and to use a pastoral letter to express personal political views on such a subject was wrong: "Don't you think, my dear Bishop, that we have enough problems at home to unite on to solve rather than you attempting to polarize our Catholic community on an issue, which most of us are without an effective means to solve?"[79]

Two parishioners at St. Charles Borromeo parish in Oklahoma City went even further. Kent Snyder reaffirmed the validity of the domino theory and reminded Reed that Catholics were always the first to suffer after a Communist takeover. "If you as a responsible member of the church hierarchy persist in this appeasement of communist activity and denunciation of the deterrent actions of the U.S.," Snyder warned Reed, "then I cannot continue to support this Diocese (and the Church itself, since you represent it) without being hypocritical. This will leave me with no other choice but to leave the Church and continue to support the morally just actions of our courageous country."[80]

For Joseph Freeh, resistance to Communism in 1970 differed in no great wise from resistance to Fascism in 1940, and he believed that massacres would follow a North Vietnamese victory. He also had little regard for the motives of the antiwar lobby: that the antiwar activists were "the very scum of our nation—the long-haired, unwashed, against-everything, dope-using, protesting, irresponsible, loud-mouthed, uncouth, foul-mouthed, flag-

78. Alfred W. Turney to Victor Reed, July 6, 1970, Reed Papers.
79. Nancy Dastalik to Victor Reed, June 22, 1970, Thomas B. Clary to Reed, June 28, 1970, Reed Papers.
80. J. Kent Synder to Victor Reed, June 28, 1970, Reed Papers

burning people—this alone would make me for [the war]." Margaret Clarkin of Tulsa, meanwhile, reminded Reed that encouraging free people to lay down their arms and submit to Communism would be a huge blow to Catholics behind the Iron Curtain, particularly Cardinals Mindszenty of Hungary and Wyszynski of Poland.[81]

Reed did attract his share of support from the advocates of a peaceful solution. In Bartlesville, parishioners of St. James's parish told their pastor that they felt like applauding when the pastoral was read, and several members of Tulsa's Church of the Madalene wrote to express their appreciation.[82] A Tulsan assured Reed that his effort to relate Christian principles to the world in which they lived had helped sustain her faith, while Mel Fiegel of Weatherford reaffirmed the connection between active pacifism and other social justice issues. "These are trying times for the Church," he admitted, "and for those who speak out against racism, injustice, poverty and war."[83]

Joseph Smith of Owasso expressed appreciation for the bishop's stand against the "anti-Christian and barbarous war in Vietnam," and others echoed the praise of Reed's prophetic vision. "Material directorship has frequently been so demanding on our bishops," declared Robert and Mary Cichowski, "that moral leadership seems so often to be given second place." Perhaps the most telling letter of support came from Leo Starry of Oklahoma City who, with his wife, had attended a wake for a soldier killed in Vietnam. "I would like all the 'patriots' who criticized your action in regard to the war to have such an experience," Starry told Reed.[84]

Such appreciative comments were increasingly outstripped by criticism, however. A June 30 meeting at St. Andrew's parish in Moore resolved by thirteen votes to two that most Catholics did not share the bishop's opinion and objected to the way that he made his personal views public.[85] "If we are fighting to preserve the freedom of choice of any people," declared David Thrower of Bartlesville, "who can say so emphatically that we are wrong. In the 'new' Church where freedom of conscience is so emphasized surely we

81. Joseph P. Freeh to Victor Reed, June 29, 1970, .Margaret L. Clarkin to Reed, July 2, 1970, Reed Papers.

82. Revd. Robert T. Pickett to Victor Reed, June 28, 1970, Michael and Mary Kollar to Reed, June 22, 1970, Patricia Anthony to Reed, July 8, 1970, Reed Papers.

83. Lois A. Joyce to Victor Reed, June 30, 1970, Mel Fiegel to Reed, July 3, 1970, Reed Papers.

84. Joseph J. Smith to Victor Reed, July 3, 1970, Robert and Mary Cichowski to Reed, July 18, 1970, Leo J. Starry to Reed, July 31, 1970, Reed Papers.

85. Ruth Bruehl to Victor Reed, July 1, 1970, Reed Papers.

have the freedom to support our government."[86] A newcomer to St. Charles Borromeo parish in Oklahoma City also expressed her distress at the way in which a political point of view had been imposed on a "captive audience" at Mass. Although she preferred not to see politics in the pulpit at all, why could not the other side at least be given a chance to respond?[87] Paul Eckroat of Oklahoma City, who had walked out of Mass once he had heard the gist of Reed's letter, agreed. Many Catholics, he confided to Reed, both cradle Catholics and converts, had told him that they had had enough.[88]

CONCLUSION

"Today, even in our midst, there are too many persons who do not seem to grasp the nature of the mission of the Church," Reed told friends and relatives of the Guatemala mission team at a service of dedication in 1963. "They seem to consider their own sanctification and salvation an entirely individual affair between themselves and God. The collegiality of the Catholic bishops of the world today, the common life of members of the Mystical Body of Christ is lost to them."[89] At every step, Oklahoma's Catholics could see their ordinary leading them onward—whether to renew the spirituality of Indians in Central America or to denounce the wastage of human life that accompanied military efforts to preserve freedom in Southeast Asia. As the Church moved out into this a new phase of prophetic witness, however, some observers expressed reservations. "I'm beginning to wonder about the Catholic Church," a medical student at Southwestern State College in Duncan told Reed. "I wish that all of the church officials would keep their noses out of world affairs that don't concern them. . . . I'm sorry if what I have said has offended you. But I believe the Church's place is at the altar and not in world politics. I wish Pope Paul VI would realize this."[90]

86. David Thrower to Victor Reed, July 3, 1970, Reed Papers.
87. Mrs. B. H. Flusche to Victor Reed, July 11, 1970, Reed Papers.
88. Paul H. Eckroat to Victor Reed, July 13, 1970, Reed Papers.
89. Sermon of Victor Reed, August 11, 1963, Reed Papers.
90. Richard Grace to Victor Reed, n.d., Reed Papers.

part four

The Human Church,
1958–1971

chapter 10

From Pastor to Professional

The Catholic Priesthood in the 1960s

Exercising the office of Christ, the Shepherd and Head, and according to their share of his authority, priests, in the name of the bishop, gather the family of God together as a brotherhood enlivened by one spirit. Through Christ they lead them in the Holy Spirit to God the Father. For the exercise of this ministry, as for the other priestly duties, spiritual power is conferred upon them for the building up of the Church. In building up of the Church, priests must treat all with exceptional kindness in imitation of the Lord. They should act toward men, not as seeking to please them, but in accord with the demands of Christian doctrine and life. They should teach them and admonish them as beloved sons, according to the words of the Apostle: "Be urgent in season, out of season, reprove, entreat, rebuke in all patience and doctrine."

Second Vatican Council, Decree on the Ministry and Life of Priests,
Presbyterorum Ordinis, December 7, 1965

In February 1962, the president of the glass workers' union in Henryetta, Oklahoma (a trustee of St. Michael's parish) requested that his pastor, Monsignor Theophile Caudron, be awarded a papal honor. Three months later, Richard Lane, a Tulsa Presbyterian who had headed a 1954 fund-raising drive for St. John's Catholic Hospital, made the same request. The unusual harmony of labor and business perspectives on this issue spoke to Caudron's abilities as a strike mediator and the high standing he had enjoyed in a largely Protestant community for half a century.[1]

---

1. B. J. Lambiotti et al. to Victor Reed, February 21, 1962, Richard K. Lane to William K. Warren, May 1, 1962, St. Michael's Church, Henryetta File, box 46.1, Archives of

The following year, the *Oklahoma Courier* published a profile of Father Richard Sneed, head of religion at the high school at St. Gregory's Abbey in Shawnee. Forty-eight years Caudron's junior, Sneed had come to Oklahoma in 1939, the year Victor Reed had returned from Louvain. Caudron had been a builder in the old style, a priest who left his mark in terms of bricks and mortar. For him the priest carried the burden of office, and the role of the laity was to obey. Sneed was one of the new breed of scriptural experts, the author of a doctoral thesis on the concept of the Kingdom of God, who had embraced the scientific method of biblical exegesis—the exploration of the biblical texts in the original languages, taking into account the mode of thought of their writers and editors—from a Catholic perspective. Most Protestant Oklahomans knew of Caudron only if they were old enough to remember the strike-torn times of the Great Depression and the monsignor's attempts to negotiate compromises, but many more had heard of Sneed as a result of his appearances on the *Your Bible* television program, where experts answered questions on the Bible.[2]

Rarely was the dichotomy as sharp as between Caudron and Sneed, yet it does illustrate the profound change that the Catholic priesthood was undergoing in the early 1960s. The greater involvement of priests in activities outside the Catholic enclave necessarily involved devolution of a parish priest's traditional duties. In a 1961 letter to the *Courier*, Father John Vrana indicted contemporary parish life as constant "helter skelter." A priest had to delegate, Vrana insisted, by encouraging lay participation in worship and fostering lay leadership in a variety of areas. He also needed to devote time both to the study of contemporary theological developments and to regular meetings with fellow priests to discuss the nature of priestly life.[3]

Vrana's concerns pointed to the limitations under which most parish priests labored until the 1960s. For all practical purposes, the priest alone represented the parish and had no expectation that the laity could or would play an active role either within the parish or beyond it. This state of affairs

---

the Catholic Diocese of Tulsa (hereafter ADT). Caudron was selected as Henryettan of the Year in 1960. Protestant appreciation for the work of Catholic priests grew in the course of the decade. In 1967, four prominent non-Catholics (two senior figures at the First National Bank, the city manager, and a local attorney) signed a letter from the members of Holy Cross parish in Madill requesting that Reed reconsider and not assign the local pastor elsewhere. Holy Cross Catholic Church Congregation to Victor Reed, June 5, 1967, Reed to Holy Cross Congregation, June 15, 1967, Holy Cross Church, Madill File, Archives of the Catholic Archdiocese of Oklahoma City (hereafter AAOC).

2. *Oklahoma Courier*, March 15, 1963.   3. *Oklahoma Courier*, February 17, 1961.

was often encouraged by his episcopal superiors, who felt better able to control pastors who owed obedience to them than laymen who might be more tempted to dissent. Seminary training emphasized the sacramental side of a priest's duties and did little to address his need for training in pastoral counseling and administration, skills especially needed by those serving urban and suburban parishes.[4]

The Catholic movement into suburbia had profound consequences for the clergy. Earlier generations of priests had served as mediators between a largely blue-collar ethnic community and mainstream America, but that world was rapidly passing away. Catholic Action began the process of transforming the laity by encouraging the clergy to take on a more supportive role in the formulation of a lay apostolate, and Vatican II completed the transition by further reducing the gap between priest and people. In addition to the obvious spectacle of priest and layman standing shoulder to shoulder in various social action initiatives, the priesthood would increasingly come to be viewed less as a profoundly distinctive type of service and more as merely another professional occupation. For the first time, there was open acknowledgment that priests were equally prone to human frailty, whether in the form of alcoholism, depression, or sexual indiscretion.

At the same time, the phenomenon of the "hyphenated" priest—one who pursued an academic, literary, journalistic, or political avocation in addition to (and perhaps sometimes to the detriment of) his pastoral responsibilities—became increasingly common. Such "professionalism" was generally welcomed as reflecting a Catholic willingness to take on the secular world. All too often, though, engagement could end in accommodation. "For many," lamented midwesterner James Hitchcock in 1971, writing of those who had left the priesthood to marry, "the validation of 'the world' is simply the canonization of the banal, the exaltation of bland middle-class American values, although one of the main points of the radical critique of the Church is precisely the ease with which the Church has come to terms with society."[5]

4. Appleby, "Present to the People of God," 7–23. One contemporary critic took the majority of parish priests to task for their aversion to intellectual pursuits and their unwillingness to break away from established patterns and traditions. "It is a cliché that [seminary] administrators feel that the good average student makes the best priest," he concluded. "Unfortunately, it is but a brief step from glorifying the average to condoning the mediocre." Fr. Stafford Poole, C.M., "The Diocesan Priest and the Intellectual Life," *Commonweal*, April 9, 1965, 78–81.

5. Appleby, "Present to the People of God," 54–73; Hitchcock, *The Decline and Fall of Radical Catholicism*, 76.

Few would have predicted in 1965 the demoralizing collapse that was to afflict the Roman priesthood, least of all Bishop Reed, but some of his officials had an inkling that problems were looming. In 1965, the diocesan director of vocations warned that with only seventeen students studying in major seminaries, it would be increasingly difficult to sustain the needed replacement rate of eight to ten priests per year. Fewer than half the existing diocesan priests were native Oklahomans, he warned, nineteen counties lacked a resident Catholic priest, and twenty-one parishes were staffed by religious-order priests. With only ten seminarians hailing from out of state, it was clear that, without more vocations, any reduction in support by the religious orders coupled with natural attrition would precipitate a pastoral crisis.[6]

Reed's relations with the priestly community were ambiguous. On the one hand, he was better acquainted with his priests than most bishops since he had been appointed from within their ranks rather than from another jurisdiction. There was an obvious generation gap that separated him from many of the younger priests in his diocese, as compared to the close ties that bound him to the Catholic Action generation, but even among those priests ordained in the 1950s, there were those who regarded him with equal amounts of affection and respect.[7] While always hospitable, Reed lacked some of the gregariousness of his predecessor. To one priest's complaint that the bishop never invited visitors to join him for lunch when they visited the chancery, Reed responded with the telling admission that he wasn't Bishop McGuinness. He was always glad to invite a visitor to partake, he insisted, but it often never occurred to him to issue the invitation. He did enjoy socializing with his clerical colleagues in parochial settings, however, joining a group of them for a meal at which stories of seminary days would be exchanged and some of the bolder spirits might even indulge in a little humor at his expense.[8]

Reed was also assiduous in extending support to seminarians and young

6. *Oklahoma Courier*, March 26, 1965. Reed must have had some awareness of the problem, for in 1961 he informed the pastor of Christ the King parish in Tulsa that he could not replace the latter's assistant, who had been called to full-time duty as a military chaplain, because he was short of men. Victor Reed to Msgr. Daniel C. Fletcher, September 6, 1961, Christ the King Church, Tulsa File, box 2.1, ADT.

7. "I didn't know him," Father Charles Swett declared. "[The Catholic Action generation] were his friends." Monsignor Gregory Gier observed that younger priests who accompanied the Catholic Action stalwarts often got a warmer reception. Clergy roundtable discussion, June 23, 2005.

8. Donovan, interview.

priests in new cures. When Father Joseph Ross told him that he did not want to be absent from Oklahoma for four years while studying in Rome because of the birth of a younger brother, the bishop bent the rules to allow him to return home for a visit after two years.[9] Tensions between Father James Greiner and members of his parish in rural Hugo prompted Reed to visit the parish to say Mass. When the time came to deliver the homily, he requested Greiner to step outside and then informed the congregation that he would not tolerate further harassment of their new pastor.[10] Gestures of this sort evoked great loyalty. "While it was easy to communicate my decision [to seek laicization] to Bishop Quinn, it would have been extremely difficult to tell Bishop Reed," declared Frank Manning. "He had always treated me with kindness and concern."[11] Reed also gave his priests considerable latitude, always provided they gave him ample warning of potential problems. "If something comes up," he told attendees at a Clergy Day, "call me, call the chancery, and if we can get you permission, we will, but don't box me into a corner." When such a warning was not given, he could be uncharacteristically peremptory, as was the case when Father John Bloms, O.S.B., chose to use girl servers in his parish without prior consultation. An infuriated Reed telephoned from Rome (where he was attending the Second Vatican Council) to inform his secretary that he wanted Bloms removed from the parish. He was dissuaded from this course only when one of his diocesan consultors firmly told the bishop that if he wished to take this course he should return to Oklahoma and do it face-to-face.[12]

<h2 style="text-align:center">OKLAHOMA'S PRIESTS</h2>

Sometime in the early 1970s, Father Kenneth King delivered a paper in which he sought to explain to explain why "the very persons on whose loyalty and obedience the efficient structure [of the Church] depends are increasingly abandoning it." The problem, King insisted, was with the structure itself and the "clericalist mentality" that had until the 1960s supported it. The

9. Clergy roundtable discussion, June 19, 2005.
10. Schettler, interview.
11. Frank V. Manning, "A Religionless Priest," in Brousseau, *A Dying Breed of Brave Men*, 122.
12. Donovan, interview. Since Bloms was not a diocesan priest, Reed's ability to discipline him on his own initiative was actually rather limited. On the Bloms affair, see chapter 6.

idea of the priest being a man set apart for holiness had served to deprive the laity of *their* responsibility for the holiness of the Church: "Prayer does not create holiness, neither does education, nor do these things necessarily help one approach life more validly. By double-standarding the priests, that is, by making them represent what the whole Church should be, we are destroying the very thing we're trying to create. The priest cannot be the whole Church for the people, and they cannot wait for the gifted priest before anything Christian happens among them."[13]

Priests should be obliged to reeducate their people, King suggested (perhaps even at gunpoint!), to recognize the Mass and the parish as both their responsibility and their joy. They would come to be seen as participators *with* the people, carrying out a function that was merely a specialization of the community as a whole. "This is not a religion second-hand, accepted blindly from the priest as a sacred oracle. In this context, there is, above all, no refusal of moral responsibility as the community by accepting the off-the-rack morality from a clerical caste to which the care-taking of morals has been entrusted." Ordination had no necessary effect on a man's ability to be an administrator, a theologian, or a scholar, nor did it gift him with the grace to solve every problem that might arise. "The dilemma of the priest," King concluded, "is to be all things to all men, or professional in every field. The mark of a professional is to know his limitations. This points to specialization in the ministry, by reason of what one finds pleasant and fulfilling in his field of competence."[14]

Such analysis begs the question of the extent to which this new philosophy of ministry was internalized by Oklahoma's priestly community. In 1967, Professor Jerry Dewey of Nazareth College in Michigan revealed the results of his study of Oklahoma priests. Dewey's findings, which gave disproportionate weight to priests under forty-five in urban areas (119 out of 186 priests responded to his questions), suggested that 55 percent of priests viewed themselves as moderates, 20 percent as progressives, and 15 percent as traditionalists. Interestingly, Dewey detected very clear class cleavages in his sample. Progressives were more likely to be Oklahoma-born and from middle-class backgrounds (more than half of assistants were progressives, compared to two-fifths of administrators and only one-sixth of pastors). Most saw a con-

13. Fr. Kenneth King, "The Priesthood of the Church," n.d., St. Joseph's Monastery Archives, Tulsa, Oklahoma. This paper was delivered to members of the McAlester Deanery, probably in 1970 or 1971.
14. Ibid.

tinued value in the sacraments but tended to emphasize study, ecumenism, and social reform over such traditional priestly duties as saying daily Mass, making converts, and encouraging the laity to join parish organizations. Traditionalists were more often the product of eastern dioceses and hailed from working-class families. Two-thirds of pastors and half of administrators in the sample, however, were identified as moderates—the "vital element" in diocesan life—and were more pragmatic and issue oriented.[15]

Dewey's findings have to be seen in the context of his sample. A more subjective but universal assessment of diocesan clergy was supplied the professor by Father William Garthoeffner, who sent him a list of diocesan clergy with the chancellor's personal assessment of where they fell on the spectrum (see table 1). Garthoeffner identified fifty-three priests as "progressives" but maintained that one-third of Oklahoma's clergy were "traditional" in outlook.[16] The latter included Garthoeffner's mentor Monsignor John Connor of Our Lady of Perpetual Help Cathedral in Oklahoma City. "Catholicity is strong when it has a dedicated, zealous, holy body of clergy and religious," insisted Connor in 1962. "It is strong when it has a laity which drinks deep of the well of spirituality in the Mass, the sacraments and prayer, and makes this spirituality operative in its daily life in the marketplace of the world." Progressives might consider devotions and Marian worship passé, but Monsignor Connor pledged to continue to offer novenas to the Mother of God.[17]

Four years later, Connor's tone was, if anything, more acidulous: "We are all aware of the unfortunate stupidity of some priests who deride devotion to Mary and who have had the unbelievable gall to scorn the Rosary. . . . We'll continue to honor the Virgin because we firmly believe the Trinity first honored her—the Father chose her as His daughter, the Son as His Mother, the Holy Spirit as His Spouse. Pretty good pattern to follow." Devotions could sometimes take on a distinctly political complexion. The May 1966 sermon of a Redemptorist priest from New Orleans who led the novena provoked outrage from a more liberal member of the parish. "Last Sunday," Herb Giles told Connor, "you subjected us to the teaching of a bigoted, narrow-minded and intolerant man. A man who made libelous, slanderous and mud slinging

15. *Oklahoma Courier*, November 24, 1967. These findings appeared in published form as Dewey, "Role-Conflict."

16. Jerry Dewey to Revd. William C. Garthoeffner, December 20, 1966, Clergy List—Questionnaires, Garthoeffner to Dewey, December 22, 1966, Reed Papers.

17. Cathedral of Our Lady of Perpetual Help bulletin, October 14, 1962, Cathedral of Our Lady of Perpetual Help, Oklahoma City File, AAOC.

TABLE 1. Ideology of Oklahoma Priests in 1966

Ideology	Number	Percentage
Progressive	53	28.5
Progressive/moderate	12	6.4
Moderate	42	22.6
Moderate/traditional	9	4.8
Traditional	64	34.4
Unknown	6	3.3
Total	186	100

Source: Revd. William C. Garthoeffner to Jerry Dewey, December 22, 1966, Clergy List—Questionnaires, Reed Papers.

remarks about the religious and laymembers of the diocese. His talk reminded me of the half-truths and propaganda we have recently heard from our local politicians."[18] Traditionalists also had little tolerance for the doctrine of lay initiative. After Father William Pace arrived at St. Francis Xavier parish in Stillwater in 1963, the new pastor significantly curtailed its tradition of lay activism. "Is it too much to expect," one lay member asked the bishop, "that the spirit of the Church here move with the spirit of the Ecumenical Council in encouraging, rather than discouraging, a more active and intelligent participation of the laity?"[19]

A gentler form of traditionalism was preached by Father Bernard Havlik of St. Joseph's parish in Tonkawa. In 1969, Havlik recommended the value of personal prayer to the candidates from Oklahoma offering themselves for the priesthood. "What I really wanted to write to you courageous young men (no one can deny that it takes a lot more courage to become a priest than it did twenty-five years ago)," Havlik told them, "is to urge each of you to cultivate a manly attachment to prayer, prayer that is both official and private. Such an attachment to prayer will in my estimation keep the goals of the priesthood and above all its obligations always before our minds. . . . It probably wouldn't be hard to get an admission from me that I didn't always pray the office 'attente, digne et devote,' [attentively, worthily, and devoutly]

18. Cathedral of Our Lady of Perpetual Help bulletin, April 17, 1966, Herb Giles to Msgr. John M. Connor, May 2, 1966, Cathedral of Our Lady of Perpetual Help, Oklahoma City File.
19. Katherine Nettleton to Victor Reed, April 20, 1963, Reed Papers.

but perhaps the Good Lord considered more my sense of obligation rather than the other part."[20]

Havlik's advice seemed to fall on deaf ears, for both the Divine Office and personal devotions had fallen out of favor by the late 1960s. In 1967, Father Wade Darnall of Blessed Sacrament parish in Lawton estimated that fewer than half the diocesan priests still said the Office. Darnall refused to require such a duty of his assistant pastors, believing that they would resent such "unsolicited advice," yet another indication that the days when a pastor exercised unquestioned sway over his subordinates were passing away. When Reed told the 1967 Clergy Days (the annual conference for Oklahoma's priests), that he would be willing to allow substitution of meditative reading of the Scriptures for daily recitation of the Breviary, Fathers Forrest O'Brien, Lowell Stieferman, and Louis Lamb all jumped at the chance. "I have said the Breviary for five years now," Stieferman confided, "and I realize the importance of prayer in the life of a priest; however, I find it very difficult to say the Breviary in a prayerful manner because of its length and the repetition of the psalms."[21]

A shift on other matters of pastoral concern was revealed by a poll of attendees at the 1969 Clergy Days, which revealed that 87 percent of Oklahoma priests would be willing to hold a wedding Mass on a Sunday, although only 27 percent were prepared to contemplate private homes and gardens as a suitable location, and even fewer were willing to use chapels in hospitals (21 percent) or in motherhouses (18 percent). When asked if they should be free to act as civil officials in performing the marriages of non-Catholics, three-quarters of priests favored the option for persons free to marry, but only 25 percent were willing to contemplate it in the case of divorced persons. Most supported the distribution of Communion by a designated layman where the pastor deemed it necessary (72 percent) and the development of a permanent diaconate (81 percent).[22]

20. Revd. Bernard J. Havlik to "Dear future priests for the people of God in Oklahoma," January 10, 1969, Reed Papers.

21. Revd. T. Wade Darnall to Victor Reed, March 31, 1967, Blessed Sacrament Church, Lawton File, AAOC; Revd. Forrest L. O'Brien to Reed, n.d., Reed to O'Brien, June 13, 1967, Revd. Lowell Stieferman to Reed, June 20, 1967, Reed to Stieferman, June 21, 1967, Revd. Louis Lamb to Reed, July 20, 1967, Reed to Lamb, July 21, 1967, Reed Papers.

22. Voting Results of Clergy, June 2–5, 1969, Shawnee, Oklahoma, Clergy Days— June 1967–June 1972 File, AAOC. The figures of support for a permanent diaconate are in marked contrast with Father James White's recollection of the cool response accorded his proposal for experimental use of the diaconate at the 1970 Diocesan Council. Although *Lu-*

Progressive priests sought to devolve authority to the laity without delay. "For too long we viewed the Christian life as Sunday Mass, Friday fish and the avoidance of mortal sin," wrote Father Paul Mollan of St. Barbara's parish in Lawton in 1965. "Little was asked of the layman except physical presence and financial support. The net result has been to weaken our social awareness, and to make religion strictly a matter between God and the person. . . . Only when the people of the parish have found each other in Holy Mass will they be in a position to be a 'witness and living instrument of the mission of the church.'"[23]

When Father Ramon Carlin came to St. Cornelius parish in Cherokee in 1963, he forcefully criticized his predecessors for not consulting with the parish about matters of importance and established a parish advisory board to facilitate such discussions. "Each succeeding meeting," he insisted, "has shown a gradual relaxing of its members, progressing from a seemingly suspicious reticence to a state of sincere thinking and discussing questions in some depth."[24] Pastors also sought to remove from themselves the aura of separateness that had characterized the preconciliar priest. "Father [Vincent McGouldrick] has brought our religion to us in a practical everyday way," several teenage Catholics in Henryetta declared in 1969. "He makes us feel that God really *cares* about us, that he isn't just sitting up there judging us. Because Father treats us this way, he doesn't put himself up as perfect, just because he is a priest."[25] In Idabel, a missionary priest was authorized to wear a shirt and tie at civic events in order to make him seem more approachable to residents of the state's Little Dixie region, although the bishop required him to wear a black suit and clerical collar on Sundays and at clerical conferences.[26]

The notion of openness to lay participation needs to be set against the expressed views of certain progressive priests. "Nobody underestimates the tremendous work that is being done at the ordinary level," declared Oklahoma City priest Joseph Duffy in 1960, "but only the outrageous optimist thinks that we are producing apostolic types. In many areas, our best de-

---

men Gentium had restored the permanent diaconate, that decree was not implemented until Paul VI's decree *Ministeria Quaedam* of August 15, 1972.

23. Father Paul Mollan, "The Catholic in Isolation," *Barbarian: Newsletter of St. Barbara's Parish*, June 1965, St. Barbara's Church, Lawton File, AAOC.

24. Revd. Ramon A. Carlin to Victor Reed, June 15, 1963, Reed Papers.

25. Gloria Crotty et al. to Victor Reed, February 5, 1969, Reed Papers.

26. Revd. Bob Cameron to Victor Reed, April 26, 1968, Revd. Charles H. Schettler to Cameron, May 3, 1968, St. Francis de Sales Church, Idabel File, box 50.1, ADT.

veloped form of Catholic Action is bingo, and by contrast, we all know the anemia which is the affliction of our parish organizations."[27] Many priests were also more than a little dismissive of rural Catholic communities. A rural study group concluded in 1966 that the rural population enjoyed a far more generous priest-to-person ratio than its commitment to the lay apostolate justified. Father Lee O'Neil declared that rural Oklahoma was composed of "dropouts, older persons and 'duds,'" while Father Charles White stated that in his Hobart parish he delayed confirmation until the age of fifteen and required every aspirant to make a personal profession of commitment. Some rural parishes, White concluded, deserved to be reduced to mission status.[28] What rural Catholics made of such attitudes can only be imagined.

Some progressive priests, moreover, had a generally low opinion of the readiness of most laymen for the full responsibilities of leadership. "There are few fully developed intellectually grounded authentic profound Christians in the Church (including priests, I must add)," Father William Nerin somewhat condescendingly told Reed in 1964. "You could not trust the care of the material Church to them, especially since it is so intricately connected with the spiritual mission of the Church." All too often they fell short in matters of social conscience, a spirit of poverty, and a theological background capable of reading and comprehending the work of such contemporary theologians as Karl Rahner, John Courtney Murray, and Hans Küng. Work would have to continue, Nerin concluded, on forming a body of informed laity and furthering the intellectual and spiritual development of the priests who would be their mentors.[29]

The crowning irony of Nerin's 1964 declaration was the role he subsequently played in the dissolution of the state chapter of the Christian Family Movement, supposedly the principal institution for lay empowerment within the Church. Father Nerin had been state family life director during the 1950s,

27. *Oklahoma Courier*, April 15, 1960.

28. *Oklahoma Courier*, September 16, 1966. In far-flung rural communities, a solitary pastor was often hard-pressed to celebrate Mass at every mission chapel in his jurisdiction. In one instance in Ardmore, a parishioner complained that the local pastor wanted to celebrate Mass on Saturday afternoon, even though four male parishioners worked in the oil industry, which required regular Sunday shifts. The pastor, however, already had three scheduled Sunday Masses and no assistant. Revd. Charles Schettler, Account of interview with Richard Thompson, June 13, 1967, St. Mary's Church, Ardmore File, AAOC.

29. Revd. William F. Nerin to Victor Reed, March 5, 1964, St. John the Baptist Church, Edmond File, AAOC. It is not hard, after reading this, to feel some sympathy with one of Reed's correspondents, who maintained that some of his priests were setting themselves up as "little Popes." See "A Catholic Mother" to Victor Reed, April 25, 1966, Reed Papers.

but his enthusiasm for CFM declined dramatically after 1960, as he came to consider it to be "playing" at social involvement. "The movement in Oklahoma is dead," he flatly stated in 1966, and he thought it was time for the Church at large to take up CFM's work. Nerin and other clerical activists in CFM then voted to dissolve the state chapter and release committed lay Catholics for more general social action.[30]

Progressive advocacy drew the attention of priests in dioceses where the pace of change was less dramatic. Father Robert Feeney of St. Anne's parish in Bismarck, North Dakota, sought a transfer to Oklahoma because he wished "to participate in the work of the Church in an area where the decrees and spirit of Vatican II are regarded as meaningful norms for today's Catholicism," as did Father Timothy Manello, a parish priest in the Diocese of Harrisburg. "There is just an appalling lack of appreciation of what the Church is about here," Manello told Reed. "Building up the Body of Christ seems to be a synonym for building churches. Duplicity, pettiness and ambition among the priests I know have been a surprise to me. . . . The priests who take Vatican II seriously around here are doomed to limbo."[31]

CLERICAL POLITICS

In the fall of 1968, Father Raymond Berthiaume of Idabel was invited to Paris, Texas, to address a branch of the National Council of Catholic Women. "I was rather surprised that I was asked," the Glenmary priest confessed, "since in most cases in neighboring dioceses, Oklahoma priests are suspect of heresy and radicalism."[32] The development of this reputation owed much to the formation younger Oklahoma priests received at the Theology Institute at St. Gregory's Abbey. The institute's 1966 session included presentations from Dr. Gene Fontinell, Father John O'Connell, S.J., and Father Charles Curran (the priest-psychologist, rather than the theologian). Fontinell stressed the subjectivity of much current theology and emphasized the

30. *Oklahoma Courier*, July 29, 1966; Burns, *Disturbing the Peace*, 222–23; Halpine, interview.

31. Revd. Robert E. Feeney to Victor Reed, December 17, 1966, Revd. Timothy Manello to Victor Reed, n.d. (prob. November 1966), Reed Papers.

32. Glenmary Missioner Newsletter, October 26, 1968, St. Francis de Sales Church, Idabel File, box 50.1. Father Bill Skeehan described how when he went to Los Angeles to perform his niece's wedding, the local pastor put him through a strenuous inquisition because he was convinced that Oklahoma was a "pilot church." Clergy roundtable discussion, June 23, 2005.

importance of personal conscience and the need to "restructure" the Catholic Church, while O'Connell criticized the tendency to see the world in black-and-white terms. Father Curran emphasized personalist morality in his address "Christian Morality Today," attacking "present-day Pelagianism"—the notion that one must keep busy with "holy things" or God won't bless us—and "present-day Gnosticism"—the idea that only the hierarchy knows what religion is about.[33]

Priests were not unaffected by the new orthodoxy, and their parishioners increasingly passed comment on them. Kathleen Jacobs, who had helped organize the first African American women's meeting in a state building in Muskogee, worshipped at St. Augustine's, the "colored" parish in Muskogee. The parish, she declared, "has always had a feel of religion," but by 1967 she no longer felt the sanctity: "That Sunday sermon could well have been given in a Democratic meeting—civil rights, unions, and the whole bit—with Peace and Christianity at properly paced intervals. I do not question proper subjects in proper places. Since my heart attack, I leave after the last washing of hands, or if there is one more song, after the blessing, to avoid crowding. Half way down in my genuflection, I heard the priest roar 'Mass is not over.' All things change. Of change we can be sure. So, one adjusts from the peace and tranquility of that simple lovely religious church to words."[34]

The liberal outlook of many clergy was reflected in their commitment to social activism. At the 1969 Clergy Days, a clear majority of Oklahoma priests endorsed César Chávez's effort to organize the workers in California's grape industry (85 percent) and voiced total opposition to the Nixon administration's proposed antiballistic missile system (72 percent), although thirty-five priests voted against the latter motion, compared with only nineteen who opposed support for Chávez.[35] Father Henry Kelly of Tulsa campaigned so vigorously on behalf of Democratic Party candidates that a clerical acquaintance rebuked him for risking the identification of the Church with a political

33. *Oklahoma Courier*, August 14, 1964; Glenmary Missioner Newsletter, End of August, 1966, St. Francis de Sales Church, Idabel File, box 50.1. It was difficult for orthodox Catholics like himself, William Sherry complained, to accept "the transformation in the younger clergy who we sent away to become theologians but who are turning out to be political and social workers." William J. Sherry to Victor Reed, March 5, 1969, Reed Papers.

34. Kathleen R. Jacobs to Victor Reed, November 24, 1967, Reed Papers.

35. Voting Results of Clergy, June 2–5, 1969, Shawnee, Oklahoma, Clergy Days—June 1967–June 1972 File. For a general discussion of the social attitudes of American Catholic priests, see Greeley, *Priests in the United States*, 90–117.

party; while Father Nerin engaged in correspondence with Senator Eugene McCarthy of Minnesota about the nature of the "new politics" of which Mc-Carthy was a proponent. "I feel a great amount of uneasiness of a special kind on the part of the most perceptive people," Nerin wrote. "It is the uneasiness of a creative, brooding spirit about to set in motion something truly new, new and free and thus not quite knowing what will happen. It is an uneasiness that feels that we have lived out the past and senses the human pain involved in forging such a new future."[36]

Priests who embraced the cause of social activism frequently expressed contempt for Catholics who lived conventional middle-class lives. When attorney Douglas Fox took Fathers Daniel Allen, Forrest O'Brien, and Lee O'Neil out to dinner to develop a better rapport with them, the three priests denounced Fox and south Tulsans generally for indifference to human suffering and the poor. Declared Father Allen: "Some of you will at least write checks, but that's all you ever want to do. You don't want to be involved in [our work] because it's very distasteful and unpleasant."[37] When one well-to-do Tulsan told Reed that if the Tulsa trio worked for him he would fire them, however, the bishop replied: "They don't work for me. They work for the Church."[38]

By 1968, the social activists constituted a political party within Oklahoma Catholicism. After the liberal defeats in the Little Council session, the *Oklahoma Courier* rebuked the liberals for giving up on renewal. "[W]e have the spectacle of liberals lagging badly," the editor lamented, "while the conservative element plods along, finally regaining control like the tortoise who knew all the time that the hare would get too busy taking bows." Provoked by this indictment, the progressive clergy met in Moore (where Father John Joyce was pastor of St. Andrew's parish) in June under the leadership of Father Bernard Jewitt, who invited like-minded laymen to join the "party out of power." One of their first objectives was to continue operation of the *Courier*, which the Little Council had just defunded. Other participants included John Joyce of the *Courier*, William Nerin, John Vrana, William Garthoeffner, and Monsignor Don Kanaly.[39]

Priestly politics involved not just social activism but a drive for corporate

36. Halpine, interview; Revd. William F. Nerin to Hon. Eugene J. McCarthy, September 17, 1968, Reed Papers.
37. Fox, interview.
38. Donovan, interview.
39. *Oklahoma Courier*, June 14, June 21, 1968.

recognition. In June 1965, a priests' commission was organized to discuss problems peculiar to that section of the Church. Questionnaires distributed to the priests in November 1965 revealed anxiety about the future. Priests should have a greater say in their assignments, several argued, especially when those who were doing well in a particular parish had no desire to move. Others maintained that there needed to be a greater recognition of the higher cost of living and the consequent need for higher salaries for priests as well as an adequate pension system. Priests should be encouraged to acquire a professional degree, in law, medicine, or engineering, and be allowed to practice that profession after ordination, thus lending a professional expertise to their sacred duties. Better communication at all levels was also essential. "As to priests communicating with priests," declared one respondent, "I suppose they do communicate according to ages and ordination classes; however, as far as I am concerned, none ever seems to stand still long enough to start a conversation and make it interesting."[40]

For many progressive clergy, the priests' commission was an imperfect voice. William Garthoeffner emphasized that priests needed an organization of their own that would address their specific needs and aspirations.[41] In 1967, this objective was achieved with the establishment of the College of Oklahoma Priests (CO-OP). A voluntary association of diocesan and religious priests, CO-OP was intended "to listen and speak responsibly and relevantly to the modern world by diffusing throughout our diocese the spirit of freedom, honesty, and courage, bequeathed to us by Our Lord, thereby bringing our people, through service, to full maturity in Him," as the preamble to its constitution put it. CO-OP's founders viewed it as a forum for communication among priests, between the priests and the bishop, and between the priests and the laity. It was open to all clergy on an equal basis (including assistants, chaplains, and religious priests) and had a nine-member coordinating board elected by dues-paying members. A written petition of ten members sufficed to place an item on the agenda for the annual general meeting, and a written petition of one-fourth of the membership could summon a general meeting. CO-OP also sought to foster continuing education of the clergy, to contribute to the debates over the salaries and tenure in of-

40. "Answers about topics of the questionnaire November 2, 1965; opinions, suggestions, ideas about what changes should be made in the diocese, especially changes affecting the Clergy," November 6, 1965, Reed Papers.

41. Revd. William C. Garthoeffner to Msgr. Cecil E. Finn, December 23, 1966, Reed Papers.

fice of pastors and assistants, and to obtain a voice in policy making within the diocese.[42]

One of CO-OP's earliest proposals was for a $125 increase in clerical salaries, raising compensation to $275 for pastors and assistants ordained more than six years and $250 for assistants ordained less than six years. Parishes were to continue to meet the cost of room, board, laundry, and car insurance and would pay the diocese $200 toward a priest's retirement and $150 in hospitalization insurance. In exchange, the whole process of stipends and sole fees should be ended, with any financial donations for priestly services going instead into the parish treasury. Many priests agreed that the popular perception that one "paid" for a funeral Mass was a humiliation and embarrassment. Further aggravating this situation were the twin misconceptions that the money went for the support of the Church and that, by making a Mass offering, people had adequately performed their Christian obligations, when emotional support for the family of the deceased might be of greater value. Such a situation did little to improve the perspective of non-Catholics concerning the practices of the Catholic Church.[43]

Priests were given the option of retaining the old system (in which case their salary increase was limited to $50), but pastors could make the decision only for themselves, not for their assistants. The obvious intent of these measures was to eliminate inequities in salary for priests that stemmed from their parish situation[44] and improve the status of those who remained officially "assistants" in their parishes, despite being priests with considerable experience.[45] CO-OP obtained only a $50 raise for all priests, however, since a sub-

42. Minutes of meeting of Priests' Commission, Jesuit Retreat House, Cushing, Oklahoma, January 30, 1967, Reed Papers; "Councils of Priests," n.d., Constitution of the College of Oklahoma Priests, n.d., Priest CO-OP, 1967–1970 File, AAOC.

43. "Report of the Special Committee appointed at the 1967 CO-OP meeting to look into the Questions of Salaries—Stipends—Stole Fees," n.d., Priest CO-OP, 1967–1970 File; Discussion concerning the matter of Stipends and Stole Fees, March 6, 1967, Reed Papers.

44. "There is also a serious inequality among priests in large and small parishes. All priests are required to work all the time—but the remuneration is not the same. Some have even been known to seek larger parishes—not for spiritual reasons but for the money involved. Good parishes—whatever that is—means good income. (It was decided that this point should be discussed but not published.)." Discussion concerning the matter of Stipends and Stole Fees, March 6, 1967, Reed Papers. Stipends were given that a priest might have a certain intention—such as for a deceased person—in mind while he celebrated the Eucharist, while stole fees were free-will offerings made at a time of baptism, wedding, or funeral.

45. Bishop Stephen Leven highlighted the plight of the experienced assistant pastor at the Second Vatican Council, when he spoke of the "forgotten man" of the clerical system,

Bishop Reed ratifies a trust agreement for pensions for priests in 1968.

stantial minority objected to the elimination of stole fees. A proposal at the 1969 Clergy Days that parish councils, after consulting with the pastor and his assistants, might place stipends and stole fees in the parish treasury and supplement priests' income by $75 was supported by only eighty-eight priests (58 percent) and opposed by sixty-three priests (42 percent).[46]

Personnel issues and retirement benefits were also of interest to the leaders of CO-OP. Reed was willing to accommodate some of their concerns by creating a personnel board to make determinations about the assignment of priests to new parishes. More to the point, once it was established, he rarely

---

although this mattered less in rural Oklahoma, where most priests became full pastors within ten years. Yzermans, *American Participation in the Second Vatican Council*, 496–97.

46. Voting Results of Clergy, June 2–5, 1969, Shawnee, Oklahoma, Clergy Days—June 1967–June 1972 File.

opposed its recommendations. In 1966, the board set the ordinary term for a pastor at seven years and the maximum at twelve (in large urban parishes). When priests were polled on this in 1969, most favored seven years (on a scale of seven to twelve) for when a priest *should* be moved and ten years (on a scale of ten to twelve) for when he *must* be moved.[47] The fact that the diocese lacked a funded pension plan and paid retirement packages out of operating income was also of concern to CO-OP, which argued that parishes and the diocese should be jointly responsible for priests' retirement, but that all priests should also participate in Social Security. In 1969, its leaders asked Reed to invest money raised from the sale of diocesan buildings in a retirement fund for priests.[48]

Some priests considered the personnel board to be overly legalistic and more concerned with the process than the person. "We strongly feel," Father Paul Donovan told the bishop in January 1970, "that the present attitude being expressed is too strict. While it is true we need guidelines to work with— the priests are not machines to be moved without utmost care and concern for their feelings and welfare—and the welfare of the people they serve . . . I doubt if there is a major corporation that would handle its key personnel in a manner [such as] we are seemingly treating this problem."[49] A poll conducted in November 1970 reflected a general consensus the board should only *recommend*, not make, appointments and that its members should be chosen by a *combination* of election by the priests and appointment by the bishop. Priests believed that they should have a voice in their appointments, but by a margin of sixty-eight to twelve, they rejected the idea of a parish council approving such decisions. (On the question of whether the board should have lay members, the figures were eighty-nine against and fifty-two in favor.) On the question of improvement of the policies and operations of the board between 1966 and 1970, sixty-six saw improvement, forty-two did not, and forty-nine were uncertain. Finally, a majority favored the establishment of a formal policy for those who left active ministry, including financial assistance for two or three months.[50]

47. Minutes of CO-OP meeting, June 2–5, 1969, Priest CO-OP, 1967–1970 File; Voting Results of Clergy, June 2–5, 1969, Shawnee, Oklahoma, Clergy Days—June 1967–June 1972 File.

48. Minutes of CO-OP meeting, September 18, 1967, Revd. J. Paul Donovan to Victor Reed, September 22, 1969, Priest CO-OP, 1967–1970 File.

49. Revd. J. Paul Donovan to Victor Reed, January 21, 1970, Revd. J. Paul Donovan to "Dear Fathers," January 21, 1970, Priest CO-OP, 1967–1970 File.

50. Report of the ad hoc committee for the study of personnel policies and the personnel Commission, November 23, 1970, Reed Papers.

The College of Oklahoma Priests undoubtedly drew its most active members from the progressive end of the spectrum. In 1969, seven of the fourteen candidates for three seats on the CO-OP Board were progressives, and two of the diocesan consultors elected that year were of the same mind. They followed with interest the steps leading to the establishment of the National Association of Priests' Councils, and Father Paul Donovan attended both the provincial meeting in Austin and the national meeting in Chicago in 1968. In Chicago, Donovan was struck by the attitude of representatives from the large urban dioceses, who understood how professional organizations worked. He also noted the distrust felt by some representatives from the East toward the radicals from Chicago (at one point a representative from Boston warned the hosts to remember that they weren't the only Catholics in the United States and if they didn't start behaving better, the New England delegates would leave). While CO-OP might have seemed amateurish by comparison with some of the larger diocesan groups, it did not experience the same conflict with its ordinary as occurred in Chicago.[51]

Thanks to his tolerance of freedom of expression, Reed was spared the sort of clerical agitation that engulfed many of the other dioceses in the Province of San Antonio. In 1967, unrest erupted in the Diocese of Corpus Christi between Bishop Thomas Drury and his priests' senate. The following year, dissent spread to San Antonio, where attempts to organize a priests' association comparable with that of Oklahoma saw Archbishop Lucey attempt to transfer dissidents to less appealing posts. The ensuing conflict between archbishop and priests tore the archdiocese apart and ultimately led to Lucey's resignation in May 1969. While the Catholic Action pioneer was battling for his survival, Reed was inspired to extend the protection of his diocese to the recently dismissed rector of Assumption Seminary, a move that that could have had serious consequences. "It was the right thing to do and he did it," declared Father Bill Ross, whose Norman parish hosted the rector for over a year.[52]

51. Minutes of CO-OP meeting, June 2–5, 1969, Revd. J. Paul Donovan to "Dear Father," March 7, 1968, Priest CO-OP, 1967–1970 File; Donovan, interview. For a comprehensive, though hardly unbiased, account of the struggles in Chicago, see Dahm, *Power and Authority in the Catholic Church.*

52. *Oklahoma Courier*, March 10, 1967; Bronder, *Social Justice and Church Authority*, 132–62; Clergy roundtable discussion, June 19, 2005.

CONTRACEPTION, CELIBACY, AND LAICIZATION

Agitation against Church policy by Catholic priests was a common feature of the late 1960s, as the idea of the right of personal conscience gathered strength. Perhaps the two most significant issues in this period were contraception, in which priests had a pastoral concern, and clerical celibacy, in which their concern was highly personal. Priests were often called upon to make difficult determinations about medical issues surrounding fertility, such as the use of the contraceptive Enovid for the establishment of a regular menstrual cycle (permissible because suppression of fertility was not the primary intent for its use) or the more involved question of whether two newly married students could use the rhythm method while they completed their education (permissible if their financial situation rendered them unable to raise a child).[53]

During the 1960s, many Catholics anticipated that Rome would modify its hostility to artificial contraception, at least in the case of married couples. "It was almost a given in my mind and I think in the minds of many priests that we would never go back to the traditional teaching," insisted William Garthoeffner. In light of the fact that the papal birth control commission had not yet delivered a verdict in the mid-1960s, many priests advised parishioners to follow their consciences in the years following the Second Vatican Council.[54]

A more relaxed attitude also developed toward Planned Parenthood, at least for a while. In 1965, Father Wade Darnall told Reed that he had been asked what attitude the Church would have toward a Planned Parenthood chapter in Lawton, in the light of the cooperation between Planned Parenthood and the Catholic Church in New Mexico. A year later, the diocesan family life department took the unusual step of arranging with the state chapter of Planned Parenthood to hold a clinic in their Oklahoma City offices once a month to teach indigent women about the rhythm method, arguing that it lacked the resources to staff a clinic of its own, and emphasizing that Planned Parenthood did not advocate abortion or sterilization as acceptable forms of family planning. It was "an experimental working arrangement

53. Revd. Paul F. Mollan to Revd. William C. Garthoeffner, August 28, 1961, Garthoeffner to Mollan, September 1, 1961, St. Barbara's Church, Lawton File, AAOC; Revd. Mallary Dugan to Revd. William C. Garthoeffner, n.d., Garthoeffner to Dugan, March 27, 1961, Blessed Sacrament Church, Thomas File, AAOC.

54. Garthoeffner, interview. See also Tentler, *Catholics and Contraception*, 232–47.

and in no way implies that the Catholic Church has changed its view concerning the morality of using methods of birth control that the Church considers immoral nor should it be construed as a Catholic endorsement of the Oklahoma Planned Parenthood Association," family life department officials insisted.[55]

Progressive priests drew their own conclusions from these changes. In March 1966, Father Bernard Jewitt told participants in a discussion on birth control at Immaculate Conception parish in Tulsa, which included a representative of Planned Parenthood, that he saw little difference between use of the rhythm method and the contraceptive pill. Furthermore, it was a decision that only husband and wife could make. "Even though their conscience is formed within the Church," Jewitt concluded, "it's finally their decision."[56]

Not every layman was enthused by the new pastoral strategy. Joseph Kennedy of the Church of the Madalene complained that Fathers Edward Jeep and William King, who had assisted respectively with instruction for his non-Catholic wife and premarital counseling, seemed unwilling to uphold key facets of Church teaching. Kennedy's objection to the advice of his wife's psychiatrist that she should use the contraceptive pill was treated by Jeep as being unnecessarily scrupulous, while King responded to Kennedy's expressed hope that his future wife would convert by suggesting that he was trying to "force" his faith on her, even maintaining that it might be better if there were more mixed marriages.[57]

Many priests had come to view the ban on artificial contraception as outdated and reacted with disbelief to Pope Paul VI's issuance of *Humanae Vitae* in 1968. Frank Manning, a student of Father Bernard Haring, who sat on the birth control commission, helped draft a critical letter to the American bishops signed by thirty priests pursuing graduate studies at the North American College in Rome.[58] After a visit to the diocesan mission in Guate-

55. Revd. T. Wade Darnall to Victor Reed, May 18, 1965, Blessed Sacrament Church, Lawton File; Philip A. McGuire to Revd. William C. Garthoeffner, February 11, 1966, Press release from Family Life Department to Oklahoma Courier, February 21, 1966, Reed Papers. A "fertility control clinic" had been recommended by Father Robert O'Brien as early as 1962. "The clinic would strive for the advancement of a good positive approach to the solution to be found in the human makeup according to God," O'Brien explained, "rather than remain satisfied in the negative sterile stagnation of an immoral artificial control." *Oklahoma Courier*, March 16, 1962.

56. *Oklahoma Courier*, March 4, 1966.

57. Joseph L. Kennedy to Victor Reed, n.d. (prob. February 1967), Reed Papers.

58. Manning, "A Religionless Priest," 117–18.

mala, Father Joseph Dillon became convinced that the only way to reduce the large Indian families, whose members frequently suffered from malnutrition, was for the local clinic to issue contraceptives. Along with many other Catholics, Dillon signed the massive letter of protest that was published in the *New York Times*.[59] Fifteen Tulsa priests also issued a signed statement saying that it was up to individual Catholics to make decisions about birth control, prompting Reed to warn that those who disregarded the encyclical would have to answer to God for their action.[60]

Father Henry Kelly declared that the encyclical had produced a "crisis of faith" among the members of his nonterritorial parish, the Community of the Living Christ. "It shows no awareness of the real problem of married people today," agreed Father Jewitt. Father James Greiner of St. James's parish in Oklahoma City, meanwhile, was rebuked by a visitor from Missouri who claimed the priest had misquoted the encyclical. "I cannot bring myself to believe that any priest would willfully and sanely give confusion to the faithful in opposition to clear cut statements of the Pope," complained Mark Hoffer, "when he ruled out chemical means, in fact any means that impedes the natural function of procreation."[61]

"I am afraid that the trauma connected with the Papal statement is all on the part of the priests," Chancellor William Garthoeffner reported to his ordinary in August 1968, "who have found it difficult to determine how (or if) they can follow in pastoral practice the instructions; I am getting the feeling from the people that the instruction is not going to affect them, and that they are going to continue to make their own decision about the morality of the pill in their own cases."[62] Along with Father William Ross, Garthoeffner pressed for a discussion of the issues involved by all the priests in the diocese, a proposal only reluctantly agreed to by Bishop Reed, who had already endorsed the encyclical.

At a meeting chaired by Father Paul Donovan,[63] a heated half hour's discussion involving supporters and critics of the encyclical ensued before the

59. Dillon, "Reflections on My Life," in Brousseau, *A Dying Breed of Brave Men*, 61.
60. *Tulsa Tribune*, August 9, 1968.
61. *Oklahoma Courier*, August 2, 1968; Mark Hoffer to Revd. James A. Greiner, August 28, 1968, Reed Papers.
62. Revd. William C. Garthoeffner to Victor Reed, August 4, 1968, Reed Papers.
63. Donovan had already commended Reed for his loyalty to Paul VI: "Please accept my most sincere gratitude for your statement of assent on the Pope's encyclical. I know for you, as well as for our Holy Father, this was not the easiest course of action. The Holy Spirit will guide the Church to a faithfulness greater than ever before." Revd. J. Paul Donovan to Victor Reed, August 8, 1968, Reed Papers.

bishop bluntly reminded his audience that Paul VI had refuted the notion that the principle of totality—that the whole person is worth more than the sum of its individual parts—applied to contraception, and that he had no desire to face his God with the admission that he had failed to listen to his Vicar. With that statement the meeting appeared to disperse, only for Father Donovan to subsequently discover that a rump meeting had continued the discussion and taken a vote on whether to accept the encyclical, even though many priests were no longer present. Garthoeffner and Ross then invited Donovan to speak to a local journalist whom they had invited to cover proceedings, but Donovan indignantly declined.[64] Seventy-two priests subsequently signed a statement urging that it should be left to individuals to reach an informed moral decision on birth control. Father Raymond Berthiaume, who attended the meeting with the bishop and subsequently signed the statement opposing *Humanae Vitae*, maintained that Pope Paul VI had not altered the state of practical doubt that had existed prior to the encyclical and noted that the German, Dutch, Belgian, and Canadian bishops had all embraced the principle of freedom of conscience.[65]

Complementing the debate over birth control was the very real problem of rising clerical opposition to enforced celibacy. The admission of ordained, married Anglicans into the Church in the wake of the Second Vatican Council complicated the picture considerably, since these were men raised in the Western Catholic tradition. While Reed sent a former Anglican priest with five children to Marquette University to obtain a doctorate, he carefully refrained from rushing him through the ordination process.[66] In 1963, Father Donald Smith of Christ the King parish in Tulsa opined that relaxing the rules might bring more Protestant clergy into the Church, but still defended celibacy as liberating.[67] The bishop himself embraced this view in 1968:

For all those who ask the meaning of it, celibacy is a sign. Not of a scorn for the flesh but of a will to give witness in favour of the absolute transcendence of the Lord, His love and His work. But this witnessing will be rather weak if it does not involve a certain asceticism. Celibacy should not be accompanied by the defects of egoism, harshness, moodiness, self-satisfaction, obsessions. The equilibrium of the celibate consti-

---

64. Donovan, interview. Garthoeffner was aware that he was on potentially shaky ground, given the treatment meted out to dissenters in other dioceses, although he expected Reed would be fairly lenient. Garthoeffner, interview.

65. *Oklahoma Courier*, August 16, 1968; Glenmary Missioner Newsletter, October 26, 1968, St. Francis de Sales Church, Idabel File, box 50.1.

66. Revd. William C. Garthoeffner to Revd. Richard Korzinek, January 4, 1967, Reed Papers.

67. *Tulsa Tribune*, June 29, 1963.

tutes a problem for each one, which demands special study if one wishes to have success. And the extreme difficulty of this equilibrium demands, on the part of all the faithful, in case of failure, kindness and understanding and endless patience.[68]

Kindness, understanding, and patience were in short supply in the late 1960s, though all but Reed's harshest critics admitted that he made every effort to solve his priests' difficulties. Part of the problem was that the bishop never personally experienced the sense of loss from his celibacy that many of those who left the priesthood considered to detract from the effective exercise of their ministry. "If we ever got married priests, that [sense of community] would disappear," he once remarked after an evening of conviviality with some of his clergy.[69]

Many of his younger priests did not share their bishop's enthusiasm for the celibate. The 1965 priest questionnaire revealed a growing desire for relaxation of the rules. Change was long overdue, argued one respondent, of a practice "which is of another world and of other centuries; and which, as a Msgr. told me should have never existed in the first place." Another bluntly stated that continuation of clerical celibacy could only result in a fall in vocations: "If freedom of choice concerning celibacy would be given to anyone 'before and after ordination without any discrimination,' many more men would look into that vocation; now as it stands, they would rather work for the Peace Corps, etc., etc., or other welfare agencies for work and devotedness, because they don't feel under obligation, which some day, might become a burden."[70] In 1970, the National Federation of Priests' Councils openly condemned the stance of the American bishops on clerical celibacy and was particularly incensed by the treatment of dissident clergy by Cardinal O'Boyle, archbishop of Washington.[71]

Younger men in the discernment process found celibacy an overly de-

68. Victor J. Reed, "Sacrificial Character of the Priesthood," Serra Meeting, Galveston, Texas, October 5, 1968, Reed Papers.

69. Donovan, interview.

70. "Answers about topics of the questionnaire November 2, 1965; opinions, suggestions, ideas about what changes should be made in the diocese, specially changes affecting the Clergy," November 6, 1965, Reed Papers. The *Courier* also editorialized in favor of clerical marriage: "Marriage alone is not the only answer, but it would help force the priest to live in the world he ministers to. When he preaches and counsels, he would speak from the experience common to most of mankind, rather than from the highly protected and sterile rectory." *Oklahoma Courier*, February 24, 1967.

71. Revd. Dennis C. Dorney to Victor Reed, March 13, 1970, Clergy Days—June 1967–June 1972 File. On national attitudes to celibacy, see Greeley, *Priests in the United States*, 77–89.

manding requirement. Seminarian Robert Fetsch abandoned the ordination process because of "personal loneliness aggravated by obligatory celibacy and the debilitating pressures I presently find in this life."[72] Father Frank Manning concluded that only a few of his colleagues had actually found the "charism" of celibacy. The great majority, he believed, had either broken their commitment to sexual abstinence or found compensation in alcohol, material things, or the exercise of power over their parishioners.[73]

The cultivation of romantic relationships by Oklahoma priests was an ever-increasing problem. Some, like Robert Brousseau, recount their experiences with a palpable bitterness toward the Church, arguing that John XXIII's pronouncements gave an assurance of pending change that was rudely interrupted by Paul VI. "I became less guarded," he writes, "since I firmly and foolishly believed clerical celibacy would be revoked sooner than later. Most priests did." After several short-term relationships, Brousseau fell in love with a woman twenty years his junior, the daughter of a parish family. Brousseau makes no apologies for cultivating their relationship while still in holy orders and although he left the priesthood in 1967, he was not married until the following year.[74]

Joseph Dillon, by contrast, first became acquainted with Carole Molyneaux, a Sister of Charity, in 1964, when both were students at Marquette University. In 1968, Dillon hired her to join the Tulsa branch of the Catholic Religious Education Office, though he had left for St. Patrick's before she arrived in Oklahoma. Dillon insists that initially their relationship was entirely platonic. By June of 1971, however, his feelings had changed, and in August he gave up his ministry at St. Patrick's. In his farewell sermon, Dillon assured parishioners that he continued to value the priestly ministry, but he was no longer willing to accept the idea that ministry and marriage could not be reconciled. His experience, he said, testified to the centrality of human love as expressed in marriage to the Gospel message.[75]

Although both men would have denied it strongly, their relationships were not and could not be treated as purely private matters. "We also thank God that some of the drop-out priests that got married are now getting divorces, having found that after all that was not the life for them," declared

72. Robert Fetsch to Victor Reed, May 12, 1971, Reed Papers.
73. Manning, "A Religionless Priest," 120.
74. Robert J. Brousseau, "My Quest for Freedom," in Brousseau, *A Dying Breed of Brave Men,* 178–88, 194–95 (quotation on 180). The sense of Paul VI's "betrayal" is not peculiar to Brousseau. See Garthoeffner, interview.
75. Dillon, "Reflections on My Life," 58, 61, 65–66.

Guatemala missionary Joseph Trimble in 1968. "[N]o doubt such will help to prevent others from going astray."[76] The ripple effect only strengthened as more and more priests sought laicization. "The day I was ordained a priest, eight priests left the [Oklahoma] priesthood," recalled Monsignor Gregory Gier, who became a priest in 1967. The following year, fourteen priests, including Gier's former vocation director, followed suit. When Gier moved from his first assignment to St. Patrick's in Oklahoma City, he told Reed that the bishop was "sending him home to mother," for Gier's parents lived in the neighboring parish. "I'm sure you'll be able to handle the situation, Gregory," Reed told him.[77]

It was not the proximity of family that proved most unsettling, however, but the clerical relationships that prevailed in the rectory, for Gier soon discovered that three priests in the parish were dating. In 1969, Father Joseph Dillon, the new pastor of St. Patrick's, officiated at the wedding of Father Edward Jeep. Although this troubled Gier, Jeep had at least left the priesthood before his marriage. The final straw came a year later, when Father Donald Hanley, who had succeeded Jeep as the adult education director for the diocese, announced that he was engaged and planned to marry as soon as his bride-to-be was released from her religious vows. What concerned Gier was that Hanley seemed to assume that after marriage he would simply continue not only to pursue his diocesan work but also to exercise his functions as a priest. Gier therefore told Dillon, albeit with some trepidation, that he refused to share the altar with Hanley:

I said: "When I walk to that altar and I have a collar around my neck and I say Mass, I say out loud to all the people in that church that I am a living, celibate priest. That's what the collar means in the Roman Catholic Church. And if Don Hanley walks to that altar and performs the same service to these people that I am performing, it is assumed that he is a living, celibate priest. And I am not going to live through a lie. So I don't really care how you handle this, but next Sunday if you don't announce to the people that Father Hanley is engaged, I'm going to, because I'm not going to live through another year like last year. And I think the integrity of this Church and the integrity of that altar demands that the people know what's going on."[78]

In 1962, there had been 189 Oklahoma seminarians studying at St. Francis de Sales Seminary, St. Gregory's College, and out-of-state seminaries. Five years later, that figure had fallen to 99, and by 1969 it stood at 52. A similar

76. Joseph and Kay Trimble to Victor Reed, February 23, 1968, Reed Papers.
77. Gier, interview.
78. Ibid.; Dillon, "Reflections on My Life," 60.

trend was evident among those already in holy orders. The high point for diocesan priests had been reached in 1966, when there were 193 active in the diocese. Over the next two years the diocese suffered a net loss of 12 priests. After a slight rally between 1968 and 1969, a more dramatic slump took place in 1970, when a net loss of 18 priests was recorded.[79]

Between 1966 and 1970, the diocese lost about one priest in eight, even as the pool of potential replacements steadily shrank; the hemorrhage would continue into the 1970s. In one extreme case, the pastor of St. Teresa's Church in Harrah simply walked out of his church one day without warning or permission and was discovered a month later working at a Sears Roebuck store in Oklahoma City.[80] These losses were catastrophic for the Catholic community of Oklahoma, already traumatized by so many changes in the life of the Church, and they deprived those priests who stayed of much of the moral authority with the laity that they had previously enjoyed. "You have to establish your own identity and credibility," said Monsignor Gier, current rector of Holy Family Cathedral. "We cannot be angry with the people in their thirties, forties and fifties who say: 'Well, I'm not going to do that' [when the Church proclaims difficult moral teachings], because the boys in the club are the ones that created the credibility gap."[81]

In Gier's view, the departing priests constituted two separate categories. The first were those priests who had been sent to conduct advanced study in European and American seminaries. These men were the cream of the crop, well-educated, highly motivated clergy filled with the sense of mission—those for whom the conveners of the council had prayed. At the same time, they were filled with the assurance of their personal prophetic vision, which seemed to them as infallible as the pope. An observer of Father Louis Lamb of St. Mary's parish, Tulsa, described with alarm how in a sermon the priest had declared that Pope Paul VI "is an interim Pope—that we are all waiting for him to die so that we can get going!"[82]

Another group identified by Gier were those whose seminary training proved insufficiently rigorous to resist the climate of change. Caught up in the revolutionary moment, they ultimately went down in flames. Monsignor James Halpine offered a less involved but equally plausible rationale. "I

79. *Official Catholic Directory* (hereafter *OCD*) (1962), 580; *OCD* (1966), 635; *OCD* (1967), 655; *OCD* (1968), 575; *OCD* (1969), 590; *OCD* (1970), 587; Halpine, interview.

80. Rt. Revd. Philip Berning, O.S.B., to Victor Reed, n.d. (prob. August 1967), St Teresa's Church, Harrah File, AAOC.

81. Gier, interview.

82. James E. Martin to Victor Reed, August 20, 1967, Reed Papers.

think we lost so many [priests]," he said, "because they had no one to fight against, no bishop to fight against, they could never leave saying they were persecuted . . . there were no such boundaries." For those who stayed, Gier and Halpine among them, resentment toward those who left could not be entirely avoided. "The fact that they were leaving betrayed you," explained Gier, "but you could hardly allow that to surface emotionally."[83] For Reed, the departures were scarcely comprehensible. "They're leaving the Church," he once remarked about those seeking to be laicized, "Why do they care what the Church says?" The pain he experienced was considerable, however, for he felt that he had personally failed them.[84]

CONCLUSION

Viewed from a purely clerical perspective, Oklahoma in 1971 presented a sad commentary on renewal. All the assurances that the new life of the Church included an enhanced role for those in holy orders seemed to have come to nothing. The more priests sought to engage with the world on its own terms, the less there seemed the need for them to form a special apostolate defined by what were dismissed by activists as archaic rules and practices. Many, too, seemed to forget that the people whom they served were at different states of readiness to receive the new conciliar teachings. As progressive clergy pressed on with the work of renewal, they frequently neglected to carry their people with them, seeming more ready to serve as leaders of a particular faction within the Church than as pastors responsible for the entire Body of Christ. When the pace of reform slowed, it was inevitable that some would interpret this as an institutional failure and seek an escape through laicizations.

For those priests who clung on desperately in the maelstrom, many of the anchors that had helped keep them stable in their calling seemed to have been swept away. Some, unsurprisingly, reacted to these unfamiliar times by developing an understandable concern with the material conditions of their employment, which only served to accentuate the transformation of the priesthood into simply another professional organization, the remaking of the Catholic priesthood into something more akin to its American Protestant counterpart, a provider of services as much as an administrator of sacraments.

83. Gier, interview; Halpine, interview. For other reasons for priestly resignation, see Greeley, *Priests in the United States*, 164–92.
84. Gallatin, interview.

chapter 11

The Cost of Discipleship

Catholic Sisters and Modernity

Common life, fashioned on the model of the early Church where the body of believers was united in heart and soul, and given new force by the teaching of the Gospel, the sacred liturgy and especially the Eucharist, should continue to be lived in prayer and the communion of the same spirit. As members of Christ living together as brothers, religious should give pride of place in esteem to each other and bear each other's burdens. For the community, a true family gathered together in the name of the Lord by God's love which has flooded the hearts of its members through the Holy Spirit, rejoices because He is present among them. Moreover love sums up the whole law, binds all together in perfect unity and by it we know that we have crossed over from death to life. Furthermore, the unity of the brethren is a visible pledge that Christ will return and a source of great apostolic energy.

Second Vatican Council, Decree on the Adaptation and Renewal of
Religious Life, *Perfectae Caritatis*, October 28, 1965

On Palm Sunday 1964, Victor Reed brought a message of encouragement to members of the orders of religious women based in Oklahoma. "We are living in an era of remarkable change," he told them. "The changes are affecting the whole Church in all its parts, viz., the bishops, the clergy, the religious, and the laity, so that each Catholic must now rethink his role in the light of the reorganized mind of the Church." The bishop encouraged the sisters to cooperate more closely with his diocesan clergy. "Priests and sisters must learn to work together as never before," he told them, "at least as they have not worked together perhaps since those holy women acted as helpers to the apostles." Direct involvement in the work of spiritual renewal was essential. "Read, study, discuss what is going on and how this will affect you and how you can bring all this to bear in your witnessing to the Word of God in our times," the bishop insisted.[1]

The religious communities needed all the moral reinforcement they could get. Several reports in the diocesan newspaper in 1963 had already drawn attention to the process of change as it related to women religious, none of which caused more controversy than an article on postulants to the Benedictine community in Tulsa. Such women, the *Oklahoma Courier* reported, "think that instead of building an aura of sanctity around themselves, these nuns would do better to come down to earth and depict life in the convent as a continual striving for perfection and charity in which the nuns never completely succeed." As representative of the views of the laity, the article quoted Jerry Funk, who thought it would be "a great mistake to let my child join any community which can't see beyond the rosary," and his wife, Jill, who preferred that her daughter enter a lay apostolate.[2]

Sister Marie de Paul of the Sisters of Charity denounced the religious life series for suggesting that the Benedictines condescended toward other communities, especially cloistered ones, which was far from the case. Some laymen were equally concerned about the way in which the active life had been elevated over the contemplative. One Oklahoma City resident emphasized the prayerful contribution made by the cloistered Discalced Carmelite Sisters, whose convent had been in the city since 1939. A Norman woman, meanwhile, offered a more generalized defense of contemplation: "While all the orders do good and most important work, I have always thought the contemplative made the most complete sacrifice; that he or she chose the better part. To say that a life of prayer and penance for the sins of the world, is wasted and unchristian is nonsense. Surely we need these cloistered souls to bind up our moral wounds as much as we need good teachers and expert medical care."[3]

The religious life series also attracted unfavorable attention beyond the diocese. Mother Mary Susan Sevier, O.S.B., a Benedictine and president of the Congregation of St. Scholastica, roundly denounced the *Courier*, while Father Lawrence Spencer, O.S.B., of St. Benedict's parish in Shawnee,

1. Bishop Reed's address to the Sisters on Palm Sunday, 1964, St. Joseph's Monastery Archives, Tulsa, Oklahoma.
2. *Oklahoma Courier*, February 8, 1963.
3. *Oklahoma Courier*, February 15, February 22, 1963.

warned that it could only discourage female vocations and sow confusion among the laity.[4] The bishop, however, largely refrained from passing judgment until August, when he personally responded to a complaint from a Dominican sister about the press coverage. "The appearance of such [articles] are an evidence of the freedom which I feel should be allowed to our Catholic lay writers," he told her, "in order that they may progress in worthwhile service to the Church. We are bound to encounter some criticism, bishops as well as priests, but it will serve to sharpen our awareness of faults and then our progress toward a more perfect fulfillment of the ideal service we owe Christ and his Church."[5]

Press freedom was all very well, but the fears of the *Courier*'s critics were not groundless. Religious orders of women had played a vital role in Catholic education and medical care in Oklahoma for over half a century. During Reed's episcopate, the number of sisters in Oklahoma peaked in 1959 at 792. Over the next three years, the diocese suffered a net loss of 72. Dramatic losses of 58 sisters between 1965 and 1966 and 46 sisters between 1968 and 1969 contributed to the picture of an institution in free fall. In the last year of Reed's life, the worst loss of all, amounting to 84 sisters, occurred. In 1971, the total number of women religious stood at 546, a net loss of 246 sisters since 1959 and a mean loss of 20 per year.[6] At issue was the question of whether the process of renewal of the religious orders contributed to that decline or helped prevent an even higher rate of attrition than was actually experienced.[7] By the late 1960s, many observers had come to the conclusion that, whatever the merits of stressing the active life, it was doing little to attract a new generation of postulants.

EDUCATION

From the earliest days of a Catholic presence in Oklahoma, religious orders of women played a key role in education. It was perhaps symbolic of their growing difficulties that Tulsa's Benedictine community, which supplied

4. Mother Mary Susan Sevier, O.S.B., to Victor Reed, March 9, 1963, Revd. Lawrence Spencer to Reed, July 18, 1963, Reed Papers.
5. Victor Reed to Sr. Mary Benedicta, O.P., August 17, 1963, Corpus Christi Church, Oklahoma City File, Archives of the Catholic Archdiocese of Oklahoma City (hereafter AAOC).
6. *Official Catholic Directory* (hereafter *OCD*) (1959), 563; *OCD* (1962), 580; *OCD* (1965), 624; *OCD* (1966), 635; *OCD* (1968), 575; *OCD* (1969), 590; *OCD* (1971), 590.
7. For a discussion of this, see Ebaugh, *Out of the Cloister*.

teaching sisters for parochial schools that served one quarter of Oklahoma's
Catholic children, should suffer the abrupt collapse of its flagship institution—Benedictine Heights College. During the late 1950s, the college's enrollment had swelled from 167 to 321, and the student body contained representatives of fifteen states and seven foreign countries. The college employed
some extremely talented faculty, including eight recipients of National Science Foundation summer stipends in 1963. Overshadowing such academic achievements, however, was a swelling burden of debt, which exceeded
$2.5 million by 1960. "The Order is hopelessly bankrupt," declared the bish-
op's board of control in March 1960. "If this situation is not courageously
met, acknowledged as a fact, and a solution found, the Benedictine Order
will cease to exist, and the Diocese will be prostrate by a mountainous obligation which could immobilize it for a quarter of a century."[8]

The board limited scholarships to tuition only, blocked renewal of the
contracts of several secular faculty, and requested other faculty members, secular and religious, to accept voluntary pay cuts. It also mothballed the college's air-conditioning equipment. For a time, there was optimism that the
college could be saved, and local pastors were urged to encourage attendance by their high school pupils.[9] By the end of 1960, such optimism had
faded. Reed authorized students and lay faculty to try to raise money to continue operations, but suspended all teaching in November, except for members of the community and seniors scheduled to graduate in 1961. Although
the question of reopening the college was resurrected in 1964, when the idea
of establishing two junior colleges in the diocese was briefly contemplated,
Benedictine Heights College was never again to serve as an educational establishment for Catholic laity.[10]

The failure of Benedictine Heights College was a serious blow to the morale of the community and, as we shall see, it fostered divisions that would
lead to a constitutional crisis later in the decade. To some extent, this educa-

8. J. A. Padon to the Ford Foundation, February 3, 1960, Minutes of the Second Meeting of the Board of Control of the Institutions of the Benedictine Sisters in Oklahoma,
February 26, 1960, Minutes of the Fourth Meeting of the Board of Control of the Institutions of the Benedictine Sisters in Oklahoma, March 11, 1960 (quotation), Reed Papers. The National Science Foundation summer stipends are reported in *St. Joseph's Convent News*, May 15, 1963.

9. Minutes of the Fourth Meeting of the Board of Control of the Institutions of the
Benedictine Sisters in Oklahoma, March 11, 1960 (quotation), Reed Papers.

10. Sr. Jane Marie Luecke to Victor Reed, February 22, 1961, Mother Marie Denise
Mohr to Reed, May 22, 1964, Reed Papers.

tional failure was offset by the commitment of other religious communities to state university Newman programs. In May 1964, Father Clement Pribil reported that an Ursuline sister was joining the staff of the Catholic Center at Oklahoma State University in Stillwater. She had a master of arts degree in political science and was working on a doctorate at Notre Dame University. Pribil asserted—on the strength of the presence of one Catholic sister—that this was the first Catholic center in the nation to have a "convent" built into it and that it was far from being a "ping pong and pool" apostolate. "I feel that this is a very important DIALOGUE *within* the Church," he told Reed, "which has been overlooked by most Religious Orders until recently."[11] The following month, the bishop welcomed an expression of interest from the Sisters of Charity of the Blessed Virgin Mary in a university apostolate and invited them to consider the University of Oklahoma as well as Oklahoma State University, noting that sisters could be most effective witnesses.[12]

Sisters were not present on campuses solely to serve their Newman centers. As the educational requirements for teacher accreditation steadily increased, more and more communities found it necessary for them to obtain their bachelor of arts degree within the normal four-year period, rather than during summer sessions over many years (as had frequently been the case). In 1961, Mother Celine Carter of Oklahoma City's Carmelite community indicated that she was reluctant to take on any more parochial schools in the diocese because of the need to send more sisters to college.[13]

Higher education separated sisters from the life of their community for extended periods of time. So acute did this problem become that a group of Benedictines at Oklahoma State University sought to fashion an experimental community in which student-sisters and faculty-sisters could live their communal vows within an academic context. While acknowledging that university life inevitably imposed individual schedules and duties on its members, the sisters made arrangements for prayer, dining, and recreation in common and pooled their financial resources to gain most benefit from the motherhouse's expenditures on their behalf.[14]

11. Revd. Clement E. Pribil to Victor Reed, May 30, 1964, St. John University Church, Stillwater File, box 81.1, Archives of the Catholic Diocese of Tulsa (hereafter ADT).
12. Victor Reed to Mother Mary Consolatrice, B.V.M., June 22, 1964, St. John University Church, Stillwater File, box 81.1.
13. Revd. Ernest A. Flusche to Victor Reed, July 12, 1961, Reed Papers.
14. Mother Mary Consolatrice, B.V.M., to Victor Reed, January 16, 1964, College Community in Stillwater: Proposal for an Experiment in Community Living, n.d., Reed Papers.

The new vistas exposed by campus life transformed the expectations of many sisters. Even when they had completed their educational training, the lives that they subsequently lived were frequently extensions of their university experience. One group of Benedictine sister-teachers at Bishop McGuinness High School in Oklahoma City lived a comfortable middle-class existence in a bungalow. Teaching sisters, according to Sister Judith Tate, who held a master of arts degree from the Catholic University of America, "want to serve God as intelligent human beings and not as unthinking religious machines." The Benedictines already offered considerable freedoms not granted by other communities, including the right to attend movies and concerts, to visit private homes and drive cars, but the McGuinness teachers sought even greater freedom, including the flexibility to decide when the completion of tasks might necessitate arriving late for community prayer or even missing it altogether.[15]

The increasing need to free sisters for educational development led many communities to seek a rollback of existing commitments. "As usual," Mother Marciana of the Sister Adorers of the Most Precious Blood told Reed in January 1963, "I am in the unhappy position of not having nearly enough Sisters to fill the requests that come in; indeed, we scrape bottom just to staff adequately the schools we have." Noting that St. Mary's School in McAlester had three certified teachers for fifty-one children, she argued that it would be better to close the school and reallocate her teachers. Mother Marciana complained that the obligations imposed on the sisters to teach religious vacation schools, combined with the longer school year required for certification, meant that some of them went "from the year's classroom to the vacation school to the summer school classroom, and then into retreat, and finally back to the classroom for a year again, with sessions with dentist and doctor somehow squeezed in."[16] It was hardly a recipe for healthy minds in healthy bodies. Three years later, Mother Mercedia of the Felician Sisters declared that if members of her community were to take on a new school at Duncan, they should be freed from their current commitment to Broken Arrow. She added that, in any case, she needed a year's grace to allow for losses consequent upon death, resignation, and commitments to the Sister Formation program.[17]

15. *Oklahoma Courier*, January 25, 1963.

16. Mother M. Marciana, Ad.PP.S., to Victor Reed, January 11, 1963, Reed Papers.

17. Mother M. Mercedia, C.S.S.F., to Victor Reed, April 6, 1966, St. Anne's Church, Broken Arrow File, box 27.1, ADT.

Teaching orders were increasingly unwilling to tolerate bad treatment of their members either by the pastor or the parish. When a conflict erupted at St. Catherine's School in Tulsa in 1964 between the pastor and one of the teachers at the school, the teacher's superior made it clear that she would not allow her sisters to be "shoved around." The priest had accused the teaching sister of undue interference with parish affairs and with the liturgy, and with favoritism toward the children of parish families, but Bishop Reed took seriously the threat that the sisters would be moved if the pastor was not, and the priest left St. Catherine's parish in 1966.[18]

Religious superiors watched just as closely to see if their efforts were appreciated by the local community. In 1964, the Franciscan superior general threatened to withdraw her sisters from the mission school in Anadarko because so many local parents seemed to prefer the public school. Reed conceded that many parents did not seem to hold Christian education in high esteem, but he urged her not to abandon Anadarko. He needed every one of the seventeen orders that contributed teaching sisters to Oklahoma, he told her.[19] The bishop employed a subtler strategy to block the withdrawal of the Sisters of the Sorrowful Mother from the grade school in Broken Arrow in 1966. He pointed out that their expressed wish to start a high school at their Broken Arrow convent required accreditation from the state. Such accreditation would require a student body of at least one hundred pupils, the bishop went on, and so the parochial school would represent an essential feeder school for them.[20] The bishop's efforts to keep sisters in his beloved home parish of Holy Family Cathedral came to nothing a few months later when Mother Amata of the Sisters of Divine Providence sought to withdraw from the school with the comment that most of the pupils taught there were not Catholic. Her community was also closing schools in Texas and Arkansas, she explained, one of which they had operated since the 1870s: "It all seems heartless, especially when we have to face a reluctant pastor and parishioners," she told the bishop, "but we have to be objective enough to do what is best for the schools in general."[21]

18. Revd. William J. Meyer, C.PP.S., to Victor Reed, October 14, 1965, Reed to Vy. Revd. Daniel E. Schaefer, C.PP.S., July 14, 1966, St. Catherine's Church, Tulsa File, box 10.1 , ADT.

19. Mother Mary Agnes, O.S.F., to Victor Reed, January 14, 1964, Reed to Mother Mary Agnes, February 12, 1964, St. Patrick's Church, Anadarko File, AAOC.

20. Victor Reed to Mother Mary Regina, S.S.M., January 12, 1966, St. Anne's Church, Broken Arrow File, box 27.1.

21. Mother M. Amata, C.D.P., to Victor Reed, March 26, 1966, Reed Papers.

Reed did his best to accommodate the teaching orders. In April 1966, he told the pastor of St. Teresa's parish in Harrah that he was temporarily closing the local school while the sisters rebuilt their numbers. In contrast with some other localities, he viewed this as a temporary measure, for Harrah was a suburb of Oklahoma City that was expected to grow rapidly in the years ahead.[22] The bishop also took steps to raise the salaries of teaching sisters, a matter of increasing importance to religious communities as more of their members obtained higher degrees. An illustration of the problem of teacher compensation is demonstrated by the contrasting salaries paid to members of the Carmelite Sisters of St. Therese teaching in Oklahoma (who at the time received $75 per month) and those teaching in California (who received $225 per month plus board, lodging, and transportation). Even allowing for Oklahoma's lower cost of living, it was an unsatisfactory differential. Mother Amata of the Sisters of Divine Providence warmly praised the bishop in 1964 for a decision that she knew would require sacrifices by the parishes. That there was a significant cost was confirmed by Reed when he warned his priests that sisters' salaries would rise from $1,500 for Oklahoma-certified and $1,200 for noncertified teachers in 1968 to $1,800 and $1,500 respectively by the school year of 1971–1972.[23]

Despite such ameliorative measures, the loss of teaching personnel continued throughout the decade at an accelerating rate. Between 1960 and 1971, the number of sisters in all the religious teaching orders in Oklahoma fell from a high of 467 to 211, a net loss of 258 and a mean loss of 23 per year. In 1960, teaching sisters had represented 68 percent of the faculty in Catholic schools; eleven years later they represented just 41 percent of the faculty.[24]

HEALTH CARE

Most Oklahoma sisters not involved in teaching were health care workers at major hospitals.[25] Both the Franciscan Sisters of Maryville, Missouri, and

22. Victor Reed to Revd. Timothy P. Maloney, O.S.B., April 13, 1966, St. Teresa's Church, Harrah File, AAOC. In fact, St. Teresa's school never reopened.

23. *Oklahoma Courier*, February 1, 1963; Mother M. Amata, C.D.P., to Victor Reed, April 14, 1964, Victor Reed to "Reverend and dear Fathers," February 27, 1968, Reed Papers.

24. *OCD* (1960), 567; *OCD* (1971), 590. Nonteaching sisters were mostly engaged in hospital work, although both the Benedictines and the Carmelites also maintained cloistered communities.

25. For a general overview of hospitals in Oklahoma staffed by Catholic religious orders, see *Oklahoma Courier*, May 8, 1964.

the Sister Adorers of the Most Precious Blood had major commitments in Oklahoma. The Franciscans' primary undertaking was St. Anthony's Hospital in Oklahoma City, where thirty-five sisters maintained a 611-bed hospital.[26] With the Benedictines, many sisters expressed appreciation for the changes in community discipline that had begun to make themselves apparent even before 1965. These included a shorter Divine Office, modifications in dress, two weeks' vacation every year, and a three-day home visit every three years. Still, there was concern that the continued bar on eating with patients and student nurses and on eating meals outside the hospital would discourage future recruitment. "The educated girls whom we hope to attract have led a permissive life," one sister wrote. "As sisters and supervisors they will be expected to hold responsible jobs and to use their best judgment in their work. They want to accept religious obedience, but not a blind one."[27]

The potential for tension between the advocates of professionalism and their critics built up steadily over the next six years. During the late 1960s, St. Anthony's was criticized by the city government for failing to accept county charity cases, while its medical staff protested that the hospital was operating at only 60 percent capacity. A successful effort by the new lay administrator brought the hospital back to its first profitable showing in many months in 1969. In February 1970, the hospital took out a $21 million loan for construction and improvements, the largest ever negotiated in the county, winning it the confidence of the local business community. Credit for the change in fortunes went to Sister Teresa Nagel, the superior of the hospital, who had worked closely with the lay administrator and was responsible for the establishment of a special heart unit.[28]

To the surprise of many outside the community, Sister Teresa's achievements were not well received by her superiors in Missouri, who ended her term in office seven months early in March 1970, without even the month's notice customarily given. They ordered her to return to the motherhouse to assume new duties. Sister Teresa's termination coincided with the vacation of

26. The Franciscans also ran Alverno Heights Hospital in Guthrie, but this was a less than ideal arrangement. Local doctors conducted most of their laboratory and X-ray work in their own offices and failed to utilize their courtesy privileges at St. Anthony's when they sent their patients to hospitals in Oklahoma City. See Mother M. Vincentia, O.S.F., to James S. Petty, September 20, 1967, Reed Papers.

27. *Oklahoma Courier*, January 18, 1963.

28. Revd. Charles H. Schettler, "St. Anthony's Hospital—Oklahoma City (Sisters of St. Francis, Maryville, Mo.)," March 18, 1970, 1–2, Reed Papers.

the existing lay administrator, of whom her superiors did not approve, and she interpreted this action as a bid by the motherhouse for greater control of the hospital's board of trustees.[29]

Diocesan officials advised Sister Teresa not to resign, since any vote by the board of trustees was likely to go in her favor. On March 12, her overall superior, Mother Rosina, and her council met with the hospital's lay board of advisors. Different accounts emerged of this meeting. Mother Rosina insisted that Sister Teresa had approved her transfer, which was intended to allow her to develop coronary treatment programs in the community's other hospitals in Missouri and Nebraska. She also sought to reassure the doctors that the lay administrator would not be removed after Sister Teresa had left. At least one member of the board privately declared, however, that forcing the resignations was part of a power struggle within the community, which St. Anthony's could ill afford. He doubted the wisdom of allowing the sisters to continue to dominate the board of trustees and felt it was time to bring in lay experts to run the hospital.[30]

Mother Rosina was not about to be swayed; she instructed Sister Teresa to leave for the motherhouse the next day, "under obedience." A group of about twenty of the sisters at the hospital attempted to express their concerns to Mother Rosina and the council as a group, but the superior refused to see them except as individuals, an act that hardly smoothed relations between the two sides. The vicar of religious, called in to soothe wounded feelings, was blunt as he outlined the possible fallout to Mother Rosina. "Last evening," he wrote on March 14, "I visited with the Sisters at St. Anthony's for over an hour, and they are very upset. One of the basic problems seems to be one of communications, or the lack of it. . . . Mother, as you are well aware, this is a very serious matter. The public image of the Church in Oklahoma, the welfare of our local civic community as well as the financial stability of St. Anthony's and the Sisters of St. Francis are critically involved." Matters were only worsened by Mother Rosina's failure to honor the bishop's request to discuss the matter with the vicar of religious.[31]

The morning papers carried news of Sister Teresa's transfer and the dissatisfaction among the medical personnel. Gerald Honick urged his fellow physicians to advise the community that "the continued traumatic shuffling

29. Ibid. At the time of Sister Teresa's removal, the board of trustees consisted of six sisters from the hospital and four from the motherhouse, with one vacancy.

30. Schettler, "St. Anthony's Hospital," 3–6.

31. Revd. J. Paul Donovan to Mother Rosina, O.S.F., March 14, 1970, Reed Papers.

of people and the unrealistic decision making of those not knowledgeable of situations in our area must cease immediately." Diocesan officials, battle-hardened by internal struggles within the Oklahoma-based Benedictine and Carmelite orders (see below), sought to pour water on the flames. Sister Teresa was advised to leave the hospital but not to return to the motherhouse, while the vicar of religious urged a prompt meeting between Mother Rosina, himself, and members of the advisory board. This would address, among other things, the vexed question of the appointment of at least three lay representatives to the board of trustees.[32]

On March 18, Mother Rosina came to Tulsa to request a meeting with the vicar of religious, Paul Donovan. In the discussions that followed, it became clear that her principal fear had been that the sisters at St. Anthony's planned to secede from the order and take the hospital with them, something that came as news to most of the parties involved. The reassignments had been implemented with this concern in mind, but Mother Rosina now thanked Father Donovan for his advice to Sister Teresa not to return to the motherhouse while passions were running high. While tensions persisted, the atmosphere had become far more cordial than four days previously.[33]

Unlike the Franciscans, the Sister Adorers of the Most Precious Blood faced a problem not of internal division but of external pressure. In 1960, Tulsa oilman W. K. Warren Sr. had funded the construction of St. Francis Hospital, a state-of-the-art complex in Tulsa. Operationally, the hospital was to be held in trust by a board of three lay trustees until the sisters had accumulated sufficient cash reserves to sustain operations at times of low patient occupancy, but the sisters found the board's style of management increasingly unsatisfactory. The board controlled all personnel decisions, and some feared that it might even claim the right to remove sisters who disagreed with its decisions. The hospital was, at times, forced to accept employees from the Warren Foundation (a charitable organization funded with Warren money). Hospital vendors were selected on the basis of their personal connections to members of the board of trustees, and all hospital insurance was carried by Warren's insurance companies. While the bishop appreciated the sisters' dilemma, he was in an awkward position because of his personal friendship with Warren.[34]

32. Schettler, "St. Anthony's Hospital," 6–9, Gerald L. Honick to St. Anthony Hospital Medical Staff, n.d., Reed Papers.

33. Schettler, "St. Anthony's Hospital," 6–9.

34. Notes of meeting held at St. Francis Hospital, Tulsa, Oklahoma, January 12 and

In 1963, the sisters, with the backing of the medical staff, insisted that swift transfer of control was a necessity. In the interim, they proposed a new advisory board, selected by the sisters, and demanded the right to negotiate all hospital contracts and the freedom to apply for grants from any source, whether public or private. Warren showed no inclination to accede to their demands, although for public consumption he insisted that he opposed only the "premature" transfer of control. Should the physical plant be commingled with other assets of the sisters before it was independently viable, he argued, there was a danger that the hospital would become a financial burden on the city of Tulsa. The sisters hoped to use the unencumbered land on which the hospital was situated as security for financing future expansion. They objected to any imposed restrictions, warning that they might not continue to operate the hospital under such conditions. On December 18, 1964, however, they signed an agreement with Warren that contained this restriction. The three members of the Warren Foundation serving on the board of trustees were then replaced by three sisters.[35]

The transfer did not end what the sisters increasingly felt was undue influence exercised by Warren and his wife over details of hospital policy. Despite Warren's assurances that things would change, an attempt to obtain the dismissal of certain personnel and the appointment of others, together with a demand that the hospital accept a particular computer system against the better judgment of its staff, obliged the sisters to exercise the option of complete withdrawal from St. Francis. Naturally, William Warren portrayed the sisters' departure in the starkest possible terms in a letter to the superior of the provincial motherhouse: "Needless to say I am amazed that the members of a religious congregation such as yours, dedicated to the cause of Christ, would from any standpoint, rational or otherwise, deprive themselves of the opportunity to serve humanity in a Christian manner which your Order now enjoys in the operation of St. Francis Hospital in Tulsa, Oklahoma."[36] The sisters, however, had had enough. Hospital officials had been asked to do things by the Warren Foundation that they considered morally and legally

13, 1963, between Financial Advisors Inc. and Sister M. Marcellina, administrator, Reed Papers.

35. Charles W. Dohnalek to Victor Reed, November 21, 1963, Mother M. Marciana, Ad.P.P.S., to Reed, December 21, 1964, Reed Papers.

36. J. Francis Hesse and Bruce W. Zuercher to William K. Warren Sr., William K. Warren Jr., and the William K. Warren Foundation, January 18, 1969, Warren to Sr.Teresa Palameier, January 22, 1969, Reed Papers.

wrong, declared the assistant administrator, and they were no longer willing to tolerate such a state of affairs. The sisters had made a thorough review of the situation and had come to a necessary, though painful, conclusion.[37]

RENEWAL AND THE RELIGIOUS LIFE

"Mission now is everywhere," declared the superior of the Tulsa Benedictines in November 1965. "Mission now has a double movement. One is the familiar, teaching and baptizing of souls, in order to incorporate them more closely in the Body of Christ. Mission is also something else. Mission is working on nations as well as individuals, on political entities as well as persons, on convocations of people as well as persons. In a word, it seems, that Pope Paul VI attempted to bring to us the message of mission of the Risen Christ, namely, that we are sent to teach all nations and all people."[38]

Renewal of the religious life could initially be traced to the Sister Formation movement, which had begun in the 1950s at the instigation of several sisters who were concerned about the lack of preparation for ministry being provided to young religious.[39] In August 1960, Father Ernest Flusche reported that most Oklahoma sisters were at least indirectly involved in the Sister Formation process. While this might add several years to the time needed to complete their education, Flusche believed that this investment would strengthen their community life.[40]

Most communities knew that the new climate of the 1960s obliged them to market the religious life to a generation accustomed to the lay apostolate and, consequently, less impressed by the need for a separate religious sphere. The Carmelite Sisters of St. Therese, for example, were one of the few communities founded in Oklahoma, but by 1963 only thirty of the ninety-seven sisters (and none of the four novices and seven postulants) were Oklahoma-born. Indeed, the eleven members of the community teaching school in California brought in many more vocations than did their Oklahoma counterparts.[41]

In 1964, the thirteen religious communities with members in the Tulsa area formed the Inter-Community Council of Religious Women, modeled on

37. *Oklahoma Courier*, February 28, 1969; E. C. Bene to "Dear Fellow Employees," March 31, 1969, Reed Papers.
38. *Tulsa Benedictines' News*, November 1965.
39. Beane, *From Framework to Freedom*.   40. *Oklahoma Courier*, August 12, 1960.
41. *Oklahoma Courier*, February 1, 1963.

the Archdiocesan Vocation Endeavor in the Archdiocese of Cincinnati. What became known as the Diocese of Oklahoma Vocation Endeavor (DOVE), with branches in both Tulsa and Oklahoma City, sought to foster a renewed sense of vocation among the young, to explain the religious apostolate to the laity, and to compile information from religious communities. A much more involved process of recruitment for postulants was instituted, involving interviews with interested young women, meetings with their parents, and public forums on the religious life where questions could be asked.[42]

Renewal intruded into all aspects of the religious life, since religious communities were expected to implement the same liturgical changes as parish pastors. The diocesan master of ceremonies urged the translation of the Carmelite ritual into English in 1962, as well as changes in the form of prostration practiced by the community and a change in the manner of profession of vows. Group profession, he declared, would be "more in keeping with the desires of the Church to emphasize the Mystical Body and Community action. . . . The fact that they mention their individual names will provide the individual or personal character that might be needed—just as the Profession of Faith made by priests on the occasion of taking up a new office." He also recommended that benediction be limited to no more than two dozen occasions during the year, given that no fewer than 160 services of benediction had been celebrated during the previous year.[43]

The vicar general urged a similar restraint on the part of the Tulsa Benedictines regarding benediction. "The Constitution on the Sacred Liturgy points out that all religious exercises should flow out of the Liturgy itself," he explained. "The sisters, since they have chosen to live a more deeply religious life, should, then, base their spiritual exercises and devotions on the Liturgy. Thus, simply pious exercises should be replaced, the purely emotional should be removed. . . . The Office should be used, as the Church proposes, for the official prayers recited to sanctify the day." Sisters from St. Joseph's Convent traveled to other Benedictine communities in Arkansas, South Dakota, and Wisconsin to observe their practices regarding the new liturgy, and in 1964 the community began to pray the hours of terce and sext in the vernacular, as a prelude to the employment of an entirely vernacular office. Reed designated St. Joseph's as an experimental community prior to the diocesanwide adoption of the Novus Ordo (the new order of the Mass)

42. *Oklahoma Courier*, February 28, May 15, 1964.
43. Revd. Joseph J. Mazaika to Victor Reed, June 15, 1962 (two letters), Reed Papers.

in November 1964 and gave permission for remodeling of the convent chapel in 1965 to conform to the Constitution of the Sacred Liturgy.[44]

Most communities also took steps to remodel their habits to make them less confining. The Oklahoma City Carmelites, for example, abandoned their black veil.[45] Some of the new designs, however, drew criticism. In December 1964, two Ursuline sisters at Bishop McGuinness High School attracted national attention with the adoption of a style of dress very far removed from the conventional habit. In defense of the change, Sisters Stephen and Immaculata argued that their foundress had not established a cloistered order but one intended to adapt to the times. The new style felt more genuine to them, they argued, made it easier for them to do housework or drive a car, and made them feel more like women.[46] Local reaction was generally positive. Several of the Benedictine sister-teachers at McGuinness praised the new style. "It's my bet," added a laywoman, "that fifty years from now, their convents will be operating at full capacity, while other orders, less far-sighted, will have gone the way of the dodo birds." Over the next three weeks, the ratio of positive to negative responses to the new habit ran at two-to-one.[47]

As the national media picked up the story, however, Catholics from outside the region began to express opinions that were far less favorable. Evelyn Estrin of Chicago declared that if this were the shape of the future then she would be sending her children to public school. A resident of Mount Pocono, Pennsylvania, warned that the drastic changes envisaged by the Ursuline Sisters would have a negative effect on the laity: "Can these Ursuline nuns really believe (deep down in their hearts) that a 'stylish hat, knee-length skirt, and *high* heels' will continue to earn for them (or for that matter, a nun of any community) the respect and admiration that has been accorded to

44. Msgr. Sylvester F. Luecke to Sr. M. Eulalia, November 6, 1964, Reed Papers; *St. Joseph's Convent News*, April 1964; Mother Marie Denise Mohr to Victor Reed, August 21, 1964, Reed Papers; Mother Marie Denise Mohr to Reed, June 22, 1965, St. Joseph's Monastery Archives. At that time, benediction of the Blessed Sacrament was regarded as a pious devotion, not as a liturgical ceremony. The ecclesiastical law on this point has since been changed.

45. *Oklahoma Courier*, February 1, 1963.

46. *Oklahoma Courier*, December 4, 1964. One defense of the changes was that it brought the sisters closer to the children whom they taught. "I think this is wonderful," declared a fifth grade student in a parochial school in Syracuse, New York. "I feel that the students will look at the Nuns as human beings. If this change does take place in our parish I think the students will ask more frequently about what they don't understand in class instead of thinking the Nuns will bite their heads off."

47. *Oklahoma Courier*, December 11, 1964, January 1, 1965.

nuns for many, many years? I regret to say here and now, I hardly think so! I do agree, however, a *modified* change might be in order, but the latest experiment has gone too far."[48] Loretto Kamerer of New York told Sister Stephen that her conduct "has not been that of a simple, childlike religious sister, but of one glamorizing a situation in a sensational way—anxious to get all the attention that cheap publicity has to offer." Any rejection of the notion of being "set apart," argued Kamerer, was contrary to the spirit of all but a few of the religious orders, and Sister Stephen should be careful of allowing herself to be treated as a spokeswoman for all women religious in the United States. "Just settle down like a good little Sister," urged Kamerer, in words that can hardly have resonated with their intended object, "say your prayers; fulfill your religious duties in the traditional way with which we in this Country are familiar and stop the show."[49]

The Ursuline controversy caused great concern both to Bishop Reed and the order's superior. After the apostolic delegate expressed his displeasure, Mother Mary Charles instructed the two sisters to resume the habit of the community, although she privately confided to Reed that she hoped the experiment would have a positive effect in the long term.[50] Other communities experimented with alterations to the style of the habit in later years, but memories of the earlier controversy evidently persisted. In 1967, when Mother Teresa Ranallo of the Oklahoma City Carmelites requested permission to adopt a simpler form of headdress, she stressed that the changes were proceeding only after extensive consultation: "We are well aware that these changes must be made slowly," she told Reed, "and made by the group as a whole; hence, the reason for submitting the matter to the entire community."[51]

Among the Benedictines, it was recognized that renewal must take place even in the active specialized apostolates. "It might be suggested that our *institutional apostolate* has either failed to be apostolic or is not *per se* sufficient for today's needs," Sister Jane Marie Luecke, O.S.B., of the Tulsa Benedictines opined in 1965. The focus had always been on institutional efficiency, not on the individuals united in a common apostolate. Luecke argued that her sisters needed to extend aspects of their present professional

48. Donovan, interview; Evelyn J. Estrin to Victor Reed, January 12, 1965, Mrs. C. Nawrocki to Reed, January 18, 1965, Reed Papers.

49. Loretto Kamerer to Reed, January 19, 1965, Reed Papers.

50. *Oklahoma Courier*, January 12, 1965; Mother M. Charles to Victor Reed, March 3, 1965, Reed Papers.

51. Mother Teresa Renallo, C.S.T., to Victor Reed, August 5, 1967, Reed Papers.

work outside their institution. Their new contacts might include the families of the children they taught or the patients they nursed; non-Catholics with whom they cooperated in civil rights activities, social work, and ecumenical dialogue; and fellow professionals in medicine and education. "A sense of individual and apostolic responsibility," Luecke concluded, "affects radically not so much what work is done, but how it is done."[52]

One of the consequences of the embrace of the active life was the expectation on the part of many sisters that they be given a voice in the work of diocesan renewal. Mother Marie Denise Mohr of the Benedictines rebuked the bishop for initially failing to include a commission for women religious as part of the structure of the Little Council. "To omit representatives of one of the modes of Christian life," she chided, "a mode that has proven to be a real impact in our modern world today, from a framework that surely will have influence on the diocese, is more than disappointing." The Benedictine community sent a representative to the National Committee on Research and Renewal of Religious Life and also began to explore nontraditional work environments for its sisters, including secretarial work, Montessori teaching, practical nursing, and Newman clubs.[53]

Reed took Mother Marie Denise's advice, and the first meeting of the sisters' commission was held in December 1965, when Sister Mary Angelia of Blackwell General Hospital was elected commission chairwoman.[54] Two months later, an extended meeting with Bishop Reed, Bishop Charles Buswell of Pueblo, and Sister Mary Luke, S.L., superior general of the Sisters of Loretto, took place at the University of Oklahoma, where Sister Luke recounted her experiences as one of fourteen women present for the third and fourth sessions of the council. Her invitation, she maintained, was a sign that there was no area of Church renewal to which sisters could not profitably contribute: "This is the asceticism of the modern sister," she told her audience, "to step into her place among the people of God, going forward, feeling inadequate, making mistakes and feeling embarrassed. There is really not going to be much privacy in religious life in the future; sisters must be willing to share ideas and time with others, preparing themselves to be always more competent in this area."[55]

---

52. Luecke, "The Sister in Secular Life," 269, 270.

53. Mother Marie Denise Mohr to Victor Reed, April 17, 1965, Ecumenical Council and Council of Churches Papers, AAOC; *Tulsa Benedictines' News*, November 1965.

54. Minutes of the Sisters' Commission, December 6, 1965, Reed Papers.

55. Summary of Session of Sisters' Commission, Diocese of Oklahoma City and Tulsa,

Reed echoed Sister Luke's assertion with a promise that the priests' and sisters' commissions would ultimately include representatives of the laity. He also promised that the role of the sisters would change, with more emphasis on teaching parents how to instruct their children in the faith, a process he hoped would also serve to revivify the religious commitment of adults. Teachers needed greater involvement with the world, the bishop said, so that they would know and understand the problems faced by parents. Bishop Buswell described a project run by the Sisters of Loretto in his own diocese, intended to infuse a sense of community into an underprivileged and nominally Catholic area of Pueblo. One sister taught in a job-opportunity program, another built up a religious education program where none had previously existed, while a third worked on the campus of a secular university. In this sense, they became a bridge between the Church and the wider community, and their labors *outside* the confines of their former religious life should not be viewed as spiritually enervating.[56] Sister Luke reiterated that renewal went beyond simple "adaptation." It involved religious communities fully participating in the changes sweeping through the wider Church. Among other things, it required religious superiors to seek "consultation and collaboration" with those under their authority and a recognition that the Holy Spirit could work through even the lowliest member of a community. "Sisters must make suggestions and an atmosphere of dissent must be tolerated," she insisted. "Sisters still are not talking to each other well enough; all must learn to listen, to hear out one another in religious communities."[57]

Discussion of the manner in which the sisters' commission should operate focused on interaction with the bishop, communication between the major superiors of communities working in the diocese and, finally, direct contact with sisters in the diocese to learn what they considered to be their needs and problems in the work of renewal. All agreed that knowledge and understanding of the conciliar documents was a necessary prerequisite to good thinking. Sister Luke warned those present not to follow the example of their European counterparts, who had lost connection with the parishes and priests and consequently had become largely irrelevant to the life of the Church.[58]

---

with Bishop Victor J. Reed, Diocese of Oklahoma City and Tulsa, Bishop Charles Buswell, Diocese of Pueblo, Colorado, and Sister Mary Luke, S.L. Superior General, Sisters of Loretto, and Chairman of Major Superiors of Women, Kellogg Center for Continuing Education, University of Oklahoma, Norman, Oklahoma, February 8, 1966, Reed Papers.

56. Ibid., 2–3.   57. Ibid., 4.
58. Ibid., 5–6.

The ways in which the sisters might assist the cause of renewal were further developed during the spring of 1966. Layman James Cockrell argued that they should play a significant role in lay teacher formation, adult education—especially for women—and the apostolate to the poor. There was, he said, a prophetic role for female religious, who could bring insights different from those of priests or the laity. By April, many sisters had returned a questionnaire distributed to them in January. One of the problems, as the commission itself noted, was trying to harmonize all the calls for new programs with sisters' existing responsibilities to their communities and the diocese. There was general agreement that a liaison structure between the diocese and the various religious communities was desirable, as was greater interaction between different religious communities through recreation days, shared services, and cultural activities.[59]

Renewal of individual communities, however, was agreed to be a matter for the members of that community to undertake. "Problems we will always have with us," members of the sisters' commission concluded. "No commission or structure will ever eliminate the tensions, misunderstandings, and difficulties inevitable in human relations and indeed indispensable to the growth of any Christian worthy of the name. Many situations can be improved only by openness, acceptance, confrontation with the problems, and genuine Christian love." The commission nevertheless took heart from the fact that 250 sisters had participated in the first series of discussions regarding Bishop Reed's pastoral letters on the Constitution of the Church, and 150 of them had done so in the context of a parish discussion group. Clearly the Spirit was at work uniting the sisters to the rest of the Body of Christ.[60]

By the late 1960s, however, the process of renewal had begun to be affected by the steady stream of sisters out of the traditional religious life. Many considered Reed to be sympathetic to their desire to make the active spiritual life a more meaningful experience, and some sought a transfer from the jurisdiction of their order to direct episcopal oversight. In April 1964, three Sisters of Mercy asked to become diocesan sisters, complaining that their order was more concerned with its buildings and finances than with the work of the Church. "It seems to us," they told Reed, "that the very 'bigness' of the Institute of the Sisters of Mercy of the Union militates against an effective

59. Minutes of the Sisters' Commission, April 15, 1966, Reed Papers.
60. The Sisters' Commission to "Dear Sisters of the Diocese," April 25, 1966, Reed Papers.

apostolate. It also seems that vested interests and joint debts would prevent
the breaking down of our community into smaller units (those in authority
have in fact told us this)."[61]

Many sisters moved on to initiatives like Sister Nativity Heiliger's Seventh Street Project, which provided numerous social action programs, particularly childhood literacy, in a rundown Oklahoma City neighborhood.[62]
The Seventh Street Project attracted nationwide attention. In 1967, two Iowa
Franciscan Sisters who had taught in the Dubuque school system left the religious life after requests to work in the Dubuque slums had been turned
down: "The reasons for refusal are quite complex," they explained to Reed,
"but can be reduced to a lack of trust in us, fear of taking a risk on a community scale, and lack of understanding the importance or need for such
experimenting if we are ever to come to a realization of what real community can be." Hearing of Sister Nativity's work in Oklahoma City, these ex-
sisters sought the bishop's permission to move to Oklahoma, where they
could combine service to the underprivileged with involvement in the life of
the Church.[63]

A few sisters tried to form new religious communities that were more
contemplative in nature. "[We] spent five days in Oklahoma City during the
Easter vacation—living in our hermitages, getting acquainted with one another, and participating in the beautiful Holy Week services in the little Chapel at Bella Maria," two sisters told Reed in April 1967. "It was the most
wonderful experience for both of us, and we are looking forward with joyous
anticipation to the day when we can come to stay. . . . It will be a great joy
to become a part of this truly Christian community in the diocese of Oklahoma City."[64]

One group that emerged from the fallout surrounding the removal of
Mother Marie Denise Mohr as head of the Tulsa Benedictines (see below)
was the Sisters for Christian Service, a group of six sisters who left in protest
at the Holy See's action. Two were teachers in the public schools, three at
Bishop McGuinness High School, and one was a professor at Notre Dame
University. They chose no superior, committed themselves to annual vows

61. Sr. Mary Vincenz Schmidlkofer, Sr. Mary Nativity Helliger, and Sr. Mary de Porres
Loughlin to Victor Reed, April 4, 1964, Reed Papers.
62. *Oklahoma Courier*, June 25, 1967. Sister Nativity had requested permission to leave
her community as early as 1953, but she was not formally released until 1964.
63. Sr. Enid and Sr. Mary Rochelle to Victor Reed, May 1, 1967, Reed Papers.
64. Sr. M. Vincentia, Ad.P.P.S., to Victor Reed, April 23, 1967, Reed Papers.

(which the bishop witnessed in his own chapel), and held common prayer every evening followed by discussion. "I rather think," declared Sister Suzanne Kelly in November 1967, "that each of us is learning to live with the uncertainty that will probably characterize our lives from now on."[65]

The question of how the bishop should handle requests for official recognition of such groups was one that deeply concerned diocesan officials. Father William Garthoeffner favored trying to organize some type of program to channel ex-religious into suitable environments, but vicar of religious Father Paul Donovan was not so sure.[66] Christian commitment, argued Donovan, interpreted in the light of recent developments, did not imply employment by the institutional Church: "If they wish the institutional and canonical security and the 'advantages' of working for the Church (being able to wear a badge of being a 'professional Christian' and doing something superior to the 'ordinary lay person') then I do not see how we can escape from involving them in the structure they feel so oppressive. . . . A person who has been in religious life and even taken final vows and then wishes to be dispensed from those vows and rededicate themselves in another manner—what is really being said is, they must decide what is best for them. This, of course, is excellent; but I feel in this notion, that obedience to human, fallible and sinful people is not what they are looking for."[67]

A RETURN TO MONASTICISM?

The optimistic belief that renewal could be effected by a simple dialogue between religious superiors and ordinary sisters was not borne out in the case of either of the two principal motherhouses located in Oklahoma. At St. Joseph's Convent in Tulsa, Mother Mary Paula Bartmeier, Benedictine prioress until 1960, was believed by the teaching sisters of Benedictine Heights College strongly to favor the monastic lifestyle. "One group in our community is almost markedly suited to monastic life," Sister Mary Immaculata told Reed in April 1958 (when the bishop had been in office little more

65. *Oklahoma Courier*, November 10, 1967. Another member, Sister Judith Tate, claimed in a panel discussion that a Precious Blood sister told her that her community had speeded up its process of renewal because of the fallout over the Mother Marie Denise affair. *Oklahoma Courier*, October 27, 1967.
66. Revd. William C. Garthoeffner to Sr. M. Nativity, May 6, 1967, Reed Papers.
67. Revd. J. Paul Donovan to Revd. William C. Garthoeffner, May 8, 1967, Reed Papers.

than a month). "Others of us are suited to the kind of secularization in which we would carry out the work given us to do. With the demands of the active life as strong as they are today, new definitions are needed in regard to religious life." Such criticisms foreshadowed a later cleavage between advocates of an "active" religious life and their critics. "Mother has kept a control at the College which has been detrimental to its growth," Sister Immaculata concluded. "The lay faculty, a truly able and dedicated group, has become discouraged, and most of its members are seeking more security than their present position affords."[68]

In the fall of 1958, a community visitation echoed some of Sister Immaculata's concerns and concluded that many members of the community were distressed by their inability to bring problems to Mother Paula. Archabbot Dennis Strittmatter recommended the implementation of a uniform policy for home visits, one that was not contingent on a sister securing financial support from friends or relatives. He also urged greater recourse to chapter meetings for reaching important decisions, especially those concerned with finance, and the establishment of a planning board to deal with matters related to Benedictine Heights College. At the same time, Strittmatter was careful to remind the sisters of the value of submission to duly appointed superiors: "We are inclined to confuse the field of legislation with that of administration, and when we are given administrative work we feel we should legislate a little too especially for ourselves. We joined the Benedictine Order to live according to the Rule of St. Benedict, to adjust ourselves to the Rule, and not to try to change the Rule to fit our own convenience. We promised to reform ourselves, not to reform the Rule. . . . There is too much talking to the neighbors, lay and clergy. . . . We live as a family, why do we not keep the family problems at home. Talk them over with your Superior and Confrere, not with neighbors."[69]

Discontent with Mother Paula's approach led to her resignation at the end of 1960. Bishop Reed recommended that, in preference to elections in

68. Sr. Mary Immaculata to Victor Reed, April 22, 1958, Reed Papers. The conflicts described below also occurred in more conservative dioceses. For the situation in Los Angeles, see Mark Massa, "'To Be Beautiful, Human and Christian': The IHM Nuns and the Routinization of Charisma," in *Catholics and American Culture*, 172–94.

69. Rt. Revd. Dennis Strittmatter, O.S.B., to Victor Reed, September 12, 1958, Recessus of the Visitation conducted at St. Joseph Convent, Tulsa, Oklahoma, August 27–September 3, 1958: Report to Reverend Mother Paula, O.S.B.; Report to the Members of the Community, Reed Papers.

Rita Vessels

Agnes Arvin

Paul Barthecer

Bishop Reed with principal members of the Benedictine community of St. Joseph's Convent, Tulsa. Mother Marie Denise Mohr, O.S.B., is second from left.

a divisive atmosphere, a sister be appointed as administrator, and the Holy See appointed Sister Marie Denise Mohr to that office in 1961.[70] To Mother Marie Denise fell the task of implementing the community restructuring demanded by the board of control appointed by Reed after the failure of the college.[71] The new superior established Fathers and Brothers of Benedictine Sisters (a support group composed of the male relatives of the sisters), which organized an annual reunion and picnic for sisters and their families, an approach that reflected a more relaxed attitude toward those in monastic com-

70. Victor Reed to Ildebrando Cardinal Antoniutti, June 12, 1967, Reed Papers.
71. Mother Marie Denise Mohr to Victor Reed, May 8, 1961, Reed to Mohr, May 17, 1961, St. Joseph's Monastery Archives.

munities retaining ties to their blood relations. She also became a charter member of the Tulsa branch of the Theresians, a movement of laywomen dedicated to the strengthening of spiritual life and encouragement of vocations among adult women.[72]

Mother Marie Denise's encouragement of the renewal process proved most unwelcome to the community's "monastic" faction, for whom the idea of nontraditional work environments was extremely unpalatable. When Mother Marie Denise persuaded the community to sell the original motherhouse at Guthrie—a course prescribed by the board of control—her critics, who included her predecessor, sensed an opening. In a letter to Reed, they accused the prioress of forcing the issue through chapter while several opponents were absent. "Mother is young and does not have the regard for the older Sisters that one would expect in a Superior," they insisted. "Besides she has lived most of her religious life in sophisticated surroundings and has forgotten the simplicity of her own childhood and of our life in Guthrie. As you well know it is this simplicity that is most conducive to Religious life." They pointed out that the Guthrie convent had been an excellent place for retreats and that it contained the community's cemetery and shrines. They also cultivated allies outside Oklahoma, including the head of the Congregation of St. Scholastica, Mother Susan Sevier (whom Reed suspected of fomenting disorder within the community).[73]

In the spring of 1967, Mother Marie Denise was instructed to implement a "renewal program" within the community, which seemed to yield some positive results. On April 6, the prioress assured the bishop that the sisters wished "to strengthen their convictions about the value of religious life and to arrive at more definite and unified objectives regarding our work in the Church of Oklahoma."[74] Barely two months later, however, Mother Marie Denise was abruptly removed from office by the Sacred Congregation for Religious in Rome and instructed to leave Tulsa. A chorus of protest erupted from Catholics in the city. Admirers praised her financial acumen and her contributions to ecumenical and civic causes, while the members of the board of control accused the congregation of acting in "an undignified manner, certainly not in keeping with the spirit of the Church."[75] Dissension within the community

72. *Tulsa Tribune*, October 6, 1962; *St. Joseph's Convent News*, November 19, 1962; *Tulsa Daily World*, January 5, 1964.

73. Sr. Mary Paula Bartmeier, Sr. Mary Dorothea Semotan, and Sr. Mary Stanislaus Abernathy to Victor Reed, March 28, 1966, Reed Papers.

74. Mother Marie Denise Mohr to Victor Reed, April 6, 1967, Reed Papers.

75. *Oklahoma Courier*, June 16, 1967; Alfred A. Aaronson to Victor Reed, June 12, 1967,

was no less fierce. Father Paul Donovan had to be recalled from study at the Catholic University of America, because he was the one priest with whom the sisters were willing to talk. "[They] wouldn't let Father Garthoeffner in the house," Donovan recalled in an interview.[76]

Reed was no happier about the manner in which the affair had been conducted. Pointing out that since the financial debacle involving the college the relationship between the community and the ordinary had become a very close one—not least because of the warm relations between himself and Mother Marie Denise—he objected to the manner in which outsiders sought to dictate the affairs of the Tulsa community. He viewed the appointment of Sister Mary Fabian Garrett from St. Scholastica Convent in Chicago as administrator of the community as a disservice to its members. He urged that a visitation be undertaken and that, based on its findings, consideration should be given to the separation of the convent from the Congregation of St. Scholastica. The twelve sisters who subsequently requested legal severance from the community shared the bishop's concern. "We feel that this action [the removal of Mother Marie Denise]," they declared, "represents the kind of interference from Rome which should cease."[77] Powerful Tulsa laymen echoed their protest. "While we are cognizant of internal problems in the community," Robert LaFortune wrote on behalf of several family members, "we are confident that the community can resolve these areas of disagreement by itself. We, therefore, strongly protest the appointment of an outside administrator in this instance."[78]

The new administrator proved unable to reconcile the contending factions and the question consequently arose as to what should be done with the minority "academic faction." After some debate as to the mechanics of separation, a group of thirty-three sisters, including Sister Marie Denise, agreed to give up any right to the community's property and moved to Oklahoma City, where they organized the Sisters of Benedict at Red Plains Priory. In return, the majority who remained in Tulsa agreed to take on responsibility for the community's debts and the care of any retired sisters.[79]

Advisory Board of the Congregation of the Benedictine Sisters of the Sacred Hearts to Reed, June 14, 1967, Ray H. Siegfried to Reed, June 20, 1967, Reed Papers.

76. Donovan, interview.

77. Victor Reed to Ildebrando Cardinal Antoniutti, June 12, 1967, Reed Papers; *Oklahoma Courier*, June 30, 1967.

78. Robert J. LaFortune to Victor Reed, June 21, 1967, Reed Papers.

79. Revd. J. Paul Donovan to Victor Reed, September 26, 1968, Reed Papers; Donovan, interview.

A similar pattern of community dissonance unfolded among the Carmelite Sisters of St. Therese at Villa Teresa in Oklahoma City. (The cloistered Carmelite convent of St. Joseph in Oklahoma City was largely unaffected by the turmoil of the 1960s.) Initially, this had more to do with contending personalities than disagreements over renewal.[80] Mother Celine Carter, first elected in 1951, had proved a shrewd and capable administrator but had had a stormy relationship with Bishop McGuinness. "He was a pretty tough Irishman but she used to rattle his chain," was Paul Donovan's view. "Whatever he said, she kind of did her own thing."[81] In 1963, she was approaching the end of her second and final term. Some within the community believed that progress could continue only under her leadership. "She does have very promising and great administrative ability," attested one Carmelite sister, "and since she has done so much for the progress of the Community, it seems that any future plans could only be accomplished by her." The sister did, however, concede: "I know that many things that she does do not please most of the members but I try to believe that she has her reasons for them and cannot give them to us."[82]

To secure an unprecedented third term, Mother Celine was obliged to petition her ecclesiastical superiors through postulation and then obtain twice the normal number of votes required for election. Bishop Reed, her immediate superior, was far from convinced of the wisdom of such a move, an opinion for once shared by the Sacred Congregation for Religious. Word came to him from the sisters that Mother Celine was undertaking serious politicking among the American Carmelites generally and hinting that there were those in Rome willing to raise the Oklahoma community, which was of diocesan status and responsible to the local bishop, to pontifical rank, placing it directly under the Congregation for Religious in Rome.[83] Moreover, she kept secret from the sisters the results of canonical visitations ordered by Reed. "The Council in this Community serves no purpose," Sister Bernadette told Reed. "If it can not function as it should, then there is no reason for its existence. I often have wondered how some of our transactions could be legal,

---

80. Mother Celine made various changes in the community's lifestyle in the 1960s, including a two-week home visit every five years, no religious exercises during the two-week annual vacation, and the virtual elimination of seniority. She also ended the requirement for sewing or knitting during recreation periods, something that she had always personally detested. *Oklahoma Courier*, February 1, 1963.

81. Donovan, interview.

82. Sr. Rita Teresa to Victor Reed, February 21, 1963, Reed Papers.

83. Sr. Teresa to Victor Reed, February 22, 1963, Reed Papers.

valid, licit; they can't possibly be. Yet, it is thus we continue and can do little or nothing about it. . . . It is thought that with time and a new superior some of our difficulties will disappear. With what we see going on, it is hard to believe. Time will tell."[84]

Mother Celine would not be denied an election but, to the chagrin of her supporters, two ballots showed a majority insufficient for postulation and on the third ballot, as required by canon law, the candidate with the next highest number of votes—Sister Teresa Renallo, C.S.T.—was elected.[85] "I think that in due time matters will clear up," the new superior told Reed in January 1964, "but I cannot say this with certainty. There are some individuals who are quite unhappy about the outcome of the elections and who will continue to be instigators of rebellion and hate, particularly if they do not get what they desire. This is a saddening and disheartening thing and one that certainly must grieve the heart of Jesus. Again I repeat I shall do all in my power to heal wounds and to bring peace, harmony and unity to the community."[86]

The damage to the community was considerable. Sister Celine initially took her supporters to the Diocese of Dallas, where they asked Bishop Thomas Gorman for permission to establish a new community, but Gorman declined to accommodate them. Shortly afterward, about thirty members (over one-third of the community) followed Sister Celine to California. Despite the fact that her actions had added considerably to his problems, Reed took the time to write her a letter of appreciation for the work that she had done in building up the Carmelite community.[87]

In Oklahoma City, some sisters continued to evince sympathy for their former prioress. In October 1964, Sister Miriam Teresa Guibault, C.S.T., wrote to Reed with concerns about Mother Teresa's style of leadership that echoed those directed at the Benedictine Mother Paula Bartmeier. Mother Teresa "is inclined to live a contemplative life," she reported, "and she believes that the answer to all our problems is silence and solitude. . . . She believes in the *letter of the law* which may well be God's Will for her but most spiritual directives in the present day exhort the *spirit of the law* which is *CHARITY*."[88]

84. Sr. Bernadette to Victor Reed, April 11, 1963, Reed Papers.
85. Donovan, interview.
86. Mother Teresa Renallo to Victor Reed, January 4, 1964, Reed Papers.
87. Donovan, interview.
88. Sr. Miriam Teresa Guibault to Victor Reed, October 15, 1964, Reed Papers.

Sister Guibault further criticized Mother Teresa's "authoritarian" tendencies and revealed that she herself had been branded "a source of discontent" for questioning her superior's decision not to open a planned center for the retarded. She denounced the new requirement that Holy Child School, founded by the community because it had no charitable project of its own, must become financially independent within a year. She was further distressed that a planned hospital, for which personnel had already been trained, should no longer be pursued.[89] As among the Benedictines, so among the Carmelites a division had opened between advocates of the active life and those who favored a return to contemplation. Within a year, Sister Miriam Teresa Guibault had left the community.

CONCLUSION

"This is nothing against you sister," Bishop Reed once told Sister Mary Joseph Mies, A.S.C., "because I love the Precious Blood sisters, but my greatest cross was the Benedictines and the Carmelites."[90] The precipitate decline of religious vocations in Oklahoma—and elsewhere—is surely one of the greatest tragedies of the conciliar era. Under pressure to professionalize their callings, Oklahoma's sisters struggled during the late 1950s and early 1960s to find a formula that would preserve the essential features of community life without confining an increasingly well-educated and sophisticated body of religious women.

As in so many other areas, that formula proved unable to cope with the winds of change that carried many sisters beyond the immediate confines of convent, school, and hospital. As vocations fell away, the tension between older sisters devoted to a more monastic existence and younger sisters who interpreted the council as a mandate to go out and preach the Good News erupted into open warfare. The human cost for the Benedictine and the Carmelite communities, as we have seen, was considerable, but perhaps the spiritual cost was even greater. A generation of Catholic schoolchildren would grow up without the presence of a Catholic sister in the classroom to remind them of what vocation, at its greatest, can mean. For Victor Reed, this must truly have been a bitter fruit of the council into which he had entered with such high hopes.

89. Ibid.
90. Mies, conversation.

chapter 12

Out of the Ghetto

The Conscience of the Catholic Layman

The declaration of this Vatican Council on the right of man to religious freedom has its foundation in the dignity of the person, whose exigencies have come to be fully known to human reason through centuries of experience. What is more, this doctrine of freedom has roots in divine revelation, and for this reason Christians are bound to respect it all the more conscientiously. Revelation does not indeed affirm in so many words the right of man to immunity from external coercion in matters religious. It does, however, disclose the dignity of the human person in its full dimensions. It gives evidence of the respect which Christ showed toward the freedom with which man is to fulfill his duty of belief in the word of God and it gives us lessons in the spirit which disciples of such a Master ought to adopt and continually follow. Thus further light is cast upon the general principles upon which the doctrine of this declaration on religious freedom is based. In particular, religious freedom in society is entirely consonant with the freedom of the act of Christian faith.

Second Vatican Council, Declaration on Religious Freedom,
Dignitatis Humanae, December 7, 1965

On March 11, 1960, the *Oklahoma Courier* published an editorial entitled "Rights without Fear." American Catholics, the editor concluded, needed to take a stand based on their own experience, not that of Catholics in Europe: "We Catholics know that our full rights as citizens are not being respected. One of the great tasks we face is to find a method for making these rights respected—a method not based on favor, but on the fairness of our position and our ability to sweat out our demands. This could be a significant contribution to a Christian development of Church-State relations."[1]

The notion that the American Catholic experience had been somehow unique was to be an essential ingredient in the transformation of the perceptions of the laity. Such a notion had been reinforced by the writings of theologians like George Tavard of Assumption College in Worcester, Massachusetts, who warned in 1959 of the dangers of seeking to transplant the European model of Catholic Action to American soil. Catholic Action in Europe, Tavard declared, had derived from a set of national traditions in which the Church had, until recent years, been a powerful social force and where the laity had, for some time, been performing a variety of important social functions within the Church. The American lay movement, by contrast, "is made up of small, informal groups, loosely connected by their reading of Catholic lay periodicals like *Jubilee* or *Commonweal*. It exists in the exact measure in which sound theology has become available to the laity. In other words, the lay movement in the United States is not yet marked, as in Europe, by a special method of evangelization, the apostolate to laymen by laymen of the same milieu. It is rather characterized by a strong desire for a deeper, more vital, more existential grasp of the faith."[2]

During the 1940s and 1950s, a shift took place both in the institutional Church's perception of the role of the laity and in the laity's perception of the authority of the Church. With the end of mass immigration in 1924, educated American Catholics became increasingly aware of the popular perception that their faith tradition neglected personal intellectual development. Such non-Catholic condescension fueled the steady expansion of Catholic higher education and the emergence of journals like *Commonweal* and *Orate Fratres*. After Pope Pius XI championed Catholic Action in 1929, the layman was provided with an organizational framework that—whatever the intent of its clerical founders—frequently operated independently of established Church structures. "Members of the small-group social apostolates," writes historian Debra Campbell, "along with their clerical midwives gained a sense of critical distance from mainstream 'parish Catholicism' that empow-

1. *Oklahoma Courier*, March 11, 1960.
2. Tavard, *The Church, the Layman, and the Modern World*, 8–10 (quotation on 10). At the Second Vatican Council, it was clear that classical Catholic Action remained more popular with the prelates of the Latin countries than those of northern Europe and the English-speaking world. See Rynne, *Vatican Council II*, 323–28.

ered them to dream new dreams and glean a new vision of the responsibilities of the laity."[3]

The postwar material affluence and enhanced social status of suburban American Catholics and their greater interaction with the non-Catholic community prompted a reassessment of what it meant to be both Catholic and American.[4] In this respect, the pattern of suburban growth and rural depopulation was no different in Oklahoma than in other parts of the United States. By the early 1950s, there were 18,249 Catholics in Oklahoma City and another 16,185 in Tulsa, meaning that 43.2 percent of the state's Catholic population now resided in Oklahoma's metropolitan centers. The university towns of Stillwater (Payne County) and Norman (Cleveland County) enjoyed a Catholic presence, as did Lawton (Comanche County), with its military establishment at Ft. Sill, while growing towns in the central part of the state, such as Enid (Garfield County), Ponca City (Kay County), and Shawnee (Pottawatomie County) all drew Catholics from the declining rural periphery. In rural Oklahoma, by contrast, Catholic numbers continued to decline, with the fifty counties with fewer than one thousand Catholics accounting for only 15.7 percent of the Catholic population.[5]

Higher levels of education were also associated with a reduced deference to clerical authority and a greater likelihood that a lay Catholic would make an appeal to personal conscience on moral questions (a stance encouraged by increasing numbers of priests in the pulpit). As Catholics moved into the suburbs, the complex network of relationships that had characterized the insulated ethnic Catholic parish was replaced with a more amorphous suburban Catholic culture that emphasized the mutual responsibility of Catholics to shape the moral and cultural atmosphere of their communities in *association* with their Protestant and Jewish neighbors. "I have found," declared Father James Halpine in 1960, "in my small experience in the community of Oklahoma City that I, and parishioners that I know of who have taken steps into the community, have always been received cordially and even respectfully."[6]

3. Campbell, "The Struggle to Serve," 252; Callahan, *The Mind of the Catholic Layman*, 79–90.

4. On the increased social mobility of American Catholics, see Kosa, "The Emergence of a Catholic Middle Class."

5. National Council of the Churches, *Churches and Church Membership in the United States.*

6. Callahan, *The Mind of the Catholic Layman*, 91–100; *Oklahoma Courier*, May 20, 1960.

In his assessment of the situation in Chicago during the late 1950s, Father Andrew Greeley stressed that the newfound affluence and education of the suburban Catholic left him or her with a much greater confidence to question authority, whether secular or religious. "If an executive of a large corporation cannot be treated [by Church officials] in the same fashion as his grandfather," he wrote, "it would follow that something more than the Baltimore Catechism is required for a graduate of a college and professional school." But, Greeley cautioned, suburban Catholics ran the risk of becoming too American. There was far less to insulate them from the surrounding culture than had been the case during the era of ghetto Catholicism.[7]

Suburban life, however insulated from the rest of the world it might be, fostered new transdenominational understandings. The early 1950s witnessed a final effort by the fading Protestant establishment to call into question the commitment of American Catholics to the nation on issues ranging from the funding of parochial schools to the appointment of an American ambassador to the Vatican.[8] In response to these efforts to represent Catholicism as a religious analogue to the secular totalitarian threat posed by Communism, middle-class Catholics made great efforts to repudiate those aspects of their religious culture that continued to separate them from the American mainstream. Perhaps most reflective of this middle-class transition was John F. Kennedy's election as the first Catholic president in 1960, which proved, in the words of Daniel Callahan, "that the first requirement for American Catholic social and cultural ascendancy lies in triumphing over one's cultural origins."[9] While he won the presidency, the manner of Kennedy's victory contributed to an inevitable secularization of the public square. It is notable that in 1963, Bishop Reed authorized the renaming of a school in Lawton after the soon-to-be martyred Kennedy.[10] The use of a contemporary—and, as it turned out, not particularly saintly—figure as titular of a Catholic school suggests the degree to which many Catholics had bought into the surrounding culture.

7. Greeley, The Church and the Suburbs, 51–60 (quotation on 60).
8. Curry, Protestant-Catholic Relations in America, 36–60; Fogarty, SJ, The Vatican and the American Hierarchy, 313–45, 364–67; McGreevy, "Thinking on One's Own."
9. Callahan, The Mind of the Catholic Layman, 149. See also Mark Massa, "A Catholic for President? JFK, Peter Berger, and the 'Secular' Theology of the Houston Speech, 1960," in Catholics and American Culture, 128–47.
10. Revd. T. Wade Darnall to Victor Reed, July 16, 1963, Reed to Darnall, July 18, 1963, Blessed Sacrament Church, Lawton File, Archives of the Catholic Archdiocese of Oklahoma City (hereafter AAOC).

As educated Catholics entered public life, so the pressure increased to scale back or eliminate specifically Catholic organizations that, at least in the eyes of progressives, only reinforced the ghetto mentality, and to join non-denominational fraternities.[11] In 1961, Bishop Reed expressed reservations about the wisdom of establishing a Catholic war veterans' group in Hennessey, suggesting that the small numbers involved made it more appropriate for them to affiliate with the local branch of the American Legion.[12] While Reed may well have meant only that it was a waste of resources to organize a small fraternity, his attitude could also have reinforced the sentiment that occupational and social groups need not be organized on confessional lines.

The prevailing Church ban on membership in the YMCA excited the ire of some Oklahomans, particularly since it seemed to imply that Catholics could not even visit the Y's facilities.[13] Unlike some bishops, however, Reed refrained from taking a formal position on membership, leaving it to the discretion of parish priests. When it came to young Catholics in Bartlesville, Cushing, and Dewey participating in Hi-Y, a subordinate unit of the YMCA that taught teenagers the principles of good government, he was prepared to look the other way.[14]

A similar problem arose later in the decade with regard to the Church bar on participation in secular fraternal societies. Philip Vorderlander, a member of the Knights of Columbus, reported that his parish priest had told him that it was now permissible to join the Elks (which he had done) but not the Odd Fellows. Since the Elks required an oath (the reason given for the proscription of the Odd Fellows), he was puzzled as to the discrepancy, but all Fa-

11. Declared the editors of *Commonweal*: "But far from turning out independent Catholics, many of these organizations retain the tight dependence of layman on priest that prevents the maturity which the groups aim at. . . . The problems of lay groups taking off on their own without correctly understanding Catholic principles are obvious, but so is the danger that lay groups which are lay in name only will alienate some of the best prospective members and fail in their mission." *Commonweal*, March 20, 1964, 737–38.

12. Revd. William C. Garthoeffner to Revd. M. Joseph Griffin, January 10, 1961, St. Joseph's Church, Hennessey File, AAOC.

13. *Oklahoma Courier*, February 7, 1964.

14. Revd. Philip Wilkiemeyer to Victor Reed, June 8, 1960, Revd. William C. Garthoeffner to Wilkiemeyer, June 9, 1960, Sts. Peter and Paul Church, Cushing File, box 36.1, Archives of the Catholic Diocese of Tulsa (hereafter ADT); Revd. Thomas G. Litsch to Revd. Charles H. Schettler, October 15, 1961, Schettler to Litsch, October 25, 1961, St. James Church, Bartlesville File, box 23.1, ADT. In the words of Father Schettler: "The Bishop has not taken an official or semi-official stand on the Y.M.C.A., so in the meantime, assistants should act in accord with the thinking of their pastor on the Y.M.C.A."

ther Charles Schettler could tell him was that the ban against the Odd Fellows was still in force. In 1971, Schettler had the arguably more embarrassing task of confirming that the prohibition against membership in Masonic organizations included such apparently innocuous bodies as the International Order of the Rainbow for Girls, whose international headquarters was located in McAlester, Oklahoma.[15]

THE TRANSFORMATION OF CATHOLIC ACTION

The educated Catholic not only wished to participate in American life, but to bring "American" principles to bear on the institution that had previously defined his existence. In this he was aided by those scholarly writings of the 1950s that developed the idea of the engaged layman, most notably Yves Congar's *Lay People in the Church*. A controversial theologian and French Dominican who would later be a *peritus* at the Second Vatican Council, Congar vigorously asserted the concept of the "lay priesthood" in relation to eucharistic worship, Catholic Action, and evangelization. In so doing, he directly challenged clerical paternalism in favor of an essential parity between the ordained and the unordained. While accepting that the power of decision making rested with the hierarchy, Congar emphasized that the process of Catholic Action often demanded the prudent determination of God's will in a given set of circumstances by the informed layman. A superficial reading of such a text might easily leave the layman with the impression that his sphere of autonomy was considerably wider than many of the leading Church authorities had, until now, been willing to countenance.[16]

The same small group of educated Catholics who would rush to peruse the new conciliar documents in the mid-1960s, with a view to applying them in everyday life, had spent the previous decade exposed—both in college and outside it—to the new currents in biblical criticism, liturgical and ecumenical initiatives, and the insights of anthropology and psychology. An increasingly professionalized Catholic press, inclined more to criticism than to praise of the established Church, and a network of forthright Catholic publishers gave

15. Philip H. Vorderlander to Victor Reed, n.d., Revd. Charles H. Schettler to Vorderlander, August 27, 1969, Sts. Peter and Paul Church, Kingfisher File, AAOC; Revd. Charles H. Schettler to Revd. Joseph C. Kolb, August 6, 1971, St. Peter's Church, Guymon File, AAOC.

16. Lakeland, *The Liberation of the Laity*, 49–77; Congar, *Lay People in the Church*, 190–233.

readers access to a new Catholic theology that stressed the full apostolate of the laity.

Such exposure led many laymen to expect the same influence over matters ecclesiastical enjoyed by their Protestant counterparts.[17] James Cockrell, head of diocesan Catholic Action, urged the Church to have faith in the laity, and a 1962 survey of American expectations for the Second Vatican Council revealed that 98 out of 114 respondents from Oklahoma thought that there was a need for greater lay participation.[18] While some bishops might have been willing partially to accommodate such expectations by appointing lay representatives to diocesan synods, ecumenical boards, and educational commissions, there was considerable potential for friction between the Church and an activist laity. What might have begun as a request for greater freedom of speech to discuss Church practice and policy seemed inevitably to lead to demands for a *say* in that practice and policy. The editor of *Commonweal* argued in 1963 that the educated layman did not see himself as taken seriously as a full and active member of the Church. By the mid-1960s, such men and women would increasingly find themselves at odds with the Church authorities.[19]

At the start of the decade, however, the Young Christian Workers and the Christian Family Movement continued to absorb much of the energy of young Catholic couples. "The YCW is a game for warriors, not flabby-footed people," Father Robert Brousseau told the state Young Christian Workers' convention in 1960. The organization existed to apply Catholic principles to politics, economics and working life, leisure time, parish life, and marriage. The father of Oklahoma Catholic Action, Monsignor Don Kanaly, reminded those attending that many Catholic leaders had received their early training in YCW, while the bishop emphasized that Catholic Action groups had a vital role to play in implementing the Church's teachings.[20] National repre-

17. In 1968, a Bartlesville resident proposed that parishes should be consulted before any redrawing of parish boundaries. She also suggested that, rather than create new parishes, new churches might be allowed to be satellites of the original foundation, with the right to use the facilities of the mother parish. The first suggestion implied a right of congregational consultation; the second challenged the Catholic principle of the territorial parish. Grace Donaldson to Victor Reed, March 18, 1968, Reed Papers.

18. *Oklahoma Courier*, May 27, 1960, September 28, 1962. The 1962 survey, carried out by the periodical *Eucharist*, achieved a response rate of 1 reader in 214 from Oklahoma compared to 1 reader in 265 nationally.

19. Callahan, *The Mind of the Catholic Layman*, 103–23.

20. *Oklahoma Courier*, February 19, 1960.

sentatives of the YCW were extremely impressed by the situation in Oklahoma and praised the "solidarity, spirit, intelligence and progressiveness of the Catholic minority." Unlike Father Brousseau, they noted that YCW sought to find solutions to the pressures on family life posed by early and mixed marriages and a process of extended higher education.[21]

Concern for the family was, first and foremost, a priority of the Christian Family Movement, an institution that Bishop Reed felt was still relevant to the modern era. "[Your members'] adoption of the challenge of anti-Christian thought and materialistic living in their community will witness to the guidance of the Holy See and will surely be blessed by God," he told Father Stephen MacAulay in 1962, after Our Lady of Fatima parish in Oklahoma City formed a new Catholic Action Club.[22] Only one year earlier, twenty-three parishes (about one-fifth of the diocese) maintained units of CFM, involving 420 couples and twenty-four priests, of which 55 percent were located in the western half of the state. Considerable growth was taking place in Oklahoma City, Tulsa, and Lawton, but work was also under way in north central Stillwater and Blackwell. The state federation's officers maintained that the movement's effectiveness was not confined to the metropolitan regions and that it emphasized the personal spiritual growth of their members.[23] "CFM really Americanized the structure [of Catholic Action]," Father Paul Gallatin testified, "and it did so by providing the group with a very clear outline . . . and it took the priest out of the process."[24]

CFM was also much involved in marital and premarital counseling. In June 1960, the first couples' retreat in the region, sponsored by the CFM unit of Christ the King parish in Oklahoma City, was conducted in Guthrie by Father Walter Imbriorski.[25] Two of the most active CFM chaplains in the early 1960s were Father William Nerin in Oklahoma City and Father William Ross in Tulsa, both of whom favored greater reliance on secular methods of counseling. Nerin proposed that CFM chaplains hold group discussions about the techniques employed by psychologists, psychiatrists, and counsel-

21. *Oklahoma Courier*, February 26, 1960.
22. Victor Reed to Revd. Stephen A. MacAulay, March 9, 1962, Our Lady of Fatima Church, Oklahoma City File, AAOC.
23. CFM report to the Bishop's Catholic Action Committee, March 9, 1961, Reed Papers.
24. Gallatin, interview.
25. *Oklahoma Courier*, June 10, 1960. A Chicago priest, Imbriorski was the one of the principal architects of the Cana Movement, which encouraged counseling among married couples.

ors to improve their marriage counseling skills. In a revealing choice of authorities, Nerin expressed his appreciation of Abbé Marc Oraison's *Union in Marital Love*.[26] In 1955, Oraison's *Vie chrétienne et problèmes de la sexualité* had been placed on the Index of Forbidden Books.

There was no lack of demand for marital counseling. Between 1962 and 1965, the diocesan family life department helped organize eighteen Cana conferences, in which a total of more than eighteen hundred people participated. The department offered a series of five programs for a parish Cana Day—two presentations on husband-wife relationships, two on parent-child relationships, and one on family-world relationships. For a cost to the parish of $25, the department supplied a priest-director and arranged for a Cana couple to help with preparations for the conference.[27]

The shift toward a more lay-centered ministry in the Oklahoma CFM became clear in 1963 when Reed directed that all Catholic Action organizations should henceforth be headed by lay members, with the priest serving solely as a chaplain. In November, Robert and Ann Buck of Oklahoma City succeeded Father Nerin as lay directors of the family life department. "I realize this is somewhat new to the Family Life program," Nerin conceded. "But if I understand this correctly, it means that at these Director meetings the Bucks will be the only laymen among all the priests who are Directors. This will be disconcerting to many of the priest directors who believe that only we priests should discuss together the problem of marriage."[28] Lay leaders took the initiative in other areas. At Corpus Christi parish in Oklahoma City, the chair couple proposed a series on "Children, Family Economics, and Leisure Time" in 1965, which they hoped would serve as an introduction to and source of recruits for CFM.[29]

In May 1960, the diocesan CFM organized a lay organization congress with the theme "Christ in International Life," which replicated that of the national CFM. Monsignor Reynold Hillenbrand, the architect of CFM in Chicago, addressed 150 leaders of lay organizations, whom he urged to raise

26. Revd. William Nerin to "Father," September 17, 1960, Reed Papers.

27. Mr. and Mrs. Robert P. Buck to "Dear Father," January 24, 1966, Reed Papers. Pre-Cana (for engaged couples) was the preferred form of marriage preparation among Oklahoma priests.

28. Revd. William Nerin to Msgr. Christopher Knott, November 7, 1963, Reed Papers. Although Nerin addressed his letter to Monsignor Christopher Knott, he may have confused him with Monsignor John Knott, who worked in the national family life department.

29. Manse and Mary Sharp to Victor Reed, September 8, 1965, Corpus Christi Church, Oklahoma City File, AAOC.

their sights above the local level. "We all live in the shadow of nuclear destruction," Hillenbrand reminded them, as he called for bilateral disarmament and a world court. Bishop Reed added a plea for the laity to institute a program of international action. Each diocesan group was invited to select from a variety of plans, including refugees, foreign students, migrant workers, and missions, and then provide monthly reports of their activities; CFM took up the cause of foreign students, while YCS favored migrant workers.[30] After the congress, the various diocesan deaneries each selected a region of the third world with which to engage in a process of social and cultural exchange.[31]

The high hopes and expectations with which CFM had entered into this process of dialogue with the outside world steadily degenerated over the next decade. The approach of the national convention to the same subject drew the criticism of conservatives who feared a radical politicization of the movement. When demands for a return to a more basic family apostolate were rejected, one hundred couples from the Archdiocese of Los Angeles departed the movement with the enthusiastic endorsement of Cardinal James McIntyre, the conservative archbishop.

For those who remained, the deliberations of the Second Vatican Council seemed at first to be a validation of everything for which they had worked. As the movement's chronicler puts it: "The council called for greater lay participation. CFM was ready. The council sought to reform the liturgy and to encourage greater lay participation. CFM was ready. The council told Catholics to engage the world and its problems. CFM was ready. The council called for greater openness on the part of the Church. CFM was ready. Not only was CFM ready, it had been espousing and pursuing just these goals since its inception. The council seemed to be a clear vindication of CFM's vision and method."[32]

Paradoxically, the very success of lay empowerment ultimately drained CFM and other Catholic Action groups of much of their power. As its members focused their efforts on parish governance and adult education, so the organization lost its raison d'être, while many CFM chaplains saw less and less value in an exclusively Catholic structure.[33] "We desired to become ac-

30. *Oklahoma Courier*, May 6, 1960. This congress attracted considerable attention throughout the United States.
31. *Oklahoma Courier*, July 1, 1960.
32. Burns, *Disturbing the Peace*, 118.
33. Ibid., 93–118. Father William Nerin declared CFM "dead" in 1966.

tivists," Father Gallatin admitted, "It would have been more valuable had I continued to form people."[34] In May 1967, a group of Tulsa teenagers commented that the Young Christian Students movement lacked leadership. There was too much discussion, they insisted, apparently unaware of the basis on which Catholic Action had first emerged, and too little action.[35]

THE PUBLIC SQUARE

One area in which CFM activists did not shirk their responsibilities was in instructing their coreligionists in the political process. At Tulsa's Sts. Peter and Paul parish, as part of a study of political life, the CFM unit sponsored a debate between a state senator and a Tulsa attorney in 1960 on the governor's proposals to reapportion the legislature and reform the funding arrangements for state highways.[36] Other CFM groups carried out similar initiatives. St. Mary's parish in Ardmore encouraged voter registration, while St. Patrick's parish in Oklahoma City prepared maps of precinct locations and put forward ten members of the parish to serve on precinct organizations.[37]

The Catholic laity had only to look to their Church leaders to see that the Church now considered itself qualified to make pronouncements on political issues. Bishop Reed provided the most obvious example with his extensive public testimony on behalf of civil rights measures, as well as his contributions to the 1959 debate on state liquor control and the 1968 amendment to the state constitution that was intended to end the political appointment of judges.[38] Where Reed was always careful to avoid public identification with a political party, the Kennedy campaign of 1960 inevitably associated Catholicism with Democratic Party politics. In October 1960, the Forum—a group of progressive priests and laymen who met from time to time at McGuinness High School—brought Senator Eugene McCarthy of Minnesota, another product of Catholic Action and a future presidential candidate, to speak in Oklahoma City.[39]

34. Gallatin, interview.   35. *Oklahoma Courier*, May 19, 1967.
36. *Oklahoma Courier*, March 4, 1960. 37. *Oklahoma Courier*, March 18, 1960.
38. For Reed's part in the civil rights debate, see chapter 8; for liquor control, see Victor Reed to George Miskovsky, April 14, 1959, Reed Papers; for the constitutional amendment on judicial appointments, see Reed to "Reverend and Dear Father (Monsignor)," September 6, 1968, Reed Papers.
39. *Oklahoma Courier*, October 14, 1960.

The entry of Catholic candidates into the political mainstream represented a shift of no small order. "When I was a child," Monsignor James Halpine
recalled, "[Catholic involvement in politics] would be absolutely impossible,
never would you trust a Catholic, so when the dam broke, it was amazing
how it broke."[40] From 1960 onward, church newsletters carried details of
candidates for office, with special reference to their own members. That year,
Christ the King parish in Oklahoma City announced the candidacy of one of
its members as state representative for Oklahoma County, while a member of
the St. Eugene's parish CFM was a candidate for local councilman.[41]

Some observers recognized the dangers inherent in the new "Catholic" politics. They fiercely asserted in 1960 that their Church had no aspirations to temporal power. "The Catholic Church," declared Rex Whistler,
"disclaims any control over strictly civil matters. It does point out however
that membership in a political party does not abridge our duty to abide by
the ten commandments and other moral precepts given by Christ. The only
control which the Catholic Church exercises over an office holder is that she
insists that he conduct his office with honesty and integrity."[42] W. L. Kreps
of Oklahoma City warned in 1964 that candidates should avoid identifying
themselves in the religious press as "member of the parish of . . ." since this
implied that their Catholic affiliation was a reason to vote for them, something that worked against the argument raised four years earlier to defend
support for Kennedy on the basis of his program.[43] James Hayden of Tulsa
addressed the same argument from a slightly different perspective: "Is there
really only one solution to the complex issues facing us today? Do all priests,
most bishops, agree on right to work, unionism, the U.N. and so on? Are
Catholics who are against some forms of welfarism or a stronger and more
centralized Federal Government considered John Birchers? Are those Catholics who are for Goldwater less Catholic than the Johnson voters? Has Catholic dialogue on social questions been closed?"[44]

These were all good questions, particularly since the most dramatic
"Catholic" victory of the period was the election, in 1966, of Dewey Bartlett

40. Halpine, interview.
41. *Oklahoma Courier*, March 18, 1960. See also the paid political advertisements for
the Democratic candidates for county offices that appeared in the parish newsletter of St.
John's parish, Yukon. *What's New from Hill's View*, September 1968, Reed Papers.
42. Rex Whistler to Victor Reed, September 14, 1960, Reed Papers.
43. *Oklahoma Courier*, May 8, 1964.
44. *Oklahoma Courier*, September 4, 1964.

Bishop Reed delivers the invocation at the inauguration of Dewey Bartlett, Oklahoma's first elected Catholic governor, in 1967.

as Oklahoma's second Republican chief executive and its first elected Catholic governor. Bartlett was a parishioner at Christ the King parish in Tulsa and an active member of the Christian Family Movement, but his political views were nevertheless far removed from many of the CFM-trained political activists who were now entering the political arena.[45] The bishop, however, viewed Bartlett's election as a triumphant vindication of the new Catholic political strategy. "Like the victory of John F. Kennedy, I believe yours in Oklahoma will accomplish much towards eliminating religious bias among

45. Christ the King proved to be an equal opportunity source of political talent. Democrat James R. Jones (U.S. congressman from Tulsa from 1971 to 1987) was also a parishioner of Christ the King, as would later be Oklahoma's third Catholic governor, Frank Keating. White, *This Far by Faith*, 44. For a profile of Dewey Bartlett, see *Oklahoma Courier*, August 14, 1964.

our people," Reed told the governor-elect. "I was happy to see that religion did not become a public issue in the campaign."[46]

Religion remained a public issue in one key area of Oklahoma life—the relationship between the public and parochial schools.[47] Problems arose in Cushing in 1961, when the state attorney general ruled that children from Sts. Peter and Paul parish could not eat at the public school cafeteria. Opposition to including Catholic students in the program was led by a Church of Christ preacher who made his protest as a private citizen, but relied upon Protestants and Other Americans United for the Separation of Church and State for his information. Most Cushing residents, however, were well disposed to their Catholic neighbors and many sent their children to the parochial school. One non-Catholic father, whose children attended the school, pointed out that Catholics had already paid for the cafeteria through their taxes. Moreover, many Catholic parishes, including St. Francis Xavier in Stillwater, participated in hot lunch programs for the benefit of public school students.[48]

Tensions next flared in Midwest City, just outside Oklahoma City, when a local resident, John Antone, filed a legal objection to allowing Catholic students to ride in public school buses, and the community responded by imposing a ban on the transport of pupils at nonpublic schools. Many local Protestants disagreed with Antone, recognizing that Catholic citizens helped sustain the local public school system in a variety of ways. They were also well aware of the dangers to which Catholic children were likely to be exposed as a result of any ban, given the heavy traffic on local roads that stemmed from the presence of a military base. The case was ultimately appealed to the state supreme court, which ruled in July 1963 that the ban was constitutional.[49]

Vastly different solutions to the school problem were proposed within the Catholic community. Omer Schnoebelen, who belonged to a mission parish in Mooreland, suggested that all denominations that maintained re-

46. Victor Reed to Governor-elect and Mrs. Dewey F. Bartlett, November 9, 1966, Reed Papers; Goble, "Oklahoma Politics and the Sooner Electorate," 166–72.
47. Interestingly, the Catholic sociologist Father Andrew Greeley concluded in 1966 that most Catholic schools appeared to be producing very Americanized and tolerant Catholics, especially on civil liberties issues, perhaps as a consequence of the Second Vatican Council and the debates that preceded it. Greeley and Rossi, *The Education of Catholic Americans*, 114–37.
48. *Oklahoma Courier*, September 29, 1961. St Joseph's parish in Tonkawa also hosted a hot lunch program for public school students. See Revd. Bernard J. Havlik to Revd. William C. Garthoeffner, October 17, 1966, St. Joseph's Church, Tonkawa File, AAOC.
49. *Oklahoma Courier*, October 20, November 3, December 8, 1961, July 12, 1963.

ligious schools should together announce the immediate closure of their facilities. When the general public was informed about the additional burden
on the public school system posed by the influx of parochial schoolchildren,
Schnoebelen argued, they would begin to reassess the situation. Douglas
Fox, by contrast, denied the virtue of crying discrimination in such a case,
pointing out that government funding was a two-edged sword. A Catholic
child remained free to attend a public school, Fox declared, but if Catholics wanted to keep their schools going, they must be prepared to dig deeper
into their own pockets. "Let's look for answers," the Tulsa attorney concluded, "instead of playing the miscast role of martyrs."[50] In some communities, the disputes over church-state relationships played out rather different-
ly. In Tulsa, parishioner Vincent Sposato, assisted by a Presbyterian lawyer,
sought to overturn the school board's policy barring the admission of parochial school pupils to remedial reading classes. In May 1962, the state attorney general overturned the ban.[51]

The bus controversy spread to a number of other communities. One of
these was the town of Okarche, which had an unusual population profile—
60 percent Catholic and 35 percent Lutheran—rather than the heavy Baptist
and Methodist presence that characterized most small towns in Oklahoma.
The Okarche public school had 125 pupils, compared to 300 in the Catholic schools and 50 in the Lutheran school, and the public school buses trans-
ported 75 public school students and 118 Catholics. Even the public school
board was transdenominational, consisting of two Catholics, two Lutherans,
and one other. It was not surprising that a compromise solution was reached
in Okarche.[52]

Many Protestants responded with sympathy to Catholic efforts to assert
their civic rights. The mayor of Midwest City, who had watched the unfolding
fight over school buses with dismay, designated March 3, 1962 as "St. Philip
Neri Appreciation Day." He praised local Catholics for their community service and for building a school cafeteria that conformed to the standards required for a public fallout shelter, which they had promised to make available
to the general public.[53] Several years later, when the Glenmary Missioners

50. *Oklahoma Courier*, December 29, 1961.
51. *Oklahoma Courier*, December 15, 1961, May 25, 1962.
52. *Oklahoma Courier*, December 22, 1961.
53. *Oklahoma Courier*, March 2, 1962. The Catholic parish in Medford also offered its
facilities to the town for use as a potential fallout shelter. See Revd. Albert W. Stephan to
Victor Reed, March 31, 1962, St. Mary's Church, Medford File, AAOC.

proposed the closure of St. Henry's mission in Plunkettville, Father Robert Valenza issued an eloquent dissent. "Many Plunkettville people see the Catholic Church as a good influence in their community," he told the bishop. "It supports the image of the [public] school. The school [and] the church in the middle of the community conveys a wholesome image to all. Leaving the community might be consider [sic] a type of desertion since it would weaken the image of the community and the position of the school."[54]

Good relations between Protestants and Catholics were fostered by other forms of contact. Campaigns against licentious films and books during the late 1950s and early 1960s became increasingly pan-Christian efforts, particularly in Tulsa, where a united effort to regulate movies and proscribe indecent literature left many Protestants with a greater respect for the Church than they had previously entertained. In February 1960, Citizens for Decent Literature, Inc. was incorporated in Oklahoma City, with the aim of targeting pornography by requiring strict enforcement of existing laws. Although a Methodist served as president, Monsignor John Walde was a member of the executive committee, while Bishop Reed served on the advisory committee.[55] Another quasi-ecumenical undertaking was Tulsa's joint campaign for community observance of Holy Week. In 1963, the city's Council of Churches and the Catholic Information Center issued a joint declaration inviting all local businesses to close on Good Friday between noon and three o'clock to allow their employees to attend church.[56]

CATHOLIC VALUES OR AMERICAN VALUES?

As Catholics came to perceive themselves as *both* people of their Church and American citizens, the threat of conflict between Church teachings and the interests of a pluralist society loomed ever larger. "The layman is, at one and the same time, a member of an authoritarian—but not monolithic— Church and the member of a democratic society mediating a pluralism of values," averred Daniel Callahan, editor of *Commonweal*. The scope of that pluralism would place ever-increasing burdens on the institutional Church. While pluralism could sometimes be used to the Church's advantage, as

54. Revd. Robert Valenza to Victor Reed, May 3, 1967, Reed Papers.

55. Mrs. S. H. Brandt to Victor Reed, May 20, 1958, Reed Papers; *Oklahoma Courier*, February 12, 1960.

56. "Citizen's Good Friday Observance," 1963, Raymond J. Schaefer to Victor Reed, n.d., Reed Papers.

in a campaign for federal aid to parochial schools, a pluralistic framework on issues as diverse as ecumenism, civil rights, or Vietnam inevitably created as many divisions within the Catholic community as within society as a whole.[57]

The steady accrual of authority by Catholic laymen within the Church and outside it inevitably prompted a reassessment of relationships with both parish priests and bishops. Lay Catholics were more intellectually advanced than ever before, wrote church historian John Tracy Ellis in 1962: "With this heightened intellectual and cultural prestige, with the deepening knowledge that accompanies a superior education, there has inevitably appeared a closer scrutiny of all that pertains to the Church, a sharper and more critical turn of mind, which makes the educated Catholic layman of this second half of the twentieth century a quite different person than his unlettered immigrant grandparents of two or three centuries ago."[58]

Oklahomans increasingly voiced such sentiments. "The Church isn't Roman!" declared Jeanie Gassen of Okarche. "I'm not Roman! My nationality is American! I hope my *being* is becoming Universal in awareness of the importance of love for All Man." Arliss Olds of the Church of the Madalene interpreted the "American" focus as requiring a greater degree of democratic accountability on the part of the Church toward its members. "We, the laity, are the Church," she told Reed. "Pursuing that thought, when a parish community begins to evolve into a thinking, acting organism, others notice and ask why? Most assuredly, the answer comes from the laymen, who have been infected with purpose, confidence and awakened to a meaningful offering of the Holy Eucharist."[59] In a letter to the apostolic delegate defending Bishop Reed against the charges of conservatives, Mary Kropp insisted that her bishop was providing teaching appropriate to the needs of the time: "I hope

57. Callahan, *The Mind of the Catholic Layman*, 160–70 (quotation on 153). For a typical example of cultural accommodation, see the *Courier* editorial commending the Legion of Decency's decision to pass the film *La Dolce Vita* with reservations: "With such a responsible approach to film ratings, the Legion of Decency clearly demonstrates value and should gain the cooperation of film makers and the American public alike. Such commentaries dealing with the shades of grey do much to assist all of us to a better understanding of the national concern over 'censorship' vs. 'unlimited license.'" *Oklahoma Courier*, May 26, 1961.

58. John Tracy Ellis, "The Catholic Layman in America Today," *Commonweal*, June 22, 1962, 319–22 (quotation on 320).

59. *Oklahoma Courier*, May 6, 1966; Arliss Olds to Victor Reed, June 20, 1966, Reed Papers.

this letter will help you to understand that not all the people in Oklahoma are unhappy with Bishop Reed only a few who are not willing to believe that this is the 20th Century and we are no longer riding in horse and buggy but riding in space ships landing on the moon. Rules of the Church in the 15th Century were just great and fulfilled their needs, but now it is not senisble [sic] to keep the old laws when everything around us today is new and modern, please don't take Bishop Reed from this growing society, both spirtually [sic] and economically."[60]

The implications of this new philosophical outlook were initially unclear. Some social issues—the debate over civil rights and opposition to the Vietnam War—produced the same divisions among lay Catholics as in American society generally, but the principles animating them, if not the methods employed to achieve them, did not necessarily conflict with Church teaching. The true cultural divide related to the development of ideas of radical personal freedom and the basic equality of the sexes, and Catholic laymen and laywomen who found aspects of these intellectual currents appealing were far more likely to come into direct conflict with the magisterial teaching of the Catholic Church. Some laymen seem to have concluded that the promulgation of *Dignitatis Humanae* implied that the new Church was willing to surrender determination of the morality of many issues to the exercise of individual conscience. In this, they were seriously mistaken.[61]

Perhaps unsurprisingly, the defining issue of the new era was artificial birth control. Most people understood that the issue had much deeper philosophical implications. One anonymous correspondent from Tulsa praised Father Louis Janssens of Louvain for advocating the use of the contraceptive pill for those for whom the rhythm method did not work.[62] Parents, the writer pointed out, were rarely willing to bring up what for them was a delicate subject and many of them feared that expression of pro-contraceptive

60. Mary J. Kropp to Abp. Egidio Vagnozzi, n.d., Reed Papers. Oklahoman Gordon Cooper was one of the first seven astronauts, and several more Sooners have followed him into space.

61. Tentler, *Catholics and Contraception*, 210–32.

62. Louis Janssens was born in Belgium in 1908. He matriculated as a doctoral student in the Faculty of Theology at Louvain in 1933 and completed his doctorate in 1937. He became a full-time professor at Louvain in 1942, where he lectured on moral theology. His personalist theology led him to an interest in marriage, the regulation of fertility, and the use of chemical contraceptives in a wider ethical context, and his views on this were featured in *Time*. He played a leading role in the drafting of several council documents, and one of his books was later translated into English as *Freedom of Conscience and Religious Freedom* (1966).

views might reflect on their children. "God made me, and He also made animals," the writer concluded. "But God gave only me the use of reason. The use of reason therefore is a part of the natural law. We people are here to use that reason to the best of our ability in harmony with Christ's basic teaching and example of brotherly love."[63]

Many of those who favored a change in the Church's official position emphasized the negative relational aspects of using rhythm. Another anonymous Tulsa correspondent with six children reported that her "fear" of conception and consequent reluctance to engage in intercourse was interpreted by her husband as a lack of love for him.[64] A Del City resident reported that after reading reports in the *Courier* she had concluded that she was the best and only judge about whether to take the pill. Those Catholics with scruples, however, could only take aspirin to counteract the headaches their children gave them and "hang on to their calendar until the church comes up with some non-ambiguous answers."[65]

Increasingly, the right of conscience took center stage as the Roman authorities continued their silence on the matter of chemical birth control. A doctor in Oklahoma City stated that as long as the diocese did not forbid him from doing so he would prescribe birth control pills where medically necessary, though with the proviso that such prescribing was approved by the clergy. Doctor Bodine evidently still saw a role for the confessor in his medical practice.[66] Not so, many of the laity. A parishioner at the Church of the Madalene—and mother of eight—demanded that the bishop effect a change in the rules. Educated people, she insisted, ought to know better than to have too many children, and it was unrealistic to expect married couples to live a chaste existence. Why should Catholics be denied the right to benefit from chemical means to limit family size, if they were able to take advantage of other aspects of medical science? "Wouldn't you know it—the priests and theologians who have decided that contraception is so wrong have never borne that first child much less half a dozen or more little ones. I trust that God understands my position and if I get thru this confinement with my life and sanity I refuse to go on this way any longer. I will not increase the size of my family several times more. So the only alternative seems to be to make use of contraceptive devices and leave the Church."[67] Such views were

63. *Oklahoma Courier*, April 10, 1964.   64. *Oklahoma Courier*, May 8, 1964.
65. *Oklahoma Courier*, June 12, 1964.   66. *Oklahoma Courier*, March 11, 1965.
67. Mrs. Duane Hogsett to Victor Reed, August 29, 1965, Church of the Madalene, Tulsa File, box 5.1, ADT.

shared by many within the Christian Family Movement, including its founders, Pat and Patty Crowley. Building on the more positive view of marriage
commended by Pope John XXIII, national CFM sought to make the case for
change with impassioned accounts of improved family life consequent upon
use of the pill, together with the negative experiences of married Catholics
who relied on the rhythm method, which they submitted to the birth control commission convened by Pope Paul VI.[68]

There is no doubt that the *Oklahoma Courier* helped foster a climate in
which birth control came to be viewed as a legitimate recourse for married
couples. One of the periodic polls of *Courier* readers in July 1966 revealed
that 95 percent of readers hoped that the Church would take a new stand on
artificial birth control. Catholic Oklahomans reflected the sea change in outlook that characterized the nation, with only 7 percent (the poll obviously
had some internal contradictions, given that 95 percent supposedly sought
a new outlook on the part of the Church) viewing the use of birth control as a mortal sin and 40 percent considering it an entirely personal matter
that should not be discussed in the confessional (two-thirds considered that a
couple must make the ultimate decision). Almost one-third of Oklahomans,
however, expected no change (5 percent because the Church had already
made its view clear and 27 percent because of internal disagreements), while
44 percent expected slight changes, and only 24 percent expected a major
change.[69] Perhaps even more significant was a *Courier* editorial praising the
work of Margaret Sanger, the heroine of the birth control movement, which
appeared two months later.[70]

Under such conditions, the promulgation of Paul VI's encyclical *Humanae Vitae* in 1968 came as a severe shock to those members of the laity who
had expected some modification. Gerald Murphy, recently arrived from New
England, commended Reed for an open and conciliatory policy that treated liberals and conservatives alike, but regretted that he had raised no objection to the encyclical. "You have made your decision and I don't want to
argue or degrade your motives," Murphy told the bishop. "Nevertheless, I

---

68. Burns, *Disturbing the Peace*, 174–83. In an undated letter to Reed, a group of married couples and married women from Oklahoma complained that the rhythm method was
unreliable and that use of birth control tended to increase expressions of love between
husband and wife. "Regarding the Recent Encyclical 'Humane Vitae': A Letter to Bishop
Reed," n.d., Reed Papers.

69. *Oklahoma Courier*, July 8, 1966.

70. *Oklahoma Courier*, September 9, 1966.

do not think you have made it as an independently thinking man, but as a Bishop of an overly structured Church and I express my sympathy for your lonely bishopric."[71] Paul Sprehe, chairman of the diocesan finance committee and a member of the Community of John XXIII (Oklahoma City's non-territorial parish), felt that support for the position embraced by *Humanae Vitae* "would indeed be unfortunate."[72] Dorothy Tabata of St. Mary's parish in Ponca City offered an even more negative view of the encyclical: "I have decided that if the Pope can be so dangerously wrong on the issue of birth-control, then many other Catholic issues may also be completely wrong. Perhaps many other mortal sins were invented to control the Catholic population and are not the teaching of God, but of man. In order that I may follow my own conscience, I intent [*sic*] to use birth-control and to speak for birth-control whenever I get the chance."[73]

While artificial birth control was the dominant subject of discussion, some laymen expressed dissenting views on other matters of ecclesiastical discipline, including mandatory clerical celibacy and a solely male priesthood. Francis Heinz of Chilocco suggested that clergy be allowed to marry, insisting that a wife could be a source of spiritual inspiration. Grace Donaldson of Bartlesville favored allowing older married men to enter the priesthood while their wives were still living, something partly addressed at the end of the decade when the American Church began to experiment with a married permanent diaconate.[74]

A more radical proposal came from Lynn Rehkopf, a high school senior at Ft. Sill, who urged episcopal support for the ordination of women to the priesthood. She insisted that the Pauline injunction so often invoked on the subject had to be seen in its cultural context. "Tradition doesn't make anything right," she insisted. "The Catholic Church is breaking away from a lot of traditions and it is for the better. . . . You also may think that I'm just

71. Gerald W. Murphy and Margaret C. Murphy to Victor Reed, August 10, 1968, Reed Papers. See the discussion of the public reaction to *Humanae Vitae* in Tentler, *Catholics and Contraception*, 264–75.

72. Sprehe insisted to Reed that his off-the-record comment in an interview with the *Oklahoma Journal* had been misrepresented, but the damage was already done. Paul F. Sprehe to Victor Reed, July 30, 1968, Reed Papers.

73. Dorothy Tabata to Pope Paul VI, July 6, 1971, St. Mary's Church, Ponca City File, AAOC.

74. Francis W. Heinz to Victor Reed, May 1, 1966, Grace Donaldson to Reed, March 18, 1968, Reed Papers. The permanent diaconate was actually authorized in 1965, but the first permanent deacon was not ordained in Oklahoma until 1977.

some neurotic female and that my almost hopeless dream will pass. But, Father, it won't. I realize that you alone can't do much about this change in the Church so I've written to most of the archdioceses and dioceses in the United States." What was most revealing about Rehkopf's correspondence was that she believed such a matter could be resolved within the context of a *national* episcopal forum. Reed gently attempted to make her aware of her error when, while thanking her for her interest and promising to keep the issue in prayer, he reminded her that female ordination would be a matter for the pope or a general council of the Church to decide.[75]

CONCLUSION

The transformation of the status of Catholic laity was seen as one of the great triumphs of the Second Vatican Council. Under the auspices of their permissive bishop, Oklahoma Catholics of all persuasions enjoyed the freedom to compete in the marketplace of ideas, to contribute directly to the upbuilding of the Church, and to be treated as social equals in the wider society. Full participation in public life, including entry into mainstream politics, gave Oklahoma Catholics a new sense of accomplishment and acceptance. It emboldened them to assert their right to protest that they be allowed to make use of certain public facilities in a sectarian context on the principle that they deserved to be treated with the same consideration as other taxpayers. To be Catholic was no longer something to be concealed in certain public contexts but to be proudly affirmed in this corner of the Bible Belt.

While Catholic identity was now being vigorously affirmed, it was not necessarily the identity embraced by the institutional Church. Americanized Catholics were now "thinking for themselves" and creating their own definitions of what constituted Catholic teaching. For many laymen, *Humanae Vitae* did not constitute part of that identity. The challenge to individual episcopal authority in the years ahead was evidently to come not only from the new collegial authority espoused by the National Conference of Catholic Bishops but also from a newly empowered laity which, five years after Reed's death, would unsuccessfully seek even an even greater lay voice in the government of the Church at the 1976 Call to Action conference.[76]

75. Lynn Rehkopf to Abp. James McIntyre, August 1, 1968, Victor Reed to Rehkopf, August 8, 1968, Reed Papers. Rehkopf's letter was forwarded to Reed as the responsible bishop.
76. Manning. *A Call to Action.*

chapter 13 ⌒⟀

An Enduring
Sense of Separation

Catholic Identity in Crisis

But the college or body of bishops has no authority unless it is understood together with the Roman Pontiff, the successor of Peter as its head. The pope's power of primacy over all, both pastors and faithful, remains whole and intact. In virtue of his office, that is as Vicar of Christ and pastor of the whole Church, the Roman Pontiff has full, supreme and universal power over the Church. And he is always free to exercise this power. The order of bishops, which succeeds to the college of apostles and gives this apostolic body continued existence, is also the subject of supreme and full power over the universal Church, provided we understand this body together with its head the Roman Pontiff and never without this head. This power can be exercised only with the consent of the Roman Pontiff. For our Lord placed Simon alone as the rock and the bearer of the keys of the Church, and made him shepherd of the whole flock. . . . A council is never ecumenical unless it is confirmed or at least accepted as such by the successor of Peter; and it is the prerogative of the Roman Pontiff to convoke these councils, to preside over them and confirm them.

Second Vatican Council, Dogmatic Constitution on the Church, *Lumen Gentium*, November 12, 1964

While most Catholics welcomed the greater sense of social inclusion that they experienced during the 1960s, they were well aware that anti-Catholic prejudices lurked beneath the surface of society. Suspicion of Catholic intentions had produced its own brand of intolerance, and stories of convent abuses had been a staple of early-twentieth-century Oklahoma discourse. Even during the 1960 presidential campaign, members of Protestants and Other Americans United for the Separation of Church and State had enlisted the services of former priest Emmet McLaughlin, who traveled through the small towns of Oklahoma denouncing his former coreligionists for their supposed hostility to the public school system.[1]

As late as 1965, a survey of two small Oklahoma communities revealed that 68 percent of Protestants believed that Catholics voted as a political bloc (26 percent of Catholics agreed) and that 91 percent of Catholics believed that there were active efforts to exclude them from public office (69 percent of Protestants agreed). That same year, Father Lee O'Neil of St. William's parish in Skiatook held a protest meeting. He accused the town's board of education of discriminating against Catholic applicants for positions in public school teaching. (The school superintendent was reputed to have said: "I wouldn't consider hiring a Catholic teacher because this is a Baptist town.")[2]

Some Catholics responded to such blatant examples of religious prejudice by asserting their rights to equal treatment as American citizens. Key to such a strategy was a conscious effort to dispel notions entertained by many Protestants about Catholicism, despite the minimal differences between Protestant and Catholic conceptions of the supernatural.[3] Many Oklahoma Catholics believed that Protestants often attacked "Catholic" doctrines without any awareness of what the latter actually were, and that they spread false rumors about the behavior of priests and sisters (three quarters of Protestants admitted the first charge and more than half the second).[4] Some parishes sought to follow up on the 1956 program "Operation Understanding," during which

1. Donald F. Sullivan to T. Austin Gavin and Leo Morrison, September 20, 1960, Reed Papers.

2. Davidson and Schlangen, "Cultural and Structural Assimilation among Catholics in the Southwest," 446–47; *Oklahoma Courier*, June 11, 1965.

3. In the 1965 survey previously cited, the only significant differences in supernatural belief were that Catholics reported a slightly higher belief in the necessity of baptism and in the existence of the devil, while Protestants laid a slightly greater emphasis on the necessity of a commitment to Christ. Davidson and Schlangen, "Cultural and Structural Assimilation among Catholics in the Southwest," 448–49.

4. Ibid., 446. Community hostility to the presence of members of religious orders may well have depended on whether they undertook religious instruction or performed corporate acts of mercy. In Cherokee, the Sisters of St. Francis, who assisted with the care of the sick and dying at the local Masonic hospital, enjoyed strong community support, including from the Chamber of Commerce, the county judge, and the local sheriff. Report of Sisters of St. Francis at St. Cornelius Catechetical Center, n.d., St. Cornelius Church, Cherokee File, Archives of the Catholic Archdiocese of Oklahoma City (hereafter AAOC).

every Catholic parish in the state held an open house and invited its non-Catholic neighbors to visit the church, see the furnishings—which were labeled and were accompanied by parishioners trained to speak about each item—and ask questions. In 1958, parishioners at one Tulsa parish invited their non-Catholic neighbors to attend a lecture series on "The Catholic Way of Living," and two years later, as the presidential election loomed, St. Catherine's parish in Tulsa sponsored a lecture series to defuse "myths" about Catholicism relating to marriage, confession, the Mass, and the place of Mary and the saints.[5]

In practice, Catholic priests were sometimes able to exploit internecine strife within the Protestant community to build their own congregations. When the Protestant community of Cherokee was traumatized by the divorce of the local Methodist preacher and the excommunication of many locals who had gone into the liquor business in 1959, the local priest saw interest in instruction in the Catholic faith rise dramatically. "Father," a Cherokee resident him, "you're going to have more excommunicated Masons on your hands than you realize."[6]

The assertion of a separatist Catholic identity was often at its strongest among the laity in rural parishes and missions. In Mooreland, there had been an active mission in the town since 1904, with a regular attendance of around twenty families. When it was proposed that the mission be closed in 1967, local residents complained that the number of communicants was generally underreported by the assigned priests. Furthermore, since a weekly devotion was still promised for Mooreland and clerical obligations for sick calls and family visitations remained unchanged, all the priest was spared was a Sunday trip to the town. At least eighteen automobiles would be needed, however, to bring the Mooreland Catholics to the nearest community with a church. "When I see every trend being toward large centers or big cities," declared Omer Schnoebelen, "I also see every evil consequence of such congestion of population. I think it just as reasonable to require that the Woodward people come to Oklahoma City or to Tulsa as to require our people of the Mooreland Mission to go to Woodward or Alva or Enid—and some of them will not, because they deem it an imposition to take from us the thing that we have worked for and sustained all these years."[7]

5. *Tulsa Tribune*, August 29, 1958; *Tulsa Daily World*, September 18, 1960.
6. Revd. Richard F. Dolan to Victor Reed, September 17, 1959, St. Cornelius Church, Cherokee File.
7. Mooreland Sacred Heart Congregation to Victor Reed, June 13, 1967, Omer Schnoebelen to Reed, June 13, 1967, Reed Papers.

Certain Catholic values necessarily stood in sharp relief against secular cultural orthodoxy. The tumult over *Humanae Vitae* worked against the encyclical among most Oklahoma laymen (see chapter 12), but some voices could still be heard endorsing Paul VI's teaching. Typical of such an approach were Mr. and Mrs. Frank Prichard of Krebs who, two years before the encyclical, sounded a solidly countercultural note: "Why such a 'I hate babies' campaign? Why soften the truth any: Our nation is fast becoming a nation full of self-centered, over-indulged, sex-for-sex-sake individuals! The pleasures of married life are fine, as long as there is no risk of being faced with the possible responsibilities that might result from them. . . . The fact that children are blessings in a home is overlooked—sad, but true."[8]

After the promulgation of *Humanae Vitae* and the negative reaction it provoked, other papal loyalists took up the gauntlet. The chief of staff at Tulsa's St. Francis Hospital bluntly observed those who disagreed with the encyclical should leave the Church rather than stay and provoke controversy.[9] Leon Lykes, a convert living in Oklahoma City, agreed that the issue was not whether Catholics agreed or disagreed with Paul VI's views. "The thing that is important is that this rule was made and as practicing Catholics we must accept it."[10] Leonard Landell of Lawton dispatched a tongue-in-cheek missive thanking the *Oklahoma Courier* for publishing the names of the seventy-two diocesan priests who had signed a statement in defense of private conscience. "This will certainly eliminate a lot of 'shopping around' for the right confessor," he concluded. "You could help us a lot by publishing a list of 'right doctors' to go with your 'right priests.' It is very important that everyone you list be a Catholic in good standing."[11] Charles Von Dracek of Alva complained that too many priests were trying to find a moral defense for birth control. If conscience became the guide to the Church's stance on birth control, it would lead to marriage based on a couple's feelings rather than a commitment to eternal truth. "Individual conscience as a guide for true morality," he concluded, "would result in the same disastrous results that have come from private interpretation of the Bible: over 300 religions instead of one that Christ founded."[12]

8. *Oklahoma Courier*, July 15, 1966. The Prichards had eight children and were strong supporters of Bishop Reed.
9. Robert G. Tompkins to Victor Reed, August 16, 1968, Reed Papers.
10. *Oklahoma Courier*, September 20, 1968.
11. *Oklahoma Courier*, August 23, 1968.
12. Charles Von Dracek to Victor Reed, December 12, 1968, Reed Papers.

Birth control was a debate between the laity and the hierarchy, which ended in effective defeat for the latter, as the former largely ceased to accept official pronouncements on this—and eventually on other—subjects after *Humanae Vitae*. On the related issue of abortion, however, the Church still found it possible to assert a countercultural theology acceptable to the laity. By the mid-1960s, the prospect of legalized abortion in certain jurisdictions had made it a matter of heated public debate. Oklahoma City's Catholic community received a rude awakening in 1964, when administrators at Bishop McGuinness High School set as a topic for three senior speech classes the question of whether or not the United States should legalize abortion. While Father David Monahan insisted that it had been explained to the students that the proposition was a purely hypothetical one from a Catholic standpoint and that the principal objective was debating technique rather than the merits of the issue, he suggested that since abortion was a much-debated subject in the popular periodicals (he listed articles in eleven journals, including *Time* and *Newsweek*), it was well for Catholic students to be exposed to the strength of the Catholic position and the weakness of the non-Christian one.[13]

Traditionalist Catholics viewed such reasoning as an exercise in semantics. Leading the charge was Tom Costello, the Catholic traditionalist leader in Oklahoma City, who had children at McGuinness, though not in the speech classes in question. Costello complained that an April 14 poll of *all* the children at McGuinness contradicted Monahan's assurances that the debate was confined to seniors (all the speech classes were for seniors) and that it would not hurt or confuse them. The poll reported that while 396 children opposed legalization of abortion, another 66 were undecided, and 113 supported it. Was it the education system or the home that had produced such a departure from Catholic principles, Costello wondered, and if the latter, why had teachers at McGuinness not corrected it? "For any Catholic student to have answered 'yes' or to have been 'undecided' would have been evidence of a flaw in his (or her) Catholic schooling," Costello concluded. "For 187 out of 609 students to be in these two categories is prima facie evidence of gross incompetence on the part of the school in fulfilling it's [sic] most important function, that of providing proper religious training in the principles and doctrine of Catholicism."[14]

13. Revd. David Monahan to Msgr. Sylvester S. Luecke, April 13, 1964, Reed Papers.
14. Tom Costello to Revd. David Monahan, May 11, 1964, Reed Papers. For more on Costello, see below.

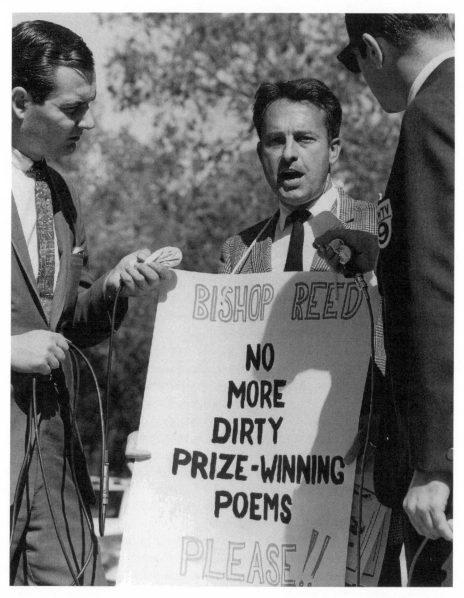

Conservative activist Tom Costello protests outside the diocesan chancery in 1966.

Costello upped the ante by circulating his complaints to parents of children at McGuinness. Many of those who replied to him threw light on the cultural cleavages that now divided the Catholic community into progressive and traditionalist factions. Costello viewed the issue through the lens of magisterial teaching. For him, making something a matter of *debate* implied that there were legitimate differences of interpretation as to Catholic doctrine, something that he would have denied in relation to abortion. His critics disputed his reading of the *meaning* of debates and polls. "I see no harm in the poll or the debate held by the student council," Robert Ferioli told Father Monahan. "For a student to answer 'yes' to such a question gives us no right to assume that this is the undying belief of the student who will actually practice this belief in life. We are training our children to be 'thinkers' who will soon meet the challenges of the world and make the decisions of leaders. For them to know both sides of a story is the only way to find a true answer." Ferioli took Costello to task, demanding to know the value of hiding controversial topics from his children. Would Costello conceal a copy of *Reader's Digest* from his children because it contained an article on the ongoing controversy over birth control in Rome? he demanded. Ferioli also repeated his objections to taking the "yes" vote on the poll as evidence of serious doctrinal slippage. Had Costello ascertained how many "yes" votes were from non-Catholic students? he wondered.[15]

Other parents expressed similar sentiments. Upholding the new spirit of Catholic Americanism, George Thompson and his wife denounced the idea that Catholicism could simply be reduced to rote propositions: "Today Catholic education cannot be a series of pat answers like it was in our day. Catholics are now a part of every phase of American life. Our ghetto thinking cannot accomplish the things Christ expects of us. Catholic education must furnish the tools and mechanics so that our Catholic citizens can think, judge and act on any subject at any time." Rita Clarkson echoed Monahan's insistence that the young adults would soon be on college campuses where issues of morality would be everyday topics of conversation. Some precollege preparation, she declared, was essential. Perhaps the most intriguing response came from Gerard Rosenthal, whose daughter had given one of the "don't know" responses on the abortion question. Rosenthal, who had grown up in Nazi Germany, had been raised in a liberal family in which many

15. Robert Ferioli to Revd. David Monahan, May 26, 1964, Ferioli to Tom Costello, May 27, 1964, Reed Papers.

viewpoints were discussed "openly and in a moral manner," a practice he had adopted in his own household. Rosenthal had gone over his daughter's answers with her to discover why she answered as she did:

As for the specific question involved, she answered according to the best of her ability and according to the limited knowledge she had of this issue. She was aware of the great problem, which confronted parents of "Thalidomide" babies, as they were called and the very difficult decisions they faced. Remember dear Sir that these people, who were in the public limelight at that time, did not have the grace of our Holy Faith and did not have the spiritual strength we have as children of God and members of Christ's Holy Church . . . this is a mind of a Catholic child, which is being enriched every day of the week by the Catholic teaching in her fine school, by her Catholic home, where her parents in their struggling, human ways are trying to cooperate with God, to make of their children true disciples of Christ and world citizens of their society in which they must be able to function to the best of their ability.[16]

While the debate probably changed few minds on either side, within a few years abortion had ceased to be a purely theoretical proposition. Seven years prior to the *Roe v. Wade* decision legalizing abortion throughout the United States (January 22, 1973), Oklahoma legislators were already introducing bills to legalize abortion, of which the most prominent—drafted by State Representative Curtis Lawson—defined protection of the "health" of the mother in terms of prevention of physical or mental distress to the mother or the presence of physical or mental handicaps in the fetus. If passed, Bishop Reed pointed out, it would give Oklahoma some of the most liberal abortion laws in the country: "[This argument] may prove to be more persuasive with legislators and those of other faiths than to assume a hard line against the bill simply because we as Catholics believe that all abortion is wrong."[17]

Leading the fight in the trenches was Catholic layman Ed Story, a member of St. Matthew's parish in Elk City, who urged lay Catholics to write letters to their state representatives. Story set them an example by inquiring of Representative Lawson why his legislation had not included a provision to permit euthanasia for the elderly, crippled, and handicapped. "Better respect for God, and family and country," Story concluded, "and there would be no thought of abortion and other forms of legalized murder. Why don't you

16. Mr. and Mrs. George H. Thompson to Tom Costello, May 26, 1964, Rita Clarkson to Revd. David Monahan, May 28, 1964, Gerard M. Rosenthal to Costello, June 7, 1964, Reed Papers.
17. Victor Reed to Priests of the Diocese, March 10, 1967, Reed Papers.

get all the preachers and teachers and leading citizens of church and state to propose better lives, and also set the good example yourselves." Story's campaigning won him a letter of appreciation from Democratic representative Jerry Sokolosky, a staunch opponent of the Lawson bill.[18]

Interestingly, the abortion debate proved to be one of the rare occasions on which progressive Catholics embraced the more traditionalist viewpoint. Father William Nerin, then the administrator of the Community of John XXIII, appeared at the legislative committee hearing on the Lawson bill and spoke against it, in opposition to a minister from the United Campus Church Fellowship at the University of Oklahoma. Addressing the proposition that termination was the better course with severely handicapped children, Nerin spoke in the explicitly Catholic idiom that has defined the Church's pro-life stance since 1973. "I contend that it is a greater good for society to bring these defective children into the world," he told legislators, "and then take care of them as we care for others who are already alive."[19] Parish units of the Christian Family Movement also mobilized to oppose the Lawson bill, including the chapter of the generally progressive parishioners at Tulsa's Church of the Madalene.[20] Such activism contrasted with an initial silence from more traditionalist elements, prompting Emerson Pyne of Yukon to comment acidly that when it came to speaking out, only the bishop and the "ultra liberals" were in evidence. "Where were all you pastors, mothers, defenders and traditionalists?" he asked. "Is the only 'change' that you favor the one legalizing abortion?"[21]

Despite Pyne's criticism, it began to be clear in the late 1960s that a growing number of Catholics were following in the footsteps of many mainstream Protestants and beginning to see a place for selective abortion alongside a full-fledged program of contraception. In October 1967, there was concern regarding a proposed forum on abortion at Immaculate Conception parish in Tulsa that was scheduled to include the appearance of a doctor who had been imprisoned for performing criminal abortions. Since the Church regarded abortion as immoral and the state considered it illegal, one observer commented, why discuss it?[22] Four years later, the chief of staff at Tulsa's St. Francis Hospital complained about Sally Brown, who said she was the

18. Ed Story to Curtis L. Lawson, March 30, 1967, Jerry Sokolosky to Story, April 4, 1967, Story to Revd. William C. Garthoeffner, April 8, 1967, Reed Papers.
19. *Oklahoma Courier*, March 10, 1967.   20. *Oklahoma Courier*, April 14, 1967.
21. *Oklahoma Courier*, March 24, 1967.
22. C. E. White to Victor Reed, October 2, 1967, Reed Papers.

chair of the social action committee at the Community of John XXIII and
had been reported as supporting a bill that would allow abortion on demand
for the first three months of pregnancy. "While recognizing the right of individual conscience for any Catholic," he observed, "I deeply resent any person
presenting such a viewpoint as representing that of a Catholic parish. This is
particularly unfortunate as we work with so many good Protestants against
this pernicious movement."[23] That same month, the board of directors of
St. John's Hospital in Tulsa issued a statement opposing abortion and euthanasia. "We support those educational, social and economic measures carried
on by public and private agencies and other interested person[s]," it concluded, "which aim to correct conditions that lead persons to seek measures
not in conformity with a Christian perception of man's dignity."[24]

THE CONCILIAR LABORATORY

"When we compare our progress with that of friends and relatives in
other parts of the country," Catholics in Midwest City told Reed in May
1966, "we know we are indeed fortunate and blessed to have your leadership
and wisdom during this period of transition."[25] Another Oklahoma laywoman expressed equally fulsome sentiments. "I am merely reading the various
Catholic newspapers and magazines," she declared, "about other dioceses still struggling with renewal in liturgy (truly an accepted *basic* here) and
from talking with Catholics who have moved here from Chicago, New York
and other places, I am convinced that the freedoms you allow to the priests
and the people have resulted in a growth in the Spirit of Christ that is un-
paralleled."[26]

The idea of Oklahoma as a place in which the full potential of the renewal process was being realized was shared by many, but was not a source
of universal rejoicing. For some Oklahoma Catholics, the practitioners of
change seemed in danger of confusing liberty with license, a suspicion only
heightened by the fact that liberals who had welcomed the teaching authority of a papal reformer like John XXIII showed every inclination to disregard

23. Robert G. Tompkins to Victor Reed, April 12, 1971, Reed Papers.
24. St. John's Hospital and School of Nursing, Inc., "Statement on Respect for Life,"
April 1971, Reed Papers.
25. William J. Vetter et al. to Victor Reed, May 10, 1966, Reed Papers.
26. Mrs. John N. Steinard to Victor Reed, January 5, 1968, Reed Papers.

the injunctions of Pope Paul VI when these failed to conform with what they had hoped and expected.

Traditionalist Catholics in Oklahoma, like those across the United States, were rarely more realistic or consistent than their liberal adversaries, but they were equally passionate. They yearned for the halcyon days of the 1940s and 1950s, when practicing Catholicism seemed so simple, and they reacted with anger to the pronouncements of clerical sophisticates who seemed more interested in liturgical change for its own sake than in obtaining a better understanding of the theology that sustained it.[27]

An early target of conservative wrath was the *Oklahoma Courier* and its progressive editor (see chapter 3). Initially, traditionalists accused the *Courier* of pursuing a "Communistic line." In the spring of 1962, fifteen prominent Oklahoma Catholics endorsed a 125-page booklet consisting of a lengthy introduction and twenty selected articles reproduced from the *Courier*, with accompanying comments. Copies of the booklet were sent to Bishop Reed, Archbishop Lucey of San Antonio, the cardinals of the United States, and the apostolic delegate, but no official response was forthcoming. Detecting a link between the editorial line of the *Courier* and the "subversive" activities of certain priests, traditionalists turned to the *Wanderer*, a publication from the far right of the spectrum of opinion. (It was, and still is, headquartered in St. Paul, Minnesota.) They took out a subscription for every priest in the Oklahoma diocese.[28]

Conservatives directly targeted priests who delivered what they considered to be objectionable speeches or sermons. Father Patrick Quirk was abused at a Knights of Columbus meeting in 1961 for comments he had made on the pro–civil liberties film *Operation Abolition*, while several critics attended two speeches given by Father Charles Schettler at the Oklahoma City Serra Club, during which they spent most of the time glaring at the speaker and taking copious notes. Such intimidatory techniques were also employed against perceived radicals among the Oklahoma City clergy, such as Father David Jones of Christ the King parish. Sometimes those present would conspicuously leave the church for the duration of the sermon, while at other times they would take notes of statements with which they disagreed.[29]

In 1964, traditionalists responded to the absence of official condemnation

27. On the conservative backlash, see Cuneo, *The Smoke of Satan*, 21–58.
28. "Extreme Right Wingism in Oklahoma," 1–3, Reed Papers.
29. Ibid., 6–8.

of the *Courier* by launching a publication dedicated to driving a wedge between the older generation of priests and laity and the younger modernizers. Consisting of a page of editorial comment printed on yellow paper—the *Yellow Sheet*—this new journalistic endeavor shifted the focus of the debate from secular politics to the validity of the whole process of aggiornamento. Its targets included the vernacular Mass, the relaxed rules on abstinence, folk Masses, discussion of birth control, and the Little Council. The participation of priests in civil rights and antiwar demonstrations and the decision of Father Nerin to replace the altar crucifix in his church in Edmond with a banner of Christ Triumphant were welcome grist to its mill. The *Yellow Sheet* also descended to more unsavory depths by reporting unfounded allegations of psychiatric disorders or sexual indiscretion against its clerical bêtes noires. While it was at one time estimated to have been seen by as many as one in six Oklahoma Catholics, it failed to sway either Reed or most of his clergy and laity from the course.[30]

In the aftermath of the Second Vatican Council, Oklahoma traditionalists were able to tap into a much broader body of sympathizers around the country. First out of the gate was Father Gommar De Pauw's Catholic Traditionalist Movement, which sought to rally the foes of liturgical innovation.[31] In April 1965, De Pauw, who was in conflict with his superior, Archbishop (and later Cardinal) Lawrence Shehan of Baltimore, wrote to Reed inviting him to endorse a proposal that, for Easter and the three Sundays following, equal numbers of "vernacularized noisy" and "Latin quiet" Masses be celebrated across the nation and that a national referendum then be held to allow the people to determine the future of both liturgies. Reed made no reply; it is unlikely that he could have had much influence, even had he been sympathetic to De Pauw.[32]

Father Paul Donovan, one of De Pauw's former pupils at Mount St. Mary's Seminary in Maryland, expressed his irritation about De Pauw's Dam-

30. *St. Louis Review*, May 13, 1966. The traditionalists also published the *Catholic Heritage Newsletter*, which launched bitter attacks on the teaching philosophy of faculty at McGuinness High School. This was distributed to the clergy and parents of students at the school. In 1963, they criticized efforts by school officials to affiliate with the national Parent-Teacher Association and also raised objections to the way in which various religion teachers dealt with matters of social justice and reform of the liturgy. "Extreme Right Wingism in Oklahoma," 4–6; *Oklahoma Courier*, May 14, 1965.

31. Father De Pauw was a Belgian priest who taught at Mount St. Mary's Seminary in Maryland. At one point he was in charge of the Belgian Bureau, an office in New York whose ostensible purpose was to aid Belgian immigrants. This had been important in Bishop Meerschaert's day, when Father Joseph Stillemans of Oklahoma was its director.

32. Revd. Gommar De Pauw to Victor Reed, April 5, 1965, Reed Papers.

ascene conversion to the notion of freedom of speech and of conscience, since he had consistently displayed contempt for laymen and affirmed the superior nature of the priesthood. "What amazes me," he declared to one of the seminary's administrators, "is that this man is now using his 'rights' of free expression to attack what he doesn't like. I can remember so well in fundamental dogma, Father De Pauw stating that there would never be another Council, since Vatican I we didn't need one. . . . I would say let him spew his ignorance elsewhere and not sully the halls of an institution that has been graced by great and learned Churchmen of past ages."[33]

Traditionalists like Tom Costello would certainly not have endorsed Donovan's assessment of De Pauw. A real estate salesman and parishioner of Christ the King parish in Oklahoma City (he later moved to St. Eugene's parish), Costello was the most vocal Oklahoma campaigner against change in all its forms. "He was a brash kind of Irish guy," Monsignor James Halpine recalled of his time at Christ the King during the 1950s, "who would say [to me]: 'Where are you going? I hear you're going to be going on vacation for three weeks. I don't get a vacation like that.' And I said, 'Now listen Tom . . . I'm sure that when you were young some nun was after you all the time to become a priest and you didn't do it, so shut up with griping and enjoy your vacation. I'm going to enjoy mine.' And he would laugh."[34]

Such badinage was replaced by outright hostility toward much of the clerical establishment as the diocese entered the 1960s. Costello's doubts increasingly took the form of open hostility toward Bishop Reed, whom he viewed as failing to exercise proper authority over "dissidents" under his care and displaying a lack of commitment toward the institutional Church. In 1960, he demanded that Reed take a stand on the question of public schooling after a fellow member of the Knights of Columbus enrolled his child at a non-Catholic school where, Costello believed, there would be "a steady diet of anti-Catholic training."[35] Four years later, he openly asserted Reed's unfitness to hold the office of bishop and the need to have him removed before serious harm was inflicted upon the diocese, a pronouncement that led to a scuffle with one of Reed's admirers at a Knights of Columbus' meeting.[36]

33. Revd. J. Paul Donovan to Msgr. George Mulcahy, April 8, 1965, Reed Papers. *Commonweal* objected to De Pauw's stance, but defended his right to criticize the vernacular liturgy. *Commonweal*, April 30, 1965, 181.
34. Halpine, interview.
35. Tom Costello to Victor Reed, April 12, 1960, Reed Papers.
36. "Extreme Right Wingism in Oklahoma," 10–11.

While he always refused to confirm or deny that he was the editor of the
Yellow Sheet, most observers credited Costello with a leading role in its production. During the conflict over the abortion debate at McGuinness High
School, Costello reported that he had had an argument with Father James
Ross of St. Eugene's parish, who told him not to interfere with the freedom
of his (Costello's) children's developing minds. "I advised Father Ross,"
Costello explained, "that that was the very reason that I was concerned—
they were not adults, they were formative minds, that I as a parent had a
spiritual obligation to the formation of my children and that I resented the
activities of the school and his unclerical attitude regarding the subject." The
McGuinness case, Costello forcefully declared, was symptomatic of a wider
problem in the diocese—namely, that "the older and more profound priests
have either lost heart or are frightened to do battle against the young liberals
who apparently are 'running the show.'"[37]

In their struggle, Costello and his associates recognized that they had
a valuable ally in the person of the apostolic delegate, Archbishop Egidio
Vagnozzi, who strongly upheld the "Roman" position in his dealings with
the American hierarchy and had endeavored to restrict the public activities
of the *periti*, notably the Jesuit John Courtney Murray, at the Second Vatican Council.[38] From 1962 onward, the Oklahoma traditionalists directed a
steady stream of complaints to Washington. In one case, they sent a complaint about Bishop Reed directly to the Sacred Consistorial Congregation in
Rome, the body concerned with the appointment of bishops (the congregation promptly returned it to Washington for investigation). Costello also understood the nature of power politics when, in a letter to Vagnozzi, he described a conversation with Father Joseph La Barge of Christ the King parish
about the nature of authority in the Church. Costello sought to elicit from
La Barge a declaration as to the authorities over Bishop Reed *in the United
States*, which the priest gave as Archbishop Lucey (as head of the Province of
San Antonio) and Cardinal Spellman (as the senior American cardinal). Then
who, enquired Costello with deceptive innocence, is the authority over Cardinal Spellman? "He replied 'The Pope in Rome' and I asked 'Who, in *this*
country has any authority over Cardinal Spellman?' and he very fluently went
into the double talk which I uncoded as meaning that in his opinion there

37. Tom Costello to Revd. David F. Monahan, April 16, 1964, Reed Papers.
38. Fogarty, *The Vatican and the American Hierarchy*, 387, 394–95; Jones, *John Cardinal Krol*, 31–34.

was no authority over the Bishop except that they were responsible to 'each other,' (Collegiality you know) etc. etc. and that the office of the Apostolic delegate was more or less old stuff and of no present authority."[39]

Costello had shrewdly understood how to elicit a response calculated to antagonize Vagnozzi. The American hierarchy was self-evidently in a very different position from where it had been even twenty years before. The personalist episcopalism of the Spellman era had begun to give way to the collectivist approach of the National Conference of Catholic Bishops, and the apostolic delegate was no longer supposed to play such an intrusive role as Vagnozzi often imagined, yet La Barge's answer summoned up an image of an American Church that had not merely reshaped its leadership structure but thrown in the towel in matters of discipline. Such an image was unlikely to sit well with an Italian prelate of Vagnozzi's stamp.

LAY ACTIVISM, CONSERVATIVE STYLE

By the spring of 1966, supporters of renewal had become fully aware of the conservative campaign and had begun also to communicate with the apostolic delegate. James Fulton, a professor of chemical engineering at Oklahoma State University, sought to turn the tables on Costello and his supporters by arguing that the real problem in the diocese was "a small but vociferous group of willful people who are attempting to discredit Bishop Victor J. Reed and nullify the changes set forth by Vatican II."[40] Paul Sprehe sought to reinforce the notion that the critics represented a small minority. "The changes in the Church may appear to some to be extreme," he told Vagnozzi, "but to any knowledgeable Christian they are only man's feeble attempt to praise, reverence and serve God in a manner which will insure our's [sic] and our children's salvation."[41] Conservatives had no intention of abandoning their crusade, however, and soon turned their attention to those institutions in Oklahoma charged with the formation and education of priests. A 1961 meeting of the board of St. Francis de Sales Seminary was transformed into a forum for the denunciation of the "communistic" tendencies of diocesan priests, and at least one traditionalist made a visit to the seminary to obtain incriminating information about its operation. In

---

39. "Extreme Right Wingism in Oklahoma," 11, Tom Costello to "Apostolic Delegate," December 6, 1965, Reed Papers.

40. James W. Fulton to Abp. Egidio Vagnozzi, April 24, 1966, Reed Papers.

41. Paul F. Sprehe to Abp. Egidio Vagnozzi, April 28, 1968, Reed Papers.

1966, Tom Costello and one of his associates fixed their sights on the Theology Institute at St. Gregory's College in Shawnee, which provided instruction to priests of the diocese. "They seemed to be unfamiliar with the sciences of theology and philosophy," Father Richard Sneed reported to Reed of their meeting with him, "and yet anxious to judge currents in these disciplines. They visited for about an hour. I must say that what disturbed me most was their singular lack of humor."[42] For Costello, of course, the topic was hardly one for humor, and when Father Thomas Litsch—an assistant at St. Eugene's Church—delivered a sermon contending that simply keeping the Ten Commandments and the laws of the Church was inadequate for salvation and that people must also be open to the workings of God's love on such issues as open housing, Costello blamed the institute for disseminating "New Theology."[43]

From a small group of well-to-do dissidents, traditionalists steadily widened their following to include a much more diverse body of supporters. Having previously placed great emphasis on Tridentine liturgy, traditionalists now sought to recruit all those who had problems with the Novus Ordo. Some liberals, like *Commonweal* journalist John Leo, even showed a degree of sympathy for their position on liturgy. "[Father De Pauw's] plea for one Mass a day in the old liturgy," wrote Leo in January 1966, "taken in itself, shouldn't be dismissed out of hand. . . . The Liturgical Constitution leaves plenty of room for options, and Father De Pauw's comment that liberals only support freedom for the things they already favor ought to be taken to heart."[44]

Costello himself criticized relative fast laws because people failed to observe them, demanding instead an *objective* standard incumbent on all Catholics. His fellow conservatives made it a point of principle to refuse to participate in the new liturgy in the way desired by the reformers. Although the *Courier* continued to play down the numbers involved, it finally made a public acknowledgment of the existence of dissent in April 1966, when a group of over fifty traditionalist women held a meeting in Oklahoma City from which the *Courier*'s reporter was banned. A new organization, known as the Society for the Preservation of the Faith, emerged to harness the energies of dissident traditionalists. The organization picketed the bishop's house and

42. "Extreme Right Wingism in Oklahoma," 9–10, Revd. Richard Sneed to Victor Reed, August 12, 1966, Reed Papers.
43. Tom Costello to Revd. James Ross, August 30, 1966, Reed Papers.
44. John Leo, "Father De Pauw Returns," *Commonweal*, January 21, 1966, 458–59.

encouraged members to gather examples of unorthodox statements made in Catholic meetings, talks, and sermons. One traditionalist paid a visit to the *Courier* offices and blamed recent changes on disobedience to Church authority. "I was raised in a fundamentalist atmosphere," he declared. "I believe that if we do not follow Rome we are lost. We don't have that. We will *not* have that."[45]

That same month, Bishop Reed expressed his own views on traditionalist dissent. "Today," he told the *Oklahoma City Times*, "because of the difficult nature of the post-conciliar era of change and adjustment, great confidence in the responsibility and judgment of the bishop is necessary on the part of the people. I do wish to believe that these dissenting people have the right end in view (i.e., the welfare of the Church)—but their assumption of personal authority as a means to the end cannot be viewed by true Catholics but as mistaken judgment."[46]

Liberals rushed to confirm their bishop's judgment. "I know Tom Costello personally," one Texas Catholic told Reed, "and have argued with him, if that is possible, concerning The New Church. He did impress upon me one thing. How drastically the church needed and needs to update its teaching and its approach to teaching. If The Old Church produced Tom Costello's [*sic*], it made an awful lot of mistakes. I grieve for Tom as I'm sure you do and it grieves me that I could not turn him away from his fanatical course."[47] A woman who had served with Costello on the Oklahoma City deanery board declared that people had been excommunicated for doing less harm than the editors of the *Yellow Sheet* and questioned Costello's vaunted concern with morality, having heard him tell a risqué story in mixed company.[48]

Further proofs of support for Reed flooded into the chancery throughout the spring and summer of 1966. "Never in our lifetime so far have we found the faith of our birth 'the Catholic faith' to be in such a turbulent state with all the problems of centuries begging to be solved," declared one couple, "but also never in our experience have we found a faith that goes deeper and embraces more people than our faith does today."[49] Similar sentiments were

45. "Extreme Right Wingism in Oklahoma," 9, 11–12; *Rocky Mountain News*, August 13, 1966; *Oklahoma Courier*, April 22, 1966 (quotation).
46. "Statement of Bishop Reed re. 'right wing' activities given to *Oklahoma City Times* on April 22, 1966," Reed Papers.
47. James R. Steichen to Victor Reed, April 29, 1966, Reed Papers.
48. Roynetta Fredgren to Victor Reed, n.d., Reed Papers.
49. Mr. and Mrs. John Steward to Victor Reed, April 24, 1966, Reed Papers.

forthcoming from parishioners of St. John's, Yukon; Sts. Peter and Paul, Tulsa; Blessed Sacrament, Lawton; Our Lady of Fatima, Nicoma Park; St. Francis Xavier, Del City; Our Lady of Victory, Purcell; Sacred Heart, Oklahoma City; and St. Joseph's, Buffalo.[50] "We know of no one in our parish, who are not satisfied and not co-operating fully," declared Ed Story in Elk City, "and only one or two in this area who seem to be angry and are with-holding support. One of them has never been very co-operative, and the other loves his money, so I was told?"[51]

As time passed, it became clear that one of the distinguishing features of traditionalism—respect for duly constituted ecclesiastical authority—had begun to break down under the strain of the renewal process. Conservatives were beginning to choose their "authorities" according to their own private judgment as to what was "orthodox," much as liberals were doing on the basis of what was "authentic."[52] Charles Reeves of Norman, invited by some of his friends to sign a petition to the apostolic delegate in support of Reed, pointed out that the expression of a vote of confidence in a Catholic prelate stood contrary to the principles on which the Church was organized. While the *Yellow Sheet* left "something to be desired in elegance and courtesy of expression," Reeves was not convinced that it was more inclined to innuendo and rumormongering than the *Oklahoma Courier*, and he wondered why there was such agitation against an insignificant minority. Perhaps this was an attempt, he said, to keep rumors of the truth from Reed in order that he should not intervene to reimpose order. Reeves concluded with a flourish that exposed the inconsistency of some liberals when it came to the question of episcopal authority. "I might have been more hesitant to withhold my signature," he told his friends, "if I had any evidence of a similar concern on your part for the authority and comfort of the archbishops of Los Angeles,

50. Petition of Holy Name Society, St. John's Parish, Yukon, May 1, 1966, Petition of Members of Sts. Peter and Paul Parish, Tulsa, May 1, 1966, Petition of Little Council Discussion Group, Blessed Sacrament Parish, Lawton, May 4, 1966, Parishioners of Our Lady of Fatima Parish, Nicoma Park to Victor Reed, May 12, 1966, Petition of Members of St. Francis Xavier Parish, Del City, May 15, 1966, Group I of Little Council, Our Lady of Victory Parish to Reed, May 24, 1966, Walter P. Lane to Reed, July 14, 1966, Petition from St. Joseph's Church, Buffalo to Reed, August 31, 1966, Reed Papers.

51. Ed Story to Victor Reed, April 22, 1966, Reed Papers.

52. An illustrative example from outside Oklahoma is provided by James Carroll on the dissent by his military father from the antiwar sentiments expressed by Pope Paul VI in 1965: "I was incapable of hearing it but my father's dispassionate response included the seeds of dissent from papal teaching that would infuriate him a few years later when the issue had shifted to birth control." Carroll, *An American Requiem*, 161.

Milwaukee and Boston in their recent efforts at obtaining the obedience of certain priests, nuns, and seminarians in their own dioceses."[53]

The speed with which traditionalists lost faith in Reed was dramatic. In June 1966, the bishop attended a Knights of Columbus banquet in Norman, where one of his more prominent critics, Francis Kovach, a philosophy professor at the University of Oklahoma, delivered a keynote address entitled "Anti-Intellectualism: A Crisis in the Church." Kovach painted what an aide to the bishop called "a dismal picture of conditions in the world today, of the young people, their skepticism, lack of learning, the poor quality of training in high schools, the folly of the new math, and of modern education in general," and conveyed the impression that no one could be a true Catholic unless instructed in theology as taught by St. Thomas Aquinas. Furthermore, the presence of several conservative couples who were not members of the Knights of Columbus gave "the appearance and smell of John Birch tactics." Reed gave only a brief response to Kovach and sought to leave as soon as grace had been said. As he approached the door, it was announced that "The Star Spangled Banner" would be sung, and although the bishop turned back for the anthem, it was clear from the number of people present who looked to see if he would remain that the announcement was a calculated one intended to place him in a poor patriotic light.[54]

Kovach remained a constant thorn in the bishop's side. In March 1968, he wrote to complain about an offertory prayer used at the university chapel that supposedly expressed regret to God for not having aided the Communists in the past and the fact that the priests had recited "a neo-Arian parody of the Apostle's Creed and, in the last line, even expressed their doubts about the traditional meaning of the Resurrection." Reed had stated the previous year that he permitted only moderate and ecclesiastically sanctioned changes in the liturgy, Kovach noted, and the innovations described were far from moderate. He could only conclude that the priests had flagrantly disobeyed Reed but had counted on his "permissiveness" to escape sanction.[55]

Other conservatives turned their attention toward more separatist activi-

53. Charles H. Reeves to Mr. and Mrs. Edwin H. Klehr, Mr. and Mrs. Francis J. Schmitz, and Mrs. Hugo Martines, May 3, 1966, Reed Papers.

54. "Right Wing Talk," June 18, 1966, Knights of Columbus Hall, Oklahoma City, Reed Papers; *Oklahoma Courier*, June 24, 1966. Kovach had his own response to the notion that conscience should be the ultimate guide: "Now that sounds fine, but that's how Luther started Protestantism."

55. Francis J. Kovach to Victor Reed, March 17, 1968, St. Thomas More Church, Norman File, AAOC.

ties in the final years of Reed's episcopate. Father Francis Fenton spoke in Oklahoma City in January 1967, delivering a powerful diatribe against Communism and the Catholic press. Two years later, the Movement to Restore Decency sought to invite him to speak in Duncan. Since Fenton, a member of the John Birch Society, would in 1970 organize the Orthodox Roman Catholic Movement—a separatist group based in Connecticut—one can conclude that some Oklahoma traditionalists were looking very far afield from the orthodoxy of their childhood.[56]

"Somewhere our past leadership in the church has evidently failed miserably in teaching to many Catholics the distinction between an institution and the objectives necessarily precedent to the institution," declared Helen Canfield in June 1966. "Christ-following, and all this implies, got lost in the shuffle and we are only just beginning to see the proper emphases in Church actions and teachings. One can only marvel, and grieve, that Dr. Kovach and his fellow protesters have, as sincere Catholics, been so misled as to arrive at such strange misunderstandings of what our religion really involves."[57] What was truly ironic was that in December 1967, Reed had extended his opponents a very real olive branch when he gave the traditionalists the opportunity to run traditional catechism classes at Our Lady of Perpetual Help Cathedral in Oklahoma City and Holy Family Cathedral in Tulsa. Although they were supposed to allow visitations from the diocesan director of education, Reed permitted them to use a revised version of the Baltimore Catechism rather than *Word and Worship*, used in most parishes.[58]

CONCLUSION

The introduction of concepts like "personal conscience" and "church democracy" inevitably brought about conflicts with constituted authority and reaction from those who had varying degrees of reservation about the conciliar revolution. For traditionalists, if "personal conscience" was allowed free rein, the Church ran the risk of accepting the principles of the prevailing cul-

56. *Oklahoma Courier*, January 27, 1969; Gerald L. Beasley Jr. to Victor Reed, July 18, 1969, Assumption Church, Duncan File, AAOC. Catholic separatism is discussed in Cuneo, *The Smoke of Satan*, 81–119.

57. Helen Canfield to Victor Reed, June 24, 1966, Reed Papers.

58. *Oklahoma Courier*, December 15, 1967. The *Courier* defended Reed's action as a form of Catholic pluralism comparable with the nonterritorial parishes, but this was not an analogy that the traditionalists would have welcomed.

ture. Furthermore, the actual progress of renewal seemed, all too often, to lead to an elimination of what was distinctively Catholic. It was one thing to make liturgy comprehensible or to seek better understanding between Catholics and Protestants, but should these developments lead ultimately to yet another "denomination" in the United States? Tom Costello and Francis Kovach might not speak for more than a tiny fraction of Oklahoma's Catholic community, but they articulated the fears of many that the Church as it had been in its heyday (at least as that time existed in their own range of memory) was being replaced by a necessarily inferior substitute. Lay empowerment cut both ways and could embolden those on the traditionalist side of the tracks who had previously deferred to episcopal authority. In the final analysis, Reed would bequeath to John Quinn a diocese racked by the tensions that the forces of renewal had unleashed.

Perhaps the most poignant verdict on the changes was rendered by Monsignor Theophile Caudron seven months before his death in his Belgian homeland, as he surveyed the transformation of the parish in Henryetta over which he had stood guard for so long. "I had a letter written," he told Reed in 1969, "asking you to spare the gym as it was a memorial of the young Catholic men of Henryetta who had given their lives in World War II. I hear though that it has been destroyed already. My last plea is please spare the Church [building]. Tradition is a good thing for people to hold onto in times of chaos [such] as the present. Why destroy all the roots of the past for the present generations who need such to keep their balance?"[59]

59. Msgr. Theophile F. Caudron to Victor Reed, June 15, 1969, Reed Papers.

Conclusion

Aggiornamento Completed

The meeting on March 1, 1971, at Bishop Kelley High School in Tulsa had all the elements of grand drama: a wealthy businessman willing to spend millions of dollars to build a new cathedral for the city, a bishop desirous of moving his seat from the crumbling infrastructure of the downtown area to the expanding neighborhoods of the city's south side, a militant social action priest, and the energized congregation of an experimental parish.

The story of the abortive attempt to build a new cathedral serves as an illustrative paradigm for the evolution of the renewal process in Oklahoma. The Church of the Resurrection had been established in 1968 as an experimental parish, under the leadership of Father Bill Skeehan but without a permanent building. Its parish office and small chapel were located in a shopping center, and Sunday Mass was offered in a public high school gymnasium. In 1969, the parish accepted the offer of five acres of land from W. K. Warren Sr. for $50,000, but problems subsequently developed with the Warren Foundation, and Bishop Reed indicated that he wished to handle matters himself. In the spring of 1970, Father Skeehan was informed privately that the Warrens had offered to build a debt-free church in southeast Tulsa. The pastor was also instructed not to divulge this information to his parishioners. In January 1971, however, Resurrection parishioners visiting Denver came across a newsletter penned by the former editor of the now-defunct Oklahoma diocesan newspaper that described the prospective new edifice as a cathedral.[1]

---

1. "The Status of the Church," transcript of meeting in Bishop Kelley gym, March 1, 1971, 2–3, Resurrection Church, Tulsa File, box 7.1, Archives of the Catholic Diocese of Tulsa (hereafter ADT).

"For several years," the newsletter commented, "the accusation has been made by Tulsa Catholics that the Church there has generally ignored the needs of the poor on the northside, and concentrated its efforts overwhelmingly on the wealthy southside. The establishment of two very large and costly hospitals on Tulsa's southside, and the total neglect of the medical needs of the poor on the northside is the most frequently mentioned example. Another example is the placing of all Tulsa's present Catholic high schools on the southside."[2]

Many members were perturbed that discussions appeared to have gone so far without even a hint of consultation with the supposed beneficiaries. Under the leadership of parishioner J. Robert Pielsticker, they prepared to fight the Warren proposal and defend their pastor, whom the Warrens regarded as "inimical" to their interests, desiring that he be assigned elsewhere. In a letter to Warren, Pielsticker conceded that some of Skeehan's statements against the Warrens had been "in bad taste and unjustified," but he rebuked both Warren and "Our 'Brick and Mortar' Bishop" for hindering the wishes of the Resurrection community to erect a church building with no strings attached. "Throughout this conflict," he told Warren, "the people of this parish seem to have been ignored. I believe that the church is the people of God and that the desires of the parishioners should be considered. An effective church is not a unilateral agreement between you and the Bishop."[3]

Father Skeehan rehearsed several of the complaints of the opponents of the Warren plan in a general memorandum that he prepared on February 20 and distributed to parishioners: the unilateral nature of the negotiation (which was "in open conflict with the collegial spirit of Vatican II"), the erection of another large church on the south side when the poor on the north side were in want, and the implication that the Warrens would have some say in the appointment of the rector of the new cathedral. Skeehan warned that while he considered himself to have been generally loyal to Reed, the nature of the negotiation now obliged him to take a stand for his people and against the bishop. The dissenters in the parish agreed, and on Sunday, Feb-

2. "Anybody Want a Cathedral?" *Perspective*, January 15, 1971, Resurrection Church, Tulsa File, box 7.1, ADT. The St John Medical Center, established in 1926 by the Sisters of the Sorrowful Mother, had 579 beds in 2003, while St Francis Hospital, owned and operated by the Warren Foundation since 1960, had 589 beds. These two are the largest of Tulsa's five hospitals. Tulsa has two Catholic high schools—Kelley and Cascia Hall—located on the south side but near the center of the city's population.

3. J. Robert Pielsticker to William K. Warren Sr., February 20, 1971, Resurrection Church, Tulsa File, box 7.1.

ruary 21, a member of the parish rose after the Gospel at each Mass to ask Father Skeehan to respond to the issue of the cathedral rather than deliver his regular homily. The next day, twenty-seven parishioners met to organize the opposition. Father Skeehan, meanwhile, sent letters to every priest in the diocese and to the *National Catholic Reporter.* On February 25, Father John Sullivan, episcopal vicar for the eastern part of the diocese, informed the committee of Reed's desire to obtain a sense of the parish's feelings on the matter, and a meeting was hastily arranged for the following Monday.[4]

The response from the diocesan priests strongly favored Skeehan. Father Raymond Berthiaume, a Glenmary priest in Idabel in the far southeast corner of Oklahoma, told Reed that the proposal represented a violation of the moratorium the latter had imposed on church building and that building a new cathedral in the "right" neighborhood would have a negative impact on ecumenical endeavors. "And how, in these days," he asked, "can such a decision be made unilaterally? What of the people on the local scene—priest and laity? What of the Diocese as a whole?"[5] A meeting of diocesan priests in Oklahoma City was equally unsympathetic to the project. Father Joseph Ross, the most junior priest there, told Reed as he left that he was shocked that the issue was even under consideration. The bishop gave him a pained look, but made no response. "My head tells me to do one thing," he later confided to Father Charles Schettler, the diocesan chancellor, "and my heart tells me to do something else."[6]

The priestly divisions were still evident at a meeting of the diocesan consultors (a group of priests who advised the bishop), which endorsed the plan by the narrow margin of six to five, provided no strings were attached. They conceded that the sale of Holy Family Cathedral (whose parochial school received an annual subsidy of $20,000) would raise $1.5 million and that Warren was prepared to donate twenty acres and spend at least $1 million to build the new edifice.[7]

---

4. "The Status of the Church," 4–5, Father Bill Skeehan to "Whom it may concern," February 20, 1971, Minutes of organizational meeting of members of Resurrection Parish, February 22, 1971, Resurrection Church, Tulsa File, box 7.1. Father Skeehan has testified that despite the tensions between them, Reed never told him to cease active campaigning: "Nowhere during the whole process did he say no." Clergy roundtable discussion, June 23, 2005.

5. Revd. Raymond Berthiaume to Victor Reed, February 25, 1971, Resurrection Church, Tulsa File, box 7.1.

6. Clergy roundtable discussion, June 19, 2005.

7. Consultors' Meeting, March 1, 1971, Resurrection Church, Tulsa File, box 7.1.

For Reed, the issue ran deeper than the future of one parish, however vibrant. Already in discussions about the possible division of the state into two dioceses, he considered that a future Tulsa-based diocese should enjoy an episcopal seat of suitable dignity. Holy Family Cathedral, where he had served as rector from 1947 to 1957, lay in the downtown area, originally a residential neighborhood but now deserted as the population moved toward the southeastern, more suburban areas of the city. The prospect of a new cathedral in the heart of the new Catholic neighborhoods, for which neither the bishop nor ordinary Catholics would be financially liable, seemed almost too good to be true. It was not irrelevant to the issue that, despite considerable political differences, Victor Reed and W. K. Warren Sr. had been close friends since the bishop had arrived at Holy Family a quarter of a century before. For all the accusations that later swirled around the issue, it seems safe to assume that the new cathedral was at least as much his project as Warren's.[8]

The bishop's preliminary statement at the March 1 meeting indicated that Warren had given the bishop an oral promise to give part of the land he owned for a church in southeast Tulsa back in the late 1950s, but it was only in 1970 that the idea had been revived. Warren's recent offer to build a debt-free church and rectory was simply an offer, the bishop insisted, and the land in question was physically in St. Mary's parish. Admitting that the Church at that time could not contemplate the sort of financial expenditure needed for a cathedral, given the other demands on its resources, Reed pointed out that what Warren ("one of the old school") wished to do with his money was his concern alone. The Church would be freer to use its money for needed social action. He emphasized that it had been *his* thought that Skeehan might not be the best fit as rector of the new cathedral. The Warrens had laid down no conditions in this regard. He was willing to reconsider and appoint Skeehan if that seemed the best course.[9]

As Reed outlined his view of things, many in the audience listened unconvinced. Most had deliberately chosen to join Resurrection precisely because of its unconventional pastor and its determination to make the Christian life one that was active in the world. Talk of great buildings and wealthy benefactors left them cold. "We are trying to live the Gospel and this is what we want to maintain," one told Reed. "We feel that a large church would de-

8. These are the conclusions of Father James D. White, archivist of the Diocese of Tulsa, based on correspondence with W. K. Warren in 1978. Clergy roundtable discussion, June 23, 2005.

9. "The Status of the Church," 6–12.

stroy it." The bishop responded with sympathy. "In regard to things of the old school, I am sort of, maybe, in between," he said. "I am not as old as [Warren] is and perhaps hear a great deal more, I mean, you know, [about] new ideas in regard to the Church, a formation of the Christian Community than he does, but I feel quite certain in speaking to him that he considers his purpose, you see, of building a Church is a very good one."[10]

Given his obvious interest in the project, Reed was perhaps a little disingenuous in response to the inevitable questions about the appropriateness of expending a large sum on one building when more basic facilities were needed in north Tulsa that would cost only a fraction of that. It was Warren's offer, he insisted, and his reasons were his own. The bishop endeavored to defend the principle of an ornate church building as "a symbol of the presence of God in the world." Communities need buildings to be most effective, he argued, though he acknowledged that it was possible to exist without a permanent structure, as indeed Resurrection had done. To build a church was a good thing, not necessarily the best, but still a good thing.[11]

Although Father Skeehan kept largely silent during the proceedings, he did enter the dialogue toward the end of the debate. He had been charged with maintaining an experimental community of three hundred families, he said, but he believed in a wide diversity of parish life. He encouraged those who lived in the area but were not drawn to Resurrection to find a nearby parish where they could acquire whatever spiritual sustenance they were seeking. What he feared was a large parish: "With a large church it becomes a matter of me becoming Ecclesiastical caretaker. I will not be that." While he had nothing against buildings, he accepted that he and the bishop differed on the necessity of a church building: "I believe the church then has to be a server of the community not itself. If a church is just serving itself then I can not accept it. If it is serving the community, the neighbors or the whole city of Tulsa then I say the church is alive. That's my particular philosophy of churches. So the building will look like a people who serve the community." Such a building, Skeehan insisted, would cost no more than $200,000 and would be composed not of marble or steel but prestressed concrete. He reiterated his concern that money was being spent among the affluent when food and medicine were needed on the north side.[12]

Summing up, Reed assured those present that he was still open to hear-

---

10. Ibid., 15–16.   11. Ibid., 21–22, 26–27.
12. Ibid., 35–41.

ing from those who wished to express an opinion. "I don't believe that I'm autocratic," he declared, "in fact, I'm criticized for not being autocratic enough . . . [but] I've found out you know it is an impossibility for the Bishop to please everybody."[13] The next three weeks demonstrated the truth of that statement. W. K. Warren reacted to the climate of publicity with a marked reduction in enthusiasm for the project. Resurrection parishioners, meanwhile, planned for a future that might not include any Warren money at all.[14] On March 21, the parish gathered for a meeting on the Warren proposal and voted 169 to 56 against it. While 225 of the roughly 260 present agreed a permanent building was needed, over 220 preferred an "aesthetic multi-purpose building," compared to 44 who endorsed a traditional church building. The parish agreed to reactivate its building committee to consider proposals after learning that the Warren offer had been withdrawn.[15] It was the end of the line for the cathedral.

The battle for Resurrection, which became a more or less conventional parish in the 1970s, embodied many of the conflicts that had emerged in Oklahoma during the 1960s. On the one hand could be found preconciliar Catholics like Warren, who hewed to the vision of the "Church Triumphant," a top-down hierarchical institution with its army of priests and religious sisters and brothers, its hospitals and schools, and its unique access to salvation. Opposing them was the postconciliar generation, with its social action advocates like Skeehan, whose philosophy could best be seen as that of the "Church Militant," with its rejection of clerical "authoritarianism" and embrace of the apostolate of the laity, its refusal to contemplate salvation through institutions, and an ecumenical ethos that was deeply troubled by any claim to Catholic exclusivity. Standing between the two fires, in the Resurrection affair and throughout the 1960s, was Victor Reed (arguably the standard-bearer of the "Church Expectant"), who had lived through it all and was now called upon to try to resolve the issues to everyone's satisfaction.

This would be the final act in the drama of the renewal process in Oklahoma under Victor Reed's leadership. On September 7, 1971, Father Paul

13. Ibid., 31.
14. Minutes of organizational meeting of members of Resurrection Parish, March 11, 1971, Resurrection Church, Tulsa File, box 7.1.
15. Resurrection Parish Poll, March 21, 1971, Resurrection Church, Tulsa File, box 7.1; *Tulsa Tribune*, March 22, 1971; *Tulsa Daily World*, March 22, 1971; Joseph Dillon, "Reflections on My Life," in Brousseau, ed., *A Dying Breed of Brave Men*, 64–65.

Gallatin visited the chancery, where he encountered his ordinary. He told the bishop that he and Monsignor Don Kanaly planned to attend a showing of the film of *Billy Jack* later in the evening. "I haven't been to a movie in years," the delighted bishop told him. "I would love to go to a movie." Gallatin promised that he and Kanaly would come by later in the evening after the pastoral board meeting was over. They found the bishop in high spirits about a recent victory over the city council, so much so that he offered to pay for the movie. Only when they reached the theater did they discover that the bishop had no money with him.[16]

The three settled in, and when Gallatin stole a glance at the bishop he seemed to be asleep. A few minutes later, he realized that what he had initially mistaken for the snores of a sleeping man were actually the gasps of someone fighting for air. The two priests pulled Reed into the lobby and summoned an ambulance. Gallatin gave Reed absolution but lacked the oil necessary for extreme unction. By the time they reached Baptist Hospital, the bishop was still alive, but subsequent efforts to revive him proved in vain. Just after midnight on September 8, Victor Reed passed away, eighty years to the day after the consecration of Theophile Meerschaert as vicar apostolic of the Indian Territory. He was just sixty-five years old.[17]

As word spread, more and more of the state's priests arrived at the hospital. "The place was absolutely packed with priests," Gallatin recalled. "I thought it was a beautiful moment, I don't know if it will ever be repeated, but they needed to be together."[18] One of the first to express his sympathies was the spokesman of the radical priestly fringe, Father William Nerin. "[Bishop Reed] was a man to take forward looking steps before others did," he declared. "He was a man who was willing to put his body on the line for what he believed."[19]

Non-Catholic religious leaders concurred. "His tireless dedication to the cause of Jesus Christ, his openness to others who were not of his church and his continuing spirit of grace and kindness endeared him to us all," declared Hugh Nelson of the United Presbyterian Church. "He opened doors through which many of us have walked." Harold Brockwolf, president of the Oklahoma district of the Lutheran Church–Missouri Synod agreed: "The Most Rev. Victor J. Reed walks with the saints in the glory of His Lord. We share with you in this moment of loss. Bishop Reed's work during the por-

---

16. Gallatin, interview.
18. Ibid.

17. Ibid.
19. *Tulsa Tribune*, September 8, 1971.

tion of his lifetime in this world has demonstrated the greater values and pointed ahead to the world which is to come. We join you in thanking God for His use of His servant during his lifetime." Perhaps the most touching tribute came from Rabbi David Novak of Oklahoma City's Emmanuel Synagogue. "I regarded him as one of the 'saintly of the world,'" he declared, "whom our Talmudic tradition assures us join God's company in the World-to-Come." [20]

The body was borne to Tulsa, where it lay in state in Holy Family Cathedral in a walnut casket between two rows of gold tapers and surrounded by purple-stained wreaths and white chrysanthemums. On Saturday, September 11, the press reported the death of Nikita Khrushchev, but for Tulsans, the funeral of their late bishop carried far more weight. At the funeral, a special section had been reserved for ministers of other denominations while, in another ecumenical touch, the recessional hymn was Isaac Watts's "O God Our Help in Ages Past." "All of the people of Oklahoma have lost a friend," declared Father John Sullivan, the celebrant, "and the Catholic Church has lost one of its outstanding leaders of modern times. . . . Bishop Reed was a servant of God's people. He was always available to the priests and laity or willing to drive to Boise City or Idabel."[21] Others who shared in the obsequies included Bishop Charles Buswell, who preached both in Tulsa and at the parallel ceremony in Oklahoma City on September 13; John Cardinal Carberry, archbishop of St. Louis, Reed's classmate at the North American College in Rome, who presided in Oklahoma City; and Bishop Stephen Leven of San Angelo, Texas, who spoke at the wake.[22]

Studies of the Vatican II era tend to emphasize conflict over consideration of the actual dynamics of change. This tendency has been enhanced by an inclination to view the period from 1899 to 1962 as a single era in U.S. Catholic history and thus to overstate the revolutionary impact of the Second Vatican Council on Catholic life.[23] Do the judgments of Reed's contem-

20. Revd. Hugh D. Nelson to "Colleagues in Ministry," September 8, 1971, Revd. Harold Brockwolf to "Brethren," September 9, 1971, Rabbi David Novak to Msgr. Raymond F. Harkin, September 10, 1971, Reed Papers.

21. In 1972, Father Sullivan was named bishop of Grand Island, Nebraska, by the Holy See. His ordination took place in Tulsa. In 1977, he became bishop of Kansas City–St. Joseph, Missouri. He retired in 1993 and died in 2001.

22. *Tulsa Tribune*, September 11, 1971; *Tulsa Daily World*, September 9, September 11, September 12, 1971.

23. See Kelly, *Battle for the American Church*, 3–20 (chap. 1, "Vatican II: Aftershocks of an Ecclesiastical Revolution"); Hennesey, *American Catholics*, 307–31 (chap. 21, "A Revo-

poraries reflect or refute such a perspective? On balance, they suggest that he handled conflict more deftly, or at any rate less high-handedly, than many of his contemporaries. He was "the right man at the right time," declared a leading Tulsa layman. "Had there been an old-fashioned ecclesiastic and personal conservative [in Oklahoma] I think we would have had far more confrontation and far more adverse results than we did. His willingness to be a lightning rod actually defused some of it, more than he probably thought."[24] He guided the Oklahoma Church through a difficult time, agreed one Oklahoma priest, and achieved a balance of contending forces. He avoided the dissolution into open conflict between bishop and clergy that characterized so many American dioceses during this period.[25] Another priest identifies Reed's principal legacy as the association of the Church in Oklahoma with the needs of the poor and destitute.[26]

That said, it must be admitted that many of the forces at work in society during Reed's episcopate enjoyed a momentum of their own. Change in Oklahoma, remarked Monsignor James Halpine, was "more than I ever dreamed I would see.... I had no idea that every generation could be switching back and forth as rapidly as it does." The forces unleashed by the pronouncements of the council proved to be more even than a diocesan bishop could fully control. "We had a superficial view to my mind of what it took to renew the Church," admitted William Garthoeffner. "We thought if we made some structural changes, if we gave people a chance to express themselves and make known their feelings and beliefs, it would help—I still think that—but we also became intolerant of people.... Reform of the Church meant reform of ourselves." A movement intended to more fully integrate the Body of Christ ended with the alienation of a substantial minority. "I look at myself and my brothers growing up," declared Father Paul Donovan. "Even though we grew up here in Protestant Oklahoma ... I don't think we could ever have left the Church. We might have quit going to it, but we could never have been anything but Catholic. It would have been impossible. I don't think that's true today."[27]

Perhaps the most significant postscript to the Reed years came fifteen

---

lutionary Moment"); Dolan, *The American Catholic Experience*, 421–54 (chap. 15, "A New Catholicism"). On the "myth" of the papal revolution, promoted by liberals and conservatives alike, see Komonchak, "Interpreting the Council."

24. Fox, interview. 25. Gallatin, interview.
26. Gier, interview.
27. Halpine, interview; Garthoeffner, interview; Donovan, interview.

months after the bishop's death. On April 30, 1971, the bishop had announced that the state's board of consulters had recommended the division
of the diocese, a recommendation that he endorsed, but it was not until December 19, 1972 that the Holy See raised Oklahoma City to the status of an
archdiocese and created the separate Diocese of Tulsa.[28] The symbolic nature of this division loomed large in the divided world that was postconciliar
Oklahoma. Bishop Kelley's dream of a separate Tulsa diocese was finally a reality, but at a price that even he might have baulked at paying.

28. *Tulsa Daily World*, August 1, 1971. According to Father James D. White, a committee composed of Father John Sullivan (vicar for eastern Oklahoma), Father William Garthoeffner (vicar for western Oklahoma), and Father Charles Schettler (chancellor) discussed
the new boundaries, although Reed made the final decision. The initial plan proposed *three*
dioceses: Oklahoma City and the parishes to its south in the center, Tulsa (the eastern third
of the state), and another diocese—with its cathedral at either Enid or Lawton—that would
take in everything else, including the counties north of Guthrie. It was decided that financial support for even two dioceses would be hard enough to maintain, and a revised plan
was adopted.

Appendix of maps

Parishes and Missions in Northwest Oklahoma, 1965

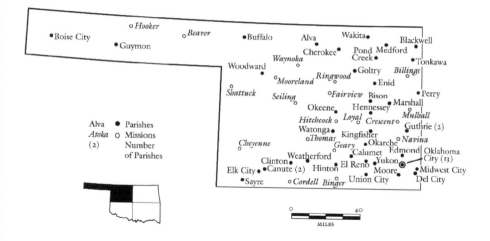

Prepared by Michael Larson, coordinator of cartography, Department of Geography, Oklahoma State University at Stillwater.

Parishes and Missions in Northeast Oklahoma, 1965

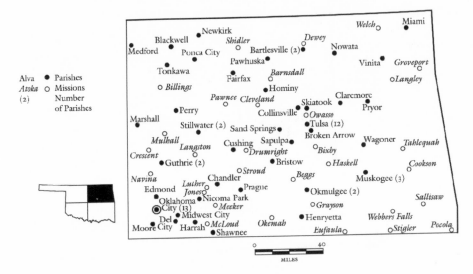

Alva   ● Parishes
Atoka   ○ Missions
(2)   Number
          of Parishes

Parishes and Missions in Southeast Oklahoma, 1965

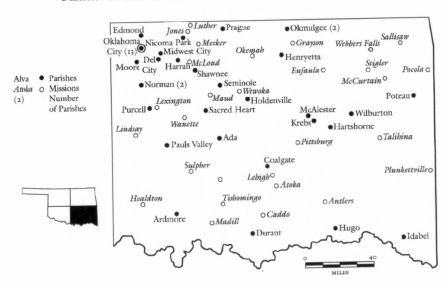

Alva   ● Parishes
Atoka   ○ Missions
(2)   Number
          of Parishes

Parishes and Missions in Southwest Oklahoma, 1965

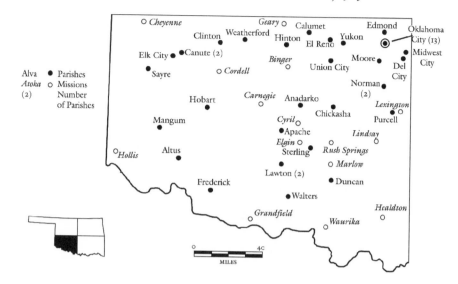

Alva ● Parishes
Atoka ○ Missions
(2) Number
of Parishes

Cheyenne ○ Geary ○ Calumet ○ Edmond ● Oklahoma City (13)
Clinton ● Weatherford ● Hinton ● Yukon ● Midwest City
Elk City ● ●Canute (2) El Reno ●
Sayre ● Cordell ○ Binger ● Moore ● Del City
Hobart ● Carnegie ○ Union City ○ Norman ● (2)
Mangum ● Anadarko ● Chickasha ● Lexington ○ Purcell ○
Hollis ○ Altus ● Cyril ○ Lindsay ○
Apache ● Elgin ○ Rush Springs ●
Sterling ● Marlow ○
Frederick ● Lawton (2) Duncan ●
Walters ● Healdton ○
Grandfield ○ Waurika ○

4C
MILES

Parishes and Institutions in Oklahoma City

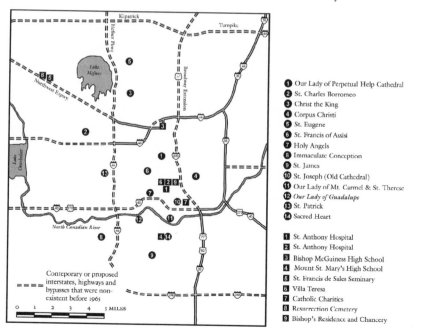

❶ Our Lady of Perpetual Help Cathedral
❷ St. Charles Borromeo
❸ Christ the King
❹ Corpus Christi
❺ St. Eugene
❻ St. Francis of Assisi
❼ Holy Angels
❽ Immaculate Conception
❾ St. James
❿ St. Joseph (Old Cathedral)
⓫ Our Lady of Mt. Carmel & St. Therese
⓬ Our Lady of Guadalupe
⓭ St. Patrick
⓮ Sacred Heart

1 St. Anthony Hospital
2 St. Anthony Hospital
3 Bishop McGuiness High School
4 Mount St. Mary's High School
5 St. Francis de Sales Seminary
6 Villa Teresa
7 Catholic Charities
8 Resurrection Cemetery
9 Bishop's Residence and Chancery

Contemporary or proposed
interstates, highways and
bypasses that were non-
existent before 1965

0 1 2 3 4 5 MILES

Appendix of Maps

Parishes and Institutions in Tulsa

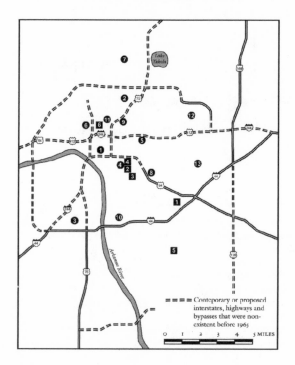

❶	Holy Family Co-Cathedral	⓫	St. Monica
❷	St. Augustine	⓬	Sts. Peter and Paul
❸	St. Catherine	⓭	St. Pius X
❹	Christ the King		
❺	St. Francis Xavier	▪1	Bishop Kelley High School
❻	Immaculate Conception	▪2	Cascia Hall
❼	St. Jude	▪3	Monte Cassino School, St. Joseph Convent
❽	The Madalene		Benedictine Heights College
❾	*Our Lady of Guadalupe*	▪4	St. John Hospital
❿	St. Mary	▪5	St. Francis Hospital
		▪6	Associated Catholic Charities

Contemporary or proposed interstates, highways and bypasses that were non-existent before 1965

Bibliography

Archival Sources

Archives of the Benedictine Order, St. Joseph's Monastery, Tulsa, Oklahoma.

Catholic Action File, Archives of the Catholic Archdiocese of Oklahoma City, Oklahoma.

Diocesan Congress of Catholic Action File, Archives of the Catholic Archdiocese of Oklahoma City, Oklahoma.

Ecumenical Council and Council of Churches Papers, Archives of the Catholic Archdiocese of Oklahoma City, Oklahoma.

Holy Family Cathedral Papers, Holy Family Cathedral, Tulsa, Oklahoma.

Parish Files, Archives of the Catholic Archdiocese of Oklahoma City, Oklahoma.

Parish Files, Archives of the Catholic Diocese of Tulsa, Oklahoma.

Victor Reed Papers, Archives of the Catholic Archdiocese of Oklahoma City, Oklahoma.

Oral History Sources

Clergy roundtable discussion with author. June 19, 2005, Oklahoma City, Oklahoma.

Clergy roundtable discussion with author. June 23, 2005, Tulsa, Oklahoma.

Donovan, Father J. Paul. Interview by author. May 8, 2004, Owasso, Oklahoma.

Flusche, Father Ernest. Interview by Father James D. White. July 25, 2005, Enid, Oklahoma.

Fox, G. Douglas. Interview by author. May 10, 2004, Tulsa, Oklahoma.

Gallatin, Father Paul H. Interview by author. June 24, 2005, Sand Springs, Oklahoma.

Garthoeffner, William C. Interview by author. November 16, 2004, Oklahoma City, Oklahoma.

Gier, Monsignor Gregory. Interview by author. May 10, 2004, Tulsa, Oklahoma.

Halpine, Monsignor James F. Interview by author. May 8, 2004, Tulsa, Oklahoma.

Harkin, Monsignor Raymond F. Interview by Father James D. White. May 18, 1971, Oklahoma City, Oklahoma.

Markey, Veronica (daughter of Victor Reed's sister Veronica). Reminiscences, as reported to Father James D. White. In author's possession.

Meiser, Charles A. Interview by author. June 20, 2005, Oklahoma City, Oklahoma.

Mies, Sister Mary Joseph. Conversation with author. June 20, 2005, Oklahoma City, Oklahoma.

Reed, Julia. Conversation with author. May 6, 2004, Tulsa, Oklahoma

Schettler, Father Charles H. Interview by author. March 30, 2004, Oklahoma City, Oklahoma.
Swift, Father William J. Interview by author. May 6, 2004, Tulsa, Oklahoma.

Printed Primary Sources

Brousseau, Robert J., ed. *A Dying Breed of Brave Men: The Self-Written Stories of Nine Married Priests.* Bloomington, Ind.: 1stBooks, 2003.
Doherty, Martin W. *The House on Humility Street: Memories of the North American College in Rome.* New York: Longman's, Green, 1942.
Leven, Stephen A. *Go Tell It in the Streets.* N.p.: n.p., 1984.
Reed, Julia. Reed Family History. N.d. In author's possession.
White, James D. "Personal Memories of Bishop Reed." In author's possession.

Newspapers and Periodicals

American College Bulletin
Commonweal
Crusader
Oklahoma Courier
St. Joseph's Convent News
Southwest Courier
Spires
Tulsa Benedictines' News
Tulsa Daily World
Tulsa Tribune

Secondary Sources

Adams, Richard N. *Essays on Guatemalan National Social Structure, 1944–1966.* Austin: University of Texas Press, 1970.
Alexander, Charles C. *The Ku Klux Klan in the Southwest.* Lexington: University of Kentucky Press, 1965.
Appleby, R. Scott. "Present to the People of God: The Transformation of the Roman Catholic Parish Priesthood." In Jay P. Dolan, R. Scott Appleby, Patricia Byrne, and Debra Campbell, eds., *Transforming Parish Ministry: The Changing Role of Catholic Clergy, Laity, and Women Religious,* 3–108. New York, Crossroad, 1989.
Avella, Steven M. *In the Richness of the Earth: A History of the Archdiocese of Milwaukee, 1843–1958.* Milwaukee: Marquette University Press, 2002.
———. *This Confident Church: Catholic Leadership and Life in Chicago, 1940–1965.* Notre Dame, Ind.: University of Notre Dame Press, 1992.
Beane, Marjorie N. *From Framework to Freedom: A History of the Sister Formation Conference.* Lanham, Md.: University Press of America, 1993.
Bible, Life, and Worship. Twenty-second Annual North American Liturgical Week. Washington, D.C.: Liturgical Conference, 1961.
Black, Gregory D. *The Catholic Crusade against the Movies, 1940–1975.* New York: Cambridge University Press, 1998.

Blantz, Thomas E. *A Priest in Public Service: Francis J. Haas and the New Deal*. Notre Dame, Ind.: University of Notre Dame Press, 1982.

Branch, Taylor. *Parting the Waters: America in the King Years, 1954–1963*. New York: Simon and Schuster, 1988.

———. *Pillar of Fire: America in the King Years, 1963–65*. New York: Simon and Schuster, 1998.

Brinkley, Alan. *Voices of Protest: Huey Long, Father Coughlin, and the Great Depression*. New York: Vintage, 1982.

Broderick, Francis L. *Right Reverend New Dealer, John A. Ryan*. New York: Macmillan, 1963.

Bronder, Saul, *Social Justice and Church Authority: The Public Life of Archbishop Robert E. Lucey*. Philadelphia: Temple University Press, 1982.

Brown, Robert M. *The Ecumenical Revolution: An Interpretation of the Protestant-Catholic Dialogue*. Garden City, N.Y.: Doubleday, 1967.

Brown, Robert M., and Gustave Weigel, S.J. *An American Dialogue: A Protestant Looks at Catholicism and a Catholic Looks at Protestantism*. Garden City, N.Y.: Doubleday, 1960.

Brown, Thomas E. *Bible Belt Catholicism: A History of the Roman Catholic Church in Oklahoma, 1905–1945*. New York: United States Catholic Historical Society, 1977.

Bryant, Keith L. Jr. "Oklahoma and the New Deal." In John Braeman, Robert H. Bremner, and David Brody, eds., *The New Deal: The State and Local Levels*, 166–81. Columbus: Ohio State University Press, 1975.

Bugnini, Annibale. *The Reform of the Liturgy, 1948–1975*. Collegeville, Minn.: Liturgical Press, 1990.

Burns, Jeffrey M. *Disturbing the Peace: A History of the Christian Family Movement, 1949–1974*. Notre Dame, Ind.: Notre Dame University Press, 1999.

Burtchaell, James T. *The Dying of the Light: The Disengagement of Colleges and Universities from Their Christian Connections*. Grand Rapids, Mich.: William B. Eerdmans, 1998.

Callahan, Daniel *The Mind of the Catholic Layman*. New York: Charles Scribners Sons, 1963.

Campbell, Debra. "The Struggle to Serve: From the Lay Apostolate to the Ministry Experience." In Jay P. Dolan, R. Scott Appleby, Patricia Byrne, and Debra Campbell, eds., *Transforming Parish Ministry: The Changing Role of Catholic Clergy, Laity, and Women Religious*, 201–80. New York, Crossroad, 1989.

Carey, Patrick W. *An Immigrant Bishop: John England's Adaptation of Irish Catholicism to American Republicanism*. Yonkers, N.Y.: U.S. Catholic Historical Society, 1982.

———. *People, Priests, and Prelates: Ecclesiastical Democracy and the Tensions of Trusteeism*. Notre Dame, Ind.: University of Notre Dame Press, 1987.

Carroll, James *An American Requiem: God, My Father, and the War That Came between Us*. New York: Houghton Mifflin, 1996.

Cavert, Samuel M. *The American Churches in the Ecumenical Movement, 1900–1968*. New York: Association Press, 1968.

Chinnici, Joseph P., O.F.M. "The Catholic Community at Prayer, 1926–1976." In James M. O'Toole, ed., *Habits of Devotion: Catholic Religious Practice in Twentieth Century America*, 9–87. Ithaca, N.Y.: Cornell University Press, 2004.

Cohen, Lizabeth. *Making a New Deal: Industrial Workers in Chicago, 1919–1939*. New York: Cambridge University Press, 1990.

Congar, Yves, O.P. *Lay People in the Church*. Westminster, Md.: Newman, 1963.

Cooney, John. *The American Pope: The Life and Times of Francis Cardinal Spellman*. New York: Times Books, 1984.

Cross, Richard W., and Eugene L. Zoeller. *The Story of the American College.* (Extract from *American College Bulletin*, 1957.)

Cuneo, Michael W. *The Smoke of Satan: Conservative and Traditionalist Dissent in Contemporary American Catholicism.* New York: Oxford University Press, 1997.

Curran, Robert E. *Michael Augustine Corrigan and the Shaping of Conservative Catholicism in America, 1878–1902.* New York: Arno, 1978.

Curry, Lerond. *Protestant-Catholic Relations in America: World War I through Vatican II.* Lexington: University of Kentucky Press, 1972.

Dahm, Charles W. *Power and Authority in the Catholic Church: Cardinal Cody in Chicago.* Notre Dame, Ind.: University of Notre Dame Press, 1981.

Davidson, James B., and John P. Schlangen. "Cultural and Structural Assimilation among Catholics in the Southwest." In William T. Liu and Nathaniel J. Pallone, eds., *Catholics/U.S.A.: Perspectives on Social Change,* 435–55. New York: John Wiley and Sons, 1970.

Debo, Angie. *Prairie City: The Story of an American Community.* New York: Alfred A. Knopf, 1944.

Decade of Change: A Supplement to the Oklahoma Courier (March 1, 1968).

Dewey, Gerald J. "Role-Conflict: The Priest in a Post-conciliar Church." In William T. Liu and Nathaniel J. Pallone, eds., *Catholics/U.S.A.: Perspectives on Social Change,* 75–110. New York: John Wiley and Sons, 1970.

Dolan, Jay P. *The American Catholic Experience: A History from Colonial Time to the Present.* Garden City, N.Y.: Doubleday, 1985.

Dolan, Timothy M. *Some Seed Fell on Good Ground: The Life of Edwin V. O'Hara.* Washington, D.C.: The Catholic University of America Press, 1992.

Ebaugh, Helen R. *Out of the Cloister: A Study of Organizational Dilemmas.* Austin: University of Texas Press, 1977.

Faherty, William B., S.J. *Dream by the River: Two Centuries of St. Louis Catholicism.* St. Louis, Mo.: Piraeus, 1973.

Falla, Ricardo. *Quiché Rebelde: Religious Conversion, Politics and Ethnic Identity in Guatemala.* Translated by Philip Berryman. Austin: University of Texas Press, 2001.

Findlay, James F. Jr. *Church People in the Struggle: The National Council of Churches and the Black Freedom Movement, 1950–1970.* New York: Oxford University Press, 1993.

Fogarty, Gerald P., S.J. *The Vatican and the American Hierarchy from 1870 to 1965.* Wilmington, Del.: Michael Glazier, 1985.

Fortin, Roger. *Faith and Action: A History of the Archdiocese of Cincinnati, 1821–1996.* Columbus: Ohio State University Press, 2002.

Friedland, Michael B. *Lift Up Your Voice Like a Trumpet: White Clergy and the Civil Rights and Antiwar Movements, 1954–1973.* Chapel Hill: University of North Carolina Press, 1998.

Gaffey, James P. *Francis Clement Kelley and the American Catholic Dream.* Wilmington, N.C.: McGrath, 1979.

Garneau, James F. "The First Inter-American Episcopal Conference, November 2–4, 1959: Canada and the United States Called to the Rescue of Latin America." *Catholic Historical Review* 87:4 (2001): 662–87.

Gavin, Thomas F. *Champion of Youth: A Dynamic Story of a Dynamic Man, Daniel A. Lord, S. J.* Boston: St. Paul, 1977.

Glasscock, Carl B. *Then Came Oil: The Story of the Last Frontier.* New York: Bobbs-Merrill, 1938.

Gleason, Philip. *Contending with Modernity: Catholic Higher Education in the Twentieth Century.* New York: Oxford University Press, 1995.

Goble, Danney. "Oklahoma Politics and the Sooner Electorate." In Anne H. Morgan and H. Wayne Morgan, eds., *Oklahoma: New Views of the Forty-sixth State*, 133–74. Norman: University of Oklahoma Press, 1982.

Greeley, Andrew M. *The Church and the Suburbs*. New York: Sheed and Ward, 1959.

———. *Priests in the United States: Reflections on a Survey*. Garden City, N.Y.: Doubleday, 1972.

Greeley, Andrew M., and Peter H. Rossi. *The Education of Catholic Americans*. Chicago: Aldine, 1966.

Greene, Michael J. "The Catholic Press in America." In William T. Liu and Nathaniel J. Pallone, eds., *Catholics/U.S.A.: Perspectives on Social Change*, 227–53. New York: John Wiley and Sons, 1970.

Gregory, James N. *American Exodus: The Dust Bowl Migration and Okie Culture in California*. New York: Oxford University Press, 1989.

Hale, Douglas. "The People of Oklahoma: Economics and Social Change." In Anne H. Morgan and H. Wayne Morgan, eds., *Oklahoma: New Views of the Forty-sixth State*, 31–92. Norman: University of Oklahoma Press, 1982.

Heineman, Kenneth J. *A Catholic New Deal: Religion and Reform in Depression Pittsburgh*. University Park: Pennsylvania State University Press, 1999.

Hennesey, James, S.J. *American Catholics: A History of the Roman Catholic Community in the United States*. New York: Oxford University Press, 1981.

Higham, John. *Strangers in the Land: Patterns of American Nativism, 1860–1925*. New Brunswick, N.J.: Rutgers University Press, 1955.

Hitchcock, James. *The Decline and Fall of Radical Catholicism*. Garden City, N.Y.: Image, 1971.

Hovda, Robert W. "Sunday Mass—Dullsville." In Robert W. Hovda, ed., *Sunday Morning Crisis: Renewal in Catholic Worship*, 30–44. Baltimore: Helicon, 1963.

Hynes, Emerson. "The Parish in the Rural Community." In C. J. Nuesse and Thomas J. Harte, C.Ss.R., eds., *The Sociology of the Parish: An Introductory Symposium*, 100–32. Milwaukee: Bruce, 1951.

Jones, E. Michael. *John Cardinal Krol and the Cultural Revolution*. South Bend, Ind.: Fidelity, 1995.

Kantowicz, Edward R. *Corporation Sole: Cardinal Mundelein and Chicago Catholicism*. Notre Dame, Ind.: University of Notre Dame Press, 1983.

Kelly, George A. *Battle for the American Church*. Garden City, N.Y.: Doubleday, 1979.

———. *Inside My Father's House*. New York: Doubleday, 1989.

Komonchak, Joseph A. "Interpreting the Council: Catholic Attitudes towards Vatican II." In Mary Jo Weaver and R. Scott Appleby, eds., *Being Right: Conservative Catholics in America*, 17–36. Bloomington: Indiana University Press, 1995.

Kosa, John. "The Emergence of a Catholic Middle Class." In William T. Liu and Nathaniel J. Pallone, eds., *Catholics/U.S.A.: Perspectives on Social Change*, 15–24. New York: John Wiley and Sons, 1970.

Lakeland, Paul. *The Liberation of the Laity: In Search of an Accountable Church*. New York: Continuum International, 2002.

Lay, Shawn, ed. *The Invisible Empire in the West: Toward a New Historical Appraisal of the Ku Klux Klan of the 1920s*. Urbana: University of Illinois Press, 1992.

Lichtman, Allan J. *Prejudice and the Old Politics: The Presidential Election of 1928*. Chapel Hill: University of North Carolina Press, 1979.

Lindsey, William, and Mark Silk, eds. *Religion and Public Life in the Midwest: America's Common Denominator?* Lanham, Md.: AltaMira, 2004.

Liptak, Dolores, R.S.M. *Immigrants and Their Church*. New York: Macmillan, 1989.

Luecke, Sr. Jane Marie, O.S.B. "The Sister in Secular Life." In Sr. M. Charles Borromeo Muckenhirn, ed., *The Changing Sister*, 263–94. Notre Dame, Ind.: Fides, 1965.

MacGregor, Morris J. *Steadfast in the Faith: The Life of Patrick Cardinal O'Boyle*. Washington, D.C.: The Catholic University of America Press, 2006.

Manning, Frank V. *A Call to Action*. Notre Dame, Ind.: Fides, 1977.

Marlett, Jeffrey. "'There Is a Church West of Buffalo!' Catholic Studies and Regional Identity." *Cushwa Center Newsletter*, Fall 2004, 1, 8–10.

Massa, Mark. *Catholics and American Culture: Fulton Sheen, Dorothy Day, and the Notre Dame Football Team*. New York: Crossroad, 1999.

McAvoy, Thomas T., C.S.C. *The Great Crisis in American Catholic History, 1895–1900*. Chicago: Henry Regnery, 1957.

McGreevey, John T. *Parish Boundaries: The Catholic Encounter with Race in the Twentieth Century*. Chicago: University of Chicago Press, 1996.

———. "Thinking on One's Own: Catholicism in the American Intellectual Imagination, 1928–1960." *Journal of American History* 84:1 (1997): 97–131.

McGuinness, Margaret M. "Let Us Go to the Altar: American Catholics and the Eucharist, 1926–1976." In James M. O'Toole, ed., *Habits of Devotion: Catholic Religious Practice in Twentieth Century America*, 187–235. Ithaca, N.Y.: Cornell University Press, 2004.

McNamara, Robert F. *The American College in Rome, 1855–1955*. Rochester, N.Y.: Christopher, 1956.

McShane, Joseph M. *Sufficiently Radical: Catholicism, Progressivism, and the Bishops' Program of 1919*. Washington, D.C.: The Catholic University of America Press, 1986.

Morgan, H. Wayne, and Anne H. Morgan, eds.. *Oklahoma: A Bicentennial History*. New York: W. W. Norton, 1977.

Murdick, Olin J. *The Parish School Board*. Dayton, Ohio: National Catholic Educational Association, 1967.

National Council of the Churches of Christ in the U.S.A. *Churches and Church Membership in the United States: An Enumeration and Analysis by Counties, States, and Regions*. Series C, no. 46–47. New York, 1952.

Nelson, Charles E. "Modest and Humble Crosses: A History of the Catholic Parish in the South Central Region." In Jay P. Dolan, ed., *The American Catholic Parish: A History from 1850 to the Present*, 1:235–323. Mahwah, N.J.: Paulist, 1987.

Norton-Taylor, Duncan. "The Catholic Layman Confronts His Changing Church." *Fortune*, December 1966, 172–75, 220, 224, 227–28.

O'Brien, David J. *American Catholics and Social Reform: The New Deal Years*. New York: Oxford University Press, 1968.

———. *Public Catholicism*. New York: Macmillan, 1989.

———. "When It All Came Together: Bishop John J. Wright and the Diocese of Worcester, 1950–1959." *Catholic Historical Review* 85:2 (1999): 175–94.

O'Connell, Marvin R. *John Ireland and the American Catholic Church*. St. Paul: Minnesota Historical Society Press, 1988.

Official Catholic Directory. New York: P. J. Kenedy and Sons, 1940–71.

One Family, One Century: A Photographic History of the Catholic Church in Oklahoma, 1875–1975. Oklahoma City: Archdiocese of Oklahoma City, 1977.

Orsi, Robert A. *The Madonna of 115th Street: Faith and Community in Italian Harlem, 1880–1950*. New Haven, Conn.: Yale University Press, 1985.

Pardo, Henry A. "Parish Finances." In Marvin Bordelon, ed., *The Parish in a Time of Change*, 187–94. Notre Dame, Ind.: Fides, 1967.

Pecklers, Keith F. *The Unread Vision: The Liturgical Movement in the United States of America, 1926–1955*. Collegeville, Minn.: Liturgical Press, 1998.

Piehl, Mel. *Breaking Bread: The Catholic Worker and the Origin of Catholic Radicalism in America.* Philadelphia: Temple University Press, 1982.

Reese, Thomas J., S.J. *A Flock of Shepherds: The National Conference of Catholic Bishops.* Kansas City, Mo.: Sheed and Ward, 1992.

Rynne, Xavier. *Vatican Council II.* New York: Farrar, Straus and Giroux, 1968.

Schirber, Martin E., O.S.B. "Catholic Rural Life." In Leo R. Ward, C.S.C., ed., *The American Apostolate: American Catholics in the Twentieth Century,* 133–48. Westminster, Md.: Newman, 1952.

Scott, Vaile J. *Catholic Adult Education.* Dayton, Ohio: National Catholic Education Association, 1968.

Shannon, James P. *Reluctant Dissenter.* New York: Crossroads, 1998.

Shaw, Stephen J. "The Cities and the Plains, a Home for God's People: A History of the Catholic Parish in the Midwest." In Jay P. Dolan, ed., *The American Catholic Parish: A History from 1850 to the Present,* 2:277–380. Mahwah, NJ: Paulist Press, 1987.

Shelley, Thomas J. *Paul J. Hallinan: First Archbishop of Atlanta.* Wilmington, Del.: Michael Glazier, 1989.

Slade, Joseph W., and Judith Y. Lee, eds. *The Greenwood Encyclopedia of American Regional Cultures: The Midwest.* Westport, Conn.: Greenwood, 2004.

Slawson, Douglas J. *The Foundation and First Decade of the National Catholic Welfare Council.* Washington, D.C.: The Catholic University of America Press, 1992.

Spalding, Thomas W. *The Premier See: A History of the Archdiocese of Baltimore, 1789–1989.* Baltimore, Md.: Johns Hopkins University Press, 1989.

Strakhovsky, Leonid I. "The Louvain Concept of a University." *Catholic Historical Review* 25:2 (1939): 179–83.

Tavard, George H. *The Church, the Layman, and the Modern World.* New York: Macmillan, 1959.

Tentler, Leslie W. *Catholics and Contraception: An American History.* Ithaca, N.Y.: Cornell University Press, 2004.

———. *Seasons of Grace: A History of the Catholic Archdiocese of Detroit.* Detroit: Wayne State University Press, 1990.

Van Allen, Rodger. *"The Commonweal" and American Catholicism: The Magazine, the Movement, the Meaning.* Philadelphia: Fortress, 1974.

Ward, Leo R. C.S.C. *Catholic Life, U.S.A.: Contemporary Lay Movements.* New York: B. Herder, 1959.

Weisbrot, Robert. *Freedom Bound: A History of America's Civil Rights Movement.* New York: Norton, 1990.

Whetten, Nathan L. *Guatemala: The Land and the People.* New Haven, Conn.: Yale University Press, 1961.

White, James D., ed. *Diary of a Frontier Bishop: The Journals of Theophile Meerschaert.* Tulsa: Sarto, 1994.

———. *This Far by Faith, 1875–2004: 125 Years of Catholic Life in Oklahoma.* N.p.: Editions du Signe, 2000.

———. *The Souls of the Just: A Necrology of the Catholic Church in Oklahoma.* Tulsa: Sarto, 1983.

White, Joseph M. *The Diocesan Seminary in the United States: A History from the 1780s to the Present.* Notre Dame, Ind.: University of Notre Dame Press, 1989.

Worster, Donald. *Dustbowl: The Southern Plains in the 1930s.* New York: Oxford University Press, 1979.

Yzermans, Vincent A. *American Participation in the Second Vatican Council.* New York: Sheed and Ward, 1967.

Index

Abortion, 377, 379–82

African Americans, Oklahoma, 239, 248, 249–54

Albany, diocese of, 40, 244n28

Allen, Daniel, 143–44, 173, 257, 308

Alter, Karl, 71, 80, 84–85, 183, 283

Alverno Heights Hospital, Guthrie, 331n26

Americanization, Catholic: and Christian Family Movement, 358; decline of confessionalism, 2, 62–63, 65; and education, 117–18, 124; and Little Council, 108; Newman apostolate, 144–45; popular culture, 367–68, 379; rise of middle class, 6–7; role of the press, 100, 103–4; and St. Gregory's College, 138–39; and suburban churches, 151, 354–55; theological developments, 14; traditionalists, 132; and worship, 185, 207

An American Dialogue, 212

Anti-Catholicism, 4, 28, 143, 373–74

Arledge, Jerry, 271

Association for Christian Development, 174–75

Baltimore, archdiocese of, 231–32

Bartlett, Dewey, 93–94, 258, 362–63

Bartmeier, Mary Paula, 343–44, 346

Beauduin, Lambert, 182

Beckerle, Frederick, 105, 162, 205

Belgium, influence on American Catholicism, 5, 26, 51. *See also* Louvain

Benedictine Heights College, 73, 74, 93, 139, 325–26, 343–44

Benedictine Sisters of Guthrie and Tulsa: Benedictine Heights College, 325–26; conflict, 343–47; and education, 135, 327–28; and renewal, 336–37, 338–39; response to criticism, 324. *See also* Benedictine Heights College; Sisters of Benedict

Berning, Philip, 262

Berthiaume, Raymond, 195, 227, 228, 306, 317, 397

Birth control, 314–17, 368–71

Bishop, Howard, 60

Bloms, John, 202–3, 223, 225n55, 299

Brooks, Donald, 197, 245, 252

Brousseau, Robert, 31, 72, 217, 319, 357

Bryce, Mary Charles, 172

Buck, Robert and Ann, 359

Buswell, Charles: on liturgical innovation, 183, 187; at North American Liturgical Conference, 214; at Our Lady of Perpetual Help, Oklahoma City, 72; at Reed's funeral, 402; at Second Vatican Council, 80, 82, 86; at Sisters' Conference, 340

Cantwell, Daniel, 237

Carberry, John, 402

Cardijn, Joseph, 51

Carlin, Ramon: and criticism of parochial education, 117, 129; and lay initiative, 304; mission oversight, 276–80; profile, 273; rejects proposed mission site, 271

Carmelite Sisters of St. Therese: conflict, 348–50; and Guatemala mission school, 270; liturgical renewal, 336, 337, 338, 348n80; and parochial schools, 327, 300

Carter, Celine, 270, 327, 348–49

Catholic Action: in Belgium, 51; Catholic Action Congress (1934), 42–45; Catholic Action Congress (1941), 55–56; Catholic Activities of Tulsa, 57; early phase, 5, 39–41, 352–53; rural potential, 53–54. *See also* Christian Family Movement; Young Christian Students; Young Christian Workers

parish councils, 160, 163–70; parish school boards, 122, 128; rural setting, 149–50; suburban setting, 151–52; urban setting, 151

Paul VI, 11, 85, 203, 193, 283, 317, 319, 321, 370

Peace movement, 282–83, 283–84, 288

Philadelphia, archdiocese of, 14, 131

Pittsburgh, diocese of, 91

Pius IX, 32

Pius XI, 5, 30, 34, 38, 48, 52

Pius XII, 183, 186, 238, 241

Planned Parenthood, 314–15

Politics: in election of 1921, 28–29; in Great Depression, 37; in the 1960s, 307–8, 354, 361–64, 374, 380–81

Pribil, Clement, 142–43, 230–31, 327

Priests: and adult Christian education, 176–78; and birth control, 314–17; and celibacy, 317–20; and civil rights, 239, 240–41, 242–45, 247, 248–49, 308; College of Oklahoma Priests, 309–13; and conservatives, 157–58; criticism of, 383–84; decline in vocations, 141, 298, 320–21; devotional life, 301–3; Dewey study, 300–301; and ecumenism, 212, 215, 216, 217, 230, 233–34; and Guatemala mission, 274; and integration, 251, 252, 253; liberals, 300–302, 303–6, 307, 313; and liturgical renewal, 183–84, 187–88, 190, 192, 193, 195–99, 204–5; married priests, 317–18, 320; and mixed marriages, 221–25, 315; and new cathedral, 397; and parish conflict, 162, 164–65, 165–66, 166–69; and parochial school closings, 134; and peace movement, 284, 286, 288; personnel board, 311–12; and politics, 254, 307–8, 313; priests' commission, 309; priest-to-people ratio, 149; professionalization, 158, 296–97, 299–300, 309–13; and St. Francis de Sales Seminary, 139–40; salaries, 310–11; sense of vocation before 1960, 64, 71–72, 296–97; and tithing, 160–61; traditionalists, 300–302; view of the laity, 158, 160, 304–6, 312

Primeau, Ernest, 279

Project Equality, 257–58

Protestants: and Bishop Kelley, 29; and Extension Lay Volunteers, 171, 172; impact of Catholic Action upon, 40, 41, 42–43; interaction with Catholics, 2–3, 210, 216–17; and John XXIII, 213; and North American Liturgical Conference, 214; opposition to ecumenism, 219–20; support for ecumenism, 233; and Victor Reed, 55; view of Catholics, 295–96, 310, 352, 374; view of Catholic schools, 135, 364–66; and wartime services, 57. See also Anti-Catholicism

Pyeatt, Patrick, 275, 276

Quadragesimo Anno, 38

Race, in Oklahoma: and African American parishes, 251–54; and Association for Christian Development, 175; and Catholic institutions, 239–40, 249, 250; and Catholic Interracial Council, 242–43; and civil rights protests, 240–41; and Community of the Living Christ, 156; legislation, 245–47; neighborhood integration, 254–55; and pre-1960 Catholic parish, 237; social outreach, 256–58, 263–65

Reed, Henrietta, 24, 26, 30, 66n73

Reed, Victor: on abortion, 380; aesthetic sensibility, 10–11, 26; and Albert Outler, 229; and American College at Louvain, 47–50, 52; appointed monsignor, 74; as army chaplain, 57–58; and Benedictine Heights College, 74; birth, 24; and birth control, 316–17; and Catholic Action, 40–41, 45; on Christian Family Movement, 358, 359, 360; and church-building moratorium, 149, 397; and civil rights, 239, 241, 243, 245, 246–47, 257–58; on clerical celibacy, 317–18, 322; on closing of Oklahoma Courier, 106; consecration and installation as bishop, 74–76; and Council of Churches, 229; death, 401; devotional life, 11; as diocesan administrator, 90, 92; on diocesan finance, 95, 97; early ecumenism, 55, 59; and ecumenical partners, 401–2; on ecumenism, 84n13, 85, 214, 217–19, 227, 235; on education, 147; and federal poverty programs, 255–56; on fraternity membership, 355; funeral, 402; on Guatemala mission, 275, 276; on Heritage Hall, 258; as honorary Caddo Indian, 262; and John Bloms, 202; legacy, 403; liberal admirers, 387, 389–90; liberal critics, 10, 12–13; on liberals, 13; on Little Council, 107–8, 109, 112, 114; on liturgy, 83, 184, 186, 188, 191, 192, 198, 200–201, 203–4, 205, 208; membership of Citizens for Decent Literature, 366; on mixed marriages, 221–24; and National Catholic Rural Life Conference, 59–60; and new cathedral, 397, 398, 399–400; on Newman Society apostolate, 141, 143; on nonterritorial parishes, 156; and North American College, 32–34; ordination, 34; on parish autonomy, 165–65; on parish closures, 178; on parish councils, 165; on parish life, 152; on parish transfers, 152–54; on the Parks affair, 130; on parochial education, 120, 249, 250; social connections, 12; permissive approach to renewal process, 8, 13, 18–19, 391; politics, 12, 13, 361, 363–64; on

The Road to Renewal: Victor Joseph Reed & Oklahoma Catholicism, 1905–1971,
was designed and typeset in Galliard by Kachergis Book Design of Pittsboro,
North Carolina. It was printed on 60-pound House Natural Smooth
and bound by Sheridan Books, Inc., of Ann Arbor, Michigan.